THE COMPLETE WORKS

OF

SAINT ALPHONSUS DE LIGUORI,

DOCTOR OF THE CHURCH,

Bishop of Saint Agatha, and Founder of the Congregation of the Most Holy Redeemer.

TRANSLATED FROM THE ITALIAN.

EDITED BY

REV. EUGENE GRIMM,

Priest of the Congregation of the Most Holy Redeemer.

THE ASCETICAL WORKS.

Volumes VII and VIII in One

THE GLORIES OF MARY.

FOURTH REPRINT REVISED

THE COMPLETE ASCETICAL WORKS

OF

ST. ALPHONSUS DE LIGUORI.

Each book is complete in itself, and any volume will be sold separately.

THE GLORIES OF MARY.

BY

St. ALPHONSUS de LIGUORI

Doctor of the Church.

EDITED BY

REV. EUGENE GRIMM,

Priest of the Congregation of the Most Holy Redeemer.

Two Volumes in One

FOURTH REPRINT REVISED

REDEMPTORIST FATHERS

BROOKLYN

ST. LOUIS   TORONTO

Nihil obstat.
Arthur J. Scanlan, S.T.D.,
Censor Librorum.

Imprimatur.
† Patritius Cardinalis Hayes,
Archiepiscopus Neo-Eboracensis

Neo-Eboraci
Die 16 Aprilis, 1931

APPROBATION.

By virtue of the authority granted me by the Most Rev. Patrick Murray, Superior General of the Congregation of the Most Holy Redeemer, I hereby sanction the publication of the work entitled "THE GLORIES OF MARY", which combines Volumes VII and VIII of the complete edition of the works of St. Alphónsus de Liguori.

Andrew B. Kuhn, C.SS.R.,
Provincial

Brooklyn, N. Y., January 1, 1931.

Introduction

This book has been reprinted here in the Philippines so that it can be made available to everyone at a most reasonable price and in order that even the poor may be able to afford the book. It is our hope to soon print other titles of St. Alphonsus' works.

We know as Christians that our Lord has told us in St. Matthews Gospel that we must let our light shine before men. We don't hide our light under a basket but let it shine for everyone to see.

So to let our light shine before men we won't put this beautiful book in a drawer or on a book shelf or under a basket; we will let others see it by lending it to our poor neighbor who can't afford to buy a copy of it. It is better to lend the book than give it away, or they may just put it on a shelf and only one more person reads the book.

By lending it we can reach many people over a period of time. In fact, it is a zealous idea for everyone to buy extra copies of our favorite religious books and set up a small lending library to spread the light of the faith far and wide.

St. John Bosco said that only God knows the good that can come about by reading one good Catholic book.

Surely, this is so. I was given a vocation to the priesthood by reading a small book on the Blessed Virgin. My brother decided to become a priest also by reading a beautiful Catholic book called the Way of Divine Love.

St. Jerome says that when we pray we speak to God; but when we read; God speaks to us. St. Augustine, St. Ignatius of Loyola, and St. John Colombino all left the world and dedicated their lives completely to God after reading a good spiritual book. Maybe the person to whom you lend this book will also dedicate his life to God or develop a deeper love of Him and His Mother. It will be your generosity and sacrifice which will have helped God accomplish this.

St. Alphonsus tells us that without good books and spiritual reading it will be morally impossible to save our souls.

So let us realize the importance of good reading materials and buy some extra copies for our friends and the poor or at least lend our copy to someone else.

The price has been held to the minimum so that you yourself can become an apostle and spread the good news and let your light shine before men.

Young men interested in serving God in the religious life as a brother or priest may contact me. Partial or full scholarship is still available for poor candidates who want to live a life of total consecration to the Mother of God and Her Divine Son. Our Blessed Mother loves the poor and has provided the means for those who lack the funds for the long years of seminary formation. High School graduates may apply.

Fr. Ronald Tangen
O.B.L. Victory Mission
R.R. #2 Box 25
Brookings S.D. 57006
Tel. 605-693-3983

CONTENTS

PART THE FIRST.

EXPLANATION OF THE SALVE REGINA.

CHAPTER I.

Salve Regina, Mater misericordiae.

MARY, OUR QUEEN, OUR MOTHER.

CHAPTER II.

Vita, Dulcedo.

MARY, OUR LIFE, OUR SWEETNESS.

Contents.

6

Contents.

Chapter VIII.

Et Jesum, benedictum Fructum ventris tui nobis post hoc exilium ostende.

MARY, OUR SALVATION.

Chapter IX.

O Clemens, O Pia!

CLEMENCY AND COMPASSION OF MARY.

Chapter X.

O dulcis Virgo Maria.

SWEETNESS OF THE NAME OF MARY.

PART THE SECOND.

DISCOURSES ON THE PRINCIPAL FEASTS OF MARY.

DISCOURSE I.

MARY'S IMMACULATE CONCEPTION.

8 *Contents.*

PART THE THIRD.

THE DOLORS OF MARY.

DISCOURSE.

MARY IS THE QUEEN OF MARTYRS.

SERMON

ON THE DOLORS OF MARY.

REFLECTIONS

ON EACH OF THE SEVEN DOLORS OF MARY.

PART THE FOURTH.

THE VIRTUES OF THE MOST BLESSED VIRGIN MARY

Contents.

NOTICE.

First Edition.

THIS work, the GLORIES OF MARY, was published in 1750, at Naples. St. Alphonsus was then fifty-four years old. , His bodily health had become exhausted by austerities and excessive labor. This made him believe that his end was approaching, as he himself declares in the dedication of his work, and did not permit him to suspect that he had yet to live nearly forty years in the service of God. It is known that this indefatigable apostle made a vow never to lose a moment's time. All the time that he did not employ in the exercise of the ministry he divided between prayer and study, hardly allowing his body the rest and the care that it absolutely required. His zeal at the same time embraced all that might serve to promote the welfare of souls. It is thus that during many years he amassed an ample supply of materials destined to form so many useful works, which it was his intention to publish in order to convert sinners, or enlighten and nourish the piety of the faithful, or to aid those that were charged with the duty of laboring in behalf of souls:—a twofold end that he always kept in view, and that he specially proposed to himself by publishing the Glories of Mary, as may be seen in the Introduction.

There are books which, though not voluminous, are yet sufficient to render a name popular and immortal; and such undoubtedly is the book entitled the GLORIES OF MARY. This work is not only a source of glory to its author, but it is much more—it is a great benefit that God bestows upon all. Heartily welcomed by all those that love good books, and especially by souls that hunger and thirst after justice, or need consolation and encouragement, translated afterwards into all languages, printed and reprinted in every country of the world, the GLORIES OF MARY has up to the present time produced incalculable good, and what good should it not produce in the future?

In the original, the GLORIES OF MARY is divided only into two parts, no doubt because it was printed at first in two volumes, the first of which contained the explanation of the *Salve*

Regina, and the second all the rest. In it, however, we find five Parts that are very distinct, and we follow this division in order to be better able to understand the whole work in all its details.

Everything that our saint has written is, as it were, a summary of a Catholic tradition on the subject that he treats: it is not an individual author; it is, so to speak, the Church herself that speaks to us by the voice of her prophets, her apostles, her pontiffs, her saints, her fathers, her doctors, of all nations and of all ages. No other book appears to be more worthy of recommendation in this respect than the GLORIES OF MARY. We should, however, be able to rely upon the authenticity of the quotations. These we have carefully verified, and can vouch for their exactness. We found that we had to make corrections in the texts of Scripture as well as in other parts of the work; but we have made them because we are convinced that the holy author himself would have made them or would have approved them.

Cardinal Dechamps, in the preface of the little work that he has published in honor of the Blessed Virgin, entitled LA NOUVELLE EVE, "The New Eve," relates the following incident: "At a visit that we paid to a learned and pious friend, we found the GLORIES OF MARY among the books that covered his table. He saw that I had noticed the work, and taking it in his hand, he said: 'This is my spiritual thermometer, for when I am not faithful to grace, this book by the least of its pages enlightens me and sustains my confidence. When I grow negligent and become lukewarm it hardly suits my taste; it is, so to speak too much for me. Noticing this state of things, I enter into myself, and I recognize without difficulty that it is not the light that has diminished its brightness, but that it is the interior eye that is no longer able to bear its brilliancy. I then strive to restore to this eye of the soul its purity and its power, and soon the thermometer rises; I wish to say that the soul rises and finds itself in unison with the dear GLORIES OF MARY.'

"We have taken care," adds Cardinal Dechamps, "not to draw from this isolated fact a general conclusion, as this would not be justifiable, since daily experience proves that the GLORIES OF MARY touches sinners and brings them back to God, as well as consoles the just, and animates them to perseverance. Yet it is not less true that there is a certain state of the soul, unhappily too much known;—a state of languor and darkness, in which one feels the need of varying one's reading, and of being sweetly brought back to that kind of reading, which one has become almost unworthy of relishing."

St. Alphonsus has himself unintentionally bestowed praise on his work, under most touching circumstances, as is related by Father Panzuti. When the saint was almost a nonagenarian, the lay-brother who attended him was as usual making with him a spiritual reading. One day he was quite enraptured with what was read to him, and his memory having failed him, he said at the end: "Brother, who is the author of that beautiful book? Oh how well written it is! what sweetness! Tell me who wrote it?" The lay-brother reading the title of the book, answered, "The GLORIES OF MARY, by Alphonsus de Liguori." At these words the holy man became quite confused, and remained silent. His humility found itself, as it were, caught in a trap.

There is no danger of erring if we say that those persons who are fond of reading books, such as those of our saint, and especially the GLORIES OF MARY, are in God's friendship or are on the point of attaining it; and if they persevere in such a disposition their salvation will be assured. The GLORIES OF MARY is a book that contains a selection of fine pearls, skilfully set in a frame that enhances yet more their beauty and their value: it is a mosaic of precious stones, the sight of which attracts and delights the eye, elevates and purifies it, without ever fatiguing it, provided it is not yet injured; it is a cloud that illumines and protects, a water that refreshes and heals, a celestial manna that sustains our life in this arid and perilous desert, and aids us to reach safely the promised land, by giving as a foretaste of the goods with which it abounds. Read a page of the GLORIES OF MARY, no matter which, and you will experience these effects.—ED.

SOME PRELIMINARY OBSERVATIONS.

I

Objections have been raised against some of the examples employed by St. Alphonsus in his edition of the Glories of Mary. The following observations will therefore not seem amiss.

The examples quoted by our Saint are taken from various sources: some are from post mediaeval writers, some from his own experience, and others from the legends of the middle ages. The word "legend" meant at that time, not fable or fictitious narrative, but event or occurrence; things to be read, *"res legendae"* as the Latin expresses it.

The nature of these narratives bears witness to the simplicity and sincerity of the times in which they were written. May we not say that sincerity and simplicity were equally characteristic of St. Alphonsus and his Neapolitan people. In that spirit only can they be rightly understood and appreciated.

To quote the Saint's own words: "When an opinion tends in any way to the honor of the most Blessed Virgin, when it has some foundation, and is not repugnant to the faith, nor to the decrees of the Church, nor to truth, the refusal to hold it, or to oppose it because the reverse may be true, shows little devotion to the Mother of God. Of the number of such as these I do not choose to be, nor do I wish my reader to be so, but rather of the number of those who fully and firmly believe all that can without error be believed of the greatness of Mary, according to the Abbot Rupert, who, amongst the acts of homage most pleasing to this good Mother, places that of firmly believing all that redounds to her honor. If there was nothing else to take away our fear of exceeding in the praises of Mary, St.

Augustine should suffice; for he declares that whatever we may say in praise of Mary is little in comparison with that which she deserves, on account of her dignity of Mother of God; and, moreover, the Church says, in the Mass appointed for her festivals, 'Thou art happy, O sacred Virgin Mary, and most worthy of all praise'."

During the ages of which we speak the people were noted for a childlike confidence in God joined to an intimate whole-souled love for Christ and His Blessed Mother. Little wonder then that God's goodness should manifest itself in exceptional favors bestowed on these fervent souls. The accounts of extraordinary graces were readily accepted and put to good purpose in sermons and public discourses. Without doubt many of the stories have a foundation in fact. Others contain merely an historical kernel that must needs be viewed in its proper setting. Other stories again were handed down from generation to generation and served to embody important truths. Some writer or preacher of distinction may have narrated a story as an allegory or parable such as our Lord Himself employed. The same was repeated by others, embellished and passed on from one to another.

The fundamental idea of all these stories was practically the same. Their object was to depict in graphic coloring the mercy of the Mother of God, and the power of her intercession for the repentant sinner. They serve to bring home perhaps more forcibly than a long doctrinal discourse could do, the mediation of Christ's Blessed Mother, the truth universally accepted, that all God's graces come to us through the hands of the Blessed Virgin Mother.

It would be far from the truth to say that people of the middle ages were influenced merely by sentiment and were only too eager to give credence to the seemingly miraculous. Men like Vincent of Beauvais, James de Voragine, noted for their profound investigations and scientific experiments, could hardly be accused of childish credulity, and yet they employed the narrative of which we speak. Caesarius of

Heisterbach was the object of much unmerited abuse, but he is acknowledged even by Protestant authorities as holding a place in the front rank of the world's historians. Cfr. Dialogus Miraculorum.

There were in those days, as in ours, falsifications, forgeries, exaggerations and historical errors. But would it be just, on that account to demolish everything at one fell swoop as the skeptic is prone to do? A story may not be based on historical fact, but it may nevertheless serve a worthy purpose. Often we discover in such narratives a mine of information which throws light on the history, culture and religious life of the times. Cf. "Analecta Bollandiana" and "Studien zu den mittelalterlichen Marienlegenden" by Mussafia.

The authorities referred to by St. Alphonsus when quoting his various narratives were looked upon in their day, as approved and reliable sources of information. "A critical examination of all he quotes from others would often have been very difficult, and at times impossible," says Cardinal Capecelatro. He wrote for the benefit of the people of his day, and his large experience in directing consciences guided him in selecting matter that would appeal to his reading public. Were he writing for the people of today, no doubt he would omit some of the stories he narrates. The same may be said of St. Augustine, and St. Ambrose, and St. Bernard and St. Francis de Sales. (Vie de St. Alph., tr. by le Monnier.) With this in mind therefore, a number of the original stories have been omitted, and others also quoted by St. Alphonsus put in their place. These substitutions are designated by an asterisk. After a rigorous examination of all the writings of our saint, the Sacred Congregation of Rites declared that "nothing in them was deserving of censure." In the Bull of Canonization we find these words: "The faithful may read his works without any harm whatsoever."

THE STYLE OF THE NARRATIVES

A few words as to the style the saint employs. In the

Introduction to the GLORIES OF MARY we find these words of the holy author: "I have tried to gather together within a brief compass from all the writers at my disposal, the most beautiful and most significant sayings of the Fathers and theologians of the church." These few words gave rise to the opinion in the minds of some that the work was little more than a compilation of choice quotations. Of this opinion the distinguished writer Romano has the following to say: "Far from being a mere compilation, the book resembles a work in mosaic executed by a clever artist; or to use another simile, it is like a work done in enamel, adorned with sparkling jewels so arranged as to exhibit a beautiful harmony of light and shade and color. Such an achievement reveals the skill of the master who planned the work and executed it with consummate skill. The numberless passages culled with remarkable diligence and prodigious labor are fused in the heart of the holy author as in a crucible aglow with the fire of love for the Blessed Mother. Alphonsus lives in his work, proclaiming until the end of time, in accordance with his vow, the glories, and prerogatives of his beloved queen. Not only are the outline of the work and the arrangement of matter to be attributed to St. Alphonsus, but his thoughts, considerations and affections are so interwoven with the text as to impart to the whole his spirit and his life.

Listen to the words of the celebrated Jesuit Lehmkuhl: "His [St. Alphonsus] humble disregard of self appears in almost every line of his writings. We are almost tempted to believe that the Saint purposely tried, by his unassuming style, to keep his remarkable talents and extraordinary knowledge in the background. But this very artifice only discloses to the observant reader his keenness of intellect and his acuteness of judgment. From his ascetical writings there breathes a sacred unction that irresistibly draws the reader to God and His holy love." Stimmen aus Maria-Laach 1887 II. p. 359.

The illustrious Cardinal Dechamps says: "St. Alphonsus

is a holy and learned theologian, and the faithful echo of Tradition for our modern times. His great learning coupled with a prodigious store of useful information render him eminently suited for such a task. He shows an astonishing familiarity with Sacred Scripture and the writings of the Fathers and Doctors of the Church. His very language is redolent of the unction so characteristic of the sources whence his quotations are drawn, and withal it is simple and childlike. Witness the words he addresses to the Virgin Mother. It is the language of the heart, and no one misunderstands that." Cf. L'Infaillibilite etc. C. 8.

Let us conclude these observations with the words of the celebrated Alibrandi quoted in the Acts of Conferring the Doctorate: "St. Alphonsus has given us an excellent work and perfect from every point of view. It is worthy of a man of his great intellectual gifts and profound knowledge. Not only does it serve to promote piety among the faithful, but it provides ample material for theologians and preachers of the Word of God. A cursory reading may convey the impression that it is just an ordinary book. But an attentive study of the contents will reveal a veritable mine of ecclesiastical lore and Marian theology. Often a single sentence or a prayer will exemplify a doctrine that other theologians use a lengthy discourse to explain. The manna of Sacred Scripture seemed to have the property of adapting itself to the taste of him who ate it. The same seems to be true of the GLORIES OF MARY. It satisfies the needs and the taste of the most diverse readers."

When the grave of Alphonsus was opened at Nocera, three fingers of his right hand were taken and sent to Rome. This was the wish of Pope Pius VII. who said: "Let those three fingers that have written so well for the honor of God, of the Blessed Virgin and of religion, be carefully preserved and sent to Rome."

EDITOR.

Salve, Regina, Mater misericordiae! Vita, Dulcedo, et Spes nostra! salve. Ad te clamamus, exsules filii Evae. Ad te suspiramus, gementes et flentes in hac lacrymarum valle. Eia ergo, Advocata nostra! illos tuos misericordes oculos ad nos converte. Et Jesum, benedictum Fructum ventris tui, nobis post hoc exsilium ostende, o clemens, o pia, o dulcis Virgo Maria!

Hail, O Queen, O Mother of mercy! hail our life, our comfort, and our hope. We, the banished children of Eve, cry out unto thee. To thee we send up our sighs, groaning, and weeping in this vale of tears. Come, then, our advocate, and look upon us with those thy pitying eyes. And after this our banishment, show us Jesus, the blessed fruit of thy womb; O merciful, O compassionate, O sweet Virgin Mary.

To Jesus and Mary.

My most loving Redeemer and Lord Jesus Christ. I, Thy miserable servant, well knowing what pleasure he gives Thee who endeavors to exalt Thy most holy Mother, whom Thou lovest so much; knowing, too, how much Thou desirest to see her loved and honored by all, have determined to publish this work of mine, which treats of her glories. I know not, however, to whom I could better recommend it than to Thee, who hast her glory so much at heart. To Thee, therefore, do I dedicate and commend it. Accept this little homage of the love I bear Thee and Thy beloved Mother. Do Thou protect it by showering down on all that read it the light of confidence and flames of love towards this Immaculate Virgin in whom Thou hast placed the hope and whom Thou hast made the refuge of all the redeemed. And as a reward for my poor labor, grant me, I beseech Thee, that love towards Mary, which, by the means of this book, I desire to see enkindled in all that read it.

And now I turn to thee, O my most sweet Lady and Mother Mary. Thou well knowest that, after Jesus, I have placed my entire hope of salvation in thee; for I acknowledge that everything good—my conversion, my vocation to renounce the world and all the other graces that I have received from God—all were given me through thy means. Thou knowest that in order to see thee loved by all as thou deservest, and also as some mark of gratitude for the many benefits thou hast conferred upon me, I have always endeavored in my sermons, in public and in private, to insinuate into all thy sweet and salutary devotion. I hope to continue doing so until my last breath, but my advanced years and feeble health admonish me that I am near the end of my pilgrimage and my entry into eternity; and therefore I wish, before dying, to leave this book to the world, in order that in my place it may continue to preach thee, and encourage others to announce thy glories, and the tender compassion thou showest to thy clients. I trust, my most beloved Queen, that this little gift, which is one of love, though far beneath thy merits, will yet be acceptable to thy most gracious heart. Extend, then, that most sweet hand with which thou hast drawn me from the world and delivered me from hell, and accept it and protect it as thine own. But at the same time thou must know that I expect a reward for my little offering; and that is, that from this day forward I may love thee more than ever, and that every one into whose hands this work may fall may at once be inflamed with love of thee; and that his desire of loving thee, and of seeing thee loved by others, may be increased, so that he may labor with all affection to preach and promote, as far as he can, thy praises, and confidence in thy most powerful intercession. Amen.

Thy most loving though unworthy servant,

ALPHONSUS DE LIGUORI.

TO THE READER.

In order that my present work may not be condemned by the over-critical, I think it well to explain certain propositions that will be found in it, and which may seem hazardous, or perhaps obscure. I have noticed some, and should others attract your attention, charitable reader, I beg that you will understand them according to the rules of sound theology and the doctrine of the holy Roman Catholic Church, of which I declare myself a most obedient son.

In the Introduction, page 32, referring to the fifth chapter of this work, I say that it is the will of God that all graces should come to us by the hands of Mary. Now, this is indeed a most consoling truth for souls tenderly devoted to our most Blessed Lady, and for poor sinners who wish to repent.

Nor should this opinion be looked upon as contrary to sound doctrine, since the Father of theology, St. Augustine,[1] in common with most writers, says, that Mary co-operated by her charity in the spiritual birth of all members of the Church. A celebrated writer, and one who cannot be accused of exaggeration or of misguided devotion, says,[2] "that it was, properly speaking, on Mount Calvary that Jesus formed his Church;" and then it is evident that the Blessed Virgin co-operated in

[1] "Mater quidem spiritu, non capitis nostri, quod est ipse Salvator, ex quo magis illa spiritaliter nata est; quia omnes, qui in eum crediderint, in quibus et ipsa est, recte filii Sponsi appellantur; sed plane mater membrorum ejus, quod nos sumus, quia cooperata est charitate, ut fideles in ecclesia nascerentur, quæ illius capitis membra sunt." —*Lib. de Sancta Virginitate*, cap. vi.

[2] *Nicole, Instr. sur la Sal. Ang.* ch. 2.

2

a most excellent and especial manner in the accomplish-ment of this work. And in the same way it can be said, that though she brought forth the Head of the Church, Jesus Christ, without pain, she did not bring forth the body of this Head without very great suffering; and so it was on Mount Calvary that Mary began, in an espe-cial manner, to be the Mother of the whole Church. And now, to say all in a few words: God, to glorify the Mother of the Redeemer, has so determined and dis-posed that of her great charity she should intercede in behalf of all those for whom his divine Son paid and offered the superabundant price of his precious blood in which alone ? is our salvation, life, and resurrection."[1]

On this doctrine, and on all that is in accordance with it, I ground my propositions[2]—propositions which the saints have not feared to assert in their tender colloquies with Mary and fervent discourses in her honor. Hence St. Sophronius says, as quoted by the celebrated Vin-cent Contenson, that "the plenitude of all grace which is in Christ came into Mary, though in a different way;"[3] meaning that the plenitude of grace was in Christ, as the Head from which it flows, as from its source; and in Mary, as in the neck through which it flows. This opinion is clearly confirmed and taught by the angelic Doctor, St. Thomas, who says: "Of the three ways in which the Blessed Virgin is full of grace, the third is that she is so for its transfusion into all men; and then he adds: "This plenitude is great in any saint when there is as much grace as would suffice for the sal-vation of many, but it is in its highest degree when

[1] "In quo est salus, vita et resurrectio nostra."—*Off. de Exalt. SS. Cruc.*

[2] In chapters vi., § 2; vii.; viii., § 2; ix.

[3] "In Christo fuit plenitudo gratiæ, sicut in capite influente; in Maria vero, sicut in collo transfundente."—*Theol. ment. et cord.* L. 10, d. 6. c. 1. SD. 2.

there is as much as would suffice for the salvation of the world; and it was in this degree in Christ and in the Blessed Virgin: for in all dangers thou canst obtain salvation of this glorious Virgin; and therefore it is said in the sacred Canticles that *a thousand bucklers*, that is to say, means of protection against dangers, *hang upon it.* Also, in every work of virtue thou canst have her for thy helper, for she says in the words of Ecclesiasticus, *In me is all hope of life and virtue.*[1]

[1] " Dicitur autem beata Virgo plena gratiæ, quantum ad tria . . . Tertio, quantum ad refusionem in omnes homines. Magnum enim est in quolibet sancto, quando habet tantum de gratia, quod sufficit ad salutem multorum: sed quando haberet tantum, quod sufficeret ad salutem omnium hominum de mundo, hoc esset maximum, et hoc est in Christo et in Beata Virgine. Nam in omni periculo potes salutem obtinere ab ipsa Virgine gloriosa. Unde Canticorum iv. 4, 'mille clypei,' id est, remedia contra pericula, 'pendent ex ea.' Item, in omni opere virtutis potes eam habere in adjutorium, et ideo dicit ipsa Ecclesiastici xxiv. 25: 'In me omnis spes vitæ et virtutis.'"—*Expos. in Salut. Ang.*

INTRODUCTION

WHICH SHOULD BE READ.

My beloved reader and brother in Mary : Since the devotion that led me to write, and moves you to read, this book makes us happy children of the same good Mother, should you hear it remarked that I might have spared myself the labor, as there are already so many celebrated and learned works on the same subject, I beg that you will reply, in the words of the Abbot Francone, that "the praise of Mary is an inexhaustible fount: the more it is enlarged the fuller it gets, and the more you fill it so much the more is it enlarged."[1] In short, this Blessed Virgin is so great and so sublime that the more she is praised the more there remains to praise; so much so, says an ancient writer, "that if all the tongues of men were put together, and even if each of their members was changed into a tongue, they would not suffice to praise her as much as she deserves."[2]

I have seen innumerable works of all sizes which treat of the Glories of Mary; but finding that they were rare, voluminous, or did not answer the object I had in view, I endeavored to collect, from as many authors as I could lay my hands on, the choicest passages, extracted from Fathers and theologians, and those which seemed to me to be the most to the point, and have put them together in this book, in order that the devout may with little trouble and expense be able to inflame themselves with

[1] "Laus Mariæ fons est indeficiens, qui, quanto longius extenditur, tanto amplius impletur, et quanto amplius impletur, tanto latius dilatatur."—*De Grat. Dei*, lib. vii.

[2] "Etsi omnium nostrum membra verterentur in linguas, eam laudare sufficeret nullus."—*Serm*. 208, *E. B. App.*

the love of Mary, and more particularly to furnish priests with matter for their sermons, wherewith to excite others to devotion towards this divine Mother.

Worldly lovers often speak of those whom they love, and praise them, in order that the object of their affections may be praised and extolled by others. There are some who pretend to be lovers of Mary, and yet seldom either speak of her or endeavor to excite others to love her: their love cannot be great. It is not thus that true lovers of this amiable Lady act; they desire to praise her on all occasions, and to see her loved by the whole world, and never lose an opportunity, either in public or in private, of enkindling in the hearts of others those blessed flames of love with which they themselves burn towards their beloved Queen.

That every one may be persuaded how important it is, both for his own good and that of others, to promote devotion towards Mary, it is useful to know what theologians say on the subject.

St. Bonaventure says that those who make a point of announcing to others the glories of Mary are certain of heaven; and this opinion is confirmed by Richard of St. Laurence, who declares "that to honor this Queen of Angels is to gain eternal life;"[1] and he adds, "that this most gracious Lady will honor in the next world those who honor her in this."[2] And who is ignorant of the promise made by Mary herself, in the words of Ecclesiastes, to those who endeavor to make her known and loved here below, *they that explain me shall have life everlasting ;*[3] for this passage is applied to her by the Church, in the office of the Immaculate Conception. "Rejoice, then," exclaims St. Bonaventure (who did so much to

---

[1] "Honorare Mariam, thesaurizare est sibi vitam æternam."—*De Laud. B. M. V.* l. 2, p. 1.

[2] "Glorificabit in futuro honorificantes se in præsenti."—*Ib.*

[3] "Qui elucidant me, vitam æternam habebunt."—*Ecclus.* xxiv. 31.

make the glories of Mary known), "rejoice, my soul, and be glad in her; for many good things are prepared for those who praise her;"[1] and he says that the whole of the sacred Scriptures speak in praise of Mary: let us therefore always with our hearts and tongues honor this divine Mother, in order that we may be conducted by her into the kingdom of the blessed.[2]

We learn from the revelations of St. Bridget, that the blessed Bishop Emingo was in the habit of always beginning his sermons with the praises of Mary. One day the Blessed Virgin herself appeared to the saint, and desired her to tell him that in consequence of his pious practice, "she would be his mother, that he would die a holy death, and that she would herself present his soul to God;"[3] he died like a saint in the act of praying, and in the most heavenly peace. Mary also appeared to a Dominican friar, who always concluded his sermons by speaking of her; when on his deathbed the Blessed Virgin defended him from the devils, consoled him, and then she herself carried off his happy soul.[4] The devout Thomas à Kempis represents to us Mary recommending a soul who had honored her to her Son, and saying, "My most loving Son, have mercy on the soul of this servant of Thine, who loved and extolled me."[5]

Next, as to the advantage of this devotion for all, St. Anselm says, that as the most sacred womb of Mary was the means of salvation for sinners, the hearing of her praises must necessarily convert them, and thus also be

[1] "Exsulta, anima mea, et lætare in illa; quia multa bona sunt laudatoribus præparata."—*Psalt. B. V.* ps. 43.

[2] "Si enim omnes Scripturæ loquuntur de ea, Deiparam perpetuo contemplemur corde, et lingua celebremus, ut ab ipsa ad gaudia perpetua perducamur."—*Paciucch. in Ps.* 86, *exe.* 25.

[3] *Rev. extr.* c. 104.—*Rev.* l. 4, c. 125.

[4] *Auriem. Aff. scamb.* p. 1, c. 13.

[5] "Fili mi amantissime, miserere animæ famuli tui, amatoris et laudatoris mei."—*Ad Nov.* s. 21.

a means of their salvation; "how can it be otherwise than that the salvation of sinners should come from the remembrance of her praises, whose womb was made the way through which the Saviour came to save sinners ?"[1] And if the opinion is true, and I consider it as indubitably so (as I shall show in the fifth chapter), that all graces are dispensed by Mary, and that all who are saved are saved only by the means of this divine Mother, it is a necessary consequence that the salvation of all depends upon preaching Mary, and exciting all to confidence in her intercession. It is well known that it was thus that St. Bernardine of Sienna sanctified Italy, and that St. Dominic converted so many provinces. St. Louis Bertrand never omitted in his sermons to exhort all to love Mary; and many others have done the same.

I find that Father Paul Segneri the younger, who was a very celebrated missioner, in every mission preached a sermon on devotion to Mary, and always called it his beloved sermon. And in our own missions, in which it is an inviolable rule to do the same, we can attest, with all truth, that in most cases no sermon is more profitable, or produces so much compunction in the hearts of the people, as the one on the mercy of Mary. I say, on her mercy; for, in the words of St. Bernard, "we praise her virginity, we admire her humility; but because we are poor sinners, mercy attracts us more and tastes sweeter; we embrace mercy more lovingly; we remember it oftener, and invoke it more earnestly;"[2] and for this reason I here leave other authors to describe the other prerogatives of Mary, and confine myself for the most part to that of her mercy and powerful interces-

---

[1] "Quomodo fieri potest, ut ex memoria laudis ejus salus non proveniat peccatorum, cujus uterus factus est via ad sanandum peccatores ?"—*De Excell. V.* c. 1.

[2] "Laudamus virginitatem, humilitatem miramur; sed miseris sapit dulcius misericordia; misericordiam amplectimur carius, recordamur sæpius, crebrius invocamus."—*In Assumpt.* s. 4.

sion; having collected, as far as I was able, and with the labor of many years, all that the holy Fathers and the most celebrated writers have said on this subject; and as I find that the mercy and power of the most Blessed Virgin are admirably portrayed in the prayer "Salve Regina," the recital of which is made obligatory for the greater part of the year on all the clergy, secular and regular, I shall divide and explain this most devout prayer in separate chapters. In addition to this, I thought that I should be giving pleasure to Mary's devout clients, by adding discourses on the principal festivals and virtues of this divine Mother, and by placing at the end of the work the devotions and pious practices most used by her servants, and most approved of by the Church.

Devout reader, should this work, as I trust it will, prove acceptable to you, I beg that you will recommend me to the Blessed Virgin, that she may give me great confidence in her protection. Ask this grace for me; and I promise you, whoever you may be, that I will ask the same for you who do me this charity. O, blessed are they who bind themselves with love and confidence to these two anchors of salvation, Jesus and Mary. Certainly, they will not be lost. Let us then both say, devout reader, with the pious Alphonsus Rodriguez, "Jesus and Mary, my most sweet loves, for you may I suffer, for you may I die; grant that I may be in all things yours and in nothing mine." [1] Let us love Jesus and Mary, and become saints; we can neither expect nor hope anything better. Farewell, then, until we meet in Paradise, at the feet of this most sweet Mother and of this most loving Son; there to praise them, to love them face to face for all eternity. Amen.

[1] "Jesu et Maria, amores mei dulcissimi! pro vobis patiar, pro vobis moriar; sim totus vester, sim nihil meus."

PART THE FIRST.

Explanation of the Salve Regina.

THE MANY AND ABUNDANT GRACES DISPENSED BY THE MOTHER OF GOD TO HER DEVOUT CLIENTS.

CHAPTER I.

Salve, Regina, Mater Misericordiæ!

HAIL, HOLY QUEEN, MOTHER OF MERCY!

MARY, OUR QUEEN, OUR MOTHER.

I.

How great should be our Confidence in Mary, who is the Queen of Mercy.

As the glorious Virgin Mary has been raised to the dignity of Mother of the King of kings, it is not without reason that the Church honors her, and wishes her to be honored by all, with the glorious title of Queen.

"If the Son is a king," says St. Athanasius, "the Mother who begot him is rightly and truly considered a Queen and Sovereign." [1]   "No sooner had Mary," says St. Bernardine of Sienna, "consented to be Mother of the Eternal Word, than she merited by this consent to be made Queen of the world and of all creatures." [2]

---

[1] "Si ipse Rex est, qui natus est de Virgine, Mater quæ eum genuit, Regina et Domina proprie ac vere censetur."—*Serm. de Deip.*

[2] "Hæc autem Virgo, in illo consensu, meruit primatum orbis dominium mundi, sceptrum regni super omnes creaturas."—*Pro fest. V. M.* s. 5 c. 3.

"Since the flesh of Mary," remarks the Abbot Arnold of Chartres, " was not different from that of Jesus, how can the royal dignity of the Son be denied to the Mother?"[1] "Hence we must consider the glory of the Son, not only as being common to his Mother, but as one with her."[2]

And if Jesus is the King of the universe, Mary is also its Queen. "And as Queen," says the Abbot Rupert, "she possesses, by right, the whole kingdom of her Son."[3]   Hence St. Bernardine of Sienna concludes that " as many creatures as there are who serve God, so many they are who serve Mary: for as angels and men, and all things that are in heaven and on earth, are subject to the empire of God, so are they also under the dominion of Mary!"[4]   The Abbot Guerricus, addressing himself to the divine Mother on this subject, says: " Continue, Mary, continue to dispose with confidence of the riches of thy Son; act as Queen, Mother and Spouse of the King: for to thee belongs dominion and power over all creatures!"[5]

Mary, then, is a Queen: but, for our common consolation, be it known that she is a Queen so sweet, clement, and so ready to help us in our miseries, that the holy Church wills that we should salute her in this prayer under the title of Queen of Mercy.

---

[1] " Nec a dominatione et potestate filii Mater potest esse sejuncta: una est Mariæ et Christi caro."— *De Laud. B. Virg.*

[2] " Filii gloriam cum Matre non tam communem judico, quam eamdem."—*Ibid.*

[3] " Regina cœlorum, totum jure possidens Filii regnum."—*In Cant.* l. 3

[4] " Tot creaturæ serviunt gloriosæ Virgini, quot serviunt Trinitati; omnes nempe creaturæ, sive angeli sive homines, et omnia quæ sunt in cœlo et in terra, quia omnia sunt divino imperio subjugata, gloriosæ Virgini sunt subjectæ."—*Pro Fest. V. M.* s. 5, c. 6.

[5] " Perge, Maria! perge secura in bonis filii tui; fiducialiter age tamquam Regina, Mater regis et sponsa; tibi debetur regnum et potestas."—*In Ass. B. M.* s. 3.

"The title of Queen," remarks Blessed Albert the Great,[1] "differs from that of Empress, which implies severity and rigor, in signifying compassion and charity towards the poor." "The greatness of kings and queens," says Seneca, "consists in relieving the wretched,"[2] and whereas tyrants, when they reign, have their own good in view, kings should have that of their subjects at heart. For this reason it is that, at their consecration, kings have their heads anointed with oil, which is the symbol of mercy, to denote that, as kings, they should, above all things, nourish in their hearts feelings of compassion and benevolence towards their subjects.

Kings should, then, occupy themselves principally in works of mercy, but not so as to forget the just punishments that are to be inflicted on the guilty. It is, however, not thus with Mary, who, although a Queen, is not a queen of justice, intent on the punishment of the wicked, but a queen of mercy, intent only on commiserating and pardoning sinners. And this is the reason for which the Church requires that we should expressly call her "the Queen of Mercy." The great Chancellor of Paris, John Gerson, in his commentary on the words of David, *These two things have I heard, that power belongeth to God, and mercy to thee, O Lord,*[3] says that the kingdom of God, consisting in justice and mercy, was divided by our Lord: the kingdom of justice he reserved for himself, and that of mercy he yielded to Mary, ordaining at the same time that all mercies that are dispensed to men should pass through the hands of Mary, and be disposed of by her at will. These are Gerson's own words: "The kingdom of God consists in power and mercy; reserving

---

[1] *Super Miss.* q. 162.

[2] "Hoc reges habent magnificum, prodesse miseris."—*Medea,* act. 2.

[3] "Duo hæc audivi; quia potestas Dei est, et tibi, Domine, misericordia."—*Ps.* lxi. 12.

power to himself, he, in some way, yielded the empire
of mercy to his Mother."[1]   This is confirmed by St.
Thomas, in his preface to the Canonical Epistles, saying,
"that when the Blessed Virgin conceived the Eternal
Word in her womb, and brought him forth, she obtained
half the kingdom of God; so that she is Queen of Mercy,
as Jesus Christ is King of Justice."[2]

The Eternal Father made Jesus Christ the King of
justice, and consequently universal Judge of the world:
and therefore the royal prophet sings: *Give to the King
Thy judgment, O God, and to the King's Son Thy justice.*[3]
Here a learned interpreter takes up the sentence, and
says: "O Lord, Thou hast given justice to Thy Son, because Thou hast given mercy to the King's Mother."[4]
And, on this subject, St. Bonaventure, paraphrasing the
words of David, thus interprets them: "Give to the
King Thy judgment, O God, and Thy mercy to the
Queen his Mother."[5]   Ernest, Archbishop of Prague,
also remarks, "that the Eternal Father gave the office of
judge and avenger to the Son, and that of showing mercy
and relieving the necessitous to the Mother."[6]   This was
foretold by the prophet David himself; for he says that
God (so to speak) consecrated Mary Queen of mercy,
anointing her with the oil of gladness: *God hath anointed*

[1] "Regnum Dei consistit in potestate et misericordia: potestate
Domino remanente, cessit quodammodo misericordiæ pars Christi
Matri regnanti."—*Super Magn.* tr. 4.

[2] "Quando filium Dei in utero concepit, et postmodum peperit, sic
dimidiam partem regni Dei impetravit, ut ipsa sit Regina misericordiæ, cujus Filius est Rex justitiæ."

[3] "Deus, judicium tuum Regi da, et justitiam tuam filio Regis."—
Ps. lxxi. 2

[4] "Quia misericordiam tuam dedisti Matri Regis."

[5] "Deus judicium tuum Regi da, et misericordiam tuam Reginæ,
Matri ejus."

[6] "Pater omne judicium dedit Filio, misericordiæ vero officium
dedit Matri."—*Marial.* c. 127.

thee with the oil of gladness.[1]   In order that we miserable
children of Adam might rejoice, remembering that in
heaven we have this great Queen, overflowing with the
unction of mercy and compassion towards us; and thus
we can say with St. Bonaventure, "O Mary, thou art full
of the unction of mercy and of the oil of compassion;"[2]
therefore God has anointed thee with the oil of gladness.

And how beautifully does not Blessed Albert the Great
apply to this subject the history of Queen Esther, who
was herself a great type of our Queen Mary!

We read, in the fourth chapter of the Book of Esther,
that in the reign of Assuerus, a decree was issued, by
which all Jews were condemned to death. Mardochai,
who was one of the condemned, addressed himself to
Esther, in order that she might interpose with Assuerus,
and obtain the revocation of the decree, and thus be the
salvation of all. At first Esther declined the office, fearing that such a request might irritate the king still more;
but Mardochai reproved her, sending her word that she
was not to think only of saving herself, for God had
placed her on the throne to obtain the salvation of all
the Jews: *Think not that thou mayest save thy life only, because
thou art in the king's house, more than all the Jews.*[3] Thus did
Mardochai address Queen Esther. And so can we poor
sinners address our Queen Mary, should she show any
repugnance to obtain of God our delivery from the chastisement we have justly deserved: "Think not, O Lady,
that God has raised thee to the dignity of Queen of the
world, only to provide for thy good; but in order that,
being so great, thou mightest be better able to compassionate and assist us miserable creatures."

[1] "Unxit te Deus . . . oleo lætitiæ."—*Ps.* xliv. 8.

[2] "Maria plena unctione misericordiæ, plena oleo pietatis."—*Spec.
B. M. V. lect.* 7.

[3] "Ne putes, quod animam tuam tantum liberes, quia in domo regis
es præ cunctis Judæis."—*Esth.* iv. 13.

As soon as Assuerus saw Esther standing before him, he asked her, with love, what she came to seek. *What is thy request?* The Queen replied, *If I have found favor in thy sight, O King, give me my people, for which I request.*[1] Assuerus granted her request, and immediately ordered the revocation of the decree. And now, if Assuerus, through love for Esther, granted, at her request, salvation to the Jews, how can God refuse the prayers of Mary, loving her immensely as he does, when she prays for poor miserable sinners, who recommend themselves to her, and says to him, " My King and my God, if ever I have found favor in Thy sight" (though the divine Mother well knows that she was the blessed, the holy one, the only one of the human race who found the grace lost by all mankind; well does she know that she is the beloved one of her Lord, loved more than all the saints and angels together), *give me my people for which I ask.* If thou lovest me, she says, "give me, O Lord, these sinners, for whom I entreat Thee." Is it possible that God should refuse her? And who is ignorant of the power of the prayers of Mary with God? *The law of clemency is on her tongue.*[2] Each of her prayers is, as it were, an established law for our Lord, that he should show mercy to all for whom she intercedes. St. Bernard asks why the Church calls Mary " the Queen of Mercy"? And he replies, that " it is because we believe that she opens the abyss of the mercy of God to whomsoever she wills, when she wills, and as she wills; so that there is no sinner, however great, who is lost if Mary protects him."[3]

[1] " Quæ est petitio tua? . . . Si inveni gratiam in oculis tuis, o rex! Dona mihi . . . populum meum pro quo obsecro."—*Esth.* vii. 2, 3.

[2] " Lex clementiæ in lingua ejus."—*Prov.* xxxi. 26.

[3] " Quod divinæ pietatis abyssum, cui vult, quando vult, et quomodo vult, creditur aperire; ut quivis enormis peccator non pereat, cui Sancta Sanctorum patrocinii sui suffragia præstat."—*In Salve Reg.* s. I.

But perhaps we may fear that Mary would not deign
to interpose for some sinners, because they are so over-
loaded with crimes? Or perhaps we ought to be over-
awed at the majesty and holiness of this great Queen?
" No," says St. Gregory VII.; "for the higher and more
holy she is, the greater is her sweetness and compassion
towards sinners, who have recourse to her with the desire to amend their lives." [1] Kings and queens, with their
ostentation of majesty, inspire terror, and cause their
subjects to fear to approach them: but what fear, says
St. Bernard, can the miserable have to approach this
Queen of Mercy, for she inspires no terror, and shows no
severity, to those who come to her, but is all sweetness
and gentleness. " Why should human frailty fear to go
to Mary? In her there is no austerity, nothing terrible:
she is all sweetness, offering milk and wool to all." [2]
Mary is not only willing to give, but she herself offers
milk and wool to all: the milk of mercy to animate our
confidence, and the wool of her protection against the
thunderbolts of divine justice.

Suetonius [3] relates of the Emperor Titus that he could
never refuse a favor, so much so that he sometimes
promised more than he could grant, and when admon-
ished of this he replied, that a prince should never send
away any person whom he admitted to his audience dissatisfied. Titus spoke thus, but in reality he must often
have deceived or failed in his promises. Our Queen
cannot deceive, and can obtain all that she wills for her
clients. Moreover, " our Lord has given her so benign
and compassionate a heart," says Lanspergius, " that she

---

[1] " Maria, quanto altior et sanctior, tanto clementior et dulcior circa
conversos peccatores."—*Lib.* i. *Ep.* 47.

[2] " Quid ad Mariam accedere trepidet humana fragilitas? nihil austerum in ea, nihil terribile; tota suavis est, omnibus offerens lac et
lanam."—*In Sign. Magn.*

[3] *Tit.* c. 8.

3

cannot send away any one dissatisfied who prays to her."[1] But how, to use the words of St. Bonaventure, canst thou, O Mary, who art the Queen of Mercy, refuse to succor the miserable? And "who," asks the saint, "are the subjects for mercy, if not the miserable? And since thou art the Queen of Mercy," he continues, "and I am the most miserable of sinners, it follows that I am the first of thy subjects. How, then, O Lady, canst thou do otherwise than exercise thy mercy on me?"[2] Have pity on us, then, O Queen of Mercy, and take charge of our salvation.

"Say not, O holy Virgin," exclaims St. George of Nicomedia, "that thou canst not assist us on account of the number of our sins, for thy power and thy compassion are such, that no number of sins, however great, can outweigh them. Nothing resists thy power, for our common Creator, honoring thee as his Mother, considering thy glory as his own:" and the Son, "exulting in it, fulfils thy petitions as if he were paying a debt;"[3] meaning thereby, that although Mary is under an infinite obligation to the Son for having chosen her to be his Mother, yet it cannot be denied that the Son is under great obligation to her for having given him his humanity; and therefore Jesus, to pay as it were what he owes to Mary, and glorying in her glory, honors her in a special manner by listening to and granting all her petitions.

How great, then, should be our confidence in this

---

[1] "Ita benigna est, ut neminem a se redire tristem sinat."—*Alloq.* l. 1, p. 4, *can.* 12.

[2] "Tu es Regina misericordiæ, et qui misericordiæ subditi nisi miseri? Tu Regina misericordiæ es, et ego miserrimus peccatorum, subditorum maximus; rege nos ergo, o Regina misericordiæ!"— *Paciucch. In Salve Reg. exc.* 2.

[3] "Habes vires insuperabiles, ne clementiam tuam superet multitudo peccatorum. Nihil tuæ resistit potentiæ; tuam enim gloriam Creator existimat esse propriam. Et Filius in ea exsultans, quasi exsolvens debitum, implet petitiones tuas."—*Or. de Ingr. B. V.*

Queen, knowing her great power with God, and that she is so rich and full of mercy, that there is no one living on the earth who does not partake of her compassion and favor. This was revealed by our Blessed Lady herself to St. Bridget, saying, "I am the Queen of heaven and the Mother of Mercy; I am the joy of the just, and the door through which sinners are brought to God. There is no sinner on earth so accursed as to be deprived of my mercy; for all, if they receive nothing else through my intercession, receive the grace of being less tempted by the devils than they would otherwise have been."[1] "No one," she adds, "unless the irrevocable sentence has been pronounced" (that is, the one pronounced on the damned), "is so cast off by God that he will not return to him, and enjoy his mercy, if he invokes my aid."[2] "I am called by all the Mother of Mercy, and truly the mercy of my Son towards men has made me thus merciful towards them;"[3] and she concludes by saying, "and therefore miserable will he be, and miserable will he be to all eternity, who, in this life, having it in his power to invoke me, who am so compassionate to all, and so desirous to assist sinners, is miserable enough not to invoke me, and so is damned."[4]

Let us, then, have recourse, and always have recourse, to this most sweet Queen, if we would be certain of salvation; and if we are alarmed and disheartened at the

[1] " Ego sum Regina cœli, ego mater misericordiæ: ego justorum gaudium, et aditus peccatorum ad Deum. Nullus est adeo maledictus, qui, quamdiu vivit, careat misericordia mea; quia propter me levius tentatur a dæmonibus quam aliter tentaretur."

[2] " Nullus ita alienatus est a Deo, nisi omnino fuerit maledictus, qui, si me invocaverit, non revertatur ad Deum; et habebit misericordiam."—*Rev.* l. 6, c. 10.

[3] " Ego vocor ab omnibus mater misericordiæ; vere, misericordia Filii mei misericordem me fecit."—*Ibid.* l. 2, c. 23.

[4] " Ideo miser erit, qui ad misericordiam, cum possit, non accedit." —*Ibid.*

sight of our sins, let us remember that it is in order to save the greatest and most abandoned sinners, who recommend themselves to her, that Mary is made the Queen of Mercy. Such have to be her crown in heaven; according to the words addressed to her by her Divine Spouse: *Come from Libanus, my spouse ; come from Libanus, come : thou shalt be crowned ; . . . from the dens of the lions from the mountains of the leopards.*[1] And what are these dens of beasts, but miserable sinners, whose souls have become the home of sin, the most frightful monster that can be found. "With such souls," says the Abbot Rupert, addressing our Blessed Lady, " saved by thy means, O great Queen Mary, wilt thou be crowned in heaven; for their salvation will form a diadem worthy of, and well-becoming, a Queen of Mercy."[2] On this subject read the following

EXAMPLE.

We read, in the life of Sister Catharine of St. Augustine, that in the place where she resided, there was a woman, of the name of Mary, who in her youth was a sinner, and in her old age continued so obstinate in wickedness, that she was driven out of the city, and reduced to live in a secluded cave; there she died, half consumed by disease, without the sacraments, and was consequently interred in a field like a beast. Sister Catharine, who always recommended the souls of those who departed from this world, with great fervor to God, on hearing the unfortunate end of this poor, poor old woman, never thought of praying for her, and she looked upon her (as did every one else) as irrevocably lost. One day, four years afterwards, a suffering soul

---

[1] " Veni de Libano, Sponsa mea, veni de Libano, veni, coronaberis . . . . de cubilibus leonum, de montibus pardorum."—*Cant.* iv. 8.

[2] " De talium leonum cubilibus tu coronaberis; . . eorum salus corona tua erit."—*In Cant.* l. iii.

appeared to her, and exclaimed: "How unfortunate is my lot, Sister Catharine! thou recommendest the souls of all those that die to God: on my soul alone thou hast not compassion." "And who art thou?" asked the servant of God. "I am," she replied, "that poor Mary who died in the cave." "And art thou saved?" said Catharine. "Yes," she answered, "by the mercy of the Blessed Virgin Mary." "And how?" "When I saw myself at the point of death, loaded with sins, and abandoned by all, I had recourse to the Mother of God, saying, 'Lady, thou art the refuge of abandoned creatures; behold me, at this moment, abandoned by all; thou art my only hope; thou alone canst help me: have pity on me.' The Blessed Virgin obtained, for me the grace to make an act of contrition. I died, and am saved; and besides this, she my Queen obtained for me another favor, that my purgatory should be shortened, by enduring, in intensity, that which otherwise would have lasted for many years: I now want only a few masses to be entirely delivered; I beg thee to have them said; and on my part, I promise always to pray for thee to God and to Mary." Sister Catharine immediately had the masses said; and after a few days that soul again appeared to her, shining like the sun, and said: "I thank thee, Catharine: behold, I go to Paradise, to sing the mercies of my God, and to pray for thee."

Prayer

O, Mother of my God, and my Lady Mary; as a beggar, all wounded and sore, presents himself before a great queen, so do I present myself before thee, who art the Queen of heaven and earth. From the lofty throne on which thou sittest, disdain not, I implore thee, to cast thine eyes on me, a poor sinner. God has made thee so rich that thou mightest assist the poor, and has constituted thee Queen of Mercy in order that thou mightest relieve the miserable. Behold me then, and pity me: behold me and abandon me not, until thou seest me changed from a sinner into a saint. I know well that I merit nothing ; nay more, that I deserve, on account of my ingratitude, to be deprived of the graces that, through thy means, I have already received from God. But thou, who art the Queen of Mercy, seekest not merits, but miseries, in order to help the needy. But who is more needy than I ? O, exalted Virgin, well do I know that thou, who art Queen of the universe, art already my queen ; yet am I determined to dedicate myself more especially to thy service, in order that thou mayest dispose of me as thou pleasest. Therefore do I address thee in the words of St. Bonaventure : "Do thou govern me, O my Queen, and leave me not to myself."[1] Command me ; employ me as thou wilt, and chastise me when I do not obey ; for the chastisements that come from thy hands will be to me pledges of salvation. I would rather be thy servant than the ruler of the earth. *I am thine ; save me.*[2] Accept me, O Mary, for thine own, and as thine, take charge of my salvation. I will no longer be mine; to thee do I give myself. If, during the time past I have served thee ill, and lost so many occasions of honoring thee, for the future I will be one of thy most loving and faithful servants. I am determined that from this day forward no one shall surpass me in honoring and loving thee, my most amiable Queen. This I promise ; and this, with thy help, I hope to execute. Amen.

II.

How much our Confidence in Mary should be Increased because she is our Mother.

It is not without a meaning, or by chance, that Mary's clients call her Mother; and indeed they seem unable to invoke her under any other name, and never tire of calling her Mother. Mother, yes! for she is truly our Mother; not indeed carnally, but spiritually; of our souls and of our salvation.

Sin, by depriving our souls of divine grace, deprived

---

[1] "Domina, me tuæ dominationi committo, ut me plenarie regas et gubernes; non mihi me relinquas."—*Stim. div. Am.* p. 3, c. 19.

[2] "Tuus sum ego, salvum me fac."—*Ps.* cxviii. 94.

them also of life. Jesus our Redeemer, with an excess
of mercy and love, came to restore this life by his own
death on the cross, as he himself declared: *I am come
that they may have life, and may have it more abundantly.*[1]
He says more abundantly; for, according to theologians,
the benefit of redemption far exceeded the injury done
by Adam's sin. So that by reconciling us with God he
made himself the Father of souls in the law of grace, as
it was foretold by the prophet Isaias: *He shall be called
the Father of the world to come, the Prince of Peace.*[2] But
if Jesus is the Father of our souls, Mary is also their
Mother; for she, by giving us Jesus, gave us true life;
and afterwards, by offering the life of her Son on Mount
Calvary for our salvation, she brought us forth to the
life of grace.

On two occasions, then, according to the holy Fathers,
Mary became our spiritual Mother.

The first, according to Blessed Albert the Great,[3] was
when she merited to conceive in her virginal womb the
Son of God. St. Bernardine of Sienna says the same
thing more distinctly, for he tells us, "that when at the
Annunciation the most Blessed Virgin gave the consent
which was expected by the Eternal Word before becoming her Son, she from that moment asked our salvation
of God with intense ardor, and took it to heart in such
a way, that from that moment, as a most loving mother,
she bore us in her womb."[4]

In the second chapter of St. Luke, the Evangelist,

---

[1] "Ego veni ut vitam habeant, et abundantius habeant."—*John*,
x. 10.

[2] "Pater futuri sæculi, princeps pacis."—*Is.* ix. 6.

[3] *De Laud. B. M.* l. 6, c. 1.

[4] "Virgo per hunc consensum, in Incarnatione filii omnium electorum salutem viscerosissime expetiit et procuravit; et omnium salva-
tioni per hunc consensum se dedicavit, ita ut ex tunc omnes in suis
visceribus bajularet, tanquam verissima mater filios suos."—*Pro Fest.
V. M.* s. 8, a. 2, c. 2.

speaking of the birth of our Blessed Redeemer, says
that Mary *brought forth her first-born son.*[1]   Then, remarks
an author, "since the Evangelist asserts that on this
occasion the most Holy Virgin brought forth her first-
born, must we suppose that she had afterwards other
children ?"   But then he replies to his own question,
saying, "that as it is of faith that Mary had no other
children according to the flesh than Jesus, she must
have had other spiritual children, and we are those children."   This was revealed by our Lord to St. Gertrude,[2]
who was one day reading the above text, and was per-
plexed and could not understand how Mary, being only
the Mother of Jesus, could be said to have brought forth
her first-born.   God explained it to her, saying, that
Jesus was Mary's first-born according to the flesh, but
that all mankind were her second-born according to the
spirit.[3]

From what has been said, we can understand that passage of the sacred Canticles: *Thy belly is like a heap of
wheat, set about with lilies,*[4] and which applies to Mary.
And it is explained by St. Ambrose, who says: "That
although in the most pure womb of Mary there was but
one grain of corn, which was Jesus Christ, yet it is
called a heap of wheat, because all the elect were vir-
tually contained in it;" and as Mary was also to be their
Mother, in bringing forth Jesus, he was truly and is
called the first-born of many brethren.[5]   And the Abbot

[1] "Peperit Filium suum primogenitum."—*Luke,* ii. 7.

[2] "Si primogenitus, ergo alii filii secuti sunt secundogeniti . . .
Carnales nullos habuit Beata Virgo præter Christum; ergo spirituales
habeat necesse est."—*Spann. Polyanth. litt. m.* t. 6.

[3] *Insin.* l. 4, c. 3.

[4] "Venter tuus sicut acervus tritici, vallatus liliis."—*Cant.* vii. 2.

[5] "Unum granum frumenti fuit in utero Virginis, Christus Dominus; et tamen 'acervus tritici' dicitur, quia granum hoc virtute omnes
electos continet, 'ut sit ipse primogenitus in multis fratribus.' "—*Ap.
Novar. Umbra V.* c. 63.

St. William writes in the same sense, saying, "that Mary, in bringing forth Jesus, our Saviour and our life, brought forth many unto salvation; and by giving birth to life itself, she gave life to many." [1]

The second occasion on which Mary became our spiritual Mother, and brought us forth to the life of grace, was when she offered to the Eternal Father the life of her beloved Son on Mount Calvary, with so bitter sorrow and suffering. So that St. Augustine declares, that "as she then co-operated by her love in the birth of the faithful to the life of grace, she became the spiritual Mother of all who are members of the one Head, Christ Jesus." [2] This we are given to understand by the following verse of the sacred Canticles, and which refers to the most Blessed Virgin: *They have made me the keeper in the vineyards; my vineyard I have not kept.* [3] St. William says, that "Mary, in order that she might save many souls, exposed her own to death;" [4] meaning, that to save us, she sacrificed the life of her Son. And who but Jesus was the soul of Mary? He was her life, and all her love. And therefore the prophet Simeon foretold that a sword of sorrow would one day transpierce her own most blessed soul. [5] And it was precisely the lance which transpierced the side of Jesus, who was the soul of Mary. Then it was that this most Blessed Virgin brought us forth by her sorrows to eternal life: and thus we can all call ourselves the children of the sorrows of

[1] "In illo uno fructu, in uno Salvatore omnium Jesu, piurimos Maria peperit ad salutem; pariendo Vitam, multos peperit ad vitam." —*Delrio, In Cant.* iv. 13.

[2] "Mater membrorum ejus, quia cooperata est charitate, ut fideles in Ecclesia nascerentur."—*De S. Virginitate*, c. vi.

[3] "Posuerunt me custodem in vineis; vineam meam non custodivi." —*Cant.* i. 5.

[4] "Ut multas animas salvas faceret, animam suam morti exposuit." —*Delrio, In Cant.* i. 6.

[5] "Et tuam ipsius animam pertransibit gladius."—*Luke*, ii. 35.

Mary. Our most loving Mother was always, and in all, united to the will of God. "And therefore," says St. Bonaventure, "when she saw the love of the Eternal Father towards men to be so great that, in order to save them, he willed the death of his Son; and, on the other hand, seeing the love of the Son in wishing to die for us: in order to conform herself to this excessive love of both the Father and the Son towards the human race, she also with her entire will offered, and consented to, the death of her Son, in order that we might be saved."[1]

It is true that, according to the prophecy of Isaias, Jesus, in dying for the redemption of the human race, chose to be alone. *I have trodden the winepress alone;*[2] but, seeing the ardent desire of Mary to aid in the salvation of man, he disposed it so that she, by the sacrifice and offering of the life of her Jesus, should co-operate in our salvation, and thus become the Mother of our souls. This our Saviour signified, when, before expiring, he looked down from the cross on his Mother and on the disciple St. John, who stood at its foot, and, first addressing Mary, he said, *Behold thy Son;*[3] as it were saying, Behold, the whole human race, which by the offer thou makest of my life for the salvation of all, is even now being born to the life of grace. Then, turning to the disciple, he said, *Behold thy Mother.*[4] "By these words," says St. Bernardine of Sienna, "Mary, by reason of the love she bore them, became the Mother, not only of St. John, but of all men."[5] And Silveira remarks, that St. John himself, in stating this fact in his Gospel,

[1] "Nullo modo est dubitandum, quin Mariæ animus voluerit tradere etiam Filium suum pro salute generis humani, ut Mater per omnia conformis esset Patri et Filio."—*In Sent.* l. i. d. 48, a. 2, q. 2.

[2] "Torcular calcavi solus."—*Is.* lxiii. 3.

[3] "Ecce filius tuus."—*John,* xix. 26.

[4] "Ecce mater tua."—*John,* xix. 26.

[5] "Intelligimus in Joanne omnes, quorum, per dilectionem, Beata Virgo facta est Mater."—*T. I.* s. 51. a. 1. c. 3.

says: "Then he said to the disciple, *Behold thy Mother.*"
Here observe well that Jesus Christ did not address
himself to John, but to the disciple, in order to show
that he then gave Mary to all who are his disciples, that
is to say, to all Christians, that she might be their
Mother. "John is but the name of one, whereas the
word disciple is applicable to all; therefore our Lord
makes use of a name common to all, to show that Mary
was given as a Mother to us."[1]

The Church applies to Mary these words of the sacred
Canticles: *I am the Mother of fair love;*[2] and a commenta-
tor explaining them, says, that the Blessed Virgin's love
renders our souls beautiful in the sight of God, and also
makes her as a most loving mother receive us as her
children, "she being all love towards those whom she
has thus adopted."[3] And what mother, exclaims St.
Bonaventure, loves her children, and attends to their
welfare, as thou lovest us and carest for us, O most
sweet Queen! "For dost thou not love us and seek our
welfare far more without comparison than any earthly
mother?"[4]

O blessed are they who live under the protection of
so loving and powerful a mother! The prophet David,
although she was not yet born, sought salvation from
God by dedicating himself as a son of Mary, and thus
prayed: *Save the son of thy handmaid.*[5] "Of what handmaid?" asks St. Augustine; and he answers, "Of her

---

[1] "Joannes nomen est particulare; . . . Discipulus, commune; ut
denotetur, quod Maria dabatur omnibus in Matrem."—*In Evang.* l.
viii. c. 17, q. 14.

[2] "Ego mater pulchræ dilectionis."—*Ecclus.* xxiv. 24.

[3] "Quia tota est amor erga nos, quos in filios recepit."—*Paciucch.
In Ps.* 86, exc. 22.

[4] "Nonne plus sine comparatione nos diligis, ac bonum nostrum
procuras, quam mater carnalis?"—*Stim. div. am.* p. 3, c. 19.

[5] "Salvum fac filium ancillæ tuæ."—*Ps.* lxxxv. 16.

who said, Behold the handmaid of the Lord."[1] "And who," says Cardinal Bellarmine, "would ever dare to snatch these children from the bosom of Mary, when they have taken refuge there? What power of hell, or what temptation, can overcome them, if they place their confidence in the patronage of this great Mother, the Mother of God, and of them?"[2] There are some who say that when the whale sees its young in danger, either from tempests or pursuers, it opens its mouth and swallows them. This is precisely what Novarinus asserts of Mary: "When the storms of temptations rage, the most compassionate Mother of the faithful, with maternal tenderness, protects them as it were in her own bosom until she has brought them into the harbor of salvation."[3]

O most loving Mother! O most compassionate Mother! be thou ever blessed; and ever blessed be God, who has given thee to us for our mother, and for a secure refuge in all the dangers of this life. Our Blessed Lady herself, in a vision, addressed these words to St. Bridget: "As a mother, on seeing her son in the midst of the swords of his enemies, would use every effort to save him, so do I, and will do for all sinners who seek my mercy."[4] Thus it is that in every engagement with the infernal powers, we shall always certainly conquer by having recourse to the Mother of God, who is also our Mother, saying and repeating again and again: "We fly to thy patronage, O holy Mother of God: we fly to thy patronage, O holy

[1] "Cujus ancillæ? quæ ait: Ecce ancilla Domini."

[2] "Quam bene nobis erit sub præsidio tantæ Matris? Quis nos detrahere audebit de sinu ejus? Quæ nos tentatio, quæ tribulatio superare poterit, confidentes in patrocinio Matris Dei et nostræ?"— *De Sept. Verb.* l. i. c. 12.

[3] "Fidelium piissima Mater, furente tentationum tempestate, materno affectu eos velut intra viscera propria receptos protegit, donec in beatum portum reponat."

[4] "Ita ego facio, et faciam omnibus peccatoribus, misericordiam meam petentibus."—*Rev.* l. iv. cap. 138.

Mother of God." [1]   Oh, how many victories have not the faithful gained over hell, by having recourse to Mary with this short but most powerful prayer! Thus it was that the great servant of God, Sister Mary Crucified, of the Order of St. Benedict, always overcame the devils.

Be of good heart, then, all you who are children of Mary. Remember that she accepts as her children all those who choose to be so. Rejoice! Why do you fear to be lost, when such a Mother defends and protects you? " Say, then, O my soul, with great confidence: I will rejoice and be glad; for whatever the judgment to be pronounced on me may be, it depends on and must come from my Brother and Mother." [2]   " Thus," says St. Bonaventure, " it is that each one who loves this good Mother, and relies on her protection, should animate himself to confidence, remembering that Jesus is our Brother, and Mary our Mother." The same thought makes St. Anselm cry out with joy, and encourage us, saying: " O, happy confidence! O safe refuge! the Mother of God is my Mother. How firm, then, should be our confidence, since our salvation depends on the judgment of a good Brother and a tender Mother." [3]   It is, then, our Mother who calls us, and says, in these words of the Book of Proverbs: *He that is a little one, let him turn to me.* [4]   Children have always on their lips their mother's name, and in every fear, in every danger, they immediately cry out, Mother! mother! Ah, most sweet Mary! ah, most loving Mother! this is precisely what thou desirest: that we should become children, and call

[1] "Sub tuum præsidium confugimus, sancta Dei genitrix !"

[2] " Dic, anima mea, cum magna fiducia exsultabo et lætabor, quia quidquid judicabitur de me, pendet ex sententia Fratris et Matris meæ."—*Solil.* c. 1.

[3] "O beata fiducia! O tutum refugium! Mater Dei est Mater nostra; qua igitur certitudine debemus sperare, quorum salus, de boni Fratris et piæ Matris pendet arbitrio!"—*Or.* 51.

[4] " Si quis est parvulus, veniat ad me."—*Prov.* ix. 4.

on thee in every danger, and at all times have recourse to thee, because thou desirest to help and save us, as thou hast saved all who have had recourse to thee.

EXAMPLE.

In the history of the foundation of the Society of Jesus in the kingdom of Naples,[1] we read the following account of a young Scotch nobleman, named William Elphinstone. He was related to King James, and lived for some time in the heresy in which he was born. Enlightened by divine grace, he began to perceive his errors. Having gone to France, with the help of a good Jesuit Father, who was also a Scotchman, and still more by the intercession of the Blessed Virgin, he at last discovered the truth, abjured his heresy, and became a Catholic. From France he went to Rome, and there a friend, finding him one day weeping and in great affliction, inquired the cause of his grief. He answered that during the night his mother, who was lost, appeared to him, and said: " It is well for thee, son, that thou hast entered the true Church; for as I died in heresy, I am lost." From that moment he redoubled his devotions towards Mary, choosing her for his only Mother, and by her he was inspired with the thought of embracing the religious state, and he bound himself to do so by vow. Being in delicate health, he went to Naples for a change of air, and there it was the will of God that he should die, and die as a religious; for shortly after his arrival, finding himself at the last extremity, by his prayers and tears he moved the Superiors to accept him, and in presence of the Most Blessed Sacrament, when he received it as viaticum, he pronounced his vows, and was declared a member of the Society of Jesus. After this it was most touching to hear with what tenderness he thanked his Mother Mary for having snatched him from heresy, and

[1] *Schinosi*, l. 5, ch. 7.

led him to die in the true Church, and in the house of God, surrounded by his religious brethren. This made him exclaim: " Oh, how glorious is it to die in the midst of so many angels!" When exhorted to repose a little, "Ah," he replied, " this is no time for repose, now that I am at the close of my life." Before expiring, he said to those who surrounded him: " Brothers, do you not see the angels of heaven here present who assist me?" One of the religious having heard him mutter some words, asked him what he said. He answered, that his guardian angel had revealed to him that he would remain but a very short time in purgatory, and that he would soon go to heaven. He then entered into a colloquy with his sweet Mother Mary, and like a child that abandons itself to rest in the arms of its mother, he exclaimed, "Mother, mother!" and sweetly expired. Shortly afterwards a devout religious learnt by revelation that he was already in heaven.

Prayer.

O most holy Mother Mary, how is it possible that I, having so holy a mother, should be so wicked? a mother all burning with the love of God, and I loving creatures; a mother so rich in virtue, and I so poor? Ah, amiable Mother, it is true that I do not deserve any longer to be thy son, for by my wicked life I have rendered myself unworthy of so great an honor. I am satisfied that thou shouldst accept me for thy servant; and in order to be admitted amongst the vilest of them, I am ready to renounce all the kingdoms of the world. Yes, I am satisfied. But still thou must not forbid me to call thee mother. This name consoles and fills me with tenderness, and reminds me of my obligation to love thee. This name excites me to great confidence in thee. When my sins and the divine justice fill me most with consternation, I am all consoled at the thought that thou art my mother. Allow me then to call thee mother, my most amiable mother. Thus do I call thee, and thus will I always call thee. Thou, after God, must be my hope, my refuge, my love in this valley of tears.　Thus do I hope to die, breathing forth my soul into thy holy hands, and saying, My Mother my Mother Mary, help me, have pity on me!　Amen.

III.

The Greatness of the Love which this Mother bears us.

Since Mary is our Mother, we may consider how great is the love she bears us; love towards our children is a necessary impulse of nature; and St. Thomas[1] says that this is the reason why the divine law imposes on children the obligation of loving their parents; but gives no express command that parents should love their children, for nature itself has so strongly implanted it in all creatures, that, as St. Ambrose remarks, " we know that a mother will expose herself to danger for her children," and even the most savage beasts cannot do otherwise than love their young.[2]　It is said that even tigers, on hearing the cry of their cubs taken by hunters, will go into the sea and swim until they reach the vessel in which they are.　Since the very tigers, says our most loving Mother Mary, cannot forget their young, how can I forget to love you, my children?　And even, she adds, were such a thing possible as that a mother should forget to love her child, it is not possible that I should cease to love a soul that has become my child: *Can a woman forget her infant, so as not to have pity on the son of her womb? And if she should forget, yet will I not forget thee.* [3]

Mary is our Mother, not, as we have already observed, according to the flesh, but by love; *I am the Mother of*

---

[1] *De Dil. Chr.* c. 13.

[2] " Natura hoc bestiis infundit, ut catulos proprios ament."—*Hexam.* l. 6. c. 4.

[3] " Numquid oblivisci potest mulier infantem suum, ut non misereatur filio uteri sui?　Et si illa oblita fuerit, ego tamen non obliviscar tui."—*Is.* xlix. 15.

fair love; [1] hence it is the love only that she bears us that makes her our mother; and therefore some one remarks, "that she glories in being a mother of love, because she is all love towards us whom she has adopted for her children." [2] And who can ever tell the love that Mary bears us miserable creatures? Arnold of Chartres tells us that "at the death of Jesus Christ, she desired with immense ardor to die with her Son, for love of us;" [3] so much so, adds St. Ambrose, that whilst "her Son was hanging on the cross, Mary offered herself to the executioners," [4] to give her life for us.

But let us consider the reason of this love; for then we shall be better able to understand how much this good mother loves us.

The first reason for the great love that Mary bears to men, is the great love that she bears to God; love towards God and love towards our neighbor belong to the same commandment, as expressed by St. John : *this commandment we have from God, that he who loveth God, love also his brother;* [5] so that as the one becomes greater the other also increases. What have not the saints done for their neighbor in consequence of their love towards God! Read only the account of the labors of St. Francis Xavier in the Indies, where, in order to aid the souls of these poor barbarians and bring them to God, he exposed himself to a thousand dangers, clambering amongst the mountains, and seeking out these poor creatures in the caves in which they dwelt like wild beasts. See a

---

[1] " Ego mater pulchræ dilectionis."—*Ecclus.* xxiv. 24.

[2] " Se dilectionis esse Matrem merito gloriatur, quia tota est amor erga nos, quos in filios recepit."—*Paciucch. In Ps.* 86, *Exc.* 22.

[3] " Flagrabat tunc Virgo æstuanti charitate incensa, ut, pro humani generis salute, simul cum prole sua profunderet vitam."—*Ibid. Exc.* 1.

[4] " Pendebat in cruce Filius, Mater se persecutoribus offerebat."—*Inst. Virg.* c. 7.

[5] " Hoc mandatum habemus a Deo, ut, qui diligit Deum, diligat et fratrem suum."—1 *John,* iv. 21.

4

St. Francis de Sales, who, in order to convert the heretics of the province of Chablais, risked his life every morning, for a whole year, crawling on his hands and feet over a frozen beam, in order that he might preach to them on the opposite side of a river; a St. Paulinus, who delivered himself up as a slave, in order that he might obtain liberty for the son of a poor widow; a St. Fidelis, who, in order to draw the heretics of a certain place to God, persisted in going to preach to them, though he knew it would cost him his life. The saints, then, because they loved God much, did much for their neighbor; but who ever loved God as much as Mary? She loved him more in the first moment of her existence than all the saints and angels ever loved him, or will love him; but this we shall explain at length, when treating of her virtues. Our Blessed Lady herself revealed to Sister Mary the Crucified, that the fire of love with which she was inflamed towards God was such, that if the heavens and earth were placed in it, they would be instantly consumed; so that the ardors of the seraphim, in comparison with it, were but as fresh breezes. And as amongst all the blessed spirits, there is not one that loves God more than Mary, so we neither have nor can have any one who, after God, loves us as much as this most loving Mother; and if we concentrate all the love that mothers bear their children, husbands and wives one another, all the love of angels and saints for their clients, it does not equal the love of Mary towards a single soul. Father Nieremberg[1] says that the love that all mothers have ever had for their children is but a shadow in comparison with the love that Mary bears to each one of us; and he adds, that she alone loves us more than all the angels and saints put together.

Moreover, our Mother loves us much, because we were recommended to her by her beloved Jesus, when

[1] *De Aff. erga B. V.* c. 14.

he before expiring said to her, *Woman, behold thy son!* for we were all represented in the person of St. John, as we have already observed: these were his last words; and the last recommendations left before death by persons we love are always treasured and never forgotten.

But again, we are exceedingly dear to Mary on account of the sufferings we cost her. Mothers generally love those children most, the preservation of whose lives has cost them the most suffering and anxiety; we are those children for whom Mary, in order to obtain for us the life of grace, was obliged to endure the bitter agony of herself offering her beloved Jesus to die an ignominious death, and had also to see him expire before her own eyes in the midst of the most cruel and unheard-of torments. It was then by this great offering of Mary that we were born to the life of grace; we are therefore her very dear children, since we cost her so great suffering. And thus, as it is written of the love of the Eternal Father towards men, in giving his own Son to death for us, that *God so loved the world as to give His only-begotten Son.*[1] "So also," says St. Bonaventure, "we can say of Mary, that she has so loved us as to give her only-begotten Son for us."[2] And when did she give him? She gave him, says Father Nieremberg, when she granted him permission to deliver himself up to death; she gave him to us, when, others neglecting to do so, either out of hatred or from fear, she might herself have pleaded for the life of her Son before the judges. Well may it be supposed that the words of so wise and loving a mother would have had great weight, at least with Pilate, and might have prevented him from sentencing a man to death whom he knew and had declared to be innocent. But no, Mary would not say a word in favor

[1] "Sic Deus dilexit mundum, ut filium suum unigenitum daret."— *John*, iii. 16.

[2] "Sic Maria dilexit nos, ut Filium suum unigenitum daret."

of her Son, lest she might prevent that death on which
our salvation depended.   Finally, she gave him to us a
thousand and a thousand times, during the three hours
preceding his death, and which she spent at the foot of
the cross; for during the whole of that time she unceasingly offered, with the extreme of sorrow and the extreme of love, the life of her Son in our behalf, and this
with such constancy, that St. Anselm and St. Antoninus
say,[1] that if executioners had been wanting, she herself
would have crucified him, in order to obey the Eternal
Father who willed his death for our salvation.   If Abraham had such fortitude as to be ready to sacrifice with
his own hands the life of his son, with far greater fortitude would Mary (far more holy and obedient than
Abraham) have sacrificed the life of hers.   But let us
return to the consideration of the gratitude we owe to
Mary, for so great an act of love as was the painful sacrifice of the life of her Son, which she made to obtain
eternal salvation for us all.   God abundantly rewarded
Abraham for the sacrifice he was prepared to make of
his son Isaac; but we, what return can we make to
Mary for the life of her Jesus, a Son far more noble and
beloved than the son of Abraham?   "This love of Mary,"
says St. Bonaventure, "has indeed obliged us to love
her; for we see that she has surpassed all others in love
towards us, since she has given her only Son, whom she
loved more than herself, for us."[2]

From this arises another motive for the love of Mary
towards us; for in us she beholds that which has been
purchased at the price of the death of Jesus Christ.   If a
mother knew that a servant had been ransomed by a beloved son at the price of twenty years of imprisonment

[1] P. 4, t. 15, c. 41, § 1.

[2] "Nulla post eam creatura ita per amorem nostrum exardescet,
quæ Filium suum unicum, quem multo plus se amavit, nobis dedit, et
pro nobis obtulit."—*De B. V. M.* s. 1.

and suffering, how greatly would she esteem that servant on this account alone! Mary well knows that her
Son came into the world only to save us poor creatures,
as he himself protested, *I am come to save that which was
lost.*[1] And to save us he was pleased even to lay down
his life for us, *Having become obedient unto death.*[2] If, then,
Mary loved us but little, she would show that she valued
but little the blood of her Son, which was the price of our
salvation. To St. Elizabeth of Hungary it was revealed
that Mary, from the time she dwelt in the Temple, did
nothing but pray for us, begging that God would hasten
the coming of his Son into the world to save us. And
how much more must we suppose that she loves us, now
that she has seen that we are valued to such a degree by
her Son, that he did not disdain to purchase us at such a
cost.

Because all men have been redeemed by Jesus, therefore Mary loves and protects them all. It was she who
was seen by St. John in the Apocalypse, clothed with
the sun: *And a great sign appeared in heaven: a woman
clothed with the sun.*[3] She is said to be clothed with the
sun, because as there is no one on earth who can be
hidden from the heat of the sun—*There is no one that
can hide himself from his heat.*[4] So there is no one living
who can be deprived of the love of Mary. *From its heat,*
that is, as Blessed Raymond Jordano applies the words,
" from the love of Mary."[5] " And who," exclaims St.
Antoninus, " can ever form an idea of the tender care

---

[1] " Venit enim Filius hominis quærere et salvum facere quod peri-
rat."—*Luke.* xix. 10.

[2] " Factus obediens usque ad mortem."—*Phil.* ii. 8.

[3] " Et signum magnum apparuit in cœlo, mulier amicta sole."—
Apoc. xii. 1.

[4] " Nec est qui se abscondat a calore ejus."—*Ps.* xviii. 7.

[5] " A calore ejus, id est, a dilectione Mariæ."—*Contempl. de V. M.
in prol.*

that this most loving mother takes of all of us," [1] "offering and dispensing her mercy to every one;" [2] for our good mother desired the salvation of all, and coöperated in obtaining it. "It is evident," says St. Bernard, "that she was solicitous for the whole human race." [3] Hence the custom of some of Mary's clients, spoken of by Cornelius a Lapide, and which consists in asking our Lord to grant them the graces that our Blessed Lady seeks for them, succeeds most advantageously. They say, Lord, grant me that which the most Blessed Virgin Mary asks for me. "And no wonder," adds the same writer, "for our Mother desires for us better things than we can possibly desire ourselves." [4] The devout Bernardine de Bustis says, that Mary "loves to do us good, and dispense graces to us far more than we to receive them." [5] On this subject Blessed Albert the Great applies to Mary the words of the Book of Wisdom: *She preventeth them that covet her, so that she first showeth herself unto them.* [6] Mary anticipates those who have recourse to her by making them find her before they seek her. "The love that this good Mother bears us is so great," says Richard of St. Laurence, "that as soon as she perceives our want, she comes to our assistance. She comes before she is called." [7]

And now, if Mary is so good to all, even to the ungrateful and negligent, who love her but little, and seldom have recourse to her, how much more loving will she be to

[1] "Oh! quanta est cura B. Virgini Matri de nobis !"

[2] "Omnibus aperit sinum misericordiæ suæ."—P. 4, t. 15, c. 2.

[3] "Constat pro universo genere humano fuisse sollicitam."—*In Assumpt.* s. 4.

[4] "Ipsa enim majora optat, quam nos optare possumus."

[5] "Plus desiderat ipsa facere tibi bonum et largiri gratiam, quam tu accipere concupiscas."—*Marial.* p. 2, s. 5.

[6] "Præoccupat qui se concupiscunt, ut illis se prior ostendat."—*Wisd.* vi. 14.

[7] "Velocius occurrit ejus pietas, quam invocetur."—*In Cant.* c. 23.

those who love her and often call upon her ! *She is easily found by them that seek her.*[1] "O, how easy," adds the same Blessed Albert, "is it for those who love Mary to find her, and to find her full of compassion and love !" In the words of the Book of Proverbs, *I love them that love me,*[2] she protests that she cannot do otherwise than love those who love her. And although this most loving Lady loves all men as her children, yet, says St. Bernard, "she recognizes and loves,"[3] that is, she loves in a more special manner, those who love her more tenderly. Blessed Raymond Jordano asserts that these happy lovers of Mary are not only loved but even served by her; for he says that those who find the most Blessed Virgin Mary, find all; for she loves those who love her, nay more, she serves those who serve her.[4]

In the chronicles of the Order of St. Dominic it is related that one of the friars named Leonard used to recommend himself two hundred times a day to this Mother of Mercy, and that when he was attacked by his last illness he saw a most beautiful queen by his side, who thus addressed him: "Leonard, wilt thou die, and come and dwell with my Son and with me ?" And who art thou ?" he replied. "I am," said the most Blessed Virgin, for she it was, "I am the Mother of Mercy: thou hast so many times invoked me, behold, I am now come to take thee; let us go together to Paradise." On the same day Leonard died, and, as we trust, followed her to the kingdom of the blessed.

"Ah, most sweet Mary !" exclaimed the Venerable

---

[1] "Facile videtur ab his qui diligunt eam, et invenitur ab his qui quærunt illam."—*Wisd.* vi. 13.

[2] "Ego diligentes me diligo."—*Prov.* viii. 17.

[3] *In Salve Reg.* s. 1.

[4] "Inventa Virgine Maria, invenitur omne bonum; ipsa namque diligit diligentes se, imo sibi servientibus servit."—*Contempl. de V. M. in prol.*

John Berchmans, of the Society of Jesus, " blessed is he who loves thee ! If I love Mary, I am certain of perseverance, and shall obtain whatever I wish from God." Therefore the devout youth was never tired of renewing his resolution, and of repeating often to himself: " I will love Mary; I will love Mary."

O, how much does the love of this good Mother exceed that of all her children! Let them love her as much as they will, Mary is always amongst lovers the most loving, says St. Ignatius the Martyr.[1]

Let them love her as did St. Stanislaus Kostka, who loved this dear mother so tenderly, that in speaking of her he moved all who heard him to love her. He had made new words and new titles with which to honor her name. He never did anything without first turning to her image to ask her blessing.   When he said her office, the Rosary, or other prayers, he did so with the same external marks of affection as he would have done had he been speaking face to face with Mary; when the *Salve Regina* was sung, his whole soul, and even his whole countenance, was all inflamed with love.   On being one day asked by a Father of the Society who was going with him to visit a picture of the Blessed Virgin, how much he loved Mary,— " Father," he answered, " what more can I say? she is my mother." " But," adds the Father," the holy youth uttered these words with such tenderness in his voice, with such an expression of countenance, and at the same time it came so fully from his heart, that it no longer seemed to be a young man, but rather an angel speaking of the love of Mary."

Let us love her as Blessed Hermann loved her. He called her the spouse of his love, for he was honored by Mary herself with this same title. Let us love her as did St. Philip Neri, who was filled with consolation at

[1] " Cum devotis devotior, id est, cum amantibus amantior.."—*Auriemma, Aff Scamb.* p. 1, c. 1.

the mere thought of Mary, and therefore called her his delight. Let us love her as did St. Bonaventure, who called her not only his Lady and mother, but to show the tenderness of his affection, even called her his heart and soul: "Hail, my Lady, my Mother; nay, even my heart, my soul!"[1]

Let us love her like that great lover of Mary, St. Bernard, who loved this his sweet Mother so much that he called her the ravisher of hearts;[2] and to express the ardent love he bore her, added: "for hast thou not ravished my heart, O Queen?"[3]

Let us call her beloved, like St. Bernardine of Sienna, who daily went to visit a devotional picture of Mary, and there, in tender colloquies with his Queen, declared his love; and when asked where he went each day, he replied that he went to visit his beloved.

Let us love her as did St. Aloysius Gonzaga, whose love for Mary burnt so unceasingly, that whenever he heard the sweet name of his Mother mentioned, his heart was instantly inflamed, and his countenance lighted up with a fire that was visible to all.

Let us love as much as St. Francis Solano did, who, maddened as it were (but with a holy madness), with love for Mary, would sing before her picture, and accompany himself on a musical instrument, saying, that, like worldly lovers, he serenaded his most sweet Queen.

Finally, let us love her as so many of her servants have loved her, who never could do enough to show their love. Father John of Trexo, of the Society of Jesus, rejoiced in the name of slave of Mary; and as a mark of servitude, went often to visit her in some church dedicated in her honor. On reaching the church he poured out abun-

---

[1] "Ave, Domina mea; Mater mea; imo cor meum et anima mea." —*Stim. div. am.* p. 3, c. 16.

[2] "Raptrix cordium!"—*Ib.*

[3] "Nonne rapuisti cor meum?"—*Med. in Salve Reg.*

dant tears of tenderness and love for Mary; then, prostrating, he licked and rubbed the pavement with his tongue and face, kissing it a thousand times, because it was the house of his beloved Lady. Father James Martinez, of the same Society, who for his devotion for our blessed Lady on her feasts was carried by angels to heaven to see how they were kept there, used to say, "Would that I had the hearts of all angels and saints, to love Mary as they love her—would that I had the lives of all men, to give them all for her love!"

O that others would come to love her as did Charles, the son of St. Bridget, who said that nothing in the world consoled him so much as the knowledge that Mary was so greatly loved by God. And he added, that he would willingly endure every torment rather than allow Mary to lose the smallest degree of her glory, were such a thing possible; and that if her glory was his, he would renounce it in her favor, as being far more worthy of it.

Let us, moreover, desire to lay down our lives as a testimony of our love for Mary, as Alphonsus Rodriguez desired to do. Let us love her as did those who even cut the beloved name of Mary on their breasts with sharp instruments, as did Francis Binanzio and Radagundis, wife of King Clothaire, or as did those who could imprint this loved name on their flesh with hot irons, in order that it might remain more distinct and lasting; as did her devout servants Baptist Archinto and Augustine d'Espinosa, both of the Society of Jesus, impelled thereto by the vehemence of their love.

Let us, in fine, do or desire to do all that it is possible for a lover to do, who intends to make his affection known to the person loved. For be assured that the lovers of Mary will never be able to equal her in love. "I know, O Lady," says St. Peter Damian, "that thou art most loving, and that thou lovest us with an invincible love." [1]

[1] "Scio, Domina, quia benignissima es, et amas nos amore invincibili."—*In Nat. B. V.* s. 1.

I know, my Lady, that among those that love thee thou lovest the most, and that thou lovest us with a love that can never be surpassed.

The Blessed Alphonsus Rodriguez, of the Society of Jesus, once prostrate before an image of Mary, felt his heart inflamed with love towards this most Holy Virgin, and burst forth into the following exclamation: "My most beloved Mother, I know that thou lovest me, but thou dost not love me as much as I love thee." Mary, as it were offended on the point of love, immediately replied from the image: "What dost thou say, Alphonsus—what dost thou say? O, how much greater is the love that I bear thee, than any love that thou canst have for me! Know that the distance between heaven and earth is not so great as the distance between thy love and mine."

St. Bonaventure, then, was right in exclaiming: Blessed are they who have the good fortune to be faithful servants and lovers of this most loving Mother. "Blessed are the hearts of those who love Mary; blessed are they who are tenderly devoted to her." [1] Yes; for "in this struggle our most gracious Queen never allows her clients to conquer her in love. She returns our love and homage, and always increases her past favors by new ones." [2] Mary, imitating in this our most loving Redeemer Jesus Christ, returns to those who love her their love doubled in benefits and favors.

Then will I exclaim, with the enamoured St. Anselm, "May my heart languish and my soul melt and be consumed with your love, O my beloved Saviour Jesus, and my dear Mother Mary! But, as without your grace I

---

[1] "Beati quorum corda te diligunt. Virgo Maria. Beati qui devote ei famulantur."—*Psalt. B. V. ps.* xxxi., cxviii.

[2] "Numquam tamen in hoc certamine a nobis ipsa vincetur; amorem redhibet, et præterita beneficia novis semper adauget."—*Paciucch. in Ps.* lxxxvi. *Exc.* 2.

cannot love you, grant me, O Jesus and Mary, grant my soul, by your merits and not mine, the grace to love you as you deserve to be loved. O God, lover of men, Thou couldst love guilty men even unto death. And canst Thou deny Thy love and that of Thy Mother to those who ask it?" [1]

EXAMPLE.

Father Auriemma [2] relates that there was a certain poor shepherdess, whose sole delight was to go to a little chapel of our Blessed Lady, situated on a mountain, and there, whilst her flocks were browsing, she conversed with her dear Mother and rendered honor to her. Seeing that the little image of Mary (which was carved in relief) was unadorned, she set to work to make her a mantle. One day, having gathered a few flowers in the fields, she made a garland, and climbing on the altar of the little chapel, placed it on the head of the image, saying, " My Mother, I would place a crown of gold and precious stones on thy brow, but, as I am poor, receive this crown of flowers, and accept it as a mark of the love that I bear thee." With this and other acts of homage, the pious maiden always endeavored to serve and honor our beloved Lady. But let us now see how the good Mother on her part recompensed the visits and the affection of her child. The latter fell ill, and was at the point of death. It so happened that two religious were passing that way, and, fatigued with their journey, sat down under a tree to rest : one fell asleep, and the other remained awake; but

---

[1] " Vestro continuo amore langueat cor meum: liquefiant omnia ossa mea. Date itaque supplicanti animæ meæ, non propter meritum meum, sed propter meritum vestrum, date illi, quanto digni estis. amorem vestrum. . . . O Amator hominum! tu potuisti reos tuos et usque ad mortem amare : et poteris te roganti amorem tui et Matris tuæ negare ?"—*Orat.* 51.

[2] *Aff. Scamb.* p. 2, c. 8.

both had the same vision. They saw a multitude of most beautiful young women, and amongst these was one who in beauty and majesty far surpassed them all. One of the religious addressed himself to her: "Lady, who art thou, and where art thou going by these rugged ways?" "I am," she replied, "the Mother of God, and am going with these holy virgins to a neighboring cottage to visit a dying shepherdess who has so often visited me." Having said these words, all disappeared. At once these two good servants of God said, "Let us go also to see her." They immediately started, and having found the cottage of the dying virgin, they entered it and found her stretched on a little straw. They saluted her, and she said, "Brothers, ask our Lord to let you see the company that is assisting me." They immediately knelt, and saw Mary by the side of the dying girl, holding a crown in her hand and consoling her. All at once the virgins began to sing, and at the sound of this sweet harmony her blessed soul left her body. Mary placed the crown on her head, and taking her soul, led it with her to Paradise.*

Prayer.

O Lady, O ravisher of hearts![1] I will exclaim with St. Bonaventure: "Lady, who with the love and favor thou showest thy servants dost ravish their hearts, ravish also my miserable heart, which desires ardently to love thee. Thou, my Mother, hast enamoured a God with thy beauty, and drawn him from heaven into thy chaste womb; and shall I live without loving thee? "No, I will say to thee with one of thy most loving sons, John Berchmans of the Society of Jesus, I will never rest until I am certain of having obtained thy love; but a constant and tender

[1] "O Domina, quæ rapis corda."

---

* This account bears much resemblance to the account of the circumstances of the life and death of St. Germaine Cousin, deceased in 1601 at Pibrac, near Toulouse, aged about twenty two years, beatified May 7, 1854, canonized June 29, 1867.—ED.

love towards thee, my Mother, who hast loved me with so much tenderness,"[1] even when I was ungrateful towards thee. And what should I now be, O Mary, if thou hadst not obtained so many mercies for me? Since, then, thou didst love me so much when I loved thee not, how much more may I not now hope from thee, now that I love thee? I love thee, O my Mother, and I would that I had a heart to love thee in place of all those unfortunate creatures who love thee not. I would that I could speak with a thousand tongues, that all might know thy greatness, thy holiness, thy mercy, and the love with which thou lovest all who love thee. Had I riches, I would employ them all for thy honor. Had I subjects, I would make them all thy lovers. In fine, if the occasion presented itself I would lay down my life for thy glory. I love thee, then, O my Mother; but at the same time I fear that I do not love thee as I ought; for I hear that love makes lovers like the person loved. If, then, I see myself so unlike thee, it is a mark that I do not love thee. Thou art so pure, and I defiled with many sins; thou so humble, and I so proud; thou so holy, and I so wicked. This, then, is what thou hast to do, O Mary; since thou lovest me, make me like thee. Thou hast all power to change hearts; take, then, mine and change it. Show the world what thou canst do for those who love thee. Make me a saint; make me thy worthy child. This is my hope.

IV.

Mary is the Mother of penitent Sinners.

Our Blessed Lady told St. Bridget that she was the mother not only of the just and innocent, but also of sinners, provided they were willing to repent.[2] O how prompt does a sinner (desirous of amendment, and who flies to her feet) find this good mother to embrace and help him, far more so than any earthly mother! St. Gregory VII. wrote in this sense to the princess Matilda,

[1] " Nunquam quiescam, donec habuero tenerum amorem erga Matrem meam, Mariam "

[2] " Ego sum quasi Mater omnium peccatorum se volentium emendare."—*Rev.* l. iv. c. 138.

saying: "Resolve to sin no more, and I promise that undoubtedly thou wilt find Mary more ready to love thee than any earthly mother."[1]

But whoever aspires to be a child of this great mother, must first abandon sin, and then may hope to be accepted as such. Richard of St. Laurence, on the words of Proverbs, *up rose her children*,[2] remarks that the words "up rose" come first, and then the word "children," to show that no one can be a child of Mary without first endeavoring to rise from the fault into which he has fallen; for he who is in mortal sin is not worthy to be called the son of such a mother.[3] And St. Peter Chrysologus says that he who acts in a different manner from Mary, declares thereby that he will not be her son. "He who does not the works of his mother, abjures his lineage."[4] Mary humble, and he proud; Mary pure, and he wicked; Mary full of love, and he hating his neighbor. He gives thereby proof that he is not, and will not be, the son of his holy Mother. The sons of Mary, says Richard of St. Laurence, are her imitators, and this chiefly in three things; in "chastity, liberality, and humility; and also in meekness, mercy, and such like."[5]

Whilst disgusting her by a wicked life, who would dare even to wish to be the child of Mary? A certain sinner once said to Mary, "Show thyself a Mother;" but the Blessed Virgin replied, "Show thyself a son."[6] Another

[1] "Pone finem in voluntate peccandi, et invenies Mariam, indubitanter promitto, promptiorem carnali matre in tui dilectione."—*Lib.* i. *ep.* 47.

[2] "Surrexerunt filii ejus."—*Prov.* xxxi. 28.

[3] "Nec dignus est, qui in mortali peccato est, vocari filius tantæ Matris."—*De Laud. B. V.* lib. ii. p. 5.

[4] "Qui genitoris opera non facit, negat genus."—*Serm.* 123.

[5] "Filii Mariæ, imitatores ejus in castitate, humilitate, mansuetudine, misericordia.—*Loco cit.*

[6] "Monstra te esse matrem. . . . Monstra te esse filium."—*Aurem. Aff. Scamb.* p. 3, c. 12.

invoked the divine Mother, calling her the Mother of
mercy, and she answered: " You sinners, when you want
my help, call me Mother of mercy, and at the same time
do not cease by your sins to make me a Mother of sorrows and anguish." [1]   *He is cursed of God*, says Ecclesiasticus, *that angereth his mother.* [2]   " That is Mary," [3] says
Richard of St. Laurence.   God curses those who by their
wicked life, and still more by their obstinacy in sin,
afflict this tender mother.

I say, by their obstinacy; for if a sinner, though he
may not as yet have given up his sin, endeavors to do
so, and for this purpose seeks the help of Mary, this
good mother will not fail to assist him, and make him
recover the grace of God.   And this is precisely what St.
Bridget heard one day from the lips of Jesus Christ, who,
speaking to his mother, said, " Thou assistest him who
endeavors to return to God, and thy consolations are
never wanting to any one." [4]   So long, then, as a sinner
is obstinate, Mary cannot love him; but if he (finding
himself chained by some passion which keeps him a
slave of hell) recommends himself to the Blessed Virgin,
and implores her, with confidence and perseverance, to
withdraw him from the state of sin in which he is, there
can be no doubt but this good mother will extend her
powerful hand to him, will deliver him from his chains,
and lead him to a state of salvation.

The doctrine that all prayers and works performed in
a state of sin are sins was condemned as heretical by the
sacred Council of Trent. [5]   St. Bernard says, [6] that al-

[1] *Pelb. Stell.* l. xii. p. ult. c. 7.

[2] " Maledictus a Deo, qui exasperat matrem."—*Ecclus.* iii. 18.

[3] " Matrem, id est Mariam."—*De Laud. B. M.* l. 2, p. 1.

[4] " Conanti surgere ad Deum tribuis auxilium, et neminem reliquis
vacuum a consolatione tua."—*Rev.* l. 4, c. 19.

[5] *Sess.* vi. *can.* 7.

[6] *De Div.* s. 81.

though prayer in the mouth of a sinner is devoid of
beauty, as it is unaccompanied with charity, nevertheless
it is useful, and obtains grace to abandon sin; for, as St.
Thomas teaches,[1] the prayer of a sinner, though without
merit, is an act which obtains the grace of forgiveness,
since the power of impetration is founded not on the
merits of him who asks, but on the divine goodness, and
the merits and promises of Jesus Christ, who has said,
Every one that asketh, receiveth.[2] The same thing must be
said of prayers offered to the divine mother. "If he who
prays," says St. Anselm, "does not merit to be heard, the
merits of the mother, to whom he recommends himself,
will intercede effectually."[3]

Therefore, St. Bernard exhorts all sinners to have recourse to Mary, invoking her with great confidence; for
though the sinner does not himself merit the graces
which he asks, yet he receives them, because this Blessed
Virgin asks and obtains them from God, on account of
her own merits. These are his words, addressing a
sinner: "Because thou wast unworthy to receive the
grace thyself, it was given to Mary, in order that,
through her, thou mightest receive all."[4] "If a mother,"
continues the same saint, "knew that her two sons bore
a mortal enmity to each other, and that each plotted
against the other's life, would she not exert herself to
her utmost in order to reconcile them? This would be
the duty of a good mother. And thus it is," the saint
goes on to say, "that Mary acts; for she is the mother
of Jesus, and the mother of men. When she sees a sinner at enmity with Jesus Christ, she cannot endure it,

---

[1] 2. 2, q. 178, a. 2.

[2] "Omnis enim qui petit, accipit."—*Luke*, xi. 10.

[3] "Si merita invocantis non merentur, merita tamen Matris intercedunt, ut exaudiatur."—*De Excell. Virg.* c. 6.

[4] "Quia indignus eras, cui donaretur, datum est Mariæ, ut per
illam acciperes quidquid haberes."—*In Vig. Nat.* s. 3.

and does all in her power to make peace between them. O happy Mary, thou art the Mother of the criminal, and the Mother of the judge; and being the Mother of both, they are thy children, and thou canst not endure discords amongst them." [1]

This most benign Lady only requires that the sinner should recommend himself to her, and purpose amendment. When Mary sees a sinner at her feet, imploring her mercy, she does not consider the crimes with which he is loaded, but the intention with which he comes; and if this is good, even should he have committed all possible sins, the most loving mother embraces him, and does not disdain to heal the wounds of his soul; for she is not only called the Mother of Mercy, but is so truly and indeed, and shows herself such by the love and tenderness with which she assists us all. And this is precisely what the Blessed Virgin herself said to St. Bridget: "However much a man sins, I am ready immediately to receive him when he repents; nor do I pay attention to the number of his sins, but only to the intention with which he comes: I do not disdain to anoint and heal his wounds; for I am called, and truly am, the Mother of Mercy." [2]

Mary is the mother of sinners who wish to repent, and as a mother she cannot do otherwise than compassionate them; nay more, she seems to feel the miseries of her poor children as if they were her own. When the Canaanitish woman begged our Lord to deliver her daughter from the devil who possessed her, she said, *Have*

[1] "O Maria! tu Mater rei, tu Mater judicis: cum sis Mater utriusque, discordias inter tuos filios nequis sustinere."—*Ap. S. Bonav. Spec. B. V. lect.* 3.

[2] "Quantumcumque homo peccet, si ex vera emendatione ad me reversus fuerit, statim parata sum recipere revertentem; nec attendo quantum peccaverit, sed cum quali voluntate venit; nam non dedignor ungere et sanare plagas ejus, (quia) vocor (et vere sum) Mater misericordiæ."—*Rev.* l. 2, c. 23.—l. 6, c. 117.

mercy on me, O Lord, thou Son of David, my daughter is grievously troubled by a devil.[1] But since the daughter, and not the mother, was tormented, she should rather have said, "Lord, take compassion *on my daughter:*" and not, Have mercy on me; but no, she said, "Have mercy on me," and she was right; for the sufferings of children are felt by their mother as if they were their own. And it is precisely thus, says Richard of St. Laurence, that Mary prays to God when she recommends a sinner to him who has had recourse to her; she cries out for the sinful soul, "Have mercy on *me !*" "My Lord," she seems to say, "this poor soul that is in sin is my daughter, and therefore, pity not so much her as me, who am her mother."[2]

Would that all sinners had recourse to this sweet mother! for then certainly all would be pardoned by God. "O Mary," exclaims St. Bonaventure in rapturous astonishment, "thou embracest with maternal affection a sinner despised by the whole world, nor dost thou leave him until thou hast reconciled the poor creature with his judge;"[3] meaning that the sinner, whilst in the state of sin, is hated and loathed by all, even by inanimate creatures; fire, air, and earth would chastise him, and avenge the honor of their outraged Lord. But if this unhappy creature flies to Mary, will Mary reject him? Oh, no: provided he goes to her for help, and in order to amend, she will embrace him with the affection of a mother, and will not let him go, until,. by her powerful intercession, she has reconciled him with God, and reinstated him in grace.

[1] "Miserere mei, Domine, Fili David! filia mea male a dæmonio vexatur."—*Matt.* xv. 22.

[2] "Maria clamat pro peccatrice anima: Miserere mei."—*De Laud. B. M.* l. 6.

[3] "O Maria! peccatorem toti mundo despectum materno affectu complecteris; nec deseris, quousque horrendo Judici miserum reconcilies."--*In Spec. B. V.* lect. 5.

In the second book of Kings,[1] we read that a wise woman of Thecua addressed King David in the following words: "My lord, I had two sons, and for my misfortune, one killed the other; so that I have now lost one, and justice demands the other, the only one that is left; take compassion on a poor mother, and let me not be thus deprived of both." David, moved with compassion towards the mother, declared that the delinquent should be set at liberty and restored to her. Mary seems to say the same thing when God is indignant against a sinner who has recommended himself to her. "My God," she says, "I had two sons, Jesus and man; man took the life of my Jesus on the cross, and now Thy justice would condemn the guilty one. O Lord, my Jesus is already dead, have pity on me, and if I have lost the one, do not make me lose the other also."

Most certainly God will not condemn those sinners who have recourse to Mary, and for whom she prays, since he himself commended them to her as her children. The devout Lanspergius supposes our Lord speaking in the following terms: "I recommended all, but especially sinners, to Mary, as her children, and therefore is she so diligent and so careful in the exercise of her office, that she allows none of those committed to her charge, and especially those who invoke her, to perish; but as far as she can, brings all to me."[2] "And who can ever tell," says the devout Blosius, "the goodness, the mercy, the compassion, the love, the benignity, the clemency, the fidelity, the benevolence, the charity, of this

---

[1] 2 *Kings,* xiv. 5.
[2] "Mariæ . . . peccatores in filios commendavi; . . . propterea adeo est sedula, ut, officio suo satisfaciens, neminem eorum. quantum in se est, qui sibi commissi sunt, præcipue se invocantium, perire sinat, sed, quantum valet, omnes mihi reducat."—*Alloq.* l. I, p. 4, can. 12.

Virgin Mother towards men? It is such that no words can express it."[1]

"Let us, then," says St. Bernard, "cast ourselves at the feet of this good mother, and embracing them, let us not depart until she blesses us, and thus accepts us for her children."[2] And who can ever doubt the compassion of this mother? St. Bonaventure used to say; "Even should she take my life, I would still hope in her; and, full of confidence, would desire to die before her image, and be certain of salvation." And thus should each sinner address her when he has recourse to this compassionate Mother; he should say:

"My Lady and Mother, on account of my sins I deserve that thou shouldst reject me, and even that thou shouldst thyself chastise me according to my deserts; but shouldst thou reject me, or even take my life, I will still trust in thee, and hope with a firm hope that thou wilt save me. In thee is all my confidence; only grant me the consolation of dying before thy picture, recommending myself to thy mercy, then I am convinced that I shall not be lost, but that I shall go and praise thee in heaven, in company with so many of thy servants who left this world calling on thee for help, and have all been saved by thy powerful intercession."[3] Read the following example, and then say if any sinner can doubt of the mercy and love of this good mother.

---

[1] " Hujus Matris bonitas, misericordia, fidelitas, charitas erga homines, tanta est, ut nullis verbis explicari possit."—*Sacell. an.* p. 3, c. 5.

[2] "Beatis illius pedibus provolvamur; teneamus eam, nec dimittamus, donec benedixerit nobis."—*In Sign. magn.*

[3] "Etiamsi occiderit me, sperabo in eam; et totus confidens, juxta ejus imaginem mori desidero, et salvus ero."—*Paciucchelli, In Ps.* 86, exc. 3.

EXAMPLE.*

A noble youth named Eskil was sent by the prince, his
father, to Hildesheim, a city of Saxony, to study; but he
gave himself up to a disorderly life.. He afterwards fell
so dangerously ill that he received Extreme Unction. While
in this state he had a vision: he found himself shut up in a
fiery furnace, and believed himself already in hell; but he
then seemed to escape from it by a hole, and took refuge
in a great palace, in an apartment of which he saw the most
Blessed Virgin Mary, who said to him: "Presumptuous
man that thou art, dost thou dare to appear before me?
Depart hence, and go to that fire which thou hast deserved."
The young man then besought the Blessed Virgin to have
mercy on him; and then addressed himself to some persons
who were there present, and entreated them to recommend
him to Mary. They did so, and the divine Mother replied,
"But you do not know the wicked life which he leads, and
that he does not even deign to salute me with a Hail Mary."
His advocates replied: "But, lady, he will change his life";
and the young man added, "Yes, I promise in good earnest
to amend, and I will be thy devout client." The Blessed
Virgin's anger was then appeased, and she said to him,
"Well, I accept thy promise; be faithful to me, and mean-
while, with my blessing, be delivered from death and hell."
With these words the vision disappeared. Eskil returned
to himself, and, blessing Mary, related to others the grace
which he had received: and from that time he led a holy
life, always preserving great devotion to our Blessed Lady.
He became archbishop of Lunden in Sweden, where he converted many to the faith. Towards the end of his life, on
account of his age, he renounced his archbishopric, and became a monk in Clairvaux, where he lived for four years,
and died a holy death. Hence he is numbered by some
authors amongst the Cistercian saints.[1]

---

[1] *Manriquez, Ann. Cisterc.* 1151, c. 13; 1181, c 2.

Prayer.

O my sovereign Queen and worthy Mother of my God, most holy Mary; I seeing myself, as I do, so despicable and loaded with so many sins, ought not to presume to call thee Mother, or even to approach thee; yet I will not allow my miseries to deprive me of the consolation and confidence that I feel in calling thee mother; I know well that I deserve that thou shouldst reject me; but I beseech thee to remember all, that thy Son Jesus has endured for me, and then reject me if thou canst. I am a wretched sinner, who, more than all others, have despised the infinite majesty of God: but the evil is done. To thee have I recourse; thou canst help me; my Mother, help me. Say not that thou canst not do so; for I know that thou art all-powerful, and that thou obtainest whatever thou desirest of God; and if thou sayest that thou wilt not help me, tell me at least to whom I can apply in this my so great misfortune. "Either pity me," will I say with the devout St. Anselm. "O my Jesus, and forgive me, and do thou pity me, my Mother Mary, by interceding for me, or at least tell me to whom I can have recourse, who is more compassionate, or in whom I can have greater confidence than in thee." [1] Oh, no; neither on earth nor in heaven can I find any one who has more compassion for the miserable, or who is better able to assist me, than thou canst, O Mary. Thou, O Jesus, art my Father, and thou, Mary, art my Mother. You both love the most miserable, and go seeking them in order to save them. I deserve hell, and am the most miserable of all. But you need not seek me, nor do I presume to ask so much. I now present myself before you with a certain hope that I shall not be abandoned. Behold me at your feet; my Jesus, forgive me; My Mother Mary, help me.

[1] "Aut miseremini miseri, tu parcendo, tu interveniendo; aut ostendite, ad quos tutius fugiam misericordiores; et monstrate, in quibus certius confidam potentiores."—*Orat.* 50.

CHAPTER II.

Vita, Dulcedo.

OUR LIFE, OUR SWEETNESS.

I.

MARY, OUR LIFE, OUR SWEETNESS.

Mary is our Life, because she obtains for us the Pardon of our Sins.

To understand why the holy Church makes us call Mary our life, we must know, that as the soul gives life to the body, so does divine grace give life to the soul; for a soul without grace has the name of being alive but is in truth dead, as it was said of one in the Apocalypse, *Thou hast the name of being alive, and thou art dead.*[1] Mary, then, in obtaining this grace for sinners by her intercession, thus restores them to life.

See how the Church makes her speak, applying to her the following words of Proverbs : *They that in the morning early watch for me shall find me.*[2] They who are diligent in having recourse to me in the morning, that is, as soon as they can, will most certainly find me. In the Septuagint the words *shall find me* are rendered *shall find grace.* So that to have recourse to Mary is the same thing as to find the grace of God. A little further on she says, *He that shall find me shall find life, and shall have salvation from the Lord.*[3] " Listen," exclaims St. Bonaventure on these words, " listen, all you who desire the

---

[1] " Nomen habes quod vivas, et mortuus es."—*Apoc.* iii. 1.

[2] " Qui mane vigilant ad me, invenient me."—*Prov.* viii. 17.

[3] " Qui me invenerit, inveniet vitam, et hauriet salutem a Domino."

kingdom of God: honor the most Blessed Virgin Mary, and you will find life and eternal salvation." [1]

St. Bernardine of Sienna says, that if God did not destroy man after his first sin, it was on account of his singular love for this holy Virgin, who was destined to be born of this race. And the saint adds, " that he has no doubt but that all the mercies granted by God under the old dispensation were granted only in consideration of this most Blessed Lady." [2]

Hence St. Bernard was right in exhorting us " to seek for grace, and to seek it by Mary ;" [3] meaning, that if we have had the misfortune to lose the grace of God, we should seek to recover it, but we should do so through Mary ; for though we may have lost it, she has found it ; and hence the saint calls her " the finder of grace." [4] The angel Gabriel expressly declared this for our consolation, when he saluted the Blessed Virgin saying, *Fear not, Mary, thou hast found grace.* [5] But if Mary had never been deprived of grace, how could the archangel say that she had then found it ? A thing may be found by a person who did not previously possess it ; but we are told by the same archangel that the Blessed Virgin was always with God, always in grace, nay, full of grace. *Hail, full of grace, the Lord is with thee.* [6] Since Mary, then, did not find grace for herself, she being always full of it, for whom did she find it ? Cardinal Hugo, in his commentary on the above text, replies that she found it for sinners who had lost it. " Let sinners,

---

[1] " Audite qui ingredi cupitis regnum Dei: Virginem Mariam honorate, et invenietis vitam et salutem perpetuam."—*Psalt. B. V. ps.* 48.

[2] "Omnes indulgentias factas in Veteri Testamento non ambigo Deum fecisse propter hujus benedictæ Puellæ reverentiam et amorem."—*Pro Fest. V. M.* s. 5, c. 2.

[3] " Quæramus gratiam, et per Mariam quæramus."—*De Aquæd.*

[4] " Inventrix gratiæ."—*In Adv. D.* s. 2.

[5] " Ne timeas, Maria: invenisti enim gratiam."—*Luke,* i. 30.

[6] " Ave, gratia plena! Dominus tecum."

then," says this devout writer, " who by their crimes
have lost grace, address themselves to the Blessed Virgin, for with her they will surely find it ; let them humbly salute her, and say with confidence, " Lady, that
which has been found must be restored to him who has
lost it ; restore us, therefore, our property which thou
hast found."[1]   On this subject, Richard of St. Laurence
concludes, " that if we hope to recover the grace of God,
we must go to Mary, who has found it, and finds it always."[2]   And as she always was and always will be
dear to God, if we have recourse to her, we shall certainly succeed.

Again, Mary says, in the eighth chapter of the sacred
Canticles, that God has placed her in the world to be
our defence : *I am a wall: and my breasts are as a tower.*[3]
And she is truly made a mediatress of peace between
sinners and God ; *Since I am become in His presence as one
finding peace.* On these words St. Bernard encourages
sinners, saying, " Go to this Mother of Mercy, and show
her the wounds which thy sins have left on thy soul; then
will she certainly entreat her Son, by the breasts that
gave him suck, to pardon thee all.   And this divine Son,
who loves her so tenderly, will most certainly grant her
petition."[4]   In this sense it is that the holy Church, in
her almost daily prayer, calls upon us to beg our Lord
to grant us the powerful help of the intercession of Mary
to rise from our sins : " Grant Thy help to our weakness,

[1] "Currant igitur peccatores ad Virginem, qui gratiam amiserunt
peccando, et eam invenient apud ipsam; secure dicant: Redde nobis
rem nostram, quam invenisti."

[2] "Cupientes invenire gratiam, quæramus inventricem gratiæ, quæ,
quia semper invenit, frustrari non poterit."—*De Laud. V.* 1. 2, p. 5.

[3] "Ego murus, et ubera mea sicut turris, ex quo facta sum coram
eo quasi pacem reperiens."—*Cant.* viii. 10.

[4] "Vade ad Matrem misericordiæ, et ostende illi tuorum plagas
peccatorum, et illa ostendet pro te ubera; exaudiet utique Matrem
Filius."

O most merciful God ; and that we, who are mindful of the holy Mother of God, may by the help of her intercession rise from our iniquities." [1]

With reason, then, does St. Laurence Justinian call her "the hope of malefactors;" [2] since she alone is the one who obtains them pardon from God. With reason does St. Bernard call her "the sinners' ladder;" [3] since she, the most compassionate Queen, extending her hand to them, draws them from an abyss of sin, and enables them to ascend to God. With reason does an ancient writer call her "the only hope of sinners;" for by her help alone can we hope for the remission of our sins. [4]

St. John Chrysostom also says "that sinners receive pardon by the intercession of Mary alone." [5] And therefore the saint, in the name of all sinners, thus addresses her : "Hail, Mother of God and of us all, 'heaven,' where God dwells, 'throne,' from which our Lord dispenses all grace, 'fair daughter, Virgin, honor, glory and firmament of our Church,' assiduously pray to Jesus that in the day of judgment we may find mercy through thee, and receive the reward prepared by God for those who love him." [6]

With reason, finally, is Mary called, in the words of the sacred Canticles, the dawn; *Who is she that cometh forth as the morning rising ?* [7] Yes, says Pope Innocent

[1] "Concede, misericors Deus, fragilitati nostræ præsidium; ut qui sanctæ Dei Genitricis memoriam agimus, intercessionis ejus auxilio a nostris iniquitatibus resurgamus."

[2] "Delinquentium spes."—*S. de Nat. V. M.*

[3] "Peccatorum scala."—*De Aquæd.*

[4] "Tu es spes unica peccatorum, quia per te speramus veniam omnium delictorum."—*Serm.* 194, *E. B. app.*

[5] "Per hanc peccatorum veniam consequimur."

[6] "Ave igitur, Mater, Cœlum, Thronus, Ecclesiæ nostræ decus; assidue precare Jesum, ut per te misericordiam invenire in die judicii, et, quæ reposita sunt iis, qui diligunt Deum, bona consequi possimus."—*Off. B. M. lect.* 6.

[7] "Quæ est ista, quæ progreditur quasi aurora consurgens ?"—*Cant.* vi. 9.

III.; "for as the dawn is the end of night, and the beginning of day, well may the Blessed Virgin Mary, who was the end of vices, be called the dawn of day." [1] When devotion towards Mary begins in a soul, it produces the same effect that the birth of this most Holy Virgin produced in the world. It puts an end to the night of sin, and leads the soul into the path of virtue. Therefore, St. Germanus says, "O Mother of God, thy protection never ceases, thy intercession is life, and thy patronage never fails." [2] And in a sermon the same saint says, that to pronounce the name of Mary with affection is a sign of life in the soul, or at least, that life will soon return there.

We read in the Gospel of St. Luke, that Mary said, *Behold, from henceforth all generations shall call me blessed.* [3] "Yes, my Lady," exclaims St. Bernard, "all generations shall call thee blessed, for thou hast begotten life and glory for all generations of men." [4] For this cause all men shall call thee blessed, for all thy servants obtain through thee the life of grace and eternal glory. "In thee do sinners find pardon, and the just perseverance and eternal life." [5] "Distrust not, O sinner," says the devout Bernardine de Bustis, "even if thou hast committed all possible sins : go with confidence to this most glorious Lady, and thou wilt find her hands filled with mercy and bounty." And, he adds, for "she desires

[1] "Cum aurora sit finis noctis et origo diei, merito per auroram designatur Virgo Maria, quæ fuit finis vitiorum."—*In Assumpt.* s. 2.

[2] *In Dorm. B. V.* s. 2.

[3] "Ecce enim ex hoc beatam me dicent omnes generationes."—*Luke*, i. 48.

[4] "Ex hoc Beatam te dicent omnes generationes, quæ omnibus generationibus vitam et gloriam genuisti."—*In Pentec.*

[5] "In te justi gratiam, peccatores veniam, invenerunt in æternum." *In Pentec.* s. 2.

more to do thee good than thou canst desire to receive favors from her." [1]

St. Andrew of Crete calls Mary the pledge of divine mercy; [2] meaning that, when sinners have recourse to Mary, that they may be reconciled with God, he assures them of pardon and gives them a pledge of it ; and this pledge is Mary, whom he has bestowed upon us for our advocate, and by whose intercession (by virtue of the merits of Jesus Christ) God forgives all who have recourse to her. St. Bridget heard an angel say, that the holy Prophets rejoiced in knowing that God, by the humility and purity of Mary, was to be reconciled with sinners, and to receive those who had offended him to favor. "They exulted, foreknowing that our Lord himself would be appeased by thy humility, and the purity of thy life, O Mary, thou supereffulgent star, and that he would be reconciled with those who had provoked his wrath." [3]

No sinner, having recourse to the compassion of Mary, should fear being rejected; for she is the Mother of Mercy, and as such desires to save the most miserable. Mary is that happy ark, says St. Bernard, "in which those who take refuge will never suffer the shipwreck of eternal perdition." [4] At the time of the deluge even brutes were saved in Noah's Ark. Under the

---

[1] "O peccator ! non diffidas, etiamsi commisisti omnia peccata, sed secure ad istam gloriosissimam Dominam recurras; invenies enim eam in manibus plenam misericordia et largitate. Plus enim desiderat ipsa facere tibi bonum, et largiri gratiam, quam tu accipere concupiscas."—*Marial.* p. 2, s. 5.

[2] "Fidejussio divinarum reconciliationum, quæ dato pignore fit."—*In Dorm. B. V.* s. 3.

[3] "Exsultabant autem prænoscentes, quod ipse Dominus, ex tua humilitate, et vitæ puritate, o Maria, stella præfulgida ! placaretur, et quod reciperet eos in suam gratiam, qui ipsum ad iracundiam provocaverant."—*Serm. Ang.* c. 9.

[4] "Arca in qua naufragium evadimus."—*S. de B. V. M. Deip.*

mantle of Mary even sinners obtain salvation. St. Gertrude once saw Mary with her mantle extended, and under it many wild beasts—lions, bears, and tigers—had taken refuge.[1] And she remarked that Mary not only did not reject, but even welcomed and caressed them with the greatest tenderness. The saint understood hereby that the most abandoned sinners who have recourse to Mary are not only not rejected, but that they are welcomed and saved by her from eternal death. Let us, then, enter this ark, let us take refuge under the mantle of Mary, and she most certainly will not reject us, but will secure our salvation.

EXAMPLE.

Father Bovio[2] relates that there was a wicked woman, named Ellen, who entered a church, and by chance heard a sermon on the Rosary. On leaving the church she purchased a set of beads, but wore them concealed, as she did not wish it to be known that she had them. She began to recite them, and though she did so without devotion, our most Blessed Lady poured such sweetness and consolation into her soul during the whole time, that she could not cease repeating the Hail Marys. At last she was filled with such a horror for her wicked life, that she could no longer find repose, and was obliged to go to confession. She accomplished this duty with such contrition that the priest was filled with astonishment. After her confession, she went to the foot of an altar of the most Blessed Virgin, and there, as a thanksgiving to her advocate, said the Rosary. The divine mother then addressed her from the image in the following words: "Ellen, thou hast already too much offended God and me; from this moment

[1] *Insin.* l. 4, c. 50.
[2] *Es. e Mir.* p. 1, *es.* 2.

change thy life, and I will bestow a large share of my graces upon thee." The poor sinner, in the deepest confusion, replied: "Ah! most Holy Virgin, it is true that hitherto I have been a wicked sinner; but thou canst do all, help me; on my part I abandon myself to thee, and will spend the remainder of my life in doing penance for my sins." With the assistance of Mary, she distributed all her goods among the poor, and began a life of rigorous mortification. She was tormented with dreadful temptations, but constantly recommended herself to the Mother of God, and thus was always victorious. She was favored with many extraordinary graces, with visions, revelations, and even the gift of prophecy. Finally, before her death, which was announced to her by Mary some days before it took place, the most Blessed Virgin came herself, with her divine Son, to visit her; and when she expired, her soul was seen flying towards heaven in the form of a beautiful dove.

Prayer.

Behold, O Mother of my God, my only hope, Mary, behold at thy feet a miserable sinner, who asks thee for mercy. Thou art proclaimed and called by the whole Church, and by all the faithful, the refuge of sinners. Thou art consequently my refuge; thou hast to save me. I will say with William of Paris, Thou knowest, most sweet Mother of God, how much thy Blessed Son desires our salvation.[1] Thou knowest all that Jesus Christ endured for this end. I present thee, O my Mother, the sufferings of Jesus: the cold that he endured in the stable, his journey into Egypt, his toils, his sweat, the blood that he shed, the anguish which caused his death on the cross, and of which thou wast thyself a witness. O, show that thou lovest thy beloved Son, and by this love I implore thee to assist me. Extend thy hand to a poor creature who has fallen, and asks thy help. Were I a saint, I would not need seek thy

[1] "Tu . . . enim, dulcissima Dei Mater, nosti quantum placeat benedicto Filio tuo salus nostra."—*Rhet. Div.* c. 18.

mercy; but because I am a sinner, I fly to thee, who art the Mother of Mercies. I know that thy compassionate heart finds its consolation in assisting the miserable, when thou canst do so, and dost not find them obstinate. Console, then, thy compassionate heart, and console me this day; for now thou hast the opportunity of saving a poor creature condemned to hell; and thou canst do so, for I will not be obstinate. I abandon myself into thy hands, only tell me what thou wouldst have me do, and obtain for me strength to execute it. for I am resolved to do all that depends on me to recover the divine grace. I take refuge under thy mantle. Jesus wills that I should have recourse to thee, in order not only that his blood may save me, but also that thy prayers may assist me in this great work; for thy glory, and for his own, since thou art his Mother. He sends me to thee, that thou mayst help me. O Mary, see, I have recourse to thee; in thee do I confide. Thou prayest for so many others, pray also for me; say only a word. Tell our Lord that thou willest my salvation, and God will certainly save me. Say that I am thine, and then I have obtained all that I ask, all that I desire.

II.

Mary is also our Life, because she obtains for us Perseverance.

Final perseverance is so great a gift of God, that (as it was declared by the Holy Council of Trent) it is quite gratuitous on his part, and we cannot *merit* it. Yet we are told by St. Augustine, that all who seek for it obtain it from God; and, according to Father Suarez, they obtain it infallibly, if only they are diligent in asking for it to the end of their lives. For, as Bellarmin well remarks, "that which is daily required must be asked for every day."[1] Now, if it is true (and I hold it as certain, according to the now generally received opinion, and which I shall prove in the fourth chapter of this work) that all the graces that God dispenses to men pass through the hands of Mary, it will be equally

[1] "Quotidie petenda est, ut quotidie obtineatur."

6

true that it is only through Mary that we can hope for this greatest of all graces,—perseverance. And we shall obtain it most certainly, if we always seek it with confidence through Mary. This grace she herself promises to all who serve her faithfully during life, in the following words of Ecclesiasticus; and which are applied to her by the Church,[1] on the Feast of her Immaculate Conception ; *They that work by me shall not sin. They that explain me shall have life everlasting.*[2]

In order that we may be preserved in the life of grace, we require spiritual fortitude to resist the many enemies of our salvation. Now this fortitude can be obtained only by the means of Mary, and we are assured of it in the book of Proverbs, for the Church applies the passage to this most Blessed Virgin. *Strength is mine ; by me kings reign;*[3] meaning, by the words "strength is mine," that God has bestowed this precious gift on Mary, in order that she may dispense it to her faithful clients. And by the words, *By me kings reign*, she signifies that by her means her servants reign over and command their senses and passions, and thus become worthy to reign eternally in heaven. Oh, what strength do the servants of this great Lady possess, to overcome all the assaults of hell ! Mary is that tower spoken of in the sacred Canticles: *Thy neck is as the tower of David, which is built with bulwarks ; a thousand bucklers hang upon it, all the armor of valiant men.* She is as a well defended fortress in defence of her lovers, who in their wars have recourse to her. In her do her clients

---

[1] *Off. Imm. Conc.*

[2] "Qui operantur in me, non peccabunt; qui elucidant me, vitam æternam habebunt."—*Ecclus.* xxiv. 30.

[3] "Mea est fortitudo; per me reges regnant."—*Prov.* viii. 14.—*Off. B. V.*

[4] "Sicut turris David collum tuum. quæ ædificata est cum propugnaculis: mille clypei pendent ex ea, omnis armatura fortium."—*Cant.* iv. 4.

find all shields and arms, to defend themselves against hell.

And for the same reason the most Blessed Virgin is called a plane-tree in the words of Ecclesiasticus: *As a plane-tree by the water in the streets was I exalted.*[1] Cardinal Hugo explains them, and says that the "plane-tree has leaves like shields,"[2] to show how Mary defends all who take refuge with her. Blessed Amedeus gives another explanation, and says that this holy Virgin is called a plane-tree, because, as the plane shelters travellers under its branches from the heat of the sun and from the rain, so do men find refuge under the mantle of Mary from the ardor of their passions and from the fury of temptations.[3] Truly are those souls to be pitied who abandon this defence, in ceasing their devotion to Mary, and no longer recommending themselves to her in the time of danger. If the sun ceased to rise, says St. Bernard, how could the world become other than a chaos of darkness and horror? And applying his question to Mary, he repeats it. "Take away the sun, and where will be the day? Take away Mary, and what will be left but the darkest night?"[4] When a soul loses devotion to Mary, it is immediately enveloped in darkness, and in that darkness of which the Holy Ghost speaks in the Psalms: *Thou hast appointed darkness, and it is night; in it shall all the beasts of the woods go about.*[5] When the light of heaven ceases to shine in a soul, all

[1] "Quasi platanus exaltata sum juxta aquas in plateis."—*Ecclus.* xxiv. 19.

[2] "Platanus habet folia scutis similia."

[3] "Virgo ramorum extensione se ubique expandit, ut filios Adæ ab æstu. et a turbine, et a pluvia, umbra desiderabili protegeret."—*De Laud. B. V. hom.* 8.

[4] "Tolle corpus hoc solare, ubi dies? Tolle Mariam, quid nisi tenebræ relinquentur?"—*De Aquæd.*

[5] "Posuisti tenebras, et facta est nox; in ipsa pertransibunt omnes bestiæ silvæ."—*Ps.* ciii. 20.

is darkness, and it becomes the haunt of devils and of every sin. St. Anselm says, that " if any one is disregarded and condemned by Mary, he is necessarily lost," and therefore we may with reason exclaim, "Woe to those who are in opposition to this sun ?" [1] Woe to those who despise its light ! that is to say, all who despise devotion to Mary.

St. Francis Borgia always doubted the perseverance of those in whom he did not find particular devotion to the Blessed Virgin. On one occasion he questioned some novices as to the saints towards whom they had special devotion, and perceiving some who had it not towards Mary, he instantly warned the Master of novices, and desired him to keep a more attentive watch over these unfortunate young men, who all, as he had feared, lost their vocation and renounced the religious state.

It was, then, not without reason that St. Germanus called the most Blessed Virgin the breath of Christians; for as the body cannot live without breathing, so the soul cannot live without having recourse to and recommending itself to Mary, by whose means we certainly acquire and preserve the life of divine grace within our souls. But I will quote the saint's own words: " As breathing is not only a sign but even a cause of life, so the name of Mary, which is constantly found on the lips of God's servants, both proves that they are truly alive, and at the same time causes and preserves their life, and gives them every succor." [2]

Blessed Allan was one day assaulted by a violent temptation, and was on the point of yielding, for he had not recommended himself to Mary, when the most

---

[1] " Væ eis qui Solem istum aversantur!"

[2] " Sic respiratio non solum est signum vitæ, sed etiam causa; sic Mariæ nomen, quod in servorum Dei ore versatur, simul argumentum est quod vere vivunt, simul etiam hanc vitam efficit et conservat. omnemque eis opem impertitur."—*De Zona Deip.*

Blessed Virgin appeared to him; and in order that another time he might remember to invoke her aid, she
gave him a blow, saying, "If thou hadst recommended
thyself to me, thou wouldst not have run into such
danger."

On the other hand, Mary says in the following words
of the Book of Proverbs, which are applied to her by
the Church: *Blessed is the man that heareth me, and that
watcheth daily at my gates, and waiteth at the posts of my
doors*,[1]—as if she would say, Blessed is he that hears my
voice and is constantly attentive to apply at the door of
my mercy, and seeks light and help from me.   For
clients who do this, Mary does her part, and obtains
them the light and strength they require to abandon sin
and walk in the paths of virtue.   For this reason Innocent III. beautifully calls her "the moon at night, the
dawn at break of day, and the sun at mid-day."[2]   She
is a moon to enlighten those who blindly wander in the
night of· sin, and makes them see and understand the
miserable state of damnation in which they are; she is
the dawn (that is, the forerunner of the sun) to those
whom she has already enlightened, and makes them
abandon sin and return to God, the true sun of justice;
finally, she is a sun to those who are in a state of grace,
and prevents them from again falling into the precipice
of sin.

Learned writers apply the following words of Ecclesiasticus to Mary: *Her bands are a healthful binding.*[3]
"Why bands?" asks St. Laurence Justinian, "except
it be that she binds her servants, and thus prevents them

---

[1] " Beatus homo qui audit me, et qui vigilat ad fores meas quotidie,
et observat ad postes ostii mei."—*Prov.* viii. 34.—*Off. B. V.*

[2] " Luna lucet in nocte, aurora in diluculo, sol in die."—*In Assumpt.*
s. 2.

[3] " Vincula illius alligatura salutaris."—*Ecclus.* vi. 31.

from straying into the paths of vice." [1] And truly this is the reason for which Mary binds her servants. St. Bonaventure also, in his commentary on the words of Ecclesiasticus, frequently used in the office of Mary, *My abode is in the full assembly of saints,* [2] says that Mary not only has her abode in the full assembly of saints, but also preserves them from falling, keeps a constant watch over their virtue, that it may not fail, and restrains the evil spirits from injuring them. Not only has she her abode in the full assembly of the saints, but she keeps the saints there, by preserving their merits that they may not lose them, by restraining the devils from injuring them, and by withholding the arm of her Son from falling on sinners. [3]

In the Book of Proverbs we are told that all Mary's clients are clothed with double garments. *For all her domestics are clothed with double garments.* [4] Cornelius à Lapide explains what this double clothing is: he says that it "consists in her adorning her faithful servants with the virtues of her Son and with her own;" [5] and thus clothed they persevere in virtue.

Therefore St. Philip Neri, in his exhortations to his penitents, used always to say: "My children, if you desire perseverance, be devout to our Blessed Lady." The Venerable John Berchmans, of the Society of Jesus, used also to say: "Whoever loves Mary will have persever-

[1] " 'Vincula illius,' id est, exempla et servitia quibus ligamur, ne discurramus per campos licentiæ."—*De Laud. B. M.* l. 2, p 3.

[2] " In plenitudine sanctorum detentio mea."—*Ecclus.* xxiv. 16.

[3] " Ipsa quoque, non solum in plenitudine sanctorum detinetur, sed etiam in plenitudine sanctos detinet, ne eorum plenitudo minuatur; detinet nimirum virtutes, ne fugiant; detinet merita, ne pereant; detinet dæmones, ne noceant."—*Spec B. V. M lect.* 7.

[4] "Omnes enim domestici ejus vestiti sunt duplicibus."—*Prov.* xxxi. 21.

[5] " Duplici veste ipsa ornat sibi devotos, quia tam Christi quam suis virtutibus eos induit."

ance." Truly beautiful is the reflection of the Abbot Rupert on this subject in his commentary on the parable of the prodigal son. He says, "That if this dissolute youth had had a mother living, he would never have abandoned the paternal roof, or at least would have returned much sooner than he did;"[1] meaning thereby that a son of Mary either never abandons God, or, if he has this misfortune, by her help he soon returns.

O, did all men but love this most benign and loving Lady, had they but recourse to her always, and without delay, in their temptations, who would fall? who would ever be lost? He falls and is lost who has not recourse to Mary. St. Laurence Justinian applies to Mary the words of Ecclesiasticus, *I have walked in the waves of the sea :*[2] and makes her say, "I walk with my servants in the midst of the tempests to which they are constantly exposed, to assist and preserve them from falling into sin."[3]

Bernardine de Bustis relates that a bird was taught to say "Hail, Mary!" A hawk was on the point of seizing it, when the bird cried out "Hail, Mary!" In an instant the hawk fell dead. God intended to show thereby that if even an irrational creature was preserved by calling on Mary, how much more would those who are prompt in calling on her when assaulted by devils, be delivered from them. We, says St. Thomas of Villanova, need only, when tempted by the devil, imitate little chickens, which, as soon as they perceive the approach of a bird of prey, run under the wings of their mother for protection. This is exactly what we should do whenever we are assaulted by temptation : we should not

---

[1] "Si Prodigus Filius viventem matrem habuisset, vel a paterna domo nunquam discessisset, vel forte citius rediisset."

[2] "In fluctibus maris ambulavi."—*Ecclus.* xxiv. 8.

[3] "Cum familiaribus meis, ut ipsos eriperem a naufragio peccatorum."—*De Laud. B. M.* l. 2, p. 1.

stay to reason with it, but immediately fly and place ourselves under the mantle of Mary. I will, however, quote the saint's own words addressed to Mary : " As chickens when they see a kite soaring above, run and find refuge under the wings of the hen, so are we preserved under the shadow of thy wings." [1] " And Thou," he continues, " who art our Lady and Mother, hast to defend us ; for, after God, we have no other refuge than thee, who art our only hope and our protectress, towards thee we all turn our eyes with confidence." [2]

Let us then conclude in the words of St. Bernard : " O man, whoever thou art, understand that in this world thou art tossed about on a stormy and tempestuous sea, rather than walking on solid ground ; remember that if thou wouldst avoid being drowned, thou must never turn thine eyes from the brightness of this star, but keep them fixed on it, and call on Mary. In dangers, in straits, in doubts, remember Mary, invoke Mary." [3] Yes, in dangers of sinning, when molested by temptations, when doubtful as to how you should act, remember that Mary can help you ; and call upon her, and she will instantly succor you. " Let not her name leave thy lips, let it be ever in thy heart." Your hearts should never lose confidence in her holy name, nor should your lips ever cease to invoke it. " Following her, thou wilt certainly not go astray." O, no, if we fol-

---

[1] " Sicut pulli, volitantibus desuper milvis, ad gallinæ alas occurrunt, ita nos sub velamento alarum tuarum abscondimur."—*De Nat. V. conc.* 3.

[2] " Nescimus aliud refugium nisi te ; tu sola es unica Spes nostra ; tu sola Patrona nostra, ad quam omnes aspicimus."—*De Nat. V. conc.* 3.

[3] " O quisquis te intelligis in hujus sæculi profluvio magis inter procellas et tempestates fluctuare, quam per terram ambulare ! ne avertas oculos a fulgore hujus Sideris, si non vis obrui procellis. Respice stellam, voca Mariam. In periculis, in angustiis, in rebus dubiis Mariam cogita, Mariam invoca."—*De Laud. V. M. hom.* 2.

low Mary, we shall never err from the paths of salvation. "Imploring her, thou wilt not despair." Each time that we invoke her aid, we shall be inspired with perfect confidence. "If she supports thee, thou canst not fall;" "if she protects thee thou hast nothing to fear, for thou canst not be lost:" "with her for thy guide, thou wilt not be weary; for thy salvation will be worked out with ease." "If she is propitious, thou wilt gain the port." [1] If Mary undertakes our defence, we are certain of gaining the kingdom of heaven. *This do, and thou shalt live.* [2]

EXAMPLE.

The history of St. Mary of Egypt, in the first book of the lives of the Fathers, is well known. At the age of twelve years she fled from the house of her parents, went to Alexandria, where she led an infamous life, and was a scandal to the whole city. After living for sixteen years in sin, she took it into her head to go to Jerusalem. At the time the feast of the holy cross was being celebrated, and, moved rather by curiosity than by devotion, she determined on entering the church; but when at the door, she felt herself repelled by an invisible force. She made a second attempt, and was again unable to enter; and the same thing was repeated a third and a fourth time. Finding her efforts in vain, the unfortunate creature withdrew to a corner of the porch, and there, enlightened from above, understood that it was on account of her infamous life that God had repelled her even from the church. In that moment she

---

[1] "Non recedat ab ore, non recedat a corde. Ipsam sequens, non devias; ipsam rogans, non desperas. Ipsa tenente, non corruis; ipsa protegente, non metuis; ipsa duce, non fatigaris; ipsa propitia, pervenis."—*De Laud V. M. hom.* 2.

[2] "Sic fac, et vives."—*Luke.* x 28

fortunately raised her eyes and beheld a picture of Mary. No sooner did she perceive it, than, sobbing, she exclaimed, " O Mother of God, pity a poor sinner ! I know that on account of my sins I deserve not that thou shouldst cast thine eyes upon me. But thou art the refuge of sinners ; for the love of thy Son Jesus, help me. Permit me to enter the church, and I promise to change my life, to go and do penance in whatever place thou pointest out to me." She immediately heard an internal voice, as it were that of the Blessed Virgin, replying : "Since thou hast recourse to me, and wishest to change thy life, go—enter the church, it is no longer closed against thee." The sinner entered, adored the cross, and wept bitterly. She then returned to the picture, and said, " Lady, behold I am ready where wilt thou that I should go to do penance ?" " Go," the Blessed Virgin replied, " cross the Jordan, and thou wilt find the place of thy repose." She went to confession and Communion, and then passed the river, and finding herself in the desert, she understood that it was in that place she should do penance for her sinful life. During the first seventeen years the assaults of the devil, by which he endeavored to make the saint again fall into sin, were terrible. And what were her means of defence? She constantly recommended herself to Mary, and this most Blessed Virgin obtained for her strength to resist during the whole of this time, after which her combats ceased. After fifty-seven years spent in the desert, and having attained the age of eighty-seven years she was by a disposition of Providence met by the Abbot Zosimus ; to him she related the history of her life, and entreated him to return the following year, and to bring her the holy Communion. The saintly Abbot did so, and gave her the bread of angels. She then requested that he would again return to see her. This also he did, but he found her dead. Her body was encompassed by a bright light, and at her head these words were written, " Bury my body here—it is that of a poor sinner, and intercede with God for me." A lion came and made a grave with his claws. St. Zosimus buried her, returned to his monastery, and related the wonders of God's mercy towards this happy sinner.

Prayer.

O compassionate Mother, most sacred Virgin, behold at thy feet the traitor, who, by paying with ingratitude the graces received from God through thy means, has betrayed both thee and him. But I must tell thee, O most blessed Lady, that my misery, far from taking away my confidence, increases it ; for I see that thy compassion is great in proportion to the greatness of my misery. Show thyself, O Mary, full of liberality towards me ; for thus thou art towards all who invoke thy aid. All that I ask is that thou shouldst cast thine eyes of compassion on me, and pity me. If thy heart is thus far moved, it cannot do otherwise than protect me ; and if thou protectest me, what can I fear ? No, I fear nothing ; I do not fear my sins, for thou canst provide a remedy ; I do not fear devils, for thou art more powerfull than the whole of hell ; I do not even fear thy Son, though justly irritated against me, for at a word of thine he will be appeased. I only fear lest, in my temptations, and by my own fault, I may cease to recommend myself to thee, and thus be lost. But I now promise thee that I will always have recourse to thee ; O, help me to fulfil my promise. Lose not the opportunity which now presents itself of gratifying thy ardent desire to succor such poor wretches as myself. In thee, O Mother of God, I have unbounded confidence. From thee I hope for grace to bewail my sins as I ought, and from thee I hope for strength never again to fall into them. If I am sick, thou, O heavenly physician, canst heal me. If my sins have weakened me, thy help will strengthen me. O Mary, I hope all from thee ; for thou art all-powerful with God. Amen.

III.

Mary our Sweetness; she renders Death sweet to her Clients.

He that is a friend loveth at all times; and a brother is proved in distress,[1] says the Book of Proverbs. We can never know our friends and relatives in the time of prosperity; it is only in the time of adversity that we see them in their true colors. People of the world never abandon a friend as long as he is in prosperity; but should misfortunes overtake him, and more particularly should he be at the point of death, they immediately forsake him. Mary does not act thus with her clients. In their afflictions, and more particularly in the sorrows of death, the greatest that can be endured in this world, this good Lady and Mother not only does not abandon her faithful servants, but as, during our exile, she is our life, so also is she, at our last hour, our sweetness, by obtaining for us a calm and happy death. For from the day on which Mary had the privilege and sorrow of being present at the death of Jesus her Son, who was the head of all the predestined, it became her privilege to assist also at their deaths. And for this reason the holy Church teaches us to beg this most Blessed Virgin to assist us, especially at the moment of death: Pray for us sinners, now and at the hour of our death![2]

O how great are the sufferings of the dying! They suffer from remorse of conscience on account of past sins, from fear of the approaching judgment, and from the uncertainty of their eternal salvation. Then it is that hell arms itself, and spares no efforts to gain the soul which is on the point of entering eternity; for it knows

---

[1] "Omni tempore diligit, qui amicus est; et frater in angustiis comprobatur."—*Prov.* xvii. 17.

[2] "Ora pro nobis peccatoribus, nunc et in hora mortis nostræ."

that only a short time remains in which to gain it, and that if it then loses it, it has lost it forever. *The devil is come down unto you, having great wrath, knowing that he hath but a short time.*[1] And for this reason the enemy of our salvation, whose charge it was to tempt the soul during life, does not choose at death to be alone, but calls others to his assistance, according to the prophet Isaias: *Their houses shall be filled with serpents.*[2] And indeed they are so; for when a person is at the point of death, the whole place in which he is, is filled with devils, who all unite to make him lose his soul.

It is related of St. Andrew Avellino, that ten thousand devils came to tempt him at his death. The conflict that he had in his agony with the powers of hell was so terrible that all the good religious who assisted him trembled. They saw the saint's face swelled to such a degree from agitation, that it became quite black, every limb trembled and was contorted; his eyes shed a torrent of tears, his head shook violently; all gave evidence of the terrible assault he was enduring on the part of his infernal foes. All wept with compassion, and redoubled their prayers, and at the same time trembled with fear on seeing a saint die thus. They were, however, consoled at seeing, that often, as if seeking for help, the saint turned his eyes towards a devout picture of Mary; for they remembered that during life he had often said that at death Mary would be his refuge. At length God was pleased to put an end to the contest by granting him a glorious victory; for the contortions of his body ceased, his face resumed its original size and color, and the saint, with his eyes tranquilly fixed on the picture, made a devout inclination to Mary (who it is believed then appeared to him), as if in the act of thanking her, and with

[1] "Descendit diabolus ad vos, habens iram magnam, sciens quod modicum tempus habet."—*Apoc.* xii. 12.

[2] "Replebuntur domus eórum draconibus."—*Is.* xiii. 21.

a heavenly smile on his countenance tranquilly breathed forth his blessed soul into the arms of Mary. At the same moment, a Capuchiness, who was ·in her agony, turning to the nuns who surrounded her, said, "Recite a Hail Mary; for a saint has just expired."

Ah, how quickly do the rebellious spirits fly from the presence of this queen! If at the hour of death we have only the protection of Mary, what need we fear from all our infernal enemies? David, fearing the horrors of death, encouraged himself by placing his reliance on the death of the coming Redeemer and on the intercession of the Virgin Mother. *For though*, he says, *I should walk in the midst of the shadow of death, . . . thy rod and thy staff, they have comforted me.*[1] Cardinal Hugo, explaining these words of the royal prophet, says that the staff signifies the cross, and the rod is the intercession of Mary; for she is the rod foretold by the prophet Isaias: *And there shall come forth a rod out of the root of Jesse, and a flower shall rise up out of his root.*[2] "This divine Mother," says St. Peter Damian, "is that powerful rod with which the violence of the infernal enemies is conquered."[3] And therefore does St. Antoninus encourage us, saying, "If Mary is for us, who shall be against us?"[4]

When Father Emanuel Padial, of the Society of Jesus, was at the point of death, Mary appeared to him, and to console him she said: "See at length the hour is come when the angels congratulate thee, and exclaim: O happy labors, O mortifications well requited! And in the same moment an army of demons was seen taking its flight, and crying out in despair: Alas! we can do

[1] " Et si ambulavero in medio umbræ mortis . . . virga tua, et baculus tuus, ipsa me consolata sunt."—*Ps.* xxii. 4.

[2] " Egredietur virga de radice Jesse, et flos de radice ejus ascendet." —*Is.* xi. 1.

[3] " Hæc est virga illa, qua retunduntur impetus adversantium dæmoniorum."—*S. de Assumpt.*

[4] " Si Maria pro nobis, quis contra nos ?"

nought, for she who is without stain defends him." In like manner, Father Gaspar Haywood was assaulted by devils at his death, and greatly tempted against faith ; he immediately recommended himself to the most Blessed Virgin, and was heard to exclaim, "I thank thee, Mary; for thou hast come to my aid." [1]

St. Bonaventure tells us that Mary sends without delay the prince of the heavenly court, St. Michael, with all the angels, to defend her dying servants against the temptations of the devils, and to receive the souls of all who in a special manner and perseveringly have recommended themselves to her. The saint, addressing our Blessed Lady, says, "Michael, the leader and prince of the heavenly army, with all the administering spirits, obeys thy commands, O Virgin, and defends and receives the souls of the faithful who have particularly recommended themselves to thee, O Lady, day and night." [2]

The prophet Isaias tells us that when a man is on the point of leaving the world, hell is opened and sends forth its most terrible demons, both to tempt the soul before it leaves the body, and also to accuse it when presented before the tribunal of Jesus Christ for judgment. The prophet says, *Hell below was in an uproar to meet thee at thy coming; it stirred up the giants for thee.* [3] But Richard of St. Laurence remarks that when the soul is defended by Mary, the devils dare not even accuse it, knowing that the judge never condemned, and never will condemn, a soul protected by his august Mother. He asks, " Who would dare accuse one who is patronized by the Mother

[1] *Menol.* 28 *Apr.*–9 *Jan.*

[2] " Michael, dux et princeps militiæ cœlestis, cum omnibus spiritibus administratoriis, tuis, Virgo, paret præceptis, in defendendis in corpore et suscipiendis de corpore animabus fidelium, specialiter tibi, Domina. die ac nocte se commendantium."—*Spec. B. V. lect.* 3.

[3] " Infernus subter conturbatus est in occursum adventus tui; suscitabit tibi gigantes."—*Is.* xiv. 9

of Him who is to judge?"[1] Mary not only assists her beloved servants at death and encourages them, but she herself accompanies them to the tribunal-seat of God.

As St. Jerome says, writing to the virgin Eustochia, "What a day of joy will that be for thee, when Mary the Mother of our Lord, accompanied by choirs of virgins, will go to meet thee."[2] The Blessed Virgin assured St. Bridget of this; for, speaking of her devout clients at the point of death, she said, "Then will I, their dear Lady and Mother, fly to them, that they may have consolation and refreshment."[3] St. Vincent Ferrer says, that not only does the most Blessed Virgin console and refresh them, but that "she receives the souls of the dying."[4] This loving Queen takes them under her mantle, and thus presents them to the judge, her Son, and most certainly obtains their salvation. This really happened to Charles, the son of St. Bridget,[5] who died in the army, far from his mother. She feared much for his salvation on account of the dangers to which young men are exposed in a military career; but the Blessed Virgin revealed to her that he was saved on account of his love for her, and that in consequence she herself had assisted him at death, and had suggested to him the acts that should be made at that terrible moment. At the same time the saint saw Jesus on his throne, and the devil bringing two accusations against the most Blessed Virgin: the first was, that Mary had prevented him from tempting Charles at the moment of death; and the second

[1] "Quis apud Filium accusare audeat, cui viderit Matrem patrocinantem?"—*De Laud. V.* l. 2, p. 1.

[2] "Qualis erit illa dies, quum tibi Maria, Mater Domini, choris occurret comitata virgineis?"—*De Cust. virg.*

[3] "Ideo, ego carissima domina eorum et Mater, occurram eis in morte, ut etiam in ipsa morte consolationem et refrigerium habeant."—*Rev.* l. i. c. 29.

[4] "Beata Virgo animas morientium suscipit."

[5] *Rev.* l. 7, c. 13.

was, that this Blessed Virgin had herself presented his
soul to the judge, and so saved it without even giving
him the opportunity of exposing the grounds on which
he claimed it. She then saw the judge drive the devil
away, and Charles's soul carried to heaven.

Ecclesiasticus says, that *her bands are a healthful binding*,[1] and that *in the latter end thou shalt find rest in her*.[2]
O, you are indeed fortunate, my brother, if at death you
are bound with the sweet chains of the love of the Mother
of God! These chains are chains of salvation; they are
chains that will insure your eternal salvation, and will
make you enjoy in death that blessed peace which will
be the beginning of your eternal peace and rest. Father
Binetti, in his book on the perfections of our blessed
Lord, says, "that having attended the death-bed of a
great lover of Mary, he heard him, before expiring, utter
these words: 'O my Father, would that you could know
the happiness that I now enjoy from having served the
most holy Mother of God; I cannot tell you the joy that
I now experience.'"[3] Father Suarez (in consequence of
his devotion to Mary, which was such that he used to
say that he would willingly exchange all his learning for
the merit of a single "Hail Mary") died with such peace
and joy, that in that moment he said "I could not have
thought that death was so sweet;"[4] meaning, that he
could never have imagined that it was possible, if he had
not then experienced it, that he could have found such
sweetness in death.

You, devout reader, will, without doubt, experience
the same joy and contentment in death, if you can then
remember that you have loved this good mother, who
cannot be otherwise than faithful to her children who

---

[1] "Vincula illius, alligatura salutaris."—*Ecclus.* vi. 31.
[2] "In novissimis invenies requiem in ea."—*Ibid.* 29.
[3] *Chef-d'œuvre de D.* p. 3, ch. 6.
[4] "Non putabam tam dulce esse mori."

7

have been faithful in serving and honoring her, by their visits, rosaries, and fasts, and still more by frequently thanking and praising her, and often recommending themselves to her powerful protection. Nor will this consolation be withheld, even if you have been for a time a sinner, provided that, from this day, you are careful to live well, and to serve this most gracious and benign Lady. In your pains, and in the temptations to despair which the devil will send you, she will console you, and even come herself to assist you in your last moments.

Such also will be your death, beloved reader, if you are faithful to Mary. Though you may have hitherto offended God, she will procure you a sweet and happy death. And if by chance at that moment you are greatly alarmed and lose confidence at the sight of your sins, she will come and encourage you, as she did Adolphus, Count of Alsace, who abandoned the world, and embraced the Order of St. Francis. In the Chronicles of that Order, we are told that he had a tender devotion to the Mother of God; and that when he was at the point of death, his former life and the rigors of divine justice presented themselves before his mind, and caused him to tremble at the thought of death, and fear for his eternal salvation. Scarcely had these thoughts entered his mind, when Mary (who is always active when her servants are in pain), accompanied by many saints, presented herself before the dying man, and encouraged him with words of the greatest tenderness, saying: "My own beloved Adolph, thou art mine, thou hast given thyself to me, and now why dost thou fear death so much?" On hearing these words, the servant of Mary was instantly relieved, fear was banished from his soul, and he expired in the midst of the greatest peace and joy.[1]

Let us then be of good heart, though we be sinners, and feel certain that Mary will come and assist us at death, and comfort and console us with her presence, provided only that we serve her with love during the remainder of

[1] *Auriemma, Aff. scamb. p. 2, c. 8.*

the time that we have to be in this world. Our Queen, one day addressing St. Matilda, promised that she would assist all her clients at death, who, during their lives, had faithfully served her. "I, as a most tender Mother, will faithfully be present at the death of all who piously serve me, and will console and protect them." [1] O God, what a consolation will it be at that last moment of our lives, when our eternal lot has so soon to be decided, to see the Queen of Heaven assisting and consoling us with the assurance of her protection.

Besides the cases already given in which we have seen Mary assisting her dying servants, there are innumerable others recorded in different works. This favor was granted to St. Clare; to St. Felix, of the Order of Capuchins; to St. Clare of Montefalco; to St. Teresa; to St. Peter of Alcantara. But, for our common consolation, I will relate the following: Father Crasset [2] tells us, that Mary of Oignies saw the Blessed Virgin at the pillow of a devout widow of Willembroc, who was ill with a violent fever. Mary stood by her side, consoling her, and cooling her with a fan. Let us close this subject with another example, in which we shall see how great is the tenderness of this good Mother towards her children at death.

EXAMPLE.*

Of St. John of God, who was tenderly devoted to Mary, it is related that he fully expected that she would visit him on his deathbed; but not seeing her arrive, he was afflicted, and perhaps even complained. But when his last hour had come, the divine Mother appeared, and gently reproving him for his little confidence, addressed him in the following tender words, which may well encourage all servants of

---

[1] "Ego omnibus, qui mihi pie et sancte deserviunt, volo in morte fidelissime tamquam mater piissima, adesse, eosque consolari ac protegere."—*Apud Blos. Concl. an. fid. c.* 12.

[2] *Vér. Dév.* p. I, tr. I, q. II.

Mary: "John, it is not in me to forsake my clients at such a moment." As though she had said: "John, of what wast thou thinking? Didst thou imagine that I had abandoned thee? And dost thou not know that I never abandon my clients at the hour of death? If I did not come sooner, it was that thy time was not yet come; but now that it is come, behold me here to take thee; let us go to Heaven." Shortly afterwards the saint expired, and fled to that blessed kingdom, there to thank his most loving Queen for all eternity.

---

¹ 'Hæc est hora qua devotis meis famulis deesse nunquam soleo."
—*Boll.* 8 *Mart. Vit.* 2, c. 8.

Prayer.

O my most sweet Mother, how shall I die, poor sinner that I am? Even now the thought of that important moment when I must expire, and appear before the judgment seat of God, and the remembrance that I have myself so often written my condemnation by consenting to sin, makes me tremble. I am confounded, and fear much for my eternal salvation. O Mary, in the blood of Jesus, and in thy intercession, is all my hope. Thou art the Queen of Heaven, the mistress of the universe; in short, thou art the Mother of God. Thou art great, but thy greatness does not prevent, nay even it inclines thee to greater compassion towards us in our miseries. Worldly friends, when raised to dignity, disdain to notice their former friends who may have fallen into distress. Thy noble and loving heart does not act thus, for the greater the miseries it beholds, the greater are its efforts to relieve. Thou, when called upon, dost immediately assist; nay more, thou dost anticipate our prayers by thy favors; thou consolest us in our afflictions; thou dissipatest the storms by which we are tossed about; thou overcomest all enemies; thou, in fine, never losest an occasion to promote our welfare. May that divine hand which has united in thee such majesty and such tenderness, such greatness and so much love, be forever blessed! I thank my Lord for it, and congratulate myself in having so great an advantage; for truly in thy felicity do I place my own, and I consider thy lot as mine. O comfortress of the afflicted, console a poor creature who recommends himself to thee. The remorse of a conscience overburdened with sin fills me with affliction. I am in doubt as to whether I have sufficiently grieved for them. I see that all my actions are sullied and defective; hell awaits my death in order to accuse me; the outraged justice of God demands satisfaction. My Mother, what will become of me? If thou dost not help me, I am lost. What sayest thou, wilt thou assist me? O compassionate Virgin, console me; obtain for me true sorrow for my sins; obtain for me strength to amend, and to be faithful to God during the rest of my life. And finally, when I am in the last agonies of death, O Mary, my hope, abandon me not; then, more than ever, help and encourage me, that I may not despair at the sight of my sins, which the evil one will then place before me. My Lady, forgive my temerity; come thyself to comfort me with thy presence in that last struggle. This favor thou hast granted to many, grant it also to me. If my boldness is great, thy goodness is greater; for it goes in search of the most miserable to console them. On this I rely. For thy eternal glory, let it be said that thou hast snatched a wretched creature from hell, to which he was already condemned, and that thou hast led him to thy kingdom. O yes, sweet Mother, I hope to have the consolation of remaining always at thy feet, in heaven, thanking and blessing and loving thee eternally. O Mary, I shall expect thee at my last hour; deprive me not of this consolation. *Fiat, fiat.* Amen, amen.

CHAPTER III.

Spes nostra ! Salve.

MARY, OUR HOPE.

I.

Mary is the Hope of All.

MODERN heretics cannot endure that we should salute and call Mary our hope : "Hail, our Hope !" They say that God alone is our hope ; and that he curses those who put their trust in creatures in these words of the prophet Jeremias: *Cursed be the man that trusteth in man.*[1] Mary, they exclaim, is a creature ; and how can a creature be our hope ? This is what the heretics say ; but in spite of this, the holy Church obliges all ecclesiastics and religious each day to raise their voices, and in name of all the faithful invoke and call Mary by the sweet name of " our Hope,"—the hope of all.

The angelical Doctor St. Thomas says,[2] that we can place our hope in a person in two ways : as a principal cause, and as a mediate one. Those who hope for a favor from a king, hope it from him as lord ; they hope for it from his minister or favorite as an intercessor. If the favor is granted, it comes primarily from the king, but it comes through the instrumentality of the favorite; and in this case he who seeks the favor is right in calling his intercessor his hope. The King of Heaven, being infinite goodness, desires in the highest degree to enrich us with his graces ; but because confidence is requisite on our part, and in order to increase it in us, he has given us his own Mother to be our mother and advocate, and to her he has given all power to help us ; and therefore he wills that we should repose our hope of salva-

[1] " Maledictus homo qui confidit in homine."—*Jer.* xvii. 5.
[2] 2. 2, q. 25, a. 1, ad 3.

tion and of every blessing in her. Those who place
their hopes in creatures alone, independently of God, as
sinners do, and in order to obtain the friendship and
favor of a man, fear not to outrage his divine Majesty,
are most certainly cursed by God, as the prophet
Jeremias says. But those who hope in Mary, as Mother
of God, who is able to obtain graces and eternal life for
them, are truly blessed and acceptable to the heart of
God, who desires to see that greatest of his creatures
honored ; for she loved and honored him in this world
more than all men and angels put together. And therefore we justly and reasonably call the Blessed Virgin
our hope, trusting, as Cardinal Bellarmin says, "that
we shall obtain, through her intercession, that which we
should not obtain by our own unaided prayers." "We
pray to her," says the learned Suarez, "in order that the
dignity of the intercessor may supply for our own unworthiness; so that,"[1] he continues, "to implore the
Blessed Virgin in such a spirit, is not diffidence in the
mercy of God, but fear of our own unworthiness."[2]

It is, then, not without reason that the holy Church,
in the words of Ecclesiasticus, calls Mary *the Mother of
holy Hope.*[3] She is the mother who gives birth to holy
hope in our hearts ; not to the hope of the vain and
transitory goods of this life, but of the immense and
eternal goods of heaven.

"Hail, then, O hope of my soul!" exclaims St.
Ephrem, addressing this divine Mother ; "hail, O certain salvation of Christians ; hail, O helper of sinners ;
hail, fortress of the faithful and salvation of the world!"[4]

[1] "Ut dignitas intercessoris suppleat inopiam nostram."

[2] "Unde, virginem interpellare. non est de divina misericordia diffidere, sed de propria indignitate timere."—*De Inc.* p. 2, d. 23. s. 3.

[3] "Ego mater . . . sanctæ spei."—*Ecclus.* xxiv. 24.

[4] "Ave animæ Spes ! ave, Christianorum firma Salus ! ave, peccatorum Adjutrix ! ave, Vallum fidelium et mundi Salus !"—*De Laud.
Dei Gen.*

Other saints remind us, that after God, our only hope is Mary ; and therefore they call her, "after God, their only hope." [1]

St. Ephrem, reflecting on the present order of Providence, by which God wills (as St. Bernard says, and as we shall prove at length) that all who are saved should be saved by the means of Mary, thus addresses her : "O Lady, cease not to watch over us ; preserve and guard us under the wings of thy compassion and mercy, for, after God, we have no hope but in thee." [2] St. Thomas of Villanova repeats the same thing, calling her "our only refuge, help, and asylum." [3] St. Bernard seems to give the reason for this when he says, "See, O man, the designs of God,—designs by which he is able to dispense his mercy more abundantly to us ; for, desiring to redeem the whole human race, he has placed the whole price of redemption in the hands of Mary, that she may dispense it at will." [4]

In the book of Exodus we read that God commanded Moses to make a mercy-seat of the purest gold, because it was thence that he would speak to him. *Thou shalt make also a propitiatory of the purest gold. . . . Thence will I give orders, and will speak to thee.* [5] St. Andrew of Crete says that "the whole world embraces Mary as being this propitiatory." And commenting on his words a pious author exclaims, "Thou, O Mary, art the propitiatory of the whole world. From thee does our most compassionate Lord speak to our hearts ; from thee he

---

[1] "Post Deum, sola spes nostra."—*Cant. p. Psalt.*

[2] "Nobis non est alia quam in te fiducia, O Virgo sincerissima ! sub alis tuæ pietatis protege et custodi nos."—*De Laud. Dei Gen.*

[3] "Tu unicum refugium, subsidium, et asylum."—*In Nat. B. V. Conc.* 3.

[4] "Intuere, O homo, consilium Dei, consilium pietatis : redempturus humanum genus, pretium universum contulit in Mariam."—*De Aquæd.*

[5] "Facies et propitiatorium de auro mundissimo . . Inde præcipiam et loquar ad te."—*Exod.* xxv. 17.

speaks words of pardon and mercy ; from thee he
bestows his gifts ; from thee all good flows to us." [1]
And therefore, before the divine Word took flesh in the
womb of Mary, he sent an archangel to ask her consent :
because he willed that the world should receive the
Incarnate Word through her, and that she should be the
source of every good. Hence St. Irenæus remarks, that
as Eve was seduced, by a fallen angel, to flee from God,
so Mary was led to receive God into her womb, obeying
a good angel ; and thus by her obedience repaired Eve's
disobedience, and became her advocate, and that of the
whole human race. "If Eve disobeyed God, yet Mary
was persuaded to obey God, that the Virgin Mary might
become the advocate of the virgin Eve. And as the
human race was bound to death through a virgin, it is
saved through a Virgin." [2] And Blessed Raymond Jordano also says, "that every good, every help, every grace
that men have received and will receive from God until
the end of time, came, and will come, to them by the in-
tercesssion and through the hands of Mary." [3]

The devout Blosius, then, might well exclaim, "O
Mary, O thou who art so loving and gracious towards
all who love thee, tell me, who can be so infatuated and
unfortunate as not to love thee ? Thou, in the midst of
their doubts and difficulties, enlightenest the minds of
all who, in their afflictions, have recourse to thee. Thou
encouragest those who fly to thee in time of danger;

[1] " Te universus mundus continet commune propitiatorium : inde
pientissimus Dominus nobis loquitur ad cor ; inde responsa dat benignitatis et veniæ ; inde responsa dat benignitatis et veniæ : inde
munera largitur : inde omne nobis bonum emanat."—*Paciucch. in Sal.
Ang. Exc.* 20.

[2] " Quid est quod sine Mariæ consensu non perficitur Incarnationis
mysterium ? quia nempe vult illam Deus omnium bonorum esse principium."—*Ap. C. à Lap. In Prov.* xxxi. 29.

[3] " Per ipsam, habet mundus et habiturus est omne bonum."—*Cont.
B. M. in prol.*

thou succorest those who call upon thee ; thou, after thy divine Son, art the certain salvation of thy. faithful servants. Hail, then, O hope of those who are in despair ; O succor of those who are abandoned. O Mary, thou art all-powerful ; for thy divine Son, to honor thee, complies instantly with all thy desires." [1]

St. Germanus, recognizing in Mary the source of all our good, and that she delivers us from every evil, thus invokes her : "O, my sovereign Lady, thou alone art the one whom God has appointed to be my solace here below; thou art the guide of my pilgrimage, the strength of my weakness, the riches of my poverty, remedy for the healing of my wounds, the soother of my pains, the end of my captivity, the hope of my salvation! Hear my prayers, have pity on my tears, I conjure thee, O thou who art my queen, my refuge, my love, my help, my hope and my strength." [2]

We need not, then, be surprised that St. Antoninus applies the following verse of the Book of Wisdom to Mary: *Now all good things came to me together with her.* [3] For as this Blessed Virgin is the Mother and dispenser of all good things, the whole world, and more particularly each individual who lives in it as a devout client of this great Queen, may say with truth, that with devo-

[1] "O Maria ! quis te non amet ? tu enim in dubiis es lumen, in mœroribus solatium, in periculis refugium. Tu, post Unigenitum tuum certa fidelium salus. Ave. desperantium Spes. ave, destitutorum Adjutrix ! Cujus honori tantum tribuit Filius, ut, quidquid volueris, mox fiat."—*Par. an.* p. 2, c. 4.

[2] "O Domina mea, tu sola mihi ex Deo solatium, itineris mei directio, debilitatis meæ potentia, mendicitatis meæ divitiæ, vulnerum meorum medicina, dolorum meorum relevatio, vinculorum meorum solutio, salutis meæ spes ; exaudi orationes meas, miserere suspiriorum meorum, Domina mea, Refugium, Vita, Auxilium, Spes, et Robur meum !"—*Encom. in S. Deip.*

[3] "Venerunt autem mihi omnia bona pariter cum illa."—*Wisd* vii. 11.

tion to Mary, both he and the world have obtained
everything good and perfect The saint thus expresses
his thought : "She is the Mother of all good things, and
the world can truly say, that with her (that is, the most
Blessed Virgin) it has received all good things." [1] And
hence the Blessed Abbot of Celles expressly declares,
"that when we find Mary, we find all." [2] Whoever finds
Mary finds every good thing, obtains all graces and all
virtues; for by her powerful intercession she obtains all
that is necessary to enrich him with divine grace. In
the Book of Proverbs Mary herself tells us that she possesses all the riches of God, that is to say, his mercies,
that she may dispense them in favor of her lovers.
*With me are riches . . . and glorious riches . . . that I may en-
rich them that love me.* [3] And therefore St. Bonaventure
says: "That we ought all to keep our eyes constantly
fixed on Mary's hands, that through them we may receive the graces that we desire." [4]

O, how many who were once proud have become
humble by devotion to Mary ! how many who were passionate have become meek ! how many in the midst of
darkness have found light ! how many who were in despair have found confidence ! how many who were lost
have found salvation by the same powerful means ! And
this she clearly foretold in the house of Elizabeth, in
her own sublime canticle : *Behold, from henceforth all
generations shall call me blessed.* [5] And St. Bernard, in-
terpreting her words. says: "All generations call thee

[1] "Omnium bonorum mater est, et venerunt mihi omnia bona cum
illa scilicet virgine, potest dicere mundus."—P. 4, l. 15, c. 20, § 12.

[2] "Inventa Maria, invenitur omne bonum."—*De Cont. de V. M.
in Prol.*

[3] "Mecum sunt divitiæ, et . . . opes superbæ . . . ut ditem diligentes me."—*Prov.* viii. 18.

[4] "Oculi omnium nostrum ad manus Mariæ semper debent respi-
cere, ut per manus ejus aliquid boni accipiamus."—*Spec. B. V. lect.* 3.

[5] "Ecce enim ex hoc beatam me dicent omnes generationes."

blessed, because thou hast given life and glory to all nations,' for in thee sinners find pardon, and the just perseverance in the grace of God." [1]

Hence the devout Lanspergius makes our Lord thus address the world : "Men, poor children of Adam, who live surrounded by so many enemies and in the midst of so many trials, endeavor to honor my Mother and yours in a special manner : for I have given Mary to the world, that she may be your model, and that from her you may learn to lead good lives; and also that she may be a refuge to which you can fly in all your afflictions and trials. I have rendered this, my daughter, such that no one need fear or have the least repugnance to have recourse to her ; and for this purpose I have created her of so benign and compassionate a disposition, that she knows not how to despise any one who takes refuge with her, nor can she deny her favor to any one who seeks it. The mantle of her mercy is open to all, and she allows no one to leave her feet without consoling him." [3] May the immense goodness of our God be ever praised and blessed for having given us this so great, so tender, so loving a mother and advocate.

O God, how tender are the sentiments of confidence expressed by the enamoured St. Bonaventure towards Jesus our most loving Redeemer, and Mary our most loving advocate ! He says, "Whatever God foresees to

---

[1] "Ex hoc Beatam te dicent omnes generationes, quæ omnibus generationibus vitam et gloriam genuisti."—*In Pentec.* s. 2.

[2] "In te justi gratiam, peccatores veniam inveniunt in æternum." —*In Pent.* s. 2.

[3] "Matrem meam devotione præcipua venerate. Ego enim hanc mundo dedi, in puritatis exemplum, in præsidium tutissimum, ut sit tribulatis asylum. Quam nemo formidet, nemo ad eam accedere trepidet ; propterea namque adeo feci eam mitem, adeo misericordem, ut neminem aspernetur. nulli se neget, omnibus pietatis sinum apertum teneat; neminem a se redire tristem sinat."—*Alloq.* l. 1, p. 4. *can.* 12.

be my lot, I know that he cannot refuse himself to any one who loves him and seeks for him with his whole heart. I will embrace him with my love ; and if he does not bless me, I will still cling to him so closely that he will be unable to go without me. If I can do nothing else, at least I will hide myself in his wounds, and taking up my dwelling there, it will be in himself alone that he will find me." And the saint concludes, " If my Redeemer rejects me on account of my sins, and drives me from his sacred feet, I will cast myself at those of his beloved Mother Mary, and there I will remain prostrate until she has obtained my forgiveness ; for this Mother of Mercy knows not, and has never known, how to do otherwise than compassionate the miserable, and comply with the desires of the most destitute who fly to her for succor ; and therefore," he says, "if not by duty, at least by compassion, she will engage her Son to pardon me." [1]

"Look down upon us, then," let us exclaim, in the words of Euthymius, "look down upon us, O most compassionate Mother ; cast thine eyes of mercy on us, for we are thy servants, and in thee we have placed all our confidence." [2]

---

[1] " Quantumcumque me Deus præsciverit, scio quod seipsum negare non potest. Eum amplexabor, et, si non mihi benedixerit, nec tunc dimittam; et sine me recedere non valebit. In cavernis vulnerum suorum me abscondam, ibique extra se me invenire non poterit. Ad matris suæ pedes provolutus stabo, ut mihi veniam impetret. Ipsa enim non misereri ignorat, et miseris non satisfacere nunquam scivit. Ideoque ex compassione maxima mihi ad indulgentiam Filium inclinabit."—*Stim. div. am.* p. 3, c. 13.

[2] " Respice, O Mater misericordiosissima ! respice servos tuos ; in te enim omnem spem nostram collocavimus."—*Ap. Sur.* 31 *Aug.*

EXAMPLE.*

St. Gregory relates that there was a young woman named Musa, who was very devout to the Mother of God; to whom, when she was in great danger of·losing her innocence by the bad example of her companions, Mary appeared one day with many saints, and said: "Musa, dost thou also wish to be one of these?" On her answering "Yes," she added, "Well, withdraw from thy companions, and prepare thyself, for in a month thou shalt come." Musa did so, and related the vision. On the thirteenth day she was at the point of death, when the most Blessed Virgin again appeared, and invited her to come. She replied, "Behold, I come, O Lady," and sweetly expired.[1]

[1] *Dial.* 1. 4. c. 17.

Prayer.

O Mother of holy love, our life, our refuge, and our hope, thou well knowest that thy son Jesus Christ, not content with being himself our perpetual advocate with the eternal Father, has willed that thou also shouldst interest thyself ·with. him, in order to obtain the divine mercies for us. He has decreed that thy prayers should aid our salvation, and has made them so efficacious that they obtain all that they ask. To thee therefore, who art the hope of the miserable, do I, a wretched sinner, turn my eyes. I trust, O Lady, that in the first place through the merits of Jesus Chirst, and then through thy intercession, I shall be saved. Of this I am certain; and my confidence in thee is such, that if my eternal salvation were in my own hands, I should place it in thine, for I rely more on thy mercy and pro-tection than on all my own works. My mother and my hope,

abandon me not, though I deserve that thou shouldst do so.
See my miseries, and, being moved thereby with compassion,
help and save me. I own that I have too often closed my heart,
by my sins, against the lights and helps that thou hast procured
for me from the Lord. But thy compassion for the miserable,
and thy power with God, far surpass the number and malice of
my sins. It is well known to all, both in heaven and on earrth,
that whosoever is protected by thee is certainly saved. All may
forget me, provided only that thou dost remember me, O
Mother of an omnipotent God. Tell him that I am thy servant;
say only that thou defendest me, and I shall be saved. O
Mary, I trust in thee; in this hope I live; in it I desire and
hope to die, repeating always, "Jesus is my only hope, and
after Jesus the most Blessed Virgin Mary." [1]

II.

Mary is the Hope of Sinners.

In the first chapter of the Book of Genesis we read
that *God made two great lights; a greater light to rule the
day; and a lesser light to rule the night.* [2] Cardinal Hugo
says that "Christ is the greater light to rule the just, and
Mary the lesser to rule the sinners;" [3] meaning that the sun
is a figure of Jesus Christ, whose light is enjoyed by
the just who live in the clear day of divine grace; and
that the moon is a figure of Mary, by whose means those
who are in the night of sin are enlightened. Since Mary

[1] "Unica spes mea Jesus et post Jesum Virgo Maria."

[2] "Fecitque Deus duo luminaria magna: luminare majus, ut præesset diei, et luminare minus, ut præesset nocti."—*Gen.* i. 16.

[3] "Luminare majus, Christus, qui præest justis; luminare minus,
Beata Maria, quæ præest peccatoribus."

is this auspicious luminary, and is so for the benefit of
poor sinners, should any one have been so unfortunate
as to fall into the night of sin, what is he to do? Innocent III. replies, "Whoever is in the night of sin, let him
cast his eyes on the moon, let him implore Mary."[1] Since
he has lost the light of the sun of justice by losing the
grace of God, let him turn to the moon, and beseech
Mary; and she will certainly give him light to see the
misery of his state, and strength to leave it without delay.
St. Methodius says "that by the prayers of Mary almost
innumerable sinners are converted."[2]

One of the titles which is the most encouraging to poor
sinners, and under which the Church teaches us to invoke
Mary in the Litany of Loretto, is that of "Refuge of
Sinners." In Judea in ancient times there were cities of
refuge, in which criminals who fled there for protection
were exempt from the punishments which they had deserved. Nowadays these cities are not so numerous;
there is but one, and that is Mary, of whom the Psalmist
says *Glorious things are said of thee, O city of God.*[3] But
this city differs from the ancient ones in this respect—
that in the latter all kinds of criminals did not find
refuge, nor was the protection extended to every class
of crime; but under the mantle of Mary all sinners,
without exception, find refuge for every sin that they
may have committed, provided only that they go there
to seek for this protection. "I am the city of refuge,"
says St. John Damascene, in the name of our Queen, "to
all who fly to me."[4] And it is sufficient to have recourse

---

[1] "Qui jacet in nocte culpæ, respiciat Lunam, deprecetur Mariam."
—*In Assumpt.* s. 2.

[2] "Mariæ virtute et precibus pene innumeræ peccatorum conver-
siones fiunt."—*Paciucch. in Ps.* lxxxvi. *exc.* 17.

[3] "Gloriosa dicta sunt de te. Civitas Dei."—*Ps.* lxxxvi. 3.

[4] "Ego Civitas refugii omnium ad me confugientum."—*In Dorm.
B. V. or.* 2.

to her, for whoever has the good fortune to enter this city need not speak to be saved. *Assemble yourselves, and let us enter into the fenced city, and let us be silent there,*[1] to speak in the words of the prophet Jeremias. This city, says Blessed Albert the Great, is the most holy Virgin fenced in with grace and glory. "And let us be silent there," that is, continues an interpreter, "because we dare not invoke the Lord, whom we have offended, she will invoke and ask."[2] For if we do not presume to ask our Lord to forgive us, it will suffice to enter this city and be silent, for Mary will speak and ask all that we require. And for this reason, a devout author exhorts all sinners to take refuge under the mantle of Mary, exclaiming, "Fly, O Adam and Eve, and all you their children, who have outraged God; fly, and take refuge in the bosom of this good mother; know you not that she is our only city of refuge?"[3] "the only hope of sinners,"[4] as she is also called in a sermon by an ancient writer, found in the works of St. Augustine.

St. Ephrem, addressing this Blessed Virgin, says, "Thou art the only advocate of sinners, and of all who are unprotected." And then he salutes her in the following words: "Hail, refuge and hospital of sinners!"[5] —true refuge, in which alone they can hope for reception and liberty. And an author remarks that this was the meaning of David when he said, *For He hath hidden me in his tabernacle.*[6] And truly what can this tabernacle of God be, unless it is Mary? who is called by St. Ger-

---

[1] "Ingrediamur civitatem munitam, et sileamus ibi.—*Jer.* viii. 14.

[2] "Quia non audemus deprecari Dominum, quem offendimus, ipsa deprecetur et roget."—*Bib. Mar. Jer.* n. 3.

[3] "Fugite, O Adam et Eva! fugite ipsorum liberi, intra sinum Matris Mariæ: ipsa est Civitas refugii, spes unica peccatorum."—*B. Fernandez in Gen.* c. 3, s. 22.

[4] "Spes unica peccatorum."—*Serm.* 194, *E. B. app.*

[5] "Ave, peccatorum Refugium et Hospitium."—*De Laud. Dei gen.*

[6] "Protexit me in abscondito Tabernaculi sui."—*Ps.* xxvi. 5.

manus, " A tabernacle made by God, in which he alone entered to accomplish the great work of the redemption of man." [1]

St. Basil of Seleucia remarks, " that if God granted to some who were only his servants such power, that not only their touch but even their shadows healed the sick, who were placed for this purpose in the public streets, how much greater power must we suppose that he has granted to her who was not only his handmaid but his Mother?" We may indeed say that our Lord has given us Mary as a public infirmary,[2] in which all who are sick, poor, and destitute can be received. But now I ask, in hospitals erected expressly for the poor, who have the greatest claim to admission? Certainly the most infirm, and those who are in the greatest need.

And for this reason should any one find himself devoid of merit and overwhelmed with spiritual infirmities, that is to say, sin, he can thus address Mary : O Lady, thou art the refuge of the sick poor : reject me not ; for as I am the poorest and the most infirm of all, I have the greatest right to be welcomed by thee.

Let us then cry out with St. Thomas of Villanova, "O Mary, we poor sinners know no other refuge than thee, for thou art our only hope, and on thee we rely for our salvation." [3] Thou art our only advocate with Jesus Christ ; to thee we all turn ourselves.

In the revelations of St. Bridget, Mary is called the " Star preceding the sun," [4] giving us thereby to understand, that when devotion towards the divine Mother

---

[1] " Tabernaculum a Deo fabricatum, in quo solus Deus ingressus est, sacris mysticis occulte operaturus in te pro salute omnium."—*In Nat. S. M. or.* 2.

[2] " Aperuit nobis Deus publicum valetudinarium."

[3] " Nescimus aliud refugium, nisi te ; tu sola es unica Spes nostra, in qua confidimus ; tu sola Patrona nostra, ad quam omnes aspicimus." —*De Nat. V. M. conc.* 3.

[4] " Sidus vadens ante Solem."—*Rev. Extr.* c. 50.

begins to manifest itself in a soul that is in a state of sin, it is a certain mark that before long God will enrich it with his grace. The glorious St. Bonaventure, in order to revive the confidence of sinners in the protection of Mary, places before them the picture of a tempestuous sea, into which sinners have already fallen from the ship of divine grace ; they are already dashed about on every side by remorse of conscience and by fear of the judgments of God ; they are without light or guide, and are on the point of losing the last breath of hope and falling into despair; then it is that our Lord, pointing out Mary to them, who is commonly called the "Star of the Sea," raises his voice and says, " O poor lost sinners, despair not ; raise up your eyes, and cast them on this beautiful star ; breathe again with confidence, for it will save you from this tempest, and will guide you into the port of salvation." [1]   St. Bernard says the same thing: " If thou wouldst not be lost in the tempest, cast thine eyes on the star, and invoke Mary." [2]

The devout Blosius declares that "she is the only refuge of those who have offended God, the asylum of all who are oppressed by temptation, calamity, or persecution. This Mother is all mercy, benignity, and sweetness, not only to the just, but also to despairing sinners ; so that no sooner does she perceive them coming to her, and seeking her health from their hearts, than she aids them, welcomes them, and obtains their pardon from her Son. She knows not how to despise any one, however unworthy he may be of mercy, and therefore denies her protection to none; she consoles all, and is no sooner called upon than she helps whoever it may be that invokes her. She by her sweetness often awakens and

[1] " Respirate ad illam, perditi peccatores, et perducet vos ad portum."—*Psal. B. V. ps.* 18.

[2] " Si non vis obrui procellis, respice Stellam, voca Mariam."—*De Laud. V. M. hom.* 2.

draws sinners to her devotion who are the most at enmity
with God and the most deeply plunged in the lethargy
of sin ; and then, by the same means, she excites them
effectually, and prepares them for grace, and thus renders them fit for the kingdom of heaven. God has created this his beloved daughter of so compassionate and
sweet a disposition, that no one can fear to have recourse
to her." The pious author concludes in these words :
" It is impossible for any one to perish who attentively,
and with humility, cultivates devotion towards this
divine Mother." [1]

In Ecclesiasticus Mary is called a plane-tree : *As a
plane-tree I was exalted.* [2]   And she is so called that sinners
may understand that as the plane-tree gives shelter to
travellers from the heat of the sun, so does Mary invite
them to take shelter under her protection from the wrath
of God, justly enkindled against them.   St. Bonaventure
remarks that the prophet Isaias complained of the times
in which he lived, saying, *Behold thou art angry, and we
have sinned . . . there is none . . . that riseth up and taketh hold
of thee.* [3]   And then he makes the following commentary:
" It is true, O Lord, that at the time there was none to
raise up sinners and withhold thy wrath, for Mary was

[1] " Ipsa peccantium singulare refugium.   Ipsa omnium, quos tentatio, calamitas, aut persecutio aliqua urget, tutissimum asylum. Tota
mitis est, tota suavis, non solum justis, verum etiam peccatoribus ac
desperatis.   Quos, ut ad se ex corde clamare conspexerit, statim ad-
juvat, suscipit, et Judici reconciliat.   Nullum aspernatur, nulli se
negat ; omnes consolatur, et, vel tenuiter invocata, præsto adest. Sua
bonitate sæpe eos, qui Deo minus afficiuntur, ad sui cultum blande
allicit, potenterque excitat ut per hujuscemodi studium, præparentur
ad gratiam, et tandem apti reddantur regno cœlorum.   Talis a Deo
facta est, ut nemo ad eam accedere trepidet.   Fieri non potest, ut
pereat, qui Mariæ sedulus et humilis cultor fuerit."—*Par. an. fid.* p.
1, c. 18.

[2] " Quasi platanus exaltata sum."—*Ecclus.* xxiv. 19.

[3] " Ecce tu iratus es, et peccavimus . . .; non est qui . . . consurgat,
et teneat te."—*Is.* lxiv. 5.

not yet born ;" " before Mary," to quote the saint's own words, " there was no one who could thus dare to restrain the arm of God." But now, if God is angry with a sinner, and Mary takes him under her protection, she withholds the avenging arm of her Son, and saves him. "And so," continues the same saint, "no one can be found more fit for this office than Mary, who seizes the sword of divine justice with her own hands to prevent it from falling upon and punishing the sinner." [1] Upon the same subject Richard of St. Laurence says that " God, before the birth of Mary, complained by the mouth of the prophet Ezechiel that there was no one to rise up and withhold him from chastising sinners, but that he could find no one, for this office was reserved for our Blessed Lady, who withholds his arm until he is pacified. [2]

Basil of Seleucia encourages sinners, saying, "O sinner, be not discouraged, but have recourse to Mary in all thy necessities; call her to thine assistance, for thou wilt always find her ready to help thee; for such is the divine will that she should help all in every kind of necessity." [3] This mother of mercy has so great a desire to save the most abandoned sinners, that she herself goes in search of them, in order to help them; and if they have recourse to her, she knows how to find the means to render them acceptable to God. The patriarch Isaac, desiring to eat of some wild animal, promised his blessing to his son Esau on his procuring this food for him; but Rebecca, who was anxious that her other son Jacob should receive

[1] " Ante Mariam, non fuit qui sic detinere Dominum auderet. Detinet Filium, ne peccatores percutiat. Nemo tam idoneus, qui gladio Domini pro nobis manum objiciat, ut tu Dei amantissima."— *Spec. B. V. lect.* 7, 14.

[2] " Conquerebatur Dominus, antequam Maria nasceretur: Non est qui consurgat, et teneat me."—*De Laud. B. M.* l. 2, p. 5.

[3] " Ne diffidas, peccator; sed in cunctis Mariam sequere et invoca, quam voluit Deus in cunctis subvenire "—*Paciucch. in Salve R. exc.* 7

the blessing, called him and said, *Go thy way to the flock, bring me two kids of the best, that I may make of them meat for thy father, such as he gladly eateth.*[1] St. Antoninus says,[2] "that Rebecca was a figure of Mary, who commands the angels to bring her sinners (meant by kids), that she may adorn them in such a way (by obtaining for them sorrow and purpose of amendment) as to render them dear and acceptable to the Lord." And here we may well apply to our Blessed Lady the words of the Abbot Franco: "O truly sagacious woman, who so well knew how to dress these kids, that not only they are equal to, but often superior in flavor to real venison."[3]

The Blessed Virgin herself revealed to St. Bridget "that there is no sinner in the world, however much he may be at enmity with God, who does not return to him and recover his grace, if he has recourse to her and asks her assistance."[4] The same St. Bridget one day heard Jesus Christ address his mother, and say that "she would be ready to obtain the grace of God for Lucifer himself, if only he humbled himself so far as to seek her aid."[5] That proud spirit will never humble himself so far as to implore the protection of Mary; but if such a thing were possible, Mary would be sufficiently compassionate, and her prayers would have sufficient power to obtain both forgiveness and salvation for him from God. But that which cannot be verified with regard to the devil is verified in the case of sinners who have recourse to this compassionate mother.

Noah's ark was a true figure of Mary; for as in it all

---

[1] "Pergens ad gregem, affer mihi duos hædos."—*Gen.* xxvii. 9.

[2] P. 4, t. 15, c. 2, § 2.

[3] "Vere sapiens Mulier, quæ sic novit hædos condire, ut gratiam cervorum coæquent, aut etiam superent."—*De Grat. D.* l. 3.

[4] "Nullus ita alienatus est de Deo, qui, si me invocaverit, non revertatur ad Deum.'—*Rev.* l. 6. c. 10.

[5] "Etiam diabolo exhiberes misericordiam, si humiliter peteret."—*Rev. extr.* c. 50.

kinds of beasts were saved, so under the mantle of Mary all sinners, who by their vices and sensuality are already like beasts, find refuge; but with this difference, as a pious author remarks, that "while the brutes that entered the ark remained brutes, the wolf remaining a wolf, and a tiger a tiger—under the mantle of Mary, on the other hand, the wolf becomes a lamb, and the tiger a dove." [1] One day St. Gertrude saw Mary with her mantle open, and under it there were many wild beasts of different kinds—leopards, lions, and bears; and she saw that not only our Blessed Lady did not drive them away, but that she welcomed and caressed them with her benign hand. The saint understood that these wild beasts were miserable sinners, who are welcomed by Mary with sweetness and love the moment they had recourse to her. [2]

It was, then, not without reason that St. Bernard addressed the Blessed Virgin, saying, "Thou, O Lady, dost not reject any sinner who approaches thee, however loathsome and repugnant he may be. If he asks thy assistance, thou dost not disdain to extend thy compassionate hand to him, to extricate him from the gulf of despair." [3] May our God be eternally blessed and thanked, O most amiable Mary, for having created thee so sweet and benign, even towards the most miserable sinners! Truly unfortunate is he who loves thee not, and who, having it in his power to obtain thy assistance, has no confidence in thee. He who has not recourse to Mary is lost; but who was ever lost that had recourse to the most Blessed Virgin?

---

[1] "Quod arca animalia suscepit, animalia servavit."—*Paciucch. In Sal. Ang. exc.* 4.

[2] *Insin.* l. 4, c. 50.

[3] "Tu peccatorem, quantumlibet fœtidum non horres; si ad te suspiraverit, tu illum a desperationis barathro pia manu retrahis."—*Depr. ad B. V.*

It is related in the sacred Scriptures that Booz allowed
Ruth *to gather the ears of corn, after the reapers.*[1] St.
Bonaventure says, " that as Ruth found favor with Booz,
so has Mary found favor with our Lord, and is also
allowed to gather the ears of corn after the reapers.
The reapers followed by Mary are all evangelical laborers, missionaries, preachers, and confessors, who are
constantly reaping souls for God. But there are some
hardened and rebellious souls which are abandoned even
by these. To Mary alone it is granted to save them by
her powerful intercession."[2] Truly unfortunate are
they if they do not allow themselves to be gathered,
even by this sweet Lady. They will indeed be most
certainly lost and accursed. But, on the other hand,
blessed is he who has recourse to this good Mother.
" There is not in the world," says the devout Blosius,
" any sinner, however revolting and wicked, who is
despised or rejected by Mary ; she can, she wills, and
she knows how to reconcile him to her most beloved
Son, if only he will seek her assistance."[3]

With reason then, O my most sweet Queen, did St.
John Damascene salute and call thee the " hope of those
who are in despair."[4] With reason did St. Laurence
Justinian call thee " the hope of malefactors,"[5] and
another ancient writer " the only hope of sinners."[6] St.
Ephrem calls her " the safe harbor of all sailing on the

---

[1] " Colligebat spicas post terga metentium."—*Ruth*, ii. 3.

[2] " Ruth in oculis Booz, Maria in oculis Domini hanc gratiam
invenit, ut ipsa spicas, id est, animas a messoribus derelictas, colligere
ad veniam possit."—*Spec. B. V. M. lect.* 5.

[3] " Nullum tam exsecrabilem peccatorem orbis habet, quem ipsa
abominetur, et a se repellat, quemque dilectissimo Nato suo, modo
suam precetur opem, non possit, sciat, et velit reconciliare."—*Sac.
an. fid.* p. 3. c. 5.

[4] " Salve. Spes desperatorum !"

[5] " Delinquentium Spes."

[6] " Spes unica peccatorum."

sea of the world." [1] This last-named saint also calls her "the consolation of those who are to be condemned." [2] With reason, finally, does St. Bernard exhort even the desperate not to despair; and, full of joy and tenderness towards his most dear Mother, he lovingly exclaims: "And who, O Lady, can be without confidence in thee, since thou assistest even those who are in despair? And I doubt not, that whenever we have recourse to thee, we shall obtain all that we desire. Let him, then, who is without hope, hope in thee." [3]

EXAMPLE.*

St. Antonine relates [4] that there was a sinner who was at enmity with God, and who had a vision in which he found himself before the dread tribunal; the devil accused him, and Mary defended him. The enemy produced the catalogue of his sins; it was thrown into the scales of divine justice, and weighed far more than all his good works. But then his great advocate, extending her sweet hand, placed it on the balance, and so caused it to turn in favor of her client; giving him thereby to understand that she would obtain his pardon if he changed his life; and this he did after the vision, and was entirely converted.

---

[1] "Naufragorum Portus tutissimus."

[2] "Protectrix damnatorum."

[3] "Quis non sperabit in te, quæ etiam adjuvas desperantes? . . . Non dubito quod, si ad te venerimus, habebimus quod volemus; in te ergo speret, qui desperat."—*Med. in Salv. R.*

[4] P. 4, t. 15, c. 5, § 1.

Prayer.

O most pure Virgin Mary, I venerate thy most holy heart, which was the delight and resting-place of God, thy heart overflowing with humility, purity, and divine love. I, an unhappy sinner, approach thee with a heart all loathsome and wounded. O compassionate Mother, disdain me not on this account; let such a sight rather move thee to greater tenderness, and excite thee to help me. Do not stay to seek virtues or merit in me before assisting me. I am lost, and the only thing I merit is hell. See only my confidence in thee and the purpose I have to amend. Consider all that Jesus has done and suffered for me, and then abandon me if thou canst. I offer thee all the pains of his life; the cold that he endured in the stable; his journey into Egypt; the blood which he shed; the poverty, sweats, sorrows, and death that he endured for me; and this in thy presence. For the love of Jesus, take charge of my salvation. Ah, my Mother, I will not and cannot fear that thou wilt reject me, now that I have recourse to thee and ask thy help. Did I fear this, I should be offering an outrage to thy mercy, which goes in quest of the wretched, in order to help them. O Lady, deny not thy compassion to one to whom Jesus has not denied his blood. But the merits of this blood will not be applied to me unless thou recommendest me to God. Through thee do I hope for salvation. I ask not for riches, honors, or earthly goods. I seek only the grace of God, love towards thy Son, the accomplishment of his will, and his heavenly kingdom, that I may love him eternally. Is it possible that thou wilt not hear me? No; for already thou hast granted my prayer, as I hope; already thou prayest for me; already thou obtainest me the graces that I ask; already thou takest me under thy protection. My Mother, abandon me not. Never, never cease to pray for me, until thou seest me safe in heaven at thy feet, blessing and thanking thee forever. Amen.

CHAPTER IV.

Ad te clamamus, exsules filii Evæ.

TO THEE DO WE CRY, POOR BANISHED CHILDREN OF EVE.

I.

MARY, OUR HELP.

The Promptitude of Mary in assisting those who invoke her.

TRULY unfortunate are we poor children of Eve ; for, guilty before God of her fault, and condemned to the same penalty, we have to wander about in this valley of tears as exiles from our country, and to weep over our many afflictions of body and soul.   But blessed is he who, in the midst of these sorrows, often turns to the comfortress of the world, to the refuge of the unfortunate, to the great Mother of God, and devoutly calls upon her and invokes her !   *Blessed is the man that heareth me, and that watcheth daily at my gates.*[1]   Blessed, says Mary, is he who listens to my counsels, and watches continually at the gate of my mercy, and invokes my intercession and aid.

The holy Church carefully teaches us her children with what attention and confidence we should unceasingly have recourse to this loving protectress ; and for this purpose commands a worship peculiar to Mary.   And not only this, but she has instituted so many festivals that are celebrated throughout the year in honor of this great Queen : she devotes one day in the week, in an especial manner, to her honor : in the divine office all ecclesiastics and religious are daily obliged to invoke her in the name of all Christians ; and, finally, she de-

---

[1] " Beatus homo, qui audit me, et qui vigilat ad fores meas quotidie."—*Prov.* viii. 34.

sires that all the faithful should salute this most holy
Mother of God three times a day, at the sound of the
Angelus-bell. And that we may understand the confidence that the holy Church has in Mary, we need only
remember that in all public calamities she invariably invites all to have recourse to the protection of this divine
Mother, by novenas, prayers, processions, by visiting the
churches dedicated in her honor, and her images. And
this is what Mary desires. She wishes us always to seek
her and invoke her aid ; not as if she were begging of us
these honors and marks of veneration, for they are in no
way proportioned to her merit ; but she desires them,
that by such means our confidence and devotion may be
increased, and that so she may be able to give us greater
succor and comfort "She seeks for those," says St.
Bonaventure, "who approach her devoutly and with
reverence, for such she loves, nourishes, and adopts as
her children." [1]

This last-named saint remarks, that Ruth, whose name
signifies "seeing and hastening," was a figure of Mary ;
" for Mary, seeing our miseries, hastens in her mercy to
succor us." [2] Novarino adds, that "Mary, in the greatness of her desire to help us, cannot admit of delay, for
she is in no way an avaricious guardian of the graces
she has at her disposal as mother of mercy, and cannot
do otherwise than immediately shower down the treasures of her liberality on her servants." [3]

O how prompt is this good mother to help those who
call upon her ! *Thy two breasts*, says the sacred Canticle.

[1] " Ipsa tales quærit, qui ad eam devote et reverenter accedant ; hos
enim diligit, hos nutrit, hos in filios suos suscipit."—*Stim. Am.* p. 3,
c. 16.

[2] " Videns etiam nostram miseriam, est et festinans ad impenden-
dam suam misericordiam."—*Spec. B. M. V. lect.* v.

[3] " Nescit nectere moras, benefaciendi cupida, nec gratiarum avara
custos est ; tarda nescit molimina misericordiæ Mater, beneficentiæ
suæ thesauros in suos effusura."—*Umbr. Virg. exc.* 73.

are like two roes that are twins.[1]   Richard of St. Laurence
explains this verse, and says, that as roes are swift in
their course, so are the breasts of Mary prompt to bestow
the milk of mercy on all who ask it.   " By the light
pressure of a devout salutation and prayer they distil
large drops."[2]   The same author assures us that the
compassion of Mary is poured out on every one who asks
it, even should it be sought for by no other prayer than
a simple " Hail Mary."   Wherefore Novarino declares
that the Blessed Virgin not only runs but flies to assist
him who invokes her.   " She," says this author, "in the
exercise of her mercy, knows not how to act differently
from God ; for, as he flies at once to the assistance of
those who beg his aid, faithful to his promise, *Ask, and
you shall receive,*[3] so Mary, whenever she is invoked, is at
once ready to assist him who prays to her.   " God has
wings when he assists his own, and immediately flies
to them ; Mary also takes wing when she is about to
fly to our aid."[4]   And hence we see who the woman was,
spoken of in the following verse of the Apocalypse, to
whom two great eagle's wings were given, that she might
fly to the desert.   *And there were given to the woman two
wings of a great eagle, that she might fly into the desert.*[5]
Ribeira explains these wings to mean the love with
which Mary always flew to God.   " She has the wings
of an eagle, for she flies with the love of God."[6]   But
the blessed Amadeus, more to our purpose, remarks
that these wings of an eagle signify "the velocity, ex-

[1] " Duo ubera tua, sicut duo hinnuli capreæ."—*Cant.* iv. 5.

[2] "Compressione levissima devotæ Salutationis et orationis, larga
distillabit (Virgo) stillicidia."—*De Laud. B. M.* l. 1, c. 8.

[3] " Petite, et accipietis."—*John,* xvi. 24.

[4] " Alis utitur Deus ; ut suis opituletur. statim advolat ; alas sumit
et Virgo, in nostri auxilium advolatura."—*Umbra Virg. exc.* 73.

[5] " Et datæ sunt mulieri alæ duæ aquilæ magnæ, ut volaret in desertum."—*Apoc.* xii. 14.

[6] " Pennas habet aquilæ, quia amore Dei **volat.**"

B

ceeding that of the seraphim, with which Mary always flies to the succor of her children." [1]

This will explain a passage in the Gospel of St. Luke, in which we are told that when Mary went to visit and shower graces on St. Elizabeth and her whole family, she was not slow, but went with speed. The Gospel says, *And Mary, rising up, went into the hill country with haste.* [2] And this is not said of her return. For a similar reason, we are told in the sacred Canticles that the hands of Mary are used to the lathe : *her hands are skilful at the wheel,* [3] meaning, says Richard of St. Laurence, " that as the art of turning is the easiest and most expeditious mode of working, so also is Mary the most willing and prompt of all the saints to assist her clients." [4] And truly " she has the most ardent desire to console all, and is no sooner invoked than she accepts the prayers, and helps." [5] St. Bonaventure, then, was right in calling Mary the " salvation of all who call upon her," [6] meaning, that it suffices to invoke this divine mother in order to be saved ; for, according to Richard of St. Laurence, she is always ready to help those who seek her aid. " Thou wilt always find her ready to help thee." [7] And Bernardine de Bustis adds, " that this great Lady is more desirous to grant us graces than we are desirous to receive them." [8]

[1] " Motu celerrimo Seraphim alas excedens, ubique suis ut mater occurrit."—*De Laud. B. V. hom.* 8.

[2] " Exurgens autem Maria . . . abiit in montana cum festinatione."—*Luke.* i. 39.

[3] " Manus illius tornatiles."—*Cant.* v. 14.

[4] " Sicut ars tornandi promptior est aliis artibus, sic Maria ad benefaciendum promptior est omnibus Sanctis."—*De Laud. B. M.* l. 5.

[5] " Omnes consolatur, et, vel tenuiter invocata, præsto adest." *Par. an. fid.* p. 1, c. 18.

[6] " O salus te invocantium !"—*Cant. p. Psalt.*

[7] " Semper paratam auxiliari "—*De Laud. B. M.* l. 2. p. 1.

[8] " Plus desiderat ipsa facere tibi bonum, quam tu accipere concupiscas."—*Marial.* p. 2. s. 5.

Nor should the multitude of our sins diminish our confidence that Mary will grant our petitions when we cast ourselves at her feet. She is the mother of mercy; but mercy would not be needed did none exist who require it. On this subject Richard of St. Laurence remarks, "that as a good mother does not shrink from applying a remedy to her child infected with ulcers, however nauseous and revolting they may be, so also is our good mother unable to abandon us when we have recourse to her, that she may heal the wounds caused by our sins, however loathsome they may have rendered us." [1] This is exactly what Mary gave St. Gertrude to understand, when she showed herself to her with her mantle spread out to receive all who have recourse to her. At the same time the saint was told that "angels constantly guard the clients of this Blessed Virgin from the assaults of hell."

This good Mother's compassion is so great, and the love she bears us is such, that she does not even wait for our prayers in order to assist us; but, as it is expressed in the Book of Wisdom, *she preventeth them that covet her, so that she first showeth herself unto them.* [2] St. Anselm applies these words to Mary, and says that she is beforehand with those who desire her protection. By this we are to understand that she obtains us many favors from God before we have recourse to her. For this reason Richard of St. Victor remarks, that she is called the moon, *fair as the moon,* [3] meaning, not only that she is swift as the moon in its course, by flying to the aid of those who invoke her, but that she is still more so, for

---

[1] "Non enim Mater hæc dedignatur peccatores, sicut nec bona Mater filium scabiosum; quia propter peccatores factam se recolit Misericordiæ Genitricem; ubi enim non est miseria, misericordia non habet locum."—*De Laud. B. M.* l. 4

[2] "Præoccupat, qui se concupiscunt, ut illis se prior ostendat."—*Wisd.* vi. 14.

[3] "Pulchra ut luna."—*Cant.* vi. 9.

her love for us is so tender, that in our wants she anticipates our prayers, and her mercy is more prompt to help us than we are to ask her aid.[1] "And this arises," adds the same Richard, "from the fact that the heart of Mary is so filled with compassion for poor sinners, that she no sooner sees our miseries than she pours her tender mercies upon us. Nor is it possible for this benign Queen to behold the want of any soul without immediately assisting it."[2]

Mary, even when living in this world, showed at the marriage-feast of Cana the great compassion that she would afterwards exercise towards us in our necessities, and which now, as it were, forces her to have pity on us and assist us, even before we ask her to do so. In the second chapter of St. Luke we read that at this feast the compassionate Mother saw the embarrassment in which the bride and bridegroom were, and that they were quite ashamed on seeing the wine fail; and therefore, without being asked, and listening only to the dictates of her compassionate heart, which could never behold the afflictions of others without feeling for them, she begged her Son to console them simply by laying their distress before him: *they have no wine.*[3] No sooner had she done so, than our Lord, in order to satisfy all present, and still more to console the compassionate heart of his Mother, who had asked the favor, worked the well-known miracle by which he changed the water, brought to him in jars, into wine. From this Novarinus argues, that " if Mary, unasked, is thus prompt to succor the needy, how much

[1] "Velocitate præstat. Velocius occurrit ejus pietas, quam invocetur, et causas miserorum anticipat."

[2] " A Deo pietate replentur ubera tua, ut, alicujus miseriæ notitia tacta, lac fundant misericordiæ: nec possis miserias scire, et non subvenire."—*In Cant.* c. 23.

[3] "Vinum non habent."—*John.* ii. 3.

more so will she be to succor those who invoke her and
ask for her help ?" [1]

Should there be any one who doubts as to whether
Mary will aid him if he has recourse to her, Innocent III.
thus reproves him: " Who is there that ever, when in
the night of sin, had recourse to this sweet Lady without being relieved ?" [2]

"Who ever," exclaims the Blessed Eutychian, [3] "faithfully implored thy all-powerful aid and was abandoned
by thee ?" Indeed, no one: for thou canst relieve the
most wretched and save the most abandoned. Such a
case certainly never did and never will occur.

" I am satisfied," says St. Bernard, " that whoever has
had recourse to thee, O Blessed Virgin, in his wants, and
can remember that he did so in vain, should no more
speak of or praise thy mercy." [4]

"Sooner," says the devout Blosius, " would heaven
and earth be destroyed than would Mary fail to assist
any one who asks for her help, provided he does so with
a good intention and with confidence in her." [5]

St. Anselm, to increase our confidence, adds, that
" when we have recourse to this divine Mother, not only
we may be sure of her protection, but that often we shall
be heard more quickly, and be thus preserved, if we have
recourse to Mary and call on her holy name, than we
should be if we called on the name of Jesus our Saviour;"

---

[1] " Si tam prompta ad auxilium currit non quæsita, quid requæsita
præstitura est ?"— *Umbra Virg. exc.* 72.

[2] " Quis invocavit eam, et non est exauditus ab ipsa ?"—*De Assumpt.*
s. 2.

[3] " Quis. O Domina ! fideliter omnipotentem tuam rogavit opem,
et fuit derelictus ? revera nullus unquam."—*Vit. S. Theoph. ap. Sur.*
4 *Febr.*

[4] " Sileat misericordiam tuam, Virgo Beata, qui invocatam te in
necessitatibus suis sibi meminerit defuisse."—*De Assumpt.* s. 4.

[5] " Citius cœlum cum terra perierit. quam tu, aliquem, serio te implorantem, tua ope destituas."—*Consol. pusil.* c. 35.

and the reason he gives for it is, "that to Jesus, as a judge, it belongs also to punish; but mercy alone belongs to the Blessed Virgin as a patroness."[1] Meaning, that we more easily find salvation by having recourse to the Mother than by going to the Son—not as if Mary was more powerful than her Son to save us, for we know that Jesus Christ is our only Saviour, and that he alone by his merits has obtained and obtains salvation for us; but it is for this reason: that when we have recourse to Jesus, we consider him at the same time as our judge, to whom it belongs also to chastise ungrateful souls, and therefore the confidence necessary to be heard may fail us; but when we go to Mary, who has no other office than to compassionate us as Mother of mercy, and to defend us as our advocate, our confidence is more easily established, and is often greater. "We often obtain more promptly what we ask by calling on the name of Mary than by invoking that of Jesus. Her Son is lord and judge of all, and discerns the merits of each one; and therefore if he does not immediately grant the prayers of all, he is just. When, however, the Mother's name is invoked, though the merits of the suppliant are not such as to deserve that his prayer should be granted, those of the Mother supply that he may receive."

"Many things," says Nicephorus, "are asked from God, and are not granted: they are asked from Mary, and are obtained." And how is this? It is "because God has thus decreed to honor his Mother."[2] St. Bridget heard our Lord make a most sweet and consoling

---

[1] "Velocior est nonnunquam salus, memorato nomine Mariæ, quam invocato nomine Jesu: Filius Dominus est et Judex . . . invocato autem nomine Matris, etsi merita invocantis non merentur: merita tamen Matris intercedunt, ut exaudiatur."—*De Excell. V.* c. 6.

[2] "Multa petuntur a Deo, et non obtinentur: multa petuntur a Maria, et obtinentur; non quia potentior, sed quia Deus eam decrevit sic honorare."

promise; for in the 50th chapter of the first book of her
Revelations we read that Jesus addressed his Mother in
the following words: " Thou shalt present me with no
petition that shall be refused. My Mother, ask what
thou wilt, for never will I refuse thee anything; and
know," he added, "that I promise graciously to hear all
those who ask any favor of me in thy name, though they
may be sinners, if only they have the will to amend their
lives." [1] The same thing was revealed to St. Gertrude,
when she heard our divine Redeemer assure his Mother,
that in his omnipotence he granted her power to show
mercy to sinners who invoke her in whatever manner
she might please. [2]

Let all, then, say, with full confidence in the words of
that beautiful prayer addressed to the Mother of mercy,
and commonly attributed to St. Bernard, " Remember,
O most pious Virgin Mary, that it never was heard of in
any age that any one having recourse to thy protection
was abandoned." [3] Therefore forgive me, O Mary, if I
say that I will not be the first unfortunate creature who
has ever had recourse to thee and was abandoned.

EXAMPLE.

We read in the life of St. Francis de Sales that he experienced the efficacy of this prayer. When he was
about seventeen years of age he was living in Paris,
where he was pursuing his studies. At the same time
he devoted himself to exercises of piety and to the holy

---

[1] " Nulla erit petitio tua ad me, quæ non exaudiatur, et per te omnes,
qui petunt misericordiam cum voluntate emendandi, gratiam habebunt."—*Rev.* l. i. c. 50.

[2] " Ex omnipotentia mea, Mater, tibi concessi potestatem propitiandi
peccatis omnium qui devote invocant tuæ pietatis auxilium, qualicumque modo placet tibi."—*Inisin.* l. 4. c. 53.

[3] " Memorare, piissima Maria, a sæculo non fuisse auditum quem-
quam ad tua præsidia confugientem esse derelictum."

love of God, in which he found the joys of paradise. Our Lord, in order to try him, and to strengthen the bands which united him to himself, allowed the evil spirit to persuade him that all that he did was in vain, as he was already condemned in the eternal decrees of God. The darkness and spiritual dryness in which God was pleased at the same time to leave him (for he was then insensible to all the sweeter thoughts of the goodness of God) caused the temptation to have greater power over the heart of the holy youth: and, indeed, it reached such a pitch that his fears and interior desolation took away his appetite, deprived him of sleep, made him pale and melancholy; so much so, that he excited the compassion of all who saw him.

As long as this terrible storm lasted, the saint could only conceive thoughts and utter words of despondency and bitter grief. "Then," said he, "I am to be deprived of the grace of my God, who hitherto has shown himself so lovely and sweet to me! O love, O beauty, to which I have consecrated all my affections, I am no longer to enjoy thy consolation! O Virgin, Mother of God, the fairest amongst all the daughters of Jerusalem, then I am never to see thee in heaven! Ah, Lady, if I am not to behold thy beautiful countenance in Paradise, at least permit me not to blaspheme thee in hell!" Such were the tender sentiments of that afflicted, but at the same time loving heart. The temptation had lasted a month, when it pleased our Lord to deliver him by the means of that comfortress of the world, the most Blessed Mary, to whom the saint had some time before consecrated his virginity, and in whom, as he declared, he had placed all his hopes. One evening, on returning home, he entered a church, and saw a tablet hanging on the wall. He read it, and found the following well-known prayer, commonly called "the prayer of St. Bernard:" "Remember, O most pious Virgin Mary, that it never has been heard of in any age, that any one having recourse to thy protection was abandoned." Falling on his knees before the altar of the divine Mother, he recited this prayer with tender fervor, renewed his vow of chastity, promised to say the Rosary every day, and then added: "My Queen, be my advocate with thy Son, whom I dare not approach. My Mother, if I am so unfortunate as not to be able to love my Lord in the next world, and whom I know to be so worthy of love, at least do thou obtain that I may love him in this world as much as possible. This is the grace that I ask and hope for from thee." Having thus addressed the Blessed Virgin, he cast himself into the arms of divine mercy, and resigned himself entirely to the will of God. Scarcely had he finished his prayer, when in an instant he was delivered from his temptation by his most sweet Mother. He immediately regained the peace of his soul, and with it his bodily health; and from that time forward lived most devout to Mary, whose praises and mercy he constantly extolled, both in his sermons and writings, during the remainder of his life.

Prayer.

O Mother of God, Queen of angels and hope of men, give ear to one who calls upon thee and has recourse to thy protection. Behold me this day prostrate at thy feet: I, a miserable slave of hell, devote myself entirely to thee. I desire to be forever thy servant. I offer myself to serve and honor thee to the utmost of my power during the whole of my life. I know that the service of one so vile and miserable can be no honor to thee, since I have so grievously offended Jesus, thy Son and my Redeemer. But if thou wilt accept one so unworthy for thy servant, and by thy intercession change me, and thus making me worthy, this very mercy will give thee that honor which so miserable a wretch as I can never give thee. Receive me, then, and reject me not, O my Mother. The Eternal Word came from heaven on earth to seek for lost sheep, and to save them he became thy Son. And when one of them goes to thee to find Jesus, wilt thou despise it? The price of my salvation is already paid; my Saviour has already shed his blood, which suffices to save an infinity of worlds. This blood has only to be applied even to such a one as I am. And that is thy office, O Blessed Virgin; to thee does it belong, as I am told by St. Bernard, to dispense the merits of this blood to whom thou pleasest. To thee does it belong, says St. Bonaventure, to save whomsoever thou willest, "whomsoever thou willest will be saved." [1] Oh, then, help me, my Queen; my Queen, save me. To thee do I this day consecrate my whole soul; do thou save it. O salvation of those who invoke thee, I conclude in the words of the same saint, "O salvation of those who call upon thee, do thou save me." [2]

II.

The Greatness of the Power of Mary to defend those who invoke her when tempted by the Devil.

Not only is the most Blessed Virgin Queen of heaven and of all saints, but she is also Queen of hell and of all evil spirits; for she overcame them valiantly by her virtues. From the very beginning God foretold the victory and empire that our Queen would one day obtain over the serpent, when he announced that a woman should come into the world to conquer him: *I will put enmities between thee and the woman—she shall crush thy head.* [3]

Who could this woman, his enemy, be but Mary, who by her fair humility and holy life always conquered him and beat down his strength? The Mother of our Lord Jesus Christ was promised in the person of that woman, [4] as it is remarked by St. Cyprian, [5] and after him another

---

[1] "Quem vis, ipse salvus erit."

[2] "O Salus te invocantium!"

[3] "Inimicitias ponam inter te et mulierem . . . ipsa conteret caput tuum."—*Gen.* iii. 15.

[4] "Mater Domini nostri Jesu Christi in illa Muliere promissa est."—*De Viro perf. inter op. S. Hier.*

[5] *Test. l. 2, c. 9.*

ancient writer; and therefore God did not say, "I place," but "I will place;" lest he might seem to refer to Eve: meaning that God said, *I will place enmities between thee and the woman*, to signify that the serpent's opponent was not to be Eve, who was then living, but would be another woman descending from her, and who, as St. Vincent Ferrer observes, "would bring our first parents far greater advantages than those which they had lost by their sin."[1]   Mary, then, was this great and valiant woman, who conquered the devil and crushed his head by bringing down his pride, as it was foretold by God himself: *she shall crush thy head*. Some doubt as to whether these words refer to Mary, or whether they do not rather refer to Jesus Christ; for the Septuagint renders them, *He shall crush thy head*. But in the Vulgate, which alone was approved of by the sacred Council of Trent, we find *She*, and not *He;* and thus it was understood by St. Ambrose, St. Jerome, St. Augustine, and a great many others. However, be it as it may, it is certain that either the Son by means of the Mother, or the Mother by means of the Son, has overcome Lucifer; so that, as St. Bernard remarks, this proud spirit, in spite of himself, was beaten down and trampled under foot by this most Blessed Virgin; so that, as a slave conquered in war, he is forced always to obey the commands of this Queen. "Beaten down and trampled under the feet of Mary, he endured a wretched slavery."[2]   St. Bruno says "that Eve was the cause of death," by allowing herself to be overcome by the serpent, "but that Mary," by conquering the devil, "restored life to us."[3]

[1] "Quod ab eis procederet una Virgo sanctissima, quæ afferret majus bonum, quam ipsi perdidissent."—*Serm. de Concep. B. V. M.*

[2] "Sub Mariæ pedibus conculcatus et contritus, miseram patitur servitutem."—*In Sign. Magn.*

[3] "In Eva mors, et in Maria vita consistit; illa a diabolo victa est, hæc diabolum ligavit et vicit."—*De B. V.* s. 2.

And she bound him in such a way that this enemy cannot stir so as to do the least injury to any of her clients.

Beautiful is the explanation given by Richard of St. Laurence of the following words of the Book of Proverbs: *The heart of her husband trusteth in her, and he shall have no need of spoils.*[1] He says, applying them to Jesus and Mary: "The heart of her spouse, that is Christ, trusteth in her, and he shall have no need of spoils; for she endows him with all those whom by her prayers, merits, and example, she snatches from the devil."[2] "God has entrusted the heart of Jesus to the hands of Mary, that she may insure it the love of men," says Cornelius à Lapide; and thus he will not need spoils; that is, he will be abundantly supplied with souls; for she enriches him with those whom she has snatched from hell, and saved from the devil by her powerful assistance.

It is well known that the palm is a sign of victory; and therefore our Queen is placed on a high throne, in sight of all the powers, as a palm, for a sign of the certain victory that all may promise themselves who place themselves under her protection. *I was exalted like a palm-tree in Cades,*[3] says Ecclesiasticus: "that is, to defend," adds Blessed Albert the Great.[4] "My children," Mary seems to say, "when the enemy assails you, fly to me; cast your eyes on me, and be of good heart; for as I am your defender, victory is assured to you." So that recourse to Mary is a most secure means to conquer all the assaults of hell; for she, says St. Bernardine of Sienna, is even the Queen of hell and sovereign mistress of the devils:

---

[1] "Confidit in ea cor viri sui, et spoliis non indigebit."—*Prov.* xxxi. 11.

[2] "Quia, quoscunque suis orationibus, meritis et exemplis, liberat a diabolo, apponit et assignat dominio Sponsi sui."—*De Laud. B. M.* l. 6.

[3] "Quasi palma exaltata sum in Cades."—*Ecclus.* xxiv. 18.

[4] "Scilicet ad defendendum."—*Bibl. Marian.*

since she it is who tames and crushes them. He thus expresses his thought: "The most Blessed Virgin rules over the infernal regions. She is therefore called the ruling mistress of the devils, because she brings them into subjection."[1] For this reason Mary is said in the sacred Canticles to be *terrible* to the infernal powers *as an army in battle array;*[2] and she is called thus terrible, because she well knows how to array her power, her mercy, and her prayers, to the discomfiture of her enemies, and for the benefit of her servants, who in their temptations have recourse to her most powerful aid.

As the vine I have brought forth a pleasant odor.[3] Thus does the Holy Ghost make Mary speak in the book of Ecclesiasticus. "We are told," says St. Bernard on this passage, that "all venomous reptiles fly from flowering vines;"[4] for, as poisonous reptiles fly from flowering vines, so do devils fly from those fortunate souls in whom they perceive the perfume of devotion to Mary. And therefore she also calls herself, in the same book, a cedar: *I was exalted like a cedar in Libanus.*[5] Not only because Mary was untainted by sin, as the cedar is incorruptible, but also, as Cardinal Hugo remarks on the foregoing text, because, "like the cedar which by its odor keeps off worms, so also does Mary by her sanctity drive away the devils."

In Judea victories were gained by means of the ark. Thus it was that Moses conquered his enemies, as we learn from the Book of Numbers. *And when the ark was*

[1] "Beata Virgo dominatur in regno inferni ; merito ergo domina dicitur, quasi domans dæmonum manus."—*Pro Fest. V. M.* s. 3, a. 2, c. 2.

[2] "Terribilis ut castrorum acies ordinata."—*Cant.* vi. 3.

[3] "Ego, quasi vitis, fructificavi suavitatem odoris."—*Ecclus.* xxiv. 23.

[4] "Aiunt, florescentibus vineis, omne reptile venenatum cedere loco."—*In Cant.* s. 60.

[5] "Quasi cedrus exaltata sum in Libano."—*Ecclus.* xxiv. 17.

[6] "Cedrus odore suo fugat serpentes, et Beata Virgo dæmones."

lifted up, Moses said : Arise, O Lord, and let Thy enemies be scattered.[1] Thus was Jericho conquered; thus also the Philistines; *for the Ark of God was there.*[2] It is well known that this ark was a figure of Mary. Cornelius à Lapide says, " In time of danger, Christians should fly to the most Blessed Virgin, who contained Christ as manna in the ark of her womb, and brought him forth to be the food and salvation of the world."[3] For as manna was in the ark, so is Jesus (of whom manna was a figure) in Mary; and by means of this ark we gain the victory over our earthly and infernal enemies. "And thus," St. Bernardine of Sienna well observes, " that when Mary, the ark of the New Testament, was raised to the dignity of Queen of heaven, the power of hell over men was weak-ened and dissolved."[4]

O how the infernal spirits tremble at the very thought of Mary, and of her august name! says St. Bonaventure. "O, how fearful is Mary to the devils!"[5] The saint com-pares these enemies to those of whom Job speaks: *He diggeth through houses in the dark : if the morning suddenly appear, it is to them the shadow of death.*[6] Thieves go and rob houses in the dark; but as soon as morning dawns, they fly, as if they beheld the shadow of death. "Pre-cisely thus," in the words of the same saint, "do the devils enter a soul in the time of darkness;" meaning when the soul is in the obscurity of ignorance. They dig through the house of our mind when it is in the darkness of ignorance. But then, he adds, " if suddenly

---

[1] " Cumque elevaretur Arca, dicebat Moyses: Surge Domine, et dissipentur inimici tui."—*Num.* x. 35.

[2] " Erat enim ibi Arca Dei."—1 *Kings*, xiv. 18.

[3] " Quæ Christum quasi Manna in arca ventris sui continuit."

[4] " Quando elevata fuit Virgo gloriosa ad cœlestia regna, dæmonis potentia imminuta est et dissipata."—*Pro Fest. V. M.* s. 12, a. 1, c. 3.

[5] " O quam tremenda est Maria dæmonibus!"

[6] " Perfodit in tenebris domos . . .; si subito apparuerit aurora, ar-bitrantur umbram mortis."—*Job*, xxiv. 16.

they are overtaken by the dawn, that is, if the grace and mercy of Mary enters the soul, its brightness instantly dispels the darkness, and puts the infernal enemies to flight, as if they fled from death."[1]   O blessed is he who always invokes the beautiful name of Mary in his conflicts with hell !

In confirmation of this, it was revealed to St. Bridget "that God had rendered Mary so powerful over the devils, that as often as they assault a devout client who calls on this most Blessed Virgin for help, she at a single glance instantly terrifies them, so that they fly far away, preferring to have their pains redoubled rather than see themselves thus subject to the power of Mary."[2]

The divine Bridegroom, when speaking of this his beloved bride, calls her a lily: *As the lily is amongst the thorns. so is my beloved amongst the daughters.*[3]   On these words Cornelius à Lapide makes the reflection, "that as the lily is a remedy against serpents and venomous things, so is the invocation of Mary a specific by which we may overcome all temptations, and especially those against purity, as all find who put it in practice."[4]

St. John Damascene used to say, "While I keep my hope in thee unconquerable, O Mother of God, I shall be safe.   I will fight and overcome my enemies with no other

[1] "Perfodiunt in tenebris ignorantiæ, domos mentium nostrarum. . . Si subito apparuerit aurora, si supervenerit Mariæ gratia et misericordia, sic fugiunt, sicut homines fugiunt umbram mortis."—*Spec. B. V. lect.* 3, 11.

[2] "Super omnes etiam malignos spiritus ipsam sic Deus potentem effecit, quod. quotiescumque ipsi hominem Virginis auxilium implorantem impugnaverint, ad ipsius Virginis nutum illico pavidi procul diffugiunt, volentes potius pœnas suas multiplicari. quam ejusdem Virginis potentiam super se taliter dominari."—*Serm. Ang.* c. 20.

[3] "Sicut lilium inter spinas, sic amica mea inter filias."—*Cant.* ii. 2.

[4] "Sicut lilium valet adversus serpentes et venena, sic Beatæ Virginis invocatio singulare est remedium in omni tentatione, præsertim libidinis, uti experientia constat."

buckler than thy protection and thy all-powerful aid." [1]
And all who are so fortunate as to be the servants of this
great Queen can say the same thing. O Mother of God,
if I hope in thee, I most certainly shall not be overcome ;
for, defended by thee, I will follow up my enemies, and
oppose them with the shield of thy protection and thy
all-powerful help; and then without doubt I shall conquer. For says St. James the monk (who was a Doctor
amongst the Greeks), addressing our Lord on the subject of Mary, "Thou, O Lord, hast given us in Mary
arms that no force of war can overcome, and a trophy
never to be destroyed." [2]

It is said in the Old Testament, that God guided his
people from Egypt to the land of promise, *by day in a pillar of a cloud, and by night in a pillar of fire.* [3] This stupendous pillar, at times as a cloud, at others as fire, says
Richard of St. Laurence, was a figure of Mary fulfilling the double office she constantly exercises for our
good: as a cloud she protects us from the ardor of divine justice; and as fire she protects us from the devils.
"Behold the twofold object for which Mary is given to
us; to shelter us, as a cloud, from the heat of the sun of
justice, and, as fire, to protect us all against the devil." [4]
She protects us as a burning fire: for, St. Bonaventure
remarks: "As wax melts before the fire, so do the devils
lose their power against those souls who often remember

[1] "Insuperabilem spem tuam habens, O Deipara! servabor . . ;
persequar inimicos meos, solam habens, ut thoracem, protectionem
tuam et omnipotens auxilium tuum."—*In Ann. Dei gen.*

[2] "Tu arma omni vi belli potentiora, trophæumque invictum eam
præstitisti."—*Or. in Nat. Deip.*

[3] "Per diem in columna nubis, et per noctem in columna ignis."—
Exod. xiii. 21.

[4] "Ecce duo officia ad quæ data est nobis Maria: scilicet, ut nos
protegat fervore solis justitiæ, tamquam nubes; et tamquam ignis,
ut nos protegat contra diabolum."—*De Laud. B. Virg.* l. 7.

the name of Mary, and devoutly invoke it; and still more so, if they also endeavor to imitate her virtues."[1]

The devils tremble even if they only hear the name of Mary. St. Bernard declares that in "the name of Mary every knee bows; and that the devils not only fear but tremble at the very sound of that name."[2] And as men fall prostrate with fear if a thunderbolt falls near them, so do the devils if they hear the name of Mary. Thomas à Kempis thus expresses the same sentiment: "The evil spirits greatly fear the Queen of heaven, and fly at the sound of her name, as if from fire. At the very sound of the word Mary, they are prostrated as by thunder."[3]

Oh, how many victories have the clients of Mary gained by only making use of her most holy name! It was thus that St. Anthony of Padua was always victorious; thus the Blessed Henry Suso; thus so many other lovers of this great Queen conquered. We learn from the history of the missions in Japan, that many devils appeared under the form of fierce animals to a certain Christian, to alarm and threaten him; but he thus addressed them: "I have no arms that you can fear; and if the Most High permits it, do whatever you please with me. In the mean time, however, I take the holy names of Jesus and Mary for my defence." At the very sound of these tremendous names, the earth opened, and the proud spirits cast themselves headlong into it. St. Anselm declares that he himself "knew and had seen and

---

[1] "Fluunt sicut cera a facie ignis, ubicumque invenerint crebram hujus nominis recordationem, devotam invocationem, sollicitam imitationem."—*Spec. B. M. V.* lect. 3.

[2] "Dæmones, non solum Virginem pertimescunt, sed, audita hac voce, Maria, contremiscunt."—*Apud Lyræum, Tris. Mar.* l. 3, t. 9.

[3] "Expavescunt cœli Reginam spiritus maligni, et diffugiunt, audito nomine ejus, velut ab igne. Tanquam tonitruum de cœlo factum sit, prosternuntur ad Sanctæ Mariæ vocabulum."—*Ad Nov.* s. 23.

10

heard many who had invoked the name of Mary in time of danger, and were immediately delivered from it." [1]

"Glorious indeed, and admirable," exclaims St. Bonaventure, "is thy name, O Mary; for those who pronounce it at death need not fear all the powers of hell;" [2] for the devils on hearing that name instantly fly, and leave the soul in peace. The same saint adds, "that men do not fear a powerful hostile army as much as the powers of hell fear the name and protection of Mary." [3] "Thou, O Lady," says St. Germanus, "by the simple invocation of thy most powerful name, givest security to thy servants against all the assaults of the enemy." [4] Oh, were Christians but careful in their temptations to pronounce the name of Mary with confidence, never would they fall; for, as Blessed Allan remarks, "At the very sound of these words, Hail, Mary! Satan flies, and hell trembles." Our Blessed Lady herself revealed to St. Bridget that the enemy flies even from the most abandoned sinners, and who consequently are the farthest from God, and fully possessed by the devil, if they only invoke her most powerful name with a true purpose of amendment. "All devils on hearing this name of Mary, filled with terror, leave the soul." [5] But at the same time our Blessed Lady added, "that if the soul does not amend and obliterate its sins by sorrow, the

---

[1] " Sæpe vidimus et audivimus plurimos hominum in suis periculis recordari nominis Mariæ, et omnis periculi malum illico evasisse." —*De Excell. Virg.* c. 6.

[2] "Gloriosum et admirabile est nomen tuum, O Maria! qui illud retinent, non expavescent in puncto mortis."—*Psalt. B. V.* ps. 110.

[3] "Non sic timent hostes visibiles castrorum multitudinem copiosam, sicut aereæ potestates Mariæ vocabulum, et patrocinium."—*Spec. B. M. V.* lect. 3.

[4] " Tu hostis contra invasiones servos tuos sola tui nominis invocatione, tutos servas."—*De Zona Deip.*

[5] "Satan fugit, infernus contremiscit, cum dico: Ave Maria."—*De Psalt.* p. 4, c. 30.

devils almost immediately return and continue to possess it." [1]

EXAMPLE.

In Reichersperg, in Bavaria, there was a canon regular of the name of Arnold, surnamed the Pious on account of the sanctity of his life, and who had the most tender devotion to our Blessed Lady. When at the point of death, and having received the last sacraments, he summoned his religious brethren, and begged that they would not abandon him in his last passage. Scarcely had he uttered these words, when, in the presence of all, he began to tremble, to roll his eyes, and, bathed in a cold sweat, with a faltering voice said, " Ah, do you not see the devils who are endeavoring to drag me to hell?" He then cried out, " Brothers, implore the aid of Mary for me; in her I confide; she will give me the victory." On hearing this his brethren recited the Litany of our Blessed Lady, and as they said "Holy Mary, pray for him," the dying man exclaimed, " Repeat, repeat the name of Mary, for I am already before God's tribunal." He was silent for a moment; and then added, "It is true that I did that, but I have done penance for it." And then turning to our Blessed Lady, he said, " O Mary, I shall be delivered if thou helpest me." Again the devils attacked him; but he defended himself with his crucifix and the name of Mary. Thus was the night spent; but no sooner did morning dawn than Arnold exclaimed with the greatest calmness, and full of holy joy, "Mary, my sovereign Lady, my refuge, has obtained me pardon and salvation." Then casting his eyes on that Blessed Virgin who was inviting him to follow her, he said, "I come, O Lady, I come!" and making an effort to do so

---

[1] " Dæmones, audito nomine meo, statim relinquunt animam, quasi territi. Sed revertuntur ad eam, nisi aliqua emendatio subsequatur." —*Rev.* l. I, c. 9.

even with his body, his soul fled after her to the realms of eternal bliss, as we trust, for he sweetly expired.[1]

Prayer.

Behold at thy feet, O Mary my hope, a poor sinner, who has so many times been by his own fault the slave of hell. I know that by neglecting to have recourse to thee, my refuge, I allowed myself to be overcome by the devil. Had I always had recourse to thee, had I always invoked thee, I certainly should not have fallen. I trust, O Lady most worthy of all our love, that through thee I have already escaped from the hands of the devil, and that God has pardoned me. But I tremble lest at some future period I may again fall into the same bonds. I know that my enemies have not lost the hope of again overcoming me, and already they prepare new assaults and temptations for me. Ah, my Queen and refuge, do thou assist me. Place me under thy mantle; permit me not again to become their slave. I know that thou wilt help me and give me the victory, provided I invoke thee; but I dread lest in my temptations I may forget thee, and neglect to do so. The favor, then, that I seek of thee, and which thou must grant me, O most holy Virgin, is that I may never forget thee, and especially in time of temptation; grant that I may then repeatedly invoke thee, saying, "O Mary, help me; O Mary, help me." And when my last struggle with hell comes, at the moment of death, ah then, my Queen, help me more than ever, and thou thyself remind me to call on thee more frequently either with my lips or in my heart; that, being thus filled with confidence, I may expire with thy sweet name and that of thy Son Jesus on my lips; that so I may be able to bless thee and praise thee, and not depart from thy feet in Paradise for all eternity. Amen.

[1] *Auriemma, Aff. Scamb.* p. 2, c. 8.—*Ludewig, Chron. Reichersp. anno* 1166.

CHAPTER V.

Ad te suspiramus gementes et flentes in hac lacrymarum valle.

TO THEE DO WE SIGH, MOURNING AND WEEPING, IN THIS
VALLEY OF TEARS.

I.

MARY, OUR MEDIATRESS.

The Necessity of the Intercession of Mary for our Salvation.

THAT it is not only lawful but useful to invoke and
pray to the saints, and more especially to the Queen of
saints, the most holy and ever blessed Virgin Mary, in
order that they may obtain us the divine grace, is an
article of faith, and has been defined by general Councils,
against heretics who condemned it as injurious to Jesus
Christ, who is our only mediator; but if a Jeremias after
his death prayed for Jerusalem;[1] if the ancients of the
Apocalypse presented the prayers of the saints to God;[2]
if a St. Peter promises his disciples that after his death
he will be mindful of them ;[3] if a holy Stephen prays for
his persecutors;[4] if a St. Paul prays for his companions;[5]
if, in fine, the saints can pray for us, why cannot we
beseech the saints to intercede for us? St. Paul recommends himself to the prayers of his disciples: *Brethren,
pray for us.*[6] St. James exhorts us to pray one for
another : *Pray one for another, that you may be saved.*[7]
Then we can do the same.

---

[1] *2 Mach.* xv. 14.
[2] *Apoc.* v. 8.
[3] *2 Pet.* i. 15.
[4] *Act.* vii. 59.
[5] *Act.* xxvii. 24 ; *Eph.* ii. 16; *Phil.* i. 4; *Col.* i. 3.
[6] " Orate pro nobis."—1 *Thess.* v. 25.
[7] " Orate pro invicem. ut salvemini "—*James.* v. 16.

No one denies that Jesus Christ is our only mediator of justice, and that he by his merits has obtained our reconciliation with God. But, on the other hand, it is impious to assert that God is not pleased to grant graces at the intercession of his saints, and more especially of Mary his Mother, whom Jesus desires so much to see loved and honored by all. Who can pretend that the honor bestowed on a mother does not redound to the honor of the son? *The glory of children are their fathers.*[1] Whence St. Bernard says, " Let us not imagine that we obscure the glory of the Son by the great praise we lavish on the mother ; for the more she is honored, the greater is the glory of her Son." " There can be no doubt," says the saint, " that whatever we say in praise of the Mother is equally in praise of the Son." [2] And St. Ildephonsus also says, " That which is given to the Mother redounds to the Son; the honor given to the Queen is honor bestowed on the King." [3] There can be no doubt that by the merits of Jesus Mary was made the mediatress of our salvation; not indeed a mediatress of justice, but of grace and intercession; as St. Bonaventure expressly calls her " Mary, the most faithful mediatress of our salvation." [4] And St. Laurence Justinian asks, " How can she be otherwise than full of grace, who has been made the ladder to paradise, the gate of heaven, the most true mediatress between God and man ?" [5]

Hence the learned Suarez justly remarks, that if we

[1] " Gloria filiorum, patres eorum."—*Prov.* xvii. 6.

[2] " Non est dubium, quidquid in laudibus Matris proferimus, ad Filium pertinere."—*De Laud. V. M. hom.* 4.

[3] " Redundat ad Filium, quod impenditur Matri; transit honor in Regem, qui defertur in famulatum Reginæ."—*De Virginit. S. M* c. 12.

[4] " Maria, fidelissima Mediatrix nostræ salutis."—*Spec. B. V. M.* lect. 9.

[5] " Quomodo non est plena gratia, quæ effecta est paradisi Scala; cœli Janua, Dei et hominum verissima Mediatrix?"—*S. in Ann. B. M.*

implore our Blessed Lady to obtain us a favor, it is not because we distrust the divine mercy, but rather that we fear our own unworthiness and the absence of proper dispositions; and we recommend ourselves to Mary, that her dignity may supply for our lowliness. He says that we apply to Mary "in order that the dignity of the intercessor may supply for our misery. Hence, to invoke the aid of the most Blessed Virgin is not diffidence in the divine mercy, but dread of our own unworthiness."[1]

That it is most useful and holy to have recourse to the intercession of Mary can only be doubted by those who have not faith. But that which we intend to prove here is, that the intercession of Mary is even necessary to salvation; we say necessary—not absolutely, but morally. This necessity proceeds from the will itself of God, that all graces that he dispenses should pass through the hands of Mary, according to the opinion of St. Bernard, and which we may now with safety call the general opinion of theologians and learned men. The author of the *Reign of Mary* positively asserts that such is the case. It is maintained by Vega, Mendoza, Paciucchelli, Segneri, Poiré, Crasset, and by innumerable other learned authors. Even Father Natalis Alexander, who always uses so much reserve in his propositions, even he says that it is the will of God that we should expect all graces through the intercession of Mary. I will give his own words: "God wills that we should obtain all good things that we hope for from him though the powerful intercession of the Virgin Mother, and we shall obtain them whenever (as we are in duty bound) we invoke her."[2] In confirmation of this, he quotes the

---

[1] "Ut dignitas intercessoris suppleat inopiam nostram; unde Virginem interpellare, non est de divina misericordia diffidere, sed de propria indignitate timere."—*De Inc.* p. 2, d. 23, s. 3.

[2] "Deus vult ut omnia bona ab ipso exspectemus, potentissima Virginis Matris intercessione, cum eam, ut par est, invocamus. impetranda."—*Ep.* 50 *in calce Theol.*

following celebrated passage of St. Bernard: "Such is God's will, that we should have all through Mary."[1] Father Contenson is also of the same opinion ; for, explaining the words addressed by our Lord on the cross to St. John: *Behold thy Mother,*[2] he remarks, "That it is the same thing as if he had said: As no one can be saved except through the merits of my sufferings and death, so no one will be a partaker of the blood then shed otherwise than through the prayer of my Mother. He alone is a son of my sorrows who has Mary for his Mother. My wounds are ever-flowing fountains of grace; but their streams will reach no one but by the channel of Mary. In vain will he invoke me as a Father who has not venerated Mary as a Mother. And thou, my disciple John, if thou lovest me, love her; for thou wilt be beloved by Me in proportion to thy love for her.["][3]

This proposition (that all that we receive from our Lord comes through Mary) does not exactly please a certain modern writer,* who, although in other respects he speaks of true and false devotion with much learning and piety, yet when he treats of devotion towards the divine mother he seems to grudge her that glory which was given her without scruple by a St. Germanus, a

---

[1] "Sic est voluntas ejus, qui totum nos habere voluit per Mariam." —*De Aquæd.*

[2] "Ecce mater tua."—*John,* xix. 27

[3] "Quasi diceret : Nullus sanguinis illius particeps erit, nisi intercessione Matris meæ. Vulnera gratiarum fontes sunt; sed ad nullos derivabuntur rivi, nisi per Marianum canalem. Joannes discipule, tantum a me amaberis, quantum eam amaveris."—*Theol. mentis et cord.* t. 2, l. 10, d. 4, c. 1.

---

* This author is the celebrated Muratori. An anonymous writer having attacked St. Alphonsus on the subject of the reproach directed here against Muratori, and of the doctrine maintained in this chapter, the saint sent him a reply which will be found at the end of this work. —ED.

St. Anselm, a St. John Damascene, a St. Bonaventure, a
St. Antoninus, a St. Bernardine, the Venerable Abbot of
Celles, and so many other learned men, who had no difficulty in affirming that the intercession of Mary is not
only useful, but necessary. The same author says that
the proposition that God grants no grace otherwise than
through Mary, is hyperbolical and exaggerated, having
dropped from the lips of some saints in the heat of fervor, but which, correctly speaking, is only to be understood as meaning that through Mary we received Jesus
Christ, by whose merits we obtain all graces ; for he
adds, "To believe that God can grant us no graces without the intercession of Mary, would be contrary to faith
and the doctrine of St. Paul, who says that we acknowledge but *one God and one Mediator of God and men the man
Christ Jesus.*" [1]

But with his leave, and going upon his own admis-
sions, mediation of justice by way of merit is one thing,
and mediation by grace by way of prayer is another.
And again, it is one thing to say that God cannot, and
another that he will not, grant graces without the intercession of Mary. We willingly admit that God is
the source of every good, and the absolute master of all
graces ; and that Mary is only a pure creature, who
receives whatever she obtains as a pure favor from God.
But who can ever deny that it is most reasonable and
proper to assert that God, in order to exalt this great
creature, who more than all others honored and loved
him during her life, and whom, moreover, he had chosen
to be the Mother of his Son, our common Redeemer,
wills that all graces that are granted to those whom he
has redeemed should pass through and be dispensed by
the hands of Mary? We most readily admit that Jesus
Christ is the only Mediator of justice, according to the
distinction just made, and that by his merits he obtains

[1] I *Tim.* ii. 5.

us all graces and salvation; but we say that Mary is the mediatress of grace; and that receiving all she obtains through Jesus Christ, and because she prays and asks for it in the name of Jesus Christ, yet all the same whatever graces we receive, they come to us through her intercession.

There is certainly nothing contrary to faith in this, but the reverse. It is quite in accordance with the sentiments of the Church, which, in its public and approved prayers, teaches us continually to have recourse to this divine Mother, and to invoke her as the "health of the weak, the refuge of sinners, the help of Christians, and as our life and hope." [1] In the Office appointed to be said on the feasts of Mary, this same holy Church, applying the words of Ecclesiasticus to this Blessed Virgin, gives us to understand that in her we find all hope. *In* *her is all hope of life and of virtue!* [2] in Mary is every grace, *In me is all grace of the way and of the truth.* [3] In Mary, finally, we shall find life and eternal salvation: *Who finds me finds life, and draws salvation from the Lord.* [4] And elsewhere: *They that work by me shall not sin; they that explain me shall have everlasting life.* [5] And surely such expressions as these sufficiently prove that we require the intercession of Mary.

Moreover, we are confirmed in this opinion by so many theologians and Fathers, of whom it is certainly incorrect to say, as the above-named author does, that, in exalting Mary, they spoke hyperbolically and allowed great exaggerations to fall from their lips. To exagge-

[1] "Salus infirmorum, Refugium peccatorum, Auxilium Christianorum, Vita, Spes nostra."

[2] "In me omnis spes vitæ et virtutis."—*Ecclus.* xxiv. 25.

[3] "In me gratia omnis viæ et veritatis."—*Ib.*

[4] "Qui me invenerit, inveniet vitam, et hauriet salutem a Domino."—*Prov.* viii. 35.

[5] "Qui operantur in me, non peccabunt. Qui elucidant me, vitam æternam habebunt."—*Ecclus.* xxiv. 30, 31.

rate and speak hyperbolically is to exceed the limits of truth ; and surely we cannot say that saints who were animated by the Spirit of God, which is truth itself, spoke thus. If I may be allowed to make a short digression, and give my own sentiment, it is, that when an opinion tends in any way to the honor of the most Blessed Virgin, when it has some foundation, and is not repugnant to the faith, nor to the decrees of the Church, nor to truth, the refusal to hold it, or to oppose it because the reverse may be true, shows little devotion to the Mother of God. Of the number of such as these I do not choose to be, nor do I wish my reader to be so, but rather of the number of those who fully and firmly believe all that can without error be believed of the greatness of Mary, according to the Abbot Rupert, who, amongst the acts of homage most pleasing to this good Mother, places that of firmly believing all that redounds to her honor.[1] If there was nothing else to take away our fear of exceeding in the praises of Mary, St. Augustine[2] should suffice ; for he declares that whatever we may say in praise of Mary is little in comparison with that which she deserves, on account of her dignity of Mother of God ; and, moreover, the Church says, in the Mass appointed for her festivals, " Thou art happy, O sacred Virgin Mary, and most worthy of all praise."[3]

But let us return to the point, and examine what the saints say on the subject. St. Bernard says "that God has filled Mary with all graces, so that men may receive by her means, as by a channel, every good thing that comes to them." He says that "she is a full aque-

[1] " Ejus magnalia firmiter credere."

[2] *Serm.* 208, *E. B. app.*

[3] " Felix namque es, sacra Virgo Maria, et omni laude dignissima ; quia ex te ortus est Sol justitiæ, Christus Deus noster."—*M. Vot. a .Nat.—Resp.* 7.

duct, that others may receive of her plenitude." [1] On this the saint makes the following significant remark : "Before the birth of the Blessed Virgin, a constant flow of graces was wanting, because this aqueduct did not exist." [2] But now that Mary has been given to the world, heavenly graces constantly flow through her on all.

The devil, like Holofernes, who, in order to gain possession of the city·of Bethulia, ordered the aqueducts to be destroyed, exerts himself to his utmost to destroy devotion to the Mother of God in souls; for if this channel of grace is closed, he easily gains possession of them. And here, continues the same St. Bernard, "See, O souls, with what tender devotion our Lord wills that we should honor our Queen, by always having recourse to her protection; and by relying on it ; for in Mary he has placed the plenitude of every good, so that henceforward we may know and acknowledge that whatever hope, grace, or other advantage we possess, all comes from the hand of Mary." [3] St. Antoninus says the same thing: "All graces that have ever been bestowed on men, all came through Mary." [4] And on this account she is called the moon, according to the following remark of St. Bonaventure : "As the moon, which stands between the sun and the earth, transmits to this latter whatever it receives from the former, so does Mary pour out upon

[1] "Plenus Aquæductus, ut accipiant cæteri de ejus plenitudine."

[2] "Ideo tanto tempore humano generi fluenta gratiæ defuerunt, quia necdum intercederet is Aquæductus."—*De Aquæd.*

[3] "Intuemini quanto devotionis affectu a nobis eam voluerit honorari, qui totius boni plenitudinem posuit in Maria ; ut proinde, si quid spei in nobis est, si quid gratiæ, si quid salutis, ab ea noverimus redundare."—*De Aquæd.*

[4] "Per eam exivit de cœlis, quidquid gratiæ venit in mundum."—P. 4, tit. 15, c. 20, § 12.

us who are in this world the heavenly graces that she receives from the divine sun of justice." [1]

Again, the holy Church calls her " the happy gate of heaven;" [2] for as the same St. Bernard remarks: " As every mandate of grace that is sent by a king passes through the palace-gates, so does every grace that comes from heaven to the world pass through the hands of Mary." [3] St. Bonaventure says that Mary is called " the gate of heaven, because no one can enter that blessed kingdom without passing through her." [4]

An ancient author, probably St. Sophronius, in a sermon on the Assumption, published with the works of St. Jerome, says " that the plenitude of grace which is in Jesus Christ came into Mary, though in a different way;" [5] meaning that it is our Lord, as in the head, from which the vital spirits (that is, divine help to obtain eternal salvation) flow into us, who are the members of his mystical body; and that the same plenitude is in Mary, as in the neck, through which these vital spirits pass to the members. The same idea is confirmed by St. Bernardine of Sienna, who explains it more clearly, saying, " that all graces of the spiritual life that descend from Christ, their head, to the faithful, who are his mystical body, are transmitted through the instrumentality of

---

[1] " Quia, sicut luna inter corpora cœlestia et terrena est media, et, quod ab illis accipit, ad inferiora refundit; sic et Virgo Regia inter nos et Deum est media, et gratiam ipsa nobis refundit."—*Spann. Polyanth. litt. M.* t. 6.

[2] " Felix cœli porta."

[3] " Nulla gratia venit de cœlo ad terram, nisi transeat per manus Mariæ."—*Apud S. Bernardin. Pro Fest. V. M.* s. 5, c. 8.

[4] " Nullus potest cœlum intrare, nisi per Mariam transeat, tamquam per portam."—*In Luc.* i.

[5] " In Christo fuit plenitudo gratiæ, sicut in Capite influente; in Maria, sicut in collo transfundente."

Mary."[1] The same St. Bernardine endeavors to assign
a reason for this when he says, "that as God was pleased
to dwell in the womb of this holy Virgin, she acquired,
so to speak, a kind of jurisdiction over all graces; for
when Jesus Christ issued forth from her most sacred
womb, all the streams of divine gifts flowed from her as
from a celestial ocean."[2] Elsewhere, repeating the same
idea in more distinct terms, he asserts that "from the
moment that this Virgin Mother conceived the divine
Word in her womb, she acquired a special jurisdiction,
so to say, over all the gifts of the Holy Ghost, so that no
creature has since received any grace from God otherwise than through the hands of Mary."[3]

Another author, in a commentary on a passage of Jeremias, in which the prophet, speaking of the Incarnation
of the Eternal Word, and of Mary his Mother, says that
a woman shall compass a man,[4] remarks, that "as no line
can be drawn from the centre of a circle without passing
by the circumference, so no grace proceeds from Jesus,
who is the centre of every good thing, without passing by
Mary, who compassed him when she received him into
her womb."[5]

St. Bernardine says that for this reason, "all gifts, all
virtues, and all graces are dispensed by the hands of

[1] "Per Virginem, a Capite Christo, vitales gratiæ in ejus Corpus
mysticum transfunduntur."

[2] "Cum tota natura divina intra Virginis uterum exstiterit, non timeo
dicere quod in omnes gratiarum effluxus quamdam jurisdictiónem
habuerit hæc Virgo, de cujus utero, quasi de quodam Divinitatis
oceano, flumina emanant omnium gratiarum."

[3] "A tempore a quo Virgo Mater concepit in utero Verbum Dei,
quandam, ut sic dicam, jurisdictionem obtinuit in omni Spiritus Sancti
processione temporali ; ita quod nulla creatura aliquam a Deo obtinuit gratiam, nisi secundum ipsius piæ Matris dispensationem."—*Pro
Festo V. M.* s. 5. c. 8.

[4] *Jer.* xxxi. 22.

[5] *Crasset, Vér. Dév.* p. 1, tr. 1. q 5. § 2.

Mary to whomsoever, when, and as she pleases." [1] Richard of St. Laurence also asserts "that God wills that whatever good things he bestows on his creatures should pass through the hands of Mary." [2] And therefore the Venerable Abbot of Celles exhorts all to have recourse to "this treasury of graces" (for so he calls her); for the world and the whole human race have to receive every good that can be hoped for through her alone. "Address yourselves to the Blessed Virgin," he says; "for by her, and in her, and with her, and from her, the world receives, and is to receive, every good." [3]

It must now be evident to all that when these saints and authors tell us in such terms that all graces come to us through Mary, they do not simply mean to say that we "received Jesus Christ, the source of every good, through Mary," as the before-named writer pretends; but that they assure us that God, who gave us Jesus Christ, wills that all graces that have been, that are, and will be dispensed to men to the end of the world through the merits of Christ, should be dispensed by the hands and through the intercession of Mary.

And thus Father Suarez concludes, that it is the sentiment of the universal Church, "that the intercession and prayers of Mary are, above those of all others, not only useful, but necessary." [4] Necessary, in accordance with what we have already said, not with an absolute necessity; for the mediation of Jesus Christ alone is absolutely necessary; but with a moral necessity; for the

[1] "Ideo omnia dona, virtutes et gratiæ, quibus vult quando vult, quomodo vult, per manus ipsius dispensantur."—*Pro Fest. V. M.* s. 5, c. 8.

[2] "Deus, quidquid boni dat creaturis suis, per manus Matris Virginis vult transire."—*De Laud. B. M.* l. 2, p. 3.

[3] "Accede ad Virginem, quia per ipsam, mundus habiturus est omne bonum."—*Cont. de V. M. in prol.*

[4] "Sentit Ecclesia Virginis intercessionem esse utilem ac necessariam."—*D Inc.* p. 2, d. 23. s. 3

Church believes with St. Bernard, that God has determined that no grace shall be granted otherwise than by the hands of Mary. "God wills," says the saint, "that we should have nothing that has not passed through the hands of Mary;" [1] and before St. Bernard, St. Ildephonsus asserted the same thing, addressing the Blessed Virgin in the following terms: "O Mary, God has decided on committing all good gifts that he has provided for men to thy hands, and therefore he has intrusted all treasures and riches of grace to thee." [2] And therefore St. Peter Damian remarks, "that God would not become man without the consent of Mary; in the first place, that we might feel ourselves under great obligations to her; and in the second, that we might understand that the salvation of all is left to the care of this Blessed Virgin." [3]

St. Bonaventure, on the words of the prophet Isaias, *And there shall come forth a rod out of the root of Jesse, and a flower shall rise up out of his root, and the spirit of the Lord shall rest upon him,* [4] makes a beautiful remark, saying: "Whoever desires the sevenfold grace of the Holy Spirit, let him seek for the flower of the Holy Ghost in the rod." That is, for Jesus in Mary; "For by the rod we find the flower, and by the flower, God." [5] And in the twelfth chapter of the same work, he adds, "If you de-

[1] "Nihil nos Deus habere voluit, quod per Mariæ manus non transiret."—*In Vig. Nat. D.* s. 3.

[2] "Omnia bona quæ illic summa Majestas decrevit facere, tuis manibus voluit commendare: commissi quippe sunt tibi thesauri . . . . et ornamenta gratiarum."—*In Cor. Virg.* c. 15.

[3] *Paciucch. in Ps.* lxxxvi. *exc.* 1.

[4] "Egredietur Virga de radice Jesse, et Flos de radice ejus ascendet; et requiescet super eum Spiritus Domini."—*Is.* xi. 1.

[5] "Quicumque Spiritus Sancti gratiam adipisci desiderat, Florem in Virga quærat: per Virgam enim ad Florem, per Florem ad Spiritum, pervenimus.—Si hunc Florem habere desideras, Virgam Floris precibus flectas."—*Spec. B. M. V.* lect. 6, 12.

sire to possess this flower, bend down the rod, which bears the flower, by prayer; and so you will obtain it." The seraphical Father, in his sermon for the Epiphany, on the words of St. Matthew, *They found the child, with Mary his Mother,*[1] reminds us, that if we wish to find Jesus we must go to Mary.[2] We may, then, conclude, that in vain shall we seek for Jesus, unless we endeavor to find him with Mary.[3] And so St. Ildephonsus says, "I desire to be the servant of the Son; but because no one will ever be so without serving the Mother, for this reason I desire the servitude of Mary."[4]

EXAMPLE.*

A young nobleman who was on a sea-voyage began to read an obscene book, in which he took much pleasure. A religious noticed this, and said to him: "Are you disposed to make a present to our Blessed Lady?" The young man replied that he was. "Well," the other answered, "I wish that, for the love of the most holy Virgin, you would give up that book, and throw it into the sea." "Here it is, Father," said the young man. "No," replied the religious, "you must yourself make Mary this present." He did so; and no sooner had he returned to Genoa, his native place, than the Mother of God so inflamed his heart with divine love that he entered a religious Order.[5]

---

[1] "Invenerunt puerum cum Maria, Matre ejus."—*Matth.* ii. 11.

[2] "Si ergo hunc puerum vis invenire, ad Mariam accede."

[3] "Nunquam invenitur Christus, nisi cum Maria, nisi per Mariam. Frustra igitur quærit, qui cum Maria invenire non quærit."—*Spann. Polyanth. litt. M. t. 6.*

[4] "Ut sim servus Filii, servitutem appeto Genitricis."—*De Virginit. Mar. c.* 12.

[5] *Nadasi, Ann. Mar. S. J.* 1606.

Prayer.

O my soul, see what a sure hope of salvation and eternal life our Lord has given thee, by having in his mercy inspired thee with confidence in the patronage of his mother; and this, notwithstanding that so many times by thy sins thou hast merited his displeasure and hell. Thank thy God, and thank thy protectress Mary, who has condescended to take thee under her mantle; for of this thou mayest be well convinced, after the many graces that thou hast received by her means. O yes, I do thank thee, my most loving Mother, for all thou hast done for me who am deserving of hell. And from how many dangers hast thou not delivered me, O Queen! How many inspirations and mercies hast thou not obtained for me from God! What service, what honor, have I ever rendered thee, that thou shouldst do so much for me? I know that it is thy sole goodness that has impelled thee. Ah, too little would it be in comparison with all that I owe thee, did I shed my blood and give my life for thee; for thou hast delivered me from eternal death; thou hast enabled me, as I hope, to recover divine grace; to thee, in fine, I owe all I have. My most amiable Lady, I, poor wretch that I am, can make thee no return but that of always loving and praising thee. Ah, disdain not to accept the tender affection of a poor sinner, who is inflamed with love for thy goodness. If my heart is unworthy to love thee, because it is impure and filled with earthly affections, it is thou who must change it. Ah, change it, then. Bind me to my God, and bind me so that I may never more have it in my power to separate myself from his love. Thou askest of me that I should love thy God, and I ask of thee that thou shouldst obtain this love for me, to love him always; this is all that I desire. Amen.

II.

The same Subject continued.

St. Bernard says, "that as a man and a woman cooperated in our ruin, so it was proper that another man and another woman should coöperate in our redemption, and these two were Jesus and his Mother Mary." "There is no doubt," says the saint, "that Jesus Christ alone was more than sufficient to redeem us; but it was more becoming that both sexes should coöperate in the reparation of an evil in causing which both had shared." [1] Hence Blessed Albert the Great calls Mary, the "helper of redemption:" [2] and the Blessed Virgin herself revealed to St. Bridget, that "as Adam and Eve sold the world for an apple, so did she with her Son redeem it as it were with one heart." [3] This is confirmed by St. Anselm, who says, "that although God could create the world out of nothing, yet, when it was lost by sin, he would not repair the evil without the coöperation of Mary." [4]

Suarez says, [5] "that Mary coöperated in our salvation in three ways; first, by having merited by a merit of congruity the Incarnation of the Word; secondly, by having continually prayed for us whilst she was living in this world; thirdly, by having willingly sacrificed the life of her Son to God." For this reason our Lord has justly decreed, that as Mary coöperated in the salvation of man with so much love, and at the same time gave such glory to God, so all men through her intercession are to obtain their salvation.

Mary is called "the coöperator in our justification;" for to her God has intrusted all graces intended for us; [6] and therefore St. Bernard affirms, "that all men, past,

---

[1] "Congruum magis ut adesset nostræ reparationi sexus uterque, quorum corruptioni neuter defuisset."—*In Sign. Magn.*

[2] "Adjutrix redemptionis."—*Super Miss.* q. 29. § 3.

[3] "Sicut Adam et Eva vendiderunt mundum pro uno pomo, sic Filius meus et ego redemimus mundum quasi cum uno corde."—*Rev.* l. 1, c. 35.

[4] "Qui potuit omnia de nihilo facere, noluit ea violata sine Maria reficere."—*Orat.* 51.

[5] *De Inc.* p. 2, d. 23, s. 1.

[6] "Auxiliatrix nostræ justificationis ; Deus enim omnes gratias faciendas Mariæ commisit."—*Marial.* p. 3, s. 1.

present, and to come, should look upon Mary as the means and negotiator of the salvation of all ages." [1]

Jesus Christ says, that no one can find him unless the Eternal Father first draws him by the means of divine grace: *No one comes to me unless my Father draws him.* [2] Thus also does Jesus address his Mother, says Richard of St. Laurence: "No one comes to me unless my Mother first of all draws him by her prayers." [3] Jesus was the fruit of Mary, as St. Elizabeth told her: *Blessed art thou amongst women, and blessed is the fruit of thy womb."* [4] Whoever, therefore, desires the fruit must go to the tree; whoever desires Jesus must go to Mary; and whoever finds Mary will most certainly find Jesus.

When St. Elizabeth saw that the most Blessed Virgin had come to visit her in her own house, not knowing how to thank her, and filled with humility, she exclaimed: *And whence is this to me, that the Mother of my Lord should visit me?* [5] But how could this be? we may ask. Did not St. Elizabeth already know that not only Mary, but also Jesus, had entered her house? Why then does she say that she is unworthy to receive the Mother, and not rather, that she is unworthy to receive the Son, who had come to visit her? Ah, yes, it was that the saint knew full well that when Mary comes she brings Jesus, and therefore it was sufficient to thank the Mother without naming the Son.

---

[1] "Ad illam, sicut ad medium, sicut ad arcam Dei, sicut ad negotium sæculorum respiciunt, et qui præcesserunt, et nos qui sumus, et qui sequentur."—*In Pent.* s. 2.

[2] "Nemo potest venire ad me, nisi Pater, qui misit me, traxerit eum."—*John,* vi. 44.

[3] "Nemo potest venire ad me, nisi Mater mea suis precibus traxerit eum."—*De Laud. B. M.* i. 12, p. 2.

[4] "Benedicta tu inter mulieres, et benedictus Fructus ventris tui."—*Luke,* i. 42.

[5] "Et unde hoc mihi, ut veniat Mater Domini mei ad me?"—*Ibid.*

She is like the merchant's ship, she bringeth her bread from afar.[1] Mary was this fortunate ship that brought us Jesus Christ from heaven, who is the living bread that comes down from heaven to give us eternal life, as he himself says: *I am the living bread, which came down from heaven : if any man eat of this bread, he shall live forever.*[2] And hence Richard of St. Laurence says, " that in the sea of this world all will be lost who are not received into this ship; that is to say, all who are not protected by Mary;" and therefore he adds, "As often as we see ourselves in danger of perishing in the midst of the temptations and contending passions of this life, let us have recourse to Mary, and cry out quickly, O Lady, help us, save us, if thou wilt not see us perish."[3]

Remark, by the by, that this writer does not scruple to address these words to Mary: " Save us, we perish;" as does a certain author already noticed, and who says, that we cannot ask Mary to save us, as this belongs to God alone. But since a culprit condemned to death can beg a royal favorite to save him by interceding with the king that his life may be spared, why cannot we ask the Mother of God to save us by obtaining us eternal life? St. John Damascene scrupled not to address her in these words: " Pure and immaculate Virgin, save me, and deliver me from eternal damnation."[4] St. Bonaventure called Mary "the salvation of those who invoked her."[5]

[1] " Facta est quasi navis institoris, de longe portans panem suum." —*Prov.* xxxi 14.

[2] " Ego sum Panis vivus, qui de cœlo descendi; si quis manducaverit ex hoc Pane, vivet in æternum."—*John*, vi. 51

[3] " In mare mundi submergentur omnes illi, quos non suscipit Navis ista. Ideo, quoties videmus insurgentes super nos fluctus ejus maris, clamare debemus ad Mariam: Domina! salva nos, perimus."—*De Laud. B. M.* l. 11, c. 8.

[4] " Regina immaculata et pura! salva me, libera me ab æterna damnatione."—*Paracl. in Deip.*

[5] " O Salus te invocantium!"

The holy Church approves of the invocation by also calling her the " salvation of the weak." [1] And shall we scruple to·ask her to save us, when "the way of salvation is open to none otherwise than through Mary ?" [2] as a certain author remarks. And before him St. Germanus had said the same thing, speaking of Mary: " No one is saved but through thee." [3]

But let us now see what else the saints say of the need in which we are of the intercession of the divine Mother. The glorious St. Cajetan used to say, that we may seek for graces, but shall never find them.without the intercession of Mary. This is confirmed by St. Antoninus, who thus beautifully expresses himself: " Whoever asks and expects to obtain graces without the intercession of Mary, endeavors to fly without wings;" [4] for, as Pharaoh said to Joseph, *the land of Egypt is in thy hands*, and addressed all who came to him for food to Joseph, *Go to Joseph*, [5] so does God send us to Mary when we seek for grace: "Go to Mary;" for "He has decreed," says St. Bernard, "that he will grant no graces otherwise than by the hands of Mary." [6] "And thus," says Richard of St. Laurence, "our salvation is in the hands of Mary; so that we Christians may with much greater reason say of her than the Egyptians of Joseph, *Our salvation is in thy hands*." [7] The Venerable Raymond Jordano repeats the

[1] " Salus infirmorum."

[2] " Nemini, nisi per eam, patet aditus ad salutem."—*Paciucch. In Ps.* lxxxvi. *exc.* 1.

[3] " Nullus est qui salvus fiat, nisi per te."—*De Zona Deip*.

[4] " Qui petit sine ipsa duce, sine alis tentat volare."—P. 4, tit. 15, c. 22, § 9.

[5] " Ite ad Joseph."—*Gen.* xli. 55.

[6] " Totum nos habere voluit per Mariam."—*De Aquæd.*

[7] " Salus nostra in manu Mariæ est; ut ei dicere multo melius valeamus nos Christiani, quam dixerint Ægyptii Joseph: Salus nostra in manu tua est."—(*Gen.* xlvii. 25.)—*De Laud. B. M.* l. 2, c. 1.

same thing: "Our salvation is in her hands."[1]   Cassian speaks in still stronger terms. He says absolutely, "that the salvation of all depends on their being favored and protected by Mary."[2]   He who is protected by Mary will be saved; he who is not will be lost. St. Bernardine of Sienna thus addresses this Blessed Virgin: "O Lady, since thou art the dispenser of all graces, and since the grace of salvation can only come through thy hands, our salvation depends on thee."[3]

Therefore, Richard of St. Laurence had good reason for saying, that "as we should fall into the abyss, if the ground were withdrawn from under our feet, so does a soul deprived of the succor of Mary first fall into sin, and then into hell."[4]   St. Bonaventure says, that "God will not save us without the intercession of Mary."[5] And that "as a child cannot live without a nurse to suckle it, so no one can be saved without the protection of Mary."[6]   Therefore he exhorts us "to thirst after devotion to her, to preserve it with care, and never to abandon it until we have received her maternal blessing in heaven."[7]   "And whoever," exclaims St. Germanus, "could know God, were it not for thee, O most holy Mary? who could be saved? who would be preserved from dangers? who would receive any grace, were it not for thee, O Mother of God, O full of grace?"

[1] "Salus nostra in manu illius est."—*Cont. de V. in prol.*

[2] "Tota salus humani generis consistit in multitudine gratiæ Mariæ et favoris."—*Pelbart, Stell.* l. 12, p. 1, a. 3.

[3] "Tu Dispensatrix omnium gratiarum."—*Pro Fest. V. M.* s. 13, a. 2, c. 3.

[4] "Sic, subtracto nobis adjutorio Mariæ, statim labimur in peccatum, et inde in infernum."—*De Laud. B. M.* l. 8.

[5] "Ipse, sine ea, non salvabit te."

[6] "Quemadmodum infans, sine nutrice, non potest vivere; ita nec, sine Domina nostra, potes habere salutem."

[7] "Sitiat ergo anima tua ad ipsam; tene eam, nec dimitte, donec benedixerit tibi."—*Cant. in Psalt*

The following are the beautiful words in which he expresses himself: "There is no one, O most holy Mary, who can know God but through thee; no one who can be saved or redeemed but through thee, O Mother of God; no one who can be delivered from dangers but through thee, O Virgin Mother; no one who obtains mercy but through thee, O filled with all grace." And in another place, addressing her, he says, "No one would be free from the effects of the concupiscence of the flesh and from sin, unless thou didst open the way to him." [1]

And as we have access to the Eternal Father, says St. Bernard, only through Jesus Christ, so have we access to Jesus Christ only through Mary: "By thee we have access to the Son, O blessed finder of grace, bearer of life, and mother of salvation, that we may receive him by thee, who through thee was given to us." [2] This is the reason given by the saint why our Lord has determined that all shall be saved by the intercession of Mary; and therefore he calls her the Mother of grace and of our salvation.

"Then," asks St. Germanus, "what will become of us? what hope can we have of salvation, if thou dost abandon us, O Mary, who art the life of Christians?" [3]

"But," says the modern author already quoted, "if all graces come through Mary, when we implore the intercession of other saints, they must have recourse to the

---

[1] " Nemo est. O Sanctissima, qui ad Dei notitiam venit, nisi per te! Nemo qui salvus fiat, nisi per te, Dei Parens! Nemo liber a periculis, nisi per te, Virgo Mater! Nemo donum Dei suscipit, nisi per te, gratia Plena. Nisi euim tu iter aperires, nemo spiritualis evadcret."—*In Dorm. V. M.* s. 2.

[2] " Per te accessum habemus ad filium, O Inventrix gratiæ, Mate salutis! ut per te nos suscipiat, qui per te datus est nobis."—*De Adv Dom.* s. 2.

[3] "Si tu nos deserueris, quid erit de nobis. O Vita Christianorum?" —*De Zona Deip.*

mediation of Mary. But that," he says, "no one believes or ever dreamed."

As to believing it, I reply that in that there can be no error or difficulty. What difficulty can there be in saying that God, in order to honor his Mother, and having made her Queen of saints, and willing that all graces shall be dispensed by her hands, should also will that the saints should address themselves to her to obtain favors for their clients?

And as to saying that no one ever dreamed of such a thing, I find that St. Bernard, St. Anselm, St. Bonaventure, Suarez, and others, expressly declare it to be the case. "In vain," says St. Bernard, "would a person ask other saints for a favor, if Mary did not interpose to obtain it." [1] Some other author, explaining the words of the Psalm, *All the rich among the people shall entreat thy countenance*, [2] says, "that the saints are the rich of that great people of God, who, when they wish to obtain a favor from God for their clients, recommend themselves to Mary, and she immediately obtains it." And Father Suarez correctly remarks, "that we beg the saints to be our intercessors with Mary, because she is their Queen and sovereign Lady." "Amongst the saints," he says, "we do not make use of one to intercede with the other, as all are of the same order; but we do ask them to intercede with Mary, because she is their sovereign and Queen." [3] And this is precisely what St. Benedict promised to St. Frances of Rome, as we read in Father Marchese; for he appeared to her, and taking her under his protection, he promised that he would be her advocate with the divine Mother.

[1] "Frustra alios Sanctos oraret, quem ista non adjuvaret."

[2] "Vultum tuum deprecabuntur omnes divites plebis."—*Ps.* xliv. 13.

[3] "Inter alios Sanctos non utimur uno ut intercessore ad alium, quia omnes sunt ejusdem ordinis; ad Virginem autem, tanquam ad Reginam et Dominam, alii adhibentur intercessores."—*De Inc.* p. 2, d. 23, s. 3.

In confirmation of this, St. Anselm addresses our Blessed Lady and says, "O Lady, whatever all the saints, united with thee, can obtain, thou canst obtain alone." "And why is this?" asks the saint; "why is it that thou alone hast such great power? Ah, it is because thou alone art the Mother of our common Redeemer; thou art the spouse of God; thou art the universal Queen of heaven and earth. If thou dost not speak for us, no saint will pray for or help us. But if thou beginnest to pray for us, then will all the saints do the same and succor us." [1]

So that Father Segneri,[2] in his *Devout Client of Mary*, applying with the Catholic Church the words of Ecclesiasticus to her, *I alone have compassed the circuit of heaven*,[3] says, that "as the first sphere by its motion sets all the others in motion, so it is when Mary prays for a soul; immediately the whole heavenly court begins to pray with her." "Nay, more," says St. Bonaventure, "whenever the most sacred Virgin goes to God to intercede for us, she, as Queen, commands all the angels and saints to accompany her, and unite their prayers to hers." [4]

And thus, finally, do we understand why the holy Church requires that we should salute and invoke the divine Mother under the glorious title of "our hope." [5] The impious Luther said, "that he could not endure that the Roman Church should call Mary, who is only a crea-

---

[1] "Quod possunt omnes isti tecum, tu sola potes sine illis omnibus. Quare hoc potes? Quia Mater es Salvatoris nostri, Sponsa Dei, Regina cœli et terræ. Te tacente, nullus orabit, nullus juvabit. Te orante, omnes orabunt, omnes juvabunt."—*Orat.* 45.

[2] *Div. di M.* p. 1, c. 7, § 4.

[3] ".Gyrum cœli circuivi sola."—*Ecclus.* xxiv. 8.

[4] "Quando Sanctissima Virgo procedit ad Deum pro nobis deprecandum, imperat Angelis et Sanctis, ut eam comitentur, ut simul cum ipsa Altissimum pro nobis exorent."—*Paciucch. Super Sal. Ang. exc.* 19.

[5] "Spes nostra! salve."

ture, "our hope;" [1] "for," said he, "God alone, and
Jesus Christ as our Mediator, is our hope: and God
curses those who place their hope in a creature, according to the prophet Jeremias, *Cursed be the man that trusteth
in man.*" [2]   But the Church teaches us to invoke Mary on
all occasions, and to call her "our hope; hail, our hope!"
Whoever places his confidence in a creature independently of God, he certainly is cursed by God ; for God is
the only source and dispenser of every good, and the
creature without God is nothing, and can give nothing.
But if our Lord has so disposed it, as we have already
proved that he has done, that all graces should pass
through Mary as by a channel of mercy, we not only can
but ought to assert that she, by whose means we receive
the divine graces, is truly our hope.

Therefore St. Bernard says, "that she is his greatest
confidence, and the whole foundation of his hope." [3]
St. John Damascene says the same thing ; for he thus
addresses the most Blessed Virgin: "O Lady, in thee
have I placed all my hope; and with my eyes fixed on
thee, from thee do I expect salvation. [4] St. Thomas
says, that "Mary is the whole hope of our salvation," [5]
and St. Ephrem, addressing her, says, "O most holy
Virgin, receive us under thy protection, if thou wilt see
us saved, for we have no hope of salvation but through
thy means." [6]

Let us, then, in the words of St. Bernard, "endeavor
to venerate this divine Mother with the whole affection

---

[1] "Ferre nequeo ut Maria dicatur Spes et Vita nostra."

[2] "Maledictus homo qui confidit in homine."—*Jer.* xvii. 5.

[3] "Filioli, hæc mea maxima Fiducia est, hæc tota ratio spei meæ."
—*De Aquæd.*

[4] "In te spem meam collocavi ex animo, et intentis oculis abs te
pendeo."—*Paracl. in Deip.*

[5] "Omnis Spes vitæ."—*Exp. in Sal. Ang.*

[6] "Nobis non est alia quam in te fiducia. O Virgo sincerissima !
Sub alis tuæ pietatis protege et custodi nos."—*De Laud. Dei gen*

of our hearts; for such is the will of God, who is pleased that we should receive every good thing from her hand." [1] And therefore the saint exhorts us, whenever we desire or ask for any grace, to recommend ourselves to Mary, and to be assured that we shall receive it by her means; [2] for he says, if thou dost not deserve the favor from God, Mary, who will ask it for thee, will deserve to receive it; "because thou wast unworthy of the gift, it was bestowed on Mary, that through her thou mightest receive all that thou hast." [3] The saint then advises us to recommend all that we offer to God to the care of Mary, be they good works or prayers, if we wish our Lord to accept them. "Whatever thou mayest offer to God, be sure to recommend it to Mary, in order not to meet with a repulse." [4]

The doctrine of Mary's dignity as mediatrix of all graces is commonly accepted by theologians today, and recent pontiffs have occasionally alluded to it. We know that Benedict XIV has left these words on record: "Mary is like a celestial river by which the waters of all graces and gifts are conveyed to poor mortals." Pius IX. in speaking to the bishops of the whole world made use of the words of St. Bernard: "God wills that every grace should come to us through her." In his encyclical on the devotion of the Rosary, Sept. 22, 1891, Pope Leo XIII. says: "In a true and natural sense may we say that from the great treasury of graces that the Lord has merited for us, nothing came to us, by the will of God except through Mary." Pius X. declares: "She is the dispensatrix of the graces that Jesus Christ has merited for us by His blood and His death." The following are the words of Benedict XV.: "It has pleased God to grant us all graces through the intercession of Mary." Again: "All the graces which the Giver of all good deigns to grant to the descendants of Adam, are dispensed to us, in the disposition of a loving Providence, through the hands of the Blessed Virgin." And finally: "The

---

[1] "Totis medullis cordium Mariam hanc veneremur; quia sic est voluntas ejus, qui totum nos habere voluit per Mariam."—*De Aquaed.*

[2] "Quæramus gratiam, et per Mariam quæramus."

[3] "Quia indignus eras cui donaretur, datum est Mariæ, ut per illam acciperes quidquid haberes."—*In Vig. Nat. D. s. 3.*

[4] "Quidquid Deo offerre paras, Mariæ commendare memento, si non vis sustinere repulsam."—*De Aquaed.*

graces of all kinds that we receive from the treasury of the Redemption are dispensed by the hands of the Sorrowful Virgin."

It is worthy of note that the last four popes have directed special
attention to this teaching on the Blessed Virgin Mary. They refer
to it repeatedly, and thus place the seal of approval on the authority
of those of former times who held the doctrine and particularly of
St. Alphonsus. On the strength of these testimonies one can un-
hesitatingly subscribe to the judgment of the Apologist Bainvel, S.J.:
"The twofold cooperation of Mary in the work of the redemption,
first on earth by her life, prayer and suffering, and then in heaven
by her prayer alone is sound Catholic doctrine, beyond all dispute and worthy of being defined, i.e. of being raised to the
dignity of an article of faith." [1]

Father Jansen, C.SS.R. says that what the supreme teacher of the
Church proclaims so loudly, deserves to be made known not merely
to the students of theology in class rooms, but in pulpit and press
to the faithful of the whole world. [2]

EXAMPLE.

The history of Theophilus, written by Eutychian,
patriarch of Constantinople, and who was an eye-witness
of the fact he relates, is well known. It is attested by St.
Peter Damian, St. Bernard, St. Bonaventure, St. Antonine,
and by others quoted by Father Crasset. [3]

Theophilus was archdeacon of the church of Adana, a
city of Cilicia, and he was held in such veneration by the
people that they wished to have him for their bishop, but
he, out of humility, refused the dignity. It happened that
evil-disposed persons accused him falsely of some crime,
and for this he was deposed from his archdeaconry. He
took this so much to heart, that, blinded by passion, he
went to a Jewish magician, who made him consult Satan,
that he might help him in his misfortune. The devil told
him that if he desired to be helped by him, he must renounce Jesus and his Mother Mary, and consign him the
act of renunciation written in his own hand. Theophilus
immediately complied with the demand. The next day, the
bishop having discovered that he had been deceived, asked

[1] *Dict. Apolog. d'Hales* III, *col.* 301.
[2] *Nederl. Kath. Stemmen* 18 (1918) 273.
[3] *Vér. Dév.* p. 1, tr. 1, q. 10.

the archdeacon's pardon, and restored him to office. No sooner was this accomplished than his conscience was torn with remorse, and he could do nothing but weep. What could he do? He went to a church, and there casting himself all in tears at the feet of an image of Mary, he thus addressed her: "O Mother of God, I will not despair as long as I can have access to thee, who art so compassionate, and hast the power to help me." He remained thus weeping and praying to our Blessed Lady for forty days—when, lo, one night the Mother of mercy appeared to him, and said: "O Theophilus, what hast thou done? Thou hast renounced my friendship and that of my Son, and for whom? For his and my enemy." "O Lady," answered Theophilus, "thou must pardon me, and obtain my forgiveness from thy Son." Mary seeing his confidence, replied: "Be of good heart; I will intercede for thee with God." Theophilus, encouraged by these consoling words, redoubled his tears, mortifications, and prayers, and never left the image. At last Mary again appeared to him, and with a cheerful countenance said: "Theophilus, be of good heart; I have presented thy tears and prayers to God; he has accepted them, and has already pardoned thee; but from this day forward be grateful to him and faithful." "But, O Lady," replied Theophilus, "that is not yet enough to satisfy me entirely; the enemy still possesses that impious writing in which I renounced thee and thy Son. Thou canst oblige him to surrender it." Three days afterwards, Theophilus awoke in the night, and found the writing on his breast. On the following day he went to the church where the bishop was, and, in presence of an immense concourse of people, cast himself at his feet, and with bitter tears related all that had taken place, and delivered into his hands the infamous writing. The bishop committed it to the flames in the presence of all the people, who did nothing but weep for joy, and praise the goodness of God, and the mercy of Mary shown towards this poor sinner. But he, returning to the church of our Blessed Lady, remained there for three days, and then expired, his heart filled with joy, and returning thanks to Jesus and to his most holy Mother.*

Prayer.

O Queen and Mother of mercy, who dispensest graces to all who have recourse to thee with so much liberality, because thou art a Queen, and with so much love, because thou art our most loving Mother; to thee do I, who am so devoid of merit and virtue, and so loaded with debts to the divine justice, recommend myself this day. O Mary, thou holdest the keys of all the divine mercies; forget not my miseries, and leave me not in my poverty. Thou art so liberal with all, and givest more than thou art asked for, O, be thus liberal with me. O Lady, protect me; this is all that I ask of thee. If thou protectest me, I fear nothing. I fear not the evil spirits; for thou art more powerful than all of them. I fear not my sins; for thou by one word canst obtain their full pardon from God. And if I have thy favor, I do not even fear an angry God; for a single prayer of thine will appease him. In fine, if thou protectest me, I hope all; for thou art all-powerful. O Mother of mercy, I know that thou takest pleasure and dost glory in helping the most miserable, and, provided they are not obstinate, that thou canst help them. I am a sinner, but am not obstinate; I desire to change my life. Thou canst, then, help me; O, help me and save me. I now place myself entirely in thy hands. Tell me what I must do in order to please God, and I am ready for all, and hope to do all with thy help, O Mary—Mary my Mother, my light, my consolation, my refuge, my hope. Amen, amen, amen.

---

* The Church has enrolled this celebrated penitent among the number of the saints. His life may be read in the Bollandists, in Surius, as well as in Giry, February 4.—ED.

CHAPTER VI.

Eia ergo, Advocata nostra !

O GRACIOUS ADVOCATE.

MARY, OUR ADVOCATE.

I.

Mary is an Advocate who is able to save all.

So great is the authority that mothers possess over their sons, that even if they are monarchs, and have absolute dominion over every person in their kingdom, yet never can mothers become the subjects of their sons. It is true that Jesus now in heaven sits at the right hand of the Father, that is, as St. Thomas [1] explains it, even as man, on account of the hypostatical union with the Person of the divine Word. He has supreme dominion over all, and also over Mary; it will nevertheless be always true that for a time, when he was living in this world, he was pleased to humble himself and to be subject to Mary, as we are told by St. Luke: *And He was subject to them.* [2] And still more, says St. Ambrose, Jesus Christ having deigned to make Mary his Mother, inasmuch as he was her Son, he was truly obliged to obey her. And for this reason, says Richard of St. Laurence, "of other saints we say that they are with God; but of Mary alone can it be said that she was so far favored as to be not only herself submissive to the will of God, but even that God was subject to her will." [3] And whereas of all other virgins, remarks the same

---

[1] *De Human. J. C. a.* 23.

[2] "Et erat subditus illis."—*Luke.* ii. 51.

[3] "Cum de cæteris Sanctis dicatur, eos esse cum Deo, Maria majus aliquid sortita est, ut non solum ipsa subjiceretur voluntati Domini. sed etiam Dominus voluntati ipsius."

author, we must say that *they follow the Lamb whithersoever he goeth,*[1] of the Blessed Virgin Mary we can say that the Lamb followed her, having become subject to her.[2]

And here we say, that although Mary, now in heaven, can no longer command her Son, nevertheless her prayers are always the prayers of a Mother, and consequently most powerful to obtain whatever she asks. " Mary," says St. Bonaventure, " has this great privilege, that with her Son she above all the saints is most powerful to obtain whatever she wills."[3] And why? Precisely for the reason on which we have already touched, and which we shall later on again examine at greater length, because they are the prayers of a mother.

Therefore, says St. Peter Damian, the Blessed Virgin can do whatever she pleases both in heaven and on earth. She is able to raise even those who are in despair to confidence; and he addresses her in these words: "All power is given to thee in heaven and on earth, and nothing is impossible to thee who canst raise those who are in despair to the hope of salvation."[4] And then he adds that " when the Mother goes to seek a favor for us from Jesus Christ" (whom the saint calls the golden altar of mercy, at which sinners obtain pardon), " her Son esteems her prayers so greatly, and is so desirous to satisfy her, that when she prays it seems as if she rather commanded than prayed, and was rather a queen than a handmaid."[5] Jesus is pleased thus to honor his beloved

---

[1] " Sequuntur Agnum quocumque ierit."—*Apoc.* xiv. 4.

[2] " De Virgine autem Maria secure potest dici, quod Agnus sequebatur eam, quocunque ivit; unde Lucas: Erat subditus illis."—*De Laud. B. M.* l. i. c. 5.

[3] " Grande privilegium Mariæ, quod apud Deum potentissima est." —*Spec. B. M. V. lect.* 6.

[4] " Data est tibi omnis potestas in cœlo et in terra; nihil tibi impossibile, cui possibile est desperatos in spem beatitudinis relevare."

[5] " Accedis enim ante illud humanæ reconciliationis Altare, non solum rogans, sed imperans; Domina. non ancilla; Nam Filius, nihil negans, honorat te."—*In Nat. B. V.* s. 1.

Mother who honored him so much during her life by immediately granting all that she asks or desires. This is beautifully confirmed by St. Germanus, who addressing our Blessed Lady says: " Thou art the Mother of God, and all-powerful to save sinners, and with God thou needest no other recommendation; for thou art the Mother of true life." [1]

" At the command of Mary, all obey, even God." St. Bernardine fears not to utter this sentence; meaning, indeed, to say that God grants the prayers of Mary as if they were commands.[2] And hence St. Anselm addressing Mary says: " Our Lord, O most holy Virgin, has exalted thee to such a degree that by his favor all things that are possible to him should be possible to thee." [3] " For thy protection is omnipotent, O Mary," [4] says Cosmas of Jerusalem. " Yes, Mary is omnipotent," repeats Richard of St. Laurence; " for the queen by every law enjoys the same privileges as the king. And as," he adds, " the power of the son and that of the mother is the same, a mother is made omnipotent by an omnipotent son." [5] " And thus," says St. Antoninus, " God has placed the whole Church, not only under the patronage, but even under the dominion of Mary." [6]

Since the Mother, then, should have the same power as the Son, rightly has Jesus, who is omnipotent, made Mary also omnipotent; though, of course, it is always true that where the Son is omnipotent by nature, the

---

[1] *In Dorm V. M.* s. 2.

[2] " Imperio Virginis omnia famulantur, etiam Deus."—*Pro Fest. V. M.* s. 5, c. 6.

[3] " Te, Domina, Deus sic exaltavit, et omnia tibi secum possibilia esse donavit."—*De Excell. Virg.* c. 12.

[4] " Omnipotens auxilium tuum. O Maria !"—*Hymn.* 6.

[5] " Eisdem privilegiis secundum leges gaudent Rex et Regina. Cum autem eadem sit potestas Matris et Filii ab omnipotente Filio omnipotens Mater est effecta."— *De Laud B. M.* l. 4.

[6] " Sub protectione ejus et dominio "—*P.* 4, t. 15, c. 20, § 2.

Mother is only so by grace. But that she is so is evident from the fact, that whatever the Mother asks for, the Son never denies her; and this was revealed to St. Bridget, who one day heard Jesus talking with Mary, and thus address her: "Ask of me what thou wilt, for no petition of thine can be void." [1] As if he had said, "My Mother, thou knowest how much I love thee; therefore ask all that thou wilt of me; for it is not possible that I should refuse thee anything." And the reason that he gave for this was beautiful: "Because thou never didst deny me anything on earth, I will deny thee nothing in heaven." [2] My Mother, when thou wast in the world, thou never didst refuse to do anything for the love of me; and now that I am in heaven, it is right that I should deny thee nothing that thou askest. Mary, then, is called omnipotent in the sense in which it can be understood of a creature who is incapable of a divine attribute. She is omnipotent, because by her prayers she obtains whatever she wills.

With good reason, then, O great advocate, does St. Bernard say, "Thou willest, and all things are done." [3] And St. Anselm: "Whatever thou, O Virgin, willest can never be otherwise than accomplished." [4] Thou willest, and all is done. If thou art pleased to raise a sinner from the lowest abyss of misery to the highest degree of sanctity, thou canst do it. Blessed Albert the Great, on this subject, makes Mary say: "I have to be asked that I may will; for if I will a thing, it is necessarily done." [5]

---

[1] "Pete quod vis a me; non enim inanis potest esse petitio tua."

[2] "Quia tu mihi nihil negasti in terra, ego tibi nihil negabo in cœlo."—*Rev.* l. 6, c. 23; l. 1, c. 24.

[3] "Velis tu, et omnia fient."

[4] "Tantummodo salutem nostram, et vere nequaquam salvi esse non poterimus."—*Excell. V.* c. 12.

[5] "Roganda est, ut velit; quia, si vult, necesse est fieri."—*De Laud B. M* l. 2. c. 1.

Thus St. Peter Damian, reflecting on the great power of Mary, and begging her to take compassion on us, addresses her, saying: "O let thy nature move thee, let thy power move thee; for the more thou art powerful, the greater should thy mercy be."[1] O Mary, our own beloved advocate, since thou hast so compassionate a heart, that thou canst not even see the wretched without being moved to pity, and since, at the same time, thou hast so great power with God, that thou canst save all whom thou dost protect,—disdain not to undertake the cause of us poor miserable creatures who place all our hope in thee. If our prayers cannot move thee, at least let thine own benign heart do so; or, at least, let thy power do so, since God has enriched thee with so great power, in order that the richer thou art in power to help us, the more merciful thou mayest be in the will to assist us. But St. Bernard reassures us on this point; for he says that Mary is as immensely rich in mercy as she is in power; and that, as her charity is most powerful, so also it is most clement and compassionate, and its effects continually prove it to be so. He thus expresses himself: "The most powerful and merciful charity of the Mother of God abounds in tender compassion and in effectual succor; it is equally rich in both."[2]

From the time that Mary came into the world, her only thought, after seeking the glory of God, was to succor the miserable. And even then she enjoyed the privilege of obtaining whatever she asked. This we know from what occurred at the marriage feast of Cana in Galilee. When the wine failed, the most Blessed Virgin, being moved to compassion at the sight of the

[1] "Moveat te natura, potentia moveat; quia quanto potentior, tanto misericordior esse debebis."—*In Nat. B. V.* s. 1.

[2] "Potentissima et piissima charitas Dei Matris, et affectu compatiendi, et subveniendi abundat effectu; æque locuples in utroque.' —*In Assumpt.*

affliction and shame of the bride and bridegroom, asked her Son to relieve them by a miracle, telling him that *they had no wine.* Jesus answered: *Woman, what is that to thee and Me? My hour is not yet come.*[1] And here remark, that although our Lord seemed to refuse his Mother the favor she asked, and said, What is it to thee, O woman, and to me, if the wine has failed? This is not the time for me to work a miracle; the time will be when I begin to preach, and when miracles will be required to confirm my doctrines. And yet Mary, as if the favor had already been granted, desired those in attendance to fill the jars with water, for they would be immediately satisfied. And so it was; for Jesus, to content his mother, changed the water into the best wine. But how was this? As the time for working miracles was that of the public life of our Lord, how could it be that, contrary to the divine decrees, this miracle was worked? No; in this there was nothing contrary to the decrees of God; for though, generally speaking, the time for miracles was not come, yet from all eternity God had determined by another decree that nothing that she asked should ever be refused to the divine Mother. And therefore Mary, who well knew her privilege, although her Son seemed to have refused her the favor, yet told them to fill the jars with water, as if her request had already been granted. That is the sense in which St. John Chrysostom understood it; for, explaining these words of our Lord, *Woman, what is it to thee and Me?* he says, that "though Jesus answered thus, yet in honor of his Mother he obeyed her wish."[2] This is confirmed by St. Thomas, who says that by the words, *My hour is not yet come,* Jesus Christ intended to show, that had the request come

---

[1] "Vinum non habent. Quid mihi et tibi est, mulier? nondum venit hora mea."—*John.* ii. 3.

[2] "Et licet ita responderit, maternis tamen precibus obtemperavit." —*In Jo. hom.* 21.

from any other, he would not then have complied with
it; but because it was addressed to him by his Mother,
he could not refuse it.[1] St. Cyril and St. Jerome, quoted
by Barrada,[2] say the same thing. Also Gandavensis, on
the foregoing passage of St. John, says, that " to honor
his mother, our Lord anticipated the time for working
miracles."[3]

In fine, it is certain that no creature can obtain so
many mercies for us as this tender advocate, who is thus
honored by God, not only as his beloved handmaid,
but also as his true Mother. And this, William of
Paris says, addressing her, "No creature can obtain so
many and so great favors as thou obtainest for poor
sinners; and thus without doubt God honors thee not
only as a handmaid, but as his most true Mother."[4]
Mary has only to speak, and her Son executes all. Our
Lord conversing with the spouse in the sacred Canticles,—that is Mary,—says, *Thou that dwellest in the
gardens, the friends hearken; make me hear thy voice.*[5]
The saints are the friends, and they, when they seek a
favor for their clients, wait for their Queen to ask and
obtain it; for, as we said in the fifth chapter, "no grace
is granted otherwise than at the prayer of Mary." And
how does Mary obtain favors? She has only to let
her voice be heard,—*make me hear thy voice.* She has
only to speak, and her Son immediately grants her

[1] " Per illa verba, ' nondum venit hora mea,' ostendit se dilaturum
fuisse miraculum, si alius rogasset; quia tamen rogabat Mater, fecit."
[2] T. ii l. 3, c. 1.
[3] " Quo matrem honoraret, prævenit tempus miracula faciendi."—
In Conc. Ev. c. 18.
[4] " Nulla creatura et tot et tanta impetrare posset apud Filium
tuum miseris, quanta tu impetras eisdem; in quo procul dubio non
tamquam Ancillam, sed tamquam Matrem verissimam te honorat."—
De Rhet. div. c. 18.
[5] " Quæ habitas in hortis, amici auscultant; fac me audire vocem
tuam."—*Cant.* viii. 13.

prayer. Listen to the Abbot William explaining, in this sense, the above-mentioned text. In it he introduces the Son addressing Mary: "Thou who dwellest in the heavenly gardens, intercede with confidence for whomsoever thou wilt; for it is not possible that I should so far forget that I am thy son as to deny anything to thee, my Mother.[1] Only let thy voice be heard; for to be heard by a son is to be obeyed."[2] The Abbot Godfrey says, "that although Mary obtains favors by asking, yet she asks with a certain maternal authority, and therefore we ought to feel confident that she obtains all she desires and asks for us."[3]

Valerius Maximus[4] relates that when Coriolanus was besieging Rome, the prayers of his friends and all the citizens were insufficient to make him desist; but as soon as he beheld his mother Veturia imploring him, he could no longer refuse, and immediately raised the siege. But the prayers of Mary with Jesus are as much more powerful than those of Veturia as the love and gratitude of this Son for his most dear Mother are greater. Father Justin Micoviensis says that "a single sigh of the most Blessed Mary can do more than the united suffrages of all the saints."[5] And this was acknowledged by the devil himself to St. Dominic, who, as it is related by Father Paciucchelli,[6] obliged

---

[1] "Quæ habitas in hortis cœlestibus, fiducialiter pro quibuscumque volueris intercede; non enim possum oblivisci me Filium tuum, ut Matri quidpiam denegandum putem."

[2] "Tantum vocem proferat, a Filio audiri, exaudiri est."—*Paciucch. In Sal. Ang. exc.* 20.

[3] "Virgo Maria, ex eo quod ille Homo est, et natus ex ea, quasi quodam Matris imperio, apud ipsum impetrare quidquid voluerit, pia fide non dubitatur."—*In Fest. B. M.* s. 8.

[4] *Ex mir.* l. 5, c. 4.

[5] "Unicum suspirium ab ea oblatum superat omnium Sanctorum preces."—*Super Litan.* s 270.

[6] *In Sal. Ang. exc.* 3.

him to speak by the mouth of a possessed person; and he said that "a single sigh from Mary was worth more before God than the united suffrages of all the saints."

Saint Antoninus says that "the prayers of the Blessed Virgin, being the prayers of a Mother, have in them something of a command; so that it is impossible that she should not obtain what she asks." [1] St. Germanus, encouraging sinners who recommend themselves to this advocate, thus addresses her: "As thou hast, O Mary, the authority of a Mother with God, thou obtainest pardon for the most enormous sinners; since that Lord in all things acknowledges thee as his true and spotless Mother, he cannot do otherwise than grant what thou askest." [2] And so it was that St. Bridget heard the saints in heaven addressing our Blessed Lady: "O most blessed Queen, what is there that thou canst not do? Thou hast only to will, and it is accomplished." [3] And this corresponds with that celebrated saying, "That which God can do by his power, that canst thou do by prayer, O sacred Virgin." [4] "And perchance," says St. Augustine, "it is unworthy of the benignity of that Lord to be thus jealous of the honor of his Mother, who declares that he came into the world, not to break, but to observe the law: but this law commands us to honor our parents." [5] St. George, Archbishop of Nicomedia,

[1] "Oratio Deiparæ habet rationem imperii ; unde impossibile est eam non exaudiri."—P. 4, tit. 15, c. 17, § 4.

[2] "Tu autem materna in Deum auctoritate pollens, etiam iis qui enormiter peccant, gratiam concilias; non enim potes non exaudiri, cum Deus tibi, ut veræ et intemeratæ Matri, in omnibus morem gerat."—*In Dorm. Deip.* s. 2.

[3] "Domina benedicta! quid est quod non poteris? Quod enim tu vis, hoc factum est."—*Rev.* l. 4, c. 74.

[4] "Quod Deus imperio, tu prece Virgo, potes."

[5] "Numquid non pertinet ad benignitatem Domini, Matris hono m servare, qui Legem non solvere venerat, sed adimplere?"—*Lib de Assumpt. B. M.* c. 5.

says that Jesus Christ, even as it were to satisfy an obligation under which he placed himself towards his
Mother, when she consented to give him his human
nature, grants all she asks: "the Son, as if paying a
debt, grants all thy petitions."[1]   And on this the holy
martyr St. Methodius exclaims: "Rejoice, rejoice, O
Mary, for thou hast that Son thy debtor, who gives to
all and receives from none. We are all God's debtors
for all that we possess, for all is his gift; but God has
been pleased to become thy debtor in taking flesh from
thee and becoming man."[2]

Therefore St. Augustine says, "that Mary, having
merited to give flesh to the divine Word, and thus supply the price of our redemption, that we might be delivered from eternal death ; therefore is she more powerful than all others to help us to gain eternal life."[3]
St. Theophilus, Bishop of Alexandria, in the time of St.
Jerome, left in writing the following words : "The prayers of his Mother are a pleasure to the Son, because he
desires to grant all that is granted on her account, and
thus recompense her for the favor she did him in giving
him his body."[4]   St. John Damascene, addressing the
Blessed Virgin, says, "Thou, O Mary, being Mother of
the most high God, canst save all by thy prayers, which
are increased in value by the maternal authority."[5]

Let us conclude with St. Bonaventure, who, consider-

---

[1] "Filius quasi exsolvens debitum, petitiones tuas implet."—*Or. de Ingr. B. V.*

[2] "Euge, euge, quæ debitorem habes Filium, qui omnibus mutuatur ! Deo enim universi debemus; tibi autem etiam ille debitor est."—*Or. de Sim. et Anna.*

[3] "Neque enim dubium, quæ meruit pro liberandis proferre pretium, posse, plus Sanctis omnibus, liberatis impendere suffragium."—*Serm.* 208, *E. B. app.*

[4] *Salazar. In Prov.* viii. 18.

[5] "Potes quidem omnes salvare, ut Dei altissimi Mater, precibus materna auctoritate pollentibus."—*Men Græc.* 20 *Jan. ad Mat.*

ing the great benefit conferred on us by our Lord in giving us Mary for our advocate, thus addresses her: "O truly immense and admirable goodness of our God, which has been pleased to grant thee, O sovereign Mother, to us miserable sinners for our advocate, in order that thou, by thy powerful intercession, mayest obtain all that thou pleasest for us." [1]   "O wonderful mercy of our God," continues the same saint, "who in order that we might not fly on account of the sentence that might be pronounced against us, has given us his own Mother and the patroness of graces to be our advocate." [2]

EXAMPLE.[*]

In Germany a man fell into a grievous sin; through shame he was unwilling to confess it; but, on the other hand, unable to endure the remorse of his conscience, he went to throw himself into a river; on the point of doing so, he hesitated, and weeping, he begged that God would forgive him his sin without his confessing it. One night, in his sleep, he felt some one shake his arm, and heard a voice which said, "Go to confession." He went to the church, but yet did not confess. On another night, he again heard the same voice. He returned to the church; but when he arrived there, he declared that he would rather die than confess that sin. But before returning home he went to recommend himself to the most Blessed Virgin, whose image was in that church. He had no sooner knelt down than he found himself quite changed. He immediately arose, called a confessor, and weeping bitterly, through the grace which he had received from Mary, made an entire confession of his sins; and he afterwards declared that he experienced greater satisfaction than if he had obtained all the treasures of the world.[3]

[1] "O certe Dei nostri mira benignitas, qui suis reis te Dominam tribuit, Advocatam, ut a Filio tuo, quod volueris valeas impetrare!"

[2] "O mirabilis erga nos misericordia Dei nostri, qui, ne fugeremus pro sententia, voluit Matrem suam ac Dominam gratiæ, nostram instituere Advocatam."—*Stim. div. am.* p. 3, c. 19.

[3] *Auriemma, Aff.* p. 2, c. 7.

Prayer.

I will address thee, O great Mother of God, in the words of St. Bernard: "Speak, O Lady, for thy Son heareth thee, and whatever thou askest thou wilt obtain."[1] Speak, speak, then, O Mary, our advocate, in favor of us poor miserable creatures. Remember that it was also for our good that thou didst receive so great power and so high a dignity. A God was pleased to become thy debtor by taking humanity of thee, in order that thou mightest dispense at will the riches of divine mercy to sinners. We are thy servants, devoted in a special manner to thee; and I am one of these, I trust, even in a higher degree. We glory in living under thy protection. Since thou dost good to all, even to those who neither know nor honor thee, nay, more, to those who outrage and blaspheme thee, how much more may we not hope from thy benignity, which seeks out the wretched in order to relieve them, we who honor, love, and confide in thee? We are great sinners, but God has enriched thee with compassion and power far exceeding our iniquities. Thou canst, and hast the will to save us; and the greater is our unworthiness, the greater shall be our hope in order to glorify thee the more in heaven, when by thy intercession we get there. O Mother of mercy, we present thee our souls, once cleansed and rendered beautiful in the blood of Jesus Christ, but, alas, since that time, defiled by sin. To thee do we present them; do thou purify them. Obtain for us true conversion; obtain for us the love of God, perseverance, heaven. We ask thee for much; but what is it? perhaps thou canst not obtain all? It is perhaps too much for the love God bears thee? Ah, no! for thou hast only to open thy lips and ask thy divine Son; he will deny thee, nothing. Pray, then, pray O Mary, for us; pray; thou wilt certainly obtain all: and we shall with the same certainty obtain the kingdom of heaven.

[1] "Loquere, Domina, quia audit Filius tuus; et quæcumque petieris, impetrabis."—*Depr. ad gl. V.*

II.

Mary is so tender an Advocate that she does not refuse to defend the Cause even of the most miserable.

So many are the reasons that we have for loving this our most loving Queen, that if Mary was praised throughout the world; if in every sermon Mary alone was spoken of; if all men gave their lives for Mary; still all would be little in comparison with the homage and gratitude that we owe her in return for the tender love she bears to men, and even to the most miserable sinners who preserve the slightest spark of devotion for her.

Blessed Raymond Jordano, who, out of humility, called himself the Idiot, used to say, "that Mary knows not how to do otherwise than love those who love her; and that even she does not disdain to serve those who serve her; and in favor of such a one, should he be a sinner, she uses all her power in order to obtain his forgiveness from her Blessed Son." [1] And he adds, "that her benignity and mercy are so great, that no one, however enormous his sins may be, should fear to cast himself at her feet: for she never can reject any one who has recourse to her." [2] "Mary, as our most loving advocate, herself offers the prayers of her servants to God, and especially those who are placed in her hands; for as the Son intercedes for us with the Father, so does she intercede with the Son, and does not cease to make interest with both for the great affair of our salvation, and to obtain for us the graces we ask." [3]

[1] "Maria diligit diligentes se, imo sibi servientibus servit; ipso benedicto Filio suo irato potentissime reconciliat servos et amatores suos."

[2] "Tanta est ejus benignitas, quod nulli formidandum est ad eam accedere; tantaque misericordia, ut nemo ab ea repellatur."

[3] "Ipsa preces servorum suorum, maxime quæ sibi exhibentur, repræsentat in conspectu divinæ Majestatis; quia est Advocata nostra apud Filium, sicut Filius apud Patrem; imo apud Patrem et Filium procurat negotia et petitiones nostras."—*Cont. de V. M. in prol.*

With good reason, then, does Denis the Carthusian call the Blessed Virgin "the singular refuge of the lost, the hope of the most abandoned, and the advocate of all sinners who have recourse to her." [1]

But should there by chance be a sinner who, though not doubting her power, might doubt the compassion of Mary, fearing perhaps that she might be unwilling to help him on account of the greatness of his sins, let him take courage from the words of St. Bonaventure. "The great, the special privilege of Mary is, that she is all-powerful with her Son." [2] "But," adds the saint, "to what purpose would Mary have so great power if she cared not for us?" [3] "No," he concludes, "let us not doubt, but be certain, and let us always thank our Lord and his divine Mother for it, that in proportion as her power with God exceeds that of all the saints, so is she in the same proportion our most loving advocate, and the one who is the most solicitous for our welfare." [4]

"And who, O Mother of mercy," exclaims St. Germanus, in the joy of his heart, "who, after thy Jesus, is as tenderly solicitous for our welfare as thou art?" [5] "Who defends us in the temptations with which we are afflicted as thou defendest us? Who, like thee, undertakes to protect sinners, fighting, as it were, in their behalf?" [6] "Therefore," he adds, "thy patronage, O Mary,

---

[1] "Singulare Refugium perditorum, Spes miserorum, Advocata omnium iniquorum ad eam confugientium."—*De Laud. V.* I. 2, a. 23.

[2] "Grande privilegium Mariæ, quod apud Deum potentissima est."

[3] "Sed, quid tanta Mariæ potentia prodesset nobis, si ipsa nihil curaret de nobis?"

[4] "Carissimi, sciamus indubitanter, et pro hoc gratias agamus incessanter, quia, sicut ipsa apud Deum omnibus Sanctis est potentior, ita pro nobis omnibus est sollicitior."—*Spec. B. V. lect.* 6.

[5] "Quis, post tuum Filium, curam gerit generis humani, sicut tu?"

[6] "Quis ita nos defendit in nostris afflictionibus? Quis pugnat pro peccatoribus?"

is more powerful and loving than anything of which we can ever form an idea." [1]

"For," says the Blessed Raymond Jordano, "whilst all the other saints can do more for their own clients than for others, the divine Mother, as Queen of all, is the advocate of all, and has a care for the salvation of all." [2]

Mary takes care of all, even of sinners; indeed she glories in being called in a special manner their advocate, as she herself declared to the Venerable Sister Mary Villani, saying: "After the title of Mother of God, I rejoice most in that of advocate of sinners."

Blessed Amadeus says, "that our Queen is constantly before the divine Majesty, interceding for us with her most powerful prayers." [3] And as in heaven "she well knows our miseries and wants, she cannot do otherwise than compassionate us; and thus, with the affection of a mother, moved to tenderness towards us, pitying and benign, she is always endeavoring to help and save us." [4] And therefore does Richard of St. Laurence encourage each one, however bad he may be, to have recourse with confidence to this sweet advocate, being assured that he will always find her ready to help him; [5] "for," says the Abbot Godfrey, "Mary is always ready to pray for all." [6]

---

[1] "Propterea, patrocinium tuum majus est quam comprehendi possit."—*De Zona Deip.*

[2] "Cæteri Sancti, jure quodam patrocinii, pro sibi specialiter commissis plus possunt prodesse quam pro alienis; Beatissima vero Virgo, sicut est omnium Regina, sic et omnium Patrona et Advocata; et cura est illi de omnibus."—*Cont. de V. M. in prol.*

[3] "Adstat Beatissima Virgo vultui Conditoris, prece potentissima, semper interpellans pro nobis."

[4] "Videt enim nostra discrimina, nostrique clemens et dulcis Domina materno affectu miseretur."—*De Laud. V. hom.* 8.

[5] "Inveniet semper paratam auxiliari."—*De Laud. B. M.* 1. 2, p. 1.

[6] "Ipsa pro universo mundo paratissima est ad precandum."—*In Fest. B. M.* s. 8.

"Oh, with what efficacy and love," says St. Bernard, "does this good advocate interest herself in the affair of our salvation!"[1] St. Bonaventure, considering the affection and zeal with which Mary intercedes for us with the divine Majesty, in order that our Lord may pardon us our sins, help us with his grace, free us from dangers, and relieve us in our wants, says, addressing the Blessed Virgin, in the words of an ancient writer: "We know that we have as it were but one solicitous in heaven for us, and thou art this one, so greatly does thy solicitude for us exceed that of all the saints."[2] That is, "O Lady, it is true that all the saints desire our salvation, and pray for us; but the love, the tenderness that thou showest us in heaven, in obtaining for us by thy prayers so many mercies from God, obliges us to acknowledge that in heaven we have but one advocate, and that is thyself; and that thou alone art truly loving and solicitous for our welfare."

Who can ever comprehend the solicitude with which Mary constantly stands before God in our behalf ! "She is never weary of defending us," [3] says St. Germanus; and the remark is beautiful, meaning that so great is the compassion excited in Mary by our misery, and such is the love that she bears us, that she prays constantly, and relaxes not her efforts in our behalf; that by her prayers she may effectually defend us from evil, and obtain for us sufficient graces. "She has never done enough."

Truly unfortunate should we poor sinners be, had we not this great advocate, who is so powerful and com-

---

[1] "Advocatam præmisit peregrinatio nostra, quæ tanquam Judicis Mater et Mater misericordiæ, suppliciter et efficaciter salutis nostræ negotia pertractabit."—*In Assumpt.* s. 1.

[2] "Te solam, O Maria! pro Sancta Ecclesia sollicitam præ omnibus Sanctis scimus."—*Ap. S. Bonav. Spec. B. V.* l. 6.

[3] "Non est satietas defensionis ejus."—*De Zona Deip.*

passionate, and at the same time " so prudent and wise,
that the Judge, her Son," says Richard of St. Laurence,
" cannot condemn the guilty who are defended by her." [1]
And therefore St. John Geometra salutes her, saying,
" Hail, O court, for putting an end to litigation." [2] For
all causes defended by this most wise advocate are
gained.

For this reason is Mary called, by St. Bonaventure,
" the wise Abigail." [3] This is the woman we read of in
the second Book of Kings, who by her beautiful supplications knew so well how to appease King David when
he was indignant against Nabal ; and indeed so far as
to induce him to bless her, in gratitude for having prevented him, by her sweet manners, from avenging himself on Nabal with his own hands. [4] This is exactly
what Mary constantly does in heaven, in favor of
innumerable sinners : by her tender and unctuous
prayers, she knows so well how, to appease the divine
justice, that God himself blesses her for it, and, as it
were, thanks her for having withheld him from abandoning and chastising them as they deserved.

"On this account it was," says St. Bernard, "that the
Eternal Father, wishing to show all the mercy possible,
besides giving us Jesus Christ, our principal advocate
with him, was pleased also to give us Mary, as our advocate with Jesus Christ." "There is no doubt," the
saint adds, " that Jesus Christ is the only mediator of
justice between men and God ; that, by virtue of his
own merits and promises, he will and can obtain us
pardon and the divine favors; but because men acknowl-

[1] " Tam prudens etiam et discreta est Advocata Maria, quod non
potest Filius vindicare in eos pro quibus ipsa allegat."—*De Laud.
B. M.* l. 2, p. 1.

[2] " Salve Jus dirimens lites."—*In V. Deip. Hymn.* 4.

[3] " Abigail sapiens."—*Laus B. M.* n. 13.

[4] " Benedicta tu, quæ prohibuisti me hodie, ne . . . ulciscerer me
manu mea."—1 *Kings*, xxv. 33.

edge and fear the divine Majesty, which is in him as
God, for this reason it was necessary to assign us another
advocate, to whom we might have recourse with less
fear and more confidence, and this advocate is Mary,
than whom we cannot find one more powerful with his
divine majesty, or one more merciful towards ourselves." The saint says, " Christ is a faithful and powerful Mediator between God and men, but in him men
fear the majesty of God. A mediator, then, was needed
with the mediator himself ; nor could a more fitting one
be found than Mary." [1]

"But," continues the same saint, " should any one fear
to go to the feet of this most sweet advocate, who has
nothing in her of severity, nothing terrible, but who is
all courteous, amiable, and benign, he would indeed be
offering an insult to the tender compassion of Mary.'
And he adds, " Read, and read again, as often as you
please, all that is said of her in the Gospels, and if you
can find the least trait of severity recorded of her,
then fear to approach her. But no, this you can never
find ; and therefore go to her with a joyful heart, and
she will save you by her intercession.[3]

How beautiful is the exclamation put in the mouth of a
sinner who has recourse to Mary, by William of Paris !
" O most glorious Mother of God, I, in the miserable
state to which I am reduced by my sins, have recourse
to thee, full of confidence, and if thou rejectest me, I remind thee that thou art in a way bound to help me,

[1] " Fidelis et præpotens Mediator Dei et hominum, Christus Jesus,
sed divinam in eo reverentur homines majestatem ; . . . opus est
enim mediatore ad Mediatorem istum, nec alter nobis utilior quam
Maria."

[3] " Quid ad Mariam accedere trepidet humana fragilitas ? nihil
austerum in ea, nihil terribile; tota suavis est."

[3] " Revolve diligentius Evangelicæ historiæ seriem universam et
si quid forte durum occurrerit in Maria, accedere verearis."—*In Sign.
magn*

since the whole Church of the faithful calls thee and proclaims thee the Mother of mercy." "Thou, O Mary, art that one who, from being so dear to God, art always listened to favorably. Thy great compassion was never wanting to any one ; thy most sweet affability never despised any sinner that recommended himself to thee, however great his sins." And what ! Perhaps falsely, and for nothing, the whole Church calls thee its advocate, and the refuge of sinners. "Never, O my Mother, let my sins prevent thee from fulfilling the great office of charity which is thine, and by which thou art, at the same time, our advocate and a mediatress of peace between men and God, and who art, after thy Son, our only hope, and the secure refuge of the miserable. All that thou possessest of grace and glory, and the dignity even of Mother of God, so to speak, thou owest to sinners, for it was on their account that the divine Word made thee his Mother. Far be it from this divine Mother, who brought the source itself of tender compassion into the world, to think that she should ever deny her mercy to any sinner who has recourse to her. Since, then, O Mary, thy office is to be the peace-maker between God and men, let thy tender compassion, which far exceeds all my sins, move thee to succor me." [1]

[1] "Adibo te, imo etiam conveniam. gloriosissima Dei Genitrix, quam Matrem misericordiæ et vocat, imo clamitat omnis Ecclesia sanctorum. Tu. inquam, cujus gratiositas nunquam repulsam patitur ; cujus misericordia nulli unquam defuit, cujus benignissima humilitas nullum unquam depreçantem, quantumcumque peccatorem, despexit. An falsò et inaniter vocat te omnis Ecclesia Advocatam suam et miserorum Refugium ? Absit, ut peccata mea possint suspendere te a tam salubri officio pietatis, quo, et Advocata es, et Mediatrix hominum post Filium tuum. Spes unica et Refugium tutissimum miserorum. Totum siquidem quod habes gratiæ, totum quod habes gloriæ, et etiam hoc ipsum quod es Mater Dei, si fas est dicere, peccatoribus debes. Absit hoc a Matre Dei. quæ Fontem pietatis toti mundo peperit, ut cuiquam miserorum suæ misericordiæ subventionem unquam deneget.

"Be comforted then, O you who fear," will I say with St. Thomas of Villanova: "breathe freely and take courage, O wretched sinners; this great Virgin, who is the Mother of your God and judge, is also the advocate of the whole human race; fit for this office, for she can do what she wills with God; most wise, for she knows all the means of appeasing him; universal, for she welcomes all, and refuses to defend no one." [1]

EXAMPLE.*

In one of our missions, after the sermon on the Blessed Virgin Mary, which it is always customary in our Congregation to preach, a very old man came to make his confession to one of the Fathers. Filled with consolation he said, "Father, our Blessed Lady has granted me a grace." "What grace has she granted you?" the confessor asked. "You must know, Father," he replied, "that for five-and-thirty years I have made sacrilegious confessions, for there is a sin which I was ashamed to confess; and yet I have passed through many dangers, have many times been at the point of death, and had I then died, I should certainly have been lost; but now our Blessed Lady has touched my heart with grace to tell it." This he said weeping, and shedding so many tears, that he quite excited compassion. The Father, after hearing his confession, asked him what devotion he had practised. He replied that on Saturdays he had never failed to abstain from milk-diet in honor of Mary, and that on this account the Blessed Virgin had shown him mercy. At the same time he gave the Father leave to publish the fact.

Officium ergo tuum est mediam te interponere inter ipsum et homines; moveat ergo te gloriosa Dei Mater benignissima misericordia tua, quæ major incogitabiliter est omnibus vitiis meis et peccatis."—*De Rhet. div.* c. 18.

[1] *Dial.* l. 7, c. 35.

Prayer.

O great Mother of my Lord, I see full well that my ingratitude towards God and thee, and this too for so many years, has merited for me that thou shouldst justly abandon me, and no longer have a care of me, for an ungrateful soul is no longer worthy of favors. But I, O Lady, have a high idea of thy great goodness; I believe it to be far greater than my ingratitude. Continue, then, O refuge of sinners, and cease not to help a miserable sinner who confides in thee. O Mother of mercy, deign to extend a helping hand to a poor fallen wretch who asks thee for pity. O Mary, either defend me thyself, or tell me to whom I can have recourse, and who is better able to defend me than thou, and where I can find with God a more clement and powerful advocate than thou, who art his Mother. Thou, in becoming the Mother of our Saviour, wast thereby made the fitting instrument to save sinners, and wast given me for my salvation. O Mary, save him who has recourse to thee. I deserve not thy love, but it is thine own desire to save sinners, that makes me hope that thou lovest me. And if thou lovest me, how can I be lost? O my own beloved Mother, if by thee I save my soul, as I hope to do, I shall no longer be ungrateful. I shall make up for my past ingratitude, and for the love which thou hast shown me, by my everlasting praises, and all the affections of my soul. Happy in heaven, where thou reignest, and wilt reign forever, I shall always sing thy mercies, and kiss for eternity those loving hands which have delivered me from hell, as often as I have deserved it by my sins. O Mary, my liberator, my hope, my Queen, my advocate, my own sweet Mother, I love thee; I desire thy glory, and I love thee forever. Amen, amen. Thus do I hope.

III.

Mary is the Peace-maker between Sinners and God.

The grace of God is the greatest and the most desirable of treasures for every soul. It is called by the Holy Ghost an infinite treasure; for by the means of divine grace we are raised to the honor of being the friends of God. These are the words of the Book of

Wisdom: *For she is an infinite treasure to men ; which they that use become the friends of God.*[1] And hence Jesus, our Redeemer and God, did not hesitate to call those his friends who were in grace : *You are my friends.*[2] O accursed sin, that dissolves this friendship ! *But your iniquities,* says the prophet Isaias, *have divided between you and your God.*[3] And putting hatred between the soul and God, it is changed from a friend into an enemy of its Lord, as expressed in the Book of Wisdom : *But to God the wicked and his wickedness are hateful alike.*[4]

What, then, must a sinner do who has the misfortune to be the enemy of God ? He must find a mediator who will obtain pardon for him, and who will enable him to recover the lost friendship of God. " Be comforted, O unfortunate soul, who hast lost thy God," says St. Bernard ; "thy Lord himself has provided thee with a mediator, and this is his Son Jesus, who can obtain for thee all that thou desirest ? " He has given thee Jesus for a mediator ; and what is there that such a son cannot obtain from the Father ?"[5]

But, O God, exclaims the saint, and why should this merciful Saviour, who gave his life to save us, be ever thought severe ? Why should men believe him terrible who is all love ? O distrustful sinners, what do you fear ? If your fear arises from having offended God, know that Jesus has fastened all your sins on the cross with his own lacerated hands, and having satisfied divine justice for them by his death, he has already effaced them from your souls. Here are the words of the saint: "They

[1] " Infinitus enim thesaurus est hominibus quo, qui usi sunt, participes facti sunt amici.iæ Dei."—*Sap.* vii. 14.

[2] " Vos amici mei estis."—*John,* xv. 14.

[3] " Iniquitates vestræ diviserunt inter vos et Deum vestrum."—*Isa.* lix. 2.

[4] " Odio sunt Deo impius et impietas ejus."—*Wisd.* xiv. 9.

[5] " Jesum tibi dedit Mediatorem, quid non apud talem Patrem Filius talis obtineat ?"—*De Aquæd.*

imagine him rigorous, who is all compassion; terrible,
who is all love. What do you fear, O ye of little faith?
With his own hands he has fastened your sins to the
cross."[1] "But if by chance," adds the saint, "thou
fearest to have recourse to Jesus Christ because the majesty of God in him overawes thee—for though he became
man, he did not cease to be God—and thou desirest another advocate with this divine mediator, go to Mary, for
she will intercede for thee with the Son, who will most
certainly hear her; and then he will intercede with the
Father, who can deny nothing to such a son."[2] Thence
St. Bernard concludes, "this divine Mother, O my children,
is the ladder of sinners, by which they reascend to the
height of divine grace; she is my greatest confidence, she
is the whole ground of my hope."[3]

The Holy Ghost, in the sacred Canticles, makes the
most Blessed Virgin use the following words: *I am a
wall; and my breasts are as a tower, since I am become in his
presence as one finding peace;*[4] that is, I am the defender of
those who have recourse to me, and my mercy towards
them is like a tower of refuge, and therefore I have been
appointed by my Lord the peace-maker between sinners
and God. "Mary," says Cardinal Hugo, on the above
text, "is the great peace-maker, who finds and obtains
the reconciliation of enemies with God, salvation for
those who are lost, pardon for sinners, and mercy for

[1] "Severum imaginantur, qui pius est; terribilem, qui amabilis est.
Quid timetis modicæ fidei? peccata affixit cruci suis manibus."—*In
Cant.* s. 38.

[2] "Sed forsitan et in ipso majestatem vereare divinam, quod licet
factus sit homo manserit tamen Deus; advocatum habere vis et ad
ipsum? Ad Mariam recurre; exaudiet utique Matrem Filius, et exaudiet Filium Pater."

[3] "Filioli, hæc peccatorum scala, hæc mea maxima fiducia est, hæc
tota ratio spei meæ."—*De Aquæd.*

[4] "Ego murus, et ubera mea sicut turris; ex quo facta sum coram
eo quasi pacem reperiens."—*Cant.* viii. 10.

those who are in despair."[1] And therefore was she called by the divine bridegroom, *beautiful as the curtains of Solomon.*[2] In the tents of David, questions of war alone were treated; but in those of Solomon, questions of peace only were entertained; and thus does the Holy Spirit give us to understand that this Mother of mercy never treats of war and vengeance against sinners, but only of peace and forgiveness for them.

Mary was prefigured by the dove which returned to Noah in the Ark with an olive branch in its beak,[3] as a pledge of the peace which God granted to men. And on this idea St. Bonaventure thus addresses our Blessed Lady: "Thou art that most faithful dove; thou wast a sure mediatress between God and the world, lost in a spiritual deluge;[4] thou, by presenting thyself before God, hast obtained for a lost world peace and salvation. Mary, then, was the heavenly dove which brought to a lost world the olive-branch, the sign of mercy, since she in the first place gave us Jesus Christ, who is the source of mercy; and then, by his merits, obtained all graces for us.[5] "And as by Mary," says St. Epiphanius, "heavenly peace was once for all given to the world,[6] so by her are sinners still reconciled to God." Wherefore Blessed Albert the Great makes her say: "I am that dove of Noah, which brought the olive-branch of universal peace to the Church."[7]

[1] "Ipsa reperit pacem inimicis, salutem perditis, indulgentiam reis, misericordiam desperatis."

[2] "Formosa . . . sicut pelles Salomonis."—*Cant.* i. 4.

[3] *Gen.* viii. 11.

[4] "Tu enim es illa fidelissima Columba Noe, quæ inter Deum et mundum, diluvio spirituali submersum, Mediatrix fidelissima extitisti."—*Spec. B. M. V. lect.* 9.

[5] "Nam ipsa Christum nobis detulit, Fontem misericordiæ."—*Spinelli, Mar. Deip.* c. 16.

[6] "Per te pax cœlestis donata est."—*Hom. in Laud. B. M.*

[7] "Ego sum Columba Noe. Ecclesiæ ramum olivæ et pacis deferens universalis."—*Bibl. Mar. Cant.* 16.

Again, the rainbow seen by St. John, which encircled the throne of God, was an express figure of Mary: *And there was a rainbow round about the throne.*[1] It is thus explained by Cardinal Vitalis: "The rainbow round the throne is Mary, who softens the judgment and sentence of God against sinners;"[2] meaning, that she is always before God's tribunal, mitigating the chastisements due to sinners. St. Bernardine of Sienna says, "that it was of this rainbow that God spoke when he promised Noah that he would place it in the clouds as a sign of peace, that on looking at it he might remember the eternal peace which he had covenanted to man." *I will set My bow in the clouds, and it shall be the sign of a covenant between Me and between the earth . . . and I shall see it, and shall remember the everlasting covenant.*[3] "Mary," says the saint, "is this bow of eternal peace;[4] "for, as God on seeing it remembers the peace promised to the earth, so does he, at the prayers of Mary, forgive the crimes of sinners, and confirm his peace with them."[5]

For the same reason Mary is compared to the moon, in the sacred Canticles: *Fair as the moon.*[6] "For," says St. Bonaventure, "as the moon is between the heavens and the earth, so does Mary continually place herself between God and sinners in order to appease our Lord

---

[1] "Et iris erat in circuitu sedis."—*Apoc.* iv. 3.

[2] "Iris in circuitu sedis est Maria, quæ mitigat Dei judicium et sententiam contra peccatores."—*Spec. S. Script. de B. V. M.*

[3] "Arcum meum ponam in nubibus, et erit signum fœderis inter me et inter terram; videbo illum, et recordabor fœderis sempiterni."—*Gen.* ix. 13.

[4] "Ipsa est Arcus fœderis sempiterni."—*Pro Fest. S. M.* s. 1, a. 1, c. 3.

[5] "Fructus iridis est recordatio divini fœderis; et per Virginem gloriosam, offensa reis remittitur, fœdus stringitur."—*In Apoc.* iv.

[6] "Pulchra ut luna."—*Cant.* vi. o.

in their regard, and to enlighten them to return to him." [1]

The chief office given to Mary, on being placed in this world, was to raise up souls that had fallen from divine grace, and to reconcile them with God. *Feed thy goats,* [2] was our Lord's command to her in creating her. It is well known that sinners are understood by goats, and that as at the last judgment, the just, under the figure of sheep, will be on the right hand, so will the goats be on the left. "These goats," says the Abbot William, "are intrusted to thee, O great Mother, that thou mayest change them into sheep; and those who by their sins deserve to be driven to the left, will by thy intercession be placed on the right." [3] And therefore our Lord revealed to St. Catharine of Sienna, "that he had created this his beloved daughter to be as a most sweet bait by which to catch men, and especially sinners, and draw them to God." [4] But on this subject we must not pass over the beautiful reflection of William the Angelical on the above text of the sacred Canticles, in which he says, "that God recommended *her own* goats to Mary;" "for," adds this author, "the Blessed Virgin does not save all sinners, but those only who serve and honor her. So much so indeed, that those who live in sin, and neither honor her with any particular act of homage, nor recommend themselves to her in order to extricate themselves from sin, they certainly are not Mary's goats, but at the last judg-

---

[1] " Sicut luna inter corpora cœlestia et terrena est media, et, quod ab illis accipit ad inferiora refundit; sic et Virgo Regina inter nos et Deum est media, et gratiam ipsa nobis refundit."—*Spann. Polyanth.* litt. M. t. 6.

[2] " Pasce hædos tuos."—*Cant.* i. 7.

[3] " Pasce hædos tuos, quos convertis in oves, ut, qui a sinistris in Judicio erant collocandi, tua intercessione collocentur a dexteris.

[4] " Ipsa est a me velut esca dulcissima electa pro capiendis hominibus, et animabus præcipue peccatorum."—*Dial.* c. 139.

ment will, for their eternal misery, be driven to the left hand with the damned."[1]

A certain nobleman, despairing of his salvation, on account of his many crimes, was encouraged by a monk to have recourse to the most Blessed Virgin, and, for this purpose, to visit a devout statute of Mary in a particular church. He went there, and, on seeing the image, he felt as if she invited him to cast himself at her feet and to have confidence. He hastened to prostrate and kiss her feet, when Mary extended her hand, gave it him to kiss, and on it he saw written these words : " I will deliver thee from those who oppress thee ;"[2] as though she had said, my son, despair not, for I will deliver thee from the sins and sorrows that weigh so heavily on thee. On reading these sweet words, this poor sinner was filled with such sorrow for his sins, and, at the same time, with so ardent a love for God and his tender Mother, that he instantly expired at the feet of Mary.

O, how many obstinate sinners does not this loadstone of hearts draw each day to God ! For thus did she call herself one day, saying to St. Bridget, "As the loadstone attracts iron, so do I attract hearts."[3] Yea, even the most hardened hearts, to reconcile them with God. We must not suppose that such prodigies are extraordinary events ; they are every-day occurrences. For my own part, I could relate many cases of the kind that have occurred in our missions, where certain sinners with hearts harder than iron, continued so through all the other sermons, but no sooner did they hear the one on

[1] "Suos vocat, quia non omnes hædi vocantur Mariæ, sed qui Mariam colunt ac venerantur, licet sceleribus contaminati. Qui vero peccatis irretiti sunt, nec Beatam Virginem speciali obsequio prosequuntur, nec preces fundunt in ejus cultum, ut aliquando resipiscant, hædi profecto sunt, non Mariæ, sed ad sinistram Judicis sistendi."

[2] "Ego eripiam te de affligentibus te."

[3] "Sicut magnes attrahit ferrum, sic ego attraho Deo dura corda."
—*Rev.* l. 3, c. 32.

the mercies of Mary, than they were filled with compunction and returned to God. St. Gregory [1] says, that the unicorn is so fierce a beast, that no hunter can take it; at the voice only of a virgin crying out, will this beast approach, and without resistance allow itself to be bound by her. O, how many sinners; more savage than the wild beasts themselves, and who fly from God, at the voice of this great Virgin Mary approach and allow themselves to be sweetly bound to God by her !

St. John Chrysostom says, " that another purpose for which the Blessed Virgin Mary was made the Mother of God was, that she might obtain salvation for many who, on account of their wicked lives, could not be saved according to the rigor of divine justice, but might be so with the help of her sweet mercy and powerful intercession." [2] This is confirmed by St. Anselm, who says, " that Mary was raised to the dignity of Mother of God rather for sinners than for the just, since Jesus Christ declares that he came to call not the just, but sinners." [3] For this reason, the holy Church sings, "Thou dost not abhor sinners, without whom thou wouldst never have been worthy of such a Son." [4] For the same reason William of Paris, invoking her, says : "O Mary, thou art obliged to help sinners for all the gifts, the graces, and high honors which are comprised in the dignity of Mother of God that thou hast received ; thou owest all, so to say, to sinners ; for on their account thou wast made worthy to have a God for thy Son." [5] "If then,

[1] *Moral.* l. 31, c. 13.

[2] " Ideo mater Dei præelecta es ab æterno, ut quos justitia Filii salvare non potest, tu per tuam salvares pietatem."

[3] "Scio illam magis propter peccatores, quam propter justos, esse factam Dei Matrem; dicit enim ipse bonus Filius ejus, se non venisse vocare justos, sed peccatores."—*De Excell. V.* c. 1.

[4] " Peccatores non exhorres, sine quibus nunquam fores tali digna Filio."—*Crasset, Vér. Dév.* p. 1, tr. 1, q. 10.

[5] " Totum quod habes, si fas est discere, peccatoribus debes: omnia enim hæc propter peccatores tibi collata sunt."—*De Rhet. div.* c. 18.

Mary," concludes St. Anselm, "was made Mother of God on account of sinners, how can I, however great my sins may be, despair of pardon ?"[1]

The holy Church tells us, in the prayer said in the Mass of the vigil of the Assumption, "that the divine Mother was taken from this world that she might interpose for us with God, with certain confidence of obtaining all."[2] Hence St. Justin calls Mary an arbitratrix : "The eternal Word uses Mary," he says, "as an arbitratrix."[3] An arbitrator is one to whose hands contending parties confide their whole case; and so the saint meant to say, that as Jesus is the mediator with the Eternal Father, so also is Mary our mediatress with Jesus ; and that he puts all the reasons that he has for pronouncing sentence against us into her hands.

St. Andrew of Crete calls Mary "a pledge, a security for our reconciliation with God."[4] That is, that God goes about seeking for reconciliation with sinners by pardoning them ; and in order that they may not doubt of their forgiveness, he has given them Mary as a pledge of it, and therefore he exclaims, "Hail, O peace of God with men !"[5] Wherefore St. Bonaventure encourages a sinner; saying : "If thou fearest that on account of thy faults God in his anger will be avenged, what hast thou to do ? Go, have recourse to Mary, who is the hope of sinners ; and, if thou fearest that she may refuse to take thy part, know that she cannot do so, for God himself has imposed on her the duty of succoring the miser-

[1] "Si ipsa propter peccatores facta est Domini Mater, quomodo immanitas peccatorum meorum cogere me poterit desperare veniam ?" —*De Excell. V.* c. 1.

[2] "Quam idcirco de præsenti sæculo transtulisti, ut pro peccatis nostris apud te fiducialiter intercedat."

[3] "Verbum usum est Virgine sequestra."—*Expos. Fid. de Trin.*

[4] "Fidejussio divinarum reconciliationum, quæ dato pignore fit."— *In Dorm. B. V.* s. 2.

[5] "Salve, Divina hominibus Reconciliatio."—*In Deip. Annunt.*

able." [1]   The Abbot Adam also says, " Need that sinner fear being lost to whom the Mother of the Judge offers herself to be Mother and advocate?" [2]   " And thou, O Mary," he adds, " who art the Mother of mercy, wilt thou disdain to intercede with thy Son, who is the judge, for another son, who is a sinner? Wilt thou refuse to interpose in favor of a redeemed soul, with the Redeemer who died on a cross to save sinners?"   No, no, thou wilt not reject him, but with all affection thou wilt pray for all who have recourse to thee, well knowing that " that Lord who has appointed thy Son a mediator of peace between God and man, has also made thee mediatress between the Judge and the culprit." [4]

" Then, O sinner," says St. Bernard, " whoever thou mayest be, imbedded in crime, grown old in sin, despair not; thank thy Lord, who, that he might show thee mercy, has not only given his Son for thy advocate, but, to encourage thee to greater confidence, has provided thee with a mediatress who by her prayers obtains whatever she wills. [5] Go then, have recourse to Mary, and thou wilt be saved."

---

[1] " Si contra te, propter tuas nequitias, Dominum videris indignatum, ad Spem peccatorum confugias; sibi pro miseris satisfacere ex officio commissum est."—*Stim. div. am.* p. 3, c. 12.

[2] " Timerene debet ut pereat, cui Maria se Matrem exhibet et Advocatam?"

[3] " Tu, misericordiæ Mater, non rogabis pro filio Filium, pro redempto Redemptorem?"—*Marial.* s. 1.

[4] " Rogabis plane; quia, qui Filium tuum inter Deum et homines oosuit Mediatorem, te quoque inter reum et Judicem posuit Mediatricem."—*Marial.* s. 1.

[5] " Age gratias ei, qui talem tibi Mediatricem providit."—*In Sign Magn.*

EXAMPLE.*

In Braganza there was a young man, who, after giving up the confraternity, abandoned himself to so many crimes that one day, in despair, he went to drown himself in a river; but before doing so, he addressed our Blessed Lady, saying: "O Mary, I once served thee in the confraternity; help me." The most Blessed Virgin appeared to him and said: "Yes, and now what art thou going to do? Dost thou wish to lose thyself both in soul and body? Go, confess thy sins, and rejoin the confraternity." The young man, encouraged hereby, thanked the Blessed Virgin, and changed his life.[1]

Prayer.

O my most sweet Lady, since thy office is, as William of Paris says, that of a mediatress between God and sinners,[2] I will address thee in the words of St. Thomas of Villanova: "Fulfil thy office in my behalf, O tender advocate; do thy work.[3] Say not that my cause is too difficult to gain; for I know, and all tell me so, that every cause, no matter how desperate, if undertaken by thee, is never, and never will be, lost. And will mine be lost? Ah no, this I cannot fear. The only thing that I might fear is, that, on seeing the multitude of my sins, thou mightest not undertake my defence. But, on seeing thy immense mercy, and the very great desire of thy most sweet heart to help the most abandoned sinners, even this I cannot fear. And who was ever lost that had recourse to thee? Therefore I invoke thy aid, O my great advocate, my refuge, my hope, my mother Mary. To thy hands do I entrust the cause of my eternal salvation. To thee do I commit my soul; it was lost, but thou hast to save it. I will always thank our Lord for having given me this great confidence in thee; and which, notwithstanding my unworthiness, I feel is an assurance of salvation. I have but one fear to afflict me, O beloved Queen, and that is, that I may one day, by my own negligence, lose this confidence in thee. And therefore I implore thee, O Mary, by the love thou bearest to Jesus, thyself to preserve and increase in me more

[1] *Auriem. Aff.* p. 2, c. 4.

[2] "Officium tuum est, mediam te interponere inter Deum et homines."—*De Rhet. Div.* c. 18.

[3] "Eja ergo advocata nostra . . . officium tuum imple, tuum opus exerce."—*In Nat. B. V. con.* 3.

and more this sweet confidence in thy intercession, by which I hope most certainly to recover the divine friendship, that I have hitherto so madly despised and lost; and having recovered it, I hope, through thee, to preserve it; and preserving it by the same means, I hope at length to thank thee for it in heaven, and there to sing God's mercies and thine for all eternity.   Amen. This is my hope; thus may it be, thus will it be.

CHAPTER VII.

Illos tuos misericordes oculos ad nos converte.

TURN, THEN, THINE EYES OF MERCY TOWARDS US.

MARY, OUR GUARDIAN.

Mary is All Eyes to Pity and Succor Us in our Necessities.

ST. EPIPHANIUS calls the divine Mother many-eyed,[1] indicating thereby her vigilance in assisting us poor creatures in this world. A possessed person was once being exorcised, and was questioned by the exorcist as to what Mary did. The devil replied, "She descends and ascends." And he meant, that this benign Lady is constantly descending from heaven to bring graces to men, and re-ascending to obtain the divine favor on our prayers. With reason, then, used St. Andrew Avellino to call the Blessed Virgin the "Heavenly Commissioner," for she is continually carrying messages of mercy, and obtaining graces for all, for just and sinners. "God fixes his eyes on the just," says the royal prophet. *The eyes of the Lord are on the just.*[2] "But the eyes of the Lady," says Richard of St. Laurence, "are on the just and on the sinners."[3] "For," he adds, "the eyes of Mary are the eyes of a mother; and a mother not only watches her child to prevent it from falling, but when it has fallen, she raises it up."[4]

Jesus himself revealed this to St. Bridget, for one day he allowed her to hear him thus addressing his holy mother: "My Mother, ask me what thou wilt."[5] And

[1] "Multocula."—*Hom. in Laud. S. M.*

[2] "Oculi Domini super justos."—*Ps.* xxxiii. 16.

[3] "Oculi Dominæ super peccatores et justos."

[4] "Sicut oculi Matris super puerum, ne cadat, et si ceciderit, ut eum relevet."—*De Laud. B. M.* l. 2, p. 2.

[5] "Pete ergo quod vis."—*Lib.* vi *cap.* 23.

thus is her Son constantly addressing Mary in heaven, taking pleasure in gratifying his beloved Mother in all that she asks. But what does Mary ask? St. Bridget heard her reply: "I ask mercy for sinners."[1] As if she had said, "My Son, Thou hast made me the Mother of mercy, the refuge of sinners, the advocate of the miserable; and now thou tellest me to ask what I desire; what can I ask except mercy for them?" "I ask mercy for the miserable."

"And so, O Mary, thou art so full of mercy," says St. Bonaventure, with deep feeling, "so attentive in relieving the wretched, that it seems that thou hast no other desire, no other anxiety."[2] And as amongst the miserable, sinners are the most miserable of all, Venerable Bede declares "that Mary is always praying to her Son for them."[3]

"Even whilst living in this world," says St. Jerome, "the heart of Mary was so filled with tenderness and compassion for men, that no one ever suffered so much for his own pains as Mary suffered for the pains of others."[4] The compassion for others in affliction she well showed at the marriage-feast of Cana, spoken of in the preceding chapters, when the wine failing, without being asked, remarks St. Bernardine of Sienna, she charged herself with the office of a tender comfortress:[5] and moved to compassion at the sight of the embarrassment of the bride and bridegroom, she interposed with her

---

[1] "Misericordiam peto miseris."—*Rev.* l. i. c. 50.

[2] "Undique sollicita de miseris, undique misericordia vallaris; solum misereri tu videris appetere."—*Stim. div. am.* p. 3. c. 19.

[3] "Stat Maria in conspectu Filii sui, non cessans pro peccatoribus exorare."

[4] "Nullum in hac vita adeo poenæ torserunt propriæ, sicut Mariam alienæ."

[5] "Officium piæ Auxiliatricis assumpsit non rogata."—*Pro Fest. V. M.* s. 9. a. 3. c. 2.

Son, and obtained the miraculous change of water into wine.

"But perhaps," says St. Peter Damian, addressing Mary, "now that thou art raised to the high dignity of Queen of heaven, thou forgettest us poor creatures?" "Ah, far be such a thought from our minds," he adds; "for it would little become the great compassion that reigns in the heart of Mary ever to forget such misery as ours."[1] The proverb, that "honors change our manners,"[2] does not apply to Mary. With worldlings it is otherwise; for they, when once raised to a high dignity, become proud, and forget their former poor friends, but it is not so with Mary, who rejoices in her own exaltation, because she is thus better able to help the miserable.

On this subject St. Bonaventure applies to the Blessed Virgin the words addressed to Ruth: *Blessed art thou of the Lord, my daughter, and thy latter kindness has surpassed the former;*[3] meaning to say, "that if the compassion of Mary was great towards the miserable when living in this world, it is much greater now that she reigns in heaven."[4] He then gives the reason for this, saying, "that the divine Mother shows, by the innumerable graces that she obtains for us, her greater mercy; for now she is better acquainted with our miseries."[5] Thence he adds, "that as the splendor of the sun surpasses that of the moon, so does the compassion of Mary, now that she is in heaven, surpass the compassion she had

[1] "Numquid, O Beata Virgo! quia ita deificata, ideo nostræ humilitatis oblita es? Nequaquam Domina, non enim convenit tantæ misericordiæ, tantam miseriam oblivisci."—*In Nat. B.V.* s. 1.

[2] "Honores mutant mores."

[3] "Priorem misericordiam posteriore superasti."—*Ruth*, iii. 10.

[4] "Magna erga miseros fuit misericordia Mariæ, adhuc exsulantis in mundo, sed multo major est regnantis in cœlo."

[5] "Majorem, per beneficia innumerabilia, nunc ostendit misericordiam, quia magis nunc videt hominum miseriam."

for us when in the world." ¹   In conclusion, he asks, "who is there living in this world who does not enjoy the light of the sun? and on whom does not the mercy of Mary shine?" ²

For this reason, in the sacred Canticles she is called *bright as the sun.*³ "For no one is excluded from the warmth of this sun," says St. Bonaventure, according to the words of the Psalmist; ⁴ and the same thing was also revealed to St. Bridget, by St. Agnes, who told her "that our Queen, now that she is united to her Son in heaven, cannot forget her innate goodness; and therefore she shows her compassion to all, even to the most impious sinners; so much so, that, as the celestial and terrestrial bodies are all illumined by the sun, so there is no one in the world, who, if he asks for it, does not, through the tenderness of Mary, partake of the divine mercy." ⁵

St. Bernard says, "that Mary has made herself all to all, and opens her merciful heart to all, that all may receive of her fulness; the slave redemption, the sick health, those in affliction comfort, the sinner pardon, and God glory; that thus there may be no one who can hide himself from her warmth." ⁶   "Who can there be in the world," exclaims St. Bonaventure, "who refuses to love this most amiable Queen?   She is more beautiful than the sun, and sweeter

---

¹ "Nam quemadmodum sol lunam superat magnitudine splendoris, sic priorem Mariæ misericordiam superat magnitudo posterioris."

² "Quis est, super quem misericordia Mariæ non resplendeat?"— *Spec. B. V.* lect. 10.

³ "Electa ut sol."—*Cant.* vi. 9.

⁴ "Nec est qui se abscondat a calore ejus."—*Ps.* xviii. 7.

⁵ "Nunc autem conjuncta Filio, non obliviscitur innatæ bonitatis suæ, sed ad omnes extendit misericordiam suam, etiam ad pessimos. Sicut sole illuminantur cœlestia et terrestria, sic, ex dulcedine Mariæ, nullus est, qui non per eam, si petit, sentiat pietatem."—*Rev.* l. 3, c. 30.

⁶ Maria omnia omnibus facta est; omnibus misericordiæ sinum aperit, ut de plenitudine ejus accipiant universi, captivus redemptionem, æger curationem, tristis consolationem, peccator veniam; ut non sit qui se abscondat a calore ejus."—*In Sign. Magn.*

than honey. She is a treasure of goodness, amiable and courteous to all." [1] "I salute thee, then," continues the enraptured saint, "O my Lady and Mother, nay, even my heart, my soul. Forgive me, O Mary, if I say that I love thee; for if I am not worthy to love thee, at least thou art all-worthy to be loved by me." [2]

It was revealed to St. Gertrude, [3] that when these words are addressed with devotion to the most Blessed Virgin, "Turn, then, O most gracious advocate, thine eyes of mercy towards us," Mary cannot do otherwise than yield to the demand of whoever thus invokes her.

"Ah, truly, O great Lady," says St. Bernard, "does the immensity of thy mercy fill the whole earth." [4] "And therefore," says St. Bonaventure, "this loving Mother has so earnest a desire to do good to all, that not only is she offended by those who positively outrage her (as some are wicked enough to do), but she is offended at those who do not ask her for favors or graces." [5] So that St. Hildebert addresses her, saying: "Thou, O Lady, teachest us to hope for far greater graces than we deserve, since thou never ceasest to dispense graces far, far beyond our merits." [6]

The prophet Isaias foretold that, together with the great work of the redemption of the human race, a throne of divine mercy was to be prepared for us poor creatures: *And a throne shall be prepared in mercy.* [7] What is this throne?

[1] "Quis non te diligit, O Maria, pulchriorem sole, dulciorem melle? omnibus es amabilis, omnibus es affabilis."

[2] "Ave ergo, Domina mea, Mater mea, imo, Cor meum, Anima mea! mihi parce, Domina, quod me amare dicam te; si non sum dignus, non es indigna amari."

[3] *Insin.* l. 4, c. 53.

[4] "Latitudo misericordiæ ejus replet orbem terrarum."—*In Assumpt.* s. 4.

[5] "In te, Domina, peccant, non solum qui tibi injuriam irrogant, sed etiam qui te non rogant."

[6] "Doces nos sperare majora meritis, quæ meritis majora largiri non desistis."—*Ep.* 20, *Bibl. Patr.*

[7] "Præparabitur in misericordiæ solium."—*Is.* xiv. 5.

St. Bonaventure answers, "Mary is this throne, at which all—just and sinners—find the consolations of mercy." He then adds: "For as we have a most merciful Lord, so also we have a most merciful Lady. Our Lord is plenteous in mercy to all who call upon him, and our Lady is plenteous in mercy to all who call upon her." [1] As our Lord is full of mercy, so also is our Lady; and as the Son knows not how to refuse mercy to those who call upon him, neither does the Mother. Wherefore the Abbot Guerric thus addresses the Mother, in the name of Jesus Christ: "My Mother, in thee will I establish the seat of my government; through ·thee will I pronounce judgments, hear prayers, and grant the graces asked of me. Thou hast given me my human nature, and I will give thee my divine nature," [2] that is, omnipotence, by which thou mayest be able to help to save all whomsoever thou pleasest.

One day, when St. Gertrude was addressing the foregoing words, "Turn thine eyes of mercy towards us," to the divine Mother, she saw the Blessed Virgin pointing to the eyes of her Son, whom she held in her arms, and then said, "These are the most compassionate eyes that I can turn for their salvation towards all who call upon me." [3].

A sinner was once weeping before an image of Mary, imploring her to·obtain pardon for him from God, when he perceived that the Blessed Virgin turned towards the child that she held in her arms, and said, "My Son, shall

---

[1] "Solium divinæ misericordiæ est Maria, in quo omnes inveniunt solatia misericordiæ. Nam sicut misericordissimum Dominum, ita misericordissimam Dominam habemus; Dominus noster multæ misericordiæ est invocantibus se, et Domina nostra multæ misericordiæ est omnibus invocantibus se."—*Spec. B. M. V.* lect. 9.

[2] "In te mihi quandam regni sedem constituam; per te preces exaudiam; communicasti mihi quod homo sum: communicabo tibi quod Deus sum."—*De Assumpt.* s. 2.

[3] "Isti sunt misericordissimi oculi mei, quos ad omnes me invocantes salubriter possum inclinare."—*Insin.* l. 4, c. 53.

these tears be lost?" And he understood that Jesus Christ had already pardoned him.[1]

How, then, is it possible that any one can perish who recommends himself to this good Mother, since her Son, as God, has promised her that for her love he will show as much mercy as she pleases to all who recommend themselves to her? This our Lord revealed to St. Gertrude, allowing her to hear him make the promise to his Mother in the following words: "In my omnipotence, O revered Mother, I have granted thee the reconciliation of all sinners who devoutly invoke the aid of thy compassion, in whatever way it may please thee." [2]

On this assurance the Abbot Adam of Perseigne, considering the great power of Mary with God, and, at the same time, her great compassion for us, full of confidence, says "O Mother of mercy, thy tender compassion is as great as thy power, and thou art as compassionate in forgiving as thou art powerful in obtaining all." [3] And when, he asks, "did the case ever occur in which thou, who art the Mother of mercy, didst not show compassion? O, when was it that thou, who art the Mother of omnipotence, couldst not aid? Ah, yes, with the same facility with which thou seest our misfortunes thou obtainest for us whatever thou willest." [4]

"Satiate, O satiate thyself, great Queen," says the Abbot Guerric, "with the glory of thy Son, and out of compassion, though not for any merit of ours, be pleased to send us,

---

[1] *Sinisc. Il Mart. di M. ott.*

[2] Ex omnipotentia mea, Mater reverenda, tibi concessi potestatem propitiandi omnium peccatis, qui devote invocant tuæ pietatis auxilium, qualicumque modo placet tibi."—*Insin,* l. 4, c. 53.

[3] "Mater Misericordiæ! tanta est pietas tua, quanta potestas: tam pia es ad parcendum, quam potens ad impetrandum."

[4] "Quando non compatieris miseris, Mater Misericordiæ? aut quando illis opem conferre non poteris, cum sis Mater Omnipotentiæ, eadem facilitate obtines quodcumque vis, qua facilitate nostra innotescit miseria."—*Marial.* s. 1.

thy servants and children here below, the crumbs that fall
from thy table." [1]

Should the sight of our sins ever discourage us, let us
address the Mother of mercy in the words of William of
Paris: "O Lady, do not set up my sins against me, for I
oppose thy compassion to them. Let it never be said that
my sins could contend in judgment against thy mercy, which
is far more powerful to obtain me pardon than my sins are
to obtain my condemnation." [2]

EXAMPLE.*

In the kingdom of Valencia a great sinner resolved to
become a Mohammedan, hoping thereby to escape from the
arm of justice. On his way to the ship's landing where he
meant to set sail, he entered a church in which the Jesuit
Jerome Lopez was preaching on the Mercy of God.
Touched by the sermon, the poor sinner went to confession
to the missioner. When asked if he had practised any
special devotion to which this great grace might be attributed
he replied: "I simply prayed to Mary every day not to
abandon me."

In a certain hospital the same Father met a sinner who
had not gone to confession for fifty-five years. He had
however practised this little devotion: whenever he passed
her picture he greeted the Mother of God and asked her
for a happy end. He then related: one day while fighting
with my enemy my dagger broke. I turned to Mary and
cried out: "Alas, alas, now I shall be killed and eternally
lost; Mother of sinners, help me." Scarcely had he said
this when he found himself in safety. The poor sinner
made a general confession and died full of confidence." [3]

[1] "O Mater misericordiæ! saturare gloria Filii tui, et dimitte reliquias tuas parvulis tuis."—*De Assumpt.* s. 4.

[2] "Ne allegaveris peccata mea contra me, qui misericordiam tuam
allego contra ea; absit, ut stent in judicio peccata mea contra
misericordiam tuam, quæ omnibus vitiis fortior est."—*De Rhet. Div.*
c. 18.

[3] *Patrign. Menol. 2 Feb.*

Prayer.

O greatest and most sublime of all creatures, most sacred Virgin, I salute thee from this earth—I, a miserable and unfortunate rebel against my God, who deserve chastisements, not favors, justice, and not mercy. O Lady, I say not this because I doubt thy compassion. I know that the greater thou art the more thou dost glory in being benign. I know that thou rejoicest that thou art so rich, because thou art thus enabled to succor us poor miserable creatures. I know that the greater is the poverty of those who have recourse to thee, the more dost thou exert thyself to protect and save them. O my Mother, it was thou who didst one day weep over thy Son who died for me. Offer, I beseech thee, thy tears to God, and by these obtain for me true sorrow for my sins. Sinners then afflicted thee so much, and I, by my crimes, have done the same. Obtain for me, O Mary, that at least from this day forward I may not continue to afflict thee and thy Son by my ingratitude. What would thy sorrow avail me if I continued to be ungrateful to thee? To what purpose would thy mercy have been shown me, if again I was unfaithful and lost? No, my Queen, permit it not; thou hast supplied for all my shortcomings. Thou obtainest from God what thou wilt. Thou grantest the prayers of all. I ask of thee two graces; I expect them from thee, and will not be satisfied with less. Obtain for me that I may be faithful to God, and no more offend him, and love him during the remainder of my life as much as I have offended him.

CHAPTER VIII.

Et Jesum, benedictum Fructum ventris tui nobis post hoc exilium ostende.

AND AFTER THIS OUR EXILE SHOW UNTO US THE BLESSED
FRUIT OF THY WOMB, JESUS.

MARY, OUR SALVATION.

I.

Mary delivers her Clients from Hell.

IT is impossible for a client of Mary, who is faithful
in honoring and recommending himself to her, to be
lost. To some this proposition may appear, at first
sight, exaggerated ; but any one to whom this might
seem to be the case I would beg to suspend his judgment, and, first of all, read what I have to say on this
subject.

When we say that it is impossible for a client of Mary
to be lost, we must not be understood as speaking of
those clients who take advantage of this devotion that
they may sin more freely. And therefore, those who
disapprove of the great praises bestowed on the clemency of this most Blessed Virgin, because it causes the
wicked to take advantage of it to sin with greater freedom, do so without foundation, for such presumptive
people deserve chastisement, and not ·mercy, for their
rash confidence. It is therefore to be understood of
those clients who, with a sincere desire to amend, are
faithful in honoring and recommending themselves to
the Mother of God. It is, I say, morally impossible
that such as these should be lost. And I find that
Father Crasset,[1] in his book on devotion towards the

---

[1] *Vér. Dév.* p. 1, t. 1, q. 7.

Blessed Virgin Mary, says the same thing. As did also Vega, before him, in his Marian Theology, Mendoza, and other theologians. And that we may see that they did not speak at random, let us examine what other saints and learned men have said on this subject; and let no one be surprised if many of these quotations are alike, for I have wished to give them all, in order to show how unanimous the various writers have been on the subject.

St. Anselm says, "that as it is impossible for one who is not devout to Mary, and consequently not protected by her, to be saved, so is it impossible for one who recommends himself to her, and consequently is beloved by her, to be lost."[1] St. Antoninus repeats the same thing and almost in the same words: "As it is impossible for those from whom Mary turns her eyes of mercy to be saved, so also are those towards whom she turns these eyes, and for whom she prays, necessarily saved and glorified."[2] Consequently the clients of Mary will necessarily be saved.

Let us pay particular attention to the first part of the opinions of these saints, and let those tremble who make but little account of their devotion to this divine Mother, or from carelessness give it up. They say that the salvation of those who are not protected by Mary is impossible. Many others declare the same thing; such as Blessed Albert, who says, that "all those who are not thy servants, O Mary, will perish."[3] And St. Bonaventure: "He who neglects the service of the blessed

---

[1] "Sicut, O Beatissima! omnis a te aversus et a te despectus necesse est ut intereat, ita omnis ad te conversus et a te respectus impossibile est ut pereat."—*Orat.* 51.

[2] "Sicut impossibile est, quod illi, a quibus Maria oculos suæ misericordiæ avertit, salventur; ita necessarium quod hi, ad quos convertit oculos suos, pro eis advocans, justificentur et glorificentur."—P. 4, tit. 15, c. 14, § 7.

[3] "Gens quæ non servierit tibi peribit."—*Bibl. Mar. Is. n.* 20.

Virgin will die in his sins."[1]　Again, "He who does not invoke thee, O Lady, will never get to heaven."[2]　And, on the 99th Psalm the saint even says, "that not only those from whom Mary turns her face will not be saved, but that there will be no hope of their salvation."[3]　Before him, St. Ignatius the martyr said, "that it was impossible for any sinner to be saved without the help and favor of the most Blessed Virgin ; because those who are not saved by the justice of God are with infinite mercy saved by the intercession of Mary."[4]　Some doubt as to whether this passage is truly of St. Ignatius; but, at all events, as Father Crasset remarks, it was adopted by St. John Chrysostom.　It is also repeated by the Abbot of Celles.[5]　And in the same sense does the Church apply to Mary the words of Proverbs, *All that hate me, love death:*[6] that is, all who do not love me, love eternal death. For. as Richard of St. Laurence says on the words of the same book, *She is like the merchant's ship,*[7] "All those who are out of this ship will be lost in the sea of the world."[8] Even the heretical Œcolampadius looked upon little devotion to the Mother of God as a certain mark of reprobation: and therefore he said, "Far be it from me ever to turn from Mary."[9]

[1] "Qui neglexerit illam, morietur in peccatis suis."

[2] "Qui te non invocat in hac vita, non perveniet ad regnum Dei."

[3] "A quibus averteris vultum tuum non erit spes ad salutem."—*Psalt. B. V. ps.* 116, 86, 99.

[4] "Impossibile est aliquem salvari peccatorem, nisi per tuum, O Virgo! auxilium et favorem; quia, quos non salvat Dei justitia, salvat sua intercessione Mariæ misericordia infinita."—*Ap. Lyr. Tris. Mar.* l. ii. m. 45.

[5] *Cont. de V. M. in prol.*

[6] "Omnes qui me oderunt, diligunt mortem."—*Prov.* viii. 36.

[7] "Facta est quasi navis institoris."—*Prov.* xxxi. 14.

[8] "In mare mundi submergentur omnes illi, quos non suscepit Navis ista."—*De Laud. V.* l. 11.

[9] "Nunquam de me audietur, quasi averser Mariam, erga quam minus bene affici, reprobatæ mentis certum existimem indicium."—*S. de Laud. D. in M.*

But, on the other hand, Mary says in the words applied to her by the Church, *He that hearkeneth to me shall not be confounded;*[1] that is to say, he that listeneth to what I say shall not be lost. On which St. Bonaventure says, "O Lady, he who honors thee will be far from damnation."[2] And this will still be the case, St. Hilary observes, even should the person during the past time have greatly offended God. "However great a sinner he may have been," says the saint, "if he shows himself devout to Mary, he will never perish."[3]

For this reason the devil does his utmost with sinners in order that, after they have lost the grace of God, they may also lose devotion to Mary. When Sarah saw Isaac in company with Ismael, who was teaching him evil habits, she desired that Abraham would drive away both Ismael and his mother Agar: *Cast out this bond-woman and her son.*[4] She was not satisfied with the son being turned out of the house, but insisted on the mother going also, thinking that otherwise the son, coming to see his mother, would continue to frequent the house. The devil, also, is not satisfied with a soul turning out Jesus Christ, unless it also turns out his Mother: *Cast out this bond-woman and her son.* Otherwise he fears that the Mother will again, by her intercession, bring back her Son. "And his fears are well grounded," says the learned Paciucchelli; "for he who is faithful in serving the Mother of God will soon receive God himself by the means of Mary."[5]

St. Ephrem, then, was right in calling devotion to our

[1] "Qui audit me non confundetur."—*Ecclus.* xxiv. 30.

[2] "Qui præstat in obsequio tuo, procul fiat a perditione."—*Psalt. B. V. ps.* 118.

[3] "Quantumcumque quis fuerit peccator, si Mariæ devotus exstiterit, nunquam in æternum peribit."

[4] "Ejice ancillam hanc et filium ejus."—*Gen.* xxi. 10.

[5] "Qui Dei Genitrici perseveranter obsequitur, non multa mora, et Deum ipsum in se recipiet."—*In Salv. Reg.* exc. 5.

Blessed Lady "a charter of liberty,"[1] our safeguard
from hell.[2] The same saint also calls the divine Mother
"the only hope of those who are in despair." That
which St. Bernard says is certainly true, "that neither
the power nor the will to save us can be wanting to
Mary;"[3] the power cannot be wanting, for it is impossible that her prayers should not be heard; as St. Antoninus says, " It is impossible that a Mother of God should
pray in vain;"[4] and St. Bernard says the same thing:
"that her requests can never be refused, but that she
obtains whatever she wills."[5] The will to save us cannot be wanting, for Mary is our Mother, and desires our
salvation more than we can desire it ourselves. Since,
then, this is the case, how can it be possible for a client
of Mary to be lost? He may be a sinner, but if he recommends himself to this good Mother with perseverance
and purpose of amendment, she will undertake to obtain
him light to abandon his wicked state, sorrow for his
sins, perseverance in virtue, and, finally, a good death.
And what mother would not deliver her son from death
if it only depended on her asking the favor to obtain it
from the judge? And can we think that Mary, who
loves her clients with a mother's most tender love, will
not deliver her child from eternal death when she can do
it so easily?

Ah! devout reader, let us thank our Lord if we see
that he has given us affection for the Queen of Heaven,
and confidence in her: "for," says St. John Damascene,
"God only grants this favor to those whom he is determined to save." The following are the beautiful words
of the saint, and with which he rekindles his own and

---

[1] " Charta libertatis."—*Or. de Laud. V.*
[2] " Patrocinatrix damnatorum."
[3] " Nec facultas ei deesse poterit, nec voluntas."—*In Assump.* s. 1.
[4] " Impossibile erat Deiparam non exaudiri."—P. 4, tit. 15, c. 17.
[5] " Quod quærit, invenit; et frustrari non potest."—*De Aquæd.*

our hope: "O mother of God, if I place my confidence in thee, I shall be saved. If I am under thy protection, I have nothing to fear, for the fact of being thy client is the possession of a certainty of salvation, and which God only grants to those whom he intends to save." [1] Therefore, Erasmus salutes the Blessed Virgin in these words: "Hail! O terror of hell; O hope of Christians; confidence in thee is a pledge of salvation." [2]

O, how enraged is the devil when he sees a soul persevering in devotion to the divine Mother! We read in the Life of Blessed Alphonsus Rodriguez, who was very devout to Mary, that once when in prayer, finding himself much troubled by the devil with impure thoughts, this enemy said, "Give up thy devotion to Mary, and I will cease to tempt thee."

We read in Blosius that God revealed to St. Catharine of Sienna, "that in his goodness, and on account of the Incarnate Word, he had granted to Mary, who was his Mother, that no one, not even a sinner, who devoutly recommends himself to her should ever become the prey of hell." [3] Even the Prophet David prayed to be delivered from hell, for the sake of the love he bore to Mary. *I have loved, O Lord, the beauty of Thy house . . . take not away my soul, O God, with the wicked.* [4] He says of "Thy house," for Mary was the house that God himself constructed for his dwelling on earth, and in which he could find repose on becoming man, as it is written in the Book of Proverbs, *Wisdom hath built herself a house.* [5]

[1] *Crasset, Vér. Dév.* p. 1, tr. 1, q. 6.

[2] "Salve, inferorum Formido, Christianorum Spes! quo major est tua præcellentia, hoc certior est nostra fiducia."—*Pæan ad Virg.*

[3] "Mariæ, Filii mei Genitrici, a bonitate mea concessum est, propter incarnati Verbi reverentiam, ut quicumque etiam peccator, ad eam cum devota veneratione recurrit, nullo modo diripiatur a dæmone infernali."—*Conc. an. fid.* p. 2. c. i.

[4] "Domine, dilexi decorem Domus tuæ . . .; ne perdas cum impiis, Deus, animam meam."—*Ps.* xxv. 8

[5] "Sapientia ædificavit sibi Domum."—*Prov.* ix. 1.

"No," says St. Ignatius the martyr; "he who is devout to the Virgin Mother will certainly never be lost." [1] And St. Bonaventure confirms this, saying, "Thy lovers, O Lady, enjoy peace in this life, and will never see eternal death." [2] The devout Blosius assures us, "that the case never did and never will occur in which a humble and attentive servant of Mary was lost."

"O, how many would have remained obstinate in sin, and have been eternally lost," says Thomas à Kempis, "if Mary had not interposed with her Son, that he might show them mercy!" [4] It is also the opinion of many theologians, and of St. Thomas [5] in particular, that for many who have died in mortal sin the divine Mother has obtained from God a suspension of their sentence and a return to life to do penance.

Trustworthy authors give us many instances in which this has occurred.* Amongst others, Flodoardus, who

[1] "Numquam peribit, qui Genitrici Virgini devotus, sedulusque exstiterit."—*Lohner, Bibl.* t. 70, § 3.

[2] "Pax multa diligentibus te, Domina: anima eorum non videbit mortem in æternum."—*Psalt. B. V. ps.* 67.

[3] "Fieri non potest, ut pereat, qui Mariæ sedulus et humilis cultor fuerit."—*Par. an. fid.* p. 1, c. 18.

[4] "Quot fuissent æternaliter condemnati, vel in desperatione permansissent obstinati, nisi benignissima Virgo Maria pro eis interpellasset ad Filium!"—*Ad Nov.* s. 23.

[5] *Suppl.* q. 71, a. 5.

---

* In view of these examples and of those that we read farther on, there arises the twofold question, *De jure et de facto.* Question *de jure:* Can God hinder, and can the Blessed Virgin obtain by her prayers, that condemnation to hell be not put in execution? With these theologians, and notably with St. Alphonsus, there is no one who could not answer, Yes. Question *de facto:* Has it happened, thanks to the prayers of the Blessed Virgin, that sinners condemned to hell have not been plunged into it, and that by a good confession they have effaced the sentence of their condemnation? Yes; for the facts that I cite, says St. Alphonsus, are affirmed by trustworthy authors as real and public facts.—ED.

lived about the ninth century, relates in his Chronicles, that a certain deacon named Adelman, who was apparently dead, and was being buried, returned to life, and said "that he had seen hell, to which he was condemned, but that, at the prayers of the Blessed Virgin, he had been sent back to this world to do penance."

Surius relates a similar case[2] of a Roman citizen named Andrew, who had died impenitent, and for whom Mary obtained that he should come to life again, that he might be pardoned. Pelbertus[3] says, "that in his time, when the Emperor Sigismund was crossing the Alps with his army, a voice was heard coming from a skeleton, asking for a confessor, and declaring that the Mother of God, for whom he had had a tender devotion when a soldier, had obtained that he should thus live until he had been able to make his confession; and, having done so, the soul departed."*

These, and other such examples, however, must not encourage rash persons to live in sin, with the hope that Mary will deliver them from hell even should they die in this state; for as it would be the height of folly for any

[1] *Chron. eccl. Rem. anno* 934.   [2] 4 *Dec. S. Ann.* l. 1, c. 35.
[3] *Stellar. B. V.* l. 12, p. 2, a. 1.

---

* This is undoubtedly a very strange fact. However, who will dispute it, either by limiting the power of God or the influence of the Blessed Virgin, or by refusing to believe the authority of a writer such as Father Pelbart, who, in a book dedicated to Pope Sixtus IV., relates in detail this prodigy as having happened at his time in the presence of an illustrious emperor and the members of his court, several of whom, as they were yet living, could have convicted him of falsehood, if he had not told the truth! This reflection is made by Father Crasset: it may also be applied to other examples not less wonderful. Moreover, the miracle of which there is question here is affirmed by a great number of most respectable authors; among them Lyræus is distinguished by his most circumstantial narrative in his *Trisagion Marianum*, l. 1, son. 31. See another example, page 239. —Ed.

one to throw himself into a well with a hope that Mary would preserve his life because she has occasionally preserved some under similar circumstances, still greater folly would it be to run the risk of dying in sin, in the hope that the Blessed Virgin would save him from hell. But these examples serve to revive our confidence with the reflection, that if the divine Mother has been able to deliver from hell even some who have died in sin, how much more will she be able to preserve from a similar lot those who, during life, have recourse to her with a purpose of amendment, and who serve her faithfully.

"What, then, will be our lot, O tender Mother," let us ask with St. Germanus, "who are sinners, but desire to change, and have recourse to thee, who art the life of Christians?" [1] St. Anselm says, "that he will not be lost for whom thou once prayest." [2] O, pray, then, for us, and we shall be preserved from hell. "Who," exclaims Richard of St. Victor, "will presume to say, if I have thee to defend me, O Mother of mercy, that the Judge will be unfavorable to me when I am presented before the divine tribunal!" [3] Blessed Henry Suso used to say, " that he had placed his soul in the hands of Mary, and that if he was condemned, the sentence must pass through her hands ;" [4] being confident that if it was in such hands, this tender Virgin would certainly prevent its execution. The same do I hope for myself, O my own most holy Queen ; and therefore I will always repeat the words of St. Bonaventure : "In thee, O Lady, have I placed all my hopes ; and thus I confidently trust

---

[1] " Quid autem de nobis fiet, O Sanctissima Virgo, O Vita Christianorum !"—*De Zona Virg.*

[2] " Æternum væ non sentiet ille, pro quo semel oraverit Maria."

[3] " Si accedam ad judicium, et Matrem misericordiæ in causa habuero mecum, quis Judicem denegabit propitium ?"—*In Cant.* c. 39.

[4] "Si Judex servum suum damnare voluerit, per manus tuas piissimas hoc faciat."—*Hor. Sap. æt.* l. 1. c. 16

that I shall never be lost, but praise and love thee forever in heaven." [1]

EXAMPLE.

In the year 1604, in a city of Belgium, there were two young men, students, but who, instead of attending to their studies, gave themselves up to a life of debauchery. One night they were both in the house with an evil companion, when one of them, named Richard, returned home, leaving his companion there. After he had reached home, and had begun to undress, he remembered he had not that day said some "Hail Marys," that he was in the habit of reciting. Feeling very sleepy he was loth to say them ; he did himself violence, and repeated them, though without devotion, and half asleep. He then lay down, and had fallen into a sound slumber, when he was suddenly roused by a violent knocking at the door, and without its opening he saw his companion, deformed and hideous, standing before him. "Who art thou ?" he cried out. "What ! dost thou not know me ?" "Ah, yes ! but how thou art changed ; thou seemest to me a devil." "Truly," he exclaimed, "poor unfortunate creature that I am, I am damned ; and how ? When I was leaving that wicked house, a devil came and strangled me ; my body is in the street, and my soul in hell ; and thou must know," added he, "that the same fate awaited thee, had not the Blessed Virgin preserved thee in consideration of that little act of homage of the 'Hail Mary.' Fortunate art thou if only thou knowest how to take advantage of this warning sent thee by the Mother of God." With these words he opened his mantle, and, showing the flames and serpents by which he was tormented, he disappeared. Richard immediately burst

[1] "In te, Domina, speravi ; non confundar in æternum."—*Psalt. B. V. ps.* 30.

into sobs and tears, and, casting himself prostrate on the ground, he returned thanks to Mary, his protectress; and, whilst thinking how to change his life, he heard the bell of the Franciscan monastery ringing for matins. "Ah! it is there," says he, "that God calls me to do penance." He went immediately to the convent, and implored the Fathers to admit him. But they were hardly willing to do so, knowing his wicked life; but he, sobbing bitterly, told all that had taken place; and two Fathers being sent to the street, and having found the strangled body, which was as black as a coal, they admitted him. From that time forward Richard led a most exemplary life, and at last went to preach the Gospel in the Indies, and thence to Japan, where he had the happiness of giving his life for Jesus Christ, being burnt alive for the faith." [1] *

Prayer.

O Mary, my most dear Mother, in what an abyss of evils should I not now be, if thou hadst not so many times delivered me with thy compassionate hand! How many years ago should I not have been in hell, hadst thou not saved me by thy powerful prayers! My grievous sins already drove me there; divine justice had already condemned me; the devils already longed to execute the sentence; and thou didst fly to my aid, and save me without being even called or asked. And what return can I make to thee, O my beloved protectress, for

[1] *Lyræus, Tris. Mar. l. 3.*

* In the church of Ham-sur-Heure, in Hainault, there is a picture of the martyrdom of F. Richard of St. Anne with the following inscription: "The Blessed F. Richard of S. Anne, born at Ham-sur-Heure in 1589, made his religious profession as a Recollect at Nivelles, April 13, 1605, and having been ordained Priest in the Philippine Isles, was martyred at Nagasaki, September 10, 1622, being put to death by a slow fire." He was beatified in 1867. (See Annals of the Franciscan Missions, May, 1867.—Ed.)

so many favors and for such love? Thou also didst overcome the hardness of my heart, and didst draw me to thy love and to confidence in thee. And into how many other evils should I not have fallen, if with thy compassionate hand thou hadst not so often helped me in the dangers into which I was on the point of falling! Continue, O my hope, to preserve me from hell, and from the sins into which I may still fall. Never allow me to have this misfortune—to curse thee in hell. My beloved Lady, I love thee. Can thy goodness ever endure to see a servant of thine that loves thee lost? Ah! then, obtain that I may never more be ungrateful to thee and to my God, who for the love of thee has granted me so many graces. O Mary, tell me, shall I be lost? Yes, if I abandon thee. But is this possible? Can I ever forget the love thou hast borne me? Thou, after God, art the love of my soul. I can no longer trust myself to live without loving thee. O most beautiful, most holy, most amiable, sweetest creature in the world, I rejoice in thy happiness, I love thee, and I hope always to love thee both in time and in eternity. Amen.

II.

Mary succors her Clients in Purgatory.

Fortunate, indeed, are the clients of this most compassionate Mother; for not only does she succor them in this world, but even in purgatory they are helped and comforted by her protection. And as in that prison poor souls are in the greatest need of assistance, since in their torments they cannot help themselves, our Mother of mercy does proportionately more to relieve them. St. Bernardine of Sienna says, "that in that prison, where souls that are spouses of Jesus Christ are detained, Mary has a certain dominion and plenitude of power, not only to relieve them, but even to deliver them from their pains."[1]

And, first, with respect to the relief she gives. The

[1] "Beata Virgo in regno purgatorii dominium tenet."—*Pro Fest. V. M.* s. 3. a. 2, c. 3.

same saint, in applying those words of Ecclesiasticus, *I have walked in the waves of the sea,*[1] adds "that it is by visiting and relieving the necessities and torments of her clients, who are her children."[2] He then says "that the pains of purgatory are called waves, because they are transitory, unlike the pains of hell, which never end ; and they are called waves of the sea, because they are so bitter. The clients of Mary, thus suffering, are often visited and relieved by her." "See, therefore," says Novarinus, "of what consequence it is to be the servant of this good Lady, for her servants she never forgets when they are suffering in those flames ; for though Mary relieves all suffering souls in purgatory, yet she always obtains far greater indulgence and relief for her own clients."[3]

The divine Mother once addressed these words to St. Bridget: "I am the Mother of all souls in purgatory; for all the pains that they have deserved for their sins are every hour, as long as they remain there, in some way mitigated by my prayers."[4] The compassionate Mother even condescends to go herself occasionally into that holy prison, to visit and comfort her suffering children. St. Bonaventure, applying to Mary the words of Ecclesiasticus, *I have penetrated into the bottom of the deep,*[5] says, " the deep, that is, purgatory, to relieve by my presence the

---

[1] " In fluctibus maris ambulavi."—*Ecclus.* xxiv. 8.

[2] "Scilicet, visitans et subveniens necessitatibus et tormentis devotorum meorum: quia filii ejus sunt."

[3] "Vides quantum referat hic Virginem colere, cum cultorum suorum, in purgatorii flammis existentium, non obliviscatur ; et licet omnibus opem ac refrigerium ferat, id tamen præcipue erga suos præstat."—*Umbra Virg. exc.* 86.

[4] "Sum Mater omnium qui sunt in purgatorio; quia omnes poenæ, quæ debentur purgandis pro peccatis suis, in qualibet hora propter preces meas quodammodo mitigantur."—*Rev.* l. 4, c. 138.

[5] "Profundum abyssi penetravi."—*Ecclus.* xxiv. 8.

holy souls detained there." [1] "O, how courteous and benign is the most Blessed Virgin," says St. Vincent Ferrer, "to those who suffer in purgatory! through her they constantly receive comfort and refreshment." [2]

And what other consolation have they in their sufferings than Mary, and the relief they receive from this Mother of mercy? St. Bridget once heard Jesus say to his holy Mother, "Thou art my Mother, the Mother of mercy, and the consolation of souls in purgatory." [3] The Blessed Virgin herself told the saint, "that as a poor sick person, bedridden, suffering, and abandoned, is relieved by words of encouragement and consolation, so are the souls in purgatory consoled and relieved by only hearing her name." [4] The mere name of Mary, that name of hope and salvation, and which is frequently invoked by her beloved children in their prison, is a great source of comfort to them; "for," says Novarinus, "that loving Mother no sooner hears them call upon her than she offers her prayers to God, and these prayers, as a heavenly dew, immediately refresh them in their burning pains." [5]

Mary not only consoles and relieves her clients in purgatory, but she delivers them by her prayers. Gerson says, "that on the day of her assumption into heaven purgatory was entirely emptied." [6] Novarinus confirms this, saying, "that it is maintained by many grave au-

---

[1] "Abyssi. id est, purgatorii, adjuvans illas sanctas animas."

[2] "Maria bona animabus purgatorii; quia per eam habent suffragium "—*In Nat. B. V.* s. 2.

[3] "Tu es Mater mea, tu Mater misericordiæ, tu Consolatio eorum qui sunt in purgatorio."

[4] "Qui in purgatorio sunt, gaudent, audito nomine meo, tanquam æger in lecto jacens, si audierit ab aliquibus verbum solatii."—*Rev.* l. 1, c. 16, 9.

[5] "Virginis nomen illarum pœnarum refrigerium est. Addit Virgo preces, quibus veluti supero quodam rore, cruciatus illi magni mitigantur."—*Umbra Virg. exc.* 86

[6] *Super Magn.* tr. 4.

thors, that when Mary was going to heaven, she asked as a favor from her Son to take all the souls then in purgatory with her."[1] "And from that time forward," says Gerson, "Mary had the privilege of delivering her servants."[2] St. Bernardine of Sienna also positively asserts "that the Blessed Virgin has the power of delivering souls from purgatory, but particularly those of her clients, by her prayers, and by applying her merits for them." Novarinus says, "that by the merits of Mary, not only are the pains of those souls lessened, but the time of their sufferings is shortened through her intercession."[3] She has only to ask, and all is done.

St. Peter Damian relates, "that a lady named Marozia appeared after her death to her godmother, and told her that on the feast of the Assumption she, together with a multitude exceeding the population of Rome, had been delivered by Mary from purgatory."[4] Denis the Carthusian says, "that on the feasts of the Nativity and Resurrection of Jesus Christ Mary does the same thing; for on those days, accompanied by choirs of angels, she visits that prison and delivers very many souls from their torments."[5] Novarinus says, "that he can easily believe that on all her own solemn feasts she delivers many souls from their sufferings."[6]

[1] "Ferunt quippe bonæ notæ auctores Virginem, in cœlum ituram, a Filio hoc petiisse, ut omnes animas, quæ in purgatorio detinebantur, secum ad gloriam ducere posset."—*Loco supra cit.*

[2] "Ab iis tormentis liberat Beata Virgo maxime devotos suos."—*Pro Fest. V. M.* s. 3, a. 2, c. 3.

[3] "Crediderim omnibus qui in illis flammis purgantur, Mariæ meritis, non solum leviores fuisse redditas illas pœnas, sed et breviores, adeo ut cruciatuum tempus contractum Virginis ope illis sit."—*Loco cit.*

[4] *Opusc.* 34. c. 3.

[5] "Beatissima Virgo singulis annis, in festivitate Nativitatis Christi, ad purgatorii loca cum multitudine angelorum descendit, et multas inde animas eripit; etiam in nocte Dominicæ Resurrectionis, solet descendere ad purgatorium, pro eductione animarum."—*In Assumpt.* s. 2.

[6] "Facile autem crediderim, in quocumque Virginis solemni festo plures animas ab illis pœnis eximi."—*Loco cit.*

The promise made by our Blessed Lady to Pope John XXII. is well known. She appeared to him, and ordered him to make known to all that on the Saturday after their death she would deliver from purgatory all who wore the Carmelite scapular. This, as Father Crasset [1] relates, was proclaimed by the same Pontiff in a Bull, which was afterwards confirmed by Alexander V., Clement VII., Pius V., Gregory XIII., and Paul V.; and this latter, in a Bull of the year 1613, says, "that Christian people may piously believe that the Blessed Virgin will help them after death by her continual intercession, her merits, and special protection; and that on Saturdays, the day consecrated by the Church to her, she will in a more particular manner help the souls of the brethren of the Confraternity of our Blessed Lady of Mount Carmel who have departed this life in a state of grace, provided they have worn the habit, observed the chastity of their state, and recited her office: or, if they could not recite it, if they have observed the fasts of the Church, and abstained from meat on all Wednesdays except Christmas-day." In the solemn office of our Blessed Lady of Mount Carmel we read, that it is piously believed that the Blessed Virgin comforts the brethren of this confraternity in purgatory with maternal love, and that by her intercession she soon delivers them, and takes them to heaven. [2]

Why should we not hope for the same graces and favors, if we are devout clients of this good Mother? And if we serve her with more special love, why can we not hope to go to heaven immediately after death, without even going to purgatory? This really took place in the case of Blessed Godfrey, to whom Mary sent the fol-

---

[1] *Vér. Dév.* p. 2, tr. 6, pr. 4.

[2] "Materno plane affectu. dum igne purgatorii expiantur, solari ac in. cœlestem patriam obtentu suo quantocius pie creditur efferre."— *Die* 16 *jul. lect.* 6.

lowing message, by Brother Abondo: "Tell Brother Godfrey to endeavor to advance rapidly in virtue, and thus he
will belong to my Son and to me: and when his soul de-
parts, I will not allow it to go to purgatory, but will take
it and offer it to my Son." [1]

Finally, if we wish to relieve the holy souls in purgatory,
let us do so by imploring the aid of our Blessed Lady in all
our prayers, and especially by offering the Rosary for them,
as that relieves them greatly, as we shall see in the following
example.

EXAMPLE.*

A noble lady, who had an only son, was informed one
day that he had been killed. The murderer had by chance
taken refuge in her own palace. She then began to reflect
that Mary had forgiven the executioners of her Son; and
therefore determined that she also would pardon that criminal for the love of the sorrowful Mary. She not only did
this, but also provided him with a horse, money and clothes,
that he might escape. Her son then appeared to her, and
told her that he was saved, and that for her generous conduct to his enemy the divine Mother had delivered him from
purgatory, in which otherwise he would have had to suffer
for a long time, and that he was then going to Paradise.[2]

Prayer.

O Queen of heaven and earth! O Mother of the Lord of the
world! O Mary, of all creatures the greatest, the most exalted,
and the most amiable! it is true that there are many in this
world who neither know thee nor love thee; but in heaven
there are many millions of angels and blessed spirits, who love
and praise thee continually. Even in this world, how many
happy souls are there not who burn with thy love, and live
enamoured of thy goodness! O, that I also could love thee,
O Lady worthy of all love! O that I could always remember to
serve thee, to praise thee, to honor thee, and engage all to love

[1] *Men. Cist.* 2 Oct.
[2] *Tausch. De Matre Dol.* 1, 2, c. 8.

thee! Thou hast attracted the love of God, whom, by thy beauty, thou hast, so to say, torn from the bosom of his Eternal Father, and engaged to become man, and be thy Son. And shall I, a poor worm of the earth, not be enamoured of thee? No, my most sweet Mother, I also will love thee much, and will do all that I can to make others love thee also. Accept, then, O Mary, the desire that I have to love thee, and help me to execute it. I know how favorably thy lovers are looked upon by God. He, after his own glory, desires nothing more than thine, and to see thee honored and loved by all. From thee, O Lady, do I expect all; through thee the remission of my sins, through thee perseverance. Thou must assist me at death, and deliver me from purgatory; and finally, thou must lead me to heaven. All this thy lovers hope from thee, and are not deceived. I, who love thee with so much affection, and above all other things, after God, hope for the same favors.

III.

Mary leads her Servants to Heaven.

Oh, what an evident mark of predestination have the servants of Mary! The holy Church, for the consolation of her clients, puts into her mouth the words of Ecclesiasticus, *In all these I sought rest, and I shall abide in the inheritance of the Lord.*[1] Cardinal Hugo explains these words, and says, "blessed is he in whose house the most Holy Virgin finds repose."[2] Mary, out of the love she bears to all, endeavors to excite in all devotion towards herself; many either do not admit it into their souls, or do not preserve it. But blessed is he that receives and preserves it. *And I shall abide in the inheritance of the Lord.* "That is," adds the Cardinal, "Blessed is he whose interior offers the Blessed Virgin Mary a place of repose." Devotion towards the Blessed Virgin remains in all who are the inheritance of our Lord; that is to say, in all who will praise him eternally in heaven. Mary continues, speaking in the words of Ecclesiasticus: *He that made me rested in my*

[1] "In his omnibus requiem quæsivi, et in hæreditate Domini morabor."—*Ecclus.* xxiv. 11.

[2] "Beatus, in cujus domo Beata Virgo requiem invenerit."

tabernacle, and He said to me: Let thy dwelling be in Jacob, and thy inheritance in Israel, and take root in My elect.[1] That is, my Creator has condescended to come and repose in my bosom, and his will is, that I should dwell in the hearts of all the elect (of whom Jacob was a figure, and who are the inheritance of the Blessed Virgin), and that devotion and confidence in me should take root in all the predestined.

O, how many blessed souls are now in heaven who would never have been there had not Mary, by her powerful intercession, led them thither: *I made that in the heavens there should rise light that never faileth.*[2] Cardinal Hugo, in his commentary on the above text of Ecclesiasticus, says, in the name of Mary, "I have caused as many lights to shine eternally in heaven as I have clients;" and then he adds, "There are many saints in heaven through her intercession, who would never have been there but through her."[3]

St. Bonaventure says, "that the gates of heaven will open to all who confide in the protection of Mary."[4] Hence, St. Ephrem calls devotion to the divine Mother "the unlocking of the gates of the heavenly Jerusalem."[5] The devout Blosius also, addressing our Blessed Lady, says, "To thee, O Lady, are committed the keys and the treasures of the kingdom of heaven."[6] And therefore we ought constantly to pray to her, in the words of St. Ambrose, "Open to us, O Mary, the gates of paradise, since thou hast its

---

[1] "Qui creavit me, requievit in tabernaculo meo, et dixit mihi: In Jacob inhabita, et in Israel hæreditare, et in electis meis mitte radices."

[2] "Ego feci in cœlis ut oriretur lumen indeficiens."—*Ecclus.* xxiv. 6.

[3] "Multi Sancti sunt in cœlis intercessione ejus, qui nunquam ibi fuissent nisi per eam."

[4] "Qui speraverit in illa, porta paradisi reserabitur ei."—*Psalt. B. V. ps.* 90.

[5] "Reseramentum cœlestis Jerusalem."—*De Laud. Dei gen.*

[6] "Tibi regni cœlestis claves thesaurique commissi sunt."—*Par. an. fid.* p. 2, c. 4.

keys." [1] Nay more, the Church says, that "thou art its gate." [2]

For the same reason, again, is this great Mother called by the Church the Star of the Sea, "Hail, Star of the Sea!" "For," says the angelical St. Thomas, "as sailors are guided by a star to the port, so are Christians guided to heaven by Mary." [8]

For the same reason, finally, is she called by St. Fulgentius, "the heavenly ladder." "For," says the saint, "by Mary God descended from heaven into the world, that by her men might ascend from earth to heaven." [4] "And thou, O Lady," says St. Athanasius, "wast filled with grace, that thou mightest be the way of our salvation, and the means of ascent to the heavenly kingdom." [5]

St. Bernard calls our Blessed Lady "the heavenly chariot." [6] And St. John Geometra salutes her, saying, "Hail, resplendent car!" [7] signifying that she is the car in which her clients mount to heaven. "Blessed are they who know thee, O Mother of God," says St. Bonaventure; "for the knowledge of thee is the high road to everlasting life, and the publication of thy virtues is the way of eternal salvation." [8]

Denis the Carthusian asks, "Who is there that is saved? who is there that reigns in heaven?" And he

---

[1] "Aperi nobis, O Virgo, cœlum, cujus claves habes."

[2] "Janua cœli."

[3] "Stella maris, quia, sicut per stellam maris navigantes diriguntur ad portum, ita Christiani diriguntur per Mariam ad gloriam."—*Exp. in Sal. Ang.*

[4] "Scala cœlestis, quia per ipsam Deus descendit ad terras, ut per ipsam homines mereantur ascendere ad cœlos."—*In Annunt.* s. 1

[5] "Ave, gratia Plena, quod facta sis nobis salutis Via, Ascensusque ad superos."—*In Annunt.* s. 1

[6] "Vehiculum ad cœlum."—*De Aquaed.*

[7] "Salve clarissime Currus."—*In V. Deip.* h. 1.

[8] "Scire et cognoscere te, est radix immortalitatis; et enarrare virtutes tuas, est via salutis."—*Psalt. B. V. ps.* 85.

answers, "They are certainly saved and reign in heaven for whom this Queen of mercy intercedes."[1] And this Mary herself confirms in the book of Proverbs, *By me kings reign ;*[2] through my intercession souls reign, first in this mortal life by ruling their passions, and so come to reign eternally in heaven, where, says St. Augustine, "all are kings."[3] "Mary, in fine," says Richard of St. Laurence, "is the mistress of heaven ; for there she commands as she wills, and admits whom she wills." And applying to her the words of Ecclesiasticus, *And my power was in Jerusalem,*[4] he makes her say, "I command what I will, and introduce whom I will."[5] Our Blessed Lady, being Mother of the Lord of heaven, it is reasonable that she also should be sovereign Lady of that kingdom, according to Rupert, who says, "that by right she possesses the whole kingdom of her Son."[6]

St. Antoninus tells us "that this divine Mother has already, by her assistance and prayers, obtained heaven for us, provided we put no obstacle in the way."[7] Hence, says the Abbot Guerric, "he who serves Mary, and for whom she intercedes, is as certain of heaven as if he was already there."[8] St. John Damascene also says, "that to serve Mary and be her courtier is the greatest honor we can possibly possess; for to serve the Queen of heaven is already to reign there, and live under her

---

[1] "Quis salvatur ? quis regnat in cœlo ? Illi sane pro quibus Regina misericordiæ interpellat."—*Paciucch. Sup. Salve Reg. exc.* I.

[2] "Per me reges regnant."—*Prov.* viii. 15.

[3] "Quot cives, tot reges."

[4] "In Jerusalem potestas mea."—*Ecclus.* xxiv. 15.

[5] "Imperandi scilicet, quod volo, et, quos volo, introducendi."—*De Laud. Virg.* l. 4, c. 4.

[6] "Totum jure possidens Filii regnum."—*In Cant.* l. 3.

[7] "Cœleste nobis regnum, suo interventu, auxiliis, et precibus, impetravit."—*Paciucch. Sup. Salve Reg. exc.* I.

[8] "Qui Virgini famulatur, ita securus est de paradiso, ac si esset in paradiso."

commands is more than to govern."[1] On the other hand, he adds, "that those who do not serve Mary will not be saved; for those who are deprived of the help of this great Mother are also deprived of that of her Son and of the whole court of heaven."[2]

"May the infinite goodness of our Lord be ever praised," says St. Bernard, for having been pleased to give us Mary as our advocate in heaven, that she, being at the same time the Mother of our Judge and a Mother of mercy, may be able, by her intercession, to conduct to a prosperous issue the great affair of our eternal salvation."[3] St. James, a Doctor of the Greek Church, says, "that God destined Mary as a bridge of salvation, by using which we might with safety pass over the stormy sea of this world, and reach the happy haven of paradise."[4] Therefore St. Bonaventure exclaims, "Give ear, O ye nations; and all you who desire heaven, serve, honor Mary, and certainly you will find eternal life."[5]

Nor should those even who have deserved hell be in the least doubtful as to obtaining heaven, provided they are faithful in serving this Queen. "O, how many sinners," says St. Germanus, "have found God and have been saved by thy means, O Mary!"[6] Richard of St.

[1] "Summus honor, servire Mariæ, et de ejus esse familia; etenim ei servire, regnare est; et ejus agi frænis, summa libertas."

[2] "Gens quæ non servierit illi, peribit; gentes destitutæ tantæ Matris auxilio, destituuntur auxilio Filii et totius curiæ cœlestis."—*De Laud. B. M.* l. 4.

[3] "Advocatam præmisit peregrinatio nostra; quæ, tamquam Judicis Mater et Mater misericordiæ, suppliciter et efficaciter salutis nostræ negotia pertractabit."—*In Assumpt.* s. 1.

[4] "Eam tu Pontem fecisti, quo a mundi fluctibus trajicientes, ad tranquillum portum tuum perveniamus."—*Or. in Nat. Dei gen.*

[5] "Audite, omnes gentes; qui ingredi cupitis regnum Dei, Virginem Mariam honorate, et invenietis vitam et salutem perpetuam."—*Psalt. B. V. ps.* 48.

[6] "Peccatores per te Deum exquisierunt, et salvi facti sunt."—*In Dorm. V. M.* s. 2.

Laurence remarks, that St. John in the Apocalypse says that Mary was crowned with stars : *And on her head a crown of twelve stars.*[1] On the other hand, in the sacred Canticles, she is said to be crowned with wild beasts, lions, and leopards: *Come from Libanus, my spouse, come from Libanus, come; thou shalt be crowned . . . from the dens of the lions, from the mountains of the leopards.*[2] How is this? He answers, that "these wild beasts are sinners, who by the favor and intercession of Mary have become stars of paradise, better adapted to the head of this Queen of mercy than all the material stars of heaven."[3]

We read in the life of the servant of God, Sister Seraphina of Capri, that once during the novena of the Assumption of Mary she asked our Blessed Lady for the conversion of a thousand sinners, but afterwards thought that she had asked too much; and then the Blessed Virgin appeared to her, and corrected her for her ungrounded anxiety, saying, "Why dost thou fear? Is it that I am not sufficiently powerful to obtain from my Son the conversion of a thousand sinners? See, I have already obtained the favor." With these words, she took her in spirit to heaven, and there showed her innumerable souls which had deserved hell, but had been saved through her intercession, and were already enjoying eternal happiness.

It is true that in this world no one can be certain of his salvation: *Man knoweth not whether he be worthy of love or hatred*, says Ecclesiastes.[4] But St. Bonaventure, on the words of King David, *Lord, who shall dwell in Thy tabernacle?*[5] and on the preceding quotation, answers,

[1] "Et in capite ejus corona stellarum duodecim."—*Apoc.* xii. 1.

[2] "Coronaberis . . . de montibus pardorum."—*Cant.* iv. 8.

[3] "Et quid est hoc, nisi quod feræ, per gratiam et orationes Mariæ, fiunt stellæ, ut conveniant capiti tantæ Reginæ?"—*De Laud. B. M.* l. 3.

[4] "Nescit homo, utrum amore an odio dignus sit; sed omnia in futurum servantur incerta."—*Eccles.* ix. 1.

[5] "Domine, quis habitabit in tabernaculo tuo?"—*Ps.* xiv. 1.

"Sinners, let us follow Mary closely, and casting our-selves at her feet, let us not leave them until she has blessed us; for her blessing will insure our salvation." [1]

"It suffices, O Lady," says St. Anselm, "that thou willest it, and our salvation is certain." [2] And St. An-toninus says that "souls protected by Mary, and on which she casts her eyes, are necessarily justified and saved." [3]

"With reason, therefore," observes St. Ildephonsus, "did the most Holy Virgin predict that all generations would call her blessed;" [4] "for all the elect obtain eter-nal salvation through the means of Mary." [5] "And thou, O great Mother, says St. Methodius, "art the be-ginning, the middle, and the end of our happiness;" [6] —the beginning, for Mary obtains us the pardon of our sins ; the middle, for she obtains us perseverance in di-vine grace; and the end, for she finally obtains us heaven. "By thee, O Mary, was heaven opened," says St. Bernard; "by thee was hell emptied; by thee was paradise restored; and through thee, in fine, is eternal life given to so many miserable creatures who deserved eternal death." [7]

But that which above all should encourage us to hope

[1] "Amplectamur Mariæ vestigia peccatores, et ejus beatis pedibus provolvamur; teneamus eam fortiter, nec dimittamus, donec ab ea meruimus benedici."—*Psalt. B. V. ps.* 14.

[2] "Tantummodo velis salutem nostram, et vere nequaquam salvi esse non poterimus."—*De Excell. Virg.* c. 6.

[3] "Necessarium est quod hi, ad quos convertit oculos suos, justifi-centur et glorificentur."—P. 4, tit. 15, c. 17, § 7.

[4] "Beatam me dicent omnes generationes."

[5] "Beata jure dicitur, quia omnes ex ea beatificantur."—*De As-sumpt.* s. 3.

[6] "Tu festivitatis nostræ principium, medium, et finis."—*De Sim. et Anna.*

[7] "Per te, cœlum repletum, infernus evacuatus est, instauratæ ruinæ cœlestis Jerusalem; expectantibus miseris vita perdita data."—*In Assumpt.* s. 4.

with confidence for heaven, is the beautiful promise
made by Mary herself to all who honor her, and especially to those who, by word and example, endeavor
to make her known and honored by others: *They that
work by me shall not sin; they that explain me shall have life
everlasting.*[1]   "O happy they who obtain the favor of
Mary !" exclaims St. Bonaventure; "they will be recognized by the blessed as their companions, and whoever
bears the stamp of a servant of Mary is already enrolled
in the Book of Life." [2]

Why, then, should we trouble ourselves about the
opinions of scholastics as to whether predestination to
glory precedes or follows the prevision of merits ?   If
we are true servants of Mary, and obtain her protection,
we most certainly shall be inscribed in the Book of Life ;
for, says St. John Damascene, "God only grants devotion
towards his most Holy Mother to those whom he will
save."   This is also clearly expressed by our Lord in St.
John : *He that shall overcome . . . I will write upon him the
name of My God, and the name of the city of My God.*[3]   And
who but Mary is this city of God ? observes St. Gregory
on the words of David : *Glorious things are said of thee, O
city of God.*[4]

Correctly, then, can we here say with St. Paul, *Having
this seal, the Lord knoweth who are His ;*[5] that is to say,
whoever carries with him the mark of devotion to Mary

---

[1] "Qui operantur in me, non peccabunt; qui elucidant me, vitam
æternam habebunt."—*Ecclus.* xxiv. 30.

[2] "Qui acquirit gratiam Mariæ, agnoscetur a civibus paradisi; et
qui habuerit characterem ejus, adnotabitur in libro vitæ."—*Psalt. B.
V. ps.* 91.

[3] "Qui vicerit . . . scribam super eum nomen Dei mei, et nomen
Civitatis Dei mei."—*Apoc.* iii. 12.

[4] "Gloriosa dicta sunt de te, Civitas Dei."—*Ps.* lxxxvi. 3.

[5] "Habens signaculum hoc, cognovit Dominus qui sunt ejus."—
2 Tim. ii. 19.

is recognized by God as his. Hence St. Bernard writes, that devotion to the Mother of God is a most certain mark of eternal salvation." [1] Blessed Alan, speaking of the " Hail Mary," also says, that " whoever often honors our Blessed Lady with this angelical salutation has a very great mark of predestination." [2] He says the same thing of perseverance in the daily recital of the Rosary, " that those who do so have a very great assurance of salvation." [3] Father Nieremberg says, in the tenth chapter of his book on *Affection for Mary*, that " the servants of the Mother of God are not only privileged and favored in this world, but even in heaven they are more particularly honored." He then adds : " that in heaven they will be recognized as servants of its Queen, and as belonging to her court, by a distinguishing and richer garment," according to the words of the Proverbs, *All her domestics are clothed with double garments*. [4]

St. Mary Magdalen of Pazzi saw a vessel in the midst of the sea : in it were all the clients of Mary, and this Blessed Mother herself steered it safely into the port. By this the saint understood, that those who live under the protection of Mary are secure, in the midst of the dangers of this life, from the shipwreck of sin, and from eternal damnation ; for she guides them safely into the haven of salvation. Let us then enter this blessed ship of the mantle of Mary, and there we can be certain of the kingdom of heaven ; for the Church says : " O holy

[1] " Servire Mariæ, est signum salutis æternæ consequendæ."—*Stell. B. V.* l. 12, p. 2, a. 1.

[2] " Habentibus devotionem ad hanc, signum est prædestinationis permagnum ad gloriam."

[3] " Signum sit tibi probabilissimum æternæ salutis, si perseveranter in dies eam in suo Psalterio salutaveris."—*De Psalt.* p. 2, c. 11,—p. 4, c. 24.

[4] " Omnes enim domestici ejus vestiti sunt duplicibus."—*Prov.* xxxi. 21.

Mother of God, all those who will be partakers of eternal happiness dwell in thee, living under thy protection." [1]

EXAMPLE.*

The Franciscan Chronicles relate that a certain Brother Leo saw in a vision two ladders the one red, the other white. On the upper end of the red ladder stood Jesus and on the other stood His holy Mother. The brother saw that some tried to climb the red ladder; but scarcely had they mounted some rungs when they fell back, they tried again but with no better success. Then they were advised to try the white ladder and to their surprise they succeeded for the Blessed Virgin stretched out her hand and with her aid they reached heaven. [2]

NOTE: This apparition is by no means incredible; nor is it right to say that it makes the power of Mary superior to that of Christ. The symbolic significance of the vision must be borne in mind. The idea has been expressed repeatedly in the words of St. Bernard, and more recently by Popes Leo XIII. and Benedict XV.: "As we have no access to the Father except through the Son, so no one can come to the Son except by the Mother. As the Son is all powerful by nature, the Mother is all powerful in so far that by the merciful disposition of God she is our mediatrix of graces with Christ. Therefore says Eadmer: "Frequently our petitions are heeded sooner when we address ourselves to Mary the Queen of Mercy and Compassion than when we go directly to Jesus who as King of Justice is our Judge." [3]

---

[1] "Sicut lætantium, omnium nostrum habitatio est in te, sancta Dei Genitrix."—*Off. ad Mat.*

[2] *Wadding, Ann.* 1232 n. 28.

[3] *De Excell. V.* c. 6.

Prayer.

O Queen of heaven, Mother of holy love! since thou art the most amiable of creatures, the most beloved of God, and his greatest lover, be pleased to allow the most miserable sinner living in this world, who, having by thy means been delivered from hell, and without any merit on his part been so benefited by thee and who is filled with love for thee, to love thee. I would desire, were it in my power, to let all men who know thee not know how worthy thou art of love, that all might love and honor thee. I would desire to die for the love of thee, in defence of thy virginity, of thy dignity of Mother of God, of thy Immaculate Conception, should this be necessary, to uphold these thy great privileges. Ah! my most beloved Mother accept this my ardent desire, and never allow a servant of thine, who loves thee, to become the enemy of thy God, whom thou lovest so much. Alas! poor me, I was so for a time, when I offended my Lord. But then, O Mary, I loved thee but little, and strove but little to be beloved by thee. But now there is nothing that I so much desire, after the grace of God, as to love and be loved by thee. I am not discouraged on account of my past sins, for I know that thou, O most benign and gracious Lady, dost not disdain to love even the most wretched sinners who love thee; nay more, that thou never allowest thyself to be surpassed by any in love. Ah! Queen most worthy of love, I desire to love thee in heaven. There, at thy feet, I shall better know how worthy thou art of love, how much thou hast done to save me; and thus I shall love thee with greater love, and love thee eternally, without fear of ever ceasing to love thee. O Mary, I hope most certainly to be saved by thy means. Pray to Jesus for me. Nothing else is needed; thou hast to save me; thou art my hope. I will therefore always sing O Mary, my hope, thou hast to save me.

CHAPTER IX.

O Clemens, O Pia !

O MERCIFUL, O PIOUS.

CLEMENCY AND COMPASSION OF MARY.

How great are the Clemency and Compassion of Mary.

ST. BERNARD, speaking of the great compassion of
Mary towards us poor creatures, says, " that she is the
land overflowing with milk and honey promised by
God." [1] Hence St. Leo observes, " that the Blessed
Virgin has so merciful a heart, that she deserves not
only to be called merciful, but mercy itself." [2] St. Bonaventure also, considering that Mary was made Mother of
God on account of the miserable, and that to her is committed the charge of dispensing mercy ; considering,
moreover, the tender care she takes of all, and that her
compassion is so great that she seems to have no other
desire than that of relieving the needy ; says, that when
he looks at her, he seems no longer to see the justice of
God, but only the divine mercy, of which Mary is full.
" O Lady, when I behold thee, I can only discern mercy,
for thou wast made Mother of God for the wretched,
and then thou wast intrusted with their charge : thou
art all solicitude for them ; thou art walled in with
mercy ; thy only wish is to show it." [3]

[1] " Terra repromissionis, Maria, lacte et melle manans."—*In Salve Reg.* s. 3.

[2] " Maria adeo prædita est misericordiæ visceribus, ut, non tantum misericors, sed ipsa Misericordia dici promereatur."

[3] "Certe, Domina ! cum te aspicio, nihil nisi misericordiam cerno; nam pro miseris Mater Dei facta es, et tibi miserendi est officium com-missum ; undique sollicita de miseris, misericordia vallaris, solum misereri tu videris appetere."—*Stim div. am.* p. 3, c. 19.

In fine, the compassion of Mary is so great towards us, that the Abbot Guerric says, "that her loving heart can never remain a moment without bringing forth its fruits of tenderness."[1] "And what," exclaims St. Bernard, "can ever flow from a source of compassion but compassion itself?"[2]

Mary is also called an olive-tree : *As a fair olive-tree on the plains.*[3] For as from the olive, oil (a symbol of mercy) alone is extracted, so from the hands of Mary graces and mercy alone proceed. Hence the Venerable Father Louis de Ponte says, "that Mary may properly be called the Mother of oil, since she is the Mother of mercy."[4] And thus, when we go to this good Mother for the oil of her mercy, we cannot fear that she will deny it to us, as the wise virgins in the Gospel did to the foolish ones : *lest perhaps there be not enough for us and for you.*[5] O no! for she is indeed rich in this oil of mercy, as St. Bonaventure assures us, "Mary is filled with the oil of compassion."[6] She is called by the Church not only a prudent Virgin, but most prudent, that we may understand, says Hugo of St. Victor, that she is so full of grace and compassion, that she can supply all, without losing any herself. "Thou, O Blessed Virgin, art full of grace, and indeed so full, that the whole world may draw of this overflowing oil." "For if the prudent virgins provided oil in vessels with their lamps, thou, O most prudent Virgin, hast borne an over-

[1] "Cújus viscera nunquam desinunt fructum parturire pietatis."— *De Assumpt.* s. 1.

[2] "Quid de fonte pietatis procederet, nisi pietas?"—*Dom.* 1 *p. Epiph.* s. 1.

[3] "Quasi oliva speciosa in campis."—*Ecclus.* xxiv. 19.

[4] "Optime dici potest Mater olei ; est enim Mater misericordiæ."— *In Cant. l.* 1, *exh.* 21.

[5] "Ne forte non sufficiat nobis et vobis."—*Matt.* xxv. 9.

[6] "Maria plena est oleo pietatis."—*Spec. B. M. V. lect.* 7.

flowing and inexhaustible vessel, from which, the oil of mercy streaming, thou replenishest the lamps of all." [1]

But why, I ask, is this beautiful olive-tree said to stand in the midst of the plains, and not rather in the midst of a garden, surrounded by a wall and hedges ? The same Hugo of St. Victor tells us, that it is " that all may see her, that all may go to her for refuge ;" [2] that all may see her easily, and as easily have recourse to her, to obtain remedies for all their ills. This beautiful explanation is confirmed by St. Antoninus, who says, " that all can go to, and gather the fruit of, an olive-tree that is exposed in the midst of a plain; and thus all, both just and sinners, can have recourse to Mary, to obtain her mercy." [3] He then adds, " O how many sentences of condemnation has not this most Blessed Virgin revoked by her compassionate prayers, in favor of sinners who have had recourse to her ?" [4] And what safer refuge," says the devout Thomas a Kempis, " can we ever find than the compassionate heart of Mary ? there the poor find a home, the infirm a remedy, the afflicted relief, the doubtful counsel, and the abandoned succor." [5]

[1] " Gratia plena : in tantum plena, ut ex tuo redundante totus hauriat mundus ; si enim prudentes Virgines oleum acceperunt in vasis cum lampadibus, tu, prudentissima Virgo, gestasti vas redundans et indeficiens, ex quo, effuso oleo misericordiæ, omnium lampades illuminares."—*De Verb. Inc.* c. 3.

[2] " Ut omnes peccatores ad ipsam respiciant, ad ipsam confugiant."—*De Assumpt.* s. 2.

[3] " Ad olivam in campis, omnes possunt accedere, et accipere fructum ejus ; sic ad Mariam et justi et peccatores accedere possunt, ut inde misericordiam accipiant."

[4] " Oh, quot sententias flagellorum, quæ meruit mundus propter peccata sua, hæc Sanctissima Virgo misericorditer revocavit !"—P. 3, t. 3x, c. 4, § 3.

[5] " Non est tutior locus ad latendum, quam sinus Mariæ; ibi pauper habet domicilium ; ibi infirmus invenit remedium ; ibi tristis accipit solatium ; ibi turbatus meretur consilium ; ibi destitutus acquirit juvamentum."—*Ad Nov.* s. 24.

Wretched indeed should we be, had we not this Mother of mercy always attentive and solicitous to relieve us in our wants! *Where there is no woman, he mourneth that is in want,*[1] says the Holy Ghost. "This woman," says St. John Damascene, "is precisely the most Blessed Virgin Mary; and wherever this most holy woman is not, the sick man groans."[2] And surely it cannot be otherwise, since all graces are dispensed at the prayer of Mary; and where this is wanting, there can be no hope of mercy, as our Lord gave St. Bridget to understand in these words: "Unless the prayers of Mary interposed, there could be no hope of mercy."[3]

But perhaps we fear that Mary does not see, or does not feel for, our necessities? O no, she sees and feels them far better than we do ourselves. "There is not one amongst all the saints," says St. Antoninus, "who can ever feel for us in our miseries, both corporal and spiritual, like this woman, the most Blessed Virgin Mary."[4] So much so, that there where she sees misery, she cannot do otherwise than instantly fly and relieve it with her tender compassion.[5] Richard of St. Victor repeats the same thing; and Mendoza says, "Therefore, O most Blessed Virgin, thou dispensest thy mercies with a generous hand, wherever thou seest necessities."[6] Our good Mother herself protests that she will never cease to fulfil this office of mercy: *And unto the world to come I shall not cease to be, and in the holy dwelling-place I*

---

[1] "Ubi non est mulier, ingemiscit egens."—*Ecclus.* xxxvi. 27.

[2] "Ingemiscit infirmus, ubi non fuerit hæc sanctissima Mulier."

[3] "Nisi preces Matris meæ intervenirent, non esset spes misericordiæ."—*Rev.* l. 6, c. 26.

[4] "Non reperitur aliquem Sanctorum ita compati in infirmitatibus, sicut Mulier hæc, Beata Virgo Maria."—P. 4, tit. 15, c. 2.

[5] "Ubicumque fuerit miseria, tua et currit et succurrit misericordia."—*In Cant.* c. 23.

[6] "Itaque, O Virgo Mater! ubi nostras miserias invenis, ibi tuas misericordias effundis."—*In Reg.* c. iv. n. 11; *ann.* 12.

have ministered before him ;[1] that is, as Cardinal Hugo explains, " I will never cease until the end of the world relieving the miseries of men, and praying for sinners,"[2] that they may be delivered from eternal misery, and be saved.

Suetonius relates,[3] that the Emperor Titus was so desirous of rendering service to those who applied to him, that, when a day passed without being able to grant a favor, he used to say with sorrow, "I have lost a day ; for I have spent it without benefiting any one." It is probable that Titus spoke thus more from vanity, and the desire of being esteemed, than from true charity. But should such a thing happen to our Empress Mary, as to have to pass a day without granting a grace, she would speak as Titus did, but from a true desire to serve us, and because she is full of charity. " So much so, indeed," says Bernardine de Bustis, " that she is more anxious to grant us graces than we are to receive them."[4] " And therefore," says the same author, " whenever we go to her, we always find her hands filled with mercy and liberality." [5]

Rebecca was a figure of Mary ; and she, when asked by Abraham's servant for a little water to drink, replied, that not only would she give him plenty for himself, but also for his camels, saying, *I will draw water for thy camels, also, till they all drink.*[6] On these words St. Ber-

---

[1] " Et usque ad futurum sæculum non desinam, et in habitatione ancta coram ipso ministravi."—*Ecclus.* xxiv. 14.

[2] " Usque ad futurum sæculum, quod est sæculum Beatorum, non lesinam miseris subvenire et pro peccatoribus orare."

[3] *In Tit.* c. 8.

[4] " Plus desiderat ipsa facere tibi bonum et largiri aliquam gratiam, uam tu accipere concupiscas."

[5] "Invenies eam in manibus plenam pietate, misericordia, et irgitate."—*Marial.* p. 2, s. 5.

[6] " Quin et camelis tuis hauriam aquam, donec cuncti bibant."— *en.* xxiv. 19.

nard addresses our Blessed Lady, saying: "O Mary, thou art far more liberal and compassionate than Rebecca; and therefore thou art not satisfied with distributing the treasures of thy immense mercy only to the just, of whom Abraham's servants were types, but also thou bestowest them on sinners who are signified by the camels."[1] "The liberality of Mary," says Richard of St. Laurence, "is like that of her Son, who always gives more than he is asked for."[2] *He is*, says St. Paul, *rich unto all that call upon Him.*[3] "And the liberality of Mary is like his: she bestows more than is sought." Hear how a devout writer thus addresses the Blessed Virgin: "O Lady, do thou pray for me, for thou wilt ask for the graces I require with greater devotion than I can dare to ask for them; and thou wilt obtain far greater graces from God for me than I can presume to seek."[4]

When the Samaritans refused to receive Jesus Christ and his doctrines, St. James and St. John asked him whether they should command fire to fall from heaven and devour them; our Lord replied, *You know not of what spirit you are.*[5] As if he had said, "I am of so tender and compassionate a spirit that I came from heaven to save and not to chastise sinners, and you wish to see them lost. Fire, indeed! and punishment!—speak no more of chastisements, for such a spirit is not mine." But of Mary, whose spirit is the same as that of her Son, we can never doubt that she is all-inclined to

---

[1] "Domina! nec puero Abrahæ tantum, sed et camelis tribuas de supereffluenti hydria tua."—*In Sign. Magn.*

[2] "Largitas Mariæ assimilat largitatem Filii sui, qui dat amplius quam petatur."—*De Laud. B. M.* l. 4.

[3] "Dives in omnes qui invocant illum."—*Rom.* x. 12.

[4] "Majori devotione orabis pro me, quam ego auderem petere; et majora mihi impetrabis, quam petere præsumam."—*De Rhet. div.* c. 18.

[5] "Nescitis cujus spiritus estis."—*Luke,* ix. 55.

mercy; for, as she said to St. Bridget, she is called the Mother of mercy, and it was by God's own mercy that she was made thus compassionate and sweet towards all: "I am called the mother of mercy, and truly God's mercy made me thus merciful."[1]   For this reason Mary was seen by St. John clothed with the sun: *And a great sign appeared in heaven, a woman clothed with the sun.*[2]   On which words St. Bernard, turning towards the Blessed Virgin, says, "Thou, O Lady, hast clothed the sun, that is the Eternal Word, with human flesh; but he has clothed thee with his power and mercy."[3]

"This Queen," continues the same St. Bernard, "is so compassionate and benign, that when a sinner, whoever he may be, recommends himself to her charity, she does not question his merits, or whether he is worthy or unworthy to be attended to, but she hears and succors all."[4]   "And therefore," remarks St. Idelbert, "Mary is said to be *fair as the moon.*[5]   For as the moon enlightens and benefits the lowest creatures on earth, so does Mary enlighten and succor the most unworthy sinners."[6] And though the moon, says another writer, receives all its light from the sun, yet it works quicker than the sun; "for what this latter does in a year the moon does in a month."[7]   For this reason St. Anselm says "that we often more quickly obtain what we ask by calling on

---

[1] "Ego vocor Mater misericordiæ; vere, filia, misericordia Filii mei fecit me misericordem."—*Rev.* l. 2, c. 23.

[2] "Et signum magnum apparuit in cœlo: Mulier amicta sole."—*Apoc.* xii. 1.

[3] "Vestis Solem, et Sole ipsa vestiris."—*In Sign. Magn.*

[4] "Non discutit merita, sed omnibus sese exorabilem præbet."—*Ibid.*

[5] "Pulchra ut luna."—*Cant.* vi. 9.

[6] "Pulchra ut luna, quia pulchrum est benefacere indignis."

[7] "Quod sol facit in anno, luna facit in mense."—*Joann. a S. Gem. Summ.* l. 1, c. 3.

the name of Mary than by invoking that of Jesus."[1]
On this subject Hugo of St. Victor remarks, that
"though our sins may cause us to fear to approach the
Almighty, because it is his infinite majesty that we have
offended, we must never fear to go to Mary, for in her
we shall find nothing to terrify us. True it is that she
is holy, immaculate, and the Queen of the world; but
she is also of our flesh, and, like us, a child of Adam."[2]

"In fine," says St. Bernard, "all that belongs to Mary
is filled with grace and mercy, for she, as a Mother of
mercy, has made herself all to all, and out of her most
abundant charity she has made herself a debtor to the
wise and the foolish, to the just and sinners, and opens
to all her compassionate heart, that all may receive of
the fulness of its treasures."[3] So much so, that as *the
devil*, according to St. Peter, *goes about seeking whom he
may devour*,[4] so, on the other hand, says Bernardine de
Bustis, does Mary go about seeking whom she may
save, and to whom she may give life.[5]

We should fully understand and always bear in mind
a remark of St. Germanus, who says, "that the protection of Mary is greater and more powerful than anything of which we can form an idea."[6] "How is it,"
asks another writer, "that that Lord who under the old
dispensation was so rigorous in his punishments, now

[1] "Velocior est nonnunquam salus, memorato nomine Mariæ,
quam invocato nomine Jesu."—*De Excel. V.* c. 6.

[2] "Si pertimescis ad Deum accedere, respice ad Mariam: non illic
invenis quod timeas; genus tuum vides."—*Spinelli, M. Deip.* c. 30, n.
12.

[3] "Plena omnia pietatis et gratiæ, quæ ad eam pertinent; denique,
omnibus omnia facta est, sapientibus et insipientibus copiosissima
charitate debitricem se fecit; omnibus misericordiæ sinum aperit, ut
de plenitudine ejus accipiant universi."—*In Sign. Magn.*

[4] "Circuit, quærens quem devoret."—I *Pet.* v. 8.

[5] "Ipsa semper circuit, quærens quem salvet."—*Marial.* p. 3, s. 1.

[6] "Patrocinium tuum majus est quam comprehendi possit."—*De
Zona Deip.*

shows such mercy to persons guilty of far greater crimes?" And he answers, " that it is all for the love of Mary, and on account of her merits."[1] "O, how long since," exclaims St. Fulgentius, "would the world have been destroyed, had not Mary sustained it by her powerful intercession!"[2] "But now," says Arnold of Chartres, " that we have the Son as our mediator with the Eternal Father, and the Mother as a mediatress with the Son, we have full access, and can go to God with entire confidence and hope for every good thing. "How," he goes on to say, " can the Father refuse to hear the Son who shows him his side and wounds, the marks of his sufferings endured for sinners; and how can the Son refuse to hear his Mother when she shows him her bosom and the breasts that gave him suck?"[3] St. Peter Chrysologus says, " that a gentle maiden having lodged a God in her womb, asks as its price peace for the world, salvation for those who are lost, and life for the dead."[4]

" O, how many," exclaims the Abbot of Celles, " who deserved to be condemned by the justice of the Son, are saved by the mercy of the Mother? for she is God's treasure, and the treasurer of all graces; and thus our salvation is in her hands, and depends on her."[5]   Let

---

[1] " Quare parcit nunc mundo ipse Deus, qui olim multo his minora peccata acrius punivit? Totum hoc facit propter Beatam Virginem et ejus merita."—*Pelbart, Stell.* l. 11, p. 2, c. 2.

[2] "Cœlum et terra jamdudum ruissent; si Maria suis precibus non sustentasset."—*Pelbart, loco cit.*

[3] "Securum accessum jam habet homo ad Deum, ubi Mediatorem causæ suæ Filium habet ante Patrem, et ante Filium Matrem. Christus Patri ostendit latus et vulnera; Maria Christo pectus et ubera." —*De Laud. B. V.*

[4] " Una Puella sic Deum sui pectoris capit hospitio, ut pacem terris, cœlis gloriam, salutem perditis, vitam mortuis, pro ipsa domi exigat pensione."—*Serm.* 140.

[5] " Sæpe, quos justitia Filii potest damnare, Matris misericordia liberat; quia Thesaurus Domini est, et Thesauraria gratiarum, salus nostra in manibus illius est."—*Cont. de V. M. in prol.*

us, then, always have recourse to this compassionate
Mother, and confidently hope for salvation through her
intercession ; for she, according to the encouraging assurance of Bernardine de Bustis, " is our salvation, our
life, our hope, our counsel, our refuge, our help." [1]
" Mary," says St. Antoninus, [2] is that throne of grace to
which the Apostle St. Paul, in his epistle to the Hebrews, exhorts us to fly with confidence, that we may
obtain the divine mercy, and all the help we need for
our salvation." *Let us therefore go with confidence to the
throne of grace : that we may obtain mercy, and find grace
in seasonable aid.* [3] " To the throne of grace, that is, to
Mary," says St. Antoninus ; and for this, reason St. Catharine of Sienna called Mary " the dispenser of divine
mercy." [4]

Let us conclude with the beautiful and tender exclamation of St. Bonaventure on these words, " O merciful,
O compassionate, O sweet Virgin Mary !" " O Mary,
thou art clement with the miserable, compassionate towards those who pray to thee, sweet towards those who
love thee ; clement with the penitent, compassionate to
those who advance, sweet to the perfect. Thou showest
thyself clement in delivering us from chastisement, compassionate in bestowing graces, and sweet in giving
thyself to those who seek thee." [5]

[1] " Hæc est nostra Salus, Vita, Spes, Consilium, Refugium, Auxilium nostrum."—*Marial.* p. 1, s. 6.

[2] P. 4, t. 15, c. 14, § 7.

[3] " Adeamus ergo cum fiducia ad Thronum gratiæ, ut misericordiam consequamur, et gratiam inveniamus in auxilio opportuno."—
Hebr. iv. 16.

[4] " Administratrix misericordiæ."—*Or. in Annunt.*

[5] "O clemens indigentibus ! O pia exorantibus ! dulcis diligentibus ! O clemens pœnitentibus, pia proficientibus, dulcis contem-
plantibus, O clemens laborando, pia largiendo, dulcis te donando !"—
Med. in Salve Reg.

EXAMPLE.*

In the life of Father Anthony de Colleli we find the following occurrence narrated: "A certain unfortunate woman was having illicit relations with two young men. One of these, prompted by jealousy, stabbed the other to death. Very much frightened by what had happened, the sinful woman went to confession to Father Onofrius. She related the following: After the murder the unfortunate man appeared to her, all black, bound in chains, and surrounded by flames. He held a sword in his hand with which he attempted to kill her. Trembling with fear she cried out: 'Why do you wish to kill me? What have I done to you?' The man, filled with rage, replied: 'What, you wretch, you ask what you have done! It is your fault that I have lost my God.' Immediately the woman called on the Blessed Virgin to help her, and at the sound of the name of Mary, the apparition vanished." [1]

Prayer.

O Mother of mercy, since thou art so compassionate, and hast so great a desire to render service to us poor creatures and to grant our requests, behold I, the most miserable of all men, have now recourse to thy compassion, in order that thou mayest grant me that which I ask. Others may ask what they please of thee,—bodily health, and earthly goods and advantages; but I come, O Lady, to ask thee for that which thou desirest of me, and which is most in conformity and agreeable to thy most sacred heart. Thou art so humble; obtain for me humility and love of contempt. Thou wast so patient under the sufferings of this life; obtain for me patience in trials. Thou wast all filled with the love of God; obtain for me the gift of his pure and holy love. Thou wast all love towards thy neighbor; obtain for me charity towards all, and particularly towards those who are in any way my enemies. Thou wast entirely united to the divine will; ob-

[1] c. 32, § 5.

tain for me entire conformity to the will of God in whatever way he may be pleased to dispose of me. Thou, in fine, art the most holy of all creatures; O Mary, make me a saint. Love for me is not wanting on thy part; thou canst do all, and thou hast the will to obtain me all. The only thing, then, that can prevent me from receiving thy graces is, either neglect on my part in having recourse to thee, or little confidence in thy intercession; but these two things thou must obtain for me. These two greatest graces I ask from thee; from thee I must obtain them; from thee I hope for them with the greatest confidence, O Mary, my Mother Mary, my hope, my love, my life, my refuge, my help, and my consolation. Amen.

CHAPTER X.

O dulcis Virgo Maria.

O SWEET VIRGIN MARY.

The Sweetness of the Name of Mary during Life and at Death.

THE great name of Mary, which was given to the divine Mother, did not come to her from her parents, nor was it given to her by the mind or will of man, as is the case with all other names that are imposed in this world; but it came from heaven, and was given her by a divine ordinance. This is attested by St. Jerome,[1] St. Epiphanius,[2] St. Antoninus,[3] and others. "The name of Mary came from the treasury of the divinity,"[4] says St. Peter Damian. Ah, yes, O Mary, it was from that treasury that thy high and admirable name came forth; for the most Blessed Trinity, says Richard of St. Laurence, bestowed on thee a name above every other name after that of thy Son, and ennobled it with such majesty and power, that he willed that all heaven, earth, and hell, on only hearing it, should fall down and venerate it; but I will give the author's own words: "The whole Trinity, O Mary, gave thee a name after that of thy Son above every other name, that in thy name every knee should bow, of things in heaven, on earth, and under the earth."[5] But amongst the other privileges of the name of Mary, and which were given to it by God, we will now examine that of the peculiar sweetness found in it by the servants of this most holy Lady during life and in death.

And in the first place, speaking of the course of our

[1] *De Nat. M. V.*   [2] *Or. de Præs. Deip.*
[3] *Hist.* p. 1, t. 4, c. 6, § 10.
[4] "De thesauro Divinitatis, Mariæ nomen evolvitur."—*S. de Annunt.*
[5] "Dedit tibi, Maria, tota Trinitas nomen quod est super omne nomen, post nomen Filii sui, ut in nomine ejus omne genu flectatur cœlestium, terrestrium, et infernorum "—*De Laud. B. M.* l. 1, c. 2.

life, the holy anchorite Honorius used to say, that "this name of Mary is filled with every sweetness and divine savor;"[1] so much so, that the glorious St. Anthony of Padua found the same sweetness in the name of Mary that St. Bernard found in that of Jesus. "Name of Jesus!" exclaimed the one. "O name of Mary!" replied the other; "joy in the heart, honey in the mouth, melody to the ear of her devout clients."[2] It is narrated in the life of the Ven. Father Juvenal Ancina, Bishop of Saluzzo, that in pronouncing the name of Mary he tasted so great and sensible a sweetness, that, after doing so, he licked his lips. We read also that a lady at Cologne told the Bishop Massilius, that as often as she uttered the name of Mary she experienced a taste far sweeter than honey. The Bishop imitated her, and experienced the same thing.[3]

We gather from the sacred canticles, that on the Assumption of our Blessed Lady, the angels asked her name three times. *Who is she that goeth up by the desert as a pillar of smoke?*[4] again, *Who is she that cometh forth as the morning rising?*[5] and again, *Who is this that cometh up from the desert, flowing with delights?*[6] "And why," says Richard of St. Laurence, "do the angels so often ask the name of their Queen?" He answers, "That it was so sweet even to the angels to hear it pronounced, that they desired to hear that sweet name in reply."[7]

[1] "Hoc nomen Mariæ plenum est omni dulcedine suavitate divina." —*Ap. Lyr. Tris. Mar.* l. 2. m. 13.

[2] "Jubilus in corde, mel in ore, melos in aure."—*Dom.* 3 *Quadr.* s. 2.

[3] *Cæsarius, Dial.* l. 7. c. 50.

[4] "Quæ est ista, quæ ascendit per desertum, sicut virgula fumi?"— *Cant.* iii. 6.

[5] "Quæ est ista, quæ progreditur quasi aurora consurgens?"—*Ib.* vi. 9.

[6] "Quæ est ista, quæ ascendit de deserto, deliciis affluens?"—*Ib.* iii. 5.

[7] "Forsitan quia dulce nomen sibi desiderant responderi."—*De Laud. V. M.* l. 1, c. 2.

But here I do not intend to speak of that sensible sweetness, for it is not granted to all; I speak of that salutary sweetness of consolation, of love, of joy, of confidence, of strength, which the name of Mary ordinarily brings to those who pronounce it with devotion.

The Abbot Francone, speaking on this subject, says, "there is no other name after that of the Son, in heaven or on earth, whence pious minds derive so much grace, hope, and sweetness." [1] After the most sacred name of Jesus, the name of Mary is so rich in every good thing, that on earth and in heaven there is no other from which devout souls receive so much grace, hope, and sweetness. "For," he continues, "there is something so admirable, sweet, and divine in this name of Mary, that when it meets with friendly hearts it breathes into them an odor of delightful sweetness." And he adds, in conclusion, "that the wonder of this great name is, that if heard by the lovers of Mary a thousand times, it is always heard again with renewed pleasure, for they always experience the same sweetness each time it is pronounced." [2]

The Blessed Henry Suso, [3] also speaking of this sweetness, says, "that when he named Mary, he felt himself so excited to confidence, and inflamed with such love and joy, that between the tears and joy with which he pronounced the beloved name, he desired that his heart might leave his breast; for he declared that this most sweet name was like a honeycomb dissolving in the inmost recess of the soul;" and then he would exclaim:

[1] "Neque enim, post Filii sui nomen, aliud nomen cœlum aut terra nominat, unde tantum gratiæ, tantum spei, tantum suavitatis, piæ mentes concipiant."

[2] "Nomen namque Mariæ, mirum quid, suave, ac divinum, in se continet, ut, cum sonuerit amicis cordibus, amicæ suavitatis odorem spiret. Et mirum illud est de nomine Mariæ, ut, millies auditum, semper audiatur quasi novum."—*De Grat. D.* l. 6.

[3] *Dial.* c. 16.

"O most sweet name! O Mary, what must thou thyself be, since thy name alone is thus amiable and gracious!"

The enamoured St. Bernard, raising his heart to his good Mother, says with tenderness, "O great! O pious! O thou who art worthy of all praise! O most Holy Virgin Mary! Thy name is so sweet and amiable, that it cannot be pronounced without inflaming those who do so with love towards thee and God. It only need occur to the thought of thy lovers to move them to love thee more, and to console them." "Thou canst not be named without inflaming; thou canst not be thought of by those who love thee without filling their minds with joy."[1] "And if riches comfort the poor, because they relieve them in their distress, O how much more does thy name, O Mary," says Richard of St. Laurence, "comfort us than any earthly riches! It comforts us in the anguishes of this life." "Thy name, O Mary, is far better than riches, because it can better relieve poverty."[2]

In fine, "thy name, O Mother of God, is filled with divine graces and blessings,"[3] as St. Methodius says. So much so, that St. Bonaventure declares, "that thy name, O Mary, cannot be pronounced without bringing some grace to him who does so devoutly."[4] The Blessed Raymond Jordano says, "that however hardened and diffident a heart may be, the name of this most Blessed Virgin has such efficacy, that if it is only pronounced, that heart will be wonderfully softened." I will, how-

---

[1] "O magna, O pia, O multum amabilis Maria! tu nec nominari potes, quin accendas, nec cogitari, quin recrees affectus diligentium te." —*Depr. gl. V.*

[2] "Mariæ nomen longe melius quam divitiæ, quia melius angustiam relevat."—*De Laud. B. M.* l. 1, c. 2.

[3] "Tuum, Dei genitrix, nomen divinis benedictionibus et gratiis ex omni parte refertum."—*De Sim. et Anna.*

[4] "Nomen tuum devote nominari non potest sine nominantis utilitate."—*Spec. B. V. lect.* 9.

ever, give his own words. "The power of thy most holy
name, O ever-blessed Virgin Mary, is such that it softens the hardness of the human heart in a wonderful
manner." He then tells us that it is she who leads sinners to the hope of pardon and grace: "By thee does
the sinner recover the hope of forgiveness and of grace." [1]

Thy most sweet name, O Mary, according to St. Ambrose, "is a precious ointment, which breathes forth the
odor of divine grace." The saint then prays to the divine Mother, saying: "Let this ointment of salvation
enter the inmost recesses of our souls:" [2] that is, grant,
O Lady, that we may often remember to name thee
with love and confidence; for this practice either shows
the possession of divine grace, or else is a pledge that
we shall soon recover it. "And truly it is so, O Mary ;
for the remembrance of thy name comforts the afflicted,
recalls those who have erred to the way of salvation,
and encourages sinners, that they may not abandon themselves to despair." It is thus that Ludolph of Saxony
addresses her. [3]

Father Pelbart says, "that as Jesus Christ by his five
wounds gave a remedy for the evils of the world, so
also does Mary, by her most holy name which is composed of five letters, daily bring pardon to sinners." [4]

For this reason is the holy name of Mary likened in
the sacred canticles to oil: *Thy name is as oil poured out.* [5]

[1] "Tanta est virtus tui sacratissimi nominis, O semper benedicta
Virgo Maria! quod mirabiliter emollit duritiam cordis humani; peccator per te respirat in spe veniæ ei gratiæ."—*Cont. de V. M.* c. 5.

[2] "Unguentum, nomen tuum; descendat istud unguentum in animæ
præcordia, Sancta Maria, quod divina gratiæ spiramenta redolet."—
Instit. Virg. c. 13.

[3] "O Mariæ! tui recordatio nominis, mœstos lætificat, errantes ad
viam salutis revocat et peccatores, ne desperent, confortat."—*Vita
Chr.* p. 2, c. 86.

[4] "Sic Maria, suo sanctissimo nomine, quod quinque litteris constat, confert quotidie veniam peccatoribus."—*Stell.* l. 6, p. 1. a. 2.

[5] "Oleum effusum, nomen tuum."—*Off. B. V. resp.* 6.

On these words blessed Alan says that the glory of her name is compared to oil poured out; because oil heals the sick, sends out a sweet odor, and nourishes flames.[1] Thus also does the name of Mary heal sinners, rejoice hearts, and inflame them with divine love. Hence Richard of St. Laurence "encourages sinners to have recourse to this great name," because it alone will suffice to cure them of all their evils; and " there is no disorder, however malignant, that does not immediately yield to the power of the name of Mary." [2]

On the other hand, Thomas à Kempis affirms "that the devils fear the Queen of heaven to such a degree, that only on hearing her great name pronounced, they fly from him who does so as from a burning fire." [3] The Blessed Virgin herself revealed to St. Bridget "that there is not on earth a sinner, however devoid he may be of the love of God, from whom the devil is not obliged immediately to fly, if he invokes her holy name with a determination to repent." [4] On another occasion she repeated the same thing to the saint, saying, "that all the devils venerate and fear her name to such a degree, that on hearing it they immediately loosen the claws with which they hold the soul captive." [5] Our Blessed Lady also told St. Bridget, "that in the same

---

[1] "Gloria nominis ejus oleo effuso comparatur; oleum ægrotantem sanat, odorem parit, flammam nutrit."—*In Cant.* i.

[2] "Peccator es, ad Mariæ nomen confugias; ipsum solum sufficit ad medendum: nulla enim pestis quæ, ad nomen Mariæ, non cedat continuo."—*De Laud. B. M.* l. 1, c. 2.

[3] "Expavescunt cœli Reginam spiritus maligni, et diffugiunt, audito nomine ejus, velut ab igne."—*Ad Nov.* s. 23.

[4] "Nullus tam frigidus ab amore Dei est, nisi sit damnatus, si invocaverit hoc nomen, hac intentione, ut nunquam reverti velit ad opus solitum, quod non discedat ab eo statim diabolus."

[5] "Omnes dæmones verentur hoc nomen, et timent ; qui audientes hoc nomen, Maria, statim relinquunt animam de unguibus, quibus tenebant eam."

way as the rebel angels fly from sinners who invoke the name of Mary, so also do the good angels approach nearer to just souls who pronounce her name with devotion." [1]

St. Germanus declares, " that as breathing is a sign of life, so also is the frequent pronunciation of the name of Mary a sign either of the life of divine grace, or that it will soon come ; for this powerful name has in it the virtue of obtaining help and life for him who invokes it devoutly." Addressing the Blessed Virgin, he says, " As breathing is a sign of life in the body, so is the frequent repetition of thy most holy name, O Virgin, by thy servants, not only a sign of life and of strength, but also it procures and conciliates both." [2]

In fine, " This admirable name of our Sovereign Lady," says Richard of St. Laurence, " is like a fortified tower, in which, if a sinner takes refuge, he will be delivered from death ; for it defends and saves even the most abandoned." [3]   But it is a tower of strength, which not only delivers sinners from chastisement, but also defends the just from the assaults of hell.   Thus the same Richard says, " that after the name of Jesus, there is no other in which men find so powerful assistance and salvation as in the great name of Mary." [4]   He says, " there is not such powerful help in any name, nor is there any other name given to men, after that of Jesus, from which

[1] " Angeli boni, audito hoc nomine, statim appropinquant magis justis."—*Rev.* l. 1, c. 9.

[2] " Quomodo corpus vitalis signum operationis habet respirationem, ita etiam sanctissimum nomen tuum, O Virgo ! quod in ore servorum tuorum versatur assidue, vitæ et auxilii non solum signum est, sed etiam ea procurat et conciliat."—*De Zona Deip.*

[3] " Turris fortissima, nomen Dominæ : ad ipsam fugiet peccator et liberabitur ; hæc defendit quoslibet et quantumlibet peccatores."

[4] " Non est in aliquo alio nomine, tam potens adjutorium, nec est aliquod nomen datum hominibus, post dulce nomen Jesu, ex quo tanta salus refundatur hominibus."—*De Laud. B. M.* l. 11.

so much salvation is poured forth upon men as from the name of Mary." Moreover, it is well known, and is daily experienced by the clients of Mary, that her powerful name gives the particular strength necessary to overcome temptations against purity. The same author in his commentary on the words of St. Luke, *and the Virgin's name was Mary,*[1] remarks that these two words, Mary and Virgin, are joined together by the Evangelist, to denote that the name of this most pure Virgin should always be coupled with the virtue of chastity."[2] Hence St. Peter Chrysologus says, "that the name of Mary is an indication of chastity,"[3] meaning, that when we doubt as to whether we have consented to thoughts against this virtue, if we remember having invoked the name of Mary, we have a certain proof that we have not sinned.

Let us, therefore, always take advantage of the beautiful advice given us by St. Bernard, in these words: "In dangers, in perplexities, in doubtful cases, think of Mary, call on Mary; let her not leave thy lips; let her not depart from thy heart."[4] In every danger of forfeiting divine grace, we should think of Mary, and invoke her name, together with that of Jesus; for these two names always go together. O, then, never let us permit these two most sweet names to leave our hearts, or be off our lips; for they will give us strength not only not to yield, but to conquer all our temptations.

Consoling indeed are the promises of help made by Jesus Christ to those who have devotion to the name of Mary; for one day in the hearing of St. Bridget, he

---

[1] " Et nomen, Virginis Maria."—*Luke*, i. 27.

[2] " Nomini Mariæ virginitas et sanctitas inseparabiliter sunt adjuncta."—*Loco cit.*

[3] " Nomen hoc, indicium castitatis."—*Serm.* 146.

[4] " In periculis, in angustiis, in rebus dubiis, Mariam cogita, Mariam invoca; non recedat ab ore, non recedat a corde."—*De Laud. V. M.* hom. 2.

promised his most holy Mother that he would grant
three special graces to those who invoke that holy name
with confidence : first, that he would grant them perfect
sorrow for their sins ; secondly, that their crimes should
be atoned for ; and, thirdly, that he would give them
strength to attain perfection, and at length the glory of
paradise. And then our divine Saviour added : " For
thy words, O my Mother, are so sweet and agreeable to
me, that I cannot deny what thou askest." [1]

St. Ephrem goes so far as to say, "that the name of
Mary is the key of the gates of heaven," [2] in the hands of
those who devoutly invoke it. And thus it is not without reason that St. Bonaventure says " that Mary is the
salvation of all who call upon her :" for he addresses her,
saying : "O salvation of all who invoke thee !" [3] meaning, that to obtain eternal salvation and invoke her
name are synonymous ; and Richard of St. Laurence
affirms, "that the devout invocation of this sweet and
holy name leads to the acquisition of superabundant
graces in this life, and a very high degree of glory in
the next." [4] " If then, O brethren," concludes Thomas
à Kempis, " you desire consolation in every labor, have
recourse to Mary ; invoke the name of Mary, honor
Mary, recommend yourselves to Mary, rejoice with Mary,
weep with Mary, pray with Mary, walk with Mary, seek
Jesus with Mary ; in fine, desire to live and die with
Jesus and Mary. By acting thus you will always advance

[1] " Habitatores mundi indigent tribus : contritione pro peccatis,
satisfactione, fortitudine ad faciendum bona. Quicumque invocaverit
nomen tuum, et spem habet in te, cum proposito emendandi com-
missa, ista tria dabuntur ei, insuper et regnum cœleste. Tanta enim
est mihi dulcedo in verbis tuis, ut non possim negare quæ petis."—
Rev. l. 1, c. 50.

[2] " Nomen Mariæ est reseratorium portæ cœli."—*De Laud. Dei Gen.*

[3] " O Salus te invocantium !"

[4] " Devota invocatio nominis ejus ducit ad virorem gratiæ in præsenti, ad virorem gloriæ in futuro "—*De Laud B. M.* l. 1, c. 2.

in the ways of God, for Mary will most willingly pray for you, and the Son will most certainly grant all that his Mother asks." [1]

Thus we see that the most holy name of Mary is sweet indeed to her clients during life, on account of the very great graces that she obtains for them. But sweeter still will it be to them in death, on account of the tranquil and holy end that it will insure them.

Father Sertorius Caputo, of the Society of Jesus, exhorted all who assist the dying frequently to pronounce the name of Mary; for this name of life and hope, when repeated at the hour of death, suffices to put the devils to flight, and to comfort such persons in their sufferings.

"The invocation of the sacred names of Jesus and Mary," says Thomas à Kempis, "is a short prayer which is as sweet to the mind, and as powerful to protect those who use it against the enemies of their salvation, as it is easy to remember." [2]

"Blessed is the man who loves thy name, O Mary," [3] exclaims St. Bonaventure. "Yes, truly blessed is he who loves thy sweet name, O Mother of God! for," he continues, "thy name is so glorious and admirable, that no one who remembers it has any fears at the hour of death." [4] Such is its power, that none of those who invoke it at the hour of death fear the assaults of their enemies.

[1] "Si consolari in omni tribulatione quæritis, accedite ad Mariam. Mariam invocate, Mariam honorate, Mariæ vos commendate; cum Maria gaudete, cum Maria dolete, cum Maria orate, cum Maria ambulate, cum Maria Jesum quærite, cum Maria et Jesu vivere et mori desiderate. Fratres, si ista exercetis, proficietis; Maria libenter pro vobis orabit, et Jesus libenter Matrem suam exaudiet."—*Ad Nov.* s. 21.

[2] "Hæc sancta oratio: 'Jesus et Maria,' brevis est ad legendum, facilis ad tenendum, dulcis ad cogitandum, fortis ad protegendum."—*Vall. lil.* c. 13.

[3] "Beatus vir qui diligit nomen tuum, Maria."

[4] "Gloriosum et admirabile est nomen tuum; qui illud retinent, non expavescent in puncto mortis."—*Psalt. B. V.* ps. i. 110.

Oh, that we may end our lives as did the Capuchin Father, Fulgentius of Ascoli, who expired singing, "O Mary, O Mary, the most beautiful of creatures! let us depart together;" or according to the annals of the Order, like Blessed Henry the Cistercian, who expired in the very moment that he was pronouncing the most sweet name of Mary.[1]

Let us then, O devout reader, beg God to grant us, that at death the name of Mary may be the last word on our lips. This was the prayer of St. Germanus: "May the last movement of my tongue be to pronounce the name of the Mother of God;"[2] O sweet, O safe is that death which is accompanied and protected by so saving a name; for God only grants the grace of invoking it to those whom he is about to save.

O my sweet Lady and Mother, I love thee much, and because I love thee I also love thy holy name. I purpose and hope, with thy assistance, always to invoke it during life and at death. And to conclude with the tender prayer of St. Bonaventure: "I ask thee, O Mary, for the glory of thy name, to come and meet my soul when it is departing from this world, and to take it in thine arms."[3] "Disdain not, O Mary," the saint continues, "to come then and comfort me with thy presence. Be thyself my soul's ladder and way to heaven. Do thou thyself obtain for it the grace of forgiveness and eternal repose."[4] He then concludes saying, "O Mary, our advocate, it is for thee to defend thy clients, and to undertake their cause before the tribunal of Jesus Christ."[5]

[1] "Inter ipsam dulcissimi nominis articulationem!"

[2] "Dei Matris nomen sit mihi ultimus linguæ loquentis motus."— *In Deip. Ann.*

[3] "In exitu animæ meæ de hoc mundo, occurre illi, Domina, et suscipe eam."

[4] "Consolare eam vultu sancto tuo; esto illi scala et iter ad paradisum Dei; impetra ei indulgentiam pacis, et sedem lucis."

[5] "Sustine devotos ante tribunal Christi; suscipe causam eorum in manibus tuis."—*Psalt. B. V. ps.* 113.

EXAMPLE.*

St. Camillus de Lellis urged the members of his community to remind the dying often to utter the holy name of Jesus and Mary. Such was his custom when assisting people in their last hour. When he himself came to die he gave an edifying example of confidence in the holy names. His biographer relates that when death was approaching, the saint invoked the sweet names of Jesus and Mary with such tender devotion that all present were inflamed with love for the sacred names. With his eyes fixed on the images of Jesus and Mary, and his arms crossed on his breast, an expression of heavenly peace rested on his face when his soul took its flight. His last words were the sacred names of Jesus and Mary.

Prayer.

O great Mother of God and my Mother Mary, it is true that I am unworthy to name thee; but thou, who lovest me and desirest my salvation, must, notwithstanding the impurity of my tongue, grant that I may always invoke thy most holy and powerful name in my aid, for thy name is the succor of the living, and the salvation of the dying. Ah, most pure Mary, most sweet Mary, grant that henceforth thy name may be the breath of my life. O Lady, delay not to help me when I invoke thee, for in all the temptations which assail me, and in all my wants, I will never cease calling upon thee, and repeating again and again, Mary, Mary. Thus it is that I hope to act during my life, and more particularly at death, that after that last struggle I may eternally praise thy beloved name in heaven, O clement, O pious, O sweet Virgin Mary. Ah, Mary, most amiable Mary, with what consolation, what sweetness, what confidence, what tenderness, is my soul penetrated in only naming, in only thinking of thee! I thank my Lord and God, who, for my good, has given thee a name so sweet and deserving of love, and at the same time so powerful. But, my sovereign Lady, I am not satisfied with only naming thee, I wish to name thee with love: I desire that my love may every hour remind me to call on thee, so that I may be able to exclaim with St. Bonaventure, "O name of the Mother of God, thou art my love." [1] My own dear Mary, O my beloved Jesus, may your most sweet names reign in my heart, and in all hearts. Grant that I may forget all others to remember, and always invoke, your adorable names alone. Ah! Jesus my Redeemer, and my Mother Mary, when the moment of death comes when I must breathe forth my soul and leave this world, deign, through your merits, to grant that I may then pronounce my last words, and that they may be, "I love thee, O Jesus; I love thee, O Mary; to you do I give my heart and my soul."

[1] "O amor mei, nomen Matris Dei."—*Med. de Sal. B. V.*

Beautiful and Fervent Prayers

*ADDRESSED BY THE VARIOUS SAINTS TO THE DIVINE MOTHER.**

Prayer of St. Ephrem.

O immaculate and entirely pure Virgin Mary, Mother of God, Queen of the universe, our own good Lady; thou art above all the saints, the only hope of the patriarchs, and the joy of the saints. Through thee we have been reconciled with our God. Thou art the only advocate of sinners, and the secure haven of those who are sailing on the sea of this life. Thou art the consolation of the world, the ransom of captives, the joy of the sick, the comfort of the afflicted, the refuge, the salvation of the whole world.

O great Princess, Mother of God, cover us with the wings of thy mercy, and pity us. We hope only in thee, O most pure Virgin. We are given to thee, and consecrated to thy service; we bear the name of thy servants. O, then, permit not that Lucifer should drag us to hell. O immaculate Virgin, we are under thy protection, and therefore unitedly we have recourse to thee; and we beseech thee to prevent thy beloved Son, who is irritated by our sins, from abandoning us to the power of the devil.

O thou who art full of grace, enlighten my understanding, loosen my tongue, that it may sing thy praises; and more particularly the angelic salutation, so worthy of thee. I salute thee, O peace, O joy, O consolation of the whole world. I salute thee, O greatest of miracles, O paradise of delights, secure haven of those who are in danger, fountain of graces, mediatress between God and men.[1]

[1] *De Laud. Dei Gen.*

---

* These Prayers are put here, not only that they may be used, but also that they may show the high idea that the saints had of the power and mercy of Mary, and the great confidence they had in her patronage.

Prayer of St. Bernard.

We raise our eyes to thee, O Queen of the world. We must appear before our Judge after so many sins: who will appease him? No one can do it better than thou canst, O holy Lady, who hast loved him so much, and by whom thou art so tenderly beloved. Open, then, O Mother of mercy, thy heart to our sighs and prayers. We fly to thy protection; appease the wrath of thy Son, and restore us to his grace. Thou dost not abhor a sinner, however loathsome he may be. Thou dost not despise him, if he sends up his sighs to thee, and, repentant, asks thy intercession. Thou, with thy compassionate hand, deliverest him from despair. Thou animatest him to hope, and dost not leave him until thou hast reconciled him with his Judge. Thou art that chosen Lady in whom our Lord found repose, and in whom he has deposited all his treasures without measure. Hence the whole world, O my most holy Lady, honors thy chaste womb as the temple of God, in which the salvation of the world began. In thee was effected the reconciliation between God and man. Thou, O great Mother of God, art the enclosed garden, into which the hand of a sinner never entered to gather its flowers. Thou art the beautiful garden in which God has planted all the flowers that adorn the Church, and amongst others the violet of thy humility, the lily of thy purity, the rose of thy charity. With whom can we compare thee, O Mother of grace and beauty? Thou art the paradise of God; from thee issued forth the fountain of living water that irrigates the whole earth. O, how many benefits thou hast bestowed on the world by meriting to be so salutary a channel!

Of thee it is that the question is asked, "Who is she that cometh forth like the morning rising, fair as the moon, bright as the sun?"[1] Thou camest, then, into the world, O Mary, as a resplendent dawn, preceding with the light of thy sanctity the coming of the Sun of justice. The day on which thou camest into the world can indeed be called a day of salvation, a day of grace. Thou art fair as the moon; for as amongst all planets the moon it is that is most like the sun, so amongst all

[1] *Cant.* vi. 9.

creatures thou art the nearest in resemblance to God. The moon illumines the night with the light that it receives from the sun, and thou enlightenest our darkness with the splendor of thy virtues. But thou art fairer than the moon, for in thee there is neither spot nor shadow. Thou art bright as the sun; I mean as the Sun that created the sun; he was chosen amongst all men, and thou wast chosen amongst all women. O sweet, O great, O all-amiable Mary, no heart can pronounce thy name but thou inflamest it with thy love; nor can they who love thee think of thee without feeling themselves strengthened to love thee more.

O holy Lady, help our weakness. And who is more fit to address our Lord Jesus Christ than thou, who enjoyest in such close vicinity his most sweet converse? Speak, then, speak, O Lady; for thy Son listens to thee, and thou wilt obtain all that thou askest of him.[1]

Prayer of St. Germanus of Constantinople.

O my only and sovereign Lady, who art the sole consolation that I receive from God; thou who art the only celestial dew that gives me refreshment in my pains; thou who art the light of my soul when it is surrounded with darkness; thou who art my guide in journeyings, my strength in weakness; my treasure in poverty, the balm of my wounds, my consolation in sorrow, thou who art my refuge in miseries and the hope of my salvation; listen to my prayers, have pity on me as it becomes the Mother of a God who has such love for men.[2]

O thou who art our defence and joy, grant me all that I ask; make me worthy to enjoy with thee the great happiness that thou enjoyest in heaven. Yes, my Lady, my refuge, my life, my help, my defence, my strength, my joy, my hope, grant that I may one day be with thee in heaven. I know that, being the Mother of God, thou canst, if thou wilt, obtain it for me. O Mary, thou art omnipotent to save sinners, nor needest thou any other recommendation; for thou art the Mother of true life.[3]

[1] *Depr. ad gl. V.*   [2] *Encom. in S. Deip.*   [3] *In Dorm. V. M. s. 2.*

Prayer of Blessed Raymond Jordano, Abbot of Celles.*

Draw me after thee, O Virgin Mary, that I may run to the odor of thy ointments. Draw me, for I am held back by the weight of my sins and by the malice of my enemies. As no one goes to thy Son unless the heavenly Father draws him, so do I presume to say, in a certain manner, that no one goes to him unless thou drawest him by thy holy prayers. It is thou who teachest true wisdom, thou who obtainest grace for sinners, for thou art their advocate; it is thou who promisest glory to him who honors thee, for thou art the treasurer of graces.[1]

Thou, O most sweet Virgin, hast found grace with God, for thou wast preserved from the stain of original sin, wast filled with the Holy Ghost, and didst conceive the Son of God. Thou, O most humble Virgin, didst receive all these graces not for thyself only, but also for us, that thou mightest assist us in all our necessities. And this thou dost indeed; thou succorest the good, preserving them in grace, and the wicked thou preparest to receive divine mercy. Thou assistest the dying, protecting them against the snares of the devil; and thou helpest them also after death, receiving their souls and conducting them to the kingdom of the blessed.[2]

Prayer of St. Methodius.

Thy name, O Mother of God, is filled with all graces and divine blessings. Thou hast contained him who cannot be contained, and nourished him who nourishes all creatures. He who fills heaven and earth, and is Lord of all, was pleased to stand in need of thee, for it was thou who didst clothe him with that flesh which he had not before. Rejoice then, O Mother and handmaid of God; be glad then, with exceeding great joy, for thou hast him for thy debtor who gives their being to all creatures. We are all God's debtors, but he is a debtor to thee. Hence it is, O most holy Mother of God, that

[1] *Cont. de V. M. in prol.*   [2] *Cont. de V. M.* c. 6.

---

* Out of humility he surnamed himself the Idiot.

thou hast greater goodness and greater charity than all the other saints, and hast freer access to God than any of them, for thou art his Mother. Ah, deign, we beseech thee, to remember us in our miseries, who celebrate thy glories, and know how great is thy goodness.[1]

Prayer of St. John Damascene

I salute thee, O Mary; thou art the hope of Christians; receive the supplication of a sinner who loves thee tenderly, honors thee in a special manner, and places in thee the whole hope of his salvation. From thee I have my life. Thou dost restore me to the favor of thy Son; thou art the certain pledge of my salvation. I implore thee, then, deliver me from the burden of my sins, dispel the darkness of my mind, banish earthly affections from my heart, repress the temptations of my enemies, and so rule my whole life that by thy means and under thy guidance I may attain the eternal happiness of heaven.[2]

Prayer of St. Andrew of Crete.*

I salute thee, O full of grace, our Lord is with thee. I salute thee, O cause of our joy, through whom the sentence of our condemnation was revoked and changed into one of blessings. I salute thee, O temple of the glory of God, sacred dwelling of the King of heaven. Thou art the reconciliation of God with men. I salute thee, O Mother of our joy. Truly thou art blessed, for thou alone amongst all women wast found worthy to be the Mother of thy Creator. All nations call thee Blessed.[3]

O Mary, if I place my confidence in thee, I shall be saved; if I am under thy protection, I have nothing to fear, for the fact of being thy client is the possession of a certainty of salvation, which God only grants to those whom he will save.

O Mother of mercy, appease thy beloved Son. Whilst thou wast on earth thou didst occupy only a small part of it, but now that thou art raised above the highest heavens, the whole world considers thee as the propitiatory of all nations. I implore

---

[1] *De Sim. et Anna.*   [2] *In Nat. B. V.* s. 1.   [3] *In S. Deip. Ann.*

---

* Or of Jerusalem; for it is not known whether it was one person under the two titles, or two different persons.

thee, then, O Holy Virgin, to grant me the help of thy prayers with God; prayers which are dearer and more precious to us than all the treasures of the earth; prayers which render God propitious to us in our sins, and obtain us a great abundance of graces, both for the pardon of our offences and the practice of virtue: prayers which check our enemies, confound their designs, and triumph over their strength.[1]

Prayer of St. Ildephonsus.

I come to thee, O Mother of God, and implore thee to obtain for me the pardon of my sins, and that I may be cleansed from those of my whole life. I beseech thee to grant me the grace to unite myself in affection to thy Son and to thyself: to thy Son as my God, and to thee as the Mother of my God.[2]

Prayer of St. Athanasius.

Give ear to our prayers, O most Holy Virgin, and be mindful of us. Dispense unto us the gifts of thy riches, and the abundance of the graces with which thou art filled. The archangel saluted thee, and called thee full of grace. All nations call thee blessed. The whole hierarchy of heaven blesses thee; and we, who are of the terrestrial hierarchy, also address thee, saying, Hail, O full of grace, our Lord is with thee; pray for us, O holy Mother of God, our Lady and our Queen.[3]

Prayer of St. Anselm.

We beseech thee, O Most holy Lady, by the favor that God did thee, in raising thee so high as to make all things possible to thee with him, so to act that the plenitude of grace, which thou didst merit, may render us partakers of thy glory. Strive, O most merciful Lady, to obtain for us that for which God was pleased to become man in thy chaste womb. O, lend us a willing ear. If thou deignest to pray to thy Son for this, he will immediately grant it. It suffices that thou willest our salvation, and then we are sure to obtain it. But who can restrain thy great mercy? If thou, who art our Mother, and the

---

[1] *In Dorm. S. M.* s. 3.   [2] *De Virginit. perp. S. M.* c. 12.
[3] *In Annunt. Deip.*

Mother of mercy, dost not pity us, what will become of us when thy Son comes to judge us ?

Help us, then, O most compassionate Lady, and consider not the multitude of our sins. Remember always that our Creator took human flesh of thee, not to condemn sinners, but to save them. If thou hadst become Mother of God only for thine own advantage, we might say that it signified little to thee whether we were lost or saved ; but God clothed himself with thy flesh for thy salvation, and for that of all men. What would thy great power and glory avail us, if thou dost not make us partakers of thy happiness ? O, help us, then, and protect us : thou knowest how greatly we stand in need of thy assistance. We recommend ourselves to thee ; O, let us not lose our souls, but make us eternally serve and love thy beloved Son, Jesus Christ.[1]

Prayer of St. Peter Damian.

Holy Virgin, Mother of God, succor those who implore thy aid. O, turn towards us. Hast thou, perhaps, forgotten men, because thou hast been raised to so close a union with God ? Ah no, most certainly. Thou knowest well in what danger thou didst leave us, and the wretched condition of thy servants ; ah no, it would not become so great a mercy as thine to forget so great misery as ours is. Turn towards us, then, with thy power ; for he who is powerful has made thee omnipotent in heaven and on earth. Nothing is impossible to thee, for thou canst raise even those who are in despair to the hope of salvation. The more powerful thou art, the greater should be thy mercy.

Turn also to us in thy love. I know, O my Lady, that thou art all benign, and that thou lovest us with a love that can be surpassed by no other love. How often dost thou not appease the wrath of our Judge, when he is on the point of chastising us ? All the treasures of the mercies of God are in thy hands. Ah, never cease to benefit us ; thou only seekest occasion to save all the wretched, and to shower thy mercies upon them ; for thy glory is increased when, by thy means, penitents are forgiven, and thus reach heaven. Turn, then, towards us, that

[1] *De Excell. V.* c. 12.

we also may be able to go and see thee in heaven ; for the greatest glory we can have will be, after seeing God, to see thee, to love thee, and be under thy protection. Be pleased, then, to grant our prayer; for thy beloved Son desires to honor thee, by denying thee nothing that thou askest.[1]

Prayer of William, Bishop of Paris.

O Mother of God, I have recourse to thee, and I call upon thee not to reject me ; for the whole congregation of the faithful calls and proclaims thee the Mother of mercy. Thou art that one who, from being so dear to God, art always graciously heard; thy clemency was never wanting to any one ; thy most benign affability never despised any sinner who had recourse to thee, however enormous his crimes. Can it be falsely or in vain that the Church calls thee her advocate, and the refuge of sinners ? Never let it be said that my sins could prevent thee from fulfilling the great office of mercy, which is peculiarly thine own, by which thou art the advocate and mediatress of peace, the only hope and most secure refuge of the miserable. Never shall it be said that the Mother of God, who for the benefit of the world brought forth him who is the fountain of mercy, denied her mercy to any sinner who had recourse to her. Thine office is that of peacemaker between God and men : let, then, the greatness of thy compassion, and which far exceeds my sins, move thee to help me.[2]

[1] *In Nat. B. M.* s. 1.   [2] *De Rhet. div.* c. 18.

HYMNS.

I.

To Mary, our Queen, the Mother of Mercy.

LOOK down, O Mother Mary!
　From thy bright throne above;
Cast down upon thy children
　One only glance of love.

And if a heart so tender
　With pity flows not o'er,
Then turn away, O Mother!
　And look on us no more.

See how, ungrateful sinners,
　We stand before thy Son;
His loving heart upbraids us
　The evil we have done.

But if thou wilt appease him,
　Speak for us,—but one word;
Thou only can'st obtain us
　The pardon of our Lord.

O Mary, dearest Mother!
　If thou wouldst have us live,
Say that we are thy children,
　And Jesus will forgive.

Our sins make us unworthy
　That title still to bear;
But thou art still our Mother,
　Then show a Mother's care.

Open to us thy mantle;
  There stay we without fear:
What evil can befall us
  If, Mother, thou art near?

O sweetest, dearest Mother!
  Thy sinful children save;
Look down on us with pity,
  Who thy protection crave.

II.

To Mary our Mother.

(By Mgr. Majello.)

When I think o'er my happy lot,
  That, Mary, I am a child of thine,
  Then every sorrow, Mother mine,
Swift vanishes and is forgot.

Chos'n Mother of my God to be,
  Thou still art mine own Mother dear;
  What harm then can I ever fear,
Sweet Mary, if thou lovest me?

One only fear can make me sigh,
  'Tis lest I e'er should lose thy love;
  But while my heart shall faithful prove,
Living or dying, blest am I.

Deprived of thee, my lovely Rose,
  Each joy doth bitter grief appear;
  But pain is joy if thou wert near,
And death itself is sweet repose.

From Heaven's path he cannot stray
  Who follows thee, his safest guide;
  To serve thee and in thee confide,
Is of all good the surest way.

Oh, blest is he whose sole desire
  Is e'er to love thee tenderly;
  Yes, happy he who loveth thee,
And feels his heart with love on fire.

Then grant to me, my sweetest Queen,
  Ever to burn with love of thee,
  Until in heaven I come to see,
Unveil'd, thy loveliness serene.

III.

To Mary, our Hope.

MARY, thou art Hope the brightest,
  Love most pure and sweet;
Life and peace I find, reposing
  At Thy blessed feet!

When I call on thee, O Mary,
  When I think on thee,
Joy and pleasure all-entrancing
  Fill my heart with glee.

If anon the clouds of sadness
  Rise within my heart,
When they hear thy name, O Mary,
  Straightway they depart.

Like a star on life's dark ocean,
  Shining o'er the wave,
Thou can'st guide my bark to harbor,
  Thou my soul canst save.

Under thy protecting mantle,
  Queen belov'd, I fly;
There I wish to live securely,
  There I hope to die.

If I chance my life to finish,
  Mary, loving thee,
Then I also know, dear Lady,
  Heaven is for me.

Cast thy gentle bonds around me,
  And my heart enchain,
Prisoner of love forever
  Safe will I remain.

Thus my heart, O sweetest Mary,
  Is not mine, but thine ;
Take it ; give it all to Jesus ;
  Ne'er shall it be mine.

IV.

The Name of Mary.

MOTHER MARY, Queen most sweet !
  Joy and love my heart inflame ;
Gladly shall my lips repeat
  Every moment thy dear name.

Ah ! that name, to God so dear,
  Has my heart and soul enslaved ;
Like a seal it shall appear
  Deep on heart and soul engraved.

When the morning gilds the skies,
  I will call on Mary's name ;
When at evening twilight dies,
  Mary, still will I exclaim.

Sweetest Mary, bend thine ear :
  Thou my own dear Mother art ;
Therefore shall thy name so dear,
  Never from lips depart.

If my soul is sore oppress'd
  By a load of anxious care,
Peace once more will fill my breart
  When thy name re-echoes there.

Waves of doubt disturb my peace,
  And my heart is faint with fear;
At thy name the billows cease,
  All my terrors disappear.

When the demon hosts invade,
  When temptation rages high,
Crying, " Mary, Mother! aid!"
  I will make the tempter fly.

This shall be my comfort sweet,
  When the hand of death is nigh,
Mary! Mary! to repeat
  Once again,—and then, to die.

It must be observed that this last hymn, "The Name of Mary," is not by St. Alphonsus, but by Father Apice.—ED.

PART THE SECOND.

DISCOURSES ON THE PRINCIPAL FEASTS OF MARY.

DISCOURSE I.

MARY'S IMMACULATE CONCEPTION.

Dec. 8.

How befitting it was that each of the Three Divine Persons should preserve Mary from Original Sin.

GREAT indeed was the injury entailed on Adam and all his posterity by his accursed sin; for at the same time that he thereby, for his own great misfortune, lost grace, he also forfeited all the other precious gifts with which he had originally been enriched, and drew down upon himself and all his descendants the hatred of God and an accumulation of evils. But from this general misfortune God was pleased to exempt that Blessed Virgin whom he had destined to be the Mother of the Second Adam—Jesus Christ—who was to repair the evil done by the first. Now, let us see how befitting it was that God, and all the three divine Persons, should thus preserve her from it; that the Father should preserve her as his daughter, the Son as his Mother, and the Holy Ghost as his Spouse.

I.

In the first place, it was befitting that the Eternal Father should preserve Mary from the stain of original sin, because she was his daughter, and his first-born daughter, as she herself declares: *I came out of the mouth of the Most High, the first-born before all creatures.*[1] For this text is applied to Mary by sacred interpreters, the holy Fathers, and by the Church on the solemnity of her Conception. For whether she be the first-born inasmuch as she was predestined in the divine decrees, together with the Son, before all creatures, according to the Scotists; or the first-born of grace as the predestined Mother of the Redeemer, after the prevision of sin, according to the Thomists; nevertheless all agree in calling her the first-born of God. This being the case, it was quite becoming that Mary should never have been the slave of Lucifer, but only and always possessed by her Creator; and this she in reality was, as we are assured by herself: *The Lord possessed me in the beginning of His ways.*[2] Hence Denis of Alexandria rightly calls Mary "the one and only daughter of life."[3] She is the one and only daughter of life, in contradistinction to others who, being born in sin, are daughters of death.

Besides this, it was quite becoming that the Eternal Father should create her in his grace, since he destined her to be the repairer of the lost world, and the mediatress of peace between men and God; and, as such she is looked upon and spoken of by the holy Fathers, and in particular by St. John Damascene, who thus addresses her: "O Blessed Virgin, thou wast born that thou mightest minister to the salvation of the whole world."[4] For this reason St. Bernard says "that Noah's ark was a type of Mary; for as, by its means, men were preserved

---

[1] "Ego ex ore Altissimi prodivi, primogenita ante omnem creaturam."—*Ecclus.* xxiv. 5.

[2] "Dominus possedit me in initio viarum suarum."—*Prov.* viii. 22.

[3] "Una et sola. Filia vitæ."—*Ep. contra Paul. Sam.*

[4] "In vitam prodiisti, ut orbis universi Administram te præberes."—*De Nat. B. V.* s. 1.

from the deluge, so are we all saved by Mary from the shipwreck of sin: but with the difference, that in the ark few were saved, and by Mary the whole human race was rescued from death."[1] Therefore, in a sermon found amongst the works of St. Athanasius, she is called "the new Eve, and the Mother of life;"[2] and not without reason, for the first was the Mother of death, but the most Blessed Virgin was the Mother of true life. St. Theophanius, of Nice, addressing Mary, says, "Hail, thou who hast taken away Eve's sorrow!"[3] St. Basil of Seleucia calls her the peace-maker between men and God: "Hail thou who art appointed umpire between God and men!" and St. Ephrem, the peace-maker of the whole world: "Hail, reconciler of the whole world!"[4]

But now, it certainly would not be becoming to choose an enemy to treat of peace with the offended person, and still less an accomplice in the crime itself. St. Gregory[5] says, "that an enemy cannot undertake to appease his judge, who is at the same time the injured party; for if he did, instead of appeasing him, he would provoke him to greater wrath." And therefore, as Mary was to be the mediatress of peace between men and God, it was of the utmost importance that she should not herself appear as a sinner and as an enemy of God, but that she should appear in all things as a friend, and free from every stain.

Still more was it becoming that God should preserve her from original sin, for he destined her to crush the head of that infernal serpent, which, by seducing our first parents, entailed death upon all men: and this our

---

[1] "Sicut per illam omnes evaserunt diluvium, sic per istam peccati naufragium; per illam paucorum facta est liberatio, per istam humani generis salvatio."—*S. de B. M. Deip*

[2] "Nova Eva, Mater vitæ."—*In Annunt.*

[3] "Salve, quæ sustulisti tristitiam Evæ."—*Men. Græc.* 9 *Jan. Od.* 8.

[4] "Ave, totius orbis Conciliatrix!"—*De Laud. Dei Gen*

[5] *Past.* p. I, c. II.

Lord foretold: *I will put enmities between thee and the woman, and thy seed and her seed : she shall crush thy head.*[1] But if Mary was to be that valiant woman brought into the world to conquer Lucifer, certainly it was not becoming that he should first conquer her, and make her his slave; but it was reasonable that she should be preserved from all stain, and even momentary subjection to her opponent. The proud spirit endeavored to infect the most pure soul of this Virgin with his venom, as he had already infected the whole human race. But praised and ever blessed be God, who, in his infinite goodness, pre-endowed her for this purpose with such great grace, that, remaining always free from any guilt of sin, she was ever able to beat down and confound his pride, as St. Augustine, or whoever may be the author of the commentary on Genesis, says: "Since the devil is the head of original sin, this head it was that Mary crushed: for sin never had any entry into the soul of this Blessed Virgin, which was consequently free from all stain."[2] And St. Bonaventure more expressly says, "It was becoming that the Blessed Virgin Mary, by whom our shame was to be blotted out, and by whom the devil was to be conquered, should never, even for a moment, have been under his dominion."[3]

But, above all, it principally became the Eternal Father to preserve this his daughter unspotted by Adam's sin, as St. Bernardine of Sienna remarks, because he destined her to be the Mother of his only begotten Son: "Thou wast preordained in the mind of God, before all crea-

[1] "Inimicitias ponam inter te et mulierem, et semen tuum et semen illius; ipsa conteret caput tuum."—*Gen.* iii. 15.

[2] "Cum subjectio originalis peccati caput sit diaboli, tale caput Maria contrivit; quia nulla peccati subjectio ingressum habuit in animam Virginis, et ideo ab omni macula immunis fuit."

[3] "Congruum erat ut Beata Virgo Maria, per quam aufertur nobis opprobrium, vinceret diabolum, ut nec ei succumberet ad modicum." —*In Sent.* iii. d. 3, p. 1, a. 2, q. 1.

tures, that thou mightest beget God himself as man." [1]
If, then, for no other end, at least for the honor of his
Son, who was God, it was reasonable that the Father
should create Mary free from every stain. The angelic
St. Thomas says, that all things that are ordained for
God should be holy and free from stain: "Holiness is
to be attributed to those things that are ordained for
God." [2] Hence when David was planning the temple of
Jerusalem, on a scale of magnificence becoming a God,
he said, *For a house is prepared not for man, but for God.* [3]
How much more reasonable, then, is it not, to suppose
that the sovereign architect, who destined Mary to be
the Mother of his own Son, adorned her soul with all
most precious gifts, that she might be a dwelling worthy
of a God! Denis the Carthusian says, "that God, the
artificer of all things, when constructing a worthy dwelling for his Son, adorned it with all attractive graces." [4]
And the Holy Church herself, in the following prayer,
assures us that God prepared the body and soul of the
Blessed Virgin so as to be a worthy dwelling on earth
for his only-begotten Son: "Almighty and Eternal God,
who, by the co-operation of the Holy Ghost, didst prepare the body and soul of the glorious Virgin and Mother
Mary, that she might become a worthy habitation for
thy Son." [5]

[1] "Tu ante omnem creaturam in mente Dei præordinata fuisti, ut
Deum ipsum hominem procreares."—*Pro Fest. V. M.* s. 4, a. 3, c. 4.

[2] "Sanctitas illis rebus attribuitur, quæ in Deum ordinantur."—P.
I, q. 36, a. I.

[3] "Nec enim homini præparatur habitatio, sed Deo."—I *Par.*
xxix. I.

[4] "Omnium Artifex, Deus, Filio suo dignum habitaculum fabrica-
turus, eam omnium gràtificantium charismatum adornavit."—*De
Laud. V.* l. 2, a. 2.

[5] "Omnipotens sempiterne Deus, qui gloriosæ Virginis Matris
Mariæ corpus et animam, ut dignum Filii tui habitaculum effici mere-
retur, Spiritu Sancto cooperante, præparasti."

We know that a man's highest honor is to be born of noble parents: *And the glory of children are their fathers.*[1] Hence in the world the reputation of being possessed of only a small fortune, and little learning, is more easily tolerated than that of being of low birth; for, whilst a poor man may become rich by his industry, an ignorant man learned by study, it is very difficult for a person of humble origin to attain the rank of nobility; but, even should he attain it, his birth can always be made a subject of reproach to him. How, then, can we suppose that God, who could cause his Son to be born of a noble mother by preserving her from sin, would on the contrary permit him to be born of one infected by it, and thus enable Lucifer always to reproach him with the shame of having a mother who had once been his slave and the enemy of God? No, certainly, the Eternal Father did not permit this; but he well provided for the honor of his Son by preserving his Mother always immaculate, that she might be a Mother becoming such a Son. The Greek Church bears witness to this, saying, "that God, by a singular Providence, caused the most Blessed Virgin to be as perfectly pure from the very first moment of her existence, as it was fitting that she should be, who was to be the worthy Mother of Christ."[2]

It is a common axiom amongst theologians that no gift was ever bestowed on any creature with which the Blessed Virgin was not also enriched. St. Bernard says on this subject, "It is certainly not wrong to suppose that that which has evidently been bestowed, even only on a few, was not denied to so great a Virgin."[3] St.

---

[1] " Gloria filiorum patres eorum."—*Prov.* xvii. 6.

[2] " Providentia singulari perfecit, ut Sanctissima Virgo, ab ipso vitæ suæ principio, tam omnino existeret pura, quam decebat illam quæ Christo digna existeret."—*Menol.* 25 *Mart.*

[3] "Quod vel paucis mortalium constat fuisse collatum, fas certe non est suspicari tantæ Virgini esse negatum."—*Epist.* 174.

Thomas of Villanova says, "Nothing was ever granted to any saint which did not shine in a much higher degree in Mary from the very first moment of her existence."[1] And as it is true that "there is an infinite difference between the Mother of God and the servants of God,"[2] according to the celebrated saying of St. John Damascene, we must certainly suppose, according to the doctrine of St. Thomas, that "God conferred privileges of grace in every way greater on his Mother than on his servants."[3] And now admitting this, St. Anselm, the great defender of the Immaculate Mary, takes up the question and says, "Was the wisdom of God unable to form a pure dwelling, and to remove every stain of human nature from it?"[4] Perhaps God could not prepare a clean habitation for his Son by preserving it from the common contagion? "God," continues the same saint, "could preserve angels in heaven spotless, in the midst of the devastation that surrounded them; was he, then, unable to preserve the Mother of his Son and the Queen of angels from the common fall of men?"[5] And I may here add, that as God could grant Eve the grace to come immaculate into the world, could he not, then, grant the same favor to Mary?

Yes indeed! God could do this, and did it; for on every account "it was becoming," as the same St. Anselm says, "that that Virgin, on whom the Eternal Father intended to bestow his only-begotten Son, should be adorned with

[1] "Nihil unquam alicui Sanctorum concessum est, quod non a principio vitæ accumulatius perfulgeat in Maria."—*De Ass. conc.* I.

[2] "Matris Dei et servorum Infinitum est discrimen."—*De Dorm. B. M.* or. I.

[3] "Quod præ omnibus aliis majora privilegia gratiæ acceperit."—P. 3, q. 27, a. I.

[4] "Impotensne fuit sapientia Dei mundum sibi habitaculum condere, remota omni labe conditionis humanæ?"

[5] "Angelis aliis peccantibus, bonos a peccatis servavit; et Matrem ab aliorum peccatis exsortem servare non valuit?"—*De Conc. B. M.*

such purity as not only to exceed that of all men and
angels, but exceeding any purity that can be conceived
after that of God."[1]   And St. John Damascene speaks
in still clearer terms; for he says, "that our Lord had
preserved the soul, together with the body of the Blessed
Virgin, in that purity which became her who was to receive a God into her womb; for, as he is holy, he only
reposes in holy places."[2]   And thus the Eternal Father
could well say to his beloved daughter, *As the lily among
thorns, so is my love among the daughters*.[3]   My daughter,
amongst all my other daughters, thou art as a lily in the
midst of thorns; for they are all stained with sin, but
thou wast always immaculate, and always my beloved.

II.

In the second place, it was becoming that the Son should
preserve Mary from sin, as being his Mother.   No man
can choose his mother; but should such a thing ever be
granted to any one, who is there who, if able to choose
a queen, would wish for a slave?   If able to choose a
noble lady, would he wish for a servant?   Or if able to
choose a friend of God, would he wish for his enemy?
If, then, the Son of God alone could choose a Mother according to his own heart, his liking, we must consider,
as a matter of course, that he chose one becoming a
God.   St. Bernard says, "that the Creator of men becoming man, must have selected himself a Mother whom
he knew became him."[4]   And as it was becoming that

[1] "Decens erat ut ea puritate, qua major sub Deo nequit intelligi,
Virgo illa niteret, cui Deus Pater unicum Filium suum dare dispone-
bat."—*De Conc. Virg.* c. 18.

[2] "Sic Virginis una cum corpore animam conservasset, ut eam decebat quæ Deum in sinu suo exceptura erat; sanctus enim ipse cum
sit, in sanctis requiescit."—*De Fide Orth.* l. 4, c. 15.

[3] "Sicut lilium inter spinas, sic Amica mea inter filias."—*Cant.* ii. 2.

[4] "Factor hominum, nasciturus de homine, talem sibi debuit
eligere Matrem, qualem se decere sciebat."—*De Laud. V. M. hom.* 2.

a most pure God should have a mother pure from all sin, he created her spotless. St. Bernardine of Sienna, speaking of the different degrees of sanctification, says, that " the third is that obtained by becoming the Mother of God; and that this sanctification consists in the entire removal of original sin. This is what took place in the Blessed Virgin: truly God created Mary such, both as to the eminence of her nature and the perfection of grace with which he endowed her, as became him who was to be born of her." [1] Here we may apply the words of the Apostle to the Hebrews: *For it was fitting that we should have such a high priest; holy, innocent, undefiled, separated from sinners.* [2] A learned author observes that, according to St. Paul, it was fitting that our Blessed Redeemer should not only be separated from sin, but also from sinners; according to the explanation of St. Thomas, who says, " that it was necessary that he, who came to take away sins, should be separated from sinners, as to the fault under which Adam lay." [3] But how could Jesus Christ be said to be separated from sinners if he had a Mother who was a sinner?

St. Ambrose says, " that Christ chose this vessel into which he was about to descend, not of earth, but from heaven; and he consecrated it a temple of purity." [4] The saint refers to the text of St. Paul: *The first man was of*

[1] " Tertia fuit sanctificatio maternalis, et hæc removet culpam originalem. Hæc fuit in Beata Virgine; sane Deus talem, tam nobilitate naturæ, quam perfectione gratiæ, condidit matrem, qualem eam decebat habere suam majestatem."—*Pro Fest. V. M.* s. 4, a. 1, c. 1.

[2] " Talis enim decebat ut nobis esset Pontifex, sanctus, innocens, impollutus, segregatus a peccatoribus."—*Heb.* vii. 26.

[3] " Oportuit eum, qui peccata venerat tollere, esse a peccatoribus segregatum, quantum ad culpam cui Adam subjacuit."—P. 3, q. 4, a. 6.

[4] " Non de terra, sed de cœlo. Vas sibi hoc, per quod descenderet, Christus elegit, et sacravit Templum pudoris."—*Inst. virg.* c. 5.

the earth, earthly: the second man from heaven, heavenly.[1]
The saint calls the divine Mother "a heavenly vessel,"
not because Mary was not earthly by nature, as heretics
have dreamt, but because she was heavenly by grace;
she was as superior to the angels of heaven in sanctity
and purity, as it was becoming that she should be, in
whose womb a king of glory was to dwell. This agrees
with that which St. John the Baptist revealed to St.
Bridget, saying, "It was not becoming that the King of
Glory should repose otherwise than in a chosen vessel,
exceeding all men and angels in purity."[2] And to this
we may add that which the Eternal Father himself said
to the same saint: "Mary was a clean and an unclean
vessel: clean, for she was all fair; but unclean, because
she was born of sinners; though she was conceived
without sin, that my Son might be born of her without
sin."[3] And remark these last words, "Mary was conceived without sin, that the divine Son might be born of
her without sin." Not that Jesus Christ could have contracted sin; but that he might not be reproached with
even having a mother infected with it, who would consequently have been the slave of the devil.

The Holy Ghost says that *the glory of a man is from the
honor of his father, and a father without honor is the disgrace
of the son.*[4] "Therefore it was," says an ancient writer,
that Jesus preserved the body of Mary from corruption

---

[1] "Primus homo de terra, terrenus; secundus homo de cœlo,
cœlestis."—1 *Cor.* xv. 47.

[2] "Non decuit Regem gloriæ jacere, nisi in Vase purissimo et mundissimo et electissimo præ omnibus Angelis et hominibus."—*Rev.* l.
1, c. 31.

[3] "Maria fuit Vas mundum, et non mundum; mundum, quia tota
pulchra; sed non mundum, quia de peccatoribus nata est, licet sine
peccato concepta, ut Filius meus de ea sine peccato nasceretur."—
Rev. l. 5, r. 13, *exp.*

[4] "Gloria enim hominis, ex honore patris ejus; et dedecus filii, pater
sine honore."—*Ecclus.* iii. 13.

after death; for it would have redounded to his dishonor had that virginal flesh with which he had clothed himself become the food of worms." For he adds, "Corruption is a disgrace of human nature; and as Jesus was not subject to it, Mary was also exempted; for the flesh of Jesus is the flesh of Mary."[1] But since the corruption of her body would have been a disgrace for Jesus Christ, because he was born of her, how much greater would the disgrace have been, had he been born of a mother whose soul was once infected with the corruption of sin? For not only is it true that the flesh of Jesus is the same as that of Mary, "but," adds the same author, "the flesh of our Saviour, even after his resurrection, remained the same that he had taken from his Mother." "The flesh of Christ is the flesh of Mary; and though it was glorified by the glory of his resurrection, yet it remains the same that was taken from Mary."[2] Hence the Abbot Arnold of Chartres says, "The flesh of Mary and that of Christ are one; and therefore I consider the glory of the Son as being not so much common to, as one with, that of his Mother."[3] And now if this is true. supposing that the Blessed Virgin was conceived in sin, though the Son could not have contracted its stain, nevertheless his having united flesh to himself which was once infected with sin, a vessel of uncleanness and subject to Lucifer, would always have been a blot.

Mary was not only the Mother, but the worthy Mother of our Saviour. She is called so by all the holy Fathers. St. Bernard says, "Thou alone wast found worthy to be

[1] "Putredo namque humanæ est opprobrium conditionis. a quo cum Jesus sit alienus, natura Mariæ excipitur; caro enim Jesu, caro Mariæ est."

[2] "Caro Jesu, caro est Mariæ; et quamvis gloria resurrectionis fuerit magnificata, eadem tamen mansit, quæ suscepta est de Maria."—*Lib. de Ass.* c. 5.

[3] "Una est Mariæ et Christi caro; Filii gloriam cum Matre non tam communem judico, quam eandem.—*De Laud. B. M. V.*

chosen as the one in whose virginal womb the King of
kings should have his first abode."[1]   St. Thomas of Villanova says, " Before she conceived she was already fit
to be the Mother of God."[2]   The holy Church herself
attests that Mary merited to be the Mother of Jesus
Christ, saying, "the Blessed Virgin, who merited to bear
in her womb Christ our Lord;"[3] and St. Thomas Aquinas,
explaining these words, says, that "the Blessed Virgin
is said to have merited to bear the Lord of all; not that
she merited his incarnation, but that she merited, by the
graces she had received, such a degree of purity and
sanctity, that she could becomingly be the Mother of
God;"[4] that is to say, Mary could not merit the Incarnation of the Eternal Word, but by divine grace she merited
such a degree of perfection as to render her worthy to be
the Mother of a God; according to what St. Augustine
also writes: " Her singular sanctity, the effect of grace,
merited that she alone should be judged worthy to receive a God."[5]

And now, supposing that Mary was worthy to be the
Mother of God, " what excellency and what perfection
was there that did not become her?"[6] asks St. Thomas
of Villanova.   The angelic Doctor says, " that when God
chooses any one for a particular dignity, he renders him

[1] " Tu sola inventa es digna, ut in tua virginali aula Rex regum
primam sibi mansionem elegerit."—*Depr. ad gl. V.*

[2] " Antequam conciperet, jam idonea erat, ut esset Mater Dei."—
De Nat. V. M. conc. 3.

[3] " Beata Virgo, cujus viscera meruerunt portare Dominum Christum."—*In Nat. D. resp.* 4.

[4] " Beata Virgo dicitur meruisse portare Dominum omnium, non
quia meruit ipsum incarnari, sed quia meruit, ex gratia sibi data, illum
puritatis et sanctitatis gradum, ut congrue posset esse Mater Dei."—
P. 3, q. 2, a. 11.

[5] " Promeruit hoc singularis sanctitas ejus et singularis gratia, qua
susceptione Dei singulariter æstimata est digna."—*Lib. de Ass.* c. 4.

[6] "Quæ autem excellentia, quæ perfectio, decuit eam, ut esset
idonea Mater Dei!"—*De Nat. V. M. conc.* 3.

fit for it;" whence he adds, "that God, having chosen Mary for his Mother, he also by his grace rendered her worthy of this highest of all dignities." "The Blessed Virgin was divinely chosen to be the Mother of God, and therefore we cannot doubt that God had fitted her by his grace for this dignity; and we are assured of it by the angel: *For thou hast found grace with God; behold thou shalt conceive.*[1] And thence the saint argues that "the Blessed Virgin never committed any actual sin, not even a venial one. Otherwise," he says, "she would not have been a mother worthy of Jesus Christ; for the ignominy of the Mother would also have been that of the Son, for he would have had a sinner for his mother."[2] And now if Mary, on account of a single venial sin, which does not deprive a soul of divine grace, would not have been a mother worthy of God, how much more unworthy would she have been had she contracted the guilt of original sin, which would have made her an enemy of God and a slave of the devil? And this reflection it was that made St. Augustine utter those memorable words, that, "when speaking of Mary for the honor of our Lord," whom she merited to have for her Son, he would not entertain even the question of sin in her; "for we know," he says, "that through him, who it is evident was without sin, and whom she merited to conceive and bring forth, she received grace to conquer all sin."[3]

[1] "Beata autem Virgo fuit electa divinitus, ut esset Mater Dei; et ideo non est dubitandum quin Deus, per suam gratiam, eam ad hoc idoneam reddiderit, juxta illud: 'Invenisti gratiam apud Deum: ecce, concipies in utero et paries Filium.'"—*Luke,* i. 50.

[2] "Non fuisset idonea Mater Dei, si peccasset aliquando, quia ignominia Matris ad Filium redundasset."—P. 3, q. 27, a. 4.

[3] "Excepta itaque Sancta Vírgine Maria, de qua, propter honorem Domini, nullam prorsus, cum de peccatis agitur, haberi volo quæstionem; unde enim scimus, quod ei plus gratiæ collatum fuerit ad vincendum ex omni parte peccatum, quæ concipere ac parere meruit, quem constat nullum habuisse peccatum."—*De Nat. et Gratia,* c. 36.

Therefore, as St. Peter Damian observes, we must consider it as certain "that the Incarnate Word chose himself a becoming Mother, and one of whom he would not have to be ashamed."[1] St. Proclus also says, "that he dwelt in a womb which he had created free from all that might be to his dishonor."[2] It was no shame to Jesus Christ, when he heard himself contemptuously called by the Jews the Son of Mary, meaning that he was the Son of a poor woman: *Is not His Mother called Mary?*[3] for he came into this world to give us an example of humility and patience. But, on the other hand, it would undoubtedly have been a disgrace, could he have heard the devil say, "Was not his Mother a sinner?[4] was he not born of a wicked Mother, who was once our slave?" It would even have been unbecoming had Jesus Christ been born of a woman whose body was deformed, or crippled, or possessed by devils: but how much more would it have been so, had he been born of a woman whose soul had been once deformed by sin, and in the possession of Lucifer!

Ah! indeed, God, who is wisdom itself, well knew how to prepare himself a becoming dwelling, in which to reside on earth: *Wisdom hath built herself a house.*[5] *The Most High hath sanctified His own tabernacle. . . . God will help it in the morning early.*[6] David says that our Lord sanctified this his dwelling *in the morning early;* that is to say, from the beginning of her life, to render her worthy of himself; for it was not becoming that a holy God should

---

[1] "Talem creavit eam, ut ipse digne nasci potuisset ex ea."- *De Nat. D.* s. 3.

[2] "Intra viscera, quæ citra ullam sui dedecoris notam creaverat habitavit."—*Laudat. in S. M. or.* 1.

[3] "Nonne mater ejus dicitur Maria?"—*Matt.* xiii. 55.

[4] "Nonne mater ejus exstitit peccatrix?"

[5] "Sapientia ædificavit sibi domum."—*Prov.* ix 1.

[6] "Sanctificavit tabernaculum suum Altissimus . . . Adjuvabit eam Deus mane diluculo "—*Ps.* xlv. 5.

choose himself a dwelling that was not holy: *Ho. ress becometh Thy house.*[1] And if God declares that he will never enter a malicious soul, or dwell in a body subject to sin. *for wisdom will not enter into a malicious soul, nor dwell in a body subject to sin,*[2] how can we ever think that the Son of God chose to dwell in the soul and body of Mary, without having previously sanctified and preserved it from every stain of sin? for, according to the doctrine of St. Thomas, "the Eternal Word dwelt not only in the soul of Mary, but even in her womb."[3] The holy Church sings, "Thou, O Lord, hast not disdained to dwell in the Virgin's womb."[4] Yes, for he would have disdained to have taken flesh in the womb of an Agnes, a Gertrude, a Teresa, because these virgins, though holy, were nevertheless for a time stained with original sin; but he did not disdain to become man in the womb of Mary, because this beloved Virgin was always pure and free from the least shadow of sin, and was never possessed by the infernal serpent. And therefore St. Augustine says, "that the Son of God never made himself a more worthy dwelling than Mary, who was never possessed by the enemy, or despoiled of her ornaments."[5] On the other hand, St. Cyril of Alexandria asks, "Who ever heard of an architect who built himself a temple, and yielded up the first possession of it to his greatest enemy?"[6]

Yes, says St. Methodius, speaking on the same subject,

---

[1] " Domum tuam decet sanctitudo."—*Ps.* xcii. 5.

[2] " In malevolam animam non introibit Sapientia nec habitabit in corpore subdito peccatis."—*Wisd.* i. iv.

[3] " Dei Filius in ipsa habitavit, non solum in anima, sed etiam in utero."—P. 3, q. 27. a. 4.

[4] " Non horruisti Virginis uterum."—*Hymn. Te Deum.*

[5] " Nullam digniorem domum sibi Filius Dei ædificavit quam Mariam, quæ nunquam fuit ab hostibus capta, neque suis ornamentis spoliata."

[6] " Quis unquam audivit architectum, qui sibi domum ædificavit, in ea habitare prohibitum fuisse?"—*In Conc. Eph. hom.* 6.

that Lord who commanded us to honor our parents, would not do otherwise, when he became man, than observe it, by giving his Mother every grace and honor: "He who said, Honor thy father and thy mother, that he might observe his own decree, gave all grace and honor to his Mother."[1] Therefore the author of the book already quoted from the works of St. Augustine says, "that we must certainly believe that Jesus Christ preserved the body of Mary from corruption after death; for if he had not done so, he would not have observed the law, which, at the same time that it commands us to honor our mother, forbids us to show her disrespect."[2] But how little would Jesus have guarded his Mother's honor, had he not preserved her from Adam's sin! "Certainly that son would sin," says the Augustinian Father Thomas of Strasburg, "who, having it in his power to preserve his mother from original sin, did not do so; but that which would be a sin in us," continues the same author, "must certainly be considered unbecoming in the Son of God, who, whilst he could make his Mother immaculate, did it not." "Ah, no," exclaims Gerson, "since Thou, the supreme prince, choosest to have a Mother, certainly Thou owest her honor. But now if Thou didst permit her, who was to be the dwelling of all purity, to be in the abomination of original sin, certainly it would appear that that law was not well fulfilled."[3]

"Moreover, we know," says St. Bernardine of Sienna,

[1] "Qui dixit: 'Honora patrem tuum et matrem,' ut decretum a se promulgatum servaret, omnem Matri gratiam et honorem impendit." —*De Sim. et Anna.*

[2] "Sicut honorem matris præcipit, ita inhonorationem damnat."— *Lib. de Ass.* c. 5.

[3] "Cum tu, summus Princeps, vis habere Matrem, illi debebis honorem; nunc autem appareret illam legem non bene adimpleri, si in hujusmodi abominatione peccati aliquo tempore permitteres illam, quæ esse debet habitaculum totius puritatis."—*De Conc. B. V.* s. 1.

" that the divine Son came into the world more to redeem Mary than all other creatures." [1] There are two means by which a person may be redeemed, as St. Augustine teaches us: the one by raising him up after having fallen, and the other by preventing him from falling;" [2] and this last means is doubtless the most honorable. " He is more honorably redeemed," says the learned Suarez, " who is prevented from falling, than he who after falling is raised up;" [3] for thus the injury or stain is avoided which the soul always contracts by falling. This being the case, we ought certainly to believe that Mary was redeemed in the more honorable way, and the one which became the Mother of God, as St. Bonaventure remarks; ' for it is to be believed that the Holy Ghost, as a very special favor, redeemed and preserved her from original sin by a new kind of sanctification, and this in the very moment of her conception; not that sin was in her, but that it otherwise would have been." [4] The sermon from which this passage is taken is proved by Frassen [5] to be really the work of the holy Doctor above named. On the same subject Cardinal Cusano beautifully remarks, that " others had Jesus as a liberator, but to the most Blessed Virgin he was a pre-liberator;" [6] meaning, that all others had a Redeemer who delivered them from sin

[1] " Christus plus pro ipsa redimenda venit, quam pro omni alia creatura."—*Pro Fest. V. M.* s. 4, a. 3, c. 3.

[2] " Duplex est redimendi modus; unus, erigendo lapsum; alter, præveniendo jamjam lapsurum, ne cadat."—*De Inc.* p. 2, d. 3, s. 5.

[3] " Nobilius redimitur, cui providetur ne cadat, quam ut lapsus erigatur."—P. 1, t. 8, c. 2.

[4] " Credendum est enim quod novo sanctificationis genere, in ejus conceptionis primordio, Spiritus Sanctus eam a peccato originali, non quod infuit, sed quod infuisset redemit, atque singulari gratia præser vavit.—*De B. V.* s. 2.

[5] *Scotus Academicus, de Inc.* d. 3. a. 3. s. 3, q. 1, § 5.

[6] " Præliberatorem enim Virgo Sancta habuit, cæteri Postliberato rem."—*Excit* l. 8. *Sicut lil.*

with which they were already defiled, but that the most
Blessed .Virgin had a Redeemer who, because he was
her Son, preserved her from ever being defiled by it.

In fine, to conclude this point in the words of Hugo
of St. Victor, the tree is known by its fruits. If the
Lamb was always immaculate, the Mother must also
have been always immaculate: "Such the Lamb, such
the Mother of the Lamb; for the tree is known by its
fruit."[1]   Hence this same Doctor salutes Mary, saying:
"O worthy mother of a worthy Son;" meaning, that no
other than Mary was worthy to be the mother of such a
Son, and no other than Jesus was a worthy Son of such
a Mother: and then he adds these words, "O fair Mother
of beauty itself, O high Mother of the Most High, O
Mother of God !"[2]   Let us then address this most Blessed
Mother in the words of St. Ildephonsus, "Suckle, O
Mary, thy Creator, give milk to him who made thee,
and who made thee such that he could be made of
thee."[3]

III.

Since, then, it was becoming that the Father should
preserve Mary from sin as his daughter, and the Son as
his Mother, it was also becoming that the Holy Ghost
should preserve her as his spouse.

St. Augustine says that " Mary was that only one who
merited to be called the Mother and Spouse of God."[4]
For St. Anselm asserts that " the divine Spirit, the love
itself of the Father and the Son, came corporally into

---

[1] " Talis Agnus. qualis Mater Agni; quoniam omnis arbor ex fructu
suo cognoscitur."—*De Verbo inc.* c. 3.

[2] "O Digna Digni ! Formosa Pulchri, Excelsa Altissimi, Mater
Dei!"—*De Assumpt.* c. 3.

[3] " Lacta, Maria. Creatorem tuum ; lacta eum qui fecit te, qui
talem fecit te,ut ipse fieret ex te." —*De Nat. B. V.* s. 1.

[4] " Hæc est quæ sola meruit Mater et Sponsa vocari."—*Serm.* 208,
E. B. app.

Mary, and enriching her with graces above all creatures, reposed in her and made her his Spouse, the Queen of heaven and earth."[1] He says that he came into her corporally, that is, as to the effect: for he came to form of her immaculate body the immaculate body of Jesus Christ, as the Archangel had already predicted to her· *The Holy Ghost shall come upon thee.*[2] And therefore it is, says St. Thomas, "that Mary is called the temple of the Lord, and the sacred resting-place of the Holy Ghost: for by the operation of the Holy Ghost she became the Mother of the Incarnate Word."[3]

And now, had an excellent artist the power to make his bride such as he could represent her, what pains would he not take to render her as beautiful as possible! Who, then, can say that the Holy Ghost did otherwise with Mary, when he could make her who was to be his spouse as beautiful as it became him that she should be? Ah no! he acted as it became him to act; for this same Lord himself declares: *Thou art all fair, O my love, and there is not a spot in thee.*[4] These words, say St. Ildephonsus and St. Thomas, are properly to be understood of Mary, as Cornelius à Lapide remarks; and St. Bernardine of Sienna,[5] and St. Laurence Justinian,[6] assert that they are to be understood precisely as applying to her Immaculate Conception; whence Blessed Raymond Jordano addresses her, saying, " Thou art all fair, O most

---

[1] "Ipse Spiritus Dei, ipse Amor Patris et Filii, corporaliter venit in eam, singularique gratia præ omnibus requievit in ea, et Reginam cœli et terræ fecit eam."—*De Excell. Virg.* c. 4.

[2] "Spiritus Sanctus superveniet in te."—*Luke.* i. 35.

[3] "Unde dicitur Templum Domini, Sacrarium Spiritus Sancti, quia concepit ex Spiritu Sancto."—*Exp. in Sal. Ang.*

[4] "Tota pulchra es, Amica mea, et macula non est in te."—*Cant.* iv. 7.

[5] *Pro Fest. V. M.* s. 4, a. 2, c. 2.

[6] *In Nat. B. V.*

glorious Virgin, not in part, but wholly; and no stain of mortal, venial, or original sin is in thee." [1]

The Holy Ghost signified the same thing when he called this his spouse an enclosed garden and a sealed fountain· *My sister, my spouse, is a garden enclosed, a fountain sealed up.* [2] "Mary," says St. Sophronius, "was this enclosed garden and sealed fountain, into which no guile could enter, against which no fraud of the enemy could prevail, and who always was holy in mind and body." St. Bernard likewise says, addressing the Blessed Virgin, "Thou art an enclosed garden, into which the sinner's hand has never entered to pluck its flowers." [4]

We know that this divine Spouse loved Mary more than all the other saints and angels put together, as Father Suarez, [5] with St. Laurence Justinian, and others, assert. He loved her from the very beginning, and exalted her in sanctity above all others, as it is expressed by David in the Psalms: *The foundations thereof are in the holy mountains : the Lord loveth the gates of Sion above all the tabernacles of Jacob . . . a man is born in her, and the Highest Himself hath founded her.* [6] Words which all signify that Mary was holy from her conception. The same thing is signified by other passages addressed to her by the Holy Ghost. In Proverbs we read : *Many daughters*

[1] "Tota pulchra es, Virgo gloriosissima! non in parte, sed in toto; et macula peccati, sive mortalis, sive venialis, sive originalis, non est in te."—*Cont. de V. M.* c. 2.

[2] "Hortus conclusus, soror mea, Sponsa, Hortus conclusus, Fons signatus."—*Cant.* iv. 12.

[3] "Hæc est Hortus conclusus, Fons signatus, ad quam nulli potuerunt doli irrumpere; nec prævaluit fraus inimici, sed permansit sancta mente et corpore."—*De Assumpt.*

[4] "Hortus conclusus tu es, ad quem deflorandum manus peccatorum nunquam introivit."—*Depr. ad gl. V.*

[5] *De Inc.* p. 2. d. 18. s. 4.

[6] "Fundamenta ejus in montibus sanctis; diligit Dominus portas Sion super omnia tabernacula Jacob . . . Homo natus est in ea: et ipse fundavit eam Altissimus."—*Ps* lxxxvi. r.

have gathered together riches: thou hast surpassed them all.[1] If Mary has surpassed all others in the riches of grace, she must have had original justice, as Adam and the angels had it. In the Canticles we read, *There are . . . young maidens without number. One is my dove, my perfect one* (in the Hebrew it is *my entire, my immaculate one*) *is but one, she is the only one of her mother*.[2] All just souls are daughters of divine grace; but amongst these Mary was the *dove* without the gall of sin, the *perfect* one without spot in her origin, the *one* conceived in grace.

Hence it is that the angel, before she became the Mother of God, already found her full of grace, and thus saluted her, *Hail, full of grace ;* on which words St. Sophronius writes, that "grace is given partially to other saints, but to the Blessed Virgin all was given."[3] So much so, says St. Thomas, that "grace not only rendered the soul, but even the flesh of Mary holy, so that this Blessed Virgin might be able to clothe the Eternal Word with it."[4] Now all this leads us to the conclusion that Mary, from the moment of her conception, was enriched and filled with divine grace by the Holy Ghost, as Peter of Celles remarks, "the plenitude of grace was in her ; for from the very moment of her conception the whole grace of the divinity overflowed upon her, by the outpouring of the Holy Ghost."[5]

---

[1] "Multæ filiæ congregaverunt divitias: tu supergressa es universas."—*Prov.* xxxi. 29.

[2] "Adolescentularum non est numerus; una est columba mea, perfecta mea. una est matris suæ."—*Cant.* vi. 7.

[3] "Bene ' Plena,' quia cæteris per partes præstatur, Mariæ vero simul se tota infudit plenitudo gratiæ."—*De Assumpt.*

[4] "Anima Beatæ Virginis ita fuit plena, quod ex ea refudit gratia in carnem, ut de ipsa conciperet Deum."—*Exp. in Sal. Ang.*

[5] "Simul in ea collecta est gratiæ plenitudo, quia ab exordio suæ conceptionis, aspersione Spiritus Sancti, tota Deitatis gratia est superfusa."—*De Pan.* c. 12.

Hence St. Peter Damian says, "that the Holy Spirit was about to bear her off entirely to himself, who was chosen and preëlected by God."[1]   The saint says "to bear her off," to denote the holy velocity of the divine Spirit in being beforehand in making this Spouse his own before Lucifer should take possession of her.

CONCLUSION.

I wish to conclude this discourse, which I have prolonged beyond the limits of the others, because our Congregation has this Blessed Virgin Mary, precisely under the title of her Immaculate Conception, for its principal Patroness. I say that I wish to conclude by giving in as few words as possible the reasons which make me feel certain, and which, in my opinion, ought to convince every one of the truth of so pious a belief, and which is so glorious for the divine Mother, that is, that she was free from original sin.

There are many Doctors who maintain that Mary was exempted from contracting even the debt of sin ; for instance, Cardinal Galatino,[2] Cardinal Cusano,[3] De Ponte,[4] Salazar,[5] Catharinus,[6] Novarino,[7] Viva,[8] De Lugo,[9] Egidio,[10] Denis the Carthusian,[11] and others. And this opinion is also probable ; for if it is true that the wills of all men were included in that of Adam, as being the head of all, and this opinion is maintained as probable by Gonet,[12] Habert,[13] and others, founded on the doctrine of

---

[1] "A Deo electam et præelectam, totam eam rapturus erat sibi Spiritus Sanctus."—*De Annunt.*

[2] *De Arc.* l. 7, *passim.*

[3] *Excit.* l. 8, *Sicut lil.*

[4] *In Cant.* l. 2, *exh.* 19.

[5] *Pro Imm. Conc.* c. 7.

[6] *De Pecc. orig.* c. *ult.*

[7] *Umbra Virg. exc.* 18.

[8] P. 8, d. 1, q. 2, a. 2.

[9] *De Inc.* d. 7, s. 3, 4.

[10] *De Imm. Conc.* l. 2, q. 4, a. 5.

[11] *De Dign. M.* l. 1, a. 13.

[12] *Clyp.* p. 2, tr. 5, d. 7, a. 2.

[13] *Tr. de Vit. et Pecc.* c. 7, § 1.

St. Paul, contained in the fifth chapter to the Romans.[1] If this opinion, I say, is probable, it is also probable that Mary did not contract the debt of sin ; for whilst God distinguished her from the common of men by so many graces, it ought to be piously believed that he did not include her will in that of Adam.

This opinion is only probable, and I adhere to it as being more glorious for my sovereign Lady. But I consider the opinion that Mary did not contract the sin of Adam as certain ; and it is considered so, and even as proximately definable as an article of faith (as they express it), by Cardinal Everard, Duval,[2] Raynauld,[3] Lossada,[4] Viva,[5] and many others. I omit, however, the revelations which confirm this belief, particularly those of St. Bridget, which were approved of by Cardinal Turrecremata, and by four Sovereign Pontiffs, and which are found in various parts of the sixth book of her Revelations.[6]

But on no account can I omit the opinions of the holy Fathers on this subject, whereby to show their unanimity in conceding this privilege to the divine Mother.

St. Ambrose says, "Receive me not from Sarah, but from Mary ; that it may be an uncorrupted Virgin, a Virgin free by grace from every stain of sin."[7]

Origen, speaking of Mary, asserts that "she was not infected by the venomous breath of the serpent."[8]

St. Ephrem, that "she was immaculate, and remote from all stain of sin."[9]

[1] *Rom.* v. 12.
[2] *De Pecc.* q. *ult.* a. 7.
[3] *Piet. Lugd. erga V. Imm.* n. 20.
[4] *Disc. Thomist. de Imm. Conc.*
[5] P. 8, d. 1, q. 2, a. 2.
[6] *Rev.* l. 6, c. 12, 49. 55.
[7] "Suscipe me non ex Sara, sed ex Maria, ut incorrupta sit Virgo, sed Virgo per gratiam ab omni integra labe peccati."—*In Ps.* cxviii. s. 22.
[8] "Nec serpentis venenosis afflatibus infecta est."—*In Div. hom.* 1.
[9] "Immaculata et ab omni peccati labe alienissima."—*Orat. ad Deip.*

An ancient writer, in a sermon, found amongst the works of St. Augustine, on the words "Hail, full of grace," says, "By these words the angel shows that she was altogether (remark the word 'altogether') excluded from the wrath of the first sentence, and restored to the full grace of blessing." [1]

The author of an old work, called the Breviary of St. Jerome, affirms that "that cloud was never in darkness, but always in light." [2]

St. Cyprian, or whoever may be the author of the work on the 77th Psalm, says, "Nor did justice endure that that vessel of election should be open to common injuries; for being far exalted above others, she partook of their nature, not of their sin." [3]

St. Amphilochius, that "He who formed the first Virgin without deformity, also made the second one without spot or sin." [4]

St. Sophronius, that "the Virgin is therefore called immaculate, for in nothing was she corrupt." [5]

St. Ildephonsus argues, that "it is evident that she was free from original sin." [6]

St. John Damascene says, that "the serpent never had any access to this paradise." [7]

---

[1] "Ave 'gratia plena!' Quibus verbis ostendit ex integro iram exclusam primæ sententiæ, et plenam benedictionis gratiam restitutam."—*Serm.* 123, *E. B. app.*

[2] "Nubes illa non fuit in tenebris, sed semper in luce."—*Brev. In Ps.* 77.

[3] "Nec sustinebat justitia ut illud Vas electionis communibus lassaretur injuriis; quoniam, plurimum a cæteris differens, natura communicabat, non culpa."—*De Chr. Op. De Nat.*

[4] "Qui antiquam illam virginem sine probro condidit, ipse et secundam sine nota et crimine fabricatus est."—*In S. Deip. et Sim.*

[5] "Virginem ideo dici immaculatam, quia in nullo corrupta est."—*In Conc. Œcum.* 6, *act.* 11.

[6] "Constat eam ab omni originali peccato fuisse immunem."—*Cont. Disp. de Virginit. M.*

[7] "Ad hunc paradisum serpens aditum non habuit."—*In Dorm. Deip. or.* 2.

St. Peter Damian, that " the flesh of the Virgin, taken from Adam, did not admit of the stain of Adam." [1]

St. Bruno affirms, " that Mary is that uncorrupted earth which God blessed, and was therefore free from all contagion of sin." [2]

St. Bonaventure, " that our Sovereign Lady was full of preventing grace for her sanctification; that is, preservative grace against the corruption of original sin." [3]

St. Bernardine of Sienna argues, that " it is not to be believed that he, the Son of God, would be born of a Virgin, and take her flesh, were she in the slightest degree stained with original sin." [4]

St. Laurence Justinian affirms, " that she was prevented in blessings from her very conception." [5]

The Blessed Raymond Jordano, on the words, *Thou hast found grace*, says, " thou hast found a singular grace, O most sweet Virgin, that of preservation from original sin." [6] And many other Doctors speak in the same sense.

But, finally, there are two arguments that conclusively prove the truth of this pious belief.

The first of these is the universal concurrence of the

---

[1] " Caro Virginis, ex Adam assumpta, maculas Adæ non admisit." —*In Assumpt.*

[2] " Hæc est incorrupta terra illa cui benedixit Dominus, ab omni propterea peccati contagione libera."—*In Ps.* ci.

[3] " Domina nostra fuit plena gratia præveniente in sua sanctificatione, gratia scilicet præservativa contra fœditatem originalis culpæ." —*De B. V.* s. 2.

[4] " Non est credendum, quod ipse Filius Dei voluerit nasci ex virgine, et sumere ejus carnem, quæ esset maculata ex aliquo peccato originali."—*Quadr.* s. 49, p. 1.

[5] " Ab ipsa sui conceptione, in benedictionibus est præventa."—*In Annunt.*

[6] " ' Invenisti gratiam; ' invenisti, O dulcissima Virgo! gratiam cœlestem: quia fuit in te ab originis labe præservatio."—*Cont. de V. M.* c. 6.

faithful. Father Egidius, of the Presentation,[1] assures us that all the religious Orders follow this opinion; and a modern author tells us that though there are ninety-two writers of the order of St. Dominic against it, nevertheless there are a hundred and thirty-six in favor of it, even in that religious body. But that which above all should persuade us that our pious belief is in accordance with the general sentiment of Catholics, is that we are assured of it in the celebrated bull of Alexander VII., *Sollicitudo omnium ecclesiarum,* published in 1661, in which he says, "This devotion and homage towards the Mother of God was again increased and propagated, ... so that the universities having adopted this opinion" (that is, the pious one) "already nearly all Catholics have embraced it."[2] And in fact this opinion is defended in the universities of the Sorbonne, Alcala, Salamanca, Coimbra, Cologne, Mentz, Naples, and many others, in which all who take their degrees are obliged to swear that they will defend the doctrine of Mary's Immaculate Conception. The learned Petavius mainly rests his proofs of the truth of this doctrine on the argument taken from the general sentiment of the faithful.[3] An argument, writes the most learned bishop Julius Torni, which cannot do otherwise than convince; for, in fact, if nothing else does, the general consent of the faithful makes us certain of the sanctification of Mary in her mother's womb, and of her Assumption, in body and soul, into heaven. Why, then, should not the same general feeling and belief, on the part of the faithful, also make us certain of her Immaculate Conception ?

The second reason, and which is stronger than the

---

[1] *De Imm. Conc.* l. 3, q. 6, a. 3.

[2] " Aucta rursus et propagata fuit pietas hæc et cultus erga Deiparam. . . . ita ut, accedentibus plerisque celebrioribus academiis ad hanc sententiam, jam fere omnes Catholici eam amplectantur."

[3] *De Inc.* l. 14, c. 2.

first, that convinces us that Mary was exempt from original sin, is the celebration of her Immaculate Conception commanded by the universal Church. And on this subject I see, on the one hand, that the Church celebrates the first moment in which her soul was created and infused into her body : for this was declared by Alexander VII., in the above-named bull, in which he says that the Church gives the same worship to Mary in her Conception, which is given to her by those who hold the pious belief that she was conceived without original sin. On the other hand, I hold it as certain, that the Church cannot celebrate anything which is not holy, according to the doctrine of the holy Pope St. Leo,[1] and that of the Sovereign Pontiff St. Eusebius: " In the Apostolic See the Catholic religion was always preserved spotless." [2] All theologians, with St. Augustine,[3] St. Bernard,[4] and St. Thomas, agree on this point; and the latter, to prove that Mary was sanctified before her birth, makes use of this very argument: " The Church celebrates the nativity of the Blessed Virgin; but a feast is celebrated only for a saint: therefore the Blessed Virgin was sanctified in her mother's womb." [5] But if it is certain, as the angelic Doctor says, that Mary was sanctified in her mother's womb, because it is only on that supposition that the Church can celebrate her nativity, why are we not to consider it as equally certain that Mary was preserved from original sin from the first moment of her conception, knowing as we do that

[1] *Ep. decret.* 4, c. 2.

[2] " In Sede Apostolica, extra maculam semper et Catholica servata religio."—*Decr. causa* 24, q. 1, c. 1, c. *In sede.*

[3] *S.* 310, 314, *Ed. B.*

[4] *Epist.* 174.

[5] " Ecclesia celebrat Nativitatem Beatæ Virginis; non autem celebratur festum in Ecclesia, nisi pro aliquo Sancto: ergo Beata Virgo fuit in utero sanctificata."—*P.* 3, q. 27, a. 1.

it is in this sense that the Church herself celebrates the feast ?

Finally, in confirmation of this great privilege of Mary, we may be allowed to add the well-known innumerable and prodigious graces that our Lord is daily pleased to dispense throughout the kingdom of Naples, by means of the pictures of her Immaculate Conception.* I could refer to many which passed, so to say, through the hands of Fathers of our own Congregation;

---

* These effects of the divine mercy have shone forth in a no less wonderful manner in France and elsewhere, especially in 1832 and during the following years, by means of the miraculous medal of which every one has heard. Since the time when St. Alphonsus wrote this discourse and the dissertations that one may read on the same subject in his other works (*Theol. mor.* l. 7, c. 2.—*Opera dogm.* sess. 5), the devotion to " Mary conceived without sin" continued to grow throughout the Catholic world, being sustained and favored more and more by the Holy See, and by the signal marks of her heavenly protection. Finally, yielding to the multiplied solicitations of the Bishops, of the clergy, of the religious Orders, of the reigning sovereigns, and of the laity, Pope Pius IX., during the Pontifical Mass celebrated in the Basilica of the Vatican, December 8, 1854, in the presence of the bishops assembled from all parts of the world, solemnly pronounced the decree by which he defined as an article of faith, that the Blessed Virgin Mary had been protected and preserved from every stain of original sin from the first instant of her conception, in accordance with the text the Bull published the following day: *Definimus doctrinam, quæ tenet Beatissimam Virginem Mariam in primo instanti suæ conceptionis fuisse, singulari omnipotentia Dei gratia et privilegio, intuitu meritorum Christi Jesu, Salvatoris humani generis, ab omni originalis culpæ labe preservatam immunem, esse a Deo revelatam, atque idcirco ab omnibus fidelibus firmiter constanterque credendam.* This glorious event was hailed at Rome, as well as by the whole world, with extraordinary demonstrations of joy and gratitude. What pleasure, what delight must it have given in heaven to our saint, who during his life here below labored with so much zeal to bring about such a declaration, and who protested with an oath, as we see in the prayer that concludes this discourse, that he was ready to shed his blood in so beautiful a cause!—ED.

but I will content myself with two which are truly admirable.

EXAMPLES.

A woman came to a house of our little Congregation in this kingdom to let one of the Fathers know that her husband had not been to confession for many years, and the poor creature could no longer tell by what means to bring him to his duty; for if she named confession to him, he beat her. The Father told her to give him a picture of Mary Immaculate. In the evening the woman once more begged her husband to go to confession; but he as usual turned a deaf ear to her entreaties. She gave him the picture. Behold! he had scarcely received it, when he said, "Well, when will you take me to confession, for I am willing to go?" The wife, on seeing this instantaneous change, began to weep for joy. In the morning he really came to our church, and when the Father asked him how long it was since he had been to confession, he answered, "Twenty-eight years." The Father again asked him what had induced him to come that morning. "Father," he said, "I was obstinate; but last night my wife gave me a picture of our Blessed Lady, and in the same moment I felt my heart changed, so much so, that during the whole night every moment seemed a thousand years, so great was my desire to go to confession." He then confessed his sins with great contrition, changed his life, and continued for a long time to go frequently to confession to the same Father.

In another place, in the diocese of Salerno, in which we were giving a mission, there was a man who bore a great hatred to another who had offended him. One of our Fathers spoke to him that he might be reconciled; but he answered: "Father, did you ever see me at the sermons? No, and for this very reason, I do not go. I

know that I am damned; but nothing else will satisfy
me, I must have revenge." The Father did all that he
could to convert him; but seeing that he lost his time,
he said, " Here, take this picture of our Blessed Lady."
The man at first replied, " But what is the use of this
picture ?" But no sooner had he taken it, than, as if
he had never refused to be reconciled, he said to the
missionary, "Father, is anything else required besides
reconciliation ?—I am willing." The following morning
was fixed for it. When, however, the time came, he
had again changed, and would do nothing. The Father
offered him another picture, but he refused it; but at
length, with great reluctance, took it, when, behold! he
scarcely had possession of it than he immediately said,
Now let us be quick; where is Mastrodati ?" and he was
instantly reconciled with him, and then went to confession.

Prayer.

Ah, my Immaculate Lady! I rejoice with thee on seeing thee
enriched with so great purity. I thank, and resolve always to
thank, our common Creator for having preserved thee from
every stain of sin; and I firmly believe this doctrine, and am
prepared and swear even to lay down my life, should this be
necessary, in defence of this thy so great and singular privilege
of being conceived immaculate. I would that the whole world
knew thee and acknowledged thee as being that beautiful
" Dawn" which was always illumined with divine light; as that
chosen " Ark" of salvation, free from the common shipwreck of
sin; that perfect and immaculate "Dove" which thy divine
Spouse declared thee to be : that "enclosed Garden" which was
the delight of God; that "sealed Fountain" whose waters were
never troubled by an enemy; and finally, as that " white Lily,"
which thou art, and who, though born in the midst of the
thorns of the children of Adam, all of whom are conceived in
sin, and the enemies of God, wast alone conceived pure and
spotless, and in all things the beloved of thy Creator. Permit

me, then, to praise thee also as thy God himself has praised thee : *Thou art all fair, and there is not a spot in thee.*[1] O most pure Dove, all fair, all beautiful, always the friend of God. *O how beautiful art thou, my beloved! how beautiful art thou!*[2] Ah, most sweet, most amiable, immaculate Mary, thou who art so beautiful in the eyes of thy Lord,—ah, disdain not to cast thy compassionate eyes on the wounds of my soul, loathsome as they are. Behold me, pity me, heal me. O beautiful loadstone of hearts, draw also my miserable heart to thyself. O thou, who from the first moment of thy life didst appear pure and beautiful before God, pity me, who not only was born in sin, but have again since baptism stained my soul with crimes. What grace will God ever refuse thee, who chose thee for his daughter, his Mother, and Spouse, and therefore preserved thee from every stain, and in his love preferred thee to all other creatures? I will say, in the words of St. Philip Neri, "Immaculate Virgin, thou hast to save me." Grant that I may always remember thee ; and thou, do thou never forget me. The happy day, when I shall go to behold thy beauty in Paradise, seems a thousand years off ; so much do I long to praise and love thee more than I can now do, my Mother, my Queen, my beloved, most beautiful, most sweet, most pure, Immaculate Mary. Amen.

[1] "Tota pulchra es, Amica mea, et macula non est in te."—*Cant.* iv. 7.

[2] "Quam pulchra es, amica mea, quam pulchra es!"—*Ib.* i.

DISCOURSE II.

THE BIRTH OF MARY.

September 8.

Mary was born a saint, and a great saint; for the grace with which God enriched her from the beginning was great, and the fidelity with which she immediately corresponded to it was great.

MEN usually celebrate the birth of their children with great feasts and rejoicings; but they should rather pity them, and show signs of mourning and grief on reflecting that they are born, not only deprived of grace and reason, but worse than this—they are infected with sin and are children of wrath, and therefore condemned to misery and death. It is indeed right, however, to celebrate with festivity and universal joy the birth of our infant Mary; for she first saw the light of this world a babe, it is true, in point of age, but great in merit and virtue. Mary was born a saint, and a great saint. But to form an idea of the greatness of her sanctity, even at this early period, we must consider, first, the greatness of the first grace with which God enriched her; and secondly, the greatness of her fidelity in immediately corresponding to it.

I.

To begin with the first point, it is certain that Mary's soul was the most beautiful that God had ever created: nay more, after the work of the Incarnation of the Eternal Word, this was the greatest and most worthy of himself that an omnipotent God ever did in the world. St. Peter Damian calls it "a work only surpassed by

God." [1] Hence it follows that divine grace did not come into Mary by drops as in other saints, *but like rain on the fleece,* [2] as it was foretold by David. The soul of Mary was like fleece, and imbibed the whole shower of grace, without losing a drop. St. Basil of Seleucia says, " that the holy Virgin was full of grace, because she was elected and pre-elected by God, and the Holy Spirit was about to take full possession of her." [3] Hence she said, by the lips of Ecclesiasticus, *My abode is in the full assembly of saints ;* [4] that is, as St. Bonaventure explains it, " I hold in plenitude all that other saints have held in part." [5] And St. Vincent Ferrer, speaking particularly of the sanctity of Mary before her birth, says " that the Blessed Virgin was sanctified " (surpassed in sanctity) " in her mother's womb above all saints and angels." [6]

The grace that the Blessed Virgin received exceeded not only that of each particular saint, but of all the angels and saints put together, as the most learned Father Francis Pepe, of the Society of Jesus, proves in his beautiful work on the greatness of Jesus and Mary. And he asserts that this opinion, so glorious for our Queen, is now generally admitted, and considered as beyond doubt by modern theologians (such as Carthagena, Suarez, Spinelli, Recupito, and Guerra, who have professedly examined the question, and this was never done by the more ancient theologians). And besides this, he relates that the divine Mother sent

[1] " Videbis solum Opificem opus istud supergredi."—*In Nat. B. V.* s. 1.

[2] " Sicut pluvia in vellus."—*Ps.* lxxi. 6.

[3] " Virgo Sancta totam sibi hauserat Spiritus gratiam."—*Cat. aur. In Luc.* i. 47.

[4] " In plenitudine Sanctorum detentio mea."—*Ecclus.* xxiv. 16.

[5] " Totum teneo in plenitudine, quod alii Sancti tenent in parte."—*De B. V.* s. 3.

[6] " Virgo fuit sanctificata super omnes Sanctos et Angelos."—*De Nat. B. M.* s. 1.

Father Martin Guttierez to thank Father Suarez, on her part, for having so courageously defended this most probable opinion, and which, according to Father Segneri, in his "Client of Mary," was afterwards believed and defended by the University of Salamanca.

But if this opinion is general and certain, the other is also very probable; namely, that Mary received this grace, exceeding that of all men and angels together, in the first instance of her Immaculate Conception. Father Suarez[1] strongly maintains this opinion, as do also Father Spinelli,[2] Father Recupito,[3] and Father La Colombière.[4] But besides the authority of theologians, there are two great and convincing arguments, which sufficiently prove the correctness of the above-mentioned opinion.

I. The first is, that Mary was chosen by God to be the Mother of the divine Word. Hence Denis the Carthusian says,[5] that as she was chosen to an order superior to that of all other creatures (for in a certain sense the dignity of Mother of God, as Father Suarez asserts,[6] belongs to the order of hypostatic union), it is reasonable to suppose that from the very beginning of her life gifts of a superior order were conferred upon her, and such gifts as must have incomparably surpassed those granted to all other creatures. And indeed it cannot be doubted that when the Person of the Eternal Word was, in the divine decrees, predestined to make himself man, a Mother was also destined for him, from whom he was to take his human nature; and this Mother was our infant Mary. Now St. Thomas teaches that "God gives every one grace proportioned to the dignity for which he destines him."[7] And St. Paul teaches us the same

[1] *De Inc.* p. 2, d. 4. s. 1.   [3] *M. Deip.* c. 4.
[2] *Sign. Præd* 3.   [4] *Imm. Conc.* s. 1.
[5] *De Laud. V.* l. 1, 3, *passim.*   [6] *De Inc.* p. 2, d. 1, s. 2.
[7] "Unicuique a Deo datur gratia secundum hoc ad quod eligitur."
—P. 3 q 27, a 5.

thing when he says, *Who also hath made us fit ministers of the New Testament ;*[1] that is, the apostles received gifts from God, proportioned to the greatness of the office with which they were charged. St. Bernardine of Sienna adds, "that it is an axiom in theology, that when a person is chosen by God for any state, he receives not only the dispositions necessary for it, but even the gifts which he needs to sustain that state with decorum.[2] But as Mary was chosen to be the Mother of God, it was quite becoming that God should adorn her, in the first moment of her existence, with an immense grace, and one of a superior order to that of all other men and angels, since it had to correspond to the immense and most high dignity to which God exalted her. And all theologians come to this conclusion with St. Thomas, who says, "the Blessed Virgin was chosen to be the Mother of God ; and therefore it is not to be doubted that God fitted her for it by his grace ;"[3] so much so that Mary, before becoming Mother of God, was adorned with a sanctity so perfect that it rendered her fit for this great dignity. The holy Doctor says, " that in the Blessed Virgin there was a preparatory perfection, which rendered her fit to be the Mother of Christ, and this was the perfection of sanctification."[4]

And before making this last remark the holy Doctor had said that Mary was called full of grace, not on the

---

[1] "Qui et idoneos nos fecit ministros Novi Testamenti."—2 *Cor.* iii. 6.

[2] " Regula firma est in sacra theologia, quod, quandocunque Deus aliquem eligit ad aliquem statum, omnia dona illi dispensat, quæ illi statui necessaria sunt et illum copiose decorant."—*Pro Fest. V. M.* s. 10, a. 2, c. 1.

[3] " Virgo fuit electa Mater Dei; et ideo non est dubitandum quin Deus, per suam gratiam, eam ad hoc idoneam reddidit."

[4] "In Beata Virgine fuit perfectio quasi dispositiva, per quam reddebatur idonea ad hoc. quod esset Mater Christi, et hæc fuit perfectio sanctificationis."—P. 3 : 27 a. 4. 5.

part of grace itself, for she had it not in the highest
possible degree, since even the habitual grace of Jesus
Christ (according to the same holy Doctor) was not
such, that the absolute power of God could not have
made it greater, although it was a grace sufficient for
the end for which his humanity was ordained by the
divine Wisdom, that is, for its union with the Person of
the Eternal Word. Although the divine power could
make something greater and better than the habitual
grace of Christ, it could not fit it for anything greater
than the personal union with the only-begotten Son of
the Father, and to which union that measure of grace
sufficiently corresponds, according to the limit placed by
divine Wisdom.[1] For the same angelic Doctor teaches
that the divine power is so great, that, however much it
gives, it can always give more; and although the natural
capacity of creatures is in itself limited as to receiving,
so that it can be entirely filled, nevertheless its power to
obey the divine will is unlimited, and God can always
fill it more by increasing its capacity to receive. "As
far as its natural capacity goes, it can be filled; but it
cannot be filled as far as its power of obeying goes."[2]
But now to return to our proposition, St. Thomas says,
that the Blessed Virgin was not filled with grace, as to
grace itself, nevertheless she is called full of grace as to
herself, for she had an immense grace, one which was
sufficient, and corresponded to her immense dignity, so
much so that it fitted her to be the Mother of God: "The
Blessed Virgin is full of grace, not with the fulness of

---

[1] "Virtus divina, licet possit facere aliquid majus et melius quam
sit habitualis gratia Christi, non tamen posset facere quod ordinaretur
ad aliquid majus quam sit unio personalis ad Filium unigenitum a
Patre, cui unioni sufficienter correspondet talis mensura gratiæ,
secundum definitionem Divinæ Sapientiæ."—P. 3, q. 7, a. 12.

[2] "Potentia naturalis ad recipiendum potest tota impleri, potentia
obedientiæ non potest impleri."—*De Ver.* q. 29, a. 3, ad 3.

grace itself, for she had not grace in the highest degree of excellence in which it can be had, nor had she it as to all its effects; but she was said to be full of grace as to herself, because she had sufficient grace for that state to which she was chosen by God, that is, to be the Mother of his only-begotten Son." [1] Hence Benedict Fernandez says, "that the measure whereby we may know the greatness of the grace communicated to Mary is her dignity of Mother of God." [2]

It was not without reason, then, that David said that the foundations of this city of God, that is, Mary, are planted above the summits of the mountains: *The foundations thereof are in the holy mountains.* [3] Whereby we are to understand that Mary, in the very beginning of her life, was to be more perfect than the united perfections of the entire lives of the saints could have made her. And the Prophet continues: *The Lord loveth the gates of Sion above all the tabernacles of Jacob.* [4] And the same king David tells us why God thus loved her; it was because he was to become man in her virginal womb: *A man is born in her.* [5] Hence it was becoming that God should give this Blessed Virgin, in the very moment that he created her, a grace corresponding to the dignity of Mother of God.

Isaias signified the same thing, when he said that, in a time to come, a mountain of the house of the Lord

[1] "Beata Virgo est plena gratia, non ex parte ipsius gratiæ. quia non habuit gratiam in summa excellentia qua potest haberi, nec ad omnes effectus gratiæ; sed dicitur fuisse plena gratia per comparationem ad ipsam, quia scilicet habebat gratiam sufficientem ad statum illum ad quem erat electa a Deo, ut esset Mater Unigeniti ejus."—P 3, q 7. a. 10.

[2] "Est igitur dignitas Matris Dei regula, per quam metiendum est quidquid Virgini ab eo collatum credimus."

[3] "Fundamenta ejus in montibus sanctis."—*Ps.* lxxxvi. 1.

[4] "Diligit Dominus portas Sion super omnia tabernacula Jacob."

[5] "Homo natus est in ea."

(which was the Blessed Virgin) was to be prepared on the top of all other mountains; and that, in consequence, all nations would run to this mountain to receive the divine mercies. *And in the last days the mountain of the house of the Lord shall be prepared on the top of mountains, and it shall be exalted above the hills, and all nations shall flow unto it.*[1] St. Gregory, explaining this passage, says, " It is a mountain on the top of mountains; for the perfection of Mary is resplendent above that of all the saints."[2] And St. John Damascene, that it is "a mountain in which God was well pleased to dwell."[3] Therefore Mary was called a cypress, but a cypress of Mount Sion: she was called a cedar, but a cedar of Libanus : an olive-tree, but a fair olive-tree ;[4] beautiful, but beautiful as the sun ;[5] for as St. Peter Damian said, " As the light of the sun so greatly surpasses that of the stars, that in it they are no longer visible ; it so overwhelms them, that they are as if they were not ;"[6] "so does the great Virgin Mother surpass in sanctity the whole court of heaven."[7] So much so that St. Bernard beautifully re-marks, that the sanctity of Mary was so sublime, that "no other Mother than Mary became a God, and no other Son than God became Mary."[8]

---

[1] " Et erit in novissimis diebus præparatus mons Domus Domini in vertice montium, et elevabitur super colles; et fluent ad eum omnes gentes."—*Is.* ii. 2.

[2] " Mons quippe in vertice montium fuit, quia altitudo Mariæ supra omnes Sanctos refulsit."—*In 1 Reg.* i.

[3] " Mons in quo beneplacitum est Deo habitare in eo."—*Ps.* lxvii. 17.

[4] *Ecclus.* xxiv. 17, 19.

[5] *Cant.* vi. 9.

[6] " Siderum rapit positionem, ut sint quasi non sint."

[7] " Sic Virgo merita singulorum et omnium titulos antecedit."—*In Assumpt.*

[8] " Neque enim filius alius Virginem nec Deum decuit partus alter."—*In Assumpt.* s. 4.

II. The second argument by which it is proved that Mary was more holy in the first moment of her existence than all the saints together, is founded on the great office of mediatress of men, with which she was charged from the beginning; and which made it necessary that she should possess a greater treasure of grace from the beginning than all other men together. It is well known with what unanimity theologians and holy Fathers give Mary this title of mediatress, on account of her having obtained salvation for all, by her powerful intercession and her merit "of congruity," thereby procuring the great benefit of redemption for the lost world. I say by her merit of congruity, for Jesus Christ alone is our mediator by way of justice and by merit, "de condigno," as the scholastics say, he having offered his merits to the Eternal Father, who accepted them for our salvation. Mary, on the other hand, is a mediatress of grace, by way of simple intercession and merit of congruity, she having offered to God, as theologians say, with St. Bonaventure, her merits, for the salvation of all men; and God, as a favor, accepted them with the merits of Jesus Christ. On this account Arnold of Chartres says that "she effected our salvation in common with Christ."[1] And Richard of St. Victor says that "Mary desired, sought, and obtained the salvation of all; nay, even she effected the salvation of all."[2] So that everything good, and every gift in the order of grace, which each of the saints received from God, Mary obtained for them.

And the holy Church wishes us to understand this, when she honors the divine Mother by applying the following verses of Ecclesiasticus to her: *In me is all grace*

---

[1] "Cum Christo communem in salute mundi effectum obtinuit."—*De Laud. B. M.*

[2] "Omnium salutem desideravit, quæsivit, et obtinuit; imo salus omnium per ipsam facta est."—*In Cant.* c. 26.

of the way and the truth.[1] "Of the way," because by Mary
all graces are dispensed to wayfarers. "Of the truth,"
because the light of truth is imparted by her. *In me is
all hope of life and of virtue.*[2] "Of life," for by Mary we
hope to obtain the life of grace in this world, and that
of glory in heaven. "And of virtue," for through her
we acquire virtues, and especially the theological virtues, which are the principal virtues of the saints. *I am
the mother of fair love, and of fear, and of knowledge, and of
holy hope.*[3] Mary, by her intercession, obtains for her
servants the gifts of divine love, holy fear, heavenly
light, and holy perseverance. From which St. Bernard
concludes that it is a doctrine of the Church that Mary
is the universal mediatress of our salvation. He says :
"Magnify the finder of grace, the mediatress of salvation, the restorer of ages. This I am taught by the
Church proclaiming it ; and thus also she teaches me to
proclaim the same thing to others."[4]

St. Sophronius, Patriarch of Jerusalem, asserts that
the reason for which the Archangel Gabriel called her
full of grace, *Hail, full of grace!* was because only limited grace was given to others, but it was given to Mary
in all its plenitude : "Truly was she full ; for grace is
given to other saints partially, but the whole plenitude
of grace poured itself into Mary."[5] St. Basil of Seleucia declares that she received this plenitude that she
might thus be a worthy mediatress between men and
God : "Hail full of grace, mediatress between God and

---

[1] "In me gratia omnis vitæ et veritatis "—*Ecclus.* xxiv. 24.

[2] "In me omnis spes vitæ et virtutis."—*Ib.*

[3] " Ego mater pulchræ dilectionis, et timoris. et agnitionis, et sanctæ spei."—*Ib.*

[4] " Magnifica gratiæ Inventricem, Mediatricem salutis. Restaura-
tricem sæculorum. Hæc mihi de illa cantat ecclesia, et me eadem docuit decantare."—*Epist.* 174.

[5] " Bene ' Plena,' quia cæteris per partes præstatur, Mariæ vero se
tota infudit plenitudo gratiæ."—*De Assumpt.*

men, and by whom heaven and earth are brought together and united." [1] "Otherwise," says St. Laurence
Justinian, "had not the Blessed Virgin been full of divine grace, how could she have become the ladder to
heaven, the advocate of the world, and the most true
mediatress between men and God." [2]

The second argument has now become clear and evident. If Mary, as the already destined Mother of our
common Redeemer, received from the very beginning
the office of mediatress of all men, and consequently
even of the saints, it was also requisite from the very
beginning she should have a grace exceeding that of all
the saints for whom she was to intercede. I will explain
myself more clearly. If, by the means of Mary, all men
were to render themselves dear to God, necessarily
Mary was more holy and more dear to him than all
men together. Otherwise, how could she have inter-
ceded for all others? That an intercessor may obtain
the favor of a prince for all his vassals, it is absolutely
necessary that he should be more dear to his prince than
all the other vassals. And therefore St. Anselm concludes that Mary deserved to be made the worthy repairer of the lost world, because she was the most holy
and the most pure of all creatures. "The pure sanctity
of her heart, surpassing the purity and sanctity of all
other creatures, merited for her that she should be made
the repairer of the lost world." [3]

Mary, then, was the mediatress of men; it may be

---

[1] "'Ave, gratiæ Plena!' propterea Deum inter et homines Mediatrix intercedens."—*In Annunt.*

[2] "Quomodo non est Maria plena gratia, quæ effecta est paradisi
Scala, Interventrix mundi, Dei et hominum verissima Mediatrix?"—
De Annunt.

[3] "Pura sanctitas pectoris ejus, omnis creaturæ puritatem sive
sanctitatem transcendens, promeruit, ut Reparatrix perditi orbis dig-
nissime fieret."—*De Excell. V.* c. 9.

asked, but how can she be called also the mediatress of angels? Many theologians maintain that Jesus Christ merited the grace of perseverance for the angels also; so that as Jesus was their mediator *de condigno*, so also Mary may be said to be the mediatress even of the angels *de congruo*, she having hastened the coming of the Redeemer by her prayers. At least meriting *de congruo* to become the Mother of the Messiah, she merited for the angels that the thrones lost by the devils should be filled up. Thus she at least merited this accidental glory for them; and therefore Richard of St. Victor says, "By her every creature is repaired; by her the ruin of the angels is remedied; and by her human nature is reconciled." [1] And before him St. Anselm said, "All things are recalled and reinstated in their primitive state by this Blessed Virgin." [2]

Let us conclude that our heavenly child, because she was appointed mediatress of the world, as also because she was destined to be the Mother of the Redeemer, received, at the very beginning of her existence, grace exceeding in greatness that of all the saints together. Hence, how delightful a sight must the beautiful soul of this happy child have been to heaven and earth, although still enclosed in her mother's womb! She was the most amiable creature in the eyes of God, because she was already loaded with grace and merit, and could say, "When I was a little one I pleased the Most High." [3] And she was at the same time the creature above all others that had ever appeared in the world up to that moment, who loved God the most; so much so, that had Mary been born immediately after her most pure con-

---

[1] "Utraque creatura per hanc reparatur; et Angelorum ruina per hanc restaurata est, et humana natura reconciliata."—*In Cant.* c. 23.

[2] "Cuncta per hanc Virginem in statum pristinum revocata sunt et restituta."—*De Excell. V.* c. 11.

[3] "Cum essem parvula, placui Altissimo."—*Offic. B. V. resp.* 2.

ception, she would have come into the world richer in merits, and more holy, than all the saints united. Then let us only reflect how much greater her sanctity must have been at her nativity ; coming into the world after acquiring all the merits that she did acquire during the whole of the nine months that she remained in the womb of her mother.

II.

Now let us pass to the consideration of the second point, that is to say, the greatness of the fidelity with which Mary immediately corresponded to divine grace.

It is not a private opinion only, says a learned author, Father La Colombière,[1] but it is the opinion of all, that the holy child, when she received sanctifying grace in the womb of St. Anne, received also the perfect use of her reason, and was also divinely enlightened, in a degree corresponding to the grace with which she was enriched. So that we may well believe, that from the first moment that her beautiful soul was united to her most pure body, she, by the light she had received from the wisdom of God, knew well the eternal truths, the beauty of virtue, and above all, the infinite goodness of God ; and how much he deserved to be loved by all, and particularly by herself, on account of the singular gifts with which he had adorned and distinguished her above all creatures, by preserving her from the stain of original sin, by bestowing on her so immense grace, and destining her to be the Mother of the Eternal Word, and Queen of the universe.*

Hence from that first moment Mary, grateful to God, began to do all that she could do, by immediately and

[1] *Imm. Conc.* s. 2.

---

* The Blessed Virgin had, however, no explicit knowledge of her sublime destiny, as may be seen in the two following discourses.—ED.

faithfully trafficking with that great capital of grace which had been bestowed upon her ; and applying herself entirely to please and love the divine goodness, from that moment she loved him with all her strength, and continued thus to love him always, during the whole of the nine months preceding her birth, during which she never ceased for a moment to unite herself more and more closely with God by fervent acts of love. She was already free from original sin, and hence was exempt from every earthly affection, from every irregular movement, from every distraction, from every opposition on the part of the senses, which could in any way have hindered her from always advancing more and more in divine love : her senses also concurred with her blessed spirit in tending towards God. Hence her beautiful soul, free from every impediment, never lingered, but always flew towards God, always loved him, and always increased in love towards him.

It was for this reason that she called herself a plane-tree, planted by flowing waters: *As a plane-tree by the waters . . . was I exalted.*[1] For she was that noble plant of God which always grew by the streams of divine grace. And therefore she also calls herself a vine: *As a vine I have brought forth a pleasant odor.*[2] Not only because she was so humble in the eyes of the world, but because she was like the vine, which, according to the common proverb, " never ceases to grow." [3] Other trees —the orange-tree, the mulberry, the pear-tree—have a determined height, which they attain; but the vine always grows, and grows to the height of the tree to which it is attached. And thus did the most Blessed Virgin always grow in perfection. " Hail, then, O vine, always

---

[1] " Quasi platanus exaltata sum juxta aquam in plateis."—*Ecclus.* xxiv. 19.

[2] " Ego quasi vitis."—*Ib.* 23

[3] " Vitis nullo fine crescit."

growing !" [1] says St. Gregory Thaumaturgus; for she was always united to God, on whom alone she depended. Hence it was of her that the Holy Ghost spoke, saying, *Who is this that cometh up from the desert, flowing with delights, leaning upon her beloved?* [2] which St. Ambrose thus paraphrases: "She it is that cometh up, clinging to the Eternal Word, as a vine to a vine-stock." [3] Who is this accompanied by the divine Word, that grows as a vine planted against a great tree?

Many learned theologians say that a soul that possesses a habit of virtue, as long as it corresponds faithfully to the actual grace which it receives from God, always produces an act equal in intensity to the habit it possesses; so much so that it acquires each time a new and double merit, equal to the sum of all the merits previously acquired. This kind of augmentation was, it is said, granted to the angels in the time of their probation; and if it was granted to the angels, who can ever deny that it was granted to the divine Mother when living in this world, and especially during the time of which I speak, that she was in the womb of her mother, in which she was certainly more faithful than the angels in corresponding to divine grace? Mary, then, during the whole of that time, in each moment, doubled that sublime grace which she possessed from the first instant; for, corresponding to her whole strength, and in the most perfect manner in her every act, she subsequently doubled her merits in every instance. So that supposing she had a thousand degrees of grace in the first instance, in the second she had two thousand, in the third four thousand, in the fourth eight thousand, in the fifth six-

[1] " Ave vitis semper vigens!"—*In Ann. hom.* 1.

[2] "Quæ est ista, quæ ascendit de deserto, deliciis affluens, innixa super Dilectum suum?"—*Cant* viii. 5.

[3] " Hæc est quæ ascendit, ita ut inhæreat Dei Verbo sicut vitis propago."—*De Isaac et an.* c. 5.

teen thousand, in the sixth thirty-two thousand. And
we are as yet only at the sixth instance; but multiplied
thus for an entire day, multiplied for nine months, consider what treasures of grace, merit, and sanctity Mary
had already acquired at the moment of her birth!

Let us, then, rejoice with our beloved infant, who was
born so holy, so dear to God, and so full of grace. And
let us rejoice, not only on her account, but also on our
own; for she came into the world full of grace, not only
for her own glory, but also for our good. St. Thomas
remarks, in his eighth treatise, that the most Blessed
Virgin was full of grace in three ways: first, she was
filled with grace as to her soul, so that from the beginning her beautiful soul belonged all to God. Secondly,
she was filled with grace as to her body, so that she
merited to clothe the Eternal Word with her most pure
flesh. Thirdly, she was filled with grace for the benefit
of all, so that all men might partake of it: "She was
also full of grace as to its overflowing for the benefit of
all men." [1]   The angelical Doctor adds, that some saints
have so much grace that it is not only sufficient for
themselves, but also for the salvation of many, though
not for all men: only to Jesus Christ and to Mary was
such a grace given as sufficed to save all: "should any
one have as much as would suffice for the salvation of
all, this would be the greatest: and this was in Christ
and in the Blessed Virgin." [2]   Thus far St. Thomas. So
that what St. John says of Jesus, *And of His fulness we
all have received,* [3] the saints say of Mary. St. Thomas
of Villanova calls her " full of grace, of whose plenitude

[1] " Fuit etiam gratia plena, quantum ad refusionem in omnes
homines."

[2] " Sed quando haberet tantum quod sufficeret ad salutem omnium,
hoc esset maximum; et hoc est in Christo et in Beata Virgine."—*Exp.
in Sal. Ang.*

[3] " Et de plenitudine ejus nos omnes accepimus."—*John,* i. 16.

all receive;"[1] so much so that St. Anselm says, "that there is no one who does not partake of the grace of Mary."[2] And who is there in the world to whom Mary is not benign, and does not dispense some mercy? "Who was ever found to whom the Blessed Virgin was not propitious? Who is there whom her mercy does not reach?"[3]

From Jesus, however, it is (we must understand) that we receive grace as the author of grace, from Mary as a mediatress; from Jesus as a Saviour, from Mary as an advocate; from Jesus as a source, from Mary as a channel. Hence St. Bernard says, that God established Mary as the channel of the mercies that he wished to dispense to men; therefore he filled her with grace, that each one's part might be communicated to him from her fulness: "A full aqueduct, that others may receive of her fulness, but not fulness itself."[4] Therefore the saint exhorts all to consider, with how much love God wills that we should honor this great Virgin, since he has deposited the whole treasure of his graces in her: so that whatever we possess of hope, grace, and salvation, we may thank our most loving Queen for all, since all comes to us from her hands and by her powerful intercession. He thus beautifully expresses himself: "Behold with what tender feelings of devotion he wills that we should honor her! He who has placed the plenitude of all good in Mary; that thus, if we have any hope, or anything salu-

---

[1] "'Gratia plena,' de cujus plenitudine accipiunt universi."—*De Ann. conc.* 3.

[2] "Ita ut nullus sit, qui de plenitudine gratiæ Virginis non sit particeps."

[3] "Quis unquam reperitur, cui Virgo propitia non sit? Ad quem ejus misericordiæ non se extendunt?"—*Paciucchelli, In Salut. Ang. exc.* 15.

[4] "Plenus Aquæductus, ut accipiant cæteri de plenitudine, sed non plenitudinem ipsam."

tary in us, we may know that it was from her that it overflowed." [1]

Miserable is that soul that closes this channel of grace
against itself, by neglecting to recommend itself to Mary!
When Holofernes wished to gain possession of the city of
Bethulia, he took care to destroy the aqueducts: *He commanded their aqueduct to be cut off.*[2] And this the devil
does when he wishes to become master of a soul; he causes
it to give up devotion to the most Blessed Virgin Mary;
and when once this channel is closed, it easily loses supernatural light, the fear of God, and finally eternal salvation.
Read the following example, in which may be seen how
great is the compassion of the heart of Mary, and the destruction that he brings on himself who closes this channel
against himself, by giving up devotion to the Queen of
heaven.

EXAMPLE.*

There were two young noblemen in Madrid, of whom
the one encouraged the other in leading a wicked life, and
in committing all sorts of crimes. One of them one night
in a dream saw his friend taken by certain black men, and
carried to a tempestuous sea. They were going to take him
in a similar manner, but he had recourse to Mary, and
made a vow that he would embrace the religious state; on
which he was delivered from those blacks. He then saw
Jesus on a throne, as if in anger, and the Blessed Virgin
imploring mercy for him. After this his friend came to pay
him a visit, and he then related what he had seen; but his
companion only turned it into ridicule, and he was shortly
afterwards stabbed and died. When the young man saw

---

[1] "Intueamini, quanto devotionis affectu a nobis eam voluerit
honorari, qui totius boni plenitudinem posuit in Maria; ut proinde,
si quid spei in nobis est, si quid salutis, ab ea noverimus redundare."—*De Aquaed.*

[2] "Incidi præcepit aquæductum illorum."—*Judith,* vii. 6.

this his vision was verified, he went to confession, and renewed his resolution to enter a religious Order, and for this purpose he sold all that he had; but instead of giving it to the poor, as he had intended, he spent it in all sorts of debauchery. He then fell ill, and had another vision. He thought he saw hell open, and the divine Judge, who had already condemned him. Again he had recourse to Mary, and she once more delivered him. He recovered his health and went on worse than ever. He afterwards went to Lima in South America, where he relapsed into his former illness; and in the hospital of that place he was once more touched by the grace of God, confessed his sins to the Jesuit Father, Francis Perlino, and promised him that he would change his life; but again he fell into his former crimes. At last the same Father, going into another hospital in a distant place, saw the miserable wretch extended on the ground, and heard him cry out: "Ah, abandoned wretch that I am! for my greater torment this Father is come to witness my chastisement. From Lima I came hither, where my vices have brought me to this end; and now I go to hell." With these words he expired, without even leaving the Father time to help him.

Bovio, Es. e Mir. p. 3, *es.* 9.

Prayer.

O holy and heavenly Infant, Thou who art the destined Mother of my Redeemer and the great mediatress of miserable sinners, pity me. Behold at thy feet another ungrateful sinner who has recourse to thee and asks thy compassion. It is true, that for my ingratitude to God and to thee I deserve that God and thou should abandon me ; but I have heard, and believe it to be so (knowing the greatness of thy mercy), that thou dost not refuse to help any one who recommends himself to thee with confidence. O most exalted creature in the world ! since this is the case, and since there is no one but God above thee, so that compared with thee the greatest saints of heaven are little ; O saint of saints, O Mary ! abyss of charity, and full of grace, succor a miserable creature who by his own fault has lost the divine favor. I know that thou art so dear to God that he denies thee nothing. I know also that thy pleasure is to use thy greatness for the relief of miserable sinners. Ah, then, show how great is the favor that thou enjoyest with God, by obtaining me a divine light and flame so powerful that I may be changed from a sinner into a saint ; and detaching myself from every earthly affection, divine love may be enkindled in me. Do this, O Lady, for thou canst do it. Do it for the love of God, who has made thee so great, so powerful, and so compassionate. This is my hope. Amen.

DISCOURSE III.

THE PRESENTATION OF MARY.

November 21.

The Offering that Mary made of herself to God was prompt without delay, and entire without reserve.

THERE never was, and never will be, an offering on the part of a pure creature greater or more perfect than that which Mary made to God when, at the age of three years, she presented herself in the temple to offer him, not aromatical spices, nor calves, nor gold, but her entire self, consecrating herself as a perpetual victim in his honor. She well understood the voice of God, calling her to devote herself entirely to his love, when he said, *Arise, make haste, my love, my dove, my beautiful one, and come!* [1] Therefore her Lord willed that from that time she should forget her country, and all, to think only of loving and pleasing him: *Hearken, O daughter, and see, and incline thine ear; and forget thy people, and thy father's house.* [2] She with promptitude and at once obeyed the divine call. Let us, then, consider how acceptable was this offering which Mary made of herself to God; for it was prompt and entire. Hence the two points for our consideration are, first, Mary's offering was prompt and without delay; secondly, it was entire and without reserve.

I.

Mary's offering was prompt. From the first moment that this heavenly child was sanctified in her mother's

---

[1] " Surge, propera, Amica mea . . . et veni."—*Cant.* ii. 10.

[2] " Audi, Filia, et vide, et inclina aurem tuam ; et obliviscere populum tuum et domum patris tui."—*Ps.* xliv. 11.

womb, which was in the instant of her Immaculate Conception, she received the perfect use of reason, that she
might begin to merit. This is in accordance with the
general opinion of theologians, and with that of Father
Suarez in particular, who says, that as the most perfect
way in which God sanctifies a soul is by its own merit,
as St. Thomas also teaches,[1] it is thus we must believe
that the Blessed Virgin was sanctified : " To be sanctified by one's own act is the more perfect way. Therefore it is to be believed that the Blessed Virgin was thus
sanctified." [2]   And if this privilege was granted to the
angels, and to Adam, as the angelic Doctor says, much
more ought we to believe that it was granted to the
divine Mother, on whom, certainly, we must suppose that
God, having condescended to make her his Mother, also
conferred greater gifts than on all other creatures.
" From her," says the same holy Doctor, " He received
his human nature, and therefore she must have obtained
a greater plenitude of grace from Christ than all
others." [3]   " For being a mother," Father Suarez says,
" she has a sort of special right to all the gifts of her
Son ;" [4] and as, on account of the hypostatic union, it
was right that Jesus should receive the plenitude of all
graces, so, on account of the divine maternity, it was
becoming that Jesus should confer, as a natural debt,
greater graces on Mary than he granted to all other
saints and angels.

Thus, from the beginning of her life, Mary knew God,

---

[1] P. 3, q. 19, a. 3.

[2] "Sanctificari per proprium actum, est perfectior modus; ergo credendum est, hoc modo fuisse sanctificatam Virginem."—*De Inc.* p. 2,
d. 4. s. 8.

[3] " Ex ea accepit humanam naturam; et ideo præ cæteris majorem
debuit a Christo gratiæ plenitudinem obtinere."—P. 3, q. 27, a. 5.

[4] " Unde fit ut singulare jus habeat ad bona Filii sui."—*De Inc.* p.
2, d. 1, s. 2.

and knew him so that "no tongue" (as the angel declared to St. Bridget) "will ever express how clearly this Blessed Virgin understood his greatness in that very first moment of her existence." And thus enlightened, she instantly offered her entire self to her Lord, dedicating herself, without reserve, to his love and glory. "Immediately," the angel went on to say, "our Queen determined to sacrifice her will to God, and to give him all her love for the whole of her life. No one can understand how entire was the subjection in which she then placed her will, and how fully she was determined to do all according to his pleasure." [1]

But the immaculate child, afterwards understanding that her holy parents, Joachim and Anne, had promised God, even by vow, as many authors relate, that if he granted them issue, they would consecrate it to his service in the temple; as it was, moreover, an ancient custom amongst the Jews to take their daughters to the temple, and there to leave them for their education (for which purpose there were cells contiguous) as it is recorded by Baronius,[2] Nicephorus, Cedrenus, and Suarez, with Josephus the Jewish historian and also on the authority of St. John Damascene,[3] St. George of Nicomedia, St. Anselm, and St. Ambrose,[4] and as we may easily gather from the Second book of Machabees, where, speaking of Heliodorus, who besieged the temple, that he might gain possession of the treasures there deposited, says, *Because the place was like to come into contempt . . . and the virgins also that were shut up came forth, some to Onias.*[5]

---

[1] *Serm. Ang.* c. 14.

[2] *Appar. ad Ann.* n. 47.

[3] *De Fide Orth.* l. 4, c. 15.

[4] *De Virg.* l. 1.

[5] "Pro eo quod in contemptum locus esset venturus . . . Virgines, quæ conclusæ erant, procurrebant ad Oniam."—2 *Machab.* iii. 18.

Mary hearing this, I say, having scarcely attained the age of three years, as St. Germanus [1] and St. Epiphanius attest—the latter of whom says, "In her third year she was brought to the temple" [2]—an age at which children are the most desirous and stand in the greatest need of their parents' care, she desired to offer and solemnly to consecrate herself to God, by presenting herself in the temple. Hence, of her own accord, she requested her parents with earnestness to take her there, that they might thus accomplish their promise. And her holy mother, says St. Gregory of Nyssa, "did not long delay leading her to the temple, and offering her to God." [3]

Behold now Joachim and Anne, generously sacrificing to God the most precious treasure that they possessed in the world, and the one that was dearest to their heart, setting out from Nazareth, carrying their well-beloved little daughter in turns, for she could not otherwise have undertaken so long a journey as that from Nazareth to Jerusalem, it being a distance of eighty miles, as several authors say. They were accompanied by few relatives, but choirs of angels, according to St. George of Nicomedia, [4] escorted and served the immaculate little Virgin, who was about to consecrate herself to the divine Majesty. *How beautiful are thy steps, O prince's daughter!* [5] O, how beautiful (must the angels have sung), how acceptable to God is thy every step, taken on thy way to present and offer thyself to him! O noble daughter, most beloved of our common Lord!

"God himself, with the whole heavenly court," says

[1] *Enc. in S. Deip.*

[2] "Tertio anno, oblata est in Templo."

[3] "Anna haud cunctata est eam ad Templum adducere, ac Deo offerre."—*In Nat. Chr.*

[4] *Or. de Ingr. B. V.*

[5] "Quam pulchri . sunt gressus tui . . . Filia principis !"—*Cant.* vii. 1.

Bernardine de Bustis, " made great rejoicings on that day, beholding his spouse coming to the temple." [1] For he never saw a more holy creature, or one whom he so tenderly loved, come to offer herself to him.[2] " Go then" (says St. Germanus, archbishop of Constantinople), " go, O Queen of the world, O Mother of God, go joyfully to the house of God, there to await the coming of the divine Spirit, who will make thee the Mother of the Eternal Word. Enter with exultation the courts of the Lord, in expectation of the coming of the Holy Ghost, and the Conception of the only-begotten Son of God." [3]

When the holy company had reached the temple the fair child turned to her parents, and on her knees kissed their hands and asked their blessing; and then, without again turning back, she ascended the fifteen steps of the temple (according to Arius Montano, quoting Josephus), and as we are told by St. Germanus, presented herself to the priest, St. Zachary. Having done this, she bade farewell to the world, and renouncing all the pleasures that it promises to its votaries, she offered and consecrated herself to her Creator.

At the time of the deluge a raven sent out of the ark by Noah remained to feed on the dead bodies ; but the dove, without resting her foot, quickly *returned to him into the ark*.[4] Many who are sent by God into this world unfortunately remain to feed on earthly goods. It was not thus that Mary, our heavenly dove, acted ; she knew full well that God should be our only good, our only hope, our only love ; she knew that the world is full of dan-.

[1] " Magnam quoque festivitatem fecit Deus cum Angelis, in deductione suæ Sponsæ ad Templum."

[2] " Quia nullus unquam Deo gratior usque ad illud tempus templum ascendit."—*Marial.* p. 4, s. 1.

[3] " Abi, ergo. O Domina Mater Dei ! in atria Domini, exsultans et exspectans Sancti Spiritus adventum, et unigeniti Filii conceptionem."—*Enc. in S. Deip.*

[4] " Reversa est ad eum in arca."—*Gen.* viii. 9.

gers, and that he who leaves it the soonest is freest from
its snares : hence she sought to do this in her tenderest
years, and as soon as possible shut herself up in the
sacred retirement of the temple, where she could better
hear his voice, and honor and love him more.

Thus did the Blessed Virgin in her very first actions
render herself entirely dear and agreeable to her Lord,
as the holy Church says in her name : " Rejoice with
me, all ye who love God ; for when I was a little one I
pleased the Most High.¹ For this reason she was likened
to the moon ; for as the moon completes her course with
greater velocity than the other planets, so did Mary
attain perfection sooner than all the saints, by giving
herself to God promptly and without delay, and making herself all his without reserve.

Let us now pass to the second point, on which we
shall have much to say.

II.

The enlightened child well knew that God does not
accept a divided heart, but wills that, as he has commanded, it should be consecrated to his love without the
least reserve: *Thou shalt love the Lord thy God with thy
whole heart.*² Hence from the first moment of her life
she began to love God with all her strength, and gave
herself entirely to him. But still her most holy soul
awaited with the most ardent desire the moment when
she might consecrate herself to him in a more solemn
and public way. Let us, then, consider with what fervor
this loving and tender Virgin, on finding herself actually
enclosed in the holy place, first prostrate, kissed that
ground as the house of her Lord; and then adored his

¹ " Congratulamini mihi, omnes qui diligitis Dominum, quia, cum
essem parvula, placui Altissimo."—*Off. B. V. resp.* 2.
² " Diliges Dominum Deum tuum ex toto corde tuo."—*Deut.* vi. 5.

infinite majesty, thanked him for the favor she had received in being thus brought to dwell for a time in his house, and then offered her entire self to God, wholly, without reserving anything—all her powers and all her senses, her whole mind and her whole heart, her whole soul and her whole body; for then it was, according to many authors, that to please God "she vowed him her virginity," a vow which, according to the Abbot Rupert, "Mary was the first to make."[1] And the offering she then made of her entire self was without any reserve as to time, as Bernardine de Bustis declares: "Mary offered and dedicated herself to the perpetual service of God;"[2] for her intention was to dedicate herself to the service of his divine majesty in the temple for her whole life, should such be the good pleasure of God, and never to leave that sacred place. O, with what effusion of soul must she then have exclaimed, *My beloved to me, and I to Him!*[3] Cardinal Hugo paraphrases these words, saying, "I will live all his, and die all his."[4] "My Lord and my God," she said, "I am come here to please Thee alone, and to give Thee all the honor that is in my power; here will I live all Thine, and die all Thine, should such be Thy pleasure; accept the sacrifice which Thy poor servant offers Thee, and enable me to be faithful to Thee."

Here let us consider how holy was the life which Mary led in the temple, where, as *the morning rising*,[5] which rapidly bursts out into the full brightness of mid-day, she progressed in perfection. Who can ever tell the always-increasing brightness with which her resplendent virtues shone forth from day to day: charity, modesty, humility,

---

[1] "Deo prima vovisti votum virginitatis."—*In Cant.* l. 3.

[2] "Maria seipsam perpetuis Deo obsequiis obtulit et dedicavit."—*Marial.* p. 4, s. 1.

[3] "Dilectus meus mihi, et ego illi !"—*Cant.* ii. 16.

[4] "Ego illi tota vivam, et tota moriar."

[5] "Quasi aurora consurgens."—*Cant.* vi. 9.

silence, mortification, meekness. This fair olive-tree,
says St. John Damascene, planted in the house of God,
and nurtured by the Holy Ghost, became the dwelling-
place of all virtues; "led to the temple, and thenceforward planted in the house of God, and cultivated by the
Spirit, she as a fruitful olive-tree became the abode of
all virtues." [1] The same saint says elsewhere, "that the
countenance of the Blessed Virgin was modest, her mind
humble, her words proceeding from a composed interior
were engaging." [2] In another place he asserts that she
turned her thoughts far from earthly things, embracing
all virtues; and thus exercising herself in perfection, she
made so rapid progress in a short time, that she merited
to become a temple worthy of God. [3]

St. Anselm also speaks of the life of the Blessed Virgin
in the temple, and says that "Mary was docile, spoke
little, was always composed, did not laugh, and that her
mind was never disturbed. She also persevered in
prayer, in the study of the sacred Scriptures, in fastings,
and all virtuous works." [4]

St. Jerome and St. Bonaventure enter more into detail.
They say that Mary thus regulated her life: In the morning until the third hour she remained in prayer; from
the third hour until the ninth she employed herself with
work; and from the ninth hour she again prayed until
the angel brought her her food, as he was wont to do.
She was always the first in watchings, the most exact in
the observance of the divine law, the most profoundly
humble, and the most perfect in every virtue. No one
ever saw her angry: her every word carried such sweet-

---

[1] "Ad templum adducitur; ac deinde in domo Dei plantata atque
per Spiritum saginata, instar olivæ frugiferæ, virtutum omnium domicilium efficitur."—*De Fide Orth.* l. 4, c. 15.

[2] *De Nat. B. M.* or. 1.

[3] *De Fide, ut supra.*

[4] *Forma et Mor. B. M.*

ness with it that it was a witness to all that God was with her.[1]

We read in St. Bonaventure's *Life of Christ*, that the divine Mother herself revealed to St. Elizabeth of Hungary that "when her father and mother left her in the temple she determined to have God alone for her Father, and often thought how she could please him most."[2] Moreover, as we learn from the Revelations of St. Bridget, "she determined to consecrate her virginity to him, and to possess nothing in the world, and to give him her entire will."[3] Besides this, she told St. Elizabeth that of all the commandments to be observed she especially kept this one before her eyes : *Thou shalt love the Lord thy God ;*[4] and that at midnight she went before the altar of the temple to beg that he would grant her the grace to observe them all, and also that she might live to see the birth of the Mother of the Redeemer, entreating him at the same time to preserve her eyes to behold her, her tongue to praise her, her hands and feet to serve her, and her knees to adore her divine Son in her womb. St. Elizabeth, on hearing this, said, " But, Lady, wast thou not full of grace and virtue?" Mary replied, "Know that I considered myself most vile and unworthy of divine grace, and therefore thus earnestly prayed for grace and virtue." And finally, that we might be convinced of the absolute necessity under which we all are of asking the graces that we require from God, she added: "Dost thou think that I possessed grace and virtue without effort? Know that I obtained

---

[1] *Med. vitæ Chr.* c. 3.

[2] " Cum pater meus et mater mea me dimiserunt in Templo, statui in corde meo habere Deum in Patrem; et frequenter cogitabam, quid possem facere Deo gratum."

[3] " Vovi observare virginitatem, nihil unquam possidere in mundo; et ei (Deo) omnem voluntatem meam commisi."—*Rev.* l. 1, cap. 10.

[4] " Diliges Dominum Deum tuum."

no grace from God without great effort, constant prayer, ardent desire, and many tears and mortifications."

But above all we should consider the revelation made to St. Bridget of the virtues and practices of the Blessed Virgin in her childhood, in the following words : " From her childhood Mary was full of the Holy Ghost, and as she advanced in age she advanced also in grace. Thenceforward she determined to love God with her whole heart, so that she might never offend him, either by her words or actions; and therefore she despised all earthly goods. She gave all that she could to the poor. In her food she was so temperate, that she took only as much as was barely necessary to sustain her body. Afterwards, on discovering in the sacred Scriptures that God was to be born of a Virgin, that he might redeem the world, her soul was to such a degree inflamed with divine love, that she could desire and think of nothing but God; and finding pleasure in him alone, she avoided all company, even that of her parents, lest their presence might deprive her of his remembrance. She desired, with the greatest ardor, to live until the time of the coming of the Messiah, that she might be the servant of that happy Virgin, who merited to be his Mother." Thus far the Revelations of St. Bridget. [1]

Ah, yes, for the love of this exalted child the Redeemer did indeed hasten his coming into the world; for whilst she, in her humility, looked upon herself as unworthy to be the servant of the divine Mother, she was herself chosen to be this Mother; and by the sweet odor of her virtues and her powerful prayers she drew the divine Son into her virginal womb. For this reason Mary was called a turtle-dove by her divine Spouse : *The voice of the turtle is heard in our land.* [2] Not only because as a turtle-dove she always loved solitude, living

[1] *Rev.* l. 3, c. 8; l. 1, c. 10.
[2] " Vox Turturis audita est in terra nostra."—*Cant.* ii. 12.

23

in this world as in a desert, but also because, like a turtle-dove, which always sighs for its companions, Mary always sighed in the temple, compassionating the miseries of the lost world, and seeking from God the redemption of all. O, with how much greater feeling and fervor than the prophets did she repeat their prayers and sighs, that God would send the promised Redeemer! *Send forth, O Lord, the Lamb, the ruler of the earth.*[1] *Drop down dew, ye heavens, from above, and let the clouds rain the Just.*[2] *O that thou wouldst rend the heavens, and wouldst come down!*[3]

In a word, it was a subject of delight to God to behold this tender virgin always ascending towards the highest perfection, like a pillar of smoke, rich in the sweet odor of all virtues, as the Holy Ghost himself clearly describes her in the sacred Canticles: *Who is she that goeth up by the desert as a pillar of smoke, of aromatical spices, of myrrh and frankincense, and of all the powders of the perfumer?*[4] "This child," says St. Sophronius, "was truly God's garden of delights; for he there found every kind of flower, and all the sweet odors of virtues."[5] Hence St. John Chrysostom affirms,[6] that God chose Mary for his Mother in this world because he did not find on earth a Virgin more holy and more perfect than she was, nor any dwelling more worthy than her most sacred womb. St. Bernard also says, "that there was not on earth a more

---

[1] "Emitte agnum, Domine, Dominatorem terræ."—*Is.* xvi. 1.

[2] "Rorate, cœli, desuper, et nubes pluant Justum."—*Ib.* xlv. 8.

[3] "Utinam dirumperes cœlos, et descenderes."—*Ib.* lxiv. 1.

[4] "Quæ est ista quæ ascendit per desertum, sicut virgula fumi ex aromatibus myrrhæ, et thuris, et universi pulveris pigmentarii?"—*Cant.* iii. 6.

[5] "Vere Virgo erat Hortus deliciarum, in quo consita sunt universa florum genera et odoramenta virtutum."—*De Assumpt.*

[6] *Ap. Canis. De M. Deip.* l. 1, c. 13.

worthy place than the virginal womb."[1] This also agrees with the assertion of St. Antoninus, that the Blessed Virgin, to be chosen for, and destined to the dignity of Mother of God, was necessarily so great and consummate in perfection as to surpass all other creatures: "The last grace of perfection is that which prepared her for the conception of the Son of God."[2]

As, then, the holy child Mary presented and offered herself to God in the temple with promptitude and without reserve, so let us also present ourselves this day to Mary without delay and without reserve ; and let us entreat her to offer us to God, who will not reject us when he sees us presented by the hand of that blesssd creature, who was the living temple of the Holy Ghost, the delight of her Lord, and the chosen Mother of the Eternal Word. Let us also have unbounded confidence in this high and gracious Lady, who rewards, indeed, with the greatest love the homage that she receives from her clients, as we may gather from the following example.

EXAMPLE.

We read in the life of Sister Domenica del Paradiso, written by the Dominican Father Ignatius del Niente, that she was born of poor parents, in the village of Paradiso, near Florence. From her very infancy she began to serve the divine Mother. She fasted every day in her honor, and on Saturdays gave to the poor her food, of which she deprived herself. Every Saturday she went into the garden and into the neighboring fields, and gathered all the flowers that she could find, and presented them before an image of the Blessed Virgin with

[1] " Nec in terris locus dignior uteri virginalis templo."—*In Assumpt.* s. 1.

[2] " Ultima gratia perfectionis est præparatio ad Filium Dei concipiendum."—P. 4, t. 15, c. 6, § 2.

the Child in her arms, which she kept in the house. But let us now see with how many favors this most gracious Lady recompensed the homage of her servant. One day, when Domenica was ten years of age, standing at the window, she saw in the street a lady of noble bearing, accompanied by a little child, and they both extended their hands, asking for alms. She went to get some bread, when in a moment, without the door being opened, she saw them by her side and perceived that the child's hands and feet and side were wounded. She therefore asked the lady who had wounded the child. The mother answered, "It was love." Domenica, inflamed with love at the sight of the beauty and modesty of the child, asked him if the wounds pained him? His only answer was a smile. But, as they were standing near the statue of Jesus and Mary, the lady said to Domenica: "Tell me, my child, what is it that makes thee crown these images with flowers?" She replied, "It is the love that I bear to Jesus and Mary." "And how much dost thou love them?" "I love them as much as I can." "And how much canst thou love them?" "As much as they enable me." "Continue, then," added the lady, "continue to love them; for they will amply repay thy love in heaven." The little girl then perceiving that a heavenly odor came forth from those wounds, asked the mother with what ointment she anointed them, and if it could be bought. The lady answered, "It is bought with faith and good works." Domenica then offered the bread. The Mother said, "Love is the food of my Son: tell him that thou lovest Jesus, and he will be satisfied." The child at the word love seemed filled with joy, and turning towards the little girl, asked her how much she loved Jesus. She answered that she loved him so much, that night and day she always thought of him, and sought for nothing else but to give him as much pleasure as she possibly could." "It is well," He replied:

" love him, for love will teach thee what to do to please
him." The sweet odor which exhaled from those wounds
then increasing, Domenica cried out, " O God! this odor
makes me die of love." If the odor of a child is so sweet,
what must that of heaven be? But behold the scene now
changed; the Mother appeared clothed as a Queen, and
the child resplendent with beauty like the sun. He took
the flowers and scattered them on the head of Domenica,
who, recognizing Jesus and Mary in those personages,
was already prostrate adoring them. Thus the vision
ended. Domenica afterwards took the habit of a Dominicaness, and died in the odor of sanctity in the year
1553.

Prayer.

O beloved Mother of God, most amiable child Mary, O that,
as thou didst present thyself in the temple, and with promptitude and without reserve, didst consecrate thyself to the glory
and love of God, I could offer thee, this day, the first years of
my life, to devote myself without reserve to thy service, my holy
and most sweet Lady! But it is now too late to do this; for,
unfortunate creature that I am, I have lost so many years in the
service of the world and my own caprices, and have lived in
almost entire forgetfulness of thee and of God: *Woe to that
time in which I did not love thee!* [1] But it is better to begin
late than not at all. Behold, O Mary, I this day present myself
to thee, and I offer myself without reserve to thy service for the
long or short time that I still have to live in this world; and in
union with thee I renounce all creatures, and devote myself entirely to the love of my Creator. I consecrate my mind to thee,
O Queen, that it may always think of the love that thou deservest, my tongue to praise thee, my heart to love thee. Do thou
accept, O most holy Virgin, the offering which this miserable
sinner now makes thee; accept it, I beseech thee, by the consolation that thy heart experienced when thou gavest thyself to
God in the temple. But since I enter thy service late, it is rea-

---

[1] " Væ tempori illi, in quo non amavi te !"

sonable that I should redouble my acts of homage and love, thereby to compensate for lost time. Do thou help my weakness with thy powerful intercession, O Mother of Mercy, by obtaining me perseverance from thy Jesus, and strength to be always faithful to thee until death; that thus always serving thee in life, I may praise thee in Paradise for all eternity. Amen.

DISCOURSE IV.

THE ANNUNCIATION OF MARY.

March 25.

In the Incarnation of the Eternal Word, Mary could not have humbled herself more than she did humble herself: God, on the other hand, could not have exalted her more than he did exalt her.

Whosoever shall exalt himself shall be humbled; and he that shall humble himself shall be exalted.[1] These are the words of our Lord, and cannot fail. Therefore, God having determined to become man, that he might redeem lost man, and thus show the world his infinite goodness, and having to choose a Mother on earth, he sought amongst women for the one that was the most holy and the most humble. But amongst all, one there was whom he admired, and this one was the tender Virgin Mary, who, the more exalted were her virtues, so much the more dove-like was her simplicity and humility, and the more lowly was she in her own estimation. *There are young maidens without number : one is my dove, my perfect one.*[2] Therefore God said: This one shall be my chosen Mother. Let us now see how great was Mary's humility, and consequently how greatly God exalted her. Mary could not have humbled herself more than she did humble herself in the Incarnation of the Word; this will be the first point. That God could not have exalted Mary more than he did exalt her; this will be the second.

[1] "Qui autem se exaltaverit, humiliabitur; et qui se humiliaverit, exaltabitur."—*Matt.* xxiii. 12.

[2] "Adolescentularum non est numerus; una est Columba mea, Perfecta mea."—*Cant.* vi. 8.

I.

The Holy Spirit in the sacred Canticles, speaking precisely of the humility of the most humble Virgin, says: *While the king was at his repose, my spikenard sent forth the odor thereof.*[1]   St. Antoninus, explaining these words, says that "spikenard, being a small and lowly herb, was a type of Mary, the sweet odor of whose humility, ascending to heaven so to say, awakened the divine Word, reposing in the bosom of the Eternal Father, and drew him into her virginal womb."[2]   So that our Lord, drawn as it were by the sweet odor of this humble Virgin, chose her for his Mother, when he was pleased to become man to redeem the world.

But he, for the greater glory and merit of this Mother, would not become her Son without her previous consent. The Abbot William says, "He would not take flesh from her unless she gave it."[3]   Hence, when this humble Virgin (for so it was revealed to St. Elizabeth of Hungary) was in her poor little cottage, sighing and beseeching God more fervently than ever, and with desire more than ever ardent, that he would send the Redeemer; behold, the Archangel Gabriel arrives, the bearer of the great message.   He enters and salutes her, saying: *Hail, full of grace; the Lord is with thee; blessed art thou amongst women.*   Hail, O Virgin full of grace; for thou wast always full of grace above all other saints.

[1] "Dum esset Rex in accubitu suo, nardus mea dedit odorem suum."—*Cant.* i. 11.

[2] "Nardus est herba parva, sed significat Beatam Virginem, quæ dedit odorem suæ humilitatis; qui odor usque ad cœlum ascendit, et in cœlo accumbentem quasi evigilare fecit, et in utero suo quiescere."—P. 4. t. 15, c. 21, § 2.

[3] "Nec carnem volebat sumere ex ipsa, non dante ipsa."—*Delrio, In Cant.* i. 2.

[4] "Ave, gratia Plena!   Dominus tecum; benedicta tu in mulieribus."—*Luke*, i. 28.

The Lord is with thee, because thou art so humble. Thou art blessed amongst women, for all others fell under the curse of sin; but thou, because thou art the Mother of the blessed one, art, and always wilt be blessed, and free from every stain.

But what does the humble Mary answer to a salutation so full of praises? Nothing; she remains silent, but reflecting upon it, is troubled: *Who having heard was troubled at his saying, and thought with herself what manner of salutation this should be.*[1] Why was she troubled? Did she fear an illusion, or was it her virginal modesty which caused her to be disturbed at the sight of a man, as some suppose, in the belief that the angel appeared under a human form? No, the text is clear: *She was troubled at his saying.*[2] "Not at his appearance, but at what he said,"[3] remarks Eusebius Emissenus. Her trouble, then, arose entirely from her humility, which was disturbed at the sound of praises so far exceeding her own lowly estimate of herself. Hence, the more the angel exalted her, the more she humbled herself, and entered into the consideration of her own nothingness. Here St. Bernardine remarks, that "had the angel said, O Mary, thou art the greatest sinner in the world, her astonishment would not have been so great; the sound of so high praises filled her with fear."[4] She was troubled; for, being so full of humility, she abhorred every praise of herself, and her only desire was that her Creator, the giver of every good thing, should be praised and blessed. This Mary herself revealed to St. Bridget, when speaking of the time in which she became Mother

[1] "Quæ cum audisset, turbata est in sermone ejus, et cogitabat qualis esset ista salutatio."

[2] "Turbata est in sermone ejus."

[3] "Non in vultu, sed in sermone ejus."—*In Fer.* 4 p. *Dom.* 4 *Adv.*

[4] "Si dixisset: Tu, O Maria! es lascivior quæ sit in mundo;—non ita admirata fuisset; unde turbata fuit de tantis laudibus."—*T. III. Quadr.* s. 37, p. 3.

of God: "I desired not my own praise, but only that my Creator, the giver of all, should be glorified."[1]

The Blessed Virgin was already well aware, from the sacred Scriptures, that the time foretold by the prophets for the coming of the Messiah had arrived; that the weeks of Daniel were completed; that already, according to the prophecy of Jacob, the sceptre of Juda had passed into the hands of Herod, a strange king: she already knew that a virgin was to be the Mother of the Messiah. She then heard the angel give her praises which, it was evident, could apply to no other than to the Mother of God. Hence, may not the thought, or at least some vague impression, have entered her mind, that perhaps she was this chosen Mother of God? No, her profound humility did not even admit such an idea. Those praises only caused great fear in her: "so much so," as St. Peter Chrysologus remarks, "that as Christ was pleased to be comforted by an angel, so was it necessary that the Blessed Virgin should be encouraged by one."[2] St. Gabriel, seeing Mary so troubled and almost stupefied by the salutation, was obliged to encourage her, saying, *Fear not, Mary; for thou hast found grace with God.*[3] Fear not, O Mary, and be not surprised at the great titles by which I have saluted thee; for if thou in thine own eyes art so little and lowly, God, who exalts the humble, has made thee worthy to find the grace lost by men; and therefore he has preserved thee from the common stain of the children of Adam. Hence, from the moment of thy conception, he has honored thee with a grace greater than that of all the saints; and therefore

[1] "Nolui laudem meam, sed solius Datoris et Creatoris."—*Rev.* l. 2, c. 23.

[2] "Sicut Christus per Angelum confortari voluit, ita decuit Virginem per Angelum animari."—*Suarez, De Inc.* q. 30, a. 2.

[3] "Ne timeas, Maria; invenisti enim gratiam apud Deum."—*Luke,* i. 30.

he now finally exalts thee even to the dignity of being his Mother. *Behold, thou shalt conceive in thy womb, and shalt bring forth a Son: and thou shalt call His name Jesus.*[1]

And now, why this delay, O Mary? "The angel awaits the reply" (says St. Bernard); "and we also, O Lady, on whom the sentence of condemnation weighs so heavily, await the word of mercy;"[2] we, who are already condemned to death. "Behold, the price of our salvation is offered thee; we shall be instantly delivered if thou consentest;"[3] continues the same St. Bernard. Behold, O Mother of us all, the price of our salvation is already offered thee: that price will be the divine Word, made man in thee; in that moment in which thou acceptest him for thy Son we shall be delivered from death. "For thy Lord himself desires thy consent, by which he has determined to save the world, with an ardor equal to the love with which he has loved thy beauty."[4] "Answer then, O sacred Virgin," says St. Augustine, or some other ancient author; "why delayest thou giving life to the world?"[5] Answer quickly, O Lady; no longer delay the salvation of the world, which now depends upon thy consent.

But see, Mary already answers; she says to the angel: *Behold the handmaid of the Lord; be it done to me according to thy word.*[6] O, what more beautiful, more humble, or

[1] "Ecce concipies in utero, et paries filium, et vocabis nomen ejus Jesum."

[2] "Exspectat Angelus responsum; expectamus et nos, O Domina! verbum miserationis, quos miserabiliter premit sententia damnationis."

[3] "Ecce offertur tibi pretium salutis nostræ; statim liberabimur, si consentis."

[4] "Ipse quoque omnium Dominus, quantum concupivit decorem tuum, tantum desiderat et responsionis assensum, in qua nimirum proposuit salvare mundum."—*De Laud. V. M. hom.* 4.

[5] "Responde jam, Virgo sacra! vitam quid tricas mundo?"—*Serm.* 120, *E. B. app.*

[6] "Ecce ancilla Domini; fiat mihi secundum verbum tuum."—*Luke,* i. 38.

more prudent answer could all the wisdom of men and
angels together have invented, had they reflected for a
million years? O powerful answer, which rejoiced heaven,
and brought an immense sea of graces and blessings into
the world!—answer which had scarcely fallen from the
lips of Mary, before it drew the only begotten Son of
God from the bosom of his Eternal Father, to become
man in her most pure womb! Yes indeed; for scarcely
had she uttered these words, *Behold the handmaid of the
Lord ; be it done to me according to thy word*, when instantly
the Word was made flesh ; [1] the Son of God became also
the Son of Mary. "O powerful *Fiat !*" exclaims St.
Thomas of Villanova; " O efficacious *Fiat ! O Fiat* to be
venerated above every other *Fiat !* For with a *fiat* God
created light, heaven, earth; but with Mary's *fiat*," says
the saint, "God became man, like us." [2]

Let us, however, not wander from our point, but consider the great humility of the Blessed Virgin in this answer. She was fully enlightened as to the greatness of
the dignity of a Mother of God. She had already been
assured by the angel that she was this happy Mother
chosen by our Lord. But with all this, she in no way
rises in her own estimation, she does not stop to rejoice
in her exaltation; but seeing, on the one side, her own
nothingness, and on the other the infinite majesty of
God, who chose her for his Mother, she acknowledges
how unworthy she is of so great an honor, but will
not oppose his will in the least thing. Hence, when her
consent is asked, what does she do? what does she say?
Wholly annihilated within herself, yet all inflamed at
the same time by the ardor of her desire to unite herself
thus still more closely to God, and abandoning herself
entirely to the divine will, she answers, *Behold the hand-*

[1] "Et Verbum caro factum est, et habitavit in nobis."—*John,* i. 14.
[2] "O *fiat* potens! O *fiat* efficax! O *fiat* super omne *fiat*, perpetuo
honore venerandum!"—*De Ann. conc.* I.

maid of the Lord. Behold the slave of the Lord, obliged
to do that which her Lord commands. As if she meant
to say: Since God chooses me for his Mother, who have
nothing of my own, and since all that I have is his gift,
who can ever think that he has done so on account of
my own merits? *Behold the handmaid of the Lord.* What
merit can a slave ever have, that she should become the
Mother of her Lord? *Behold the handmaid of the Lord.*
May the goodness of God alone be praised, and not his
slave: since it is all his goodness, that he fixes his eyes
on so lowly a creature as I am, to make her so great.

"O humility!" here exclaims the Abbot Guerric; "as
nothing in its own eyes, yet sufficiently great for the divinity! Insufficient for itself, sufficient for Him whom
the heavens cannot contain."[1] O great humility of Mary!
which makes her little to herself, but great before God.
Unworthy in her own eyes, but worthy in the eyes of
that immense Lord whom the world cannot contain.
But the exclamation of St. Bernard on this subject is still
more beautiful, in his fourth sermon on the Assumption
of Mary, in which, admiring her humility, he says: "And
how, O Lady, couldst thou unite in thy heart so humble
an opinion of thyself with so great purity, with such innocence, and so great a plenitude of grace as thou didst
possess?"[2] "And how, O Blessed Virgin," continues the
saint, "did this humility and so great humility ever take
so deep root in thy heart, seeing thyself thus honored
and exalted by God? Whence thy humility, and so
great humility, O blessed one?"[3] Lucifer, seeing himself endowed with great beauty, aspired to exalt his
throne above the stars, and to make himself like God:

[1] "O humilitas, angusta sibi, ampla Divinitati! insufficiens sibi, sufficiens ei quem non capit orbis!"—*In Assumpt.* s. 3.

[2] "Quanta humilitatis virtus cum tanta puritate, cum innocentia
tanta, imo cum tantæ gratiæ plenitudine!"

[3] "Unde tibi humilitas, et tanta humilitas, O Beata?"

I will exalt my throne above the stars of God . . . I will be like the Most High.[1] O what would that proud spirit have said, and to what would he have aspired, had he ever been adorned with the gifts of Mary! The humble Mary did not act thus; the higher she saw herself raised, the more she humbled herself. Ah, Lady! concludes St. Bernard, by this admirable humility thou didst indeed render thyself worthy to be regarded by God with singular love; worthy to captivate thy king with thy beauty; worthy to draw, by the sweet odor of thy humility, the Eternal Son from his repose, from the bosom of God, into thy most pure womb. "She was indeed worthy to be looked upon by the Lord, whose beauty the King so greatly desired, and by whose most sweet odor he was drawn from the Eternal repose of his Father's bosom."[2]

Hence Bernardine de Bustis says that "Mary merited more by saying with humility, *Behold the handmaid of the Lord!* than all pure creatures could merit together by all their good works."[3] Thus, says St. Bernard, this innocent Virgin, although she made herself dear to God by her virginity, yet it was by her humility that she rendered herself worthy, as far as a creature can be worthy, to become the Mother of her Creator. "Though she pleased by her virginity, she conceived by her humility."[4] St. Jerome confirms this, saying that "God chose her to be his Mother more on account of her humility

---

[1] "Super astra Dei exaltabo solium meum . . . similis ero Altissimo."—*Is.* xiv. 13.

[2] "Digna plane quam respiceret Dominus, cujus decorem concupisceret Rex, cujus odore suavissimo ab æterno illo paterni sinus attraheretur accubitu."—*In Assumpt.* s. 4.

[3] "Beata Virgo plus meruit, dicendo humiliter: 'Ecce ancilla Domini,' quam simul mereri possent omnes puræ creaturæ."

[4] "Etsi placuit ex virginitate, tamen ex humilitate concepit."—*De Laud. V. M. hom.* I.

than all her other sublime virtues.[1] Mary herself also assured St. Bridget of the same thing, saying· "How was it that I merited so great a grace as to be made the Mother of my Lord, if it was not that I knew my own nothingness, and that I had nothing, and humbled myself."[2] This she had already declared in her canticle, breathing forth the most profound humility, when she said: *Because He hath regarded the humility of his handmaid . . . He that is mighty hath done great things to me.*[3] On these words St. Laurence Justinian remarks, that the Blessed Virgin "did not say he hath regarded the virginity, or the innocence, but only the humility: and by this humility, as St. Francis de Sales observes, Mary did not mean to praise the virtue of her own humility, but she meant to declare that God had regarded her nothingness (humility, that is nothingness),[5] and that, out of his pure goodness, he had been pleased thus to exalt her.

In fine, St. Augustine says that Mary's humility was a ladder by which our Lord deigned to descend from heaven to earth, to become man in her womb : "Mary's humility," he says, "became a heavenly ladder, by which God came into the world.".[6] This is confirmed by St. Antoninus, who says that the humility of Mary was her most perfect virtue, and the one that immediately prepared her to become the Mother of God. "The last

[1] " Maluit Deus de Beata Maria incarnari propter humilitatem, quam propter aliam quamcumque virtutem."—*Euseb. de Morte Hier.*

[2] " Unde promerui tantam gratiam, nisi quia cogitavi et scivi, me nihil a me esse vel habere ?"—*Rev.* l. 2, c. 23.

[3] " Quia respexit humilitatem ancillæ suæ . . fecit mihi magna qui potens est."

[4] "Non ait: Respexit virginitatem, innocentiam; sed humilitatem tantum."—*De Vita sol.* c. 14.

[5] " Humilitatem, id est, nihilitatem."

[6] " Facta est certe Mariæ humilitas scala cœlestis. per quam descendit Deus ad terras."—*Serm.* 208. *E. B App*

grace of perfection is preparation for the conception of the Son of God, which preparation is made by profound humility." [1] The prophet Isaias foretold the same thing: *And there shall come forth a rod out of the root of Jesse, and a flower shall rise up out of his root.* [2] Blessed Albert the Great remarks on these words, that the divine flower, that is to say, the only-begotten Son of God, was to be born, not from the summit, nor from the trunk, of the tree of Jesse, but from the root, precisely to denote the humility of the Mother: " By the root humility of heart is understood." [3] The Abbot of Celles explains it more clearly still, saying: " Remark that the flower rises, not from the summit, but out of the root." [4] For this reason God said to his beloved daughter, *Turn away thy eyes from Me, for they have made Me flee away.* [5] St. Augustine asks, " Whence have they made Thee flee, unless it be from the bosom of Thy Father into the womb of Thy Mother?" [6] On this same thought the learned interpreter Fernandez says, that the most humble eyes of Mary, which she always kept fixed on the divine greatness, never losing sight of her own nothingness, did such violence to God himself, that they drew him into her womb: " Her most humble eyes held God in such a way captive, that the Blessed Virgin, with a kind of most sweet violence, drew the Word himself of God the Father

[1] " Ultima gratia perfectionis est præparatio ad Filium Dei concipiendum ; quæ præparatio fuit per profundam humilitatem."—P. 4, t. 15, c. 6, § 2.

[2] " Et egredietur virga de radice Jesse, et flos de radice ejus ascendet."—*Is.* xi. 1.

[3] " In radice humilitas cordis intelligitur."

[4] " Nota quod non ex summitate virgæ ascendit flos."—*De Sanct.* s. 56.

[5] " Averte oculos tuos a me, quia ipsi me avolare fecerunt."—*Cant* vi. 4.

[6] " Unde avolare, nisi a sinu Patris in uterum Matris ?"—*De Ass. conc.* 3

into her womb." [1] "Thus it is that we can understand,"
says the Abbot Franco, "why the Holy Ghost praised
the beauty of this his spouse, so greatly, on account of
her dove's eyes:" *How beautiful art thou, my love! how
beautiful art thou! thine eyes are dove's eyes.* [2] For Mary,
looking at God with the eyes of a simple and humble
dove, enamoured him to such a degree by her beauty,
that with the bands of love she made him a prisoner in
her chaste womb. The Abbot thus speaks: "Where on
earth could so beautiful a Virgin be found, who could
allure the King of heaven by her eyes, and by a holy
violence lead him captive, bound in the chains of love?" [3]
So that, to conclude this point, we will remark, that in
the Incarnation of the Eternal Word, as we have already
seen at the commencement of our discourse, Mary could
not have humbled herself more than she did humble
herself. Let us now see how it was that God, having
made her his Mother, could not have exalted her more
than he did exalt her.

II.

To understand the greatness to which Mary was
exalted, it would be necessary to understand the sub-
limity and greatness of God. It is sufficient, then, to
say simply, that God made this Blessed Virgin his
Mother, to understand that God could not have exalted
her more than he did exalt her. Arnold of Chartres,
then, rightly asserts that God, by becoming the Son of
the Blessed Virgin, "established her in a rank far above

[1] "Ita illius oculi humillimi Deum tenuerunt, ut, suavissima quadam
violentia, ipsummet Dei Patris Verbum in uterum suum attraxerit."
—*In Gen.* xxiv. sect. 1.

[2] "Quam pulchra es, Amica mea! quam pulchra es! oculi tui
columbarum."—*Cant.* iv. 1.

[3] "Ubinam terrarum tam speciosa, quæ Filium Dei de sinu Patris
alliceret; ut vinculis charitatis pia violentia captivum traheret."—*De
Grat. Dei*, l. 6.

that of all the saints and angels." [1] So that, with the exception of God himself, there is no one who is so greatly exalted; [2] as St. Ephrem also asserts : "Her glory is incomparably greater than that of all the other celestial spirits." This is confirmed by St. Andrew of Crete, saying, "God excepted, she is higher than all." [3] St. Anselm also says, "No one is equal to thee, O Lady, for all are either above or beneath thee : God alone is above thee, and all that is not God is inferior to thee." [4] In fine, says St. Bernardine, "the greatness and dignity of this Blessed Virgin are such, that God alone does, and can, comprehend it." [5]

In this reflection we have more than sufficient, remarks St. Thomas of Villanova, to take away the surprise which might be caused on seeing that the sacred Evangelists, who have so fully recorded the praises of a John the Baptist and of a Magdalene, say so little of the precious gifts of Mary : "It was sufficient to say of her, 'Of whom was born Jesus.'" "What more could you wish the Evangelists to have said of the greatness of this Blessed Virgin?" continues the saint. "Is it not enough that they declare that she was the Mother of God? In these few words they recorded the greatest, the whole, of her precious gifts ; and since the whole was therein contained, it was unnecessary to enter into details." [6] And why not? St.

---

[1] "Maria constituta est super omnem creaturam."—*De Laud. B. M.*

[2] "Nulla comparatione, cæteris superis est gloriosior."

[3] "Excepto Deo, omnibus altior."—*In Dorm. S. M.* s. 3.

[4] "Nihil tibi, Domina, æquale ; omne enim quod est, aut supra te est, aut subtus te ; quod supra, solus Deus ; quod infra, omne quod Deus non est."—*De Conc. B. M.*

[5] "Tanta fuit perfectio Virginis, ut soli Deo cognoscenda reservetur."—*Pro Fest. V. M.* s. 4, a. 3, c. 1.

[6] "Sufficit quod scriptum est, quia de illa natus est Jesus. Quid ultra requiris? sufficit tibi quod Mater Dei est. Ubi ergo totum erat, pars scribenda non fuit."—*De Nat. V. conc.* 2.

Anselm replies, "that when we say of Mary she is the Mother of God, this alone transcends every greatness that can be named or imagined after that of God." [1] Peter of Celles, on the same subject, adds : "Address her as Queen of heaven, sovereign mistress of the angels, or any other title of honor you may please, but never can you honor her so much as by simply calling her the Mother of God." [2]

The reason of this is evident : for, as the angelic Doctor teaches, the nearer a thing approaches its author, the greater is the perfection that it receives from him ; and therefore Mary being of all creatures the nearest to God, she, more than all others, has partaken of his graces, perfections, and greatness. He says, " The Blessed Virgin Mary was the nearest possible to Christ; for from her it was that he received his human nature, and therefore she must have obtained a greater plenitude of grace from him than all others." [3] To this Father Suarez traces the reason for which " the dignity of Mother of God is above every other created dignity;" for he says, " It belongs in a certain way to the order of hypostatic union; for it intrinsically appertains to it; and has a necessary conjunction with it." [4] Hence Denis the Carthusian asserts, that "after the hypostatic union there is none more intimate than that of the Mother of God with

[1] " Hoc solum de Sancta Virgine prædicari, quod Dei Mater sit, excedit omnem altitudinem quæ, post Deum, dici vel cogitari potest." —*De Excell. V.* c. 2.

[2] " Si cœli Reginam, si Angelorum Dominam, vel quodlibet aliud protuleris, non assurget ad hunc honorem, quo prædicatur Dei Genitrix."—*De Pan.* c. 21.

[3] " Beata autem Virgo Maria propinquissima Christo fuit, quia ex ea accepit humanam naturam ; et ideo præ cæteris majorem debuit a Christo gratiæ plenitudinem obtinere."—P. 3, q. 27, a. 5.

[4] " Dignitas matris est altioris ordinis ; pertinet enim quodammodo ad ordinem unionis hypostaticæ ; illam enim intrinsice respicit, et cum illa necessariam conjunctionem habet."—*De Incar.* p. 2, d. 1, s. 2.

her Son."[1] This, St. Thomas teaches, is the supreme, the highest degree of union that a pure creature can have with God : "It is a sort of supreme union with an infinite person."[2] Blessed Albert the Great also asserts, that "to be the Mother of God is the highest dignity after that of being God."[3] Hence he adds, that "Mary could not have been more closely united to God than she was without becoming God."[4]

St. Bernardine says, that "to become Mother of God, the Blessed Virgin had to be raised to a sort of equality with the divine Persons by an almost infinity of graces."[5] And as children are, morally speaking, regarded one with their parents, so that their properties and honors are in common, it follows, says St. Peter Damian, that God, who dwells in creatures in different ways, dwelt in Mary in an especial way, and was singularly identified with her, making himself one and the same thing with her. "The fourth mode," he says, "in which God is in a creature is that of identity; and this he is in the Blessed Virgin Mary, for he is one with her." Thence he exclaims in those celebrated words, "Let every creature be silent and tremble, and scarcely dare glance at the immensity of so great a dignity. God dwells in the Blessed Virgin, with whom he has the identity of one nature."[6]

[1] "Post hypostaticam conjunctionem non est alia tam vicina, ut unio Matris Dei cum Filio suo."—*De Laud. V. M.* l. i. c. 35.

[2] "Est suprema quædam conjunctio cum Persona infinita."

[3] "Immediate post esse Deum, est esse Matrem Dei."—*Super Miss. r.* ad 3, q. 140.

[4] "Magis Deo conjungi, nisi fieret Deus, non potuit."

[5] "Quod femina conciperet et pareret Deum, oportuit eam elevari ad quamdam æqualitatem divinam, per quamdam infinitatem gratiarum."—*Pro Fest. V. M.* s. 5, c. 12.

[6] "Quarto modo inest Deus uni creaturæ, videlicet Mariæ Virgini, identitate, quia idem est quod illa : hic taceat et contremiscat omnis creatura, et vix audeat aspicere tantæ dignitatis immensitatem : habitat Deus in Virgine, cum qua unius naturæ habet identitatem."—*In Nat. B. V.* s. 1.

Therefore St. Thomas asserts that when Mary became Mother of God, by reason of so close a union with an infinite good, she received a dignity which Father Suarez calls "infinite in its kind." [1] The dignity of Mother of God is the greatest dignity that can be conferred on a pure creature. For although the angelic Doctor teaches that "even the humanity of Jesus Christ could have received greater habitual grace from God,—since grace is a created gift, and therefore its essence is finite; for all creatures have a determined measure of capacity, so that it is yet in God's power to make another creature whose determined measure is greater," [2]—yet since his humanity was destined to a personal union with a divine Person, it could not have for its subject anything greater; or, as the saint expresses himself in another place, "though the divine power could create something greater and better than the habitual grace of Christ, nevertheless it could not destine it to anything greater than the personal union of the only-begotten Son of the Father." [3] Thus, on the other hand, the Blessed Virgin could not have been raised to a greater dignity than that of Mother of God. "Which dignity is in a certain manner infinite, inasmuch as God is an infinite good; in this respect, then, she could not have been made greater." [4] St. Thomas of Villanova says the same thing: "There is

[1] "Dignitas Matris Dei suo genere est infinita."—*Loco supra cit.*

[2] "Cum enim gratia habitualis sit donum creatum, confiteri oportet quod habeat essentiam finitam. Est cujuslibet creaturæ determinata capacitatis mensura, quin possit aliam creaturam majoris capacitatis facere."—*Comp. theol.* c. 215.

[3] "Virtus divina, licet possit facere aliquid majus et melius, quam sit habitualis gratia Christi; non tamen posset facere, quod ordinaretur ad aliquid majus, quam sit unio personalis ad Filium unigenitum a Patre."—P. 3, q. 7, a. 12.

[4] "Beata Virgo, ex hoc quod est Mater Dei, habet quandam dignitatem infinitam ex bono infinito, quod est Deus: et ex hac parte, non potest aliquid fieri melius."—P. 1, q. 25. a. 6.

something infinite in being the Mother of him who is infinite." [1] St. Bernardine also says, that "the state to which God exalted Mary in making her his Mother was the highest state that could be conferred on a pure creature : so that he could not have exalted her more." [2] This opinion is confirmed by Blessed Albert the Great, who says, that "in bestowing on Mary the maternity of God, God gave her the highest gift of which a pure creature is capable." [3]

Hence that celebrated saying of St. Bonaventure, that "to be the Mother of God is the greatest grace that can be conferred on a creature. It is such that God could make a greater world, a greater heaven, but that he cannot exalt a creature more than by making her his Mother." [4] But no one has so well expressed the greatness of the dignity to which God had raised her as the divine Mother herself whe.. she said, *He that is mighty hath done great things in me.* [5] And why did not the Blessed Virgin make known what were the great things conferred on her by God ? St. Thomas of Villanova answers, that Mary did not explain them because they could not be expressed : "She did not explain them, because they were inexplicable." [6]

Hence St. Bernard with reason says, "that for this

---

[1] "Utique habet quandam infinitatem, sse matrem Infiniti."—*De Nat. V. conc.* 3.

[2] "Status maternitatis Dei erat summus status, qui puræ creaturæ dari posset."—*Pro Fest. V. M.* s. 8, a. 3.

[3] "Deus Beatissimæ Virgini summum donum donavit, cujus pura creatura capax fuit, scilicet Dei maternitatem."—*Sup. Miss.* q. 138.

[4] "Quid mirabilius quam esse Dei Matrem ? ipsa est qua majorem Deus facere non posset: majorem mundum posset facere Deus, majus cœlum; majorem matrem quam matrem Dei non posset facere."—*Spec. B. V. lect.* 9, 10.

[5] "Fecit mihi magna qui potens est."

[6] "Non explicat quænam hæc magna fuerint, quia inexplicabilia."—*Umbra Virg. exc.* 14.

Blessed Virgin, who was to be his Mother, God created the whole world."[1]   And St. Bonaventure, that its existence depends on her will.   He says, addressing her, "The world which thou with God didst form from the beginning continues to exist at thy will, O most holy Virgin;"[2] the saint adhering in this to the words of Proverbs applied by the Church to Mary: *I was with Him forming all things.*[3]   St. Bernardine adds, that it was for the love of Mary that God did not destroy man after Adam's sin: "He preserved it on account of his most singular love for this Blessed Virgin."[4]   Hence the Holy Ghost with reason sings of Mary: *She has chosen the best part;*[5] for this Virgin Mother not only chose the best things, but she chose the best part of the best things; "God endowing her in the highest degree," as Blessed Albert the Great asserts, "with all the general and particular graces and gifts conferred on all other creatures, in consequence of the dignity granted her of the divine maternity."[6]   Thus Mary was a child, but of this state she had only the innocence, not the defect of incapacity; for from the very first moment of her existence she had always the perfect use of reason.   She was a Virgin without the reproach of sterility.   She was a Mother, but at the same time possessed the precious treasure of virginity.   She was beautiful, even most beautiful, as Richard of St. Victor asserts,[7] with St. George of Nicomedia,[8] and St. Denis the Areopagite,

[1] "Propter hanc totus mundus factus est."—*In Salve Reg.* s. 3.

[2] "Dispositione tua Virgo, perseverat mundus, quem et tu cum Deo fundasti ab initio."—*Psalt. B. V. ps.* 118.

[3] "Cum eo eram cuncta componens."—*Prov.* viii. 30.

[4] "Propter singularissimam dilectionem quam habebat ad Virginem, praeservavit."—*Pro Fest. V. M.* s. 5, c. 2.

[5] "Optimam partem elegit."—*Off. Assumpt. evang.*

[6] "Beatissima Virgo fuit gratia plena. quia omnes gratias generales et speciales in summo habuit."—*Bibl. Mar. Luc.* n. 13.

[7] *In Cant.* s. 26.

[8] *Or. de Ingr. B. V.*

who (as it is believed) had the happiness of once beholding her beauty; and he declared that had not faith taught him that she was only a creature, he should have adored her as God. Our Lord himself also revealed to St. Bridget that the beauty of his Mother surpassed that of all men and angels. Allowing the saint to hear him addressing Mary, he said : " Thy beauty exceeds that of all angels, and of all created things." [1] She was most beautiful, I say ; but without prejudice to those who looked upon her, for her beauty banished all evil thoughts, and even enkindled pure ones, as St. Ambrose attests : " So great was her grace, that not only it preserved her own virginity, but conferred that admirable gift of purity on those who beheld her.[2] This is confirmed by St. Thomas, who says, " that sanctifying grace not only repressed all irregular motions in the Blessed Virgin herself, but was also efficacious for others ; so that, notwithstanding the greatness of her beauty, she was never coveted by others."[3] For this reason she was called myrrh, which prevents corruption, in the words of Ecclesiasticus, applied to her by the Church : *I yielded a sweet odor like the best myrrh.*[4] The labors of active life, when engaged in them, did not interrupt her union with God. In her contemplative life she was wrapped in him, but not so as to cause her to neglect her temporal affairs and the charity due to her neighbor. She had to die,

[1] " Omnes angelos, et omnia quæ creata sunt, excessit pulchritudo tua."—*Rev.* l. i. c. 51.

[2] " Tanta erat ejus gratia, ut, non solum in se virginitatis gratiam reservaret, sed etiam his, quos viseret, integritatis insigne conferret."—*Inst. Virg.* c. 7.

[3] " Gratia sanctificationis non tantum repressit in Virgine motus illicitos, sed etiam in aliis efficaciam habuit ; ita ut, quamvis esset pulchra corpore, a nullo unquam concupisci potuit."—*In Sent.* iii. d. 3, q. 1, a. 2, s. 1.

[4] " Quasi myrrha electa, dedi suavitatem odoris."—*Ecclus.* xxiv. 20: *Off. B. V. resp.* 4.

but her death was unaccompanied by its usual sorrows, and not followed by the corruption of the body.

In conclusion, then, this divine Mother is infinitely inferior to God, but immensely superior to all creatures; and as it is impossible to find a Son more noble than Jesus, so is it also impossible to find a Mother more noble than Mary. This reflection should cause the clients of so great a Queen not only to rejoice in her greatness, but should also increase their confidence in her powerful patronage.; for, says Father Suarez, as she is the Mother of God; ".she has a certain peculiar right to his gifts,"[1] to dispense them to those for whom she prays. St. Germanus, on the other hand, says, "that God cannot do otherwise than grant the petitions of this Mother ; for he cannot but acknowledge her for his true and immaculate Mother." Here are his words addressed to this Blessed Virgin : For thou, who by thy maternal authority hast great power with God, obtainest the very great grace of reconciliation even for those who have been guilty of grievous crimes. It is impossible that thou shouldst not be graciously heard ; for God in all things complies with thy wishes as being those of his true and spotless Mother."[2]

Therefore power to succor us is not wanting to thee, O Mother of God, and Mother of us all. The will is not wanting : "neither the power nor the will can fail her."[3] For thou well knowest (will I say, addressing thee in the words of thy servant the Abbot of Celles) that "God did not create thee for 'himself only ; he gave thee to

---

[1] "Unde fit, ut singulare jus habeat ad bona Filii sui.'—*De Inc.* p. 2, d. 1, s. 2.

[2] "Tu autem, quæ materna in Deum auctoritate polles, etiam iis qui enormiter peccant, eximiam remissionis gratiam concilias ; non enim potes non exaudiri, cum Deus tibi, ut veræ ac immaculatæ Matri suæ, in omnibus morem gerat."—*In Dorm. V. M.* s. 2.

[3] "Nec facultas ei deesse poterit, nec voluntas."—*In Assumpt.* s. 1

the angels as their restorer, to men as their repairer, to the devils as their vanquisher; for through thy means we recover divine grace, and by thee the enemy is conquered and crushed." [1]

If we really desire to please the divine Mother, let us often salute her with the "Hail Mary." She once appeared to St. Mechtilde, [2] and assured her that she was honored by nothing more than by this salutation. By its means we shall certainly obtain even special graces from this Mother of mercy, as will be seen in the following example.

EXAMPLE.

The event recorded by Father Paul Segneri, in his "Christian Instructed," [3] is justly celebrated. A young man, of vicious habits and laden with sins, went to confession to Father Nicholas Zucchi in Rome. The confessor received him with charity, and, filled with compassion for his unfortunate state, assured him that devotion to our Blessed Lady could deliver him from the accursed vice to which he was addicted; he therefore imposed on him as his penance, that he should say a "Hail Mary," to the Blessed Virgin, every morning and evening, on getting up and on going to bed, until his next confession; and, at the same time, that he should offer her his eyes, his hands, and his whole body, beseeching her to preserve them as something belonging to herself, and that he should kiss the ground three times. The young man performed the penance, but at first there was only slight amendment. The Father, however, continued to inculcate the same practice on

---

[1] "Non solum sibi ipsi te fecit; sed te Angelis dedit in instaurationem, hominibus in reparationem, dæmonibus in hostem: per te, Deus homini pacificatur, diabolus vincitur et conteritur."—*Cont. de V. M.* c. 4.

[2] *Spir. Grat.* l. 1. c. 67.

[3] *Crist. istr.* p. 3, r. 34, § 2.

him, desiring him never to abandon it, and at the same time encouragèd him to confide in the patronage of Mary. In the mean time the penitent left Rome with other companions, and during several years travelled in different parts of the world. On his return he again sought out his confessor, who, to his great joy and admiration, found that he was entirely changed, and free from his former evil habits. " My son," said he, " how hast thou obtained so wonderful a change from God ? The young man replied, " Father, our Blessed Lady obtained me this grace on account of that little devotion which thou taughtest me." Wonders did not cease here. The same confessor related the above fact from the pulpit ; a captain heard it who for many years had carried on improper intercourse with a certain woman, and determined that he also would practise the same devotion, that he too might be delivered from the horrible chains which bound him a slave of the devil (for it is necessary that sinners should have this intention, in order that the Blessed Virgin may be able to help them), and he also gave up his wickedness and changed his life.

But still more. After six months he foolishly, and relying too much on his own strength, went to pay a visit to the woman, to see if she also was converted. But on coming up to the door of the house, where he was in manifest danger of relapsing into sin, he was driven back by an invisible power, and found himself as far from the house as the whole length of the street, and standing before his own door. He was then clearly given to understand that Mary had thus delivered him from perdition. From this we may learn how solicitous our good Mother is, not only to withdraw us from a state of sin, if we recommend ourselves to her for this purpose, but also to deliver us from the danger of relapsing into it.

Prayer.

O immaculate and holy Virgin! O creature the most humble and the most exalted before God! Thou wast so lowly in thine own eyes, but so great in the eyes of thy Lord, that he exalted thee to such a degree as to choose thee for his Mother, and then made thee Queen of heaven and earth. I therefore thank God who so greatly has exalted thee, and rejoice in seeing thee so closely united with him, that more cannot be granted to a pure creature. Before thee, who art so humble, though endowed with so precious gifts, I am ashamed to appear, I who am so proud in the midst of so many sins. But miserable as I am, I will also salute thee, *Hail, Mary, full of grace.* Thou art already full of grace; impart a portion of it to me. *Our Lord is with thee.* That Lord who was always with thee from the first moment of thy creation, has now united himself more closely to thee by becoming thy Son. *Blessed art thou amongst women.* O Lady, blessed amongst all women, obtain the divine blessing for us also. *And blessed is the fruit of thy womb.* O blessed plant which hath given to the world so noble and holy a fruit! "Holy Mary, Mother of God!" O Mary, I acknowledge that thou art the true Mother of God, and in defence of this truth I am ready to give my life a thousand times. *Pray for us sinners.* But if thou art the Mother of God, thou art also the Mother of our salvation, and of us poor sinners; since God became man to save sinners, and made thee his Mother, that thy prayers might have power to save any sinner. Hasten, then, O Mary, and pray for us, *now, and at the hour of our death.* Pray always: pray now, that we live in the midst of so many temptations and dangers of losing God; but still more, pray for us at the hour of our death, when we are on the point of leaving this world, and being presented before God's tribunal; that, being saved by the merits of Jesus Christ and by thy intercession, we may come one day, without further danger of being lost, to salute thee and praise thee with thy Son in heaven for all eternity. Amen.

DISCOURSE V.

THE VISITATION OF MARY.

July 2.

Mary is the Treasurer of all Divine Graces; therefore, who-
ever desires Graces must have recourse to Mary; and he who
has recourse to Mary may be sure of obtaining the Graces
that he desires.

FORTUNATE does that family consider itself which is
visited by a royal personage, both on account of the
honor that redounds from such a visit, and the advantages that may be hoped to accrue from it. But still
more fortunate should that soul consider itself that is
visited by the Queen of the world, the most holy Virgin
Mary, who cannot but fill with riches and graces those
blessed souls whom she deigns to visit by her favors.
The house of Obededom was blessed when visited by
the ark of God : *And the Lord blessed his house.*[1] But
with how much greater blessings are those persons enriched who receive a loving visit from this living ark of
God, for such was the divine Mother ! " Happy is that
house which the Mother of God visits," [2] says Engelgrave. This was abundantly experienced by the house
of St. John the Baptist ; for Mary had scarcely entered
it when she heaped graces and heavenly benedictions on
the whole family ; and for this reason the present feast
of the Visitation is commonly called that of " Our Blessed
Lady of Graces." Hence we shall see in the present
discourse that the divine Mother is the treasurer of all
graces. We shall divide the subject into two parts. In

---

[1] " Benedixit Dominus domui ejus."—1 *Par.* xiii. 14.
[2] " Felix illa domus quam Mater Dei visitat."—*Cœl. Panth. in Vis.*
§ 2.

the first we shall see that whoever desires graces must have recourse to Mary. In the second, that he who has recourse to Mary should be confident of receiving the graces he desires.

I.

After the Blessed Virgin had heard from the archangel Gabriel that her cousin St. Elizabeth had been six months pregnant, she was internally enlightened by the Holy Ghost to know that the Incarnate Word, who had become her Son, was pleased then to manifest to the world the riches of his mercy in the first graces that he desired to impart to all that family. Therefore, without interposing any delay, according to St. Luke, *Mary, rising up, . . . went into the hill-country with haste.*[1] Rising from the quiet of contemplation to which she was always devoted, and quitting her beloved solitude, she immediately set out for the dwelling of St. Elizabeth ; and because *charity beareth all things,*[2] and cannot support delay, as St. Ambrose remarks on this Gospel, " the Holy Ghost knows not slow undertakings,"[3] without even reflecting on the arduousness of the journey, this tender Virgin, I say, immediately undertook it. On reaching the house, she salutes her cousin : *And she entered into the house of Zachary, and saluted Elizabeth.*[4] St. Ambrose here remarks that Mary was " the first to salute "[5] Elizabeth. The visit of Mary, however, had no resemblance to those of worldlings, which, for the greater part, consist in ceremony and outward demonstrations, devoid of all sincerity; for it brought with it an accumulation of

[1] " Exsurgens autem, Maria . . . abiit in montana cum festinatione."—*Luke*, i. 39.

[2] " Charitas omnia suffert."—1 *Cor.* xiii. 7.

[3] " Nescit tarda molimina Sancti Spiritus gratia."—*In Luc.* i.

[4] " Et intravit in domum Zachariæ, et salutavit Elizabeth."—*Luke*, i. 40.

[5] " Prior salutavit."

graces. The moment she entered that dwelling, on her first salutation, Elizabeth was filled with the Holy Ghost ; and St. John was cleansed from original sin, and sanctified ; and therefore gave this mark of joy by leaping in his mother's womb, wishing thereby to manifest the grace that he had received by the means of the Blessed Virgin, as St. Elizabeth herself declared : *As soon as the voice of thy salutation sounded in my ears, the infant in my womb leaped for joy.*[1] Thus, as Bernardine de Bustis remarks, by virtue of Mary's salutation St. John received the grace of the divine Spirit which sanctified him : "When the Blessed Virgin saluted Elizabeth, the voice of the salutation, entering her ears, descended to the child, and by its virtue he received the Holy Ghost."[2]

And now, if all these first-fruits of Redemption passed through Mary as the channel through which grace was communicated to the Baptist, the Holy Ghost to Elizabeth, the gift of propecy to Zachary and so many other blessings to the whole house, the first graces that to our knowledge the Eternal Word had granted on earth after his Incarnation, it is quite correct to believe that thenceforward God made Mary the universal channel, as she is called by St. Bernard, through which all the other graces that our Lord is pleased to dispense to us should pass, as we have already declared in the fifth chapter of the first part of this work.[3]

With reason, then, is this divine Mother called the treasure, the treasurer, and the dispenser of divine

---

[1] "Ut facta est vox salutationis tuæ in auribus meis, exsultavit in gaudio infans in utero meo."

[2] "Christus fecit Mariam salutare Elizabeth, ut sermo procedens de utero Matris, ubi habitabat Dominus. per aures Elizabeth ingressus, descenderet ad Joannem : ut illic eum ungeret in prophetam."— *Marial.* p. 6, s. 1.

[3] Chap. 5, page 155.

graces. She is thus called by the Venerable Abbot of Celles, "the Treasure of God, and the Treasurer of graces;"[1] by St. Peter Damian, "the Treasure of divine graces;"[2] by Blessed Albert the Great, "the Treasurer of Jesus Christ;"[3] by St. Bernardine, "the Dispenser of graces;"[4] by a learned Greek, quoted by Petavius, "the storehouse of all good things."[5] So also by St. Gregory Thaumaturgus, who observes that "Mary is said to be thus full of grace, for in her all the treasures of graces were hidden."[6] Richard of St. Laurence also says that "Mary is a treasure, because God has placed all gifts of graces in her as in a treasury; and thence he bestows great stipends on his soldiers and laborers."[7] She is a treasury of mercies, whence our Lord enriches his servants.

St. Bonaventure, speaking of the field in the Gospel, in which a treasure is hidden, and which should be purchased at however great a price, *the kingdom of heaven is like unto a treasure hidden in a field, which a man having found hid it, and for joy thereof goeth and selleth all that he hath and buyeth that field,*[8] says that "our Queen Mary is this field, in which Jesus Christ, the treasure of God the Father, is hid,"[9] and with Jesus Christ the source and

---

[1] "Thesaurus Domini est, et Thesauraria gratiarum."—*Cont. de V. M. in prol.*

[2] "Thesaurus divinarum gratiarum."

[3] "Thesauraria Jesu Christi."

[4] "Dispensatrix gratiarum."

[5] "Promptuarium omnium bonorum."

[6] "Maria sic gratia plena dicitur, quod in illa totus gratiæ thesaurus reconditus erat."—*In Annunt. hom.* 1.

[7] "Maria est thesaurus, quia in ea, ut in gazophylacio, reposuit Dominus omnia dona gratiarum, et de hoc thesauro ipse largitur larga stipendia suis militibus et operariis."—*De Laud. B. M.* l. 4.

[8] "Simile est regnum cœlorum thesauro abscondito in agro; quem qui invenit homo, abscondit. et præ gaudio illius vadit, et vendit universa quæ habet et emit agrum illum."—*Matt.* xiii. 44.

[9] "Ager iste est Maria, in qua Thesaurus Dei Patris absconditus est."—*Spec. B. V.* lect. 7.

flowing fountain of all graces. St. Bernard affirms that our Lord "has deposited the plenitude of every grace in Mary, that we may thus know that if we possess hope, grace, or anything salutary, that it is from her that it came."[1] Of this we are also assured by Mary herself, saying, *In me is all grace of the way and of the truth ;*[2] in me are all the graces of real blessings that you men can desire in life.

Yes, sweet Mother and our Hope, we know full well, says St. Peter Damian, "that all the treasures of divine mercies are in thy hands."[3] Before St. Peter Damian, St. Ildephonsus asserted the same thing in even stronger terms, when, speaking to the Blessed Virgin, he said, "O Lady, all the graces that God has decreed for men he has determined to grant through thy hands ; and therefore to thee has he committed all the treasures and ornaments of grace,"[4] so that, O Mary, concludes St. Germanus, no grace is dispensed to any one otherwise than through thy hands ; "there is no one saved but by thee ; no one who receives a gift of God but through thee."[5]

Blessed Albert the Great makes a beautiful paraphrase of the words of the angel addressed to the most Blessed Virgin, *Fear not, Mary, for thou hast found grace with God.*[6]

[1] "Totius boni plenitudinem posuit in Maria ; ut proinde si quid spei in nobis est, si quid gratiæ, si quid salutis, ab ea noverimus redundare."—*De Aquæd.*

[2] "In me gratia omnis viæ et veritatis."—*Ecclus.* xxiv. 25.

[3] "In manibus tuis thesauri miserationum Domini."—*In Nat. B. V.* s. 1.

[4] "Omnia bona, quæ illic summa Majestas decrevit facere, tuis manibus voluit commendare ; commissi quippe sunt tibi thesauri et ornamenta gratiarum."—*De Corona V.* c. 15.

[5] "Nullus, qui salvus fiat, nisi per te, nemo cui donum concedatur, nisi per te."—*De Zona Deip.*

[6] "Ne timeas, Maria! invenisti enim gratiam apud Deum."—*Luke,* i. 30.

"Fear not, O Mary, for thou hast found, not taken grace, as Lucifer tried to take it; thou hast not lost it as Adam lost it; thou hast not bought it as Simon Magus would have bought it; but thou hast found it because thou hast desired and sought it. Thou hast found uncreated grace; that is, God himself become thy Son; and with that grace thou hast found and obtained every created good." [1] St. Peter Chrysologus confirms this thought, saying, "This great Virgin and Mother found grace to restore thereby salvation to all men." [2] And elsewhere he says that Mary found a grace so full that it sufficed to save all: "Thou hast found grace, but how great a grace! It was such that it filled thee; and so great was its plenitude, that it could be poured down as a torrent on every creature." [3] So much so indeed, says Richard of St. Laurence, "that as God made the sun, that by its means light might be diffused through the whole earth, so he made Mary, that by her all divine mercies may be dispensed to the world." [4] St. Bernardine adds, that "from the time that the Virgin Mother conceived the divine Word in her womb, she obtained a kind of jurisdiction, so to say, over all the temporal manifestations of the Holy Ghost; so that no creature can obtain any grace from God that is not dispensed by this tender and compassionate mother." [5]

[1] "Ne timeas, quia invenisti; non rapuisti, ut primus angelus, non perdidisti, ut primus parens; non emisti, ut Simon Magus; sed invenisti, quia quæsivisti. Invenisti Gratiam increatam, et in illa omnem creatam."—Sup. Miss. q. 204.

[2] "Hanc gratiam accepit Virgo, salutem sæculis redditura."—Serm. 143.

[3] "Invenisti gratiam; quantam? quantam superius dixerat, plenam, et vere plenam, quæ largo imbre totam infunderet creaturam."—S. 142.

[4] "Sicut sol factus est, ut illuminet totum mundum, sic Maria facta est, ut misericordiam impetret toti mundo."—De Laud. B. M. l. 7.

[5] "A tempore quo Virgo Mater concepit in utero Verbum Dei, quamdam, ut sic dicam, jurisdictionem obtinuit in omni Spiritus Sancti processione temporali; ita quod nulla creatura aliquam a Deo

Hence let us conclude this point in the words of Richard of St. Laurence, who says, "that if we wish to obtain any grace, we must have recourse to Mary, the finder of grace, who cannot but obtain all that she asks for her servants ; for she has recovered the divine grace which was lost, and always finds it."[1] This thought he borrowed from St. Bernard, who says, "Let us seek for grace, and seek it by Mary ; for that which she seeks she finds, and cannot be frustrated."[2] If we, then, desire graces, we must go to this treasurer and dispenser of graces ; for it is the sovereign will of the giver of every good thing ; and we are assured of it by the same St. Bernard, that all graces should be dispensed by the hands of Mary : "for such is his will, who is pleased that we should have all by Mary."[3] *All, all ;* and he who says *all* excludes nothing.

II.

But because confidence is necessary to obtain graces, we will now consider how sure we ought to feel of obtaining them when we have recourse to Mary.

Why did Jesus Christ deposit all the riches of mercy that he intends for us in the hands of his Mother, unless it was that she might therewith enrich all her clients who love her, who honor her, and who have recourse to her with confidence ? *With me are riches . . . that I*

obtinuit gratiam, nisi secundum ipsius piæ Matris dispensationem."— *Pro Fest. V. M.* s. 5, c. 8.

[1] "Cupientes invenire gratiam, quæramus Inventricem gratiæ, quæ, quia semper invenit, frustrari non poterit."—*De Laud. B. M.* l. 2, p. 5.

[2] "Quæramus gratiam, et per Mariam quæramus ; quia, quod quærit, invenit, et frustrari non potest."—*De Aquæd.*

[3] "Quia sic est voluntas ejus, qui *totum* nos habere voluit per Mariam."

may enrich them that love me.[1] Thus the Blessed Virgin herself assures us that it is so in this passage, which the Holy Church applies to her on so many of her festivals. Therefore for no other purpose than to serve us, says the Abbot Adam, are those riches of eternal life kept by Mary, in whose breast our Lord has deposited the treasure of the miserable, and that the poor being supplied from it may become rich: "The riches of salvation are in custody of the Blessed Virgin for our use. Christ has made Mary's womb the treasury of the poor; thence the poor are enriched."[2] And St. Bernard says, "that she is a full aqueduct, that others may receive of her plenitude."[3] Mary was therefore given to the world that her graces might continually descend from heaven upon men.

Hence the same holy Father goes on to ask, "But why did St. Gabriel, having found the divine Mother already full of grace, according to his salutation, *Hail, full of grace!* afterwards say, that the Holy Ghost would come upon her to fill her still more with grace? If she was already full of grace, what more could the coming of the divine spirit effect?" The saint answers, "Mary was already full of grace; but the Holy Ghost filled her to overflowing, for our good, that from her superabundance we miserable creatures might be provided."[4] For this

---

[1] "Mecum sunt divitiæ . . . ut ditem diligentes me."—*Prov.* viii. 18, 21.

[2] "Divitiæ salutis penes Virginem nostris usibus reservantur. Christus in Virginis utero pauperum gazophylacium collocavit ; inde pauperes spiritu locupletati sunt."—*Tilman, Alleg. utr. Test. in Ecclus.* xxiv.

[3] "Ad hoc enim data est ipsa mundo quasi Aquæductus, ut per ipsam a Deo ad homines dona cœlestia jugiter descenderent."

[4] "Ad quid, nisi ut, adveniente jam Spiritu plena sibi, eodem superveniente, nobis quoque superplena et supereffluens fiat?"—*In Assumpt.* s. 2.

same reason Mary was called the moon, of which it is said, " She is full for herself and others." [1]

He that shall find me shall find life, and shall have salvation from the Lord. [2] Blessed is he who finds me by having recourse to me, says our Mother. He will find life, and will find it easily ; for as it is easy to find and draw as much water as we please from a great fountain, so it is easy to find graces and eternal salvation by having recourse to Mary. A holy soul once said, "We have only to seek graces from our Blessed Lady to receive them." St. Bernard also says, " That it was because the Blessed Virgin was not yet born that in ancient times the great abundance of grace which we now see flow on the world was wanting; for Mary, this desirable channel, did not exist." [3] But now that we have this Mother of mercy, what graces are there that we need fear not to obtain when we cast ourselves at her feet ? " I am the city of refuge" (thus St. John Damascene makes her speak) "for all those who have recourse to me." "Come, then, to me, my children; for from me you will obtain graces, and these in greater abundance than you can possibly imagine." [4]

It is true that that which the Venerable Sister Mary Villani saw in a celestial vision is experienced by many. This servant of God once saw the divine Mother as a great fountain, to which many went, and from it they carried off the waters of grace in great abundance. But what then happened ? Those who had sound jars preserved the graces they received; but those who brought

[1] " Luna plena sibi et aliis."

[2] " Qui me invenerit, inveniet vitam, et hauriet salutem a Domino." —*Prov.* viii. 35

[3] " Propterea tanto tempore humano generi fluenta gratiarum defuerunt, quod necdum intercederet is Aquæductus."—*De Aquæd.*

[4] " Ego Civitas refugii, iis qui ad me confugiunt; accedite, et gratiarum dona affluentissime haurite."—*De Dorm. B. M.* s. 2.

broken vessels, that is to say, those whose souls were burdened with sin, received graces, but did not long preserve them. It is, however, certain that men, even those who are ungrateful sinners and the most miserable, daily obtain innumerable graces from Mary. St. Augustine, addressing the Blessed Virgin, says, " Through thee do the miserable obtain mercy, the ungracious grace, sinners pardon, the weak strength, the worldly heavenly things, mortals life, and pilgrims their country."[1]

Let us then, O devout clients of Mary, rouse ourselves to greater and greater confidence each time that we have recourse to her for graces. That we may do so, let us always remember two great prerogatives of this good Mother; her great desire to do us good, and the power she has with her Son to obtain whatever she asks.

To be convinced of the desire that Mary has to be of service to all, we need only consider the mystery of the present festival, that is, Mary's visit to St. Elizabeth. The journey from Nazareth, where the most Blessed Virgin lived, to the city of Hebron, which St. Luke calls a city of Judea, and in which according to Baronius[2] and other authors St. Elizabeth resided, was at least sixty-nine miles long, as we learn from Brother Joseph of Jesus Mary, the author of a life of the Blessed Virgin,[3] Bede, and Brocardus; but, notwithstanding the arduousness of the undertaking, the Blessed Virgin, tender and delicate as she then was, and unaccustomed to such fatigue, did not delay her departure. And what was it that impelled her? It was that great charity with which her most tender heart was ever filled that drove her, so to say, to go and at once begin her great office of dispenser

---

[1] " Per te hæreditamus misericordiam miseri, ingrati gratiam, veniam peccatores, sublimia infirmi, cœlestia terreni, mortales vitam, et patriam peregrini."

[2] *Appar. ad Ann.* n. 77.

[3] L. 3. ch. 22.

of graces. Precisely thus does St. Ambrose speak of her journey: "She did not go in incredulity of the prophecy, but glad to do what she had undertaken; it was joy that hastened her steps, in the fulfilment of a religious office;"[1] the saint thereby meaning, that she did not undertake the journey to inquire into the truth of what the angel had pronounced to her of the pregnancy of St. Elizabeth, but exulting in the greatness of her desire to be of service to that family, and hastening for the joy she felt in doing good to others, and wholly intent on that work of charity: *Rising, she went with haste.* Here, let it be observed, the Evangelist, in speaking of Mary's departure for the house of Elizabeth, says, that she went with haste; but when he speaks of her return, he no longer says anything of haste, but simply that *Mary abode with her about three months; and she returned to her own house.*[2] What other object, then, asks St. Bonaventure, could the Mother of God have had in view, when she hastened to visit the house of St. John the Baptist, if it was not the desire to render service to that family? "What caused her to hasten in the performance of that act of charity but the charity which burnt in her heart?"[3]

This charity of Mary towards men certainly did not cease when she went to heaven; nay more, it greatly increased there, for there she better knows our wants, and has still greater compassion for our miseries. Bernardine de Bustis writes, "that Mary desires more earnestly to do us good and grant us graces than we desire to receive them."[4] So much so, that St. Bonaventure says,

[1] "Non quasi incredula de oraculo, sed quasi læta pro voto, religiosa pro officio, festina præ gaudio, in montana perrexit."—*In Luc.* i.

[2] "Mansit autem Maria cum illa quasi mensibus tribus: et reversa est in domum suam."—*Luke,* i. 56.

[3] "Quid eam ad officium charitatis festinare cogebat, nisi charitas, quæ in corde ejus fervebat?"—*Spec. B. V.* lect. 4.

[4] "Plus desiderat ipsa facere tibi bonum, et largiri gratiam, quam tu accipere concupiscas."—*Marial.* p. 2, s. 5.

that she considers herself offended by those who do not ask her for graces: "Not only those, O Lady, offend thee who outrage thee, but thou art also offended by those who neglect to ask thy favors."[1] For Mary's desire to enrich all with graces is, so to say, a part of her nature, and she superabundantly enriches her servants, as blessed Raymond Jordano affirms: "Mary is God's treasure, and the treasurer of his graces; she plentifully endows her servants with choice gifts."[2]

Hence the same author says, that "he who finds Mary finds every good."[3] And he adds, that every one can find her, even the most miserable sinner in the world; for she is so benign that she rejects none who have recourse to her: "Her benignity is such, that no one need fear to approach her. And her mercy is so great, that no one meets with a repulse."[4] Thomas à Kempis makes her say: "I invite all to have recourse to me; I expect all, I desire all, and I never despise any sinner, however unworthy he may be, who comes to seek my aid."[5] Richard of St. Laurence says, that whoever goes to ask graces from Mary "finds her always prepared to help;"[6] that is, she is always ready and inclined to help us, and to obtain for us every grace of eternal salvation by her powerful prayers.

I say, by her powerful prayers; for another reflection, which should increase our confidence, is, that we know

[1] "In te, Domina, peccant non solum qui tibi injuriam irrogant, sed etiam qui te non rogant."

[2] "Maria thesaurus Domini est, et Thesauraria gratiarum ipsius; donis spiritualibus ditat copiosissime servientes sibi."

[3] "Inventa Maria, invenitur omne bonum."

[4] "Tanta est ejus benignitas, quod nulli formidandum est ad eam accedere; tantaque misericordia, quod ab ea nemo repellitur."—*Cont. de B. V. in prol.*

[5] "Omnes invito, omnes exspecto, omnes venire desidero; nullum peccatorem despicio."—*Solil. an.* c. 24.

[6] "Inveniet semper paratam auxiliari."—*De Laud. B. M.* l. 2, p. 1.

and are certain that she obtains from God all that she asks for her clients. Observe especially, says St. Bonaventure, in this visit of Mary to St. Elizabeth, the great power of her words. According to the Evangelist, at the sound of her voice the grace of the Holy Ghost was conferred on St. Elizabeth, as well as on her son St. John the Baptist: *And it came to pass, that when Elizabeth heard the salutation of Mary, the infant leaped in her womb, and she was filled with the Holy Ghost.*[1] On this text St. Bonaventure says, "See how great is the power of the words of our lady; for no sooner has she pronounced them, than the Holy Ghost is given."[2]

Theophilus of Alexandria says, "that Jesus is greatly pleased when Mary intercedes with him for us; for all the graces which he is, so to say, forced to grant through her prayers, he considers as granted not so much to us as to herself."[3] And remark the words, "forced by the prayers of his Mother." Yes, for, as St. Germanus attests, Jesus cannot do otherwise than graciously accede to all that Mary asks; wishing, as it were, in this to obey her as his true Mother. Hence the saint says, that "the prayers of this Mother have a certain maternal authority with Jesus Christ; so that she obtains the grace of pardon even for those who have been guilty of grievous crimes, and commend themselves to her;" and then he concludes: "for it is not possible that thou shouldst not be graciously heard; for God in all things acts towards

---

[1] "Et factum est, ut audivit salutationem Mariæ Elizabeth, exsultavit infans in utero ejus; et repleta est Spiritu Sancto Elizabeth." —*Luke,* i. 41.

[2] "Vide quanta virtus sit in verbis Dominæ; quia ad eorum pronuntiationem confertur Spiritus Sanctus."—*Med. vit. Christi,* c. 5.

[3] "Gaudet Filius, orante Matre; quia omnia quæ nobis, precibus suæ Genitricis evictus, donat, ipsi Matri se donasse putat."—*Salazar, in Prov.* viii. 18.

thee as his true and spotless Mother." [1] This is fully confirmed, as St. John Chrysostom observes, by what took place at the marriage-feast of Cana, when Mary asked her Son for wine which had failed: *They have no wine.* Jesus answered: *Woman, what is that to Me and to thee? My hour is not yet come.* [2] But though the time for miracles was not yet come, as St. Chrysostom and Theophylact explain it, yet, says St. Chrysostom, "the Saviour, notwithstanding his answer, and to obey his Mother, worked the miracle she asked for," [3] and converted the water into wine.

Let us go, therefore, with confidence to the throne of grace, says the Apostle, exhorting us, *that we may obtain mercy, and find grace in seasonable aid.* [4] "The throne of grace is the Blessed Virgin Mary," [5] says Blessed Albert the Great. If, then, we wish for graces, let us go to the throne of grace, which is Mary; and let us go with the certain hope of being heard; for we have Mary's intercession, and she obtains from her Son all whatever she asks. "Let us seek for grace," I repeat with St. Bernard, "and let us seek it through Mary," [6] trusting to what the Blessed Virgin Mother herself said to St. Mechtilde, that the Holy Ghost, filling her with all his sweetness, has rendered her so dear to God, that whoever seeks

[1] "Tu autem materna in Deum auctoritate pollens, etiam iis qui enormiter peccant, eximiam remissionis gratiam concilias; non enim potes non exaudiri, cum Deus tibi, ut veræ et intemeratæ Matri, in omnibus morem gerat."—*In Dorm. V. M.* s. 2.

[2] "Vinum non habent. Quid mihi et tibi est, mulier? nondum venit hora mea."—*John,* ii. 3, 4.

[3] "Et licet ita responderit, maternis tamen precibus obtemperavit."

[4] "Adeamus ergo cum fiducia ad Thronum gratiæ, ut misericordiam consequamur, et gratiam inveniamus in auxilio opportuno."—*Heb.* iv. 16.

[5] "Thronus gratiæ est Beata Virgo Maria."—*De Sanctis,* s. 53.

[6] "Quæramus gratiam, et per Mariam quæramus."

graces through her intercession is certain to obtain them." [1]

And if we credit that celebrated saying of St. Anselm, "that salvation is occasionally more easily obtained by calling on the name of Mary than by invoking that of Jesus;" [2] we shall sometimes sooner obtain graces by having recourse to Mary than by having directly recourse to our Saviour Jesus himself; not that he is not the source and Lord of all graces, but because, when we have recourse to the Mother, and she prays for us, her prayers have greater efficacy than ours, as being those of a mother. Let us then never leave the feet of this treasurer of graces; but ever address her in the words of St. John Damascene: "O Blessed Mother of God, open to us the gate of Mercy; for thou art the salvation of the human race." [3] O Mother of God, open to us the door of thy compassion, by always praying for us; for thy prayers are the salvation of all men. When we have recourse to Mary, it would be advisable to entreat her to ask and obtain us the graces which she knows to be the most expedient for our salvation; this is precisely what the Dominican Brother Reginald did, as it is related in the chronicles of the Order. [4] This servant of Mary was ill, and he asked her to obtain him the recovery of his health. His sovereign Lady appeared to him, accompanied by St. Cecily and St. Catharine, and said with the greatest sweetness, "My son, what dost thou desire of me?" The religious was confused at so gracious an offer on the part of Mary, and knew not

[1] " Spiritus Sanctus, tota sua dulcedine me penetrando, tam gratiosam effecit, ut omnis qui per me gratiam quærit, ipsam inveniet."— *Spir. Grat.* l. 1, c. 67.

[2] " Velocior est nonnunquam salus, memorato nomine ejus Mariæ, quam invocato nomine Jesu."— *De Excell. V.* c. 6.

[3] " Misericordiæ januam aperi nobis, benedicta Deipara! tu enim es salus generis humani."— *In Annunt.*

[4] *De Castill. Hist. Præd.* p. 1, l. 1. c. 33.

what to answer. Then one of the saints gave him this advice: Reginald, I will tell thee what to do; ask for nothing, but place thyself entirely in her hands, for Mary will know how to grant thee a greater grace than thou canst possibly ask. The sick man followed this advice, and the divine Mother obtained the re-establishment of his health.

But if we also desire the happiness of receiving the visits of this Queen of heaven, we should often visit her by going before her image, or praying to her in churches dedicated to her honor. Read the following example, in which you will see with what special favors she rewards the devout visits of her clients.

EXAMPLE.*

A certain cavalier named Ansald of the city of Dole in France, received in battle a wound from an arrow, which entered so deep into the jaw-bone that it was not possible to extract the iron point which remained. After four years, the poor man, unable any longer to endure the torment, and being besides very ill, thought of having the wound reopened, that the surgeons might again try to extract the iron. He recommended himself to the Blessed Virgin, and made a vow that he would every year visit a devout image of Mary, which was in that place, and make an offering of a certain sum of money, should she grant his prayer. He had no sooner made the vow than he felt the iron drop of its own accord in his mouth. On the following day, ill as he was, he went to visit the image, and scarcely had he placed his offering on the altar when he found himself entirely restored to health.

Chron. Dol. 1550, ap. Labb. Bibl. man.

Prayer.

Immaculate and Blessed Virgin, since thou art the universal dispenser of all divine graces, thou art the hope of all, and my hope. I will ever thank my Lord for having granted me the grace to know thee, and for having shown me the means by which I may obtain graces and be saved. Thou art this means, O great Mother of God; for I now understand that it is principally through the merits of Jesus Christ, and then through thy intercession, that my soul must be saved. Ah! my Queen, thou didst hasten so greatly to visit, and by that means didst sanctify the dwelling of St. Elizabeth; deign, then, to visit, and visit quickly, the poor house of my soul. Ah! hasten, then, for thou well knowest, and far better than I do, how poor it is, and with how many maladies it is afflicted; with disordered affections, evil habits, and sins committed, all of which are pestiferous diseases, which would lead it to eternal death. Thou canst enrich it, O treasurer of God; and thou canst heal all its infirmities. Visit me, then, in life, and visit me especially at the moment of death, for then I shall more than ever require thy aid. I do not indeed expect, neither am I worthy, that thou shouldst visit me on this earth with thy visible presence, as thou hast visited so many of thy servants; but they were not unworthy and ungrateful as I am. I am satisfied to see thee in thy kingdom of heaven, there to be able to love thee more, and thank thee for all that thou hast done for me. At present I am satisfied that thou shouldst visit me with thy mercy; thy prayers are all that I desire.

Pray, then, O Mary, for me, and commend me to thy Son. Thou, far better than I do, knowest my miseries and my wants. What more can I say? Pity me; I am so miserable and ignorant, that I neither know nor can I seek for, the graces that I stand the most in need of. My most sweet Queen and Mother, do thou seek and obtain for me from thy Son those graces which thou knowest to be the most expedient and necessary for my soul. I abandon myself entirely into thy hands, and only beg the divine Majesty, that by the merits of my Saviour Jesus he will grant me the graces which thou askest him for me. Ask, ask, then, O most Holy Virgin, that which thou seest best for me; thy prayers are never rejected, they are the prayers of a Mother addressed to a Son, who loves thee, his Mother, so much, and rejoices in doing all that thou desirest, that he may honor thee more, and at the same time show thee the great love that he bears thee. Let us make an agreement, O Lady, that while I live confiding in thee, thou on thy part wilt charge thyself with my salvation. Amen.

DISCOURSE VI.

THE PURIFICATION OF MARY.

February 2.

The great Sacrifice which Mary made on this day to God in offering Him the Life of her Son.

IN the old law there were two precepts concerning the birth of the first-born sons: one was, that the mother should remain as unclean, retired in her house for forty days; after which she was to go to purify herself in the temple. The other was, that the parents of the first-born son should take him to the Temple, and there offer him to God. On this day the most Blessed Virgin obeyed both these precepts. Although Mary was not bound by the law of purification, since she was always a virgin and always pure, yet her humility and obedience made her wish to go like other mothers to purify herself. She at the same time obeyed the second precept, to present and offer her Son to the Eternal Father. *And after the days of her purification, according to the law of Moses, were accomplished, they carried him to Jerusalem to present him to the Lord.*[1] But the Blessed Virgin did not offer him as other mothers offered their sons. Others offered them to God; but they knew that this oblation was simply a legal ceremony, and that by redeeming them they made them their own, without fear of having again to offer them to death. Mary really offered her son to death, and knew for certain that the sacrifice of the life of Jesus which she then made was one day to be actually

[1] " Et postquam impleti sunt dies purgationis ejus, secundum legem Moysi, tulerunt illum in Jerusalem, ut sisterent eum Domino."—*Luke*, ii. 22.

consummated on the altar of the cross; so that Mary, by offering the life of her Son, came, in consequence of the love she bore this Son, really to sacrifice her own entire self to God. Leaving, then, aside all other considerations into which we might enter on the many mysteries of this festival, we will only consider the greatness of the sacrifice which Mary made of herself to God in offering him on this day the life of her Son. And this will be the whole subject of the following discourse.

The Eternal Father had already determined to save man, who was lost by sin, and to deliver him from eternal death. But because he willed at the same time that his divine justice should not be defrauded of a worthy and due satisfaction, he spared not the life of his Son already become man to redeem man, but willed that he should pay with the utmost rigor the penalty which men had deserved. *He that spared not even His own Son, but delivered Him up for us all.*[1] He sent him, therefore, on earth to become man. He destined him a mother, and willed that this mother should be the blessed Virgin Mary. But as he willed not that his divine Word should become her Son before she by an express consent had accepted him, so also he willed not that Jesus should sacrifice his life for the salvation of men without the concurrent assent of Mary; that, together with the sacrifice of the life of the Son, the mother's heart might also be sacrificed. St. Thomas teaches that the quality of a mother gives her a special right over her children; hence, Jesus being in himself innocent and undeserving of punishment, it seemed fitting that he should not be condemned to the cross as a victim for the sins of the world without the consent of his Mother, by which she should spontaneously offer him to death.

But although from the moment she became the

[1] " Qui etiam proprio Filio suo non pepercit, sed pro nobis omnibus tradidit illum."—*Rom.* viii. 32.

Mother of Jesus, Mary consented to his death, yet God willed that on this day she should make a solemn sacrifice of herself, by offering her Son to him in the Temple, sacrificing his precious life to divine justice. Hence St. Epiphanius calls her "a priest." [1] And now we begin to see how much this sacrifice cost her, and what heroic virtues she had to practise when she herself subscribed the sentence by which her beloved Jesus was condemned to death.

Behold Mary is actually on her road to Jerusalem to offer her Son; she hastens her steps towards the place of sacrifice, and she herself bears the beloved victim in her arms. She enters the Temple, approaches the altar, and there, beaming with modesty, devotion, and humility, presents her Son to the Most High. In the mean time the holy Simeon, who had received a promise from God that he should not die without having first seen the expected Messiah, takes the divine child from the hands of the Blessed Virgin, and, enlightened by the Holy Ghost, announces to her how much the sacrifice which she then made of her Son would cost her, and that with him her own blessed soul would also be sacrificed.

Here St. Thomas of Villanova contemplates the holy old man becoming troubled and silent at the thought of having to give utterance to a prophecy so fatal to this poor Mother. The saint then considers Mary, who asks him, "Why, O Simeon, art thou thus troubled in the midst of such great consolations?" "O royal Virgin," he replies, "I would desire not to announce thee so bitter tidings; but since God thus wills it for thy greater merit, listen to what I have to say. This child, which is now such a source of joy to thee—and, O God, with how much reason?—this child, I say, will one day be a source of so bitter grief to thee that no creature in the world

---

[1] "Virginem appello velut sacerdotem."—*Hom. in Laud. S. M.*

has ever experienced the like; and this will be when thou seest him persecuted by men of every class, and made a butt upon earth for their scoffs and outrages; they will even go so far as to put him to death as a malefactor before thine own eyes. Thou so greatly rejoicest in this infant; but, behold, he is placed for a sign which shall be contradicted. Know that after his death there will be many martyrs, who for the love of this Son of thine will be tormented and put to death; their martyrdom, however, will be endured in their bodies; but thine, O divine Mother, will be endured in thy heart. O, how many thousands of men will be torn to pieces and put to death for the love of this child! and although they will all suffer much in their bodies, thou, O Virgin, wilt suffer much more in thy heart." [1]

Yes, in her heart; for compassion alone for the sufferings of this most beloved Son was the sword of sorrow which was to pierce the heart of the Mother, as St. Simeon exactly foretold: *And thy own soul a sword shall pierce.* [2] Already the most blessed Virgin, as St. Jerome says, was enlightened by the sacred Scriptures, and knew the sufferings that the Redeemer was to endure in his life, and still more at the time of his death. She fully understood from the prophets that he was to be betrayed by one of his disciples: *For even the man of my peace, in whom I trusted, who ate my bread, hath greatly supplanted me,* [3] as David foretold: that he was to be abandoned by them: *Strike the shepherd, and the sheep shall be*

[1] "Unde tibi tanta turbatio? O Virgo regia! nollem tibi talia nuntiare. sed audi: Nimium nunc pro isto Infante lætaris; Ecce positus est hic . . . in signum, cui contradicetur a multis . . . O quot millia hominum pro isto puero laniabuntur, jugulabuntur! sed, et si omnes patiantur in corpore, tu, Virgo, amplius in animo patieris."—*De Purif. B. V.*

[2] "Et tuam ipsius animam pertransibit gladius."—*Luke,* ii. 35.

[3] "Qui edebat panes meos, magnificavit super me supplantationem."—*Ps.* xl. 10.

scattered.[1] She well knew the contempt, the spitting, the blows, the derisions that he was to suffer from the people: *I have given my body to the strikers, and my cheeks to them that plucked them: I have not turned away my face from them that rebuked me and that spit upon me.*[2] She knew that he was to become the reproach of men, and the outcast of the most degraded of the people, so as to be saturated with insults and injuries: *But I am a worm, and no man: the reproach of men, and the outcast of the people.*[3] *He shall be filled with reproaches.*[4] She knew that at the end of his life his most sacred flesh would be torn and mangled by scourges: *But He was wounded for our iniquities, He was bruised for our sins.*[5] And this to such a degree that his whole body was to be disfigured, and become like that of a leper—all wounds, and the bones appearing. *There is no beauty in Him nor comeliness . . . and we have thought Him, as it were, a leper.*[6] *They have numbered all my bones.*[7] She knew that he was to be pierced by nails: *They have dug my hands and feet.*[8] To be ranked with malefactors: *And was reputed with the wicked.*[9] And that finally, hanging on a cross, he was to die for the salvation of men: *And they shall look upon Me, whom they have pierced.*[10]

[1] "Percute pastorem, et dispergentur oves."—*Zach.* xiii. 7.

[2] "Corpus meum dedi percutientibus, et genas meas vellentibus; faciem meam non averti ab increpantibus et conspuentibus in me."— *Is.* l. 6.

[3] "Ego autem sum vermis, et non homo, opprobrium hominum et abjectio plebis."—*Ps.* xxi. 7.

[4] "Saturabitur opprobriis."—*Lam.* iii. 30.

[5] "Ipse autem vulneratus est propter iniquitates nostras, attritus est propter scelera nostra."—*Is.* liii. 5.

[6] "Non est species ei, neque decor; . . . et nos putavimus eum quasi leprosum."—*Ibid.* 2.

[7] "Dinumeraverunt omnia ossa mea."—*Ps.* xxi. 18.

[8] "Foderunt manus meas et pedes meos."—*Ps.* xxi. 17.

[9] "Et cum sceleratis reputatus est."—*Is.* liii. 12.

[10] "Et aspicient ad me, quem confixerunt."—*Zach.* xii. 10.

Mary, I say, already knew all these torments that her Son was to endure; but, in the words addressed to her by Simeon : *And thy own soul a sword shall pierce,* all the minute circumstances of the sufferings, internal and external, that were to torment her Jesus in his Passion, were made known to her, as our Lord revealed to St. Teresa.[1] She consented to all with a constancy which filled even the angels with astonishment; she pronounced the sentence that her Son should die, and die by so ignominious and painful a death, saying, " Eternal Father, since Thou willest that it should be so, *not my will, but Thine be done.*[2] I unite my will to Thy most holy will, and I sacrifice this my Son to Thee. I am satisfied that he should lose his life for Thy glory and the salvation of the world. At the same time I sacrifice my heart to Thee, that it may be transpierced with sorrow, and this as much as Thou pleasest: it suffices me, my God, that Thou art glorified and satisfied with my offering: *Not my will, but Thine be done.* O charity without measure ! O constancy without parallel ! O victory which deserves the eternal admiration of heaven and earth !

Hence it was that Mary was silent during the Passion of Jesus, when he was unjustly accused. She said nothing to Pilate, who was somewhat inclined to set him at liberty, knowing, as he did, his innocence; she only appeared in public to assist at the great sacrifice, which was to be accomplished on Calvary; she accompanied her beloved Son to the place of execution; she was with him from the first moment, when he was nailed on the cross: *There stood by the cross of Jesus His Mother,*[3] until she saw him expire, and the sacrifice was con-

---

[1] *Life, addit.*

[2] " Non mea voluntas, sed tua fiat."—*Luke,* xxii. 42.

[3] " Stabant autem juxta crucem Jesu Mater ejus."—*John,* xix. 25.

summated.   And all this she did to complete the offering which she had made of him to God in the Temple.

To understand the violence which Mary had to offer herself in this sacrifice, it would be necessary to understand the love that this Mother bore to Jesus.   Generally speaking, the love of mothers is so tender towards their children, that, when these are at the point of death, and there is fear of losing them, it causes them to forget all their faults and defects, and even the injuries that they may have received from them, and makes them suffer an inexpressible grief.   And yet the love of these mothers is a love divided amongst other children, or at least amongst other creatures.   Mary had an only Son, and he was the most beautiful of all the sons of Adam— most amiable, for he had everything to make him so: he was obedient, virtuous, innocent, holy; suffice it to say, he was God.   Again, this Mother's love was not divided amongst other objects; she had concentrated all her love in this only Son; nor did she fear to exceed in loving him; for this Son was God, who merits infinite love. This Son it was who was the victim that she of her own free-will had to sacrifice to death.

Let each one, then, consider how much it must have cost Mary, and what strength of mind she had to exercise in this act, by which she sacrificed the life of so amiable a Son to the cross.   Behold, therefore, the most fortunate of mothers, because the Mother of a God ; but who was at the same time, of all mothers, the most worthy of compassion, being the most afflicted, inasmuch as she saw her Son destined to the cross from the day on which he was given to her.   What mother would accept of a child, knowing that she would afterwards miserably lose him by an ignominious death, and that moreover she herself would be present and see him thus die ? Mary willingly accepts this Son on so hard a condition ; and not only does she accept him, but she herself on this day offers him, with her own hand, to death, sacrificing him to divine justice.

St. Bonaventure says that the Blessed Virgin would have accepted the pains and death of her Son far more willingly for herself; but to obey God she made the great offering of the divine life of her beloved Jesus, conquering, but with an excess of grief, the tender love which she bore him. "Could it have been so, she would willingly have endured all the torments of her Son; but it pleased God that his only-begotten Son should be offered for the salvation of the human race."[1] Hence it is that in this offering Mary had to do herself more violence and was more generous than if she had offered herself to suffer all that her Son was to endure. Therefore she surpassed all the martyrs in generosity; for the martyrs offered their own lives, but the Blessed Virgin offered the life of her Son, whom she loved and esteemed infinitely more than her own life. Nor did the sufferings of this painful offering end here; nay, even, they only began; for from that time forward, during the whole life of her Son, Mary had constantly before her eyes the death and all the torments that he was to endure. Hence, the more this Son showed himself beautiful, gracious, and amiable, the more did the anguish of her heart increase.

Ah, most sorrowful Mother, hadst thou loved thy Son less, or had he been less amiable, or had he loved thee less, thy sufferings in offering him to death would certainly have been diminished. But there never was, and never will be, a mother who loved her son more than thou didst love thine; for there never was, and never will be a son more amiable, or one who loved his

---

[1] " Placuit ei, quod Unigenitus suus pro salute generis humani offerretur; et tantum etiam compassa est, ut, si fieri potuisset, omnia tormenta quæ Filius pertulit, ipsa multo libentius sustinuisset."—*In Sent.* 1. d. 48, a. 2, q. 2.

mother more than thy Jesus loved thee. O God, had we beheld the beauty, the majesty of the countenance of that divine Child, could we have ever had courage to sacrifice his life for our salvation? And thou, O Mary, who wast his Mother, and a Mother loving him with so tender a love, thou couldst offer thy innocent Son, for the salvation of men, to a death more painful and cruel than ever was endured by the greatest malefactor on earth!

Ah, how sad a scene from that day forward must love have continually placed before the eyes of Mary,—a scene representing all the outrages and mockeries which her poor Son was to endure! See, love already represents him agonized with sorrow in the garden, mangled with scourges, crowned with thorns in the prætorium, and finally hanging on the ignominious cross on Calvary! "Behold, O Mother," says love, "what an amiable and innocent Son thou offerest to so many torments and to so horrible a death!" And to what purpose save him from the hands of Herod, since it is only to reserve him for a far more sorrowful end?

Thus Mary not only offered her Son to death in the Temple, but she renewed that offering every moment of her life; for she revealed to St. Bridget "that the sorrow announced to her by the holy Simeon never left her heart until her assumption into heaven."[1] Hence St. Anselm thus addresses her: "O compassionate Lady, I cannot believe that thou couldst have endured for a moment so excruciating a torment without expiring under it, had not God himself, the Spirit of Life sustained thee."[2] But St. Bernard affirms, speaking of the great

---

[1] "Dolor iste, usquedum assumpta fui corpore et anima in cœlum, numquam defuit a corde meo."—*Rev.* l. 6, c. 57.

[2] "Pia Domina! non crediderim te potuisse ullo puncto stimulos tanti cruciatus, quin vitam amitteres, sustinere, nisi ipse Spiritus vitæ te confortaret."—*De Excell. V.* c. 5.

sorrow which Mary experienced on this day, that from that time forward "she died living, enduring a sorrow more cruel than death."[1] In every moment she lived dying; for in every moment she was assailed by the sorrow of the death of her beloved Jesus, which was a torment more cruel than any death.

Hence the divine Mother, on account of the great merit that she acquired by this great sacrifice which she made to God for the salvation of the world, was justly called by St. Augustine "the repairer of the human race;"[2] by St. Epiphanius, "the redeemer of captives;"[3] by St. Anselm, "the repairer of a lost world;"[4] by St. Germanus, "our liberator from our calamities;"[5] by St. Ambrose, "the mother of all the faithful;"[6] by St. Augustine, "the mother of the living;"[7] and by St. Andrew of Crete, "the Mother of life."[8] For Arnold of Chartres says, "The wills of Christ and of Mary were then united, so that both offered the same holocaust; she thereby producing with him the one effect, the salvation of the world."[9] At the death of Jesus Mary united her will to that of her Son; so much so, that both offered one and the same sacrifice; and therefore the holy abbot says that both the Son and the mother effected human redemption, and obtained salvation for men—Jesus by satisfying for our sins, Mary by obtaining the applica-

---

[1] "Moriebatur vivens; ferens dolorem morte crudeliorem."—*Lib. de pass. D.* c. 10.

[2] "Reparatrix generis humani."

[3] "Redemptrix captivorum."

[4] "Reparatrix perditi orbis."

[5] "Restauratio calamitatum nostrarum."

[6] "Mater omnium credentium."

[7] "Mater viventium."

[8] "Mater vitæ."

[9] "Omnino tunc erat una Christi et Mariæ voluntas, unumque holocaustum ambo pariter offerebant Deo: cum Christo communem in salute mundi effectum obtinuit."—*De Laud. B. M*

tion of this satisfaction to us. Hence Denis the Carthusian also asserts "that the divine Mother can be called the saviour of the world, since by the pain that she endured in commiserating her Son (willingly sacrificed by her to divine justice) she merited that through her prayers the merits of the Passion of the Redeemer should be communicated to men." [1]

Mary, then, having by the merit of her sorrows, and by sacrificing her Son, become the Mother of all the redeemed, it is right to believe that through her hands, divine graces, and the means to obtain eternal life, which are the fruits of the merits of Jesus Christ, are given to men. To this it is that St. Bernard refers when he says, that " when God was about to redeem the human race, he deposited the whole price in Mary's hands:" [2] by which words the saint gives us to understand that the merits of the Redeemer are applied to our souls by the intercession of the Blessed Virgin ; for all graces that are the fruits of Jesus Christ were comprised in that price of which she had charge.

If the sacrifice of Abraham by which he offered his son Isaac to God was so pleasing to the divine Majesty, that as a reward he promised to multiply his descendants as the stars of heaven—*Because thou hast done this thing, and hast not spared thy only-begotten son for My sake, I will bless thee, and I will multiply thy seed as the stars of heaven* [3]—we must certainly believe that the more noble sacrifice which the great Mother of God made to him of her

---

[1] " Virgo dici potest mundi Salvatrix propter meritum suæ compassionis, quæ, patienti Filio acerbissime condolendo, excellenter promeruit, ut, per preces ejus, meritum passionis Christi communicetur hominibus."—*De Laud. V. M.* l. 2, a. 23.

[2] " Redempturus humanum genus, pretium universum contulit in Mariam."—*De Aquæd.*

[3] " Quia fecisti hanc rem, et non pepercisti filio tuo unigenito propter me, benedicam tibi, et multiplicabo semen tuum sicut stellas cœli."—*Gen.* xxii. 16, 17.

Jesus, was far more agreeable to him, and therefore that he has granted that through her prayers the number of the elect should be multiplied, that is to say, increased by the number of her fortunate children; for she considers and protects all her devout clients as such.

St: Simeon received a promise from God that he should not die until he had seen the Messiah born : *And he had received an answer from the Holy Ghost, that he should not see death before he had seen the Christ of the Lord.*[1] But this grace he only received through Mary, for it was in her arms that he found the Saviour. Hence, he who desires to find Jesus, will not find him otherwise than by Mary. Let us, then, go to this divine Mother if we wish to find Jesus, and let us go with great confidence.

Mary told her servant Prudenziana Zagnoni that every year, on this day of her purification, a great grace would be bestowed upon some sinner. Who knows but one of us may be the favored sinner of this day ? If our sins are great, the power of Mary is greater. " The Son can deny nothing to such a Mother," says St. Bernard.[2] If Jesus is irritated against us, Mary immediately appeases him. Plutarch relates that Antipater wrote a long letter to Alexander the Great, filled with accusations against his mother Olympia. Having read the letter, Alexander said, " Antipater does not know that a single tear of my mother suffices to cancel six hundred letters of accusation."[3] We also may imagine that Jesus thus answers the accusations presented against us by the devil, when Mary prays for us: " Does not Lucifer know that a prayer of my Mother in favor of a sinner suffices to make me forget all accusations of offences committed against me ?" The following example is a proof of this.

[1] " Responsum acceperat a Spiritu Sancto; non visurum se mortem, nisi prius videret Christum Domini."—*Luke*, ii. 26.

[2] " Exaudiet utique Matrem Filius."—*Serm. De Aquæd.*

[3] " Ignorare Antipatrem sexcentas epistolas una deleri matris lacrymula."

EXAMPLE.

This example is not recorded in any book, but was told me by a priest, a friend of mine, as having happened to himself. This priest was hearing confessions in a church (to compromise no one, I do not mention the name of the place, though the penitent gave him leave to publish the fact), when a young man stood before him, who seemed to wish, but at the same time to fear, to go to confession. The Father, after looking at him several times, at length called him, and asked him if he wished to confess. He replied that he did ; but as his confession was likely to be very long, he begged to be taken to a private room. The penitent there began by saying that he was a foreigner, and of noble birth, but who had led such a life that he did not believe it possible that God would pardon him. Besides the other innumerable shameful crimes and murders he had committed, he said that, having entirely despaired of salvation, he committed sins, no longer from inclination, but expressly to outrage God, out of the hatred he bore him. He said, amongst other things, that he wore a crucifix, and that he beat it out of disrespect ; and that that very morning, only a short time before, he had communicated sacrilegiously ; and for what purpose ? It was that he might trample the sacred particle under his feet. And he had indeed already received it, and had only been prevented from executing his horrible design by the people who would have seen him. He then consigned the sacred particle in a piece of paper to the confessor. Having done this, he said that, passing before the church, he had felt himself strongly impelled to enter it; that, unable to resist, he had done so. After entering, he was seized with great remorse of conscience, and at the same time a sort of confused and irresolute desire to confess his sins; and hence the reason for which he stood before the confessional; but while standing there his confusion and diffidence were so great that he endeavored to go away, but it seemed to him as if some one held him there by force. "In the mean time," he said, "Father, you called me, and now I am here making my confession, and I know not how." The Father then asked him if he ever practised any devotion during the time, meaning towards the Blessed Virgin; for such conversions only come through the powerful hands of Mary. "None, Father. Devotions, indeed! I looked on myself as damned." "But reflect again," said the Father. "Father, I did nothing," he repeated. But, putting his hand to his breast to uncover it, he remembered that he wore the scapular of Mary's dolors. "Ah, my son," said the confessor, "dost thou not see it is our Blessed Lady who has obtained thee so extraordinary a grace? And know," he added, "that to her this church is dedicated." On hearing this the young man was moved, and began to grieve, and at the same time to weep; then, continuing the confession of his sins, his compunction increased to such a degree that with a loud sob he fell fainting at the Father's feet. When he had been restored to consciousness, he finished his confession; and the Father with the greatest consolation absolved him, and sent him back to his own country entirely contrite, and resolved to change his life, giving the Father full permission to preach and publish everywhere the great mercy that Mary had shown him.

Prayer.

O holy Mother of God, and my Mother Mary, thou wast so deeply interested in my salvation as to offer to death the dearest object of thy heart, thy beloved Jesus! Since, then, thou didst so much desire to see me saved, it is right that, after God, I should place all my hopes in thee. O yes, most Blessed

Virgin, I do indeed entirely confide in thee. Ah, by the merit of the great sacrifice which thou didst offer this day to God, the sacrifice of the life of thy Son, entreat him to have pity on my poor soul, for which this Immaculate Lamb did not refuse to die on the cross. I could desire, O my Queen, to offer my poor heart to God on this day, in imitation of thee; but I fear that, seeing it so sordid and loathsome, he may refuse it. But if thou offerest it to him, he will not reject it. He is always pleased with and accepts the offerings presented to him by your most pure hands. To thee, then, O Mary, do I this day present myself, miserable as I am; to thee do I give myself without reserve. Do thou offer me as thy servant, together with Jesus, to the Eternal Father; and beseech him, by the merits of thy Son and for thy sake, to accept me and take me as his own. Ah, my sweetest Mother, for the love of thy sacrificed Son, help me always and at all times, and abandon me not. Never permit me to lose by my sins this most amiable Redeemer, whom on this day thou didst offer with so bitter grief to the cruel death of the cross. Remind him that I am thy servant, that in thee I have placed all my hope; say, in fine, that thou willest my salvation, and he will certainly graciously hear thee.

DISCOURSE VII.

THE ASSUMPTION OF MARY.*

August 15.

How precious was the death of Mary, both on account of the special graces that attended it, and on account of the manner in which it took place.

DEATH being the punishment of sin, it would seem that the divine Mother—all holy, and exempt as she was from its slightest stain—should also have been exempt from death, and from encountering the misfortunes to which the children of Adam, infected by the poison of sin, are subject. But God was pleased that Mary should in all things resemble Jesus; and as the Son died, it was becoming that the mother should also die ; because, moreover, he wished to give the just an example of the precious death prepared for them, he willed that even the most Blessed Virgin should die, but by a sweet and happy death. Let us, therefore, now consider how precious was Mary's death: first, on account of the special favors by which it was accompanied; secondly, on account of the manner in which it took place.

I.

There are three things that render death bitter: attachment to the world, remorse for sins, and the uncertainty of salvation. The death of Mary was entirely free from these causes of bitterness, and was accompanied by three special graces, which rendered it precious and joyful. She died as she had lived, entirely detached

---

* On this day the Church celebrates in honor of Mary two solemn festivals: the first is that of her happy passage from this world ; the second, that of her glorious Assumption into Heaven.

from the things of the world; she died in the most perfect peace; she died in the certainty of eternal glory.

I. And in the first place, there can be no doubt that attachment to earthly things renders the death of the worldly bitter and miserable, as the Holy Ghost says: *O death, how bitter is the remembrance of thee to a man who hath peace in his possessions!* [1] But because the saints die detached from the things of the world, their death is not bitter, but sweet, lovely, and precious; that is to say, as St. Bernard remarks, worth purchasing at any price, however great. *Blessed are the dead who die in the Lord.* [2] Who are they who, being already dead, die? They are those happy souls who pass into eternity already detached, and, so to say, dead to all affection for terrestrial things; and who, like St. Francis of Assisi, found in God alone all their happiness, and with him could say, "My God and my all." [3] But what soul was ever more detached from earthly goods, and more united to God, than the beautiful soul of Mary? She was detached from her parents; for at the age of three years, when children are most attached to them, and stand in the greatest need of their assistance, Mary, with the greatest intrepidity, left them, and went to shut herself up in the Temple to attend to God alone. She was detached from riches, contenting herself always to live poor, and supporting herself with the labor of her own hands. She was detached from honors, loving an humble and abject life, though the honors due to a queen were hers, as she was descended from the kings of Israel. The Blessed Virgin herself revealed to St. Elizabeth of Hungary, that when her parents left her in the temple, she resolved in her heart to have no father, and to love no other good than God.

[1] "O mors! quam amara est memoria tua homini pacem habenti in substantiis suis!"—*Ecclus.* xli. 1.

[2] " Beati mortui qui in Domino moriuntur."—*Apoc.* xiv. 13.

[3] " Deus meus et omnia."

St. John saw Mary represented in that woman, clothed with the sun, who held the moon under her feet. *And a great sign appeared in heaven : a woman clothed with the sun, and the moon under her feet.*[1] Interpreters explain the moon to signify the goods of this world, which, like her, are uncertain and changeable. Mary never had these goods in her heart, but always despised them and trampled them under her feet; living in this world as a solitary turtle-dove in a desert, never allowing her affection to centre itself on any earthly thing; so that of her it was said: *The voice of the turtle is heard in our land.*[2] And elsewhere: *Who is she that goeth up by the desert ?*[3] Whence the Abbot Rupert says, "Thus didst thou go up by the desert; that is, having a solitary soul."[4] Mary, then, having lived always and in all things detached from the earth, and united to God alone, death was not bitter, but, on the contrary, very sweet and dear to her; since it united her more closely to God in heaven, by an eternal bond.

II. Peace of mind renders the death of the just precious. Sins committed during life are the worms that so cruelly torment and gnaw the hearts of poor dying sinners, who, about to appear before the divine tribunal, see themselves at that moment surrounded by their sins, which terrify them, and cry out, according to St. Bernard, "We are thy works; we will not abandon thee."[5] Mary certainly could not be tormented at death by any remorse of conscience, for she was always pure, and always free from the least shade of actual or original sin; so much so,

---

[1] "Signum magnum apparuit in cœlo : Mulier amicta sole, et luna sub pedibus ejus."—*Apoc.* xii. 1.

[2] "Vox turturis audita est in terra nostra."—*Cant.* ii. 12.

[3] "Quæ est ista quæ ascendit per desertum ?"—*Ib.* iii. 6.

[4] "Talis ascendisti per desertum, id est, animum habens valde solitarium."

[5] "Opera tua sumus, non te deseremus."—*Medit.* c. 2.

that of her it was said: *Thou art all fair, O my love, and there is not a spot in thee.*[1] From the moment that she had the use of reason, that is, from the first moment of her immaculate conception in the womb of St. Anne, she began to love God with all her strength, and continue to do so, always advancing more and more throughout her whole life in love and perfection. And all her thoughts, desires, and affections were of and for God alone; she never uttered a word, made a movement, cast a glance, or breathed, but for God and his glory ; and never departed a step or detached herself for a single moment from the divine love. Ah, how did all the lovely virtues that she had practised during life surround her blessed bed in the happy hour of her death! That faith so constant ; that loving confidence in God ; that unconquerable patience in the midst of so many sufferings; that humility in the midst of so many privileges ; that modesty; that meekness; that tender compassion for souls; that insatiable zeal for the glory of God; and, above all, that most perfect love towards him, with that entire conformity to the divine will: all, in a word, surrounded her, and consoling her, said: "We are thy works; we will not abandon thee." Our Lady and Mother, we are all daughters of thy beautiful heart ; now that thou art leaving this miserable life, we will not leave thee; we also will go, and be thy eternal accompaniment and honor in Paradise, where, by our means thou wilt reign as Queen of all men and of all angels.

III. Finally, the certainty of eternal salvation renders death sweet. Death is called a passage ; for by death we pass from a short to an eternal life. And as the dread of those is indeed great who die in doubt of their salvation, and who approach the solemn moment with well-grounded fear of passing into eternal death ; thus,

[1] "Tota pulchra es, amica mea, et macula non est in te."—*Cant.* iv. 7.

on the other hand, the joy of the saints is indeed great at the close of life, hoping with some security to go and possess God in heaven. A nun of the Order of St. Teresa, when the doctor announced to her her approaching death, was so filled with joy that she exclaimed, "O, how is it, sir, that you announce to me such welcome news, and demand no fee?" St. Laurence Justinian, being at the point of death, and perceiving his servants weeping round him, said: "Away, away with your tears; this is no time to mourn."[1] Go elsewhere to weep; if you would remain with me, rejoice, as I rejoice, in seeing the gates of heaven open to me, that I may be united to my God. Thus also a St. Peter of Alcantara, a St. Aloysius Gonzaga, and so many other saints, on hearing that death was at hand, burst forth into exclamations of joy and gladness. And yet they were not certain of being in possession of divine grace, nor were they secure of their own sanctity, as Mary was.

But what joy must the divine Mother have felt in receiving the news of her approaching death! she who had the fullest certainty of the possession of divine grace, especially after the Angel Gabriel had assured her that she was full of it, and that she already possessed God. *Hail, full of grace, the Lord is with thee . . . thou hast found grace.*[2] And well did she herself know that her heart was continually burning with divine love; so that, as Bernardine de Bustis says,[3] "Mary, by a singular privilege granted to no other saint, loved, and was always actually loving God, in every moment of her life, with such ardor, that St. Bernard declares, it required a continued miracle to preserve her life in the midst of such flames."

[1] "Abite hinc cum vestris lacrymis; tempus lætitiæ est, non lacrymarum."—*Bern. Just. Vit.* c. 10.

[2] "Ave. gratia Plena! Dominus tecum; invenisti enim gratiam."—*Luke.* i. 28.

[3] *Marial.* p. 2, s. 5.

Of Mary it had already been asked in the sacred canticles, *Who is she that goeth up by the desert, as a pillar of smoke, of aromatical spices, of myrrh, and frankincense, and all the powders of the perfumer ?* [1] Her entire mortification typified by the myrrh, her fervent prayers signified by the incense, and all her holy virtues united to her perfect love for God, kindled in her a flame so great that her beautiful soul, wholly devoted to and consumed by divine love, arose continually to God as a pillar of smoke, breathing forth on every side a most sweet odor. "Such smoke, nay even such a pillar of smoke," says the Abbot Rupert, "hast thou, O Blessed Mary, breathed forth a sweet odor to the Most High." [2] Eustachius expresses it in still stronger terms: "A pillar of smoke, because burning interiorly as a holocaust with the flame of divine love, she sent forth a most sweet odor." [3] As the loving Virgin lived, so did she die. As divine love gave her life, so did it cause her death; for the Doctors and holy Fathers of the Church generally say she died of no other infirmity than pure love; St. Ildephonsus says that Mary either ought not to die, or only die of love.

II.

But now let us see how her blessed death took place. After the ascension of Jesus Christ, Mary remained on earth to attend to the propagation of the faith. Hence the disciples of our Lord had recourse to her, and she solved their doubts, comforted them in their persecutions, and encouraged them to labor for the divine glory

[1] " Quæ est ista quæ ascendit per desertum sicut virgula fumi, ex aromatibus myrrhæ, et thuris, et universi pulveris pigmentarii ?"— *Cant.* iii. 6.

[2] " Talis fumi virgula, tu, O beata Maria! suavem odorem spirasti Altissimo."

[3] " ' Virgula fumi,' quia, concremata intus in holocaustum incendio divini amoris, ex ea flagrabat suavissimus odor."—*De Assumpt.*

and the salvation of redeemed souls. She willingly remained on earth, knowing that such was the will of God, for the good of the Church; but she could not but feel the pain of being far from the presence and sight of her beloved Son, who had ascended to heaven. *Where your treasure is, there will your heart be also,*[1] said the Redeemer. Where any one believes his treasure and his happiness to be, here he always holds the love and desires of his heart fixed. If Mary, then, loved no other good than Jesus, he being in heaven, all her desires were in heaven.

Tauler says, that "Heaven was the cell of the heavenly and most Blessed Virgin Mary; for, being there with all her desires and affections, she made it her continual abode. Her school was eternity; for she was always detached and free from temporal possessions. Her teacher was divine truth; for her whole life was guided by this alone. Her book was the purity of her own conscience, in which she always found occasion to rejoice in the Lord. Her mirror was the divinity; for she never admitted any representations into her soul but such as were transformed into and clothed with God, that so she might always conform herself to his will. Her ornament was devotion; for she attended solely to her interior sanctification, and was always ready to fulfil the divine commands. Her repose was union with God; for he alone was her treasure and the resting-place of her heart."[2]

The most holy Virgin consoled her loving heart during this painful separation by visiting, as it is related, the holy places of Palestine, where her Son had been

[1] " Ubi enim thesaurus vester est, ibi et cor vestrum erit."—*Luke*, xii. 34.

[2] " Mariæ cella fuit cœlum; schola, æternitas pædagogus, divina Veritas; speculum, Divinitas; ornatus ejus, devotio; quies, unitas cum Deo; cordis illius locus et thesaurus, solus Deus."—*Serm. in Nat. V.*

during his life. She frequently visited—at one time the stable at Bethlehem, where her Son was born; at another, the workshop of Nazareth, where her Son had lived so many years poor and despised; now the Garden of Gethsemani, where her Son began his Passion; then the Prætorium of Pilate, where he was scourged, and the spot on which he was crowned with thorns; but she visited most frequently the Mount of Calvary, where her Son expired; and the Holy Sepulchre in which she had finally left him: thus did the most loving Mother soothe the pains of her cruel exile. But this could not be enough to satisfy her heart, which was unable to find perfect repose in this world. Hence she was continually sending up sighs to her Lord, exclaiming with David: *Who will give me wings like a dove, and I will fly and be at rest?* [1] Who will give me wings like a dove, that I may fly to my God, and there find my repose? *As the hart panteth after the fountains of water: so my soul panteth after Thee. my God.* [2] As the wounded stag pants for the fountain, so does my soul, wounded by Thy love, O my God, desire and sigh after Thee.

Yes, indeed, the sighs of this holy turtle-dove could not but deeply penetrate the heart of her God, who indeed so tenderly loved her. *The voice of the turtle is heard in our land.* [3] Wherefore being unwilling to defer any longer the so-much-desired consolation of his beloved, behold, he graciously hears her desire, and calls her to his kingdom.

Cedrenus,[4] Nicephorus,[5] and Metaphrastes,[6] relate that,

[1] " Quis dabit mihi pennas sicut columbæ, et volabo, et requiescam?" —*Ps.* liv. 7.

[2] " Quemadmodum desiderat cervus ad fontes aquarum, ita desiderat anima mea ad te, Deus."—*Ps.* xli. 1.

[3] " Vox turturis audita est in terra nostra."—*Cant.* ii. 12.

[4] *Comp. Histor.* n. 86.

[5] *Hist.* l. 2, c. 21

[6] *Or. de Vita et Dorm. M.*

some days before her death, our Lord sent her the Arch-angel Gabriel, the same that announced to her that she was that blessed woman chosen to be the Mother of God: "My Lady and Queen," said the angel, "God has already graciously heard thy holy desires, and has sent me to tell thee to prepare thyself to leave the earth; for he wills thee in heaven. Come, then, to take possession of thy kingdom; for I and all its holy inhabitants await and desire thee." On this happy annunciation, what else could our most humble and most holy Virgin do, but, with the most profound humility, answer in the same words in which she had answered St. Gabriel when he announced to her that she was to become the Mother of God: *Behold the handmaid of the Lord.*[1] Behold, she answered again, the slave of the Lord. He in his pure goodness chose me and made me his Mother; he now calls me to Paradise. I did not deserve that honor, nor do I deserve this. But since he is pleased to show in my person his infinite liberality, behold, I am ready to go where he pleases. *Behold the handmaid of the Lord.* May the will of my God and Lord be ever accomplished in me !

After receiving this welcome intelligence she imparted it to St. John. We may well imagine with what grief and tender feelings he heard the news ; he who for so many years had attended upon her as a son, and had enjoyed the heavenly conversation of this most holy Mother. She then once more visited the holy places of Jerusalem, tenderly taking leave of them, and especially of Mount Calvary, where her beloved Son had died. She then retired into her poor cottage, there to prepare for death.

During this time the angels did not cease their visits to their beloved Queen, consoling themselves with the

---

[1] " Ecce ancilla Domini."—*Luke,* i. 38.

thought that they would soon see her crowned in
heaven. Many authors, such as Andrew of Crete,[1] St.
John Damascene,[2] Euthymius,[3] assert that, before her
death, the apostles, and also many disciples who were
scattered in different parts of the world, were miraculously assembled in Mary's room, and that when she saw
all these her dear children in her presence, she thus addressed them : "My beloved children, through love for
you and to help you my Son left me on this earth. The
holy faith is now spread throughout the world, already
the fruit of the divine seed is grown up ; hence my
Lord, seeing that my assistance on earth is no longer
necessary, and compassionating my grief in being separated from him, has graciously listened to my desire to
quit this life and to go and see him in heaven. Do you
remain, then, to labor for his glory. If I leave you, my
heart remains with you ; the great love I bear you I
shall carry with me and always preserve. I go to Paradise to pray for you."

Who can form an idea of the tears and lamentations
of the holy disciples at this sad announcement, and at
the thought that soon they were to be separated from
their Mother ? all then, weeping, exclaimed, "Then, O
Mary, thou art already about to leave us. It is true that
this world is not a place worthy of or fit for thee ; and
as for us, we are unworthy to enjoy the society of a
Mother of God; but, remember, thou art our Mother ;
hitherto thou hast enlightened us in our doubts; thou
hast consoled us in our afflictions ; thou hast been our
strength in persecutions ; and now, how canst thou
abandon us, leaving us alone in the midst of so many
enemies and so many conflicts, deprived of thy consolation ? We have already lost on earth Jesus, our Master
and Father, who has ascended into heaven ; until now

---

[1] *In Dorm. S. M. or.* 1. [2] *De Dorm B. M. or.* 1 et 2.
[3] *Hist.* l. 3, c. 40.

we have found consolation in thee, our Mother; and now, how canst thou also leave us orphans without father or mother? Our own sweet Lady, either remain with us, or take us with thee." Thus St. John Damascene writes: " No, my children" (thus sweetly the loving Queen began to speak), " this is not according to the will of God; be satisfied to do that which he has decreed for me and for you. To you it yet remains to labor on earth for the glory of your Redeemer, and to make up your eternal crown. I do not leave you to abandon you, but to help you still more in heaven by my intercession with God. Be satisfied. I commend the holy Church to you ; I commend redeemed souls to you ; let this be my last farewell, and the only remembrance I leave you : execute it if you love me, labor for the good of souls and for the glory of my Son ; for one day we shall meet again in Paradise, never more for all eternity to be separated."

She then begged them to give burial to her body after death ; blessed them, and desired St. John, as St. John Damascene relates, to give after her death two of her gowns to two virgins who had served her for some time. She then decently composed herself on her poor little bed, where she laid herself to await death, and with it the meeting with the divine Spouse, who shortly was to come and take her with him to the kingdom of the blessed. Behold, she already feels in her heart a great joy, the forerunner of the coming of the Bridegroom, which inundates her with an unaccustomed and novel sweetness. The holy apostles, seeing that Mary was already on the point of leaving this world, renewing their tears, all threw themselves on their knees around her bed ; some kissed her holy feet, some sought a special blessing from her, some recommended a particular want, and all wept bitterly ; for their hearts were pierced with grief at being obliged to separate themselves for the rest of their lives from their beloved Lady. And

she, the most loving Mother, compassionated all, and
consoled each one ; to some promising her patronage,
blessing others with particular affection, and encouraging others to the work of the conversion of the world;
especially, she called St. Peter to her, and as head of the
Church and Vicar of her Son, recommended to him in a
particular manner the propagation of the faith, promising him at the same time her especial protection in
heaven. But more particularly did she call St. John to
her, who more than any other was grieved at this moment when he had to part with his holy Mother; and the
most gracious Lady, remembering the affection and attention with which this holy disciple had served her
during all the years she had remained on earth since
the death of her son, said: " My own John" (speaking
with the greatest tenderness)—"my own John, I thank
thee for all the assistance that thou hast afforded me;
my son, be assured of it, I shall not be ungrateful. If I
now leave thee, I go to pray for thee. Remain in peace
in this life until we meet again in heaven, where I await
thee. Never forget me. In all thy wants call me to thy
aid; for I will never forget thee, my beloved son. Son, I
bless thee. I leave thee my blessing. Remain in peace.
Farewell !"

But already the death of Mary is at hand; divine love,
with its vehement and blessed flames, had already
almost entirely consumed the vital spirits; the heavenly
phœnix is already losing her life in the midst of this fire.
Then the host of angels come in choirs to meet her, as if
to be ready for the great triumph with which they were
to accompany her to Paradise. Mary was indeed consoled at the sight of these holy spirits, but was not fully
consoled; for she did not yet see her beloved Jesus, who
was the whole love of her heart.   Hence she often
repeated to the angels who descended to salute her : *I
adjure you, O daughters of Jerusalem, if you find my Beloved,*

that you tell him that I languish with love.[1] Holy angels, O fair citizens of the heavenly Jerusalem, you come in choirs kindly to console me; and you all console me with your sweet presence. I thank you; but you do not fully satisfy me, for as yet I do not see my Son coming to console me; go, if you love me, return to Paradise, and on my part tell my Beloved that *I languish with love.* Tell him to come, and to come quickly, for I am dying with the vehemence of my desire to see him.

But, behold, Jesus is now come to take his Mother to the kingdom of the blessed. It was revealed to St. Elizabeth that her Son appeared to Mary before she expired with his cross in his hands, to show the special glory he had obtained by the redemption ; having, by his death, made acquisition of that great creature, who for all eternity was to honor him more than all men and angels. St. John Damascene relates that our Lord himself gave her the Viaticum, saying with tender love, "Receive, O My Mother, from my hands that same body that thou gavest to Me." And the Mother, having received with the greatest love that last Communion, with her last breath said, "My Son, into Thy hands do I commend my spirit. I commend to Thee this soul, which from the beginning Thou didst create rich in so many graces, and by a singular privilege didst preserve from the stain of original sin. I commend to Thee my body, from which thou didst deign to take Thy flesh and blood. I also commend to Thee these my beloved children (speaking of the holy disciples, who surrounded her); they are grieved at my departure. Do Thou, who lovest them more than I do, console them; bless them, and give them strength to do great things for Thy glory."

The life of Mary being now at its close, the most delicious music, as St. Jerome relates, was heard in the

---

[1] " Adjuro vos, filiæ Jerusalem, si inveneritis Dilectum meum, ut nuntietis ei, quia amore langueo "—*Cant.* v. 8.

apartment where she lay; and, according to a revelation of St. Bridget, the room was also filled with a brilliant light. The sweet music, and the unaccustomed splendor, warned the holy apostles that Mary was then departing. This caused them again to burst forth in tears and prayers; and raising their hands, with one voice they exclaimed, " O, Mother, thou already goest to heaven; thou leavest us; give us thy last blessing, and never forget us miserable creatures." Mary, turning her eyes around upon all, as if to bid them a last farewell, said, " Adieu, my children; I bless you; fear not, I will never forget you." And now death came; not indeed clothed in mourning and grief, as it does to others, but adorned with light and gladness. But what do we say? Why speak of death? Let us rather say that divine love came, and cut the thread of that noble life. And as a light, before going out, gives a last and brighter flash than ever, so did this beautiful creature, on hearing her Son's invitation to follow him, wrapped in the flames of love, and in the midst of her amorous sighs, give a last sigh of still more ardent love, and breathing forth her soul, expired. Thus was that great soul, that beautiful dove of the Lord, loosened from the bands of this life; thus did she enter into the glory of the blessed, where she is now seated, and will be seated, Queen of Paradise, for all eternity.

Mary, then, has left this world; she is now in heaven. Thence does this compassionate Mother look down upon us who are still in this valley of tears. She pities us, and, if we wish it, promises to help us. Let us always beseech her by the merits of her blessed death, to obtain us a happy death; and should such be the good pleasure of God, let us beg her to obtain us the grace to die on a Saturday, which is a day dedicated in her honor, or on a day of a novena, or within the octave of one of her feasts; for this she has obtained for so many of her clients, and especially for St. Stanislaus Kostka, for whom she obtained that he should die on the feast of her Assumption, as Father Bartoli relates in his life of the saint.[1]

EXAMPLE.

During his lifetime this holy youth, who was wholly dedicated to the love of Mary, happened, on the first of August, to hear a sermon preached by Father Peter Canisius, in which, exhorting the novices of the Society, he urged them all, with the greatest fervor, to live each day, as if it were the last of their lives, and the one on which they were to be presented before God's tribunal. After the sermon St. Stanislaus told his companions that that advice had been for him, in an especial manner, the voice of God ; for that he was to die in the course of that very month. It is evident, from what followed, that he said this either because God had expressly revealed it to him, or at least because he gave him a certain internal presentiment of it. Four days afterwards the blessed youth went with Father Emanuel to St. Mary Major's. The conversation fell on the approaching feast of the Assumption, and the saint said, "Father, I believe that on that day a new Paradise is seen in Paradise, as the glory of the Mother of God, crowned Queen of heaven, and seated so near to our Lord, above all the choirs of angels, is seen. And if— as I firmly believe it to be—this festival is renewed every year, I hope to see the next." The glorious martyr St. Lawrence had fallen by lot to St. Stanislaus as his patron for that month, it being customary in the Society thus to draw lots for the monthly patrons. It is said that he wrote a letter to his Mother Mary, in which he begged her to obtain him the favor to be present at her next festival in heaven. On the feast of

[1] L. i c. 12.

St. Laurence he received the holy Communion, and
afterwards entreated the saint to present his letter to
the divine Mother, and to support his petition with his
intercession, that the most Blessed Virgin might graciously accept and grant it.   Towards the close of that
very day he was seized with fever ; and though the attack was slight, he considered that certainly he had obtained the favor asked for.   This indeed he joyfully expressed, and with a smiling countenance, on going to
bed, said, "From this bed I shall never rise again."
And speaking to Father Claudius Aquaviva, he added,
"Father, I believe that St. Lawrence has already obtained me the favor from Mary to be in heaven on the
feast of her Assumption."   No one, however, took much
notice of his words.   On the vigil of the feast his illness
still seemed of little consequence, but the saint assured
a brother that he should die that night.   "O brother,"
the other answered, "it would be a greater miracle to
die of so slight an illness than to be cured."   Nevertheless in the afternoon he fell into a deathlike swoon ; a
cold sweat came over him, and he lost all his strength.
The Superior hastened to him, and Stanislaus entreated
him to have him laid on the bare floor, that he might
die as a penitent.   To satisfy him, this was granted : he
was laid on a thin mattress on the ground.   He then
made his confession, and in the midst of the tears of all
present received the Viaticum : I say, of the tears of all
present, for when the divine sacrament was brought into
the room his eyes brightened up with celestial joy, and
his whole countenance was inflamed with holy love, so
that he seemed like a seraph.   He also received extreme
unction, and in the mean while did nothing but constantly raise his eyes to heaven and lovingly press to his
heart an image of Mary.   A Father asked him to what
purpose he kept a rosary in his hand, since he could not
use it ?   He replied, "It is a consolation to me, for it is

something belonging to my Mother." "O, how much greater will your consolation be," added the Father, "when in a short time you will see her and kiss her hands in heaven!" On hearing this, the saint, with his countenance all on fire, raised his hands to express his desire soon to be in her presence. His dear Mother then appeared to him, as he himself told those who surrounded him; and shortly afterwards, at the dawn of day on the fifteenth of August, with his eyes fixed on heaven, he expired like a saint, without the slightest struggle; so much so, that it was only on presenting him the image of the Blessed Virgin, and seeing that he made no movement towards it, that it was perceived that he was already gone to kiss the feet of his beloved Queen in Paradise.

Prayer.

O most sweet Lady and our Mother, thou hast already left the earth and reached thy kingdom, where, as Queen, thou art enthroned above all the choirs of angels, as the Church sings: *She is exalted above the choirs of angels in the celestial kingdom.*[1] We well know that we sinners are not worthy to possess thee in this valley of darkness; but we also know that thou, in thy greatness, hast never forgotten us miserable creatures, and that by being exalted to so great glory thou hast never lost compassion for us poor children of Adam; nay, even that it is increased in thee. From the high throne, then, to which thou art exalted, turn, O Mary, thy compassionate eyes upon us, and pity us. Remember, also, that in leaving this world thou didst promise not to forget us. Look at us and succor us. See in the midst of what tempests and dangers we constantly are, and shall be until the end of our lives. By the merits of thy happy death obtain us holy perseverance in the divine friendship, that we may finally quit this life in God's grace; and thus we also shall one day come to kiss thy feet in Paradise, and unite with the blessed spirits in praising thee and singing thy glories as thou deservest. Amen.

[1] "Exaltata est sancta Dei Genitrix super choros angelorum ad cœlestia regna."

DISCOURSE VIII.

SECOND DISCOURSE ON THE ASSUMPTION OF MARY.

How glorious was the Triumph of Mary when she ascended to Heaven.—How exalted was the Throne to which she was elevated in Heaven.

It would seem right that on this day of the Assumption of Mary to heaven the holy Church should rather invite us to mourn than to rejoice, since our sweet Mother has quitted this world and left us deprived of her sweet presence, as St. Bernard says: " It seems that we should rather weep than rejoice." [1] But no; the holy Church invites us to rejoice: " Let us all rejoice in the Lord, celebrating a festival in honor of the Blessed Virgin Mary." [2] And justly; for, if we love our Mother, we ought to congratulate ourselves more upon her glory than on our own private consolation. What son does not rejoice, though on account of it he has to be separated from his mother, if he knows that she is going to take possession of a kingdom ? Mary, on this day, is crowned Queen of heaven; and shall we not keep it a festival and rejoice if we truly love her ? " Let us rejoice, then; let us all rejoice." And that we may rejoice, and be consoled the more by her exaltation, let us consider. first, how glorious was the triumph of Mary when she ascended to heaven; and secondly, how glorious was the throne to which she was there exalted.

[1] " Plangendum nobis, quam plaudendum, magis esse videtur."— *In Assumpt* s. 1.
[2] "Gaudeamus omnes in Domino. diem festum celebrantes sub honore beatæ Mariæ Virginis."—*Miss. Introit.*

I.

After Jesus Christ our Saviour had completed, by his death, the work of redemption, the angels ardently desired to possess him in their heavenly country; hence they were continually supplicating him in the words of David: *Arise, O Lord, into thy resting-place, Thou and the ark which Thou hast sanctified.*[1] Come, O Lord, come quickly, now that Thou hast redeemed men; come to Thy kingdom and dwell with us, and bring with Thee the living ark of Thy sanctification, Thy Mother, who was the ark which Thou didst sanctify by dwelling in her womb. Precisely thus does St. Bernardine make the angels say: "Let Mary Thy most holy Mother, sanctified by Thy conception, also ascend."[2] Our Lord was, therefore, at last pleased to satisfy the desire of these heavenly citizens by calling Mary to Paradise. But if it was his will that the ark of the old dispensation should be brought with great pomp into the city of David— *And David and all the house of Israel brought the ark of the covenant of the Lord with joyful shouting, and with sound of trumpet*[3]—with how much greater and more glorious pomp did he ordain that his Mother should enter heaven! The prophet Elias was carried to heaven in a fiery chariot, which, according to interpreters, was no other than a group of angels who bore him off from the earth. "But to conduct thee to heaven, O Mother of God," says the Abbot Rupert, "a fiery chariot was not enough; the whole court of heaven, headed by its King thy Son, went forth to meet and accompany thee."[4]

[1] "Surge, Domine, in requiem tuam, tu et arca sanctificationis tuæ."—*Ps.* cxxxi. 8.

[2] "Ascendat etiam Maria, tua sanctissima Mater, tui conceptione sanctificata."

[3] "Et David et omnis domus Israel ducebant arcam testamenti Domini, in jubilo et in clangore buccinæ."—2 *Kings.* vi. 15.

[4] "Ad transferendum te in cœlum, non unus tantum currus igneus, sed totus cum Rege suo, Filio tuo, venit atque occurrit Angelorum exercitus."—*In Cant.* l. 5.

St. Bernardine of Sienna is of the same opinion. He says, that "Jesus," to honor the triumph of his most sweet Mother, "went forth in his glory to meet and accompany her."[1] St. Anselm also says, "that it was precisely for this purpose that the Redeemer was pleased to ascend to heaven before his Mother; that is, he did so not only to prepare a throne for her in that kingdom, but also that he might himself accompany her with all the blessed spirits, and thus render her entry into heaven more glorious, and such as became one who was his Mother."[2] Hence St. Peter Damian, contemplating the splendor of this assumption of Mary into heaven, says, "that we shall find it more glorious than the ascension of Jesus Christ; for to meet the Redeemer, angels only went forth; but when the Blessed Virgin was assumed to glory, she was met and accompanied by the Lord himself of glory, and by the whole blessed company of saints and angels."[3] For this reason the Abbot Guerric supposes the divine Word thus speaking: "To honor the Father, I descended from heaven; to honor My Mother, I reascended there:"[4] that thus I might be enabled to go forth to meet her, and myself accompany her to Paradise.

Let us now consider how our Saviour went forth from heaven to meet his Mother. On first meeting her, and to console her, he said: *Arise, make haste, My love, My*

[1] "Surrexit gloriosus Jesus in occursum suæ dulcissimæ Matris."— *Pro Fest. M. V.* s. 12. a. 2.

[2] "Prudentiori consilio usus, præcedere illam volebas, quatenus ei locum in regno tuo præparares, et sic comitatus tota curia tua festivius ei occurreres, eamque sublimius, sicut decebat tuam Matrem, ad te ipsum exaltares."—*De Excell. V.* c. 7.

[3] "Invenies occursum hujus pompæ non mediocriter digniorem: soli quippe Angeli Redemptori occurrere potuerunt, Matri vero Filius ipse, cum tota curia, tam Angelorum, quam justorum, solemniter occurrens, evexit ad beatæ consistorium sessionis."—*In Assumpt.*

[4] "Ego, ut Patrem honorarem, in terram descendi; ut Matrem honorarem, in cœlum reascendi."—*In Assumpt.* s. 2

dove, My beautiful one, and come, for winter is now past and gone.[1] Come, my own dear Mother, my pure and beautiful dove; leave that valley of tears, in which, for my love, thou hast suffered so much. *Come from Libanus, My Spouse, come from Libanus, come: thou shalt be crowned.*[2] Come in, soul and body, to enjoy the recompense of thy holy life. If thy sufferings have been great on earth, far greater is the glory which I have prepared for thee in heaven. Enter, then, that kingdom, and take thy seat near me; come to receive that crown which I will bestow upon thee as Queen of the universe. Behold, Mary already leaves the earth, at which she looks with affection and compassion: with affection, remembering the many graces she had there received from her Lord; and with affection and compassion, because in it she leaves so many poor children surrounded with miseries and dangers. But see, Jesus offers her his hand, and the Blessed Mother already ascends; already she has passed beyond the clouds, beyond the spheres. Behold her already at the gates of heaven. When monarchs make their solemn entry into their kingdoms, they do not pass through the gates of the capital, for they are removed to make way for them on this occasion. Hence, when Jesus Christ entered Paradise, the angels cried out: *Lift up your gates, O ye princes, and be ye lifted up, O eternal gates; and the King of Glory shall enter in.*[3] Thus also, now that Mary goes to take possession of the kingdom of heaven, the angels who accompany her cry out to those within: "Lift up your gates, O ye princes, and be ye lifted up, O eternal gates; and the Queen of glory shall enter in."

[1] "Surge, propera, Amica mea, Columba mea, Formosa mea, et veni; jam enim hiems transiit, imber abiit, et recessit."—*Cant.* ii. 10.

[2] "Veni de Libano, Sponsa mea! veni de Libano, veni; coronaberis."—*Cant.* iv. 8.

[3] "Attollite portas, principes, vestras; et elevamini, portæ æternales; et introibit Rex gloriæ."—*Ps.* xxiii. 7.

Behold, Mary already enters that blessed country. But on her entrance the celestial spirits, seeing her so beautiful and glorious, ask the angels without, as Origen supposes it, with united voices of exultation,[1] *Who is this that cometh up from the desert, flowing with delights, leaning upon her Beloved?*[2] And who can this creature so beautiful be, that comes from the desert of the earth—a place of thorns and tribulation? But this one comes pure and rich in virtue, leaning on her beloved Lord, who is graciously pleased himself to accompany her with so great honor. Who is she? The angels accompanying her answer: "She is the Mother of our King; she is our Queen, and the blessed one among women; full of grace, the saint of saints, the beloved of God, the immaculate one, the dove, the fairest of all creatures." Then all the blessed spirits begin to bless and praise her; singing with far more reason than the Hebrews did to Judith: *Thou art the glory of Jerusalem; thou art the joy of Israel; thou art the honor of our people.*[3] Ah, our Lady and our Queen, thou, then, art the glory of Paradise, the joy of our country, thou art the honor of us all: be thou ever welcome, be thou ever blessed! Behold thy kingdom; behold us also, who are thy servants, ever ready to obey thy commands.

All the saints who were in Paradise then came to welcome her and salute her as their Queen. All the holy virgins came; *The daughters saw her, and declared her most blessed; and they praised her.*[4] "We," they said, "O most Blessed Lady, are also queens in this kingdom, but thou

---

[1] "Una omnium in cœlo erat lætantium vox."—*Paciucchelli, In Ps.* lxxxvi. exc. 15.

[2] "Quæ est ista, quæ ascendit de deserto, deliciis affluens, innixa super Dilectum suum?"—*Cant.* viii. 5.

[3] "Tu gloria Jerusalem, tu lætitia Israel, tu honorificentia populi nostri."—*Judith*, xv. 10.

[4] "Viderunt eam filiæ, et beatissimam prædicaverunt."—*Cant.* vi. 8.

art our Queen; for thou wast the first to give us the great example of consecrating our virginity to God; we all bless and thank thee for it." Then came the holy confessors to salute her as their mistress; who, by her holy life, had taught them so many beautiful virtues. The holy martyrs also came to salute her as their Queen; for she, by her great constancy in the sorrows of her Son's Passion, had taught them, and also by her merits had obtained them strength, to lay down their lives for the faith. St. James, the only one of the apostles who was yet in heaven, also came to thank her in the name of all the other apostles for all the comfort and help she had afforded them while she was on earth. The prophets next came to salute her, and said: "Ah, Lady, thou wast the one foreshadowed in our prophecies." The holy patriarchs then came, and said: "O Mary, it is thou who wast our hope; for thee it was that we sighed with such ardor and for so long a time." But amongst these latter came our first parents, Adam and Eve, to thank her with the greatest affection. "Ah, beloved daughter," they said, "thou hast repaired the injury which we inflicted on the human race; thou hast obtained for the world that blessing which we lost by our crime; by thee we are saved, and for it be ever blessed."

St. Simeon then came to kiss her feet, and with joy reminded her of the day when he received the infant Jesus from her hands. St. Zachary and St. Elizabeth also came, and again thanked her for that loving visit which, with so great humility and charity, she had paid them in their dwelling, and by which they had received such treasures of grace. St. John the Baptist came with still greater affection to thank her for having sanctified him by her voice. But how must her holy parents, St. Joachim and St. Anne, have spoken when they came to salute her! O God, with what tenderness must they have blessed her, saying: "Ah, beloved daughter, what a favor it was for us to have such a child! Be thou now our Queen; for thou art the Mother of our God, and as such we salute and adore thee."

But who can ever form an idea of the affection with which her dear spouse, St. Joseph, came to salute her? Who can ever describe the joy which the holy patriarch felt at seeing his spouse so triumphantly enter heaven and made Queen of Paradise? With what tenderness must he have addressed her: "Ah, my Lady and spouse, how can I ever thank our God as I ought, for having made me thy spouse, thou who art his true Mother! Through thee I merited to assist on earth the childhood of the Eternal Word, to carry him so often in my arms, and to receive so many special graces. Ever blessed be those moments which I spent in life in serving Jesus and thee, my holy spouse. Behold our Jesus! let us rejoice that now he no longer lies on straw in a manger, as we saw him at his birth in Bethlehem. He no longer lives poor and despised in a shop, as he once lived with us in Nazareth; he is no longer nailed to an infamous gibbet, as when he died in Jerusalem for the salvation of the world; but he is seated at the right hand of his Father, as King and Lord of heaven and earth. And now, O my Queen, we shall never more be separated from his feet; we shall there bless him and love him for all eternity."

All the angels then came to salute her; and she, the great Queen, thanked all for the assistance they had given her on earth, and more especially she thanked the archangel Gabriel, who was the happy ambassador, the bearer of all her glories, when he came to announce to her that she was the chosen Mother of God.

The humble and holy Virgin, then kneeling, adored the divine Majesty, and all absorbed in the consciousness of her own nothingness, thanked him for all the graces bestowed upon her by his pure goodness, and especially for having made her the Mother of the Eternal Word.

And then let him who can, comprehend with what love the Most Holy Trinity blessed her. Let him comprehend the welcome given to his daughter by the Eternal Father, to his Mother by the Son, to his spouse by the Holy Ghost. The Father crowned her by imparting his power to her; the Son, his wisdom; the Holy Ghost, his love. And the three divine Persons, placing her throne at the right of that of Jesus, declared her Sovereign of heaven and earth; and commanded the angels and all creatures to acknowledge her as their Queen, and as such to serve and obey her.

II.

Let us now consider how exalted was the throne to which Mary was raised in heaven.

"If the mind of man," says St. Bernard, "can never comprehend the immense glory prepared in heaven by God for those who on earth have loved him, as the Apostle tells us,[1] who can ever comprehend the glory that he has prepared for his beloved Mother, who, more than all men, loved him on earth; nay, even from the very first moment of her creation, loved him more than all men and angels united?"[2] Rightly, then, does the Church sing, that Mary having loved God more than all the angels, "the Mother of God has been exalted above them all in the heavenly kingdom."[3] Yes, "she was exalted," says the abbot Guerric, "above the angels; so that she sees none above her but her Son,"[4] who is the only-begotten of the Father.

Hence it is that the learned Gerson asserts that, as all the orders of angels and saints are divided into three

[1] 1 *Cor.* ii. 9.

[2] "Quod præparavit gignenti se, quis loquatur?"—*In Assumpt.* s. 1.

[3] "Exaltata est sancta Dei Genitrix super choros Angelorum ad cœlestia regna."—*In festo Assumpt.*

[4] "Mariam dico exaltatam super choros angelorum, ut nihil contempletur supra se Mater. nisi Filium solum."—*In Assumpt.* s. 1.

hierarchies (according to the angelic Doctor [1] and St.
Denis), so does Mary of herself constitute a hierarchy
apart, the sublimest of all, and next to that of God.[2]
And as (adds St. Antoninus) the mistress is, without
comparison, above her servants, so is "Mary, who is the
sovereign Lady of the angels, exalted incomparably above
the angelic hierarchies." [3] To understand this, we need
only know what David said: *The Queen stood on thy right
hand.*[4] And in a sermon by an ancient author, among the
works of St. Athanasius, these words are explained as
meaning that "Mary is placed at the right hand of God." [5]

It is certain, as St. Ildephonsus says, that Mary's good
works incomparably surpassed in merit those of all the
saints, and therefore her reward must have surpassed
theirs in the same proportion; for "as that which she
bore was incomprehensible, so is the reward which she
merited and received incomprehensibly greater than
that of all the saints." [6] And since it is certain that God
rewards according to merit, as the Apostle writes, *who
will render to every man according to his works,*[7] it is also
certain, as St. Thomas teaches, that the Blessed Virgin,
"who was equal to and even superior in merit to all men
and angels, was exalted above all the celestial orders." [8]
"In fine," adds St. Bernard, "let us measure the sin-

---

[1] P. 1, q. 108.

[2] "Constituit Virgo sola hierarchiam secundam, sub Deo Hierarchia primo."—*Sup. Magn.* tr. 4.

[3] "Virgo est domina Angelorum; ergo improportionabiliter est supra omnem hierarchiam exaltata."—P. 4, t. 15. c. 20, § 15.

[4] "Astitit regina a dextris tuis."—*Ps.* xliv. 10.

[5] "Collocatur Maria a dextris Dei."—*S. de S. Deip.*

[6] "Sicut incomparabile est quod gessit, ita et incomprehensibile præmium, et gloria ultra omnes Sanctos, quam promeruit."—*De Assumpt.* s. 2.

[7] "Reddet unicuique secundum opera ejus."—*Rom.* ii. 6.

[8] "Sicut habuit meritum omnium, et amplius, ita congruum fuit ut super omnes ponatur."—*S. de Ass. ex Ep.*

gular grace that she acquired on earth, and then we may measure the singular glory which she obtained in heaven;" for, "according to the measure of her grace on earth is the measure of her glory in the kingdom of the blessed." [1]

A learned author, Father La Colombière,[2] remarks that the glory of Mary, which is a full, a complete glory, differs in that from the glory of other saints in heaven. It is true that in heaven all the blessed enjoy perfect peace and full contentment; yet it will always be true that no one of them enjoys as great glory as he could have merited had he loved and served God with greater fidelity. Hence, though the saints in heaven desire nothing more than they possess, yet in fact there is something that they could desire. It is also true that the sins which they have committed, and the time which they have lost, do not bring suffering; still it cannot be denied that a greater amount of good done in life, innocence preserved, and time well employed, give the greatest happiness. Mary desires nothing in heaven, and has nothing to desire. Who amongst the saints in heaven, except Mary, says St. Augustine,[3] if asked whether he has committed sins, could say no? It is certain, as the holy Council of Trent [4] has defined, that Mary never committed any sin of the slightest imperfection. She not only never lost divine grace, and never even obscured it, but she never kept it idle; she never performed an action which was not meritorious; she never pronounced a word, never had a thought, never drew a breath, that was not directed to the greater glory of God. In fine,

[1] "Quantum enim gratiæ in terris adepta est præ cæteris, tantum et in cœlis obtinet gloriæ singularis."—*In Assumpt.* s. I.

[2] *Assompt.* s. I.

[3] *De Nat. et Gr.* c. 36.

[4] *Sess.* vi. *can.* 23.

she never cooled in her ardor or stopped a single moment in her onward course towards God; she never lost anything by negligence, but always corresponded to grace with her whole strength, and loved God as much as she could love him. "O Lord," she now says to him in heaven, "if I loved Thee not as much as Thou didst deserve, at least I loved Thee as much as I could."

In each of the saints there were different graces, as St. Paul says, *there are diversities of graces.*[1] So that each of them, by corresponding to the grace that he had received, excelled in some particular virtue—the one in saving souls, the other in leading a penitential life; one in enduring torments, another in a life of prayer: and this is the reason for which the holy Church, in celebrating their festivals, says of each, *there was not found one like him.*[2] And as in their merits they differ, so do they differ in celestial glory: *for star differeth from star.*[3] Apostles differ from martyrs, confessors from virgins, the innocent from penitents. The Blessed Virgin, being full of all graces, excelled each saint in every particular virtue: she was the Apostle of the apostles; she was the Queen of martyrs, for she suffered more than all of them; she was the standard-bearer of virgins, the model of married people; she united in herself perfect innocence and perfect mortification: in fine, she united in her heart all the most heroic virtues that any saint ever practised. Hence of her it was said that *the Queen stood on Thy right hand in gilded clothing, surrounded with variety.*[4] For all the graces, privileges, and merits of the other saints were all united in Mary, as the Abbot of Celles says:

[1] "Divisiones vero gratiarum sunt."—1 *Cor.* xii. 4.

[2] "Non est inventus similis illi."

[3] "Stella enim a stella differt in claritate."—*Ibid.* xv. 41.

[4] "Astitit Regina a dextris tuis in vestitu deaurato, circumdata va rietate."—*Ps.* xliv. 10.

" The prerogatives of all the saints, O Virgin, thou hast united in thyself." [1]

She possessed them in such a degree that, as " the splendor of the sun exceeds that of all the stars united," so, says St. Basil of Seleucia, " does Mary's glory exceed that of all the blessed." [2] St. Peter Damian adds, that " as the light of the moon and stars is so entirely eclipsed on the appearance of the sun, that it is as if it was not, so also does Mary's glory so far exceed the splendor of all men and angels, that, so to say, they do not appear in heaven." [3] Hence St. Bernardine of Sienna asserts, with St. Bernard, that the blessed participate in part in the divine glory; but that the Blessed Virgin has been, in a certain way, so greatly enriched with it, that it would seem that no creature could be more closely united with God than Mary is: " She has penetrated into the bottom of the deep, and seems immersed as deeply as it is possible for a creature in that inaccessible light." [4] Blessed Albert the Great confirms this, saying that our Queen " contemplates the majesty of God in incomparably closer promixity than all other creatures." [5] The above-named St. Bernardine moreover says, " that as the other planets are illumined by the sun, so do all the blessed receive light and an in-

[1] " Omnium Sanctorum privilegia omnia, O Virgo! habes in te congesta."—*Cont. B. V. c.* 2.

[2] " Maria universos tantum excedit, quantum sol reliqua astra."—*In Annunt.*

[3] " Sol ita sibi siderum et lunæ rapit positionem, ut sint quasi non sint; similiter et Virga Jesse utrorumque spirituum hebetat dignitatem, ut in comparatione Virginis nec possint apparere."—*In Assumpt.*

[4] " Divinæ gloriæ participatio cæteris quodammodo per partes datur; sed, secundum Bernardum, Beata Virgo Maria divinæ sapientiæ penetravit abyssum, ut, quantum creaturæ conditio patitur, illi luci inaccessibili videatur immersa."—*Pro Fest. V. M.* s. 13, a. 1, c. 10.

[5] " Visio Virginis Matris super omnes creaturas improportionabiliter contemplatur majestatem Dei."—*Sup. Missus.* q. 61, *pr.* § 5.

crease of hapiness from the sight of Mary." [1] And in another place he also asserts, that "when the glorious Virgin Mother of God ascended to heaven, she augmented the joy of all its inhabitants." [2] For the same reason St. Peter Damian says, that "the greatest glory of the blessed in heaven is, after seeing God, the presence of this most beautiful Queen." [3] And St. Bonaventure, that, "after God, our greatest glory and our greatest joy is Mary." [4]

Let us, then, rejoice with Mary that God has exalted her to so high a throne in heaven. Let us also rejoice on our own account; for though our Mother is no longer present with us on earth, having ascended in glory to heaven, yet in affection she is always with us. Nay, even being there nearer to God, she better knows our miseries; and her pity for us is greater, while she is better able to help us. "Is it possible, O Blessed Virgin," says St. Peter Damian, "because thou art so greatly exalted, thou hast forgotten us in our miseries? Ah no, God forbid that we should have such a thought! So compassionate a heart cannot but pity our so great miseries." [5] If Mary's compassion for the miserable," says St. Bonaventure, "was great when she lived upon earth, it is far greater now that she reigns in heaven." [6]

Let us, in the mean time, dedicate ourselves to the

---

[1] "Quodammodo, sicut cætera luminaria irradiantur a sole, sic tota cœlestis curia a gloriosa Virgine lætificatur."—*Loc. cit.* c. 3.

[2] "Virgo gloriosa, cœlos ascendens, supernorum gaudia civium copiosis augmentis cumulavit."—*In Assumpt.* s. 1.

[3] "Summa gloria est, post Deum, te videre."—*In Nat. B. V.* s. 1.

[4] "Post Deum major nostra gloria, majus nostrum gaudium de Maria est."—*Spec. B. V. lect.* 6.

[5] "Numquid, quia ita deificata es. ideo nostræ humanitatis oblita es? Nequaquam, domina! non convenit tantæ misericordiæ, tantam miseriam oblivisci."—*Loco supra cit.*

[6] "Magna erga miseros fuit misericordia Mariæ adhuc exsulantis in mundo, sed multo major est regnantis in cœlo."—*Spec. B. V. lect.* 10.

service of this Queen, to honor and love her as much as we can; for, as Richard of St. Laurence remarks, "she is not like other rulers, who oppress their vassals with burdens and taxes; but she enriches her servants with graces, merits, and rewards."[1] Let us also entreat her in the words of the Abbot Guerric: "O Mother of mercy, thou who sittest on so lofty a throne and in such close proximity to God, satiate thyself with the glory of thy Jesus, and send us, thy servants, the fragments that are left. Thou dost now enjoy the heavenly banquet of thy Lord; and we, who are still on earth, as dogs under the table, ask thy mercy."[2]

EXAMPLE.*

St. Peter Damian relates the following of his brother Marinus. The latter having had the misfortune to sin against the holy virtue, went shortly after before an altar of the Blessed Virgin and consecrated himself to her service. As a sign of this oblation, he put a girdle around his neck and addressed the Blessed Virgin in these words: "Dear Lady, thou mirror of purity, I poor sinner have offended God and thee. I know no other remedy but to enter thy holy service. I therefore offer myself to thee today: deign to take a poor rebel and do not reject me. At the foot of the altar he left a sum of money and promised that every year he would offer an equal amount as a mark of his servitude. When after a long and God-fearing life he came to die, he said shortly before expiring: "Arise, arise—and render homage to our loving Virgin Mother. What a favor for me, O Queen of Heaven, that thou shouldst deign to visit thy poor servant. Bless me, my Lady, and do not let me be lost after being honored by thy presence." Shortly after his brother Damian entered and the dying man told him of the appari-

---

[1] "Regina Maria largitur servis suis dona gratiarum, vestes virtutum, thesauros meritorum, et magnitudinem præmiorum."—*De Laud. M. V.* l. 6, c. 13.

[2] "O Mater misericordiæ! saturare gloria Filii tui, et dimitte reliquias tuas parvulis tuis; tu ad mensam Domina, nos sub mensa catelli."—*In Assumpt.* s. 4.

tion adding that Mary had blessed him. At the same time he complained because those present had not arisen when Mary appeared to him. In a few minutes he closed his eyes in death.[1]

Prayer.

O great, exalted, and most glorious Lady, prostrate at the foot of thy throne we adore thee from this valley of tears. We rejoice at thy immense glory, with which our Lord has enriched thee; and now that thou art enthroned as Queen of heaven and earth, ah forget us not, thy poor servants. Disdain not, from the high throne on which thou reignest, to cast thine eyes of mercy on us miserable creatures. The nearer thou art to the source of graces, in the greater abundance canst thou procure those graces for us. In heaven thou seest more plainly our miseries; hence thou must compassionate and succor us the more. Make us thy faithful servants on earth, that thus we may one day bless thee in heaven. On this day, on which thou wast made Queen of the universe, we also consecrate ourselves to thy service. In the midst of thy so great joy, console us also by accepting us as thy servants. Thou art, then, our mother. Ah, most sweet Mother, most amiable Mother, thine altars are surrounded by many people: some ask to be cured of a disorder, some to be relieved in their necessities, some for an abundant harvest, and some for success in litigation. We ask thee for graces more pleasing to thy heart: obtain for us that we may be humble, detached from the world, resigned to the divine will; obtain us the holy fear of God, a good death, and Paradise. O Lady, change us from sinners into saints; work this miracle, which will redound more to thy honor than if thou didst restore sight to a thousand blind persons, or didst raise a thousand from the dead. Thou art so powerful with God, we need only say that thou art his Mother, his beloved one, his most dear one, filled with his grace. What can he ever deny thee? O most beautiful Queen, we have no pretensions to see thee on earth, but we do desire to go to see thee in Paradise; and it is thou who must obtain us this grace. For it we hope with confidence. Amen, amen.

[1] *Opus* c. 33, c. 4.

HYMNS.

I.

The Death of Mary.

Uplift the voice and sing
 The Daughter and the Spouse,
The Mother of the King,
 To whom creation bows!

Praise to Mary, endless praise!
Raise your joyful voices, raise!
Praise to God who reigns above,
Who has made her for his love.

When Mary lingered yet
 An exile from her Son,
Like fairest lily, set
 'Mid thorns of earth alone.
     Praise to Mary, etc.

To be with God on high,
 Her heart was all on fire;
She sought and asked to die,
 With humble sweet desire.
     Praise to Mary, etc.

At length her heavenly spouse,
 Who loved her with such love,
Invites her to repose
 With him in heaven above.
     Praise to Mary, etc.

She waits till death appear,
  And let her spirit go;
But death approached with year,
  And dared not strike the blow.
              Praise to Mary, etc.

Then came sweet Love from heaven,
  And with his flaming dart
The mortal wound was given
  To Mary's stainless heart.
              Praise to Mary, etc.

Pierc'd by the deadly wound,
  She gently bowed her head;
Pining with love she swoon'd,
  And, lo, her spirit fled.
              Praise to Mary, etc.

Then did that beauteous Dove
  Spring joyfully on high;
Her Son receives with love,
  And bears her to the sky.
              Praise to Mary, etc.

And now, bright Queen of Love!
  While seated on thy throne,
High in the realms above,
  Near to thy glorious Son.
              Praise to Mary, etc.

Hear, from that blest abode,
  A sinner cries to thee:
Teach me to love that God
  Who bears such love to me.
              Praise to Mary, etc.

II.

The Same Subject.

Mary! thy heart for love
  Alone had ever sighed:
So much it loved, at length
  Of very love it died.

O happy, happy death!
  If death indeed could be,
Blest Virgin! that sweet end
  Which God bestowed on thee.

'Tis in a sweet repose,
  With smile of heavenly mirth,
Thou takest joyful flight
  To Paradise from earth.

Then speed thee, Mother mine,
  Though speeds my life from me;
Haste where thy Son awaits,
  And Heaven welcomes thee.

Oh! that my life could end,
  Sweet Mother, now with thine,
That I might soar to heaven,
  Where all thy glories shine!

Thrice fortunate, my soul,
  Yea, lot supremely blest,
To reach thy Mother's throne,
  And at her feet to rest.

But see, above the choirs
  Of saints and angels bright,
God's Mother near her Son,
  Enthroned in dazzling light.

Come then, to fetch thy child,
  O Mary, Mother dear!
And tarry by my side
  When my last hour is near.

Yes, this I hope from thee—
  Despise not my request,
To yield my soul in peace
  Upon my Mother's breast.

III.

The Assumption of Mary.

Fly, my soul, with Mary fly,
Soar beyond the golden sky,
Mount to Mary's throne on high.

Bright the queenly crown she won,
Sweet the reign she has begun,
As she stands beside her Son.
                    Fly, my soul, etc.

How endure this long delay?
Living here how can I stay
From such beauty far away?
                    Fly, my soul, etc.

Sad my lot is here below;
Who can hope or life bestow?
Who will help or pity show?
                    Fly, my soul, etc.

But though far away from me,
Still our sovereign Queen will be
Full of love and clemency.
                    Fly, my soul, etc.

With a mother's loving care
She will lift those hands so fair,
And will save us by her prayer.
    Fly, my soul, etc.

Mother's heart can ne'er forget
That we are her children yet,
By such dangers fierce beset.
    Fly, my soul, etc.

Gently, still, she bends her eyes
On the soul that longs and sighs
For her love, the heavenly prize.
    Fly, my soul, etc.

Blest that soul who, like the dove
Borne upon the wings of love,
Follows her to heaven above.
    Fly, my soul, etc.

Sermon for the Feast of the Annunciation.*

Et Verbum caro factum est.

" The Word was made flesh."—*John*, i. 14.

ST. THOMAS calls the mystery of the Incarnation of the Eternal Word "the miracle of miracles."[1] What greater prodigy could the world behold, than a woman become the Mother of God, and a God clothed in human flesh ? Let us therefore consider to-day these two prodigies.

First. Mary, by her humility, became the Mother of her Creator.

Secondly. The Creator, in his goodness, became the Son of his own creature.

I.

Mary, by her Humility, became the Mother of her Creator.

God, having determined to manifest to the world his immense goodness, by humbling himself so far as to become man, to redeem lost man, and having to choose a Virgin Mother, sought amongst virgins the one who was the most humble. He found that the Blessed Virgin Mary surpassed all others in sanctity, as greatly as she surpassed them in humility, and therefore chose her for his Mother. *He hath regarded the humility of His handmaid.*[2] "She did not say," remarks St. Laurence Jus-

[1] " Miraculum miraculorum."—*De Pot.* q. 6, a. 2.
[2] " Respexit humilitatem ancillæ suæ."

---

* This sermon does not form a part of the *Glories of Mary;* but as it happens to be isolated, it was thought proper to insert it in this place. The first point is an abridged repetition of Discourse IV., page 359.—ED.

tinian, "he hath regarded the virginity or the innocence, but only the humility, of his handmaid." [1] And before him St. Jerome had said, that "God chose her to be his Mother more on account of her humility than of all her other sublime virtues." [2]

Now we understand that Mary was that one who was spoken of in the sacred Canticles under the name of spikenard, a small and lowly plant, which, by its sweet odor, drew the King of Heaven, the Eternal Word, from the bosom of his Father, into her womb, there to clothe himself with human flesh : *While the king was at his repose, my spikenard sent forth the odor thereof ;* [3] which St. Antoninus thus explains : "Spikenard, from its being a small and lowly herb, was a type of Mary, who in the highest degree gave forth the sweet odor of her humility." [4] Before him St. Bernard had said : "She was indeed worthy to be looked upon by the Lord, whose beauty the King so greatly desired, and by whose most sweet odor he was drawn from the eternal repose of his Father's bosom." [5] So that God, attracted by the humility of the Blessed Virgin, when he became man for the redemption of man, chose her for his Mother. He would not, however, for the greater glory and merit of his Mother, become her Son without her consent. "He would not take flesh from her," says the Abbot William,

---

[1] "Non ait: Respexit virginitatem, innocentiam :—sed: Humilitatem tantum."—*De Vita sol.* c. 14.

[2] "Maluit Deus de beata Maria incarnari propter humilitatem, quam propter aliam quamcumque virtutem."—*Eusebius, De Morte Hier.*

[3] "Dum esset Rex in accubitu suo, nardus mea dedit odorem suum."—*Cant.* i. 11.

[4] "Nardus est herba parva, et significat Beatam Virginem, quæ dedit odorem suæ humilitatis."—P. 4, t. 15, c. 21, § 2.

[5] "Digna plane quam respiceret Dominus, cujus decorem concupisceret Rex, cujus odore suavissimo ab æterno illo paterni sinus attraheretur accubitu."—*In Assumpt.* s. 4.

"unless she gave it." [1] Behold, whilst this humble little Virgin was in her poor cottage, sighing and entreating the Lord, as it was revealed to St. Elizabeth of Hungary, that he would send the world its Redeemer, the archangel Gabriel came, as the bearer, on the part of God, of the great embassy, and saluted her, *Hail, full of grace; the Lord is with thee ; blessed art thou among women.*[2] Hail, O Mary, full of grace ; for thou art rich in that grace which surpasses the grace given to all men and angels. The Lord is with thee, and always was with thee, assisting thee with his grace. Thou art blessed amongst all women; for all others fell under the curse of sin; but thou, as the Mother of the Blessed One, wast preserved from every stain, and always wast, and always wilt be blessed.

What answer does the humble Mary give to a salutation so full of praises? She does not reply ; but, astonished at them, is confounded and troubled : *who having heard was troubled at his saying, and thought with herself what manner of salutation this should be.*[3] Why was she troubled? was it that she feared an illusion ? No, for she was sure that it was a celestial spirit who spoke to her. Her modesty was perhaps troubled at the sight of an angel under a human form, as some have thought ? No, the text is clear, "she was troubled at his saying:" to which Eusebius Emissenus adds, " not at his appearance, but at what he said." [4] This trouble, then, proceeded entirely from her humility, and was caused by the great praises, which were so far from her own hum-

---

[1] " Nec carnem volebat sumere ex ipsa, non dante ipsa."—*Delrio, In Cant.* i. 2.

[2] " Ave, Gratia Plena ! Dominus tecum ; benedicta tu in mulieribus."—*Luke,* i. 28.

[3] " Quæ cum audisset, turbata est in sermone ejus, et cogitabat qualis esset ista salutatio."

[4] " Non in vultu, sed in sermone ejus."—*In Fer.* 4 p. *Dom.* 4 *Adv.*

ble estimate of herself. Hence the more she heard herself praised, the more deeply did she enter into the depth of her own nothingness. St. Bernardine of Sienna writes, that " had the angel said, O Mary, thou art the greatest sinner in the world, her astonishment would not have been so great; the sound of such high praises filled her with fear." [1]

But the Blessed Virgin, I say, already understood the sacred Scriptures ; she well knew that the time foretold by the prophets for the coming of the Messiah had arrived; she knew that the seventy weeks of Daniel were completed, and that the sceptre of Juda had passed into the hands of Herod, a stranger, according to the prophecy of Jacob ; she also knew that the mother of the Messiah was to be a Virgin. She then heard the angel give her praises, which it was evident could apply to no other than a Mother of God. May not a thought or doubt have entered her mind, that she was perhaps this chosen Mother ? No ; her profound humility did not even allow her to have a doubt. Those praises only caused her so great fear, that the angel himself was obliged to encourage her not to fear, as St. Peter Chrysologus writes: "As Christ was pleased to be comforted by an angel, so had the Blessed Virgin to be encouraged by one." [2] St. Gabriel said, *Fear not, Mary ; for thou hast found grace with God.* [3] As if he had said, Why fearest thou, O Mary ? Knowest thou not that God exalts the humble ? Thou in thine own eyes art lowly and of no account, and therefore he in his goodness exalts thee to the dignity of being his Mother. *Behold, thou shalt con-*

---

[1] " Si dixisset: Tu, O Maria ! es lascivior quæ sit in mundo;—non ita admirata fuisset; unde turbata fuit de tantis laudibus."—T. iii. *Quadr.* s. 37, p. 3.

[2] " Sicut Christus per Angelum confortari voluit, ita decuit Virginem per Angelum animari."—*Suarez, De Inc.* q. 30, a. 2.

[3] " Ne timeas, Maria; invenisti enim gratiam apud Deum."

*ceive in thy womb, and shalt bring forth a Son : and thou shalt
call his name Jesus.*[1]

In the mean time the angel waits to know whether she
is willing to be the Mother of God. St. Bernard addresses her, saying, "The angel awaits thy reply ; and
we also, O Lady, on whom the sentence of condemnation
weighs so heavily, await the word of mercy."[2] "Behold,
O holy Virgin, the price of our salvation, which will be
the blood of that Son now to be formed in thy womb.
This price is offered to thee to pay for our sins, and deliver us from death; "we shall be instantly delivered if
thou consentest."[3] "Thy Lord himself desires thy consent ; for by it he had determined to save the world.
He desires it with an ardor equal to the love with which
he has loved thy beauty."[4] "Answer, O sacred Virgin,"
says St. Augustine, "why delayest thou the salvation of
the world, which depends on thy consent ?"[5]

But see, Mary already replies to the angel. *Behold the
handmaid of the Lord : be it done to me according to thy word.*[6]
O admirable answer, which rejoiced heaven, and brought
an immense treasure of good things to the world. An
answer which drew the only-begotten Son from the
bosom of his eternal Father into this world to become
man ; for these words had hardly fallen from the lips of

---

[1] "Ecce concipies in utero, et paries Filium, et vocabis nomen ejus
Jesum."

[2] "Exspectat Angelus responsum; expectamus et nos, O Domina,
verbum miserationis, quos miserabiliter premit sententia damnationis."

[3] "Ecce offertur tibi pretium salutis nostræ; statim liberabimur, si
consentis."

[4] "Ipse quoque Dominus, quantum concupivit decorem tuum, tantum desiderat et responsionis assensum, in qua nimirum proposuit
salvare mundum."—*De Laud. V. M. hom.* 4.

[5] "Responde jam, Virgo sacra ! vitam quid tricas mundo ?"—*Serm.*
120. *E. B. app.*

[6] "Ecce ancilla Domini; fiat mihi secundum verbum tuum."

Mary before *the Word was made flesh ;* [1] the Son of God became also the Son of Mary. "O powerful *fiat !*" exclaims St. Thomas of Villanova ; " O efficacious *fiat ! O fiat* to be venerated above every other *fiat !*" [2] for with that *fiat* heaven came on earth, and earth was raised to heaven.

Let us now examine Mary's answer more closely: *Behold the handmaid of the Lord.* [3] By this answer the humble Virgin meant: Behold the servant of the Lord, obliged to do that which her Lord commands; since he well sees my nothingness, and since all that I have is his, who can say that he has chosen me for any merit of my own? *Behold the handmaid of the Lord.* What merits can a servant have, for which she should be chosen to be the Mother of her Lord ? Let not the servant, then, be praised, but the goodness alone of that Lord, who is graciously pleased to regard so lowly a creature, and make her so great.

"O humility," exclaims the Abbot Guerric, "as nothing in its own eyes, yet sufficiently great for the divinity! Insufficient for itself, sufficient in the eyes of God to contain him in her womb whom the heavens cannot contain!" [4] Let us also hear the exclamations of St. Bernard on this subject. He says: "And how, O Lady, couldst thou unite in thy heart so humble an opinion of thyself with so great purity, with such innocence, and so great a plenitude of grace, as thou didst possess ?" "Whence this humility," continues the saint, "and so great humility, O blessed one ?" [5] Lucifer, seeing himself

---

[1] "Et Verbum Caro factum est."

[2] "O Fiat potens! O Fiat efficax! O Fiat super omne Fiat venerandum."—*De Annunt. conc.* I.

[3] "Ecce ancilla Domini."

[4] "O humilitas, angusta tibi, ampla Divinitati; insufficiens tibi, sufficiens ei quem non capit orbis!"—*In Assumpt.* s. 3.

[5] "Quanta humilitatis virtus cum tanta puritate, cum innocentia tanta, imo cum tanta gratiae plenitudine! Unde tibi humilitas et tanta humilitas, O Beata!"—*In Ass.* s. 4.

enriched by God with extraordinary beauty, aspired to exalt his throne above the stars, and to make himself like God: *I will exalt my throne above the stars of God. . . . I will be like the Most High.*[1] O, what would that proud spirit have said had he ever been adorned with the gifts of Mary! He, being exalted by God, became proud, and was sent to hell; but the more the humble Mary saw herself enriched, so much the more did she concentrate herself in her own nothingness; and therefore God raised her to the dignity of being his Mother, having made her so incomparably greater than all other creatures, that, as St. Andrew of Crete says, "there is no one who is not God, who can be compared with Mary."[2] Hence St Anselm also says, "there is no one who is thy equal, O Lady; for all are either above or beneath thee: God alone is above thee, and all that is not God is inferior to thee."[3]

To what greater dignity could a creature be raised than that of Mother of her Creator? "To be the Mother of God," St. Bonaventure writes, "is the greatest grace which can be conferred on a creature. It is such that God could make a greater world, a greater heaven, but he cannot exalt a creature more than by making her his Mother."[4] This the Blessed Virgin was pleased herself to express, when she said, *He that is mighty hath done great things in me.*[5] But here the Abbot of Celles reminds her: "God did not create thee for himself only;

[1] "Super astra Dei exaltabo solium meum . . . , similis ero Altissimo."—*Is.* xiv. 13.

[2] "Excepto Deo, omnibus est altior."—*In Dorm. S. M.* s. 3.

[3] "Nihil tibi, Domina, est æquale; omne enim quod est. aut supra te est, aut subtus te: quod supra, solus Deus; quod infra. omne quod Deus non est."—*De Conc. B. M.*

[4] "Quid mirabilius, quam esse Dei Matrem? ipsa est qua majorem Deus facere non posset: majorem matrem quam Matrem Dei non posset facere."—*Spec. B. V. lect.* 9, 10.

[5] "Fecit mihi magna, qui potens est."

he gave thee to the angels as their restorer, and to men as their repairer."[1] So that God did not create Mary for himself only, but he created her for man also; that is to say, to repair the ruin entailed upon him by sin. We now pass to the second point.

II.

The Creator in his Goodness became the Son of his own Creature.

Our first father Adam sinned; for, ungrateful to God for the many gifts he had received from him, he rebelled against him by eating the forbidden fruit. God was therefore obliged to drive him from before his face, and to condemn him and all his posterity to eternal death. But afterwards pitying him, and moved by the bowels of his mercy, he was pleased to come on earth to become man, and thus satisfy the divine justice, paying with his own sufferings the punishment which we deserved for our sins. This we are taught by the Holy Church: "He came down from heaven and was made man, suffered and was buried."[2]

O prodigy, O excess of the love of God,—a God became man! Did a prince of this world, seeing a worm dead in its hole, wish to restore it to life; and were he told that to do so, it would be necessary that he should himself become a worm, enter its dwelling, and there at the price of his life make it a bath in his own blood, and that thus only could its life be restored, what would the reply of such a prince be? "No," he would say: "what does it signify to me whether the worm comes to life again or not, that I should shed my blood and die to re-

---

[1] "Non solum sibi ipsi te fecit, sed te Angelis dedit in instauratonem, hominibus in reparationem."—*Cont. de V. M.* c. 4.

[2] "Descendit de cœlis . . ., et homo factus est . . . passus et sepultus est."—*Symb. Nic.*

store its life?" Of what import was it to God that men should be lost, since they had merited it by their sins? Would his happiness have been diminished thereby?

No, indeed; it was because God's love for men was so truly great that he came upon earth and humbled himself to take flesh from a Virgin; and taking the form of a servant became man,—that is, he made himself a worm like us: *He emptied Himself, taking the form of a servant, being made in the likeness of men, and in habit formed as a man.*[1] He is God as the Father,—immense, omnipotent, sovereign, and in all things equal to the Father; but when he was made man in the womb of Mary he became a creature,—a servant, weak, and less than the Father. Behold him thus humbled in the womb of Mary; there he accepted the command of his Father, who willed that after three-and-thirty years of suffering he should die cruelly executed on a cross: *He humbled Himself, becoming obedient unto death, even to the death of the cross.*[2]

Behold him as a child in the womb of his Mother. He there conformed himself in all things to the will of his Father, and, inflamed with love for us, he offered himself willingly: *He was offered because it was His own will.*[3] He offered himself, I say, to suffer all for our salvation. He then foresaw the scourging, and offered his body; he foresaw the thorns, and offered his head; he foresaw the nails, and offered his hands and feet; foresaw the cross, and offered his life. And why was he pleased to suffer so much for us ungrateful sinners? It was because he loved us: *Who hath loved us, and washed us from our sins in His own blood.*[4] He saw us soiled with sin, and prepared

---

[1] "Semetipsum exinanivit, formam servi accipiens, in similitudinem hominum factus, et habitu inventus ut homo."—*Phil.* ii. 7.

[2] "Humiliavit semetipsum, factus obediens usque ad mortem, mortem autem crucis."—*Phil.* ii. 8.

[3] "Oblatus est quia ipse voluit."—*Is.* liii. 7.

[4] "Dilexit nos, et lavit nos a peccatis nostris in sanguine suo."—*Apoc.* i. 5.

us a bath in his own blood, that we might thereby be cleansed, and become dear to God: *Christ also hath loved us, and hath delivered Himself for us.*[1] He saw us condemned to death, and prepared to die himself, that we might live; and seeing us cursed by God on account of our sins, he was pleased to charge himself with the curses which we had deserved, that we might be saved: *Christ hath redeemed us from the curse of the law, being made a curse for us.*[2]

St. Francis of Paul had, then, indeed reason in considering the mystery of a God made man and dying through love for us, to exclaim, "O charity! O charity! O charity!" Did not faith assure us of all that the Son of God did and suffered for us, who could ever believe it? Ah, Christians! the love which Jesus Christ had and has for us indeed drives and forces us to love him, *for the charity of Christ presseth us.*[3] Tender indeed are the sentiments expressed by St. Francis de Sales on these words of St. Paul: he says, "Knowing, then, that Jesus, who was truly God, has loved us, and loved us so much as to die, and to die on a cross, for us, is not this to have our hearts under a wine-press, and to feel them forced and so strongly pressed that love issues from them by the very violence with which they are pressed; and the greater this violence is with which they are pressed, the more sweet and amiable is it."[4]

But here came the tears of St. John, *He came into His own, and His own received Him not.*[5] Why did the only-begotten Son of God become man on earth, suffer and die for us, if it was not that we might love him? "God

---

[1] "Dilexit nos, et tradidit semetipsum pro nobis."—*Eph.* v. 2.
[2] "Christus nos redemit de maledicto legis, factus pro nobis maledictum."—*Gal.* iii. 13.
[3] "Charitas enim Christi urget nos."—2 *Cor.* v. 14.
[4] *Love of God*, book vii. ch. 8.
[5] "In propria venit, et sui eum non receperunt."—*John*, i. 11.

became man," says Hugo of St. Victor, "that man might love him with greater freedom." [1] "Jesus Christ," says St. Augustin, "came on earth principally that man might know how much he loved him." [2] And if a God loves us so much, he requires, with justice, that we should love him. "He made known his love," says St. Bernard, "that he might experience thine." [3] He has shown us the greatness of the love he bears us, that he may obtain our love at least out of gratitude.

Prayer.

O Eternal Word, Thou camest from heaven on earth to become man and to die for man, that Thou mightest be loved by man; how is it, then, that among men there are so few who love Thee? Ah, infinite beauty, amiable infinity, worthy of infinite love, behold me; I am one of those ungrateful creatures whom Thou hast loved so much, but have not yet known how to love Thee; nay even, instead of loving Thee, I have greatly offended Thee. But Thou becamest man and didst die to pardon sinners who detest their sins, and wish to love Thee. Lord, behold me; see, I am a sinner, it is true; but I repent of the crimes I have committed against Thee, and I desire to love Thee; pity me.

And thou, O holy Virgin, who by thy humility becamest worthy to be the Mother of God, and as such art also our mother, the refuge, the advocate of sinners, do thou pray for me, recommend me to this Son, who loves thee so much, and refuses nothing that thou askest him. Tell him to pardon me; tell him to give me his holy love; tell him to save me; that with thee I may one day love him face to face in Paradise. Amen.

[1] "Deus factus est homo, ut familiarius ab homine diligeretur."—*Misc.* l. 1, t. 87.

[2] "Maxime propterea Christus advenit, ut cognosceret homo, quantum eum diligat Deus."—*De Catech. Rud.* c. 4.

[3] "Notam fecit dilectionem suam, ut experiatur et tuam."—*De Aquæd.*

Three Meditations for the Feast of the Presentation of Mary.*

I.

Mary offers Herself to God promptly.

LET us consider how prompt Mary was in offering herself to God. In her infancy, having scarcely attained the age of three years, knowing that her parents had made a vow to consecrate her to God, she was the first to request them to accomplish their promise by assuring them that the time had already come. She also it was who by her prayers obtained from God the strength to fulfil such a promise; for certainly very great was the violence that the holy parents had to do to themselves to deprive themselves so soon of a daughter whom they had so much desired to have, and who from the tenderest age had so much charmed them by her amiability.

Behold now Joachim and Anne generously sacrificing to God that which was the dearest to their hearts, setting out from Nazareth, accompanied by few relatives, but by choirs of angels. They had to carry their well-beloved little daughter by turns, on account of the length of journey from Nazareth to Jerusalem, it being a distance of eighty miles, as several authors say.

Having reached the Temple they placed their cher-

---

* The first translation of this meditation was made in 1868 from an unpublished manuscript of St. Alphonsus, preserved by the Redemptorist Fathers at Wittem, Holland. It has been thought fit to divide it into three parts, each of which bearing its own title. Those persons who have been called to consecrate themselves to God in the religious life will find in this meditation a perfect model for imitation.—ED.

ished little daughter on the floor. The latter having immediately ascended to the first step, turned to her parents, and on her knees kissed their hands and asked them to bless her and to recommend her to God. After having received the blessing, and being fortified by the love with which she was going to serve her God, who had deigned to call her to his house, she ascended all the steps of the Temple, and ascended them with so much haste and zeal that she no more turned back, not even to look at her parents who remained there deeply afflicted, and at the same time filled with wonder at the sight of so much strength and courage in so young a child.

Prayer.

Ah! holy child, it is thou who art the happy daughter of the prince of the earth praised by Holy Scripture : *How beautiful are thy steps, O prince's daughter !* [1] Indeed, very dear and very pleasing to the eyes of thy Lord and thy God have been the generous steps that thou didst take in the tenderest years of thy life, leaving thy father, thy house, and thy relatives to go to consecrate thyself entirely to his honor and to his service. Go thou, O Sovereign Lady, will I say with St. Germanus, go with joy into the house of God, to prepare thyself for the coming of the Holy Spirit, who is to come to make thee the Mother of God himself. O happy Virgin, who didst begin so soon to serve God, and who didst always serve him so faithfully ! cast a look at me, who have returned to him with such tardiness, after so many years lost in the love of creatures, and obtain for me the grace to give him at least the remainder of my life, be it long or short. I know that I have very many times deserved to die in the state of sin ; I know that it is thou who didst obtain for me the time to do penance—a grace that has not been granted to so many others. Ah ! my most amiable Queen, may my life, so unlike to thine, excite in thee not the disgust that it merits, but rather thy compassion. Since thou hast already done so much for me, finish the work of my salvation ; do not abandon me till thou seest me safe at thy feet in paradise.

[1] " Quam pulchri sunt gressus tui, Filia Principis!"—*Cant.* vii. 1.

II.

Mary offers Herself to God entirely.

Let us consider that what was most beautiful in this offering of Mary was that she consecrated herself to the Lord not only at so early an age, but that she did this in so thorough a manner.

Already from the first moment of her existence in the womb of her mother, when by a singular privilege she received the use of reason, with its great light with which at the same time the Lord enriched it, she gave herself up to God from the bottom of her heart. Yet her very holy soul was waiting with great longing for the day in which she might consecrate herself to God more effectively and thoroughly by becoming detached from all earthly things, even from every innocent affection for her parents, who loved her so tenderly. Hence we may understand the consolation that was felt by her very pure heart when at her entrance into the Temple, by a new act of the most ardent love, she devoted herself entirely to the glory of the divine Majesty.

Let us consider that this wonderful child, as soon as she found herself in the Temple, first presented herself to her mistress, and on her knees humbly besought her to teach her all that she had to do. Afterwards she saluted her companions and begged them to condescend to admit her into their society.

After these acts of propriety and humility, the youthful Mary turned all her thoughts towards God. She prostrated herself on the floor, and kissed it as being the house of the Lord. She adored his infinite Majesty, and thanked him for the great favor that she was receiving from his hands ; namely, the favor that he had thus obliged her to come to live for a time in his house. Then it was that she offered herself entirely to God, without the least reserve, by consecrating to him all her faculties and all her senses, her whole mind and her whole heart, her whole soul and her whole body. For at this time, in order to please God the more, she made the vow of virginity, a new vow, unusual at that time, and regarded by the Jews rather as a disgrace. But if Mary was the first to make such a vow, she was not the only one to do so; for it happened as David had foretold: *After her shall Virgins be brought to the King.*[1] Oh, how many very pure virgins have followed the example of Mary their Queen!

Again, Mary offered herself thus entirely without limitation of time; for by this offering of herself she had the intention to devote herself to the service of God in the Temple during her whole life, if such should be the good pleasure of the Lord, and never to depart from this holy place. Behold me now before Thee, O Lord! this holy child must have said; I have come into Thy house only to be Thy servant; accept the desire that I have of rendering to Thee all the honor that I can render, and receive me into Thy service by giving me the grace to be faithful to Thee. The Blessed Virgin revealed to St. Elizabeth, a Benedictine nun, that when she was left in the Temple she resolved in her heart to think of nothing but of God alone.

Prayer.

O Virgin full of sweetness! when will the day come for me, on which, detached from all earthly affections, I shall give myself entirely to God, who during so many years has been waiting for me and calling me to his love? My most holy Mother! to-day at last, animated by thy example, I give myself with thee to God entirely and without reserve; I give him my soul, my body, my will; but I desire that thou first unite this offering that I make to him to that which in thy infancy thou didst make in the Temple; and then that thou present it to the Lord

[1] " Adducentur Regi virgines post eam."—*Ps.* xliv. 15.

with thy own hand. Still, this is not enough; obtain for me, besides, the grace to be faithful to God as thou hast been thyself, in order that it may never happen that by a twofold ingratitude I take back what I give to him to-day.

III.

The Life of Mary in the Temple.

Let us consider, finally, how holy and pleasing to God was the life of Mary in the Temple, in which without intermission she progressed in perfection : *As the morning rising.*[1] Who could explain how from day to day all her virtues appeared more beautiful? One especially admired in her modesty, silence, mortification, humility, sweetness. St. Anselm says that she had the habit of speaking little, of being affable and charitable towards every one, and of obliging promptly. In fact, as was revealed to St. Bridget, the virtues that she practised most in the Temple were humility, charity, and obedience.

Ah! certainly, she did not walk, but she flew in the way of the Lord. St. Jerome says that her blessed soul was the abode of every virtue. She spent a certain time, as it is related, in doing some work that had been assigned to her. But the greatest part of the day and of the night she consecrated to prayer and to close entertainments with God in solitude; for this was the most cherished and most desired occupation of her heart that was burning with love; it was her sweetest delight. Oh, how well did Mary in the Temple know how to treat with God of the great work of the redemption of the world! Seeing perfectly the miserable condition of the world, in which so many souls were lost, in which so few knew the true God, and among this number so few loved him, ah! how much better than all the patriarchs and prophets did she pray by saying: Come,

[1] " Quasi aurora consurgens."—*Cant.* vi. 9.

Lord, do not delay; show us Thy mercy; send us the Lamb that is to rule the world. Ye heavens! let your rain descend and send us the Just, that the earth may bring forth the Saviour.

Prayer.

Thou very holy child, O great mistress of virtue and of love, since it is through thy love that the Eternal Word allowed himself to be drawn from the bosom of his Father to thy own, be ever blessed and ever thanked. How many beautiful lessons dost thou give by thy example, if we are only attentive in considering the life that thou hast led in the Temple! Ah! sweet Queen, have compassion on me; thou knowest the bad use that I have made of my past life; thou knowest the great account that at the hour of death I am to render to Jesus Christ, thy Son and my Judge. My charitable mistress, since thou hast been so good to me in helping me when I little thought of imploring thy aid and thy counsel, I do not fear that thou wilt abandon me, now that I wish to obey thee, and that I ask thy assistance. Do not banish me from thy school in which thou trainest so many souls to sanctity. Teach me what I should do to belong entirely to God, and thus to repair the time that I have lost. Should I fail in my duty, O my Sovereign Lady! be so kind as to correct me and chastise me as thou mayest think fit. The chastisements coming from thy sweet hand, to make me a saint, will always be very dear to me. For pity's sake, O Mary! do not abandon me till thou seest me become thy perfect disciple in the love towards thy God and my God; for I know that it is only in order to love him that the time for me yet to live has been granted to me. My Sovereign Lady! I ask this favor of thee, and it is from thee that I hope to receive it. Amen.

PART THE THIRD.

The Dolors of Mary.

DISCOURSE.*

Mary is the Queen of Martyrs, for her Martyrdom was longer and greater than that of all the Martyrs.

Who can ever have a heart so hard that it will not melt on hearing the most lamentable event that once occurred in the world? There was a noble and holy mother who had an only son. This son was the most amiable that can be imagined—innocent, virtuous, beautiful, who loved his mother most tenderly; so much so that he had never caused her the least displeasure, but had ever shown her all respect, obedience, and affection; hence this mother had placed all her affections on earth in this son. Hear, then, what happened. This son, through envy, was falsely accused by his enemies; and though the judge knew, and himself confessed, that he was innocent, yet, that he might not offend his enemies, he condemned him to the ignominious death that they demanded. This poor mother had to suffer the grief of seeing that amiable and beloved son unjustly snatched from her in the flower of his age by a barbarous death;

---

* There are two feasts in honor of the Dolors of the Blessed Virgin, namely, the Friday of Passion week and the fifteenth of the month of September. The two points of this discourse, or those of the sermon that follows, joined to the Reflections on each of the seven dolors, may form a novena of meditations or of spiritual reading.—Ed.

for, by dint of torments and drained of all his blood, he was made to die on an infamous gibbet in a public place of execution, and this before her own eyes. Devout souls, what say you? Is not this event, and is not this unhappy mother, worthy of compassion?

You already understand of whom I speak. This son, so cruelly executed, was our loving Redeemer Jesus; and this mother was the Blessed Virgin Mary; who, for the love she bore us, was willing to see him sacrificed to divine justice by the barbarity of men. This great torment, then, which Mary endured for us—a torment that was more than a thousand deaths—deserves both our compassion and our gratitude. If we can make no other return for so much love, at least let us give a few moments this day to consider the greatness of the sufferings by which Mary became the Queen of martyrs; for the sufferings of her great martyrdom exceeded those of all the martyrs; being, in the first place, the longest in point of duration; and in the second place, the greatest in point of intensity.

I.

As Jesus is called the King of sorrows and the King of martyrs, because he suffered during his life more than all other martyrs; so also is Mary with reason called the Queen of martyrs, having merited this title by suffering the most cruel martyrdom possible after that of her son. Hence with reason was she called by Richard of St. Laurence, "the Martyr of martyrs;"[1] and of her can the words of Isaias with all truth be said, *He will crown thee with a crown of tribulation;*[2] that is to say, that that suffering itself, which exceeded the suffering of all the other martyrs united, was the crown by which she was shown to be the Queen of martyrs.

[1] " Martyr martyrum."—*De Laud. B. M.* l. 3.
[2] " Coronans coronabit te tribulatione."—*Is.* xxii. 18.

That Mary was a true martyr cannot be doubted, as Denis the Carthusian,[1] Pelbart,[2] Catharinus, and others prove; for it is an undoubted opinion that suffering sufficient to cause death is martyrdom, even though death does not ensue from it. St. John the Evangelist is revered as a martyr, though he did not die in the caldron of boiling oil, but "came out more vigorous than he went in."[3] St. Thomas says, "that to have the glory of martyrdom, it is sufficient to exercise obedience in its highest degree, that is to say, to be obedient unto death."[4] "Mary was a martyr," says St. Bernard, "not by the sword of the executioner, but by bitter sorrow of heart."[5] If her body was not wounded by the hand of the executioner, her blessed heart was transfixed by a sword of grief at the Passion of her Son, grief which was sufficient to cause her death not once, but a thousand times. From this we shall see that Mary was not only a real martyr, but that her martyrdom surpassed all others; for it was longer than that of all others, and her whole life may be said to have been a prolonged death.

"The Passion of Jesus," as St. Bernard says, "began with his birth."[6] So also did Mary, in all things like unto her Son, endure her martyrdom throughout her life. Amongst other significations of the name of Mary, as Blessed Albert the Great asserts, is that of "bitter sea."[7] Hence to her is applicable the text of Jeremias: *Great as the sea is thy destruction*[8] For as the sea is

---

[1] *De Laud. V. M.* l. 3, a. 24. [2] *Stell. B. V.* l. 3, p. 2, a. 3.

[3] "Vegetior exiverit, quam intraverit."—*Die* 6 *Maii.*

[4] "Martyrium complectitur id quod summum in obedientia esse potest, ut scilicet aliquis sit obediens usque ad mortem."—2. 2, q. 124, a. 3.

[5] "Non ferro carnificis, sed acerbo dolore cordis."—*De Serm. D. in Cœna*, s. 4.

[6] " A nativitatis exordio, passio crucis simul exorta."

[7] " Mare amarum."—*De Laud. B. M.* l. 1, c. 3.

[8] " Magna est enim velut mare contritio tua."—*Lam.* ii. 13.

all bitter and salt, so also was the life of Mary always full of bitterness at the sight of the Passion of the Redeemer, which was ever present to her mind. "There can be no doubt, that, enlightened by the Holy Ghost in a far higher degree than all the prophets, she, far better than they, understood the predictions recorded by them in the sacred Scriptures concerning the Messias."[1] This is precisely what the angel revealed to St. Bridget, and he also added, "that the Blessed Virgin, even before she became his Mother, knowing how much the Incarnate Word was to suffer for the salvation of men, and compassionating this innocent Saviour, who was to be so cruelly put to death for crimes not his own, even then began her great martyrdom."[2]

Her grief was immeasurably increased when she became the Mother of this Saviour; so that at the sad sight of the many torments that were to be endured by her poor Son, she indeed suffered a long martyrdom,[3] a martyrdom which lasted her whole life. This was signified with great exactitude to St. Bridget[4] in a vision which she had in Rome, in the church of St. Mary Major, where the Blessed Virgin with St. Simeon, and an angel bearing a very long sword, reddened with blood, appeared to her, denoting thereby the long and bitter grief which transpierced the heart of Mary during her whole life. Whence the above-named Rupert supposes Mary thus speaking: "Redeemed souls, and my beloved children, do not pity me only for the hour in which I beheld my dear Jesus expiring before my eyes; for the

---

[1] "Procul dubio est credendum, quod ex inspiratione Spiritus Sancti ipsa perfectius intellexit quidquid Prophetarum eloquia figurabant."

[2] "Ex Scripturis Deum incarnari velle intelligens, et quod tam diversis pœnis deberet cruciari, tribulationem non modicam in corde suo sustinuit."—*Serm. Ang.* c. 16.

[3] "Tu longum, præscia futuræ passionis Filii tui, pertulisti martyrium."—*In Cant.* l. 3.

[4] *Rev.* l. 7, c. :

sword of sorrow predicted by Simeon pierced my soul during the whole of my life ; when I was giving suck to my Son, when I was warming him in my arms, I already foresaw the bitter death that awaited him. Consider, then, what long and bitter sorrows I must have endured." [1]

Wherefore Mary might well say, in the words of David, *My life is wasted with grief, and my years in sighs.* [2] *My sorrow is continually before me.* [3] "My whole life was spent in sorrow and in tears ; for my sorrow, which was compassion for my beloved Son, never departed from before my eyes, as I always foresaw the sufferings and death which he was one day to endure." The divine Mother herself revealed to St. Bridget, that "even after the death and ascension of her son, whether she ate, or worked, the remembrance of his Passion was ever deeply impressed on her mind, and fresh in her tender heart." [4] Hence Tauler says, "that the most Blessed Virgin spent her whole life in continual sorrow;" [5] for her heart was always occupied with sadness and with suffering.

Therefore time, which usually mitigates the sorrows of the afflicted, did not relieve Mary; nay, even it increased her sorrows; for, as Jesus, on the one hand, advanced in age, and always appeared more and more

---

[1] "Nolite solam attendere horam illam, in qua vidi talem Dilectum mori; nam gladius, antequam pertransiret, longum per me transitum fecit. Cum igitur talem Filium sinu meo foverem, uberibus lactarem, et talem ejus mortem præ oculis haberem, quam prolixam me putatis pertulisse passionem!"—*In Cant.* l. 1.

[2] "Defecit in dolore vita mea, et anni mei in gemitibus."—*Ps.* xxx. 11.

[3] "Et dolor meus in conspectu meo semper."—*Ps.* xxxvii. 18.

[4] "Tempore quod post ascensionem Filii mei vixi, sic passio sua in corde meo fixa erat, quod sive comedebam, sive laborabam, quasi recens erat in memoria mea."—*Rev.* l. 6, c. 61.

[5] *Exc. de Vita Chr.* c. 18.

beautiful and amiable; so also, on the other hand, the time of his death always drew nearer, and grief always increased in the heart of Mary, at the thought of having to lose him on earth. So that in the words addressed by the angel to St. Bridget: "As the rose grows up amongst thorns, so the Mother of God advanced in years in the midst of suffering; and as the thorns increase with the growth of the rose, so also did the thorns of her sorrows increase in Mary, the chosen rose of the Lord, as she advanced in age; and so much the more deeply did they pierce her heart." [1]

II.

Having now considered the length of this sorrow in point of duration, let us pass to the second point—its greatness in point of intensity.

Ah, Mary is not only Queen of martyrs because her martyrdom was longer than that of all others, but also because it was the greatest of all martyrdoms. Who, however, can measure its greatness? Jeremias seems unable to find any one with whom he can compare this Mother of sorrows, when he considers her great sufferings at the death of her Son. *To what shall I compare thee? or to what shall I liken thee, O daughter of Jerusalem? . . . for great as the sea is thy destruction: who shall heal thee?* [2] Wherefore Cardinal Hugo, in a commentary on these words, says, "O Blessed Virgin, as the sea in bitterness exceeds all other bitterness, so does thy grief

---

[1] " Sicut rosa crescere solet inter spinas, ita hæc venerabilis Virgo in hoc mundo crevit inter tribulationes; et quemadmodum, quanto rosa in crescendo se plus dilatat, tanto fortior et acutior spina efficitur, ita hæc electissima Rosa, Maria, quanto plus ætate crescebat, tanto tribulationum spinis acutius pungebatur."—*Serm. Ang.* c. 16.

[2] "Cui comparabo te, vel cui assimilabo te, Filia Jerusalem? cui exæquabo te et consolabor te virgo, Filia Sion? magna est enim velut mare contritio tua; quis medebitur tui?"—*Lam.* ii. 13.

exceed all other grief."[1]   Hence St. Anselm asserts, that
"had not God by a special miracle preserved the life of
Mary in each moment of her life, her grief was such that
it would have caused her death."[2]   St. Bernardine of
Sienna goes so far as to say, "that the grief of Mary
was so great that, were it divided amongst all men, it
would suffice to cause their immediate death."[3]

But let us consider the reasons for which Mary's martyrdom was greater than that of all martyrs.

In the first place, we must remember that the martyrs
endured their torments, which were the effect of fire and
other material agencies, in their bodies; Mary suffered
hers in her soul, as St. Simeon foretold: *And thy own soul
a sword shall pierce.*[4]   As if the holy old man had said:
" O most sacred Virgin, the bodies of other martyrs will
be torn with iron, but thou wilt be transfixed, and martyred in thy soul by the Passion of thine own Son."
Now, as the soul is more noble than the body, so much
greater were Mary's sufferings than those of all the
martyrs, as Jesus Christ himself said to St. Catharine of
Sienna: "Between the sufferings of the soul and those
of the body there is no comparison."[5]   Whence the holy
Abbot Arnold of Chartres says, "that whoever had been
present on Mount Calvary, to witness the great sacrifice
of the Immaculate Lamb, would there have beheld two
great altars, the one in the body of Jesus, the other in
the heart of Mary; for, on that mount, at the same time

---

[1] "Quemadmodum mare est in amaritudine excellens, ita tuæ con-
tritioni nulla calamitas æquari potest."

[2] "Utique, Domina! non crediderim te potuisse stimulos tanti cruciatus, quin vitam amitteres, sustinere, nisi ipse spiritus Filii tui te
confortaret."—*De Excell. V.* c. 5.

[3] "Tantus fuit dolor virginis, quod, si in omnes creaturas, quæ pati
possunt, divideretur, omnes subito interirent."—*Pro Fest. V. M.* s.
13, a. 2, c. 2.

[4] "Et tuam ipsius animam pertransibit gladius."—*Luke,* ii. 35.

[5] "Inter dolorem animæ et corporis nulla est comparatio."

2

that the Son sacrificed his body by death, Mary sacrificed her soul by compassion." [1]

Moreover, says St. Antoninus,[2] while other martyrs suffered by sacrificing their own lives, the Blessed Virgin suffered by sacrificing her Son's life—a life that she loved far more than her own; so that she not only suffered in her soul all that her Son endured in his body, but moreover the sight of her Son's torments brought more grief to her heart than if she had endured them all in her own person. No one can doubt that Mary suffered in her heart all the outrages that she saw inflicted on her beloved Jesus. Any one can understand that the sufferings of children are also those of their mothers who witness them. St. Augustine, considering the anguish endured by the mother of the Machabees in witnessing the tortures of her sons, says, " she, seeing their sufferings, suffered in each one; because she loved them all, she endured in her soul what they endured in their flesh." [3] Thus also did Mary suffer all those torments, scourges, thorns, nails, and the cross, which tortured the innocent flesh of Jesus; all entered at the same time into the heart of this Blessed Virgin, to complete her martyrdom. " He suffered in the flesh, and she in the heart," [4] writes the Blessed Amadeus. " So much so," says St. Laurence Justinian, " that the heart of Mary became, as it were, a mirror of the Passion of the Son, in which might be seen, faithfully reflected, the spitting, the blows and wounds, and all that Jesus suffered." [5]

[1] "Nimirum in tabernaculo illo duo videres altaria: aliud in pectore Mariæ, aliud in corpore Christi: Christus carnem, Maria immolabat animam."—*De 7 Verbis*, tr. 3.

[2] P. 4, t. 15, c. 24, § 1.

[3] "Illa, videndo, in omnibus passa est: amabat omnes; ferebat in oculis, quod in carne omnes."—*Serm.* 300, E. B.

[4] "Ille carne, illa corde passa est."—*De Laud. B. V. hom.* 5.

[5] "Passionis Christi speculum effectum erat cor Virginis; in illo

St. Bonaventure also remarks that " those wounds which were scattered over the body of our Lord were all united in the single heart of Mary."[1] Thus was our Blessed Lady, through the compassion of her loving heart for her Son, scourged, crowned with thorns, insulted, and nailed to the cross. Whence the same saint, considering Mary on Mount Calvary, present at the death of her Son, questions her in these words: "O Lady, tell me where didst thou stand? Was it only at the foot of the cross? Ah, much more than this, thou wast on the cross itself, crucified with thy Son."[2] Richard of St. Laurence, on the words of the Redeemer, spoken by Isaias the prophet, *I have trodden the wine-press alone, and of the Gentiles there is not a man with me,*[3] says, " It is true, O Lord, that in the work of human redemption Thou didst suffer alone, and that there was not a man who sufficiently pitied Thee; but there was a woman with Thee, and she was Thine own Mother; she suffered in her heart all that Thou didst endure in Thy body."[4]

But all this is saying too little of Mary's sorrows since, as I have already observed, she suffered more in witnessing the sufferings of her beloved Jesus than if she had herself endured all the outrages and death of her Son. Erasmus, speaking of parents in general, says, that " they are more cruelly tormented by their children's sufferings than by their own."[5] This is not

agnoscebantur sputa, convicia, verbera, vulnera."—*De Tr. Chr. Ag.* c. 21.

[1] "Vulnera, per ejus corpus dispersa, sunt in corde tuo unita."— *Stim. div. am.* p. 1, c. 3.

[2] "O Domina mea, ubi stabas? numquid tantum juxta crucem? imo in cruce; cum Filio crucifixa eras."—*Ibid.*

[3] "Torcular calcavi solus, et de gentibus non est vir mecum."—*Is.* lxiii. 3.

[4] "Verum est, Domine, quod non est vir tecum; sed Mulier una tecum est, quæ omnia vulnera quæ tu suscepisti in corpore, suscepit in corde."—*De Laud. B. M.* l. 1, c. 5.

[5] " Parentes atrocius torquentur in liberis, quam in seipsis."

always true, but in Mary it evidently was so; for it is certain that she loved her Son and his life beyond all comparison more than herself or a thousand lives of her own. Therefore, Blessed Amadeus rightly affirms, that "the afflicted Mother, at the sorrowful sight of the torments of her beloved Jesus, suffered far more than she would have done had she herself endured his whole Passion." [1] The reason is evident, for, as St. Bernard says, "the soul is more where it loves than where it lives." [2] Our Lord himself had already said the same thing: *where our treasure is, there also is our heart.* [3] If Mary, then, by love, lived more in her Son than in herself, she must have endured far greater torments in the sufferings and death of her Son than she would have done, had the most cruel death in the world been inflicted upon her.

Here we must reflect on another circumstance which rendered the martyrdom of Mary beyond all comparison greater than the torments of all the martyrs: it is, that in the Passion of Jesus she suffered much, and she suffered, moreover, without the least alleviation.

The martyrs suffered under the torments inflicted on them by tyrants; but the love of Jesus rendered their pains sweet and agreeable. A St. Vincent was tortured on a rack, torn with pincers, burnt with red-hot iron plates; but, as St. Augustine remarks, "it seemed as if it was one who suffered, and another who spoke." [4] The saint addressed the tyrant with such energy and contempt for his torments, that it seemed as if one Vin-

---

[1] "Maria torquebatur magis, quam si torqueretur in se; quoniam supra se incomparabiliter diligebat id unde dolebat."—*De Laud. B. V. hom.* 5.

[2] "Anima magis est ubi amat, quam ubi animat."

[3] "Ubi enim thesaurus vester est, ibi et cor vestrum erit."—*Luke,* xii. 34.

[4] "Tanquam alius torqueretur, alius loqueretur."—*Serm.* 275, *E. B.*

cent suffered and another spoke; so greatly did God strengthen him with the sweetness of his love in the midst of all he endured. A St. Boniface had his body torn with iron hooks; sharp-pointed reeds were thrust between his nails and flesh; melted lead was poured into his mouth; and in the midst of all he could not tire saying, "I give Thee thanks, O Lord Jesus Christ."[1] A St. Mark and a St. Marcellinus were bound to a stake, their feet pierced with nails; and when the tyrant addressed them, saying, "Wretches, see to what a state you are reduced; save yourselves from these torments," they answered: "Of what pains, of what torments dost thou speak? We never enjoyed so luxurious a banquet as in the present moment, in which we joyfully suffer for the love of Jesus Christ."[2] A St. Laurence suffered; but when roasting on the gridiron, "the interior flame of love," says St. Leo, "was more powerful in consoling his soul than the flame without in torturing his body."[3] Hence love rendered him so courageous that he mocked the tyrant, saying, "If thou desirest to feed on my flesh, a part is sufficiently roasted; turn it, and eat."[4] But how, in the midst of so many torments, in that prolonged death, could the saint thus rejoice? "Ah!" replies St. Augustine, "inebriated with the wine of divine love, he felt neither torments nor death."[5]

So that the more the holy martyrs loved Jesus, the less did they feel their torments and death; and the sight alone of the sufferings of a crucified God was sufficient to console them. But was our suffering Mother

[1] "Gratias tibi ago, Domine Jesu Christe!"—*Offic. lect.* 2.

[2] "Nunquam tam jucunde epulati sumus, quam hæc libenter Jesu Christi causa perferimus."—*Ib. lect.* 3.

[3] "Segnior fuit ignis qui foris ussit, quam qui intus accendit."—*In Fest. S. Laur.*

[4] "Assatum est jam; versa et manduca."—*Offic. ant. ad Magn.*

[5] "In illa longa morte, in illis tormentis, illo calice ebrius, tormenta non sentit."—*In Jo. tr.* 27

also consoled by love for her Son, and the sight of his torments? Ah, no; for this very Son who suffered was the whole cause of them, and the love she bore him was her only and most cruel executioner; for Mary's whole martyrdom consisted in beholding and pitying her innocent and beloved Son, who suffered so much. Hence, the greater was her love for him, the more bitter and inconsolable was her grief. *Great as the sea is thy destruction; who shall heal thee?*[1] Ah, Queen of Heaven, love hath mitigated the sufferings of other martyrs, and healed their wounds; but who hath ever soothed thy bitter grief? Who hath ever healed the too cruel wounds of thy heart? "Who shall heal thee," since that very Son who could give thee consolation was, by his sufferings, the only cause of thine, and the love which thou didst bear him was the whole ingredient of thy martyrdom. So that, as other martyrs, as Diez remarks, are all represented with the instruments of their sufferings—a St. Paul with a sword, a St. Andrew with a cross, a St. Laurence with a gridiron—Mary is represented with her dead Son in her arms; for Jesus himself, and he alone, was the instrument of her martyrdom, by reason of the love she bore him. Richard of St. Victor confirms in a few words all that I have now said: "In other martyrs, the greatness of their love soothed the pains of their martyrdom; but in the Blessed Virgin, the greater was her love, the greater were her sufferings, the more cruel was her martyrdom."[2]

It is certain that the more we love a thing, the greater is the pain we feel in losing it. We are more afflicted at the loss of a brother than at the loss of a beast of bur-

[1] "Magna est enim velut mare contritio tua; quis medebitur tui?" —*Lam.* ii. 13.

[2] "In Martyribus, magnitudo amoris dolorem lenivit passionis; sed Beata Virgo, quanto plus amavit, tanto plus doluit, tantoque ipsius martyrium gravius fuit."—*In Cant.* c. 26

den; we are more grieved at the loss of a son than at
the loss of a friend. Now, Cornelius à Lapide says,
"that to understand the greatness of Mary's grief at the
death of her Son, we must understand the greatness of
the love she bore him."[1] But who can ever measure
that love? Blessed Amadeus says, that "in the heart of
Mary were united two kinds of love for her Jesus—
supernatural love, by which she loved him as her God,
and natural love, by which she loved him as her Son."[2]
So that these two loves became one; but so immense a
love, that William of Paris even says that the Blessed
Virgin "loved him as much as it was possible for a pure
creature to love him."[3] Hence Richard of St. Victor
affirms that "as there was no love like her love, so there
was no sorrow like her sorrow."[4] And if the love of
Mary towards her Son was immense, immense also must
have been her grief in losing him by death. "Where
there is the greatest love," says Blessed Albert the
Great, "there also is the greatest grief."[5]

Let us now imagine to ourselves the divine Mother
standing near her Son expiring on the cross, and justly
applying to herself the words of Jeremias, thus addressing us: *O all ye that pass by the way, attend and see if there
be any sorrow like to my sorrow.*[6] O you who spend your
lives upon earth, and pity me not, stop a while to look

[1] "Ut scias quantus fuerit dolor Virginis, cogita quantus fuerit
amor."—*In Lam.* i. 12.

[2] "Duæ dilectiones in unam convenerant, et ex duobus amoribus
factus est amor unus, cum Virgo Filio divinitatis amorem impenderet,
et in Deo amorem Nato exhiberet."—*De Laud. B. V. hom.* 5.

[3] "Quantum capere potuit puri hominis modus."

[4] "Unde, sicut non fuit amor sicut amor ejus, ita nec fuit dolor
similis dolori ejus."—*In Cant.* c. 26.

[5] "Ubi improportionabilis amor, ibi improportionabilis dolor."—
Super Miss. q. 78.

[6] "O vos omnes qui transitis per viam! attendite, et videte si est
dolor sicut dolor meus."—*Lam.* i. 12

at me, now that I behold this beloved Son dying before
my eyes; and then see if, amongst all those who are
afflicted and tormented, a sorrow is tó be found like unto
my sorrow. "No, O most suffering of all mothers,"
replies St. Bonaventure, "no more bitter grief than
thine can be found; for no son more dear than thine can
be found."[1] Ah, "there never was a more amiable son
in the world than Jesus," says Richard of St. Laurence ;
"nor has there ever been a mother who more tenderly
loved her son than Mary ! But since there never has
been in the world a love like unto Mary's love, how can
any sorrow be found like unto Mary's sorrow ?"[2]

Therefore St. Ildephonsus did not hesitate to assert,
"to say that Mary's sorrows were greater than all the
torments of the martyrs united, was to say too little."[3]
And St. Anselm adds, that "the most cruel tortures inflicted on the holy martyrs were trifling, or as nothing
in comparison with the martyrdom of Mary."[4] St. Basil
of Seleucia also writes, "that as the sun exceeds all the
other planets in splendor, so did Mary's sufferings exceed those of all the other martyrs."[5] A learned author,
Father Pinamonti,[6] concludes with a beautiful sentiment. He says that so great was the sorrow of this

[1] "Nullus dolor amarior, quia nulla proles carior."—*Off. de Comp.
B. M.*

[2] "Non fuit talis Filius, non fuit talis Mater; non fuit tanta charitas, non fuit dolor tantus; ideo, quanto dilexit tenerius, tanto vulnerata est profundius."—*De Laud. B. M.* l. 3.

[3] "Parum est Mariam in passione Filii tam acerbos pertulisse
dolores, ut omnium Martyrum collective tormenta superaret."—
Sinisc. Mart. di M. cons. 36.

[4] "Quidquid crudelitatis inflictum est corporibus Martyrum, leve
fuit, aut potius nihil, comparatione tuæ passionis."—*De Excell. V.*
c. 5.

[5] "Virgo universos Martyres tantum excedit, quantum sol reliqua
astra."—*S. in Annunt.*

[6] *Cuore di M. cons.* 6.

tender Mother in the Passion of Jesus, that she alone could compassionate adequately the death of a God made man.

But here St. Bonaventure, addressing this Blessed Virgin, says, "And why, O Lady, didst thou also go to sacrifice thyself on Calvary? Was not a crucified God sufficient to redeem us, that thou, his Mother, wouldst also go to be crucified with him?" [1] Indeed, the death of Jesus was more than enough to save the world, and an infinity of worlds; but this good Mother, for the love she bore us, wished also to help the cause of our salvation with the merits of her sufferings, which she offered for us on Calvary. Therefore, Blessed Albert the Great says, "that as we are under great obligations to Jesus for his Passion endured for our love, so also are we under great obligations to Mary for the martyrdom which she voluntarily suffered for our salvation in the death of her Son." [2] I say voluntarily, since, as St. Agnes revealed to St. Bridget, "our compassionate and benign Mother was satisfied rather to endure any torment than that our souls should not be redeemed, and be left in their former state of perdition." [3] And, indeed, we may say that Mary's only relief in the midst of her great sorrow in the Passion of her Son, was to see the lost world redeemed by his death, and men who were his enemies reconciled with God. "While grieving she rejoiced," says Simon of Cassia, "that a sacrifice was offered for the redemption of all, by which he who was angry was appeased."

[1] "O Domina! cur ivisti immolari pro nobis? numquid non sufficiebat Filii passio, nisi crucifigeretur et Mater?"—*Stim. div. am.* p. 1, c. 3.

[2] "Sicut totus mundus obligatur Deo per suam passionem, ita et Dominæ per compassionem."—*Sup. Miss.* q. 150, r. ad 148.

[3] "Sic pia et misericors fuit et est, quod maluit omnes tribulationes sufferre, quam quod animæ non redimerentur."—*Rev.* l. 3, c. 30

[4] "Lætabatur dolens, quod offerebatur sacrificium in redemptionem omnium, quo placabatur iratus."—*De Gest. D.* l. 2. c. 27.

So great a love on the part of Mary deserves our gratitude, and that gratitude should be shown by at least meditating upon and pitying her in her sorrows. But she complained to St. Bridget that very few did so, and that the greater part of the world lived in forgetfulness of them: "I look around at all who are on earth, to see if by chance there are any who pity me, and meditate upon my sorrows; and I find that there are very few. Therefore, my daughter, though I am forgotten by many, at least do thou not forget me; consider my anguish, and imitate, as far as thou canst, my grief."[1] To understand how pleasing it is to the Blessed Virgin that we should remember her dolors, we need only know that, in the year 1239 she appeared to seven devout clients of hers (who were afterwards founders of the religious Order of the Servants of Mary), with a black garment in her hand, and desired them, if they wished to please her, often to meditate on her sorrows: for this purpose, and to remind them of her sorrows, she expressed her desire that in future they should wear that mourning dress.[2] Jesus Christ himself revealed to the Blessed Veronica da Binasco, that he is, as it were, more pleased in seeing his Mother compassionated than himself; for thus he addressed her: "My daughter, tears shed for my Passion are dear to me; but as I loved my Mother Mary with an immense love, the meditation of the torments which she endured at my death is even more agreeable to me."[3]

Wherefore the graces promised by Jesus to those who are devoted to the dolors of Mary are very great. Pel-

---

[1] "Respicio ad omnes qui in mundo sunt, si forte sint aliqui qui compatiantur mihi et recogitent dolorem meum, et valde paucos invenio ; ideo, filia mea, licet a multis oblita sim, tu tamen non obliviscaris me; vide dolorem meum, et imitare quantum potes, et dole."— *Rev.* l. 2, c. 24.

[2] *Gian. Ann. S. cent.* 1, l. 1, c. 14.

[3] *Boll.* 13 *Jan. Vit.* l. 1, c. 9.

bart[1] relates that it was revealed to St. Elizabeth, that after the assumption of the Blessed Virgin into heaven, St. John the Evangelist desired to see her again. The favor was granted him; his dear Mother appeared to him, and with her Jesus Christ also appeared; the saint then heard Mary ask her Son to grant some special grace to all those who are devoted to her dolors. Jesus promised her four principal ones : 1st, that those who before death invoked the divine Mother in the name of her sorrows should obtain true repentance of all their sins ; 2d, that he would protect all who have this devotion in their tribulations, and that he would protect them especially at the hour of death ; 3d, that he would impress upon their minds the remembrance of his Passion, and that they should have their reward for it in heaven ; 4th, that he would commit such devout clients to the hands of Mary, with the power to dispose of them in whatever manner she might please, and to obtain for them all the graces that she might desire. In proof of this, let us see, in the following example, how greatly devotion to the dolors of Mary aids in obtaining eternal salvation.

EXAMPLE.

In the revelations of St. Bridget[2] we read that there was a rich man, as noble by birth as he was vile and sinful in his habits. He had given himself, by an express compact, as a slave to the devil; and for sixty successive years had served him, leading such a life as may be imagined, and never approached the sacraments. Now this prince was dying; and Jesus Christ, to show him mercy, commanded St. Bridget to tell her confessor to go and visit him and exhort him to confess his sins. The confessor went, and the sick man said that he did not require confession, as he had often approached the sacrament of

[1] *Stell.* l. 3, p. 3, a. 8.   [2] L. 6, c. 97.

penance. The priest went a second time; but this poor slave of hell persevered in his obstinate determination not to confess. Jesus again told the saint to desire the confessor to return. He did so; and on the third occasion told the sick man the revelation made to the saint, and that he had returned so many times because our Lord, who wished to show him mercy, had so ordered. On hearing this the dying man was touched, and began to weep: "But how," he exclaimed, "can I be saved; I, who for sixty years have served the devil as his slave, and have my soul burdened with innumerable sins?" "My son," answered the Father, encouraging him, "doubt not; if you repent of them, on the part of God I promise you pardon." Then, gaining confidence, he said to the confessor, "Father, I looked upon myself as lost, and already despaired of salvation; but now I feel a sorrow for my sins, which gives me confidence; and since God has not yet abandoned me, I will make my confession." In fact, he made his confession four times on that day, with the greatest marks of sorrow, and on the following morning received holy Communion. On the sixth day, contrite and resigned, he died. After his death, Jesus Christ again spoke to St. Bridget, and told her that that sinner was saved; that he was then in purgatory, and that he owed his salvation to the intercession of the Blessed Virgin his Mother; for the deceased, although he had led so wicked a life, had nevertheless always preserved devotion to the dolors, and whenever he thought of them pitied her.

Prayer.

O my afflicted Mother! Queen of martyrs and of sorrows, thou didst so bitterly weep over thy Son, who died for my salvation; but what will thy tears avail me if I am lost? By the merits, then, of thy sorrows, obtain for me true contrition for my sins, and a real amendment of life, together with constant and tender compassion for the sufferings of Jesus and thy dolors. And if Jesus and thou, being so innocent, have suffered so much for love of me, obtain that at least I, who am deserving of hell, may suffer something for your love. "O Lady," will I say with St. Bonaventure, "if I have offended thee, in justice wound my heart; if I have served thee, I now ask wounds for my reward. It is shameful to me to see my Lord Jesus wounded, and thee wounded with him, and myself without a wound." [1] In fine, O my Mother, by the grief that thou didst experience in seeing thy Son bow down his head and expire on the cross in the midst of so many torments, I beseech thee to obtain me a good death. Ah, cease not, O advocate of sinners, to assist my afflicted soul in the midst of the combat in which it will have to engage on its great passage from time to eternity. And as it is probable that I may then have lost my speech and strength to invoke thy name and that of Jesus, who are all my hope, I do so now; I invoke thy Son and thee to succor me in that last moment; and I say, Jesus and Mary, to you I commend my soul. Amen.

[1] "O Domina! . . . Si te offendi. pro justitia cor meum vulnera; si tibi servivi, nunc pro mercede peto vulnera . . . Opprobriosum est mihi videre Dominum meum Jesum vulneratum, te convulneratam. et me illæsum."—*Stim. div. am.* p. 1. c. 3.

Sermon on the Dolors of Mary.*

Stabat autem juxta crucem Jesu Mater ejus.

"Now there stood by the cross of Jesus His Mother."—*John*. xix. 25.

BEHOLD we are about to consider a new kind of martyrdom; we have to consider a Mother condemned to see her innocent Son die as a malefactor on an infamous gibbet. This Mother is Mary, who indeed, with too great reason, is called by the Church the Queen of Martyrs; yes, for Mary in the death of Jesus Christ suffered a more cruel martyrdom than all other martyrs: for

I. Her martyrdom was never equalled.

II. Her martyrdom was without relief

I.

The Martyrdom of Mary was never equalled.

The words of the prophet Jeremias explain my meaning in this point: *To what shall I compare thee? or to what shall I liken thee, O daughter of Jerusalem? . . for great as the sea is thy destruction; who shall heal thee?*[1] No, the acuteness of the sufferings of Mary are not to be compared, even with those of all the martyrs united. "The martyrdom of Mary," says St. Bernard, "was not caused

---

[1] "Cui comparabo te, vel cui assimilabo te, Filia Jerusalem? cui exæquabo te, Virgo, Filia Sion? magna est enim velut mare contritio tua; quis medebitur tui?"—*Lam.* ii. 13.

---

* This sermon does not form a part of the *Glories of Mary;* but as it is isolated, we have thought it convenient to place it here. Nearly all that it contains is found in Point II. of the preceding discourse. —ED.

by the executioner's sword, but proceeded from bitter sorrow of heart." [1] In other martyrs torments were inflicted on the body; but Mary's sorrow was in her heart and soul, verifying in her the prophecy of St. Simeon, *Thy own soul a sword shall pierce.* [2]

Arnold of Chartres writes that "whoever had been on Mount Calvary, to witness the great sacrifice of the Immaculate Lamb, would there have beheld two great altars, the one in the body of Jesus, the other in the heart of Mary; for on that Mount, when the Son sacrificed his body by death, Mary sacrificed her soul by compassion." [3] So much so, says St. Antoninus, [4] that, whereas other martyrs sacrifice their own lives, the Blessed Virgin consummated her martyrdom by sacrificing the life of her Son, a life which she loved far more than her own, and which caused her to endure a torment which exceeded all other torments ever endured by any mortal on earth.

As a general rule, the sufferings of children are also the sufferings of their mothers who are present at and witness their torments. This St. Augustine declares, when speaking of the mother of the Machabees, who witnessed the execution of her children, martyred by order of the cruel Antiochus: he says that "love caused her to endure in her soul all the torments inflicted on each of her children." [5] Erasmus adds, that "mothers suffer more at the sight of the sufferings of their chil-

---

[1] "Non ferro carnificis, sed acerbo dolore cordis."—*De Serm. D. in Cœna*, s. 4.

[2] "Et tuam ipsius animam pertransibit gladius."—*Luke*, ii. 35.

[3] "Nimirum, in tabernaculo illo duo videres altaria, aliud in pectore Mariæ, aliud in corpore Christi; Christus carnem, Maria immolabat animam."—*De 7 Verbis, tr.* 3.

[4] P. 4, t. 15, c. 24, § 1.

[5] "Illa, videndo, in omnibus passa est: amabat omnes: ferebat in oculis, quod in carne omnes."—*Serm.* 300. *E. B.*

dren than if the torments were inflicted on themselves."[1] This, however, is not always true; but in Mary it was verified; for she certainly suffered more in witnessing the sufferings of her Son than she would have done had she endured all his torments in her own person. "All the wounds," says St. Bonaventure, "which were scattered over the body of Jesus were united in the heart of Mary, to torment her in the Passion of her Son:"[2] so that, as St. Laurence Justinian writes, "the heart of Mary, by compassion for her Son, became a mirror of his torments, in which might be seen faithfully reflected the spittings, the blows, the wounds, and all that Jesus suffered."[3] We can therefore say that Mary, on account of the love she bore him, was in heart, during the Passion of her Son, struck, scourged, crowned with thorns, and nailed to the very cross of her Son.

The same St. Laurence considers Jesus, on his road to Calvary, with the cross on his shoulders, turning to Mary, and saying to her, "Alas, my own dear Mother, whither goest thou? what a scene wilt thou witness? Thou wilt be agonized by my sufferings, and I by thine."[4] But the loving Mother would follow him all the same, though she knew that, by being present at his death, she would have to endure a torment greater than any death. She saw that her Son carried the cross to be crucified upon it; and, adds Abbot William, she also took up the cross of her sorrows, and followed her Son to

[1] "Parentes atrocius torquentur in liberis, quam in seipsis."

[2] "Singula vulnera, per ejus corpus dispersa, sunt in corde tuo unita."—*Stim. Div. am.* p. 1, c. 3.

[3] "Passionis Christi speculum effectum erat cor Virginis; in illo agnoscebantur sputa, convicia, verbera, vulnera."—*De Tr. Chr. Ag.* c. 21.

[4] "Ut quid venisti, Mater mea? dolor tuus meum auget, cruciatus tuus transfigit me."—*Ibid.* c. 11

be crucified with him.[1] Hence St. Bonaventure considers Mary standing by the cross of her dying Son, and asks her, saying, " O Lady, tell me where didst thou then stand—was it near the cross? No, thou wast on the cross itself, crucified with thy Son." [2] On the words of the Redeemer, foretold by the prophet Isaias, *I have trodden the wine-press alone, and of the Gentiles there is not a man with me.*[3] Richard of St. Laurence says, "It is true, O Lord, that in the work of human redemption Thou didst suffer alone, and that there was not a man who sufficiently pitied Thee; but there was a woman with Thee, and she was Thine own Mother; she suffered in her heart all that Thou didst endure in Thy body." [4]

To show the sufferings endured by other martyrs, they are represented with the instruments of their torture; St. Andrew with a cross, St. Paul with a sword, St. Laurence with a gridiron; Mary is represented with her dead Son in her arms; for he alone was the instrument of her martyrdom, and compassion for him made her the Queen of Martyrs. On this subject of Mary's compassion in the death of Jesus Christ, Father Pinamonti gives expression to a beautiful and remarkable opinion: he says, that " the grief of Mary in the Passion of her Son was so great, that she alone compassionated in a degree by any means adequate to its merits the death of a God made man for the love of man."

---

[1] "Tollebat et ipsa crucem suam, et sequebatur eum, crucifigenda cum eo."—*Delrio, In Cant.* vii. 7.

[2] "O Domina mea! ubi stabas? numquid tantum juxta crucem? imo in cruce; cum Filio crucifixa eras."—*Stim. Div. am.* p. 1, c. 3.

[3] "Torcular calcavi solus, et de gentibus non est vir mecum."—*Isa.* lxiii. 3.

[4] "Verum est, Domine, quod non est vir tecum; sed Mulier una tecum est, quæ omnia vulnera quæ tu suscepisti in corpore, suscepit in corde."—*De Laud. B. M.* l. 1, c. 5.

Blessed Amadeus also writes, that "Mary suffered much more in the Passion of her Son than she would have done had she herself endured it ; for she loved her Jesus much more than she loved herself." [1] Hence St. Ildephonsus did not hesitate to assert, that "the sufferings of Mary exceeded those of all martyrs united together." [2] St. Anselm, addressing the Blessed Virgin, says: "The most cruel torments inflicted on the holy martyrs were trifling or as nothing in comparison with thy martyrdom, O Mary." [3] The same saint adds : "Indeed, O Lady, in each moment of thy life thy sufferings were such, that thou couldst not have endured them, and wouldst have expired under them, had not thy Son, the source of life, preserved thee." [4] St. Bernardine of Sienna even says, that "the sufferings of Mary were such, that had they been divided amongst all creatures capable of suffering, they would have caused their immediate death." [5] Who, then, can ever doubt that the martyrdom of Mary was without its equal, and that it exceeded the sufferings of all the martyrs; since, as St. Antoninus says, "they suffered in the sacrifice of their own lives; but the Blessed Virgin suffered by offering the life of her Son to God, a life which she loved far more than her own."

[1] "Maria torquebatur magis quam si torqueretur in se, quoniam supra se incomparabiliter diligebat id unde dolebat."—*De Laud. B. M. hom.* 5.

[2] "Parum est Mariam in passione Filii tam acerbos pertulisse dolores, ut omnium Martyrum collective tormenta superaret."—*Sinisc. Mart. di M. cons.* 36.

[3] "Quidquid crudelitatis inflictum est corporibus Martyrum, leve fuit, aut potuis nihil, comparatione tuæ passionis."

[4] "Utique, Domina! non crediderim te potuisse stimulos tanti cruciatus, quin vitam amitteres, sustinere, nisi ipse spiritus Filii tui te confortaret."—*De Excell. V.* c. 5.

[5] "Tantus fuit dolor Virginis, quod, si in omnes creaturas. quæ pati possunt, divideretur, omnes subito interirent."—*Pro Fest. V. M.* s. 13, a. 2, c. 2.

II.

The Martyrdom of Mary was without Relief.

The martyrs suffered under the torments inflicted on them by tyrants; but our Lord, who never abandons his servants, always comforted them in the midst of their sufferings. The love of God, which burnt in their hearts, rendered all these sufferings sweet and pleasing to them. A St. Vincent suffered, when on the rack he was torn with pincers, and burnt with hot iron plates; but St. Augustine says that " the saint spoke with such contempt of his torments, that it seemed as if it was one who spoke, and another who suffered." [1]   A St. Boniface suffered, when the flesh was torn from his body with iron hooks, sharp reeds were forced under his nails, and melted lead was poured into his mouth; but, in the midst of all, he could never cease to thank Jesus Christ, who allowed him to suffer for his love. A St. Laurence suffered, when roasting on a gridiron; " but the love which inflamed him," says St. Augustine, " did not allow him to feel the fire, or even that prolonged death itself." [2]

So that the greater was the love of the martyrs for Jesus Christ, the less did they feel their pains: and in the midst of them all, the remembrance alone of the Passion of Jesus Christ sufficed to console them. With Mary it was precisely the reverse; for the torments of Jesus were her martyrdom, and love for Jesus was her only executioner. Here we must repeat the words of Jeremias: *Great as the sea is thy destruction : who shall heal thee ?* [3]   As the sea is all bitterness, and has not within its bosom a single drop of water which is sweet, so also was the heart of Mary all bitterness, and without the

[1] " Tamquam alius torqueretur, alius loqueretur."—*Serm.* 275, *E. B.*
[2] " In illa longa morte, in illis tormentis, illo calice ebrius, tormenta non sentit."—*In Jo. tr.* 27.
[3] " Magna est velut mare contritio tua: quia medebitur tui?"

least consolation: *Who shall heal thee?* Her Son alone could console her and heal her wounds; but how could Mary receive comfort in her grief from her crucified Son, since the love she bore him was the whole cause of her martyrdom?

"To understand, then, how great was the grief of Mary, we must understand," says Cornelius à Lapide, "how great was the love she bore her Son." [1] But who can ever measure this love? Blessed Amadeus says, that "natural love towards him as her Son, and supernatural love towards him as her God, were united in the heart of Mary." [2] These two loves were blended into one, and this so great a love that William of Paris does not hesitate to assert, that Mary loved Jesus "as much as it was possible for a pure creature to love him." [3] So that, as Richard of St. Victor says, "as no other creature ever loved God as much as Mary loved Him, so there never was any sorrow like Mary's sorrow." [4]

Now there stood by the cross of Jesus His Mother. [5] Let us stay awhile to consider these words before concluding our discourse; but I entreat you to renew your attention.

There stood. When Jesus was on the cross the disciples had already abandoned him; they had done so from the moment in which he was taken in the garden of Olives: *then the disciples all leaving him fled.* [6] The disciples abandoned him; but his loving Mother did not abandon him; she remained with him until he expired.

[1] "Ut scias quantus fuerit dolor Virginis, cogita quantus fuerit amor."—*In Lam.* i. 12.

[2] "Duæ dilectiones in unam convenerant, et ex duobus amoribus factus est amor unus."—*De Laud. B. V.* hom. 5.

[3] "Quantum capere potuit puri hominis modus."

[4] "Unde, sicut non fuit amor sicut amor ejus, ita nec fuit dolor similis dolori ejus."—*In Cant.* c. 26.

[5] "Stabat autem juxta crucem Jesu Mater ejus.

[6] "Omnes, relicto eo, fugerunt."—*Matt.* xxvi. 56.

There stood by. Mothers fly when they see their children suffer much, and are unable to give them relief; they have not then strength to endure the torment, and therefore fly to a distance. Mary beheld her Son in agony on the cross; she saw that his sufferings were slowly depriving him of life; she desired to relieve him in that last extremity, but could not; but with all this she did not fly, she did not go to a distance, but drew nearer to the cross on which her Son was dying.

She stood by the cross. The cross was the hard bed on which Jesus Christ had to die. Mary, who stood by its side, never turned her eyes from him; she beheld him all torn by the scourges, thorns, and nails; she saw that her poor Son, suspended by those three iron hooks, found no repose. She, as I have already said, would have desired to give him some relief; she would have desired, at least, that he should have expired in her arms; but, no, even this is forbidden her. "Ah, cross!" she must have said, "restore me my Son; thou art a gibbet for malefactors, but my Son is innocent." But wait, O sorrowful Mother; God's will is that the cross should only restore thee thy Son when he has expired.

St. Bonaventure, considering the sorrow of Mary in the death of her Son, writes, that "no grief was more bitter than hers, because no son was as dear as her Son."[1] Since, then, there never was a son more worthy of love than Jesus, nor any mother who ever loved as Mary loved, what sorrow can be compared with the sorrow of Mary? "Ah, there never has been in the world a more amiable Son than Jesus," says Richard of St. Laurence, "nor was there ever so loving a Mother. Had there been less love between this Mother and Son, his death would have been less cruel, their griefs would have been diminished; but the more tender were their

[1] "Nullus dolor amarior, quia nulla proles carior."—*Off. de Comp B. M.*

loves, the deeper were their wounds." [1]   Mary saw that death approached her Son; therefore, casting her compassionate eyes upon him, she seemed to say, "Ah, Son, Thou already departest, already Thou leavest me; and art Thou silent? Give me a last remembrance." Yes, he did so. Jesus Christ left her a remembrance; it was this: *Woman*, He said, *behold thy son*, referring to St. John, who stood near; and with these words he bade his Mother farewell. He called her woman, that by the sweet name of Mother he might not increase her grief: *Woman, behold thy son ;* [2] he will take charge of thee when I am dead.

There stood by the cross of Jesus His Mother. Let us, in fine, observe Mary, who stood at the foot of the cross and beheld her Son expire. But, O God, what Son was it that died? It was a Son who from all eternity had chosen her for his Mother, and had preferred her in his love to all men and angels: it was a Son so beautiful, so holy, so amiable; a Son who had always obeyed her; a Son who was her only love, for he was her Son and her God; and Mary had to see him die before her eyes, of pure suffering. But, behold the hour of the death of Jesus has already come; the afflicted Mother saw her Son then enduring the last assaults of death; behold, again, his body already was sinking, his head drooped down on his breast, his mouth opened, and he expired. The people cried out, he is dead, he is dead! and Mary also said, "Ah my Jesus, my Son, Thou art now dead!"

When Jesus was dead, he was taken down from the cross. Mary received him with outstretched arms; she then pressed him to her heart, and examined that head wounded by the thorns, those hands pierced with nails,

---

[1] " Non fuit talis filius, non fuit talis mater; non fuit tanta charitas, non fuit dolor tantus; ideo, quanto dilexit tenerius, tanto vulnerata est profundius."—*De Laud. B. M.* l. 3.

[2] " Mulier, ecce filius tuus."—*John*, xix. 26.

and that body all lacerated and torn. "Ah, Son," she said, "to what has Thy love for men reduced Thee!" But the disciples, fearing that with her Son clasped in her arms she would die of grief, out of compassion approached her, and, with reverential determination, removed her Son from her arms, wrapped him in the winding sheet, and carried him away to bury him. The other holy women accompanied him, and with them the sorrowful Mother followed her son to the tomb; where, having herself deposited him with her own hands, she bade him a last farewell and retired. St. Bernard says, that "as Mary passed along the way, her sorrow and grief were such, that all who met her were thereby moved to tears;" [1] and he adds that "those who accompanied her were weeping rather for her than for our Lord." [2]

My readers, let us be devout to the dolors of Mary. Blessed Albert the Great writes, that "as we are under great obligations to Jesus Christ for His death, so also are we under great obligations to Mary for the grief which she endured when she offered her Son to God by death for our salvation." [3] This the angel revealed to St. Bridget: [4] he said that the Blessed Virgin, to see us saved, herself offered the life of her Son to the Eternal Father: a sacrifice which, we have already said, cost her greater suffering than all the torments of the martyrs, or even death itself. But the divine Mother complained to St. Bridget that very few pitied her in her sorrows, and that the greater part of the world lived in entire forgetfulness of them. Therefore she exhorted the saint, saying: "Though many forget me, do not thou, my daughter, forget me." [5] For this purpose the Blessed

---

[1] "Omnes plorabant, qui obviabant ei."—*De Lam. B. V.*

[2] "Super ipsam potius quam super Dominum plangebant."—*Ibid.*

[3] "Sicut totus mundus obligatur Deo per suam passionem, ita et Dominæ per compassionem."—*Super Miss.* q. 150, r. ad 148.

[4] *Rev.* l. 3, c. 30.

[5] "Respicio si forte sint qui compatiantur mihi et recogitent dolorem

Virgin herself appeared in the year 1239 to the founder of the Order of the Servites, or servants of Mary, to desire them to institute a religious order in remembrance of her sorrows ; and this they did.[1]

Jesus himself one day spoke to Blessed Veronica of Binasco, saying, "Daughter, tears shed over my Passion are dear to me ; but as I love my Mother Mary with an immense love, the meditation of the sorrows which she endured at my death is also very dear to me."[2] It is also well to know, as Pelbart relates it,[3] that it was revealed to St. Elizabeth of Hungary, that our Lord had promised four special graces to those who are devout to the dolors of Mary : 1st, that those who before death invoke the divine Mother, in the name of her sorrows, should obtain true repentance of all their sins : 2d, that he would protect all who have this devotion in their tribulations, and that he would protect them especially at the hour of death : 3d, that he would impress upon their minds the remembrance of his Passion, and that they should have their reward for it in heaven : 4th, that he would commit such devout clients to the hands of Mary, with the power to dispose of them in whatever manner she might please, and to obtain for them all the graces she might desire.

meum, et valde paucos invenio ; ideo, filia mea, licet a multis oblita sim, tu non obliviscaris me."—*Rev.* l. 2, c. 24.

[1] *Gian. Ann. S. cent.* 1, l. 1, c. 14.
[2] *Boll.* 13 *Jan. Vit.* l. 1, c. 9.
[3] *Stell.* l. 3, p. 3, a. 3.

Reflections on Each of the Seven Dolors of Mary.

I.

St. Simeon's Prophecy.

In this valley of tears every man is born to weep, and all must suffer, by enduring the evils which are of daily occurrence. But how much greater would the misery of life be, did we also know the future evils which await us! "Unfortunate, indeed, would his lot be," says Seneca, "who, knowing the future, would have to suffer all by anticipation."[1]

Our Lord shows us this mercy. He conceals the trials which await us, that, whatever they may be, we may endure them but once. He did not show Mary this compassion; for she, whom God willed to be the Queen of sorrows, and in all things like his Son, had to see always before her eyes and continually to suffer all the torments that awaited her; and these were the sufferings of the Passion and death of her beloved Jesus; for in the temple, St. Simeon, having received the divine Child in his arms, foretold to her that that Son would be a mark for all the persecutions and oppositions of men. *Behold, this Child is set . . . for a sign which shall be contradicted.* And therefore, that a sword of sorrow should pierce her soul: *And thy own soul a sword shall pierce.*[2]

The Blessed Virgin herself told St. Matilda, that, on this announcement of St. Simeon, "all her joy was

---

[1] "Calamitosus est animus futuri anxius, et ante miserias miser."— *Ep.* 98.

[2] "Positus est hic . . . in signum cui contradicetur: Et tuam ipsius animam pertransibit gladius."—*Luke*, ii. 34, 35.

changed into sorrow." [1] For, as it was revealed to St. Teresa,[2] though the Blessed Mother already knew that the life of her Son would be sacrificed for the salvation of the world, yet she then learnt more distinctly and in greater detail the sufferings and cruel death that awaited her poor Son.   She knew that he would be contradicted, and this in everything : contradicted in his doctrines ; for, instead of being believed, he would be esteemed a blasphemer for teaching that he was the Son of God ; this he was declared to be by the impious Caiphas, saying, *He hath blasphemed, He is guilty of death.*[3] Contradicted in his reputation ; for he was of noble, even of royal descent, and was despised as a peasant : *Is not this the carpenter's son?*[4] *Is not this the carpenter, the son of Mary?*[5] He was wisdom itself, and was treated as ignorant : *How doth this man know letters, having never learned?*[6] As a false prophet : *And they blindfolded Him, and smote His face ... saying : Prophesy, who is it that struck Thee?*[7] He was treated as a madman : *He is mad, why hear you Him?*[8] As a drunkard, a glutton, and a friend of sinners : *Behold a man that is a glutton, and a drinker of wine, a friend of publicans and sinners.*[9] As a sorcerer : *By the prince of devils He casteth out devils.*[10] As a heretic, and possessed by the evil spirit : *Do we not say well of Thee that Thou art a*

[1] " Omnis lætitia mea, ad verba Simeonis, versa est mihi in moerorem."—*Spir. Grat.* l. I, c. 16.

[2] *Life, addit.*

[3] " Blasphemavit . . . Reus est mortis."—*Matt.* xxvi. 65.

[4] " Nonne hic est fabri filius ?"—*Matt.* xiii. 55.

[5] " Nonne hic est faber, filius Mariæ ?"—*Mark*, vi. 3.

[6] " Quomodo hic litteras scit, cum non didicerit ?"—*John*, vii. 15.

[7] " Et velaverunt eum, et percutiebant faciem ejus . . , dicentes: Prophetiza, quis est, qui te percussit ?"—*Luke*, xxii. 64.

[8] " Insanit : quid eum auditis ?"—*John*, x. 20.

[9] " Ecce homo devorator et bibens vinum, amicus publicanorum et peccatorum."—*Luke*, vii. 34.

[10] " In principe dæmoniorum ejicit dæmones."—*Matt.* ix. 34.

Samaritan and hast a devil? [1] In a word, Jesus was considered so notoriously wicked, that, as the Jews said to Pilate, no trial was necessary to condemn him. *If He were not a malefactor, we would not have delivered Him up to thee.* [2] He was contradicted in his very soul; for even his Eternal Father, to give place to divine justice, contradicted him, by refusing to hear his prayer, when he said, *Father, if it be possible, let this chalice pass from Me;* [3] and abandoned him to fear, weariness, and sadness; so that our afflicted Lord exclaimed, *My soul is sorrowful unto death!* [4] and his interior sufferings even caused him to sweat blood. Contradicted and persecuted, in fine, in all his body and in his life; for he was tortured in all his sacred members, in his hands, his feet, his face, his head, and in his whole body; so that, drained of his blood, and an object of scorn, he died of torments on an ignominious cross.

When David, in the midst of all his pleasures and regal grandeur, heard from the Prophet Nathan, that his son should die,—*The child that is born to thee shall surely die,* [5]—he could find no peace, but wept, fasted, and slept on the ground. Mary with the greatest calmness received the announcement that her Son should die, and always peacefully submitted to it; but what grief must she continually have suffered, seeing this amiable Son always near her, hearing from him words of eternal life, and witnessing his holy demeanor!

Abraham suffered much during the three days he passed with his beloved Isaac, after knowing that he was to

[1] "Nonne bene dicimus nos, quia Samaritanus es tu, et dæmonium habes?"—*John*, viii. 48.

[2] "Si non esset hic malefactor, non tibi tradidissemus eum."—*John*, xviii. 30.

[3] "Pater mi, si possible est, transeat a me calix iste."—*Matt.* xxvi. 39.

[4] "Tristis est anima mea usque ad mortem."—*Ib.* 38.

[5] "Filius, qui natus est tibi, morte morietur."—2 *Kings*, xii. 14.

lose him. O God, not for three days, but for three and thirty years had Mary to endure a like sorrow ! But do I say a like sorrow ? It was as much greater as the Son of Mary was more lovely than the son of Abraham.

The Blessed Virgin herself revealed to St. Bridget, that, while on earth, there was not an hour in which this grief did not pierce her soul : "as often," she continued, "as I looked at my Son, as often as I wrapped him in his swaddling-clothes, as often as I saw his hands and feet, so often was my soul absorbed, so to say, in fresh grief ; for I thought how he would be crucified."[1]

The Abbot Rupert contemplates Mary suckling her Son, and thus addressing him: *A bundle of myrrh is my Beloved to me; He shall abide between my breasts.*[2] Ah, Son, I clasp thee in my arms, because thou art so dear to me; but the dearer thou art to me, the more dost Thou become a bundle of myrrh and sorrow to me when I think of thy sufferings. "Mary," says St. Bernardine of Sienna, "reflected that the strength of the saints was to be reduced to agony; the beauty of Paradise to be disfigured ; the Lord of the world to be bound as a criminal; the Creator of all things to be made livid with blows ; the Judge of all to be condemned ; the Glory of heaven despised; the King of kings to be crowned with thorns, and treated as a mock king."[3]

Father Engelgrave says that it was revealed to the same St. Bridget, that the afflicted Mother, already knowing what her Son was to suffer, "when suckling him, thought of the gall and vinegar ; when swathing

---

[1] "Quoties aspiciebam Filium meum, quoties involvebam pannis, quoties videbam ejus manus et pedes, toties animus meus quasi novo dolore absorptus est; quia cogitabam quomodo crucifigeretur."—*Rev.* l. 6 c. 57.

[2] "Fasciculus myrrhæ dilectus meus mihi; inter ubera mea commo rabitur."—*Cant.* i. 12.

[3] *Pro Fest. V. M.* s. 2, a. 3, c. 1.

him, of the cords with which he was to be bound; when bearing him in her arms, of the cross to which he was to be nailed; when sleeping, of his death."[1] As often as she put on him his garment, she reflected that it would one day be torn from him, that he might be crucified; and when she beheld his sacred hands and feet, she thought of the nails which would one day pierce them; and then, as Mary said to St. Bridget, "my eyes filled with tears, and my heart was tortured with grief."[2]

The Evangelist says, that as Jesus Christ advanced in years, so also did *He advance in wisdom and in grace with God and men.*[3] This is to be understood as St. Thomas[4] explains it, that he advanced in wisdom and grace in the estimation of men and before God, inasmuch as all his works would continually have availed to increase his merit, had not grace been conferred upon him from the beginning, in its complete fulness, by virtue of the hypostatic union. But, since Jesus advanced in the love and esteem of others, how much more must he have advanced in that of Mary! But, O God, as love increased in her, so much the more did her grief increase at the thought of having to lose him by so cruel a death; and the nearer the time of the Passion of her Son approached, so much the deeper did that sword of sorrow, foretold by St. Simeon, pierce the heart of his mother. This was precisely revealed by the angel to St. Bridget, saying: "That sword of sorrow was every hour

---

[1] "Eum lactans, cogitabat de felle et aceto; quando fasciis involvebat, funes cogitabat quibus ligandus erat; quando gestabat, cogitabat in cruce confixum; quando dormiebat, cogitabat mortuum."—*Lux Ev. s. infra oct. Nat.*

[2] "Oculi mei replebantur lacrymis, et cor meum quasi scindebatur præ tristitia."—*Rev.* l. 1, c. 10.

[3] "Et Jesus proficiebat sapientia, et ætate, et gratia apud Deum et homines."—*Luke,* ii. 52.

[4] P. 3, q. 7, a. 12.

approaching nearer to the Blessed Virgin, as the time for the Passion of her Son drew near." [1]

Since, then, Jesus, our King, and his most holy Mother, did not refuse, for love of us, to suffer so cruel pains throughout their lives, it is reasonable that we, at least, should not complain if we have to suffer something. Jesus, crucified, once appeared to Sister Magdalene Orsini, a Dominicaness, who had been long suffering under a great trial, and encouraged her to remain, by means of that affliction, with him on the cross. Sister Magdalene complainingly answered: "O Lord, Thou wast tortured on the cross only for three hours, and I have endured my pain for many years." The Redeemer then replied: "Ah, ignorant soul, what dost thou say? from the first moment of my conception I suffered in heart all that I afterwards endured dying on the cross." If, then, we also suffer and complain, let us imagine Jesus, and his Mother Mary, addressing the same words to ourselves.

EXAMPLE.

Father Roviglione, of the Society of Jesus, relates that a young man had the devotion of every day visiting a statue of our Lady of Sorrows, in which she was represented with seven swords piercing her heart. The unfortunate youth one night committed a mortal sin. The next morning, going as usual to visit the image, he perceived that there were no longer only seven, but eight swords in the heart of Mary. Wondering at this, he heard a voice telling him that his crime had added the eighth. This moved his heart; and, penetrated with sorrow, he immediately went to confession, and by the intercession of his advocate recovered divine grace.

[1] "Ille doloris gladius cordi Virginis omni hora tanto se propius approximabat, quanto Filius passionis tempori magis appropinquabat."—*Serm. Ang.* c. 17.

Prayer.

Ah, my Blessed Mother, it is not one sword only with which I have pierced thy heart, but I have done so with as many as are the sins which I have committed. Ah, Lady, it is not to thee, who art innocent, that sufferings are due, but to me, who am guilty of so many crimes. But since thou hast been pleased to suffer so much for me, ah, by thy merits, obtain me great sorrow for my sins, and patience under the trials of this life, which will always be light in comparison with my demerits; for I have often deserved hell. Amen.

II.

The Flight of Jesus into Egypt.

As the stag, wounded by an arrow, carries the pain with him wherever he goes, because he carries with him the arrow which has wounded him, so did the divine Mother, after the sad prophecy of St. Simeon, as we have already seen in the consideration of the first dolor, always carry her sorrow with her in the continual remembrance of the Passion of her Son. Hailgrino, explaining this passage of the Canticles, *The hairs of thy head, as the purple of the king, bound in the channel,* [1] says that these purple hairs were Mary's continual thoughts of the Passion of Jesus, which kept the blood which was one day to flow from his wounds always before her eyes: " Thy mind, O Mary, and thy thoughts, steeped in the blood of our Lord's Passion, were always filled with sorrow, as if they actually beheld the blood flowing from his wounds." [2] Thus her Son himself was

---

[1] " Et comæ capitis tui, sicut purpura regis vincta canalibus."— *Cant.* vii. 5.

[2] " Mens tua, O Maria! et cogitationes tuæ tinctæ sunt in memoria sanguinis Dominicæ passionis, et affectæ sunt quasi recentem viderent sanguinem de vulneribus profluentem."

that arrow in the heart of Mary; and the more ami-able he appeared to her, so much the more deeply did the thought of losing him by so cruel a death wound her heart.

Let us now consider the second sword of sorrow which wounded Mary, in the flight of her Infant Jesus into Egypt from the persecution of Herod.

Herod, having heard that the expected Messiah was born, foolishly feared that he would deprive him of his kingdom. Hence St. Fulgentius, reproving him for his folly, thus addresses him: "Why art thou troubled, O Herod? This King who is born comes not to con-quer kings by the sword, but to subjugate them won-derfully by his death."[1] The impious Herod, there-fore, waited to hear from the holy Magi where the King was born, that he might take his life; but finding himself deceived, he ordered all the infants that could be found in the neighborhood of Bethlehem to be put to death. Then it was that the angel appeared in a dream to St. Joseph, and desired him to *Arise, and take the Child and his Mother, and fly into Egypt.*[2] According to Gerson,[3] St. Joseph immediately, on that very night, made the order known to Mary; and taking the Infant Jesus, they set out on their journey, as it is sufficiently evident from the Gospel itself: *Who arose and took the Child and His Mother, by night, and retired into Egypt.*[4]

O God, says Blessed Albert the Great, in the name of Mary, "must he then fly from men, who came to save

---

[1] "Quid est quod sic turbaris, Herodes? Rex iste, qui natus est, non venit reges pugnando superare, sed moriendo mirabiliter sub-jugare."—*S. de Epiph. et Inn. nece.*

[2] "Surge, et accipe Puerum et Matrem ejus, et fuge in Ægyptum."—*Matt.* ii. 13.

[3] *Joseph. dist.* I.

[4] "Qui consurgens, accepit Puerum et Matrem ejus nocte, et seces-sit in Ægyptum."

men?"[1] Then the afflicted Mother knew that already the prophecy of Simeon concerning her Son began to be verified: *He is set for a sign that shall be contradicted.*[2] Seeing that he was no sooner born than he was persecuted unto death, what anguish, writes St. John Chrysostom, must the intimation of that cruel exile of herself and her Son have caused in her heart: "Flee from thy friends to strangers, from God's temple to the temples of devils. What greater tribulation than that a newborn child, hanging from its mother's breast, and she too in poverty, should with Him be forced to fly?"[3]

Any one may imagine what Mary must have suffered on this journey. To Egypt the distance was great. Most authors agree * that it was three hundred miles; so that it was a journey of upwards of thirty days. The road was, according to St. Bonaventure's description of it, "rough, unknown, and little frequented."[4] It was in the winter season; so that they had to travel in snow, rain, and wind, through rough and dirty roads. Mary was then fifteen years of age—a delicate young woman, unaccustomed to such journeys. They had no one to attend upon them. St. Peter Chrysologus says, "Joseph and Mary have no male or female servants; they were themselves both masters and servants."[5] O God, what a touching sight must it have been to have beheld that tender Virgin, with her new-born babe in her arms,

[1] "Debet fugere, qui Salvator est omnium?"—*In Matt.* 2.

[2] "Positus est hic in signum cui contradicetur."

[3] "Fuge a tuis ad extraneos, a Templo ad dæmonum fana!—Quæ major tribulatio, quam quod recens natus, a collo Matris pendens, cum ipsa Matre paupercula fugere cogatur?"

[4] "Viam silvestrem, obscuram, asperam, et inhabitatam."—*Med. vit. Chr.* c. 12.

[5] "Joseph et Maria non habent famulum, non ancillam; ipsi domini et famuli."—*Hom. de Nat. D.*

---

* *Barradas,* T. i. l. 10. c. 8.

4

wandering through the world! "But how," asks St. Bonaventure, "did they obtain their food? Where did they repose at night? How were they lodged?"[1] What can they have eaten but a piece of hard bread, either brought by St. Joseph or begged as an alms? Where can they have slept on such a road (especially on the two hundred miles of desert, where there were neither houses nor inns, as authors relate), unless on the sand or under a tree in a wood, exposed to the air and the dangers of robbers and wild beasts, with which Egypt abounded? Ah, had any one met these three greatest personages in the world, for whom could he have taken them but for poor wandering beggars?

They resided in Egypt, according to Brocard and Jansenius,[2] in a district called Maturea; though St. Anselm says[3] that they lived in the city of Heliopolis, or at Memphis, now called old Cairo. Here let us consider the great poverty they must have suffered during the seven years which, according to St. Antoninus,[4] St. Thomas, and others, they spent there. They were foreigners, unknown, without revenues, money, or relatives, barely able to support themselves by their humble efforts. "As they were destitute," says St. Basil, "it is evident that they must have labored much to provide themselves with the necessaries of life."[5] Landolph of Saxony has, moreover, written (and let this be a consolation for the poor), that "Mary lived there in the midst of such poverty that at times she had not even a bit of bread to

---

[1] "Quomodo faciebant de victu? ubi nocte quiescebant? quomodo hospitabantur?"

[2] *In Conc.* c. 11.

[3] *Enarr. in Matt.* 2.

[4] P. 4, *tit.* 15, c. 36.

[5] "Cum enim essent egeni, manifestum est quod sudores frequentabant, necessaria vitæ inde sibi quærentes."—*Const. Mon.* c. 5.

give to her Son, when, urged by hunger, He asked for it." [1]

After the death of Herod, St. Matthew relates, the angel again appeared to St. Joseph in a dream, and directed them to return to Judea. St. Bonaventure, speaking of this return, considers how much greater the Blessed Virgin's sufferings must have been on account of the pains of Jesus being so much increased, as he was then about seven years of age—an age, remarks the saint, at which "he was too big to be carried, and not strong enough to walk without assistance." [2]

The sight, then, of Jesus and Mary wandering as fugitives through the world, teaches us that we also must live as pilgrims here below; detached from the goods which the world offers us, and which we must soon leave to enter eternity: *We have not here a lasting city, but seek one that is to come.* [3] To which St. Augustine adds: "Thou art a guest: thou givest a look, and passest on." [4] It also teaches us to embrace crosses, for without them we cannot live in this world. Blessed Veronica da Binasco, an Augustinian nun, was carried in spirit to accompany Mary with the Infant Jesus on their journey into Egypt; and after it the divine Mother said, "Daughter, thou hast seen with how much difficulty we have reached this country; now learn that no one receives graces without suffering." [5] Whoever wishes to feel less the sufferings of this life must go in company with Jesus and Mary: "Take the Child and His Mother." [6]

[1] "Aliquando filius famem patiens panem petiit, nec unde daret mater habuit."— *Vit. Chr.* p. 1, c. 13.

[2] "Sic magnus est, quod portari non prævalet, et sic parvus, quod per se ire non potest."—*Med. vit. Chr.* c, 13.

[3] "Non enim habemus hic manentem civitatem, sed futuram inquirimus."—*Heb.* xiii. 14.

[4] "Hospes es, vides, et transis."

[5] *Boll.* 13 *Jan. Vit.* l. 4, c. 6.

[6] "Accipe puerum et matrem ejus

All sufferings become light, and even sweet and desirable, to him who by his love bears this Son and this Mother in his heart. Let us, then, love them; let us console Mary by welcoming in our hearts her Son, whom men even now continue to persecute by their sins.

EXAMPLE.

The most holy Virgin one day appeared to Blessed Collette, a Franciscan nun, and showed her the Infant Jesus in a basin, torn to pieces, and then said: "Thus it is that sinners continually treat my Son, renewing his death and my sorrows. My daughter, pray for them, that they may be converted." [1] To this we may add another vision, which the Venerable Sister Joanna of Jesus and Mary, also a Franciscan nun, had. She was one day meditating on the infant Jesus persecuted by Herod, when she heard a great noise, as of armed men pursuing some one; and immediately she saw before her a most beautiful child, who, all out of breath and running, exclaimed: "O my Joanna, help me, conceal me! I am Jesus of Nazareth; I am flying from sinners, who wish to kill me, and persecute me as Herod did. Do thou save me."

Prayer.

Then, O Mary, even after thy Son hath died by the hands of men, who persecuted him unto death, these ungrateful men have not yet ceased persecuting him by their sins, and continue to afflict thee, O sorrowful Mother! . And, O God, I also have been one of these. Ah, my most sweet Mother, obtain me tears to weep over such ingratitude. By the sufferings thou didst endure in that journey to Egypt, assist me in the journey in which I am now making to eternity; that thus I may at length be united to thee in loving my persecuted Saviour in the kingdom of the blessed. Amen.

[1] *Boll.* 6 *Mart. Summ. Virt.* c. 3.

III.

The Loss of Jesus in the Temple.

The Apostle St. James says that our perfection consists in the virtue of patience. *And patience hath a perfect work, that you may be perfect and entire, failing in nothing.*[1] Our Lord having, then, given us the Blessed Virgin Mary as a model of perfection, it was necessary that she should be laden with sorrows, that in her we might admire heroic patience, and endeavor to imitate it. The sorrow which we have this day to consider was one of the greatest that Mary had to endure in her life, —the loss of her Son in the temple.

He who is born blind feels but little the privation of the light of day; but he who has once enjoyed it, and loses it by becoming blind, indeed suffers much. Thus it is also with those unhappy souls who, blinded by the mire of the world, have but little knowledge of God— they suffer but little at not finding him; but, on the other hand, he who, illumined by celestial light, has become worthy to find by love the sweet presence of the supreme good, O God, how bitterly does he grieve when he finds himself deprived of it! Hence, let us see how much Mary must have suffered from this third sword of sorrow which pierced her heart, when, having lost her Jesus in Jerusalem for three days, she was deprived of his most sweet presence, accustomed as she was constantly to enjoy it.

St. Luke relates, in the second chapter of his Gospel, that the Blessed Virgin, with her spouse St. Joseph, and Jesus, was accustomed every year at the paschal solemnity to visit the temple. When her Son was twelve years of age, she went as usual, and Jesus remained in

---

[1] " Patientia autem opus perfectum habet: ut sitis perfecti et integri, in nullo deficientes."—*James.* i. 4.

Jerusalem. Mary did not at once perceive it, thinking he was in company with others. When she reached Nazareth, she inquired for her Son; but not finding him, she immediately returned to Jerusalem to seek for him, and only found him after three days.

Now let us imagine what anxiety this afflicted Mother must have experienced in those three days during which she was seeking everywhere for her Son, and inquiring for him with the spouse in the Canticles: *Have you seen him whom my soul loveth?* [1] But she could have no tidings of him. O, with how far greater tenderness must Mary, overcome by fatigue, and having not yet found her beloved Son, have repeated those words of Ruben, concerning his brother Joseph: *The boy doth not appear; and whither shall I go?* [2] "My Jesus doth not appear, and I no longer know what to do to find him; but where shall I go without my treasure?" Weeping continually, with how much truth did she repeat with David, during those three days, *My tears have been my bread day and night whilst it is said to me daily: Where is thy God?* [3] Wherefore Pelbart, with reason, says, that "during those nights the afflicted Mary did not sleep; she was constantly weeping, and entreating God that he would enable her to find her Son." [4] Frequently, during that time, according to St. Bernard, she addresses her Son in the words of the spouse in the Canticles: *Show me where thou feedest, where thou liest in the mid-day, lest I begin to*

[1] "Num, quem diligit anima mea, vidistis?"—*Cant.* iii. 3.

[2] "Puer non comparet; et ego, quo ibo?"—*Gen.* xxxvii. 30.

[3] "Fuerunt mihi lacrymæ meæ panes die ac nocte, dum dicitur mihi quotidie: Ubi est Deus tuus?"—*Ps.* xli. 4.

[4] "Illas noctes insomnes duxit in lacrymosis orationibus, Deum deprecando, ut daret sibi reperire Filium."—*Stell.* l. 3, p. 4, a. 3.

wander.[1] My Son, tell me where thou art, that I may no longer wander, seeking thee in vain.

There are some who assert, and not without reason, that this dolor was not only one of the greatest, but the greatest and most painful of all.

For, in the first place, Mary, in her other dolors, had Jesus with her: she suffered when St. Simeon prophesied to her in the temple; she suffered in the flight into Egypt; but still in company with Jesus; but in this dolor she suffered far from Jesus, not knowing where he was: *And the light of my eyes itself is not with me.*[2] Thus weeping she then said, "Ah, the light of my eyes, my dear Jesus, is no longer with me; he is far from me, and I know not whither he is gone? Origen says that through the love which this holy Mother bore her Son, "she suffered more in this loss of Jesus than any martyr ever suffered in the separation of his soul from his body."[3] Ah, too long indeed were those three days for Mary; they seemed three ages; they were all bitterness, for there was none to comfort her. And who can ever comfort me, she said with Jeremias, who can console me, since he who could alone do so is far from me? and therefore my eyes can never weep enough: *Therefore do I weep, and my eyes run down with water: because the Comforter . . . is far from me.*[4] And with Tobias she

---

[1] "Indica mihi, quem diligit anima mea, ubi pascas, ubi cubes in meridie, ne vagari incipiam."—*Cant.* i. 6.

[2] "Lumen oculorum meorum, et ipsum non est mecum."—*Ps.* xxxvii. 11.

[3] "Vehementer doluit, quia vehementer amabat. Plus doluit de ejus amissione, quam aliquis Martyr dolorem sentiat de animæ a corpore separatione."

[4] "Idciro ego plorans, et oculus meus deducens aquas, quia longe factus est a me consolator."—*Lam.* i. 16.

repeated, *What manner of joy shall be to me who sit in darkness and see not the light of heaven?* [1]

In the second place, Mary, in all her other sorrows, well understood their cause — the redemption of the world, the divine will; but in this she knew not the cause of the absence of her Son. "The sorrowful Mother," says Lanspergius, "was grieved at the absence of Jesus, because, in her humility, she considered herself unworthy to remain longer with or to attend upon him on earth, and have the charge of so great a treasure." [2] "And who knows," perhaps she thought within herself, "maybe I have not served him as I ought; perhaps I have been guilty of some negligence, for which he has left me." "They sought him," says Origen, "lest perchance he had entirely left them." [3] It is certain that, to a soul that loves God, there can be no greater pain than the fear of having displeased him. Therefore in this sorrow alone did Mary complain, lovingly expostulating with Jesus, after she had found him; *Son, why hast thou done so to us? Thy father and I have sought Thee sorrowing.* [4] By these words she had no idea of reproving Jesus, as heretics blasphemously assert, but only meant to express to him the grief proceeding from the great love she bore him which she had experienced during his absence: "It was not a rebuke," says Denis the Carthusian, "but a loving complaint." [5]

---

[1] "Quale gaudium mihi erit, qui in tenebris sedeo, et lumen cœli non video?"—*Tob.* v. 12.

[2] "Tristabatur ex humilitate, quia arbitrabatur se indignam cui tam. pretiosus commissus fuerat Thesaurus."—*Dom. 2 p. Nat. exeg. Ev.*

[3] "Quærebant eum, ne forte reliquisset eos."—*In. Luc. Hom.* 19.

[4] "Fili, quid fecisti nobis sic? ecce pater tuus et ego dolentes quærebamus te."—*Luke,* ii. 48.

[5] "Non erat increpatio, sed amorosa conquestio."—*In Luc.* a. 7.

This sorrow of Mary ought, in the first place, to serve as a consolation to those souls who are desolate, and no longer enjoy, as they once enjoyed, the sweet presence of their Lord. They may weep, but they should weep in peace, as Mary wept over the absence of her Son; and let them take courage and not fear that on this account they have lost the divine favor; for God himself assured St. Teresa, that "no one is lost without knowing it; and that no one is deceived without wishing to be deceived." If our Lord withdraws himself from the sight of a soul that loves him, he does not, therefore, depart from the heart; he often conceals himself from a soul, that it may seek him with a more ardent desire and greater love. But whoever wishes to find Jesus, must seek him, not amidst delights and the pleasures of the world, but amidst crosses and mortifications, as Mary sought him. *We sought Thee sorrowing,*[1] as Mary said to her Son. 'Learn, then, from Mary," says Origen, "to seek Jesus." [2]

Moreover, in this world she would seek no other good than Jesus. Job was not unhappy when he lost all that he possessed on earth: riches, children, health, and honors, and even descended from a throne to a dunghill; but because he had God with him, he was even then happy. St. Augustine says, "he had lost what God had given him, but he still had God Himself." [3] Truly miserable and unhappy are those souls that have lost God. If Mary wept the absence of her Son for three days, how should sinners weep, who have lost divine grace, and to whom God says: *You are not my people, and I will not be yours.*[4] For this is

---

[1] "Dolentes quærebamus te."

[2] "Disce a Maria quærere Jesum."—*In Luc. hom.* 18.

[3] "Perdiderat illa quæ dederat Deus, sed habebat ipsum Deum."—*Serm.* 34, *E. B. App.*

[4] "Vos non populus meus, et ego non ero vester!"—*Os.* i. 9.

the effect of sin; it separates the soul from God: *Your iniquities have divided between you and your God.*[1] Hence,
if sinners possess all the riches of the earth, but have lost
God, all, even in this world, becomes vanity and affliction
to them, as Solomon confessed: *Behold, all is vanity and
vexation of spirit.*[2] But the greatest misfortune of these poor
blind souls is, as St. Augustine observes, that "if they lose
an ox, they do not fail to go in search of it; if they lose a
sheep, they use all diligence to find it; if they lose a
beast of burden, they cannot rest; but when they lose
their God, who is the supreme good, they eat, drink, and
repose."[3]

EXAMPLE.*

Saint Benvenuta once asked the Blessed Virgin for the
grace to share the pain the Mother of Christ felt at the
loss of her divine Son. Mary appeared to her with the
divine Child in her arms. At the sight of the beautiful
babe St. Benvenuta fell into an ecstacy but the vision suddenly disappeared. The pain thus occasioned to the saint
was so great that she besought Mary to help her lest she
die of grief. After three days the Blessed Virgin appeared
again and said to her: "My daughter, your suffering is
only a small part of that which I endured at the loss of
my divine Son."[4]

---

[1] "Iniquitates vestræ diviserunt inter vos et Deum vestrum."—*Is.*
lix. 2.

[2] "Ecce universa vanitas et afflictio spiritus."—*Eccles. i.* 14.

[3] "Perdit homo bovem, et post eum vadit; perdit ovem, et sollicite
eam quærit; perdit asinum, et non quiescit. Perdit homo Deum, et
comedit, et bibit, et quiescit!"

[4] *Marchese, Diar.* Oct. 30.

Prayer.

O Blessed Virgin, why dost thou afflict thyself, seeking for thy lost Son? Is it that thou knowest not where He is? Knowest thou not that he is in thy heart? Art thou ignorant that he feeds amongst lilies? Thou thyself hast said it: *My Beloved to me, and I to him, who feedeth among the lilies.*[1] These, thy thoughts and affections, which are all humble, pure, and holy, are all lilies which invite thy divine Spouse to dwell in thee. Ah, Mary, dost thou sigh after Jesus, thou who lovest none but Jesus? Leave sighs to me, and to so many sinners who love him not, and who have lost him by offending him. My most amiable Mother, if through my fault thy Son is not yet returned to my soul, do thou obtain for me that I may find him. I well know that he is found by those who seek him: *The Lord is good to the soul that seeketh Him.*[2] But do thou make me seek him as I ought. Thou art the gate through which all find Jesus; through thee I also hope to find him. Amen.

IV.

The Meeting of Mary with Jesus, when He was going to Death.

St. Bernardine says,[3] that to form an idea of the greatness of Mary's grief in losing her Jesus by death, we must consider the love that this Mother bore to her Son. All mothers feel the sufferings of their children as their own. Hence, when the Canaanitish woman entreated our Saviour to deliver her daughter from the devil that tormented her, she asked him rather to pity her, the mother, than her daughter: *Have mercy on me, O Lord, Thou Son of David, my daughter is grievously troubled by a devil.*[4] But what mother ever loved her son as Mary

---

[1] "Dilectus meus mihi, et ego illi, qui pascitur inter lilia."—*Cant.* ii. 16.

[2] "Bonus est Dominus . . . animæ quærenti illum."—*Lam.* iii. 25.

[3] T. iii. s. 45, p. 2.

[4] "Miserere mei, Domine, fili David: filia mea male a dæmonio vexatur."—*Matt.* xv. 22.

loved Jesus? He was her only Son, reared amidst so many troubles; a most amiable Son, and tenderly loving his Mother; a Son who, at the same time that he was her Son, was also her God, who had come on earth to enkindle in the hearts of all the fire of divine love, as he himself declared: *I am come to cast fire on the earth, and what will I but that it be kindled?*[1] Let us only imagine what a flame he must have enkindled in that pure heart of his holy Mother, void as it was of every earthly affection. In fine, the Blessed Virgin herself told St. Bridget, "that love had rendered her heart and that of her Son but one."[2] That blending together of servant and Mother, of Son and God, created in the heart of Mary a fire composed of a thousand flames. But the whole of this flame of love was afterwards, at the time of the passion, changed into a sea of grief, when St. Bernardine declares, "that if all the sorrows of the world were united, they would not equal that of the glorious Virgin Mary."[3] Yes, because, as Richard of St. Laurence writes, "the more tenderly his Mother loved, so much the more deeply was she wounded."[4] The greater was her love for him, the greater was her grief at the sight of his sufferings; and especially when she met her Son, already condemned to death, and bearing his cross to the place of punishment. This is the fourth sword of sorrow that we have this day to consider.

The Blessed Virgin revealed to St. Bridget, that when the time of the Passion of our Lord was approaching, her eyes were always filled with tears, as she thought of

---

[1] "Ignem veni mittere in terram, et quid volo nisi ut accendatur?" —*Luke*, xii. 49.

[2] "Unum erat cor meum et cor Filii mei."

[3] "Omnes dolores mundi, si essent simul conjuncti, non essent tanti, quantus fuit dolor gloriosæ Mariæ."—T. iii. s. 45, p. 2.

[4] "Quanto dilexit tenerius, tanto vulnerata est profundius."—*De Laud. B. M.* l. 3.

her beloved Son, whom she was about to lose on earth, and that the prospect of that approaching suffering caused her to be seized with fear, and a cold sweat to cover her whole body.[1]

Behold, the appointed day at last came, and Jesus, in tears, went to take leave of his Mother, before going to death. St. Bonaventure, contemplating Mary on that night, says : " Thou didst spend it without sleep, and whilst others slept thou didst remain watching." [2] In the morning the disciples of Jesus Christ came to this afflicted Mother, the one to bring her one account, the other another ; but all were tidings of sorrow, verifying in her the prophecy of Jeremias : *Weeping, she hath wept in the night, and her tears are on her cheeks; there is none to comfort her of all them that were dear to her.*[3] Some then came to relate to her the cruel treatment of her Son in the house of Caiphas ; and others, the insults he had received from Herod. Finally—to come to our point, I omit all the rest—St. John came, and announced to Mary that the most unjust Pilate had already condemned Him to die on the cross. I say the most unjust Pilate ; for, as St. Leo remarks, " This unjust judge condemned him to death with the same lips with which he had declared him innocent." [4] " Ah ! afflicted Mother," said St. John, " thy Son is already condemned to death ; he is already gone forth, bearing himself his cross, on his way to Calvary," as the saint afterwards related in his Gospels : *and bearing His own cross, He went forth to that*

---

[1] " Imminente passione Filii mei, lacrymæ erant in oculis meis et sudor in corpore præ timore."—*Rev.* l. 4, c. 70.

[2] " Absque somno duxisti, et, soporatis cæteris, vigil permansisti." —*Off. de Comp. B. M. V.*

[3] " Plorans ploravit in nocte, et lacrymæ ejus in maxillis ejus; non est qui consoletur eam ex omnibus caris ejus."—*Lam.* i. 2.

[4] " Iisdem labiis misit ad crucem, quibus eum pronuntiaverat innocentem."—*De Pass.* s. 3.

place which is called Calvary.[1]   "Come, if thou desirest to
see him, and bid him a last farewell, in some street
through which he must pass."

Mary goes with St. John, and by the blood with which
the way is sprinkled, she perceives that her Son has already passed. This she revealed to St. Bridget : " By
the footsteps of my Son, I knew where he had passed:
for along the way the ground was marked with blood."[2]
St. Bonaventure[3] represents the afflicted Mother taking
a shorter way, and placing herself at the corner of a
street, to meet her afflicted Son as he was passing by.
" The most sorrowful Mother," says St. Bernard, " met
her most sorrowful Son."[4]   While Mary was waiting in
that place, how much must she have heard said by the
Jews, who soon recognized her, against her beloved Son,
and perhaps even words of mocking against herself.

Alas, what a scene of sorrows then presented itself before her!—the nails, the hammers, the cords, the fatal
instruments of the death of her son, all of which were
borne before him. And what a sword must the sound
of that trumpet have been to her heart, which proclaimed
the sentence pronounced against her Jesus!

But behold, the instruments, the trumpeter, and the
executioners, have already passed; she raised her eyes,
and saw, O God! a young man covered with blood and
wounds from head to foot, a wreath of thorns on his
head, and two heavy beams on his shoulders. She looked
at him, and hardly recognized him, saying, with Isaias,
and we have seen Him, and there was no sightliness.[5]   Yes,

---

[1] " Et bajulans sibi crucem, exivit in eum, qui dicitur Calvariæ,
locum."—*John.* xix. 17.

[2] " Ex vestigiis Filii mei cognoscebam incessum ejus; quo enim pro-
cedebat, apparebat terra infusa sanguine."—*Rev.* l. i, c. 10.

[3] *Med. Vit. Chr.* c. 77.

[4] " Mœstissima Mater mœstissimo Filio occurrit."

[5] " Et vidimus eum, et non erat aspectus."—*Is.* liii. 2.

for the wounds, the bruises, and the clotted blood, gave him the appearance of a leper: *we have thought Him as it were a leper ;*[1] so that he could no longer be known: *and His look was, as it were, hidden and despised ; whereupon we esteemed Him not.*[2]   But at length love revealed him to her, and as soon as she knew that it indeed was he, ah, what love and fear must then have filled her heart! as St. Peter of Alcantara says in his meditations.[3]   On the one hand she desired to behold him, and on the other she dreaded so heartrending a sight.   At length they looked at each other.   The Son wiped from his eyes the clotted blood, which, as it was revealed to St. Bridget,[4] prevented him from seeing, and looked at his Mother, and the Mother looked at her Son.   Ah, looks of bitter grief, which, as so many arrows, pierced through and through those two beautiful and loving souls.

When Margaret, the daughter of Sir Thomas More, met her father on his way to death, she could only exclaim, "O father! father!" and fell fainting at his feet. Mary, at the sight of her Son, on his way to Calvary, did not faint ; no, for it was not becoming, as Father Suarez remarks,[5] that this Mother should lose the use of her reason; nor did she die, for God reserved her for greater grief; but though she did not die, her sorrow was enough to have caused her a thousand deaths.

The Mother would have embraced him, as St. Anselm says, but the guards thrust her aside with insults, and urged forward the suffering Lord; and Mary followed him.   Ah, holy Virgin, whither goest thou ?   To Calvary. And canst thou trust thyself to behold him who is thy

[1] "Putavimus eum quasi leprosum."—*Is.* liii. 4.

[2] "Et quasi absconditus vultus ejus et despectus; unde nec reputavimus eum."—*Ibid.* 3.

[3] P. 1, c. 4, fer. 5.

[4] *Rev.* l. 1, c. 10.—l. 4, c. 70.

[5] *De Inc.* q. 51, a. 3, sect. 2.

life, hanging on a cross? *And thy life shall be, as it were, hanging before thee.*[1]

"Ah, stop, my mother" (says St. Laurence Justinian, in the name of the Son), "where goest thou? Where wouldst thou come? If thou comest whither I go, thou wilt be tortured with my sufferings, and I with thine."[2] But although the sight of her dying Jesus was to cost her so bitter sorrow, the loving Mary will not leave him: the Son advanced, and the Mother followed, to be also crucified with her Son, as the Abbot William says: "the Mother also took up her cross and followed, to be crucified with him."[3]

"We even pity wild beasts,"[4] as St. John Chrysostom writes; and did we see a lioness following her cub to death, the sight would move us to compassion. And shall we not also be moved to compassion on seeing Mary follow her immaculate Lamb to death? Let us, then, pity her, and let us also accompany her Son and herself, by bearing with patience the cross that our Lord imposes on us. St. John Chrysostom asks why Jesus Christ, in his other sufferings, was pleased to endure them alone, but in carrying his cross was assisted by the Cyrenean? He replies, that it was "that thou mayest understand that the cross of Christ is not sufficient without thine."[5]

EXAMPLE.

Our Saviour one day appeared to Sister Diomira, a nun in Florence, and said, "Think of me and love me, and I will think of thee and love thee." At the same

---

[1] "Et erit vita tua quasi pendens ante te."—*Deut.* xxviii. 66.

[2] "Ut quid venisti, Mater mea? Dolor tuus meum auget; cruciatus tuus transfigit me."—*De Tr. Chr. Ag.* c. 11.

[3] "Tollebat et ipsa crucem suam, et sequebatur eum, crucifigenda cum eo."—*Delrio, in Cant.* vii. 7.

[4] "Ferarum etiam miseremur."—*In Phil. hom.* 4.

[5] "Ut intelligas Christi crucem non sufficere sine tua."

time he presented her with a bunch of flowers and a cross, signifying thereby that the consolations of the saints in this world are always to be accompanied by the cross. The cross unites souls to God. Blessed Jerome Emilian, when a soldier, and loaded with sins, was shut up by his enemies in a tower. There, moved by his misfortunes, and enlightened by God to change his life, he had recourse to the ever-blessed Virgin; and from that time, by the help of this divine Mother, he began to lead the life of a saint, so much so that he merited once to see the very high place that God had prepared for him in heaven. He became the founder of the religious Order of the Somaschi, died as a saint, and has lately been canonized by the holy Church.

Prayer.

My sorrowful Mother, by the merit of that grief which thou didst feel in seeing thy beloved Jesus led to death, obtain me the grace, that I also may bear with patience the crosses which God sends me. Happy indeed shall I be, if I only know how to accompany thee with my cross until death. Thou with thy Jesus—and you were both innocent—hast carried a far heavier cross; and shall I, a sinner, who have deserved hell, refuse to carry mine? Ah, immaculate Virgin, from thee do I hope for help to bear all crosses with patience. Amen.

V.

The Death of Jesus.

We have now to witness a new kind of martyrdom—a Mother condemned to see an innocent Son, and one whom she loves with the whole affection of her soul, cruelly tormented and put to death before her own eyes.

There stood by the cross of Jesus his Mother.[1] St. John believed that in these words he had said enough of Mary's martyrdom. Consider her at the foot of the

[1] "Stabat autem juxta crucem Jesu Mater ejus."—*John*, xix. 25.

cross in the presence of her dying Son, and then see if there be a sorrow like unto her sorrow. Let us remain for awhile this day on Calvary, and consider the fifth sword which, in the death of Jesus, transfixed the heart of Mary.

As soon as our agonized Redeemer had reached the Mount of Calvary, the executioners stripped him of his clothes, and piercing his hands and feet " not with sharp, but with blunt nails," [1] as St. Bernard says, to torment him more, they fastened him on the cross. Having crucified him, they planted the cross, and thus left him to die. The executioners left him; but not so Mary. She then drew nearer to the cross, to be present at his death: "I did not leave him" (thus the Blessed Virgin revealed to St. Bridget), "but stood nearer to the cross." [2]

"But what did it avail thee, O Lady," says St. Bonaventure, "to go to Calvary, and see this Son expire? Shame should have prevented thee; for his disgrace was thine, since thou wert his Mother. At least, horror of witnessing such a crime as the crucifixion of a God by his own creatures should have prevented thee from going there." But the same saint answers, "Ah, thy heart did not then think of its own sorrows, but of the sufferings and death of thy dear Son," [3] and therefore thou wouldst thyself be present, at least to compassionate Him. "Ah, true Mother," says the Abbot William, "most loving Mother, whom not even the fear of death could separate from thy beloved Son !" [4]

[1] " Non acutis, sed obtusis."

[2] " Ego non separabar ab eo, et stabam vicinius cruci ejus."—*Rev.* i. 1, c. 35.

[3] "Quare, Domina, ad Calvariæ locum venisti? Cur non te tenuit verecundia virginalis, horror facinoris? Non considerabas horrorem, sed dolorem."—*Stim. div. am.* p. 1, c. 3.

[4] " Plane Mater, quæ nec in terrore mortis Filium deserebat."—*In Assumpt.* s. 4.

But, O God, what a cruel sight was it there to behold this Son in agony on the cross, and at its foot this Mother in agony, suffering all the torments endured by her Son! Listen to the words in which Mary revealed to St. Bridget the sorrowful state in which she saw her dying Son on the cross: " My dear Jesus was breathless, exhausted, and in his last agony on the cross; his eyes were sunk, half-closed, and lifeless; his lips hanging, and his ·mouth open; his cheeks hollow and drawn in; his face elongated, his nose sharp, his countenance sad; his head had fallen on his breast, his hair was black with blood, his stomach collapsed, his arms and legs stiff, and his whole body covered with wounds and blood." [1]

All these sufferings of Jesus were also those of Mary; " Every torture inflicted on the body of Jesus," says St. Jerome, " was a wound in the heart of the Mother." [2] "Whoever then was present on the Mount of Calvary," says St. John Chrysostom, "might see two altars, on which two great sacrifices were consummated; the one in the body of Jesus, the other in the heart of Mary." Nay, better still may we say with St. Bonaventure, " there was but one altar—that of the cross of the Son, on which, together with his divine Lamb, the victim, the Mother was also sacrificed;" therefore the saint asks this Mother, " O Lady, where art thou? near the cross? Nay, rather, thou art on the cross, crucified, sacrificing thyself with thy Son." [3] St. Augustine assures us of the same thing: " The cross and nails of the Son were also those of his Mother; with Christ crucified the Mother was also crucified." [4] Yes; for, as St. Bernard says,

[1] *Rev.* l. 1, c. 10.—l. 4, c. 70.

[2] " Quot læsiones in corpore Christi, tot vulnera in corde Matris."— *De 7 Verbis D. tr.* 3.

[3] " O Domina! ubi stas? Numquid juxta crucem? Imo in cruce cum Filio cruciaris."— *Stim. div. am.* p. 1, c. 3.

[4] " Crux et clavi Filii fuerunt et Matris, Christo crucifixo, crucifigebatur et Mater."

" Love inflicted on the heart of Mary the tortures caused by nails in the body of Jesus." [1] So much so, that, as St. Bernardine writes, " At the same time that the Son sacrificed his body, the Mother sacrificed her soul." [2]

Mothers ordinarily fly from the presence of their dying children; but when a mother is obliged to witness such a scene, she procures all possible relief for her child; she arranges his bed, that he may be more at ease; she administers refreshments to him; and thus the poor mother soothes her own grief. Ah, most afflicted of all Mothers ! O Mary, thou hast to witness the agony of thy dying Jesus; but thou canst administer him no relief. Mary heard her Son exclaim, *I thirst*, but she could not even give him a drop of water to refresh him in that great thirst. She could only say, as St. Vincent Ferrer remarks, " My Son, I have only the water of tears." [3] She saw that on that bed of torture her Son, suspended by three nails, could find no repose; she would have clasped him in her arms to give him relief, or that at least he might there have expired; but she could not. " In vain," says St. Bernard, " did she extend her arms; they sank back empty on her breast." [4] She beheld that poor Son, who in his sea of grief sought consolation, as it was foretold by the prophet, but in vain: *I have trodden the winepress alone; I looked about and there was none to help; I sought, and there was none to give aid.* [5] But who amongst men would console him, since all were enemies ? Even on the cross he was taunted and

[1] " Quod in carne Christi agebant clavi, in Virginis mente affectus erga Filium."

[2] " Dum ille corpus, ista spiritum immolabat."—T. i. s. 51, p. 2, a. 1, c. 3.

[3] " Fili ! non habeo nisi aquam lacrymarum."—*S. in Parasc.*

[4] " Volebat eum amplecti; sed manus frustra protensæ in se complexæ redibant."—*De Lam. V. M.*

[5] " Torcular calcavi solus. . . . Circumspexi, et non erat auxiliator; quæsivi, et non fuit qui adjuvaret."—*Is.* lxiii. 3.

blasphemed on all sides: *And they that passed by, blasphemed Him, wagging their heads.*[1] Some said to his face, *If thou be the Son of God, come down from the cross.*[2] Others, *He saved others, Himself He cannot save.*[3] Again, *If He be the King of Israel, let Him now come down from the cross.*[4] Our Blessed Lady herself said to St. Bridget,[5] "I heard some say that my Son was a thief; others, that he was an impostor; others, that no one deserved death more than he did; and every word was a new sword of grief to my heart."

But that which the most increased the sorrows which Mary endured through compassion for her Son, was hearing him complain on the cross that even his Eternal Father had abandoned him: *My God, My God, why hast Thou forsaken Me?*[6] Words which the divine Mother told the same St. Bridget could never, during her whole life, depart from her mind.[7] So that the afflicted Mother saw her Jesus suffering on every side; she desired to comfort him, but could not.

That which grieved her the most was to see that she herself, by her presence and sorrow, increased the sufferings of her Son. "The grief," says St. Bernard, "which filled Mary's heart, as a torrent flowed into and embittered the heart of Jesus."[8] "So much so," says the same saint, "that Jesus on the cross suffered more from compassion for his Mother than from his own torments." He thus speaks in the name of our Blessed Lady: "I

[1] "Prætereuntes autem blasphemabant eum, moventes capita sua." —*Matt.* xxvii. 39.

[2] "Si Filius Dei es, descende de cruce."

[3] "Alios salvos fecit, seipsum non potest salvum facere."

[4] "Si Rex Israel est, descendat nunc de cruce."

[5] *Rev.* l. 1, c. 10.

[6] "Deus meus! Deus meus! ut quid dereliquisti me?"—*Matt.* xxvii. 46.

[7] *Rev.* l. 4, c. 70.

[8] "Repleta Matre, ad Filium redundabat inundatio amaritudinis."

stood with my eyes fixed on him, and his on me, and he grieved more for me than for himself."[1] And then, speaking of Mary beside her dying Son, he says, "that she lived dying without being able to die." "Near the cross of Christ his Mother stood half-dead; she spoke not; dying she lived, and living she died; nor could she die, for death was her very life."[2]

Passino writes that Jesus Christ himself one day, speaking to blessed Baptista Varani of Camerino, assured her that when on the cross, so great was his affliction at seeing his Mother at his feet in so bitter an anguish, that compassion for her caused him to die without consolation; so much so, that the Blessed Baptista, being supernaturally enlightened as to the greatness of this suffering of Jesus, exclaimed, "O Lord, tell me no more of this Thy sorrow, for I can no longer bear it."[3]

"All," says Simon of Cassia, "who then saw this Mother silent, and not uttering a complaint in the midst of so great suffering, were filled with astonishment."[4] But if Mary's lips were silent, her heart was not so, for she incessantly offered the life of her Son to the divine justice for our salvation. Therefore, we know that by the merits of her dolors she coöperated in our birth to the life of grace; and hence we are the children of her sorrows. "Christ," says Lanspergius, "was pleased that she, the coöperatress in our redemption, and whom he had determined to give us for our Mother, should be there present; for it was at the foot of the cross that she was to bring us, her children, forth."[5] If any consola-

---

[1] "Stabam ego videns eum: et ipse videns me, plus dolebat de me quam de se."—*De Lam. V. M.*

[2] "Júxta crucem stabat Mater: vox illi non erat; vivebat moriens, moriebatur vivens; nec mori poterat, quæ vivens mortua erat."—*Ibid.*

[3] *Boll.* 31 *Maii, Vit. rev.* § 2.

[4] "Stupebant omnes qui noverant hujus Hominis Matrem, quod etiam in tantæ angustiæ pressura silentium servabat."

[5] "Voluit eam Christus Cooperatricem nostræ redemptionis sibi ad-

tion entered that sea of bitterness, the heart of Mary, the only one was this, that she knew that by her sorrows she was leading us to eternal salvation, as Jesus himself revealed to St. Bridget: "My Mother Mary, on account of her compassion and love, was made the Mother of all in heaven and on earth." [1] And indeed these were the last words with which Jesus bid her farewell before his death: this was his last recommendation, leaving us to her for her children in the person of St. John: *Woman, behold thy son.* [2] From that time Mary began to perform this good office of a mother for us; for St. Peter Damian attests, "that by the prayers of Mary, who stood between the cross of the good thief and that of her Son, the thief was converted and saved, and thereby she repaid a former service." [3] For, as other authors also relate, this thief had been kind to Jesus and Mary on their journey to Egypt; and this same office the Blessed Virgin has ever continued, and still continues, to perform.

EXAMPLE.*

Blessed Joachim Piccolomini had always a most tender devotion for Mary, and from his childhood was in the habit of visiting an image of our Blessed Lady of Sorrows, which was in the neighboring church, three times a day; and on Saturdays, in her honor, he abstained from all food; and in addition to this he always rose at midnight to meditate on her dolors. But let us see how abundantly this good Mother recompensed him. In the first place, when he was a young

stare, quam nobis constituerat dare Matrem; debebat enim ipsa sub cruce nos parere filios."—*De Pass. Chr. hom.* 48.

[1] "Maria, Mater mea, propter compassionem et charitatem, facta est Mater omnium in cœlis et in terra."—*Rev.* l. 8, c. 12.

[2] "Mulier, ecce filius tuus."—*John*, xix, 26.

[3] "Idcirco resipuit bonus latro, quia B. Virgo, inter cruces Filii et latronis posita, Filium pro latrone deprecabatur, hoc suo beneficio antiquum latronis obsequium recompensans."—*Silveira, Comm.* l. 8, c. 14, q. 8.

man she appeared to him and desired him to embrace the Order of the Servites and this the holy young man did. Again, in the latter years of his life she appeared to him with two crowns in her hands: the one was composed of rubies, and this was to reward him for his compassion for her sorrows; the other of pearls, as a recompense for his virginity, which he vowed in her honor. Shortly before his death she once more appeared to him; and then the saint begged, as a favor, that he might die on the same day on which Jesus Christ had expired. Our Blessed Lady immediately gratified him, saying: "It is well: prepare thyself; for tomorrow, Good Friday, thou shalt die suddenly as thou desirest; to-morrow thou shalt be with me in heaven." And so it was; for the next day, during the singing of the Passion according to St. John, at the words, Now there stood by the cross of Jesus His Mother, he fell into the last struggles of death; and at the words, He bowed down His head and expired, the saint also breathed his last; and in the same moment the whole church was filled with an extraordinary light and most delicious perfume.[1]

Prayer.

Ah, Mother, the most sorrowful of all mothers, thy son is, then, dead; that Son so amiable, and who loved thee so much! Weep, then, for thou hast reason to weep. Who can ever console thee? The thought alone that Jesus by his death conquered hell, opened heaven until then closed to men, and gained so many souls, can console thee. From that throne of the cross he will reign in so many hearts, which, conquered by his love, will serve him with love. Disdain not, in the mean time, O my Mother, to keep me near thee, to weep with thee, since I have so much reason to weep for the crimes by which I have offended him. Ah, Mother of Mercy, I hope, first, through the death of my Redeemer, and then through thy sorrows, to obtain pardon and eternal salvation. Amen.

[1] *Siniscalchi, Mart. di M. cons.* 28-30.

VI.

The Piercing of the Side of Jesus, and His Descent from the Cross.

O all ye that pass by the way, attend, and see if there be any sorrow like to my sorrow.[1] Devout souls, listen to what the sorrowful Mary says this day: "My beloved children, I do not wish you to console me; no, for my soul is no longer susceptible of consolation in this world after the death of my dear Jesus. If you wish to please me, this is what I ask of you; behold me, and see if there ever has been in the world a grief like mine, in seeing him who was all my love torn from me with such cruelty." But, my sovereign Lady, since thou wilt not be consoled, and hast so great a thirst for sufferings, I must tell thee that, even with the death of thy Son, thy sorrows have not ended. On this day thou wilt be wounded by another sword of sorrow, a cruel lance will pierce the side of thy Son already dead, and thou hast to receive him in thine arms after he is taken down from the cross.

Now we are to consider the sixth dolor which afflicted this poor Mother. Attend and weep. Hitherto the dolors of Mary tortured her one by one; on this day they are all, as it were, united to assail her.

It is enough to tell a mother that her son is dead, to excite all her love towards her lost child. Some persons, that they may lessen a mother's grief, remind her of the displeasure at one time caused by her departed child. But I, my Queen, did I thus wish to lighten thy grief for the death of Jesus, for what displeasure that he ever caused thee could I remind thee? No, indeed. He always loved thee, always obeyed thee, and always re-

---

[1] "O vos omnes qui transitis per viam, attendite, et videte si est dolor sicut dolor meus."—*Lam* i. 12.

spected thee. Now thou hast lost him, who can ever tell thy grief? Do thou explain it, thou who hast experienced it.

A devout author says, that when our beloved Redeemer was dead, the first care of the great Mother was to accompany in spirit the most holy soul of her Son, and present it to the eternal Father. "I present Thee, O my God," Mary must then have said, "the Immaculate soul of Thine and my Son; He has now obeyed Thee unto death; do Thou, then, receive it in Thine arms. Thy justice is now satisfied, Thy will is accomplished; behold, the great sacrifice to Thy eternal glory is consummated." Then, turning towards the lifeless members of her Jesus, "O wounds," she said, "O wounds of love, I adore you, and in you do I rejoice; for by your means salvation is given to the world. You will remain open in the body of my Son, and be the refuge of those who have recourse to you. O, how many, through you, will receive the pardon of their sins, and by you be inflamed with love for the supreme good!"

That the joy of the following Paschal Sabbath might not be disturbed, the Jews desired that the body of Jesus should be taken down from the cross; but as this could not be done unless the criminals were dead, men came with iron bars to break our Lord's legs, as they had already done those of the two thieves who were crucified with him. Mary was still weeping over the death of her Son, when she saw these armed men advancing towards her Jesus. At this sight she first trembled with fear, and then exclaimed: "Ah, my Son is already dead; cease to outrage him; torment me no more, who am his poor Mother." She implored them, writes St. Bonaventure, "not to break his legs."[1] But while she thus spoke, O God! she saw a soldier brandish a lance, and

[1] *Med. vit. Chr.* c. 80.

pierce the side of Jesus: *One of the soldiers with a spear opened His side, and immediately there came out blood and water.*[1] At the stroke of the spear the cross shook, and, as it was afterwards revealed to St. Bridget, the heart of Jesus was divided into two.[2] There came out blood and water; for only those few drops of blood remained, and even those our Saviour was pleased to shed, that we might understand that he had no more blood to give us. The injury of that stroke was inflicted on Jesus, but Mary suffered its pain. "Christ," says the devout Lanspergius, "shared this wound with his Mother; he received the insult, his Mother endured its agony."[3]

The holy Fathers maintain that this was literally the sword foretold to the Blessed Virgin by St. Simeon: a sword, not a material one, but one of grief, which transpierced her blessed soul in the heart of Jesus, where it always dwelt. Thus, amongst others, St. Bernard says: "The lance which opened his side passed through the soul of the Blessed Virgin, which could never leave her Son's heart."[4] The divine Mother herself revealed the same thing to St. Bridget: "When the spear was drawn out, the point appeared red with blood: then, seeing the heart of my most dear Son pierced, it seemed to me as if my own heart was also pierced."[5] An angel told the same saint, "that such were the sufferings of Mary, that it was only by a miraculous interposition on the part of

---

[1] " Unus militum lancea latus ejus aperuit, et continuo exivit sanguis et aqua."—*John*, xix. 34.

[2] " Ita ut ambæ partes cordis essent in lancea."—*Rev.* l. 2, c. 21.

[3] " Divisit Christus cum Matre sua hujus vulneris injuriam, ut ipse vulnerationem acciperet, Mater vero dolorem."—*De Pass. Chr. hom.* 54.

[4] "Lancea quæ ipsius aperuit latus, animam Virginis penetravit, quæ inde nequibat avelli."—*In Sign. Magn.*

[5] " Cum extraheretur hasta, apparuit cuspis rubea sanguine. Tunc mihi videbatur, quod quasi cor meum perforaretur, cum vidissem cor Filii mei carissimi perforatum "—*Rev.* l. 1, c. 10.

God that she did not die."[1] In her other dolors she at least had her Son to compassionate her; but now she has not even him to pity her.

The afflicted Mother, fearing that other injuries might still be inflicted on her Son, entreated Joseph of Arimathea to obtain the body of her Jesus from Pilate, that at least in death she might guard and protect it from further outrage. Joseph went, and represented to Pilate the grief and desires of this afflicted Mother. St. Anselm[2] believes that compassion for the Mother softened the heart of Pilate, and moved him to grant her the body of the Saviour.

Jesus then was taken down from the cross. O most sacred Virgin, after thou hast given thy Son to the world, with so great love, for our salvation, behold the world now restores him to thee; but, O God, in what state dost thou receive him? O world, said Mary, how dost thou return him to me? *My Son was white and ruddy;*[3] but thou returnest him to me blackened with bruises, and red—yes! but with the wound which thou hast inflicted upon him. He was all fair and beautiful; but now there is no more beauty in him; He is all disfigured. His aspect enamoured all: now he excites horror in all who behold him. "Oh, how many swords," says St. Bonaventure, "pierced the poor Mother's soul"[4] when she received the body of her Son from the cross! Let us only consider the anguish it would cause any mother to receive into her arms the body of her lifeless son.

It was revealed to St. Bridget,[5] that three ladders were

---

[1] "Non parvum miraculum a Deo factum est, cum Virgo Mater, tot doloribus sauciata, spiritum non emisit."—*Serm. Ang.* c. 18.

[2] *Dial. de Pass.* c. 16.

[3] "Dilectus meus candidus et rubicundus."—*Cant.* v. 10.

[4] "O quot gladii animam matris pertransierunt!"

[5] *Rev.* l. 2, c. 21.

placed against the cross to take down the sacred body ; the holy disciples first drew out the nails from the hands and feet, and, according to Metaphrastes,[1] gave them to Mary. Then one supported the upper part of the body of Jesus, and the other the lower, and thus they took it from the cross. Bernardine de Bustis describes the afflicted Mother as standing, and extending her arms to meet her dear Son ; she embraced him, and then sat at the foot of the cross. His mouth was open, his eyes were dim ; she then examined his mangled flesh and uncovered bones; she took off the crown, and saw the sad injuries which the thorns had inflicted on that sacred head ; she saw the holes in his hands and feet, and thus addressed him : " Ah, Son, to what has Thy love for men brought Thee ; and what evil hadst Thou done them, that they should thus cruelly have tormented Thee ? Thou wast my father" (continues Bernardine de Bustis, in Mary's name), " Thou wast my brother, my spouse, my delight, my glory ; Thou wast my all !"[2] My Son, see my affliction, look at me, console me; but no, Thou no longer lookest at me. Speak, say but a word, and console me; but Thou speakest no more, for Thou art dead. Then, turning to those barbarous instruments of torture, she said, O cruel thorns, O cruel nails, O merciless spear, how, how could you thus torture your Creator ? But why do I speak of thorns or nails ? Alas ! sinners, she exclaimed, it is you who have thus cruelly treated my Son.

Thus did Mary speak and complain of us. But what would she now say, were she still susceptible of suffering ? What would be her grief to see that men, notwithstanding that her Son has died for them, still continue to torment and crucify him by their sins ! Let us,

---

[1] *Ap. Sur.* 15 *Aug.*

[2] " Tu mihi pater eras; tu frater, sponsus, meæ deliciæ, mea gloria; tu mihi omnia eras."—*Mar.* p. 10, s. 1.

at least, cease to torment this afflicted Mother; and if we have hitherto grieved her by our sins, let us now do all that she desires. She says, *Return, ye transgressors, to the heart.*[1] Sinners, return to the wounded heart of my Jesus; return as penitents, and he will welcome you. "Flee from him to him," she continues to say with the Abbot Guerric; "from the Judge to the Redeemer, from the tribunal to the cross." [2] Our Blessed Lady herself revealed to St. Bridget,[3] that "she closed the eyes of her Son, when he was taken down from the cross, but she could not close his arms;" Jesus Christ giving us thereby to understand that he desired to remain with his arms extended to receive all penitent sinners who return to him. "O world," continues Mary, *behold, then, thy time is the time of lovers.*[4] "Now that my Son has died to save thee, it is no longer for thee a time of fear, but one of love—a time to love him, who to show thee the love he bore thee was pleased to suffer so much." "The heart of Jesus," says St. Bernard, "was wounded that, through the visible wound, the invisible wound of love might be seen." [5] "If, then," concludes Mary, in the words of Blessed Raymond Jordano, "my Son by excess of love was pleased that his side should be opened, that he might give thee his heart, it is right, O man, that thou in return shouldst also give him thine." [6] And if you desire, O children of Mary, to find a place in the heart

---

[1] "Redite, prævaricatores, ad cor."—*Is.* xlvi. 8.

[2] "Ab ipso fuge ad ipsum, a Judice ad Redemptorem, a tribunali ad crucem."—*In Dom. Palm.* s. 4.

[3] "Ejus brachia flectere non potui."—*Rev.* l. 4, c. 70.

[4] "Et ecce tempus tuum, tempus amantium."—*Ezek.* xvi. 8.

[5] "Propterea vulneratum est cor Christi, ut per vulnus visibile, vulnus amoris invisibile videamus."—*Lib. de Pass.* c. 3.

[6] "Præ nimio amore aperuit sibi latus, ut tibi tribuat cor suum."—*Stim. div. am.* p. I, c. I.

of Jesus, without fear of being rejected, "go," says Ubertino da Casale, "go with Mary; for she will obtain the grace for you." [1]

EXAMPLE.*

In the city of Cesena there lived two sinners who were great friends. One of them, whose name was Bartholomew, in the midst of his wickedness preserved the devotion of daily reciting the hymn "Stabat Mater" in honor of Mary in Sorrow. He was one day reciting this hymn, when he had a vision, in which he seemed to stand with his wicked friend in a lake of fire; and he saw that the most Holy Virgin moved to compassion, extended her hand to him, withdrew him from the fire, and advised him to ask pardon of Jesus Christ, who seemed to forgive him on account of the prayers of his Mother. After the vision, Bartholomew heard that his companion was dead, having been shot; and he thus knew that what he had seen was true. He then renounced the world, and entered the Order of Capuchins, where he led a most austere life, and died with the reputation of sanctity. [2]

Prayer.

O afflicted Virgin! O soul great in virtue but great also in sorrow, for the one and the other took their rise in that immense love with which thy heart was inflamed towards God, for thou couldst love Him alone; ah, Mother, pity me, for instead of loving God I have greatly offended Him. Thy sorrows encourage me to hope for pardon. But this is not enough; I wish to love my Lord; and who can better obtain me this love than thou, who art the Mother of fair love? Ah, Mary, thou comfortest all; console me also. Amen.

---

[1] "Fili hujus Matris, ingredere cum ipsa intra penetralia cordis Jesu."—*Arb. Vit.* l. 4, c. 24.

[2] *Siniscalchi, Mart. di M. cons.* 15.

VII.

The Burial of Jesus.

When a mother is by the side of her suffering and dying child, she undoubtedly feels and suffers all his pains; but after he is actually dead, when, before the body is carried to the grave, the afflicted mother must bid her child a last farewell; then, indeed, the thought that she is to see him no more is a grief that exceeds all other griefs. Behold the last sword of Mary's sorrow, which we have now to consider; for after witnessing the death of her Son on the cross, and embracing for a last time his lifeless body, this blessed Mother had to leave him in the sepulchre, never more to enjoy his beloved presence on earth.

That we may better understand this last dolor, we will return to Calvary and consider the afflicted Mother, who still holds the lifeless body of her Son clasped in her arms. O my Son, she seemed to say in the words of Job, my Son, *Thou art changed to be cruel towards me.*[1] Yes, for all Thy noble qualities, Thy beauty, grace, and virtues, Thy engaging manners, all the marks of special love which Thou hast bestowed upon me, the peculiar favors Thou hast granted me,—all are now changed into grief, and as so many arrows pierce my heart, and the more they have excited me to love Thee, so much the more cruelly do they now make me feel Thy loss. Ah, my own beloved Son, in losing Thee I have lost all. Thus does St. Bernard speak in her name: "O truly-begotten of God, Thou wast to me a father, a son, a spouse: Thou wast my very soul! Now I am deprived of my father, widowed of my spouse, a desolate, childless Mother; having lost my only Son, I have lost all."[2]

---

[1] "Mutatus es mihi in crudelem."—*Job*, xxx. 21.

[2] "O vere Dei Nate! tu mihi pater, tu mihi filius, tu mihi sponsus,

Thus was Mary, with her Son locked in her arms, absorbed in grief. The holy disciples, fearful that the poor Mother might die of grief, approached her to take the body of her Son from her arms to bear it away for burial. This they did with gentle and respectable violence, and having embalmed it, they wrapped it in a linen cloth which was already prepared. On this cloth, which is still preserved at Turin, our Lord was pleased to leave to the world an impression of his sacred body.

The disciples then bore him to the tomb. To do this, they first of all raised the sacred body on their shoulders, and then the mournful train set forth; choirs of angels from heaven accompanied it; the holy women followed, and with them the afflicted Mother also followed her Son to the place of burial. When they had reached the appointed place, "O how willingly would Mary have there buried herself alive with her Son had such been his will!" for this she herself revealed to St. Bridget.[1] But such not being the divine will, there are many authors who say that she accompanied the sacred body of Jesus into the sepulchre, where, according to Baronius,[2] the disciples also deposited the nails and the crown of thorns. In raising the stone to close up the entrance, the holy disciples of the Saviour had to approach our Blessed Lady, and say: Now, O Lady, we must close the sepulchre: forgive us, look once more at thy Son, and bid him a last farewell. Then my beloved Son (for thus must the afflicted Mother have spoken); then I shall see Thee no more? Receive, therefore, on this last occasion that I behold Thee, receive my last farewell, the farewell of thy dear Mother, and receive

tu mihi anima eras. Nunc orbor Patre, viduor Sponso, desolor Filio: omnia perdo."—*De Lam. V. M*

[1] "O quam libenter tunc posita fuissem viva cum Filio meo, si fuisset voluntas ejus!"—*Rev.* l. 1, c. 10.

[2] *Anno Chr.* 34, n. 131.

6

also my heart, which I leave buried with Thee. "The Blessed Virgin," writes St. Fulgentius, "would ardently have desired to bury her soul with the body of Christ."[1] And this Mary herself revealed to St. Bridget, saying: "I can truly say that at the burial of my Son one tomb contained as it were two hearts."[2]

Finally, the disciples raised the stone and closed up the holy sepulchre, and in it the body of Jesus, that great treasure—a treasure so great that neither earth nor heaven had a greater. Here I may be permitted to make a short digression, and remark that Mary's heart was buried with Jesus, because Jesus was her whole treasure: *Where your treasure is, there will your heart be also.*[3] And where, may we ask, are our hearts buried? In creatures—perchance in mire. And why not in Jesus, who, although he has ascended to heaven, is still pleased to remain on earth, not dead indeed, but living in the Most Holy Sacrament of the altar, precisely that our hearts may be with him, and that he may possess them?

But let us return to Mary. Before leaving the sepulchre, according to St. Bonaventure,[4] she blessed the sacred stone which closed it, saying: "O happy stone, that doth now enclose that sacred body, which for nine months was contained in my womb; I bless thee and envy thee; I leave thee the guardian of my Son, of that Son who is my whole treasure and all my love." Then, raising her heart to the Eternal Father, she said, "O Father, to thee do I recommend him—him who is thy Son at the same time that he is mine." Thus bidding

---

[1] "Animam cum corpore Christi contumulari Virgo vehementer exoptavit."

[2] "Vere dicere possum, quod, sepulto Filio meo, quasi duo corda in uno sepulchro fuerunt."—*Rev.* l. 2, c. 21.

[3] "Ubi enim thesaurus vester est, ibi et cor vestrum erit."—*Luke* xii. 34.

[4] *Med. vit. Chr.* c. 83.

her last farewell to her beloved Jesus and to the sepulchre, she left it, and returned to her own house. "This
Mother," says St. Bernard, "went away so afflicted and
sad, that she moved many to tears in spite of themselves;
and wherever she passed, all who met her wept,"[1] and
could not restrain their tears. And he adds that the
holy disciples and women who accompanied her
"mourned even more for her than for their Lord."[2]

St. Bonaventure says that her sisters covered her with
a mourning cloak: "The sisters of our Lady veiled her
as a widow, almost covering her whole face."[3] He also
says that, passing, on her return before the cross still
wet with the blood of her Jesus, she was the first to
adore it. "O holy cross," she then said, "I kiss thee, I
adore thee; for thou art no longer an infamous gibbet,
but a throne of love and an altar of mercy, consecrated
by the blood of the divine Lamb, which on thee has
been sacrificed for the salvation of the world."

She then left the cross, and returned home. When
there, the afflicted Mother cast her eyes around, and no
longer saw her Jesus; but, instead of the sweet presence
of her dear Son, the remembrance of his beautiful life
and cruel death presented itself before her eyes. She
remembered how she had pressed that Son to her bosom
in the crib of Bethlehem; the conversation she had
held with him during the many years they had dwelt
in the house of Nazareth; she remembered their mutual
affection, their loving looks, the words of eternal life
which fell from those divine lips; and then the sad scene
which she had that day witnessed again presented itself
before her. The nails, the thorns, the lacerated flesh of

---

[1] "Multos etiam invitos ad lacrymas provocabat. Omnes plorabant qui obviabant ei."—*De Lam. V. M.*

[2] "Super ipsam potius quam super Dominum plangebant."—*Ibid.*

[3] "Sorores Dominæ velaverunt eam tanquam viduam, cooperientes
quasi totum vultum."—*Med. vit. Chr.* c. 83.

her Son, those deep wounds, those uncovered bones, that open mouth, those dimmed eyes, all presented themselves before her. Ah, what a night of sorrow was that night for Mary! The afflicted Mother, turning to St. John, mournfully said: "Ah John, tell me where is thy Master?" She then asked the Magdalene: "Daughter, tell me, where is thy beloved? O God, who has taken him from us?" Mary wept, and all who were present wept with her.

And thou, my soul, weepest not! Ah, turn to Mary, and address her with St. Bonaventure, saying: "O my own sweet Lady, let me weep; thou art innocent, I am guilty."[1] Entreat her at least to let thee weep with her: "Grant that with thee I may weep."[2] She weeps for love; do thou weep through sorrow for thy sins. Thus weeping thou mayest have the happy lot of him of whom we read in the following example.

EXAMPLE.

Father Engelgrave relates[3] that a certain religious was so tormented with scruples, that he was sometimes almost driven to despair; but as he had the greatest devotion to Mary of Sorrows, he always had recourse to her in his interior agonies, and felt himself consoled whilst meditating on her dolors. Death came, and the devil then tormented him more than ever with scruples, and tempted him to despair. When, behold, the compassionate Mother seeing her poor son in such anguish, appeared to him, saying: "And thou, my son, why art thou so overcome with sorrow? why fearest thou so much? thou who hast so often consoled me by pitying me in

[1] " Sine, Domina mea, sine me flere; tu innocens es, ego sum peccator."—*Stim. Div. am.* p. 1, c. 3.

[2] " Fac ut tecum lugeam."

[3] *Lux Ev. dom. infra oct. Nat.*

my sorrows.[1] But now," she added, "Jesus sends me to console thee; be comforted, then; rejoice, and come with me to heaven." On hearing these consoling words, the devout religious, filled with joy and confidence, tranquilly expired.

Prayer.

My afflicted Mother, I will not leave thee alone to weep; no, I will accompany thee with my tears. This grace I now ask of thee: obtain that I may always bear in mind and always have a tender devotion towards the Passion of Jesus and thy sorrows, that the remainder of my days may thus be spent in weeping over thy sufferings, my own sweet Mother, and those of my Redeemer. These sorrows, I trust, will give me the confidence and strength that I shall require at the hour of death, that I may not despair at the sight of the many sins by which I have offended my Lord. They must obtain me pardon, perseverance, and heaven, where I hope to rejoice with thee, and to sing the infinite mercies of my God for all eternity. Thus do I hope; thus may it be. Amen. Amen.

Should any of my readers wish to practise the devotion of reciting the little Rosary of the Dolors of Mary, they will find it in Part V. I composed it many years ago, and now insert it for the convenience of all devout clients of Mary in Sorrow; to whom I beg that, as an act of charity, they will recommend me when they meditate on her Dolors.

[1] " Et tu, fili mi, cur mœrore conficeris, qui in mœrore meo me toties solatus es ?"

HYMNS.

I.

Words of Mary in Sorrow on Mount Calvary.

O vos omnes qui transitis per viam, attendite, et videte si est dolor sicut dolor meus.

"O all ye that pass by the way attend, and see if there be any sorrow like to my sorrow."—*Lam.* i. 12.

O ye who pass along the way
　All joyous, where with grief I pine,
In pity pause awhile, and say,
　Was ever sorrow like to mine?

See, hanging here before my eyes,
　This body, bloodless, bruis'd, and torn,—
Alas! it is my Son who dies,
　Of love deserving, not of scorn.

For know, this weak and dying man
　Is Son of Him who made the earth
And me, before the world began,
　He chose to give Him human birth.

He is my God! and since that night
　When first I saw His infant grace,
My soul has feasted on the light,
　The beauty of that heavenly face.

For He had chosen me to be
　The lov'd companion of His heart;
And ah! how that dear company
　With love transpierc'd me like a dart!

And now behold this loving Son
  Is dying in a woe so great,
The very stones are moved to moan
  In sorrow at His piteous state.

Where'er His failing eyes are bent,
  A friend to help he seeks in vain
All, all on vengeance are intent,
  And eager to increase His pain.

Eternal Father! God of love!
  Behold Thy Son! ah! see His woe!
Canst Thou look down from heaven above,
  And for Thy Son no pity show?

But, no—that Father sees His Son
  Cloth'd with the sins of guilty men;
And spares not that Belovèd One,
  Though dying on His cross of pain.

My Son! my Son! could I at least
  Console Thee in this hour of death,
Could I but lay Thee on my breast,
  And there receive Thy parting breath!

Alas! no comfort I impart;
  Nay, rather this my vain regret
But rends still more Thy loving heart,
  And makes Thy death more bitter yet.

Ah, loving souls! love, love that God
  Who all inflamed with love expires;
On you this life He has bestowed;
  Your love is all that He desires.

II.

The Same Subject.*

O YE who know love's conquering power.
Come, watch with me one dismal hour.
   My heart doth writhe with pain
   'Neath Calvary's crimson rain.
Oh, pity me, poor wilted flower.

I am the mother of the Crucified,
The Holy Spirit's anguished bride.
   My Son in woes all steeped,
   His sheaves of sorrow reaped,
The Jews in Pilate's hall deride.

Did ever burn a mother's love
As that lit by this heavenly Dove?
   But, oh, my breaking heart
   Did feel the piercing dart
Of anguish falling from above.

I saw Him clambering Calvary's steep,
With cross and crown of thorns pierced deep;
   All bound in galling chains,
   O'ercome by racking pains,
With feeble step.   I could not weep.

O ye with hearts of tender mould
Lament with me o'er hearts so cold.
   Three times He fell to earth,
   To Jews a source of mirth,
They scourged my Son by Judas sold.

They laid Him on his bed of pain,
His blood that cruel race did stain;
   They pierced his hands and feet,
   That Heart, with woes replete,
Which often on my breast had lain.

* By Father Mathew Testa.

Oh! how my heart was wrung to see
My dying Son on Calvary's tree!
  My soul I joined to His;
  To suffer then was bliss.
With Him to die, I was not free.

I lived, but felt the deathly smart
Of sorrowing love, a breaking heart.
  My murdered Son in pain
  Still, still, I see again,
Oh, love my Son and joy impart.

III.

Stabat Mater.*

Stabat Mater dolorosa	At the Cross her station keeping,
Juxta crucem lacrymosa,	Stood the mournful Mother weeping,
Dum pendebat Filius ;	Close to Jesus to the last :
Cujus animam gementem,	Through her heart his sorrow sharing,
Contristatam et dolentem,	All this bitter anguish bearing,
Pertransivit gladius.	Lo ! the piercing sword had passed.
O quam tristis et afflicta	Oh, how sad, and sore distressèd,
Fuit illa benedicta	Now was she, that Mother Blessèd
Mater Unigeniti !	Of the Sole-begotten One ;
Quæ mœrebat et dolebat,	Woe-begone, with heart's prostration,
Pia Mater, dum videbat	Mother meek, the bitter Passion
Nati pœnas inclyti !	Saw she of her glorious Son.

* In his works St. Alphonsus gives a translation of the *Stabat Mater* in Italian verse.

Quis est homo qui non fleret,	Who could mark, from tears refraining,
Matrem Christi si videret	Christ's dear Mother uncomplaining,
In tanto supplicio?	In so great a sorrow bowed?
Quis non posset contristari,	Who, unmoved, behold her anguish
Christi Matrem contemplari	Underneath His Cross of anguish,
Dolentem cum Filio?	'Mid the fierce unpitying crowd?
Pro peccatis suæ gentis,	For His people's sins rejected,
Vidit Jesum in tormentis	She her Jesus, unprotected,
Et flagellis subditum;	Saw with thorns, with scourges rent;
Vidit suum dulcem Natum,	Saw her Son from judgment taken,
Morientem, desolatum,	Her beloved in death forsaken,
Dum emisit spiritum!	Till His Spirit forth He sent.
Eia, Mater, Fons amoris!	Fount of love and holy sorrow,
Me sentire vim doloris	Mother! may my spirit borrow
Fac, ut tecum lugeam;	Somewhat of thy woe profound;
Fac, ut ardeat cor meum	Unto Christ with pure emotion,
In amando Christum Deum,	Raise my contrite heart's devotion,—
Ut sibi complaceam.	Love to read in every wound.
Sancta Mater! istud agas:	Those five wounds on Jesus smitten,
Crucifixi fige plagas	Mother! in my heart be written,
Cordi meo valide;	Deep as in thine own they be:
Tui Nati vulnerati,	Thou, my Saviour's Cross who bearest.

Tam dignati pro me pati,	Thou, thy Son's rebuke who sharest,
Pœnas mecum divide.	Let me share them both with thee!
Fac me tecum pie flere,	In the Passion of my Maker
Crucifixo condolere,	Be my sinful soul partaker,
Donec ego vixero ;	Weep till death, and weep with thee;
Juxta crucem tecum stare,	Mine with thee be that sad station,
Et me tibi sociare	There to watch the great salvation
In planctu desidero.	Wrought upon the atoning Tree.
Virgo Virginum præclara!	Virgin, thou of virgins fairest,
Mihi jam non sis amara :	May the bitter woe thou bearest
Fac me tecum plangere ;	Make on me impression deep;
Fac ut portem Christi mortem,	Thus Christ's dying may I carry,
Passionis fac consortem,	With Him in his Passion tarry,
Et plagas recolere.	And His wounds in memory keep.
Fac me plagis vulnerari,	May his wounds transfix me wholly,
Fac me cruce inebriari	May his Cross and Life-Blood holy
Et cruore Filii ;	Ebriate my heart and mind :
Flammis ne urar succensus,	Thus inflamed with pure affection,
Per te, Virgo, sim defensus In die judicii.	In the Virgin's Son protection May I at the judgment find.
Christe! cum sit hinc exire,	When in death my limbs are failing
Da per Matrem me venire	Let Thy Mother's prayer prevailing

Ad palmam victoriæ;	Lift me, Jesus! to T h y throne :
Quando corpus morietur,	To my parting soul be given
Fac, ut animæ donetur .	Entrance through the gate of heaven ;
Paradisi gloria.	There confess me for Thine own !

An indulgence of one hundred days was granted by Pope Innocent XI. to the faithful who say this hymn with devotion, in honor of the Mother of Sorrows. This indulgence was confirmed by Pope Pius IX., by a rescript, June 18, 1876 (*Raccolta*).

PART THE FOURTH.

The Virtues of the Most Blessed Virgin Mary.

SAINT AUGUSTINE says,[1] that to obtain with more certainty, and in greater abundance the favor of the saints, we must imitate them; for when they see us practise their virtues, they are more excited to pray for us. The Queen of Saints and our principal Advocate, Mary, has no sooner delivered a soul from Lucifer's grasp, and united it to God, than she desires that it should begin to imitate her, otherwise she cannot enrich it with the graces that she would wish, seeing it so opposed to her in conduct. Therefore Mary calls those blessed who with diligence imitate her life: *Now, therefore, children, hear me; blessed are they that keep my ways.*[2]

Whosoever loves, resembles the person loved, or endeavors to become like that person; according to the well-known proverb, "Love either finds or makes its like."[3] Hence St. Sophronius exhorts us to endeavor to imitate Mary, if we love her, because this is the greatest act of homage that we can offer her; "My beloved children," the saint says, "serve Mary, whom you love; for you then truly love her, if you endeavor to imitate her

------

[1] S. 225, E. B. app.

[2] "Nunc ergo, filii, audite me: beati qui custodiunt vias meas."— *Prov.* viii. 32.

[3] "Amor aut pares invenit aut facit."

whom you love." [1] Richard of St. Laurence says " that those are and can call themselves true children of Mary, who strive to imitate her life." [2] " Let the child, then," concludes St. Bernard, " endeavor to imitate his Mother, if he desires her favor; for Mary seeing herself treated as a Mother, will treat him as her child." [3]

Although there is little recorded in the Gospels of Mary's virtues in detail, yet when we learn from them that she was full of grace, this alone gives us to understand that she possessed all virtues in a heroic degree. " So much so," says St. Thomas, " that whereas other saints excelled, each in some particular virtue,—the one in chastity, another in humility, another in mercy,—the Blessed Virgin excelled in all, and is given as a model of all." [4] St. Ambrose says, " Mary was such, that her life alone was a model for all." [5] And then he concludes in the following words: " Let the virginity and life of Mary be to you as a faithful image, in which the form of virtue is resplendent. Thence learn how to live, what to correct, what to avoid, and what to retain." [6] Humility being the foundation of all virtues, as the holy Fathers teach, let us in the first place consider how great was the humility of the Mother of God.

---

[1] " Colite quam amatis; quia tunc eam vere amatis, si imitari velitis quam laudatis."—*De Assumpt.*

[2] " Filii Mariæ, imitatores ejus."—*De Laud. B. M.* l. 2, p. 5.

[3] *In Salve Reg.* s. 1.

[4] " Alii Sancti specialia opera exercuerunt: alius fuit humilis, alius castus, alius misericors; sed Beata Virgo datur in exemplum omnium virtutum."—*Expos. in Sal. Ang.*

[5] " Talis fuit Maria, ut ejus unius vita omnium sit disciplina."— *De Virginib.* l. 2.

[6] " Sit vobis tamquam in imagine descripta, virginitas vitaque Mariæ, de qua refulgeat forma virtutis. Hinc sumatis exempla vivendi, . . quid corrigere, quid effugere, quid tenere debeatis."—*Ibid*

I.

The Humility of Mary.

"Humility," says St. Bernard, ' is the foundation and guardian of virtues;[1]" and with reason, for without it no other virtue can exist in a soul. Should she possess all virtues, all will depart when humility is gone. But, on the other hand, as St. Francis de Sales wrote to St. Jane Frances de Chantal, "God so loves humility, that whenever he sees it, he is immediately drawn thither." This beautiful and so necessary virtue was unknown in the world; but the Son of God himself came on earth to teach it by his own example, and willed that in that virtue in particular we should endeavor to imitate him: *Learn of me, because I am meek and humble of heart.*[2] Mary, being the first and most perfect disciple of Jesus Christ in the practice of all virtues, was the first also in that of humility, and by it merited to be exalted above all creatures. It was revealed to St. Matilda that the first virtue in which the Blessed Mother particularly exercised herself, from her very childhood, was that of humility.[3]

The first effect of humility of heart is a lowly opinion of ourselves: "Mary had always so humble an opinion of herself, that, as it was revealed to the same St. Matilda, although she saw herself enriched with greater graces than all other creatures, she never preferred herself to any one."[4] The Abbot Rupert, explaining the passage of the sacred Canticles, *Thou hast wounded my*

---

[1] "Humilitas est fundamentum custosque virtutum."—*In Nat. D.* s. 1.

[2] "Discite a me, quia mitis sum et humilis corde."—*Matt.* xi. 29.

[3] "Respondit: Humilitas, obedientia, et amor."—*Spir. Grat.* l. 1, c. 52.

[4] "Ab infantia enim, tantæ humilitatis fui, quod nunquam me creaturæ prætuli."

heart, my sister, my spouse, . . . with one hair of thy neck,[1] says, that the humble opinion which Mary had of herself was precisely that hair of the Spouse's neck with which she wounded the heart of God.[2] Not indeed that Mary considered herself a sinner: for humility is truth, as St. Teresa remarks : and Mary knew that she had never offended God: nor was it that she did not acknowledge that she had received greater graces from God than all other creatures; for an humble heart always acknowledges the special favors of the Lord, to humble herself the more: but the divine Mother, by the greater light wherewith she knew the infinite greatness and goodness of God, also knew her own nothingness, and therefore, more than all others, humbled herself, saying with the sacred Spouse: *Do not consider that I am brown, because the sun hath altered my color.*[3] That is, as St. Bernard explains it, " When I approach him, I find myself black."[4] Yes, says St. Bernardine, for " the Blessed Virgin had always the majesty of God, and her own nothingness, present to her mind."[5] As a beggar, when clothed with a rich garment, which has been bestowed upon her, does not pride herself on it in the presence of the giver, but is rather humbled, being reminded thereby of her own poverty; so also the more Mary saw herself enriched, the more did she humble herself, remembering that all was God's gift ; whence she herself told St. Elizabeth of Hungary, that " she might rest assured that she looked upon herself as most vile and unworthy

[1] " Vulnerasti cor meum, Soror mea, Sponsa, . . . in uno crine colli tui."—*Cant.* iv. 9.

[2] " In uno crine colli tui, id est, in nimia humilitate cordis tui. Iste est crinis colli, humilis cogitatus."—*In Cant.* s. 28.

[3] " Nolite me considerare quod fusca sim, quia decoloravit me sol." —*Cant.* i. 5.

[4] " Appropinquans illi, ex eo me nigram invenio."—*In Cant.* s. 28.

[5] " Virgo continue habebat actualem relationem ad Divinam Majestatem et ad suam nihilitatem."—*Pro Fest. V. M.* s. 4, a. 3, c. 2.

of God's grace." [1] Therefore St. Bernardine says, that "after the Son of God, no creature in the world was so exalted as Mary, because no creature in the world ever humbled itself so much as she did." [2]

Moreover, it is an act of humility to conceal heavenly gifts. Mary wished to conceal from St. Joseph the great favor whereby she had become the Mother of God, although it seemed necessary to make it known to him, if only to remove from the mind of her poor spouse any suspicions as to her virtue, which he might have entertained on seeing her pregnant : or at least the perplexity in which it indeed threw him: for St. Joseph, on the one hand unwilling to doubt Mary's chastity, and on the other ignorant of the mystery, *was minded to put her away privately.* [3] This he would have done, had not the angel revealed to him that his Spouse was pregnant by the operation of the Holy Ghost.

Again, a soul that is truly humble refuses her own praise ; and should praises be bestowed on her, she refers them all to God. Behold, Mary is disturbed at hearing herself praised by St. Gabriel ; and when St. Elizabeth said, *Blessed art thou among women . . . and whence is this to me, that the Mother of my Lord should come to me ? . . . blessed art thou that hast believed,* [4] Mary referred all to God, and answered in that humble Canticle, *My soul doth magnify the Lord,* [5] as if she had said :

---

[1] " Pro firmo scias, quod me reputabam vilissimam, et gratia Dei indignam."—*Apud S. Bonav. Med. v. Chr.* c. 3.

[2] "Sicut nulla post Filium Dei creatura tantum ascendit in gratiæ dignitatem, sic nec tantum descendit in abyssum humilitatis."—*Pro Fest. V. M.* s. 4, a. 1, c. 3.

[3] "Voluit occulte dimittere eam."—*Matt.* i. 19.

[4] "Benedicta tu inter mulieres . . . Et unde hoc mihi, ut veniat Mater Domini mei ad me ? . . . Beata quæ credidisti."—*Luke*, i. 42.

[5] "Magnificat anima mea Dominum, et exsultavit spiritus meus in Deo salutari meo; quia respexit humilitatem ancillæ suæ."—*Ibid*. 46, 47.

7

" Thou dost praise me, Elizabeth; but I praise the Lord, to whom alone honor is due: thou wonderest that I should come to thee, and I wonder at the divine goodness in which alone my spirit exults :" *and my spirit hath rejoiced in God my Saviour.* Thou praisest me because I have believed ; I praise my God, because he hath been pleased to exalt my nothingness : *because He hath regarded the humility of His handmaid.* Hence Mary said to St. Bridget: " I humbled myself so much, and thereby merited so great a grace, because I thought, and knew, that of myself I possessed nothing. For this same reason I did not desire to be praised; I only desired that praises should be given to the Creator and Giver of all." [1] Wherefore an ancient author, speaking of the humility of Mary, says: " O truly blessed humility, which hath given God to men, opened heaven, and delivered souls from hell." [2]

It is also a part of humility to serve others. Mary did not refuse to go and serve Elizabeth for three months. Hence St. Bernard says, " Elizabeth wondered that Mary should have come to visit her ; but that which is still more admirable is, that she came not to be ministered to, but to minister." [3]

Those who are humble are retiring, and choose the last places ; and therefore Mary, remarks St. Bernard, when her Son was preaching in a house, as it is related by St. Matthew,[4] wishing to speak to him, would not of her own accord enter, but " remained outside, and did not avail herself of her maternal authority to interrupt

[1] " Ut quid enim ego me tantum humiliabam, aut unde promerui tantam gratiam, nisi quia cogitavi, et scivi, me nihil a me esse vel habere ? Ideo nolui laudem meam, sed solius Datoris et Creatoris." —*Rev.* l. 2, c. 23.

[2] " O vere beata humilitas, quæ Deum hominibus peperit, paradisum aperuit, et animas ab inferis liberavit !"—*S.* 208, *E. B. app.*

[3] " Venisse Mariam mirabatur Elisabeth: sed magis miretur, quod ipsa non ministrari venerit, sed ministrare."—*De Aquæd.*

[4] *Matt.* xii. 46.

him." [1]   For the same reason also when she was with the Apostles awaiting the coming of the Holy Ghost, she took the lowest place, as St. Luke relates, *All these were persevering with one mind in prayer, with the women, and Mary, the Mother of Jesus.* [2]   Not that St. Luke was ignorant of the divine Mother's merits, on account of which he should have named her in the first place, but because she had taken the last place amongst the Apostles and women; and therefore he described them all, as an author remarks, in the order in which they were. Hence St. Bernard says, "Justly has the last become the first, who being the first of all became the last." [3]

In fine, those who are humble, love to be contemned; therefore, we do not read that Mary showed herself in Jerusalem on Palm Sunday, when her Son was received by the people with so much honor: but on the other hand, at the death of her Son she did not shrink from appearing on Calvary, through fear of the dishonor which would accrue to her when it was known that she was the Mother of him who was condemned to die an infamous death as a criminal. Therefore she said to St. Bridget, "What is more humbling than to be called a fool, to be in want of all things, and to believe one's self the most unworthy of all ? Such, O daughter, was my humility ; this was my joy ; this was all my desire with which I thought how to please my Son alone." [4]

The Venerable Sister Paula of Foligno was given to

[1] " Foris stabat, nec materna auctoritate aut sermonem interrupit, aut habitationem irrupit in qua Filius loquebatur."—*In Sign. Magn.*

[2] " Hi omnes erant perseverantes unanimiter in oratione cum mulieribus et Maria, Matre Jesu."—*Acts*, i. 14.

[3] " Merito facta est novissima prima, quæ, cum prima esset omnium, sese novissimam faciebat."—*In Sign. Magn.*

[4] "Quid contemptibilius, quam vocari fatua, omnibus indigere, omnibus se credere indigniorem ? Talis, O filia, erat humilitas mea, hoc gaudium meum, hæc voluntas tota, quæ nulli nisi Filio meo placere cogitabam."—*Rev.* l 2, c. 23.

understand in an ecstasy how great was the humility of our Blessed Lady; and giving an account of it to her confessor, she was so filled with astonishment at its greatness that she could only exclaim, "O the humility of the Blessed Virgin ! O Father, the humility of the Blessed Virgin, how great was the humility of the Blessed Virgin ! In the world there is no such thing as humility, not even in its lowest degree, when you see the humility of Mary." On another occasion, our Lord showed St. Bridget two ladies. The one was all pomp and vanity. "She," he said, "is pride; but the other one whom thou seest with her head bent down, courteous towards all, having God alone in her mind, and considering herself as no one, is Humility, her name is Mary."[1] Hereby God was pleased to make known to us that the humility of his blessed Mother was such that she was humility itself.

There can be no doubt, as St. Gregory of Nyssa remarks,[2] that of all virtues there is perhaps none the practice of which is more difficult to our nature, corrupted as it is by sin, than that of humility. But there is no escape; we can never be true children of Mary if we are not humble. "If," says St. Bernard, "thou canst not imitate the virginity of this humble Virgin, imitate her humility."[3] She detests the proud, and invites only the humble to come to her: *Whosoever is a little one, let him come to me.*[4] "Mary," says Richard of St. Laurence, "protects us under the mantle of humility."[5] The Mother of God herself explained to St. Bridget what her mantle was, saying, "Come, my daughter, and hide

---

[1] *Rev.* l. 1, c. 29.

[2] *De Beatit. Hom.* 1.

[3] "Si non potes virginitatem humilis, imitare humilitatem virginis."—*De Laud. V. M. hom.* 1.

[4] "Si quis est parvulus, veniat ad me."—*Prov.* ix. 4.

[5] "Maria protegit nos . . . sub pallio humilitatis."—*De Laud. B. M.* l. 2, p. 1.

thyself under my mantle; this mantle is my humility."[1]
She then added that the consideration of her humility
was a good mantle with which we could warm ourselves;
but that as a mantle only renders this service to those
who wear it, not in thought but in deed, "so also would
her humility be of no avail except to those who endeavored to imitate it." She then concluded in these
words: "Therefore, my daughter, clothe thyself with
this humility."[2]

"O, how dear are humble souls to Mary!" says St.
Bernard; "this Blessed Virgin recognizes and loves
those who love her, and is near to all who call
upon her; and especially to those whom she sees like
unto herself in chastity and humility."[3] Hence the
saint exhorts all who love Mary to be humble: "Emul-
ate this virtue of Mary, if thou lovest her."[4] Marinus,
or Martin d'Alberto, of the Society of Jesus, used to
sweep the house, and collect the filth, through love for
this Blessed Virgin. The divine Mother one day appeared to him, as Father Nieremberg relates in his life,
and thanking him, as it were, said, "O, how pleasing
to me is this humble action done for my love!"

Then, O my queen, I can never be really thy child unless I am humble; but dost thou not see that my sins,
after having rendered me ungrateful to my Lord, have
also made me proud? O my Mother, do thou supply a
remedy. By the merit of thy humility obtain that I may
be truly humble, and thus become thy child. Amen.

---

[1] "Ergo tu, filia mea, veni, et absconde te sub mantello meo; hic
mantellus humilitas mea est."—*Rev.* l. 2, c. 23.

[2] "Nec humilitas mea proficit, nisi unusquisque studuerit eam imitari; ergo, filia mea, indue te hac humilitate."—*Ibid.*

[3] "Agnoscit Virgo et diligit diligentes se, et prope est invocantibus
se: præsertim quos videt sibi conformes factos in castitate et humilitate."—*In Salve Reg.* s. 1.

[4] "Æmulamini hanc virtutem, si Mariam diligitis."—*In Sign. Magn*

II.

Mary's Charity towards God.

St. Anselm says that "wherever there is the greatest purity, there is also the greatest charity."[1] The more a heart is pure, and empty of itself, the greater is the fulness of its love towards God. The most holy Mary, because she was all humility, and had nothing of self in her, was filled with divine love, so that "her love towards God surpassed that of all men and angels,"[2] as St. Bernardine writes. Therefore St. Francis de Sales with reason called her "the Queen of love."

God has indeed given men the precept to love him with their whole heart, *Thou shalt love the Lord thy God with thy whole heart;*[3] but, as St. Thomas declares, "this commandment will be fully and perfectly fulfilled by men only in heaven, and not on earth, where it is only fulfilled imperfectly."[4] On this subject, Blessed Albert the Great remarks, that, in a certain sense, it would have been unbecoming had God given a precept that was never to have been perfectly fulfilled. But this would have been the case had not the divine Mother perfectly fulfilled it. The saint says, "Either some one fulfilled this precept, or no one; if any one, it must have been the most Blessed Virgin."[5] Richard of St. Victor confirms this opinion, saying, "The Mother of our Emmanuel practised virtues in their very highest perfection. Who has ever fulfilled as she did that first com-

[1] "Ubi major puritas, ibi major charitas."—*Super Miss.* q. 46.

[2] "Superat . . . omnium creaturarum amores in Filium suum."—*Pro Fest. V. M.* s. 1, a. 1, c. 2.

[3] "Diliges Dominum Deum tuum ex toto corde tuo."—*Matt.* xxii. 37.

[4] "Plene et perfecte in patria implebitur hoc præceptum; in via autem impletur, sed imperfecte."—2. 2, q. 44, a. 6.

[5] "Aut aliquis implet hoc præceptum, aut nullus; si aliquis, ergo Beatissima Virgo."—*Super Miss.* q. 135.

mandment, *Thou shalt love the Lord thy God with thy whole heart?* [1] In her divine love was so ardent that no defect of any kind could have access to her." "Divine love," says St. Bernard, "so penetrated and filled the soul of Mary, that no part of her was left untouched; so that she loved with her whole heart, with her whole soul, with her whole strength, and was full of grace." [2] Therefore Mary could well say, My Beloved has given himself all to me, and I have given myself all to him: *My Beloved to me, and I to Him.* [3] "Ah! well might even the Seraphim," says Richard, "have descended from heaven to learn, in the heart of Mary, how to love God." [4]

God, who is love, [5] came on earth to enkindle in the hearts of all the flame of his divine love; but in no heart did he enkindle so much as in that of his Mother; for her heart was entirely pure from all earthly affections, and fully prepared to burn with this blessed flame. Thus St. Sophronius says that "divine love so inflamed her, that nothing earthly could enter her affections; she was always burning with this heavenly flame, and, so to say, inebriated with it." [6] Hence the heart of Mary be-

---

[1] "Emmanuelis nostri Puerpera, in omni fuit virtutum consummatione perfecta. Quis illud primum mandatum sic unquam implevit: 'Diliges Dominum Deum tuum ex toto corde tuo?' Divinus amor in ea adeo convaluit, ut qualiscunque defectus in eam incidere non posset."—*De Emman.* l. 2, c. 29, 30.

[2] "Amor Christi Mariæ animam non modo transfixit, sed etiam pertransivit, ut nullam particulam vacuam amore relinqueret, sed toto corde, tota anima, tota virtute diligeret, et esset gratia plena."—*In Cant.* s. 29.

[3] "Dilectus meus mihi, et ego illi."—*Cant.* ii. 16.

[4] "Seraphim de cœlo descendere poterant, ut amorem discerent in corde Virginis."

[5] "Deus charitas est."—1 *John,* iv. 8.

[6] "Totam incenderat divinus amor, ita ut in ea nihil esset mundanum, quod ejus violaret affectus, sed ardor continuus, et ebrietas perfusi amoris."—*De Assumpt.*

came all fire and flames, as we read of her in the sacred Canticles: *The lamps thereof are fire and flame;*[1] fire burning within through love, as St. Anselm explains it;[2] and flames shining without by the example she gave to all in the practice of virtues. When Mary, then, was in this world, and bore Jesus in her arms, she could well be called, "fire carrying fire;" and with far more reason than a woman spoken of by Hippocrates, who was thus called because she carried fire in her hand. Yes, for St. Ildephonsus said, that "the Holy Ghost heated, inflamed, and melted Mary with love, as fire does iron; so that the flame of this Holy Spirit was seen, and nothing was felt but the fire of the love of God."[3] St. Thomas of Villanova says,[4] that the bush seen by Moses,[5] which burnt without being consumed, was a real symbol of Mary's heart. Therefore with reason, says St. Bernard, was she seen by St. John clothed with the sun: *and there appeared a great wonder in heaven, a woman clothed with the sun;*[6] "for," continues the saint, "she was so closely united to God by love, and penetrated so deeply the abyss of divine wisdom, that, without a personal union with God, it would seem impossible for a creature to have a closer union with him."[7]

[1] "Lampades ejus, lampades ignis atque flammarum."—*Cant.* viii. 6.

[2] *Ap. Corn. à Lap.*

[3] "Mariam, velut ignis ferrum, Spiritus Sanctus totam ignivit; ita ut in ea Spiritus Sancti flamma tantum videatur, nec sentiatur nisi tantum ignis amoris Dei."—*De Ass.* s. 1.

[4] *In Nat. D. conc.* 2.

[5] *Exod.* iii. 2.

[6] "Signum magnum apparuit in cœlo: mulier amicta Sole."—*Apoc.* xii. 1.

[7] "Jure ergo Maria Sole perhibetur amicta, quæ divinæ sapientiæ, ultra quam credi valeat, penetravit abyssum; ut, quantum sine personali unione creaturæ conditio patitur, luci illi inaccessibili videatur immersa."—*In Sign. Magn.*

Hence St. Bernardine of Sienna asserts that the most holy Virgin was never tempted by hell; for, he says: "As flies are driven away by a great fire, so were the evil spirits driven away by her ardent love; so much so, that they did not even dare approach her." [1] Richard of St. Victor also says, that "the Blessed Virgin was terrible to the princes of darkness, so that they did not presume to tempt or approach her; for the fire of her charity deterred them." [2] Mary herself revealed to St. Bridget, that in this world she never had any thought, desire, or joy, but in and for God: "I thought," she said, "of nothing but God, nothing pleased me but God;" [3] so that her blessed soul being in the almost continual contemplation of God whilst on earth, the acts of love which she formed were innumerable, as Father. Suarez writes: "The acts of perfect charity formed by the Blessed Virgin in this life were without number; for nearly the whole of her life was spent in contemplation, and in that state she constantly repeated acts of love." [4] But a remark of Bernardine de Bustis pleases me still more: he says that Mary did not so much repeat acts of love as other saints do, but that her whole life was one continued act of it; for, by a special privilege, she always actually loved God. [5] As a royal eagle, she always kept

[1] "Sicut magnus ignis effugat muscas, sic a sua inflammata charitate dæmones pellebantur, in tantum quod non erant ausi illi appropinquare."—*Pro Fest. V. M.* s. 4, a. 3, c. 2.

[2] "Virgo principibus tenebrarum terribilis fuit, ut ad eam accedere, eamque tentare non præsumpserint; deterrebat eos flamma charitatis"—*In Cant.* c. 26.

[3] "Nihil nisi Deum cogitabam; nulla mihi, nisi Deus, placuerunt."—*Rev.* l. 1, c. 10.

[4] "Actus perfectæ charitatis, quos B. Virgo habuit in hac vita, innumerabiles fuerunt, quia fere totam vitam in contemplatione transegit, in qua hunc amoris actum frequentissime repetebat."—*De Inc.* p. 2, d. 18, s. 4.

[5] "Tamen ipsa gloriosissima Virgo de privilegio singulari continue et semper Deum amabat actualiter."—*Marial.* p. 2, s. 5.

her eyes fixed on the divine Sun of Justice: "that," as St. Peter Damian says, "the duties of active life did not prevent her from loving, and love did not prevent her from attending to those duties." [1] Therefore St. Germanus says, that the altar of propitiation, on which the fire was never extinguished day or night, was a type of Mary. [2]

Nor was sleep an obstacle to Mary's love for God; since, as St. Augustine asserts, "the dreams, when sleeping, of our first parents, in their state of innocence, were as happy as their lives when waking;" [3] and if such a privilege were granted them, it certainly cannot be denied that it was also granted to the divine Mother, as Suarez, the Abbot Rupert, and St. Bernardine fully admit. St. Ambrose is also of this opinion; for speaking of Mary, he says, "while her body rested, her soul watched," [4] verifying in herself the words of the wise man: *Her lamp shall not be put out in the night.* [5] Yes, for while her blessed body took its necessary repose in gentle sleep, "her soul," says St. Bernardine, "freely tended towards God; so much so, that she was then wrapped in more perfect contemplation than any other person ever was when awake." [6] Therefore could she well say with the Spouse in the Canticles, *I weep, and my heart watcheth.* [7] "As happy in sleep as awaking," [8] as Suarez says. In

[1] "Adeo ut nec actio contemplationem minueret, et contemplatio non desereret actionem."—*In Nat. B. V.* s. 1.

[2] *In Annunt.*

[3] "Tam felicia erant somnia dormientium, quam vita vigilantium."—*In Jul.* l. 5, c. 10.

[4] "Cum quiesceret corpus, vigilaret animus."—*De Virg.* l. 2.

[5] "Non extinguetur in nocte lucerna ejus."—*Prov.* xxxi. 18.

[6] "Anima sua libere tunc tendebat in Deum. Unde illo tempore erat perfectior contemplatrix, quam unquam fuit alius dum vigilavit."—*Pro Fest. V. M.* s. 4, a. 1, c. 2.

[7] "Ego dormio, et cor meum vigilat."—*Cant.* v. 2.

[8] "Tam felix dormiendo, quam vigilando."—*De Inc.* p. 2, d. 18, s. 2.

fine, St. Bernardine asserts, that as long as Mary lived
in this world she was continually loving God: "The
mind of the Blessed Virgin was always wrapped in the
ardor of love."[1] The saint moreover adds, "that she
never did anything that the divine Wisdom did not
show her to be pleasing to him; and that she loved God
as much as she thought he was to be loved by her."[2]

Indeed, according to Blessed Albert the Great, we can
well say that Mary was filled with so great charity, that
greater was not possible in any pure creature on earth.[3]
Hence St. Thomas of Villanova affirms, that by her ardent charity the Blessed Virgin became so beautiful, and
so enamoured of her God, that, captivated as it were by
her love, he descended into her womb and became man.[4]
Wherefore St. Bernardine exclaims, "Behold the power
of the Virgin Mother: she wounded and took captive
the heart of God."[5]

But since Mary loves God so much, there can be nothing that she so much requires of her clients as that they
also should love him to their utmost. This precisely
she one day told Blessed Angela of Foligno after Communion, saying, "Angela, be thou blessed by my Son,
and endeavor to love him as much as thou canst."[6]

---

[1] "Mens Virginis in ardore dilectionis continue tenebatur."—*Loco
cit.* a. 3, c. 2.

[2] "Nihil unquam elicere voluit nisi quod Dei sapientia præmon-
strabat; tantumque Deum dilexit, quantum a se diligendum illum
existimabat.—*Ibid.* a. 1, c. 3.

[3] "Credimus etiam, sine præjudicio melioris sententiæ, Beatam
Virginem in conceptione Filii Dei, charitatem talem et tantam acce-
pisse, qualis et quanta percipi poterat a pura creatura in statu viæ."
—*Super Miss. resp. ad* q. 61, §.2.

[4] "Hæc Virgo suâ pulchritudine Deum a cœlis allexit; amore illius
captus est, humanitatis nostræ nexibus irretitus."—*In Nat. D. conc.* 4.

[5] "O virtus Virginis Matris! una puella vulneravit et rapuit divinum cor."—*Pro Fest. V. M.* s. 5, c. 4.

[6] *Boll.* 4 *Jan. Vit.* c. 7.

She also said to St. Bridget, " Daughter, if thou desirest to bind me to thee, love my Son." [1] Mary desires nothing more than to see her beloved, who is God, loved. Novarinus asks why the Blessed Virgin, with the Spouse in the Canticles, begged the angels to make the great love she bore him known to our Lord, saying, *I adjure you, O daughters of Jerusalem, if you find my beloved, that you tell Him that I languish with love.* [2] Did not God know how much she loved him ? " Why did she seek to show the wound to her Beloved, since he it was who had inflicted it ?" The same author answers, that the divine Mother thereby wished to make her love known to us, not to God; that as she was herself wounded, so might she also be enabled to wound us with divine love. [3] And " because Mary was all on fire with the love of God, all who love and approach her are inflamed by her with this same love; for she renders them like unto herself." [4] For this reason St. Catharine of Sienna called Mary " the bearer of fire," [5] the bearer of the flames of divine love. If we also desire to burn with these blessed flames, let us endeavor always to draw nearer to our Mother by our prayers and the affections of our souls.

Ah, Mary, thou Queen of love, of all creatures the most amiable, the most beloved, and the most loving, as St. Francis de Sales addressed thee,—my own sweet Mother, thou wast always and in all things inflamed with love towards God; deign, then, to bestow at least a spark of it on me. Thou didst pray thy Son for the spouses whose wine had failed : *They have no wine.* [6] And

[1] " Si vis me tecum devincire, ama Filium meum."

[2] " Adjuro vos, filiæ Jerusalem, si inveneritis Dilectum meum, ut nuntietis ei quia amore langueo."—*Cant.* v. 8.

[3] " Ut vulnerata vulneraret."—*Umbra Virg.* exc. 28.

[4] " Quia tota ardens fuit, omnes se amantes, eamque tangentes incendit."—*De B. V. M.* s. 1.

[5] " Portatrix ignis."—*Or. in Annunt.*

[6] *John,* ii. 3.

wilt thou not pray for us, in whom the love of God, whom we are under such obligations to love, is wanting? Say also, "They have no love," and obtain us this love. This is the only grace for which we ask. O Mother, by the love thou bearest to Jesus, graciously hear and pray for us. Amen.

III.

Mary's Charity towards her Neighbor.

Love towards God and love towards our neighbor are commanded by the same precept: *And this commandment we have from God, that he who loveth God love also his brother.*[1] St. Thomas[2] says that the reason for this is, that he who loves God loves all that God loves. St. Catharine of Genoa one day said, "Lord, Thou willest that I should love my neighbor, and I can love none but Thee." God answered her in these words: "All who love me love what I love."[3] But as there never was, and never will be, any one who loved God as much as Mary loved him, so there never was, and never will be, any one who loved her neighbor as much as she did.

Father Cornelius à Lapide, on these words of the Canticles, *King Solomon hath made him a litter of the wood of Libanus . . . the midst he covered with charity for the daughters of Jerusalem,*[4] says, that "this litter was Mary's womb, in which the Incarnate Word dwelt, filling it with charity for the daughters of Jerusalem; for Christ, who is love itself, inspired the Blessed Virgin with charity in its

---

[1] "Hoc mandatum habemus a Deo, ut, qui diligit Deum, diligat et fratrem suum."—1 *John*, iv. 21.

[2] 2. 2, q. 25, a. 1.

[3] *Boll.* 15 *Sept. Vit.* c. 4.

[4] "Ferculum fecit sibi rex Salomon; media charitate constravit propter filias Jerusalem."—*Cant.* iii. 9.

highest degree, that she might succor all who had recourse to her." [1]

So great was Mary's charity when on earth, that she succored the needy without even being asked; as was the case at the marriage-feast of Cana, when she told her Son that family's distress, *They have no wine,*[2] and asked him to work a miracle. O, with what speed did she fly when there was question of relieving her neighbor! When she went to the house of Elizabeth to fulfil an office of charity, *she went into the hill-country with haste.*[3] She could not, however, more fully display the greatness of her charity than she did in the offering which she made of her Son to death for our salvation. On this subject St. Bonaventure says, "Mary so loved the world as to give her only-begotten Son." [4] Hence St. Anselm exclaims, "O blessed amongst women, thy purity surpasses that of the angels, and thy compassion that of the saints!" [5] "Nor has this love of Mary for us," says St. Bonaventure, "diminished now that she is in heaven, but it has increased; for now she better sees the miseries of men." And therefore the saint goes on to say: "Great was the mercy of Mary towards the wretched when she was still in exile on earth; but far greater is it now that she reigns in heaven." [6] St. Agnes assured St. Bridget that "there was no one who prayed without receiving

---

[1] "Beatæ Virginis sinus fuit ferculum ferens Verbum; ideoque media charitate constratum propter filias Jerusalem, quia Christus, qui est ipsa Charitas, maximam charitatem B. Virgini aspiravit, ut ipsa ad illam recurrentibus opem ferret."—*In Cant.* c. 3.

[2] "Vinum non habent."—*John*, ii. 3.

[3] "Abiit in montana cum festinatione."—*Luke*, i. 39.

[4] "Sic Maria dilexit mundum, ut Filium suum unigenitum daret !"

[5] "O Benedicta super mulieres, quæ angelos vincis puritate et sanctos superas pietate."—*Orat.* 49.

[6] "Magna erga miseros fuit misericordia Mariæ adhuc exsulantis in mundo, sed multo major est regnantis in cœlo; quia magis nunc videt hominum miseriam."—*Spec. B. M. V. lect.* 10.

grace through the charity of the Blessed Virgin." [1] Unfortunate, indeed, should we be, did not Mary intercede for us! Jesus himself, addressing the same saint, said "Were it not for the prayers of my Mother, there would be no hope of mercy." [2]

Blessed is he, says the divine Mother, who listens to my instructions, pays attention to my charity, and, in imitation of me, exercises it himself towards others: *Blessed is the man that heareth me, and that watcheth daily at my gates, and waiteth at the posts of my doors.* [3] St. Gregory Nazianzen assures us that "there is nothing by which we can with greater certainty gain the affection of Mary than by charity towards our neighbor." [4] Therefore, as God exhorts us, saying, *Be ye merciful, as your Father also is merciful,* [5] so also does Mary seem to say to all her children, "Be ye merciful, as your Mother also is merciful." It is certain that our charity towards our neighbor will be the measure of that which God and Mary will show us: *Give, and it shall be given to you. For with the same measure that you shall mete withal, it shall be measured to you again.* [6] St. Methodius used to say, "Give to the poor, and receive paradise." [7] For the apostle writes, that charity towards our neighbor renders us happy both in this world and in the next: *But piety is profitable to all*

[1] "Ex dulcedine Mariæ, nullus est, qui non per eam si petit, sentiat pietatem."—*Rev.* l. 3, c. 30.

[2] "Nisi preces Matris meæ intervenirent, non esset spes misericordiæ."—*Ibid.* l. 6, c. 26.

[3] "Beatus homo qui audit me, et qui vigilat ad fores meas quotidie, et observat ad postes ostii mei."—*Prov.* viii. 34.

[4] "Nulla res est, quæ Virginis benevolentiam conciliat ac misericordia."

[5] "Estote misericordes, sicut et Pater vester misericors est."—*Luke.* vi. 36.

"Date, et dabitur vobis . . .; eadem quippe mensura qua mensi fueritis, remetietur vobis."—*Ibid.* 38.

[7] "Da pauperi, et accipe paradisum."

things, having promise of the life that now. is, and of that which is to come.[1] St. John Chrysostom, on these words of Proverbs, *He that hath mercy on the poor lendeth to the Lord,*[2] makes a remark to the same effect, saying, " He who assists the needy makes God his debtor."[3]

O Mother of Mercy, thou art full of charity for all; forget not my miseries; thou seest them full well. Recommend me to God, who denies thee nothing. Obtain for me the grace to imitate thee in holy charity, as well towards God as towards my neighbor. Amen.

IV.

Mary's Faith.

As the Blessed Virgin is the mother of holy love and hope, so also is she the mother of faith: *I am the mother of fair love, and of fear, and of knowledge, and of holy hope.*[4] And with reason is she so, says St. Ireneus; for "the evil done by Eve's incredulity was remedied by Mary's faith."[5] This is confirmed by Tertullian, who says that because Eve, contrary to the assurance she had received from God, believed the serpent, she brought death into the world; but our Queen, because she believed the angel when he said that she, remaining a virgin, would become the mother of God, brought salvation into the world.[6] For St. Augustine says, that "when Mary con-

---

[1] " Pietas autem ad omnia utilis est, promissionem habens vitæ, quæ nunc est, et futuræ."—1 *Tim.* iv. 8.

[2] " Fœneratur Domino qui misceretur pauperis."—*Prov.* xix. 17.

[3] " Si Deo fœneramur, is ergo nobis debitor est."—*De Pœnit. hom.* 5.

[4] " Ego Mater pulchræ dilectionis, et timoris, et agnitionis, et sanctæ spei."—*Ecclus.* xxiv. 24.

[5] " Quod Eva ligavit per incredulitatem, Maria solvit per fidem."—*Adv. Hæres.* l. 3, c. 33.

[6] " Crediderat Eva serpenti, Maria Gabrieli: quod illa credendo deliquit, hæc credendo delevit."—*De Carne Chr.*

sented to the Incarnation of the Eternal Word, by means of her faith she opened heaven to men." [1]   Richard, on the words of St. Paul, *for the unbelieving husband is sancti-fied by the believing wife,* [2] also says, that " Mary is the believing woman by whose faith the unbelieving Adam and all his posterity are saved." [3]   Hence, on account of her faith, Elizabeth called the holy Virgin blessed: *Blessed art thou that hast believed, because those things shall be accomplished in thee that were spoken by the Lord.* [4]   And St. Augustine adds, that Mary was rather blessed by receiv-ing the faith of Christ than by conceiving the flesh of Christ. [5]

Father Suarez says, [6] that the most holy Virgin had more faith than all men and angels. She saw her Son in the crib of Bethlehem, and believed him the Creator of the world. She saw him fly from Herod, and yet believed him the King of kings. She saw him born and believed him eternal. She saw him poor and in need of food, and believed him the Lord of the universe. She saw him lying on straw, and believed him omnipotent. She observed that he did not speak, and she believed him infinite wisdom. She heard him weep, and believed him the joy of Paradise. In fine, she saw him in death, despised and crucified, and, although faith wavered in others, Mary remained firm in the belief that he was God.

On these words of the Gospel, *there stood by the cross of*

[1] " Fides Mariæ cœlum aperuit. cum Angelo nuntianti consensit."
—*Spinelli, M. Deip.* c. 21, n. 7.

[2] " Sanctificatus est enim vir infidelis per mulierem fidelem."—1 *Cor.* vii. 14.

[3] " Hæc est Mulier fidelis, per cujus fidem salvatus est Adam, vir infidelis, et tota posteritas."—*De Laud. B. M.* l. 6.

[4] " Beata, quæ credidisti, quoniam perficientur ea, quæ dicta sunt tibi a Domino."—*Luke,* i. 45.

[5] " Beatior Maria percipiendo fidem Christi, quam concipiendo carnem Christi."—*De S. Virginitate,* c. 3.

[6] *De Inc.* p. 2, d. 19, s. 1.

8

Jesus His Mother.[1] St. Antoninus says, "Mary stood, supported by her faith, which she retained firm in the divinity of Christ."[2] And for this reason it is, the St. adds, that in the office of *Tenebræ* only one candle is left lighted. St. Leo, on this subject, applies to our Blessed Lady the words of Proverbs, *Her lamp shall not be put out in the night.*[3] And on the words of Isaias, *I have trodden the wine-press alone,*[4] St. Thomas remarks that the prophet says "a man," on account of the Blessed Virgin, in whom faith never failed.[5] Hence Blessed Albert the Great assures us that "Mary then exercised perfect faith; for even when the disciples were doubting she did not doubt."[6]

Therefore Mary merited by her great faith to become "the light of all the faithful,"[7] as St. Methodius calls her; and the "Queen of the true faith,"[8] as she is called by St. Cyril of Alexandria. The holy Church herself attributes to the merits of Mary's faith the destruction of all heresies: "Rejoice, O Virgin Mary, for thou alone hast destroyed all heresies throughout the world."[9] St. Thomas of Villanova, explaining the words of the Holy Ghost, *Thou hast wounded my heart, my sister, my spouse . . . with one of thy eyes,*[10] says that "these eyes denoted Mary's

[1] "Stabat autem juxta crucem Jesu Mater ejus."—*John.* xix. 25.

[2] "Beata Virgo stabat fide elevata et fixa, de Christi divinitate exspectans indubie suam resurrectionem."—P. 4, t. 15, c. 41, § 1.

[3] "Non extinguetur in nocte lucerna ejus."—*Prov.* xxxi. 18.

[4] "Torcular calcavi solus, et de gentibus non est vir mecum."—*Is.* lxiii. 3.

[5] "Dicit: 'Vir,' propter Beatam Virginem, in qua fides nunquam defecit."

[6] "Fidem habuit in excellentissimo gradu, quæ, etiam discipulis dubitantibus, non dubitavit."—*In Luc.* i.

[7] "Fidelium fax."—*De Sim. et Anna.*

[8] "Sceptrum orthodoxæ fidei."—*Hom.* 4 *int. div.*

[9] "Gaude, Maria Virgo, cunctas hæreses sola interemisti in universo mundo."—*Off. B. V. noct.* 3.

[10] "Vulnerasti cor meum in uno oculorum tuorum."—*Cant.* iv. 9.

faith, by which she greatly pleased the Son of God." [1]

Here St. Ildephonsus exhorts us to imitate Mary's faith. [2] But how can we do so? Faith, at the same time that it is a gift, is also a virtue. It is a gift of God, inasmuch as it is a light infused by him into our souls; and a virtue, inasmuch as the soul has to exercise itself in the practice of it. Hence faith is not only to be the rule of our belief, but also that of our actions; therefore St. Gregory says, "He truly believes who puts what he believes into practice;" [3] and St. Augustine, "Thou sayest, I believe; do what thou sayest, and it is faith." [4] This is to have a lively faith, to live according to our belief: *My just man liveth by faith.* [5] Thus did the Blessed Virgin live very differently from those who do not live in accordance with what they believe, and whose faith is dead, as St. James declares, *Faith without works is dead.* [6]

Diogenes sought for a man on earth; but God, amongst the many faithful, seems to seek for a Christian, for few there are who have good works; the greater part have only the name of Christian. To such as these should be applied the words once addressed by Alexander to a cowardly soldier who was also named Alexander: "Either change thy name or change thy conduct." [7] But as Father Avila used to say, "It would be better to shut up these poor creatures as madmen, believing, as they do, that an eternity of happiness is pre-

[1] "Oculus fidem designat: qua Dei Filio Virgo maxime complacuit." —*In Nat. D. conc.* 4.

[2] "Imitamini signaculum fidei vestræ, Beatam Mariam."—*De Assumpt.* s. 1.

[3] "Ille vere credit, qui exercet operando quod credit."—*In Evang. hom.* 26.

[4] "Dicis, 'credo:' fac quod dicis, et fides est."—*Serm.* 49, *E. B.*

[5] "Justus meus ex fide vivit."—*Heb.* x. 38.

[6] "Fides sine operibus mortua est."—*James*, ii. 26.

[7] "Aut nomen aut mores muta."

pared for those who lead good lives, and an eternity of misery for those who lead bad ones, and who yet live as if they believed nothing. St. Augustine therefore exhorts us to see things with the eyes of Christians, that is to say, with eyes which look at all in the light of faith;[1] for, as St. Teresa often said, all sins come from a want of faith. Let us therefore entreat the most holy Virgin, by the merit of her faith, to obtain us a lively faith. "O Lady, increase our faith."

V.

Mary's Hope.

Hope takes its rise in faith; for God enlightens us by faith to know his goodness and the promises he has made, that by this knowledge we may rise by hope to the desire of possessing him. Mary then, having had the virtue of faith in its highest degree, had also hope in the same degree of excellence; and this made her say with David, *But it is good for me to adhere to my God, to put my hope in the Lord God.*[2]

Mary was indeed that faithful spouse of the Holy Ghost, of whom it was said, *Who is this that cometh up from the desert, flowing with delights, leaning on her beloved?*[3] For she was always perfectly detached from earthly affection, looking upon the world as a desert, and therefore in no way relying either on creatures or on her own merits, but relying only on divine grace, in which was all her confidence, she always advanced in the love of God. Thus Ailgrino said of her: "She ascended from the desert, that is, from the world, which she so fully renounced, and so truly considered as a desert, that she

---

[1] "Christianos oculos habete."—*In Ps.* lvi.

[2] "Mihi autem adhærere Deo bonum est, ponere in Domino Deo spem meam."—*Ps.* lxxii. 28.

[3] "Quæ est ista, quæ ascendit de deserto, deliciis affluens, innixa super dilectum suum?"—*Cant.* viii. 5.

turned all her affections from it. She leant upon her
Beloved, for she trusted not in her own merits, but in
his graces who bestows graces." [1]

The most holy Virgin gave a clear indication of the
greatness of her confidence in God, in the first place,
when she saw the anxiety of her holy spouse St. Joseph.
Unable to account for her wonderful pregnancy, he was
troubled at the thought of leaving her; *but Joseph . . .
minded to put her away privately.* [2] It appeared then necessary, as we have elsewhere remarked, that she should
discover the hidden mystery to St. Joseph; but no, she
would not herself manifest the grace she had received;
she thought it better to abandon herself to divine Providence, in the full confidence that God himself would
defend her innocence and reputation. This is precisely
what Cornelius à Lapide says, in his commentary on the
words of the Gospel quoted above: "The Blessed Virgin
was unwilling to reveal this secret to Joseph, lest she
might seem to boast of her gifts; she therefore resigned
herself to the care of God, in the fullest confidence that
he would guard her innocence and reputation." [3]

Mary again showed her confidence in God when she
knew that the time for the birth of our Lord approached,
and was yet driven even from the lodgings of the poor
in Bethlehem, and obliged to bring forth in a stable:
*and she laid Him in a manger, because there was no room for
Him in the inn.* [4] She did not then let drop a single word

---

[1] "'Ascendit de deserto,' scilicet de mundo, quem sic deseruit, et
tamquam desertum reputavit, quod ab ipso omnem suum avertit affec-
tum. 'Innixa super Dilectum suum;' nam, non suis meritis, sed ipsius
innitebatur gratiæ, qui gratiam tribuit."

[2] "Joseph autem . . . voluit occulte dimittere eam."—*Matt.* i. 19.

[3] "B. Virgo autem noluit ultro secretum hoc Josepho pandere, ne
sua dona jactare videretur; sed Dei curæ idipsum resignavit, certissime
confidens Deum suam innocentiam et famam tutaturum."

[4] "Et reclinavit eum in præsepio: quia non erat eis locus in diver-
sorio."—*Luke*, ii. 7.

of complaint, but abandoning herself to God, she trusted that he would there assist her.

The divine Mother also showed how great was her confidence in divine Providence when she received notice from St. Joseph that they must fly into Egypt. On that very night she undertook so long a journey to a strange and unknown country without provisions, without money, accompanied only by her infant Jesus and her poor spouse, *who arose and took the Child and his Mother by night, and retired into Egypt.*[1]

But much more did she show her confidence when she asked her Son for wine at the marriage-feast of Cana; for when she had said, *They have no wine,* Jesus answered her, *Woman, what is it to thee and to me? My hour is not yet come.*[2] After this answer, which seemed an evident refusal, her confidence in the divine goodness was such that she desired the servants to do whatever her Son told them; for the favor was certain to be granted: *Whatsoever He shall say to you, do ye.*[3] It indeed was so: Jesus Christ ordered the vessels to be filled with water, and changed it into wine.

Let us, then, learn from Mary to have that confidence in God which we ought always to have, but principally in the great affair of our eternal salvation—an affair in which it is true that we must coöperate; yet it is from God alone that we must hope for the grace necessary to obtain it. We must distrust our own strength, and say with the Apostle, *I can do all things in Him who strengtheneth me.*[4]

Ah, my most holy Lady, the Ecclesiasticus tells me

---

[1] "Qui consurgens, accepit Puerum et Matrem ejus nocte, et secessit in Ægyptum."—*Matt.* ii. 14.

[2] "Vinum non habent . . . . Quid mihi et tibi est, mulier? nondum venit hora mea."—*John,* ii. 3.

[3] "Quodcumque dixerit vobis, facite."

[4] "Omnia possum in eo qui me confortat."—*Phil.* iv. 13.

that thou art *the Mother of holy hope ;*[1] and the holy Church, that thou art our hope.[2] For what other hope, then, need I seek ? Thou, after Jesus, art all my hope. Thus did St. Bernard call thee; thus will I also call thee : " Thou art the whole ground of my hope;"[3] and, with St. Bonaventure, I will repeat again and again, " O salvation of all who call upon thee, save me !"[4]

VI.

Mary's Chastity.

Since the fall of Adam, the senses being rebellious to reason, chastity is of all virtues the one that is the most difficult to practise. St. Augustine says : "Of all the combats in which we are engaged, the most severe are those of chastity; its battles are of daily occurrence, but victory is rare."[5] May God be ever praised, however, who in Mary has given us a great example of this virtue.

"With reason," says Blessed Albertus Magnus, "is Mary called the Virgin of virgins; for she, without the counsel or example of others, was the first who offered her virginity to God."[6] Thus did she bring all virgins who imitate her to God, as David had already foretold: *After her shall virgins be brought . . . into the temple of the King.*[7] Without counsel and without example. Yes; for St. Bernard says: " O Virgin, who taught thee to please

---

[1] " Ego mater . . . sanctæ spei."—*Ecclus.* xxiv. 24.

[2] " Spes nostra ! salve."

[3] "Tota ratio spei meæ."

[4] " O salus te invocantium ! salva me."

[5] " Inter omnia certamina, duriora sunt prælia castitatis, ubi quotidiana est pugna, et rara victoria."—*Serm.* 293, *E. B. app.*

[6] " Virgo virginum, quia, sine præcepto, consilio, exemplo, munus virginitatis Deo obtulit, et omnes virgines, per sui imitationem, in virginitate genuit."—*Super Miss.* q. 143.

[7] " Adducentur regi virgines post eam; adducentur in templum Regis."—*Ps.* xliv. 15.

God by virginity, and to lead an angel's life on earth ?" [1] "Ah," replies St. Sophronius, "God chose this most pure virgin for his Mother, that she might be an example of chastity to all." [2] Therefore does St. Ambrose call Mary "the standard-bearer of virginity." [3]

By reason of her purity the Blessed Virgin was also declared by the Holy Ghost to be beautiful as the turtle-dove: *Thy cheeks are beautiful as the turtle-dove's.* [4] "Mary," says Aponius, "was a most pure turtle-dove." For the same reason she was also called a lily: *As the lily among the thorns, so is my love among the daughters.* [5] On this passage Denis the Carthusian remarks, that "Mary was compared to a lily amongst thorns, because all other virgins were thorns, either to themselves or to others; but that the Blessed Virgin was so neither to herself nor to others;" for she inspired all who looked at her with chaste thoughts. This is confirmed by St. Thomas, [6] who says, that the beauty of the Blessed Virgin was an incentive to chastity in all who beheld her. St. Jerome declared that it was his opinion that St. Joseph remained a virgin by living with Mary; for, writing against the heretic Helvidius, who denied Mary's virginity, he says, "Thou sayest that Mary did not remain a virgin. I say that not only she remained a virgin, but even that Joseph preserved his virginity through Mary." [7]

St. Gregory of Nyssa says, that so much did the

---

[1] " O Virgo ! quis te docuit Deo placere virginitatem et in terris angelicam ducere vitam ?"—*De Laud. V. M. hom.* 3.

[2] "Christus Matrem Virginem ideo elegit, ut ipsa omnibus esset exemplum castitatis."—*De Assumpt.*

[3] " Quæ signum virginitatis extulit."—*Instit. Virg.* c. 5.

[4] " Pulchræ sunt genæ tuæ sicut turturis."—*Cant.* i. 9.

[5] " Sicut lilium inter spinas, sic Amica mea inter filias."—*Cant.* ii. 2.

[6] " Pulchritudo Beatæ Virginis intuentes ad castitatem excitabat."— *Spinelli, M. Deip.* c. 14, n. 6.

[7] " Tu dicis Mariam Virginem non permansisse; ego mihi plus vindico, etiam ipsum Joseph virginem fuisse per Mariam."—*Adv. Helvid.*

Blessed Virgin love this virtue, that, to preserve it, she would have been willing to renounce even the dignity of Mother of God. This we may conclude from her answer to the archangel, *How shall this be done, because I know not man?*[1] and from the words she afterwards added, *Be it done to me according to thy word,*[2] signifying that she gave her consent on the condition that as the angel had assured her, she should become a Mother only by the overshadowing of the Holy Ghost.

St. Ambrose says, that " whoever has preserved chastity is an angel, and that he who has lost it is a devil."[3] Our Lord assures us that those who are chaste become angels, *They shall be as the angels of God in heaven.*[4] · But the impure becomes as devils, hateful in the sight of God. St. Remigius used to say that the greater part of adults are lost by this vice. Seldom, as we have already said with St. Augustine, is a victory gained over this vice. But why? It is because the means by which it may be gained are seldom made use of.

These means are three, according to Bellarmine and the masters of a spiritual life : fasting, the avoidance of dangerous occasions, and prayer.[5]

1. By fasting, is to be understood especially mortification of the eyes and of the appetite. Although our Blessed Lady was full of divine grace, yet she was so mortified in her eyes, that, according to St. Epiphanius and St. John Damascene, she always kept them cast down, and never fixed them on any one; and they say that from her very childhood her modesty was such,

---

[1] " Quomodo fiet istud, quoniam virum non cognosco ?"—*Luke*, i. 34.

[2] " Fiat mihi secundum verbum tuum."—*Ib.* 38.

[3] " Qui castitatem servavit, angelus est; qui perdidit, diabolus."—*De Virginib.* l. 1.

[4] " Erunt sicut angeli Dei."—*Matt.* xxii. 30.

[5] " Jejunium, periculorum evitatio, et oratio."

that it filled every one who saw her with astonishment. Hence St. Luke remarks, that, in going to visit St. Elizabeth, *she went with haste*,[1] that she might be less seen in public. Philibert relates, that, as to her food, it was revealed to a hermit named Felix, that when a baby she only took milk once a day. St. Gregory of Tours affirms that throughout her life she fasted;[2] and St. Bonaventure adds, "that Mary would never have found so much grace, had she not been most moderate in her food; for grace and gluttony cannot subsist together."[3] In fine, Mary was mortified in all, so that of her it was said *my hands dropped with myrrh*.[4]

2. The second means is to fly the occasions of sin: *He that is aware of the snares shall be secure*.[5] Hence St. Philip Neri says, that, "in the war of the senses, cowards conquer:" that is to say those who fly from dangerous occasions. Mary fled as much as possible from the sight of men; and therefore St. Luke remarks, that in going to visit St. Elizabeth, *she went with haste into the hill country*. An author observes, that the Blessed Virgin left St. Elizabeth before St. John was born, as we learn from the same Gospel, where it is said, that *Mary abode with her about three months, and she returned to her own house. Now Elizabeth's full time of being delivered was come, and she brought forth a son*.[6] And why did she not wait for this event? It was that she might avoid the conversations and visits which would accompany it.

[1] "Abiit . . . cum festinatione."

[2] "Nullo tempore Maria non jejunavit."—*Novarin. Umbra Virg.* exc. 38.

[3] "Nunquam Maria tantam gratiam invenisset, nisi gratia Mariam in cibo temperatissimam invenisset; non enim se compatiuntur gratia et gula."—*Spec. B. V. lect.* 4.

[4] "Manus meæ stillaverunt myrrham."—*Cant.* v. 5.

[5] "Qui autem cavet laqueos, securus erit."—*Prov.* xi. 15.

[6] "Mansit autem Maria cum illa quasi tribus mensibus, et reversa est in domum suam Elisabeth autem impletum est tempus pariendi, et peperit filium."—*Luke*, i. 56.

3. The third means is prayer. *And as I knew,* said the wise man, *that I could not otherwise be continent except God gave it . . . I went to the Lord and besought Him.*[1] The Blessed Virgin revealed to St. Elizabeth of Hungary, that she acquired no virtue without effort and continual prayer.[2] St. John Damascene says, that Mary "is pure. and a lover of purity."[3] Hence she cannot endure those who are unchaste. But whoever has recourse to her will certainly be delivered from this vice, if he only pronounces her name with confidence. The Venerable John d'Avila[4] used to say, "that many have conquered impure temptations by only having devotion to her Immaculate Conception."

O Mary, O most pure dove, how many are now in hell on account of this vice! Sovereign Lady, obtain us the grace always to have recourse to thee in our temptations, and always to invoke thee, saying, "Mary, Mary, help us." Amen.

VII.

Mary's Poverty.

Our most loving Redeemer, that we might learn from him to despise the things of the world, was pleased to be poor on earth : *Being rich,* says St. Paul, *He became poor for your sake, that through His poverty you might be rich.*[5] Therefore doth Jesus Christ exhort each one who desires to be his disciple, *If thou wilt be perfect, go sell what thou hast, and give to the poor . . . and come, follow Me.*[6]

[1] "Et ut scivi quoniam aliter non possem esse continens, nisi Deus det, . . adii Dominum, et deprecatus sum illum."—*Wisd.* viii. 21.

[2] *S. Bonav. Med. Vit. Chr.* c. 3.

[3] "Pura est et puritatem amans."—*De Dorm. B. M.* s. 2.

[4] *Audi fil.* c. 14.

[5] "Propter vos egenus factus est, cum esset dives, ut illius inopia vos divites essetis."—2 *Cor.* viii. 9.

[6] "Si vis perfectus esse, vade, vende quæ habes, et da pauperibus . . . et veni, sequere me."—*Matt.* xix. 21.

Behold Mary, his most perfect disciple, who indeed imitated his example. Father Canisius [1] proves that Mary could have lived in comfort on the property she inherited from her parents, but she preferred to remain poor, and reserving only a small portion for herself, distributed the rest in alms to the temple and the poor. Many authors are of opinion that Mary even made a vow of poverty ; and we know that she herself said to St. Bridget, "from the beginning I vowed in my own heart that I would never possess anything on earth." [2]

The gifts received from the holy Magi cannot certainly have been of small value ; but we are assured by St. Bernard [3] that she distributed them to the poor through the hands of St. Joseph. That the divine Mother immediately disposed of these gifts is also evident from the fact, that at her purification, in the temple she did not offer a lamb, which was the offering prescribed in Leviticus for those who could afford it, *for a son she shall bring a lamb ;* [4] but she offered two turtledoves, or two pigeons, which was the oblation prescribed for the poor: *And to offer a sacrifice, according as it was written in the law of the Lord, a pair of turtle-doves or two young pigeons.* [5] Mary herself said to St. Bridget, "All that I could get I gave to the poor, and only reserved a little food and clothing for myself." [6]

Out of love for poverty she did not disdain to marry

---

[1] *De V. M.* l. 1, c. 4; l. 4, c. 7.

[2] "A principio, vovi in corde meo nihil unquam possidere in mundo."—*Rev.* l. 1, c. 10.

[3] "Aurum sibi oblatum a Magis non modicum, prout decebat eorum regiam majestatem, non sibi reservavit, sed pauperibus per Joseph distribuit."—P. 4, t. 15, c. 32, § 2.

[4] "Pro filio . . . deferet agnum."—*Lev.* xii. 6.

[5] "Et ut darent hostiam, secundum quod dictum est in lege Domini, par turturum, aut duos pullos columbarum."—*Luke.* ii. 24.

[6] "Omnia quæ habere potui, dedi indigentibus. Nihilque, nisi victum tenuem et vestitum reservavi."—*Rev.* l. 1, c. 10.

St. Joseph, who was only a poor carpenter, and afterwards to maintain herself by the work of her hands, spinning or sewing, as we are assured by St. Bonaventure.[1] The angel, speaking of Mary, told St. Bridget that "worldly riches were of no more value in her eyes than dirt."[2] In a word, she always lived poor, and she died poor; for at her death we do not know that she left anything but two poor gowns, to two women who had served her during her life, as it is recorded by Metaphrastes[3] and Nicephorus.[4]

St. Philip Neri used to say that "he who loves the things of the world will never become a saint." We may add what St. Teresa said on the same subject, that "it justly follows that he who runs after perishable things should also himself be lost." But, on the other hand, she adds, that the virtue of poverty is a treasure which comprises in itself all other treasures. She says the "virtue of poverty;" for, as St. Bernard remarks, this virtue does not consist only in being poor, but in loving poverty.[5] Therefore did Jesus Christ say, *Blessed are the poor in spirit, for theirs is the kingdom of heaven.*[6] They are blessed because they desire nothing but God, and in God they find every good; in poverty they find their paradise on earth, as St. Francis did when he exclaimed, "My God and my all."[7]

Let us, then, as St. Augustine exhorts us, "love that one good in which all good things are found"[8] and ad-

[1] *Med. Vit. Chr.* c. 12.

[2] "Mundanæ divitiæ velut lutum sibi vilescebant."—*Serm. Ang.* c. 13.

[3] *Hom. de Vita B. M.*

[4] *Hist.* l. 2, c. 21.

[5] "Non paupertas virtus reputatur, sed paupertatis amor."—*Epist.* 100.

[6] "Beati pauperes spiritu, quoniam ipsorum est regnum cœlorum."—*Matt.* v. 3.

[7] "Deus meus, et omnia."

[8] "Ama unum bonum, in quo sunt omnia bona."—*Man.* c. 34.

dress our Lord in the words of St. Ignatius, "Give me only Thy love, with Thy grace, and I am rich enough."[1] "When we have to suffer from poverty, let us console ourselves," says St. Bonaventure, "with the thought that Jesus and his Mother were also poor like ourselves."[2]

Ah, my most holy Mother, thou hadst indeed reason to say that in God was thy joy: *and my spirit hath rejoiced in God my Saviour;*[3] for in this world thou didst desire and love no other good but God. *Draw me after thee.*[4] O Lady, detach me from the world, that I may love him alone, who alone deserves to be loved. Amen.

VIII.

Mary's Obedience.

When the angel Gabriel announced to Mary God's great designs upon her, she, through love for obedience, would only call herself a handmaid: *Behold the handmaid of the Lord.*[5] "Yes," says St. Thomas of Villanova, "for this faithful handmaid never, in either thought or word or deed, contradicted the Most High; but, entirely despoiled of her own will, she lived always and in all things obedient to that of God."[6] She herself declared that God was pleased with her obedience, when she said, *He hath regarded the humility of His handmaid;*[7] for in prompt obedience it is that the humility of a servant,

---

[1] "Amorem tui solum cum gratia tua mihi dones, et dives sum satis."

[2] "Pauper multum consolari potest de paupertate Mariæ et de paupere Christo."—*Spec. B. V. lect.* 4.

[3] "Et exsultavit spiritus meus in Deo salutari meo."

[4] "Trahe me . . . post te."

[5] "Ecce ancilla Domini."—*Luke,* i. 38.

[6] "Vere ancilla, quæ neque dicto, neque facto, neque cogitatu unquam contradixit Altissimo; . . . nihil sibi libertatis reservans, sed per omnia subdita Deo."—*De Ann. conc.* 1.

[7] "Respexit humilitatem ancillæ suæ."

properly speaking consists. St. Irenæus says that by her obedience the divine Mother repaired the evil done by Eve's disobedience: " As Eve, by her disobedience, caused her own death and that of the whole human race, so did the Virgin Mary, by her obedience, become the cause of her own salvation and of that of all mankind." [1] Mary's obedience was much more perfect than that of all other saints; since all men, on account of original sin, are prone to evil, and find it difficult to do good; but not so the Blessed Virgin. St. Bernardine writes, that, " because Mary was free from original sin, she found no obstacle in obeying God; she was like a wheel, which was easily turned by every inspiration of the Holy Ghost." [2] " Hence," continues the same saint, " her only object in this world was to keep her eyes constantly fixed on God, to discover his will, and, when she had found out what he required, to perform it." [3] Of her was said, *My soul melted when He spoke;* [4] that is, as Richard explains it, " My soul was as metal, liquefied by the fire of love, ready to be moulded into any form, according to the divine will." [5]

Mary well proved how ready she was to obey in all things, in the first place, when, to please God, she obeyed even the Roman emperor, and undertook the long journey of at least seventy miles to Bethlehem, in the

[1] " Sicut Eva inobediens, et sibi et universo generi humano causa facta est mortis; sic et Maria Virgo obediens, et sibi et universo generi humano facta est causa salutis."—*Adv. Hæres.* l. 3, c. 33.

[2] " In Virgine Beata nullum fuit omnino retardativum; proinde rota volubilis fuit, secundum omnem Spiritus Sancti nutum."—*Pro Fest. V. M.* s. 12, a. 1, c. 1.

[3] " Virgo semper habuit continuum aspectum ad Dei beneplacitum promptumque consensum."—*Ibid.* s. 4, a. 3, c. 2.

[4] " Anima mea liquefacta est, ut locutus est."—*Cant.* v. 6.

[5] " 'Anima mea liquefacta est' per incendium charitatis, parata instar metalli liquefacti decurrere in omnes modulos divinæ voluntatis."—*De Laud. B. M.* l. 4.

winter, when she·was pregnant, and in such poverty that she had to give birth to her Son in a stable.

She showed equal obedience in undertaking, on the very same night on which she had notice of it from St. Joseph, the longer and more difficult journey into Egypt. Here Silveira asks why the command to fly into Egypt was given to St. Joseph rather than to the Blessed Virgin, who was to suffer the most from it; and he answers, that it was "that Mary might not be deprived of an occasion in which to perform an act of obedience, for which she was always most ready." [1]

But above all she showed her heroic obedience when, to obey the divine will, she offered her Son to death; and this with such constancy, as St. Anselm and St. Antoninus say, that had executioners been wanting, she would have been ready herself to have crucified him. Hence Venerable Bede, explaining our Lord's answer to the woman spoken of in the Gospel, who exclaimed, *Blessed is the womb that bore Thee . . . Yea rather, blessed are they who hear the word of God and keep it,* [2] says that Mary was indeed blessed in becoming the Mother of God, but that she was much more so in always loving and obeying the divine will. [3]

For this reason, all who love obedience are highly pleasing to the Blessed Virgin. She once appeared to a Franciscan friar, named Accorso, in his cell; whilst she was still present, obedience called him to hear the confession of a sick person. He went, and on his return found that Mary had waited for him, and highly com-

---

[1] "Ne Virgini subtraheretur occasio exercendi actum obedientiæ, ad quam erat promptissima."—*Comm.* l. 2, c. 7, q. 2.

[2] "Beatus venter qui te portavit . . . Quinimo beati, qui audiunt verbum Dei, et custodiunt illud!"—*Luke.* xi. 27.

[3] "Et inde quidem beata, quia incarnandi ministra est facta; sed inde multo beatior, quia verbi ejusdem semper amandi custos manebat æterna."

mended his obedience. On the other hand, she greatly blamed another religious, who remained to finish some private devotions after the refectory-bell had rung.[1]

Our Lord, once speaking to St. Bridget on the security which is found in obeying a spiritual director, said, "Obedience brings all saints to glory;"[2] for, as St. Philip Neri[3] used to say, "God demands no account of things done by obedience, having himself said, *He that heareth you, heareth Me: and he that despiseth you, despiseth Me.*[4] The Mother of God herself revealed to St. Bridget that through the merit of her obedience she had obtained so great power that no sinner, however great were his crimes, who had recourse to her with a purpose of amendment, failed to obtain pardon."[5]

Our own sweet Queen, then, and Mother, intercede with Jesus for us; by the merit of thine obedience obtain that we may be faithful in obeying his will and the commands of our spiritual Fathers. Amen.

IX.

Mary's Patience.

This world being a place of merit, is rightly called a valley of tears; for we are all placed in it to suffer, that we may, by patience, gain our own souls unto life eternal, as our Lord himself says, *In your patience you shall possess your souls.*[6] God gave us the Blessed Virgin Mary as a model of all virtues, but more especially as an ex-

---

[1] *Novarin. Umbra Virg. exc.* 79.

[2] "Obedientia omnes introducit ad gloriam."—*Rev.* l. 6, c. 111.

[3] *Bacci,* l. 1, c. 20.

[4] "Qui vos audit, me audit: et qui vos spernit, me spernit."—*Luke,* x. 16.

[5] "Pro obedientia mea tantam potestatem obtinui, quod nullus tam immundus peccator est, si ad me cum emendationis proposito convertitur et cum corde contrito, non habebit veniam."—*Rev.* l. 1, c. 42.

[6] "In patientia vestra possidebitis animas vestras."—*Luke,* xxi. 19.

ample of patience.   St. Francis de Sales, amongst other
things, remarks, that it was precisely for this reason that
at the marriage-feast of Cana Jesus Christ gave the
Blessed Virgin an answer, by which he seemed to value
her prayers but little: *Woman, what is that to thee and
to Me?*[1]   And he did this that he might give us the
example of the patience of his most holy Mother.   But
what need have we to seek for instances of this virtue?
Mary's whole life was a continual exercise of her
patience; for, as the angel revealed to St. Bridget, "as a
rose grows up amongst thorns, so did the Blessed Virgin
grow up amongst tribulations."[2]   Compassion alone for
the Redeemer's sufferings sufficed to make her a martyr
of patience.   Hence St. Bonaventure says, "that a crucified Mother conceived a crucified Son."[3]   In speaking of
her dolors, we have already considered how much she suffered, both in her journey to Egypt, and during her
residence there, as also during the time she lived with
her Son in the house at Nazareth.   What Mary endured
when present at the death of Jesus on Calvary is alone
sufficient to show us how constant and sublime was her
patience: *There stood by the cross of Jesus His Mother.*
Then it was that precisely by the merit of her patience,
as Blessed Albert the Great says, she brought us forth to
the life of grace."[4]

If we, then, wish to be the children of Mary, we must
endeavor to imitate her in her patience: "For what,"
says St. Cyprian, "can enrich us with greater merit in
this life, and greater glory in the next, than the patient
enduring of sufferings?"[5]   God said, by the prophet

---

[1] "Quid mihi et tibi est, mulier?"—*John*, ii. 4.

[2] "Sicut rosa crescere solet inter spinas, ita hæc venerabilis virgo
in hoc mundo crevit inter tribulationes."—*Serm. Ang.* c. 16.

[3] "Crucifixa Crucifixum concepit."—*Pro Fest. V. M.* s. 8, a. 2, c. 1.

[4] "Maria facta est Mater nostra, quos genuit Filio compatiendo."—
S. Antonin. P. 4, t. 15, c. 2.

[5] "Quid utilius ad vitam, vel majus ad gloriam?"—*De Bono Pat.*

Osee, *I will hedge up thy way with thorns.*[1] To this St. Gregory adds, that " the way of the elect is hedged with thorns." [2] As a hedge of thorns protects a vineyard, so does God protect his servants from the danger of attaching themselves to the earth, by encompassing them with tribulations. Therefore St. Cyprian concludes that it is patience that delivers us from sin and from hell.[3]

It is also patience that makes saints: *Patience hath a perfect work,*[4] bearing in peace, not only the crosses which come immediately from God, such as sickness, poverty, but also those which come from men—persecutions, injuries, and the rest. St. John saw all the saints bearing palm branches—the emblem of martyrdom—in their hands; *After this I saw a great multitude, and palms were in their hands;*[5] thereby denoting that all adults who are saved must be martyrs, either by shedding their blood for Christ or by patience. " Rejoice then," exclaims St. Gregory; " we can be martyrs without the executioner's sword, if we only preserve patience." [6] " Provided only," as St. Bernard says, " we endure the afflictions of this life with patience and joy."[7] O what fruit will not every pain borne for God's sake produce for us in heaven ! Hence the Apostle encourages us, saying, *That which is at present momentary and light of our tribulation worketh for us above measure exceedingly an eternal weight of glory.*[8]

St. Teresa's instructions on this subject are beautiful.

[1] " Sepiam viam tuam spinis."—*Osee*, ii. 6.

[2] " Electorum viæ spinis sepiuntur."—*Mor.* l. 34, c. 1.

[3] " Patientia nos servat."—*De Bono Pat.*

[4] " Patientia autem opus perfectum habet."—*James*, i. 4.

[5] " Vidi turbam magnam . . . et palmæ in manibus eorum."—*Apoc.* vii. 9.

[6] " Nos sine ferro martyres esse possumus, si patientiam custodiamus."—*In Evang. hom.* 35.

[7] " Patienter et libenter."—*De Div.* s. 16.

[8] " Momentaneum et leve tribulationis nostræ . . . æternum gloriæ pondus operatur in nobis."—*2 Cor.* iv. 17.

She used to say, "Those who embrace the cross do not feel it;" and elsewhere, "that if we resolve to suffer the pain ceases." When our crosses weigh heavily upon us, let us have recourse to Mary, who is called by the Church "the Comfortress of the afflicted;" and by St. John Damascene, "the Remedy for all sorrows of the heart." [1]

Ah, my most sweet Lady, thou who wast innocent didst suffer with so much patience; and shall I, who deserve hell, refuse to suffer? My Mother, I now ask thee this favor—not, indeed, to be delivered from crosses, but to bear them with patience. For the love of Jesus, I entreat thee to obtain at least this grace for me from God; from thee do I hope for it with confidence.

X.

The Spirit of Prayer and Meditation in Mary.

There was never a soul on earth that practised in so perfect a manner as the Blessed Virgin the great lesson taught by our Saviour, *that we ought always to pray, and not to faint.*[2] From no one, says St. Bonaventure, can we better take example, and learn how necessary is perseverance in prayer, than from Mary: "Mary gave an example which we must follow and not faint;"[3] for Blessed Albert the Great asserts, that, after Jesus Christ, the divine Mother was the most perfect in prayer of all who ever have been, or ever will be."[4] Her prayer was continual and persevering. In the very first moment, in which she had the perfect use of reason, which was, as we have said in the discourse on her nativity, in the first moment of her existence, she began to pray. That she

---

[1] "Omnium dolorum cordis Medicamentum."—*De Dorm. B. M.* s. 2.

[2] "Oportet semper orare, et non deficere."—*Luke*, xviii. 1.

[3] "Maria exemplum dedit; quam oportet sequi et non deficere."— *Spec. B. M. V. lect.* 4.

[4] "Virtus orationis in B. Virgine excellentissima fuit."

might be able to devote herself still more to prayer, when only three years of age she shut herself up in the retirement of the temple; where, amongst other hours set aside for this exercise, as she herself told St. Elizabeth of Hungary, "she always rose at midnight, and went before the altar of the temple to offer her supplications." [1] For the same purpose, and that she might constantly meditate on the sufferings of Jesus, Odilo says, "she very frequently visited the places of our Lord's Nativity, Passion, and Sepulture." [2] Moreover, she prayed with the greatest recollection of spirit, free from every distraction and inordinate affection, nor did any exterior occupation ever obscure the light of her unceasing contemplation, as we are assured by Denis the Carthusian. [3]

Through love for prayer, the Blessed Virgin was so enamoured of solitude, that, as she told St. Bridget, when she lived in the temple she avoided even intercourse with her parents. [4] On the words of the prophet, Isaias, *Behold a Virgin shall conceive and bear a Son, and His name shall be called Emmanuel*, [5] St. Jerome remarks, that the word *virgin*, in Hebrew, properly signifies a *retired virgin;* so that even the prophet foretold the affection which Mary would have for solitude. Richard of St. Laurence says that the angel addressed her in these words, *The Lord is with thee*, on account of her great love for retire-

---

[1] "Surgebam semper in noctis medio, et pergebam ante altare templi . . . et petitiones Domino faciebam."—*S. Bonav. Med. vit. Chr.* c. 3.

[2] "Loca Dominicæ Nativitatis, Passionis, Sepulturæ, frequenter invisere cupiebat."—*De Assumpt.*

[3] "Nulla unquam inordinata affectio, distractio, mentem Virginis a contemplationis lumine revocavit, neque occupatio ulla exterior."—*De Laud. V.* l. 2, a. 8.

[4] *Rev.* l. 1, c. 10.

[5] "Ecce virgo concipiet, et pariet Filium, et vocabitur nomen ejus Emmanuel."—*Is.* vii. 14.

ment.[1]   For this reason St. Vincent Ferrer asserts, that the divine Mother "only left her house to go to the temple, and then her demeanor was all composed, and she kept her eyes modestly cast down."[2]   For the same reason, when she went to visit St. Elizabeth, *she went with haste.*"[3]   From this, St. Ambrose says, "that virgins should learn to avoid the world.

St. Bernard affirms that on account of Mary's love for prayer and solitude, "she was always careful to avoid the society and converse of men."[4]   She was therefore called a turtle-dove by the Holy Ghost: *Thy cheeks are beautiful as the turtle-dove's.*[5]   "The turtle-dove," says Vergello, "is a solitary bird, and denotes unitive affection in the soul."[6]   Hence it was that the Blessed Virgin always lived solitary in this world as in a desert, and that of her it was said, *Who is she that goeth up by the desert, as a pillar of smoke?*[7]   On these words the Abbot Rupert says, "Thus didst thou, indeed, loving solitude, ascend by the desert."[8]

Philo assures us that "God only speaks to souls in solitude."[9]   God himself declares the same thing by the prophet Osee: *I will lead her into the wilderness, and I will speak to her heart.*[10]   "O happy solitude!" exclaims

[1] "'Dominus tecum;' merito solitudinis, quam summe diligebat."— *De Laud. B. M.* l. 1, c. 6.

[2] "Nunquam exibat e domo, nisi quando ibat ad Templum; et tunc ibat tota composita, semper habebat oculos suos ad terram."— *In Vig. Nat. Chr.*

[3] "Abiit cum festinatione."—*Luke*, i. 39.

[4] "In proposito erat hominum fugere frequentias, vitare colloquia." —*De Laud. V. M. hom.* 3.

[5] "Pulchræ sunt genæ tuæ sicut turturis."—*Cant.* i. 9.

[6] "Turtur est solivaga, et signat mentis virtutem unitivam."

[7] "Quæ est ista, quæ ascendit per desertum sicut virgula fumi?"— *Cant.* iii. 6.

[8] "Talis ascendisti per desertum, animum habens solitarium."

[9] "Dei Sermo amat deserta."—*Quis rer. div. heres.*

[10] "Ducam eam in solitudinem, et loquar ad cor ejus."—*Osee*, ii. 14.

St. Jerome, "in which God speaks familiarly and converses with his own."[1] "Yes," says St. Bernard; "for solitude, and the silence which is there enjoyed, force the soul to leave the earth in thought, and meditate on things of heaven."[2]

Most holy Virgin, do thou obtain us affection for prayer and retirement, that, detaching ourselves from the love of creatures, we may aspire only after God and heaven, where we hope one day to see thee, to praise thee, and to love thee, together with Jesus, thy Son, for ever and ever. Amen.

———

Come over to me, all ye that desire me, and be filled with my fruits.[3] Mary's fruits are her virtues. "Thou hast had none like thee, nor shalt thou have an equal. Thou alone of women hast above all pleased Christ."[4]

[1] "O solitudo, in qua Deus cum suis familiariter loquitur et conversatur!"

[2] "Silentium, et a strepitu quies, cogit coelestia meditari."—*Epist.* 78.

[3] "Transite ad me, omnes qui concupiscitis me, et a generationibus meis implemini."—*Ecclus.* xxiv. 26.

[4] "Nec primam similem visa es, nec habere sequentem; sola sine exemplo placuisti, Femina, Christo."—*Op. pasch.* l. 2.

HYMNS.

I.

The Loveliness of Mary.

RAISE your voices, vales and mountains,
Flow'ry meadows, streams, and fountains,
Praise, oh, praise the loveliest Maiden,
    Ever the Creator made.

Murm'ring brooks, your tribute bringing,
Little birds with joyful singing,
Come with mirthful praises laden;
    To your Queen be homage paid.

Say, sweet Virgin, we implore thee,
Say what beauty God sheds o'er thee;
Praise and thanks to Him be given,
    Who in love created thee.

Like a sun with splendor glowing
Gleams thy heart with love o'erflowing;
Like the moon in starry heaven
    Shines thy peerless purity.

Like the rose and lily blooming,
Sweetly heaven and earth perfuming,
Stainless, spotless, thou appearest,
    Queenly beauty graces thee.

But to God, in whom thou livest,
Sweeter joy and praise thou givest,
When to Him in beauty nearest,
    Yet so humble thou canst be!

Lovely Maid ! to God most pleasing,
And for us His wrath appeasing,
Oh ! by all thy love for Jesus,
    Show to us thy clemency.

II.

Mary, Virgin of Virgins.

OF all virgins thou art fairest,
    Dearest Mary, heavenly Queen ;
Of all creatures thou art purest,
    Like to thee was never seen.

Thy sweet face is like the heavens,
    Full of grace and purity ;
Beauty so divine adorns it,
    God alone surpasses thee !

Thy bright eyes with love are beaming,
    Like twin stars of heaven they shine ;
And thy looks are flaming arrows,
    Wounding hearts with love divine.

Thy chaste hands, whose sight enamours,
    Are like pearls of lustre rare ;
Ever full of heavenly treasures,
    For all those who ask a share.

Queen art thou, whom all things worship,
    Earth and hell, and heaven above ;
But thy heart o'erflows with goodness,
    Just and sinners feel thy love.

When, ah, when, at length in heaven,
    May I hope thy face to see ?
When, ah, when ?—my heart keeps sighing—
    Haste—I faint—I pine for thee !

Souls unnumber'd thou dost ever
  Rescue from the Evil One :
Dearest Lady, grant me also
  Not to lose thy blessed Son.

Him who gave us such a Mother
  Let our grateful songs proclaim ;
Loving hearts and joyful voices
  Praise her great Creator's name !

Glory to the name of Mary !
  Raise your voices—louder raise !
And of Jesus, Son of Mary,
  Every creature chant the praise !

PART THE FIFTH.

Practices of Devotion in Honor of the Divine Mother.

"THE Queen of Heaven is so gracious and liberal," says St. Andrew of Crete, "that she recompenses her servants with the greatest munificence for the most trifling devotions."[1] Two conditions, however, there are:

The first is, that when we offer her our devotions our souls should be free from sin; otherwise she would address us, as she addressed a wicked soldier spoken of by St. Peter Celestine.[2] This soldier every day performed some devotion in honor of our Blessed Lady. One day he was suffering greatly from hunger, when Mary appeared to him and offered him some most delicious meats, but in so filthy a vessel that he could not bring himself to taste them. "I am the mother of God," the Blessed Virgin then said, "and am come to satisfy thy hunger." "But, O Lady," he answered, "I cannot eat out of so dirty a vessel." "And how," replied Mary, "canst thou expect that I should accept thy devotions offered to me with so defiled a soul as thine?" On hearing this the soldier was converted, became a hermit, and lived in a desert for thirty years. At death the Blessed Virgin again appeared to him and took him herself to heaven. In the first part of this work[3] we said that it

----

[1] "Cum sit magnificentissima, solet maxima pro minimis reddere."— *In Dorm. B. V.* s. 3.

[2] *Opusc.* 6, c. 23.

[3] Volume VII., Chapter VIII.

was morally impossible for a client of Mary to be lost; but this must be understood on condition that he lives either without sin, or, at least, with the desire to abandon it; for then the Blessed Virgin will help him. But should any one, on the other hand, sin in the hope that Mary will save him, he thereby would render himself unworthy and incapable of her protection.

The second condition is perseverance in devotion to Mary: "Perseverance alone," says St. Bernard, "will merit a crown."[1] When Thomas à Kempis was a young man he used every day to have recourse to the Blessed Virgin with certain prayers; he one day omitted them; he then omitted them for some weeks, and finally gave them up altogether. One night he saw Mary in a dream: she embraced all his companions, but when his turn came she said, "What dost thou expect, thou who hast given up thy devotions? Depart, thou art unworthy of my caresses." On hearing this Thomas awoke in alarm, and resumed his ordinary prayers.[2] Hence, Richard of St. Laurence with reason says, that "he who perseveres in his devotion to Mary will be blessed in his confidence and will obtain all he desires."[3] But as no one can be certain of this perseverance, no one before death can be certain of salvation. The advice given by the Venerable John Berchmans, of the Society of Jesus, deserves our particular attention. When this holy young man was dying his companions entreated him, before he left this world, to tell them what devotion they could perform which would be most agreeable to our Blessed Lady. He replied in the following remarkable words: "Any devotion, however small, provided it is constant."[4] I there-

---

[1] "Perseverantia sola meretur coronam."—*Epist.* 129.

[2] *Auriemma, Aff. Scamb.* p. 1, c. 4.

[3] "Qui tenuerit Mariam perseveranter, beatus hic erit in spe, quia omnia optata succedent ei."—*De Laud. B. M.* l. 2, p. 1.

[4] "Quidquid minimum, dummodo sit constans."

fore now give with simplicity, and in a few words, the various devotions which we can offer to our Mother, in order to obtain her favor; and this I consider the most useful part of my work. But I do not so much recommend my dear reader to practise them all as to choose those which please him most, and to persevere in them, for fear that if he omits them he may lose the protection of the divine Mother. O, how many are there now in hell who would have been saved had they only persevered in the devotions which they once practised in honor of Mary!

I.

The Hail Mary.

This angelical salutation is most pleasing to the ever-blessed Virgin; for, whenever she hears it, it would seem as if the joy which she experienced when St. Gabriel announced to her that she was the chosen Mother of God, was renewed in her; and with this object in view, we should often salute her with the "Hail Mary." "Salute her," says Thomas à Kempis, "with the angelical salutation, for she indeed hears this sound with pleasure."[1] The divine Mother herself told St. Matilda that no one could salute her in a manner more agreeable to herself than with the "Hail Mary."[2]

He who salutes Mary will also be saluted by her. St. Bernard once heard a statue of the Blessed Virgin salute him, saying, "Hail, Bernard."[3] Mary's salutation, says St. Bonaventure, will always be some grace corresponding to the wants of him who salutes her: "She willingly salutes us with grace, if we willingly salute her with a

[1] "Salutate eam angelica salutatione frequenter, quia hanc vocem audit valde libenter."—*Ad Novit.* s. 21.
[2] *Spir. Grat.* l. 1, c. 67.
[3] "Ave, Bernarde."

Hail Mary." [1] Richard of St. Laurence adds, "that if we
address the Mother of our Lord, saying, 'Hail Mary,' she
cannot refuse the grace which we ask." [2] Mary herself
promised St. Gertrude as many graces at death as she would
have said "Hail Marys." [3] Blessed Alan asserts, "that as
all heaven rejoices when the 'Hail Mary' is said, so also do
the devils tremble and take flight." [4] This Thomas a
Kempis affirms on his own experience; for he says, that once
the devil appeared to him, and instantly fled on hearing the
"Hail Mary." [5]

To practise this devotion:

1. We can every morning and evening on rising and
going to bed say three "Hail Marys" prostrate, or at least
kneeling; and add to each "Hail Mary" this short prayer:
*O Mary, by thy pure and immaculate conception, make my
body pure and my soul holy.* [6] We should then, as St.
Stanislaus always did, ask Mary's blessing as our Mother;
place ourselves under the mantle of her protection, beseeching her to guard us during the coming day or night from
sin. For this purpose it is advisable to have a beautiful
picture or image of the Blessed Virgin.

2. We can say the *Angelus* with the usual three "Hail
Marys" in the morning, at mid-day, and in the evening.
Pope John XXII. was the first to grant an indulgence for
this devotion; it was on the following occasion, as Father
Crasset relates: [7] A criminal was condemned to be burned
alive on the vigil of the Annunciation of the Mother of

[1] Libenter nos salutat cum gratia, si libenter salutamus cum Ave
Maria."—*Spec. B. V. lect.* 4.

[2] "Si quis veniat ad Matrem Domini, dicens Ave Maria, numquid
ei gratiam poterit denegare?"—*De Laud. B. M.* l. 1, c. 8.

[3] *Insin.* l. 4, c. 53.

[4] "Cœlum gaudet, Satan fugit, cum dico: Ave Maria!"—*De Psalt.*
l. 4, c. 30.

[5] *Ad Novit.* s. 21.

[6] 300 days Indulgence, morning and evening.

[7] *Vér. Dév.* p. 2, tr. 6, p. 2.

God: he saluted her with a "Hail Mary;" and in the midst of the flames. he, and even his clothes, remained uninjured. In 1724, Benedict XIII. granted a hundred days' indulgence to all who recite it, and a plenary indulgence once a month to those who during that time have recited it daily as above, on condition of going to confession and receiving the holy Communion, and praying for the usual intentions. At the end of each "Hail Mary," may be added "Thanks be to God and to Mary." Formerly, at the sound of the bell, all knelt down to say the "Angelus;" but in the present day there are some who are ashamed to do so. St. Charles Borromeo was not ashamed to leave his carriage or get off his horse to say the "Angelus" in the street, and even sometimes in the mud. It is related that there was a slothful religious who neglected to kneel at the sound of the Angelus bell; he saw the belfry bow down three times, and a voice said, "Behold, wilt thou not do that which even inanimate creatures do?" [1] Here we must remark that Benedict XIV. directed that in paschal time, instead of saying the "Angelus" we should say the "Regina cœli;" and that on Saturday evenings, and the whole of Sunday, the "Angelus" should be said standing.

We can salute the Mother of God with a "Hail Mary" every time we hear the clock strike. Blessed Alphonsus Rodriguez saluted her every hour; and at night, angels awoke him, that he might not omit this devotion.

4. In going out and returning to the house we can salute the Blessed Virgin with a "Hail Mary," that both at home and abroad she may guard us from all sin; and we should each time kiss her feet, as the Carthusian Fathers always do.

5. We should reverence every image of Mary which we pass with a "Hail Mary." For this purpose those who can do so would do well to place a beautiful image of the Blessed Virgin on the wall of their houses, that it may be venerated by those who pass. In Naples, and still more in

---

[1] *Auriemma, Aff.* p. 1, c. 3.

Rome, there are most beautiful images of our Blessed Lady placed by the wayside by her devout clients.

6. By command of the holy Church all the canonical hours are preceded by a "Hail Mary," and concluded with it; we therefore do well to begin and end all our actions with a "Hail Mary." I say all our actions, whether spiritual, such as prayer, confession, and Communion, spiritual reading, hearing sermons, and the like; or temporal, such as study, giving advice, working, going to table, to bed, etc. Happy are those actions that are enclosed between two "Hail Marys." So also should we do on waking in the morning, on closing our eyes to sleep, in every temptation, in every danger, in every inclination to anger, and the like; on these occasions we should always say a "Hail Mary."

My dear reader, do this, and you will see the immense advantage that you will derive from it. Father Auriemma relates that the Blessed Virgin promised St. Matilda a happy death if she every day recited three "Hail Marys," in honor of her power, wisdom and goodness.[1] Moreover, she herself told St. Jane Frances de Chantal that the "Hail Mary" was most acceptable to her, and especially when recited ten times in honor of her ten virtues.

II.

Novenas.

Devout clients of Mary are all attention and fervor in celebrating the novenas, or nine days preceding her festivals ; and the Blessed Virgin is all love, in dispensing innumerable and most special graces to them. St. Gertrude one day saw, under Mary's mantle, a band of souls, whom the great Lady was considering with the most tender affection; and she was given to understand that they were persons who, during the preceding days, had prepared themselves with various devotions for the Feast of the Assumption.[1] The following devotions are some of those which may be used during the novenas :

1. We may make mental prayer in the morning and evening, and a visit to the Blessed Sacrament, adding nine times the "Our Father, Hail Mary, and Glory be to the Father."

2. We may pay Mary three visits (visiting her statue or picture), and thank our Lord for the graces that he granted her: and each time ask the Blessed Virgin for some special grace: in one of these visits the prayer, which will be found after the discourse on the feast, whichever it may be, can be said.[2]

3. We may make many acts of love towards Mary (at least fifty or a hundred), and also towards Jesus; for we can do nothing that pleases her more than to love her Son, as she said to St. Bridget: "If thou wishest to bind thyself to me, love my Son."[3]

4. We may read every day of the novena, for a quarter of an hour, some book that treats of her glories.

5. We may perform some external mortification, such as wearing a hair-cloth, taking a discipline, or the like; we can also fast, or at table abstain from fruit, or some

---

[1] *Insin.* l. 4, c. 50.   [2] Part II. of this work.

[3] " Si te mihi vis devincire, ama Filium meum. Jesum."

10

favorite dish, at least a part of it, or chew some bitter herbs. On the vigil of the feast we may fast on bread and water: but none of these things should be done without the permission of our confessor. Interior mortifications, however, are the best of all to practise during these novenas, such as to avoid looking at or listening to things out of curiosity; to remain in retirement; observe silence; be obedient; not give impatient answers; bear contradictions, and such things; which can all be practised with less danger of vanity, with greater merit, and which do not need the confessor's permission. The most useful exercise is to propose, from the beginning of the novena, to correct some fault into which we fall the most frequently. For this purpose it will be well, in the visits spoken of above, to ask pardon for past faults, to renew our resolutions not to commit them any more, and to implore Mary's help. The devotion most dear and pleasing to Mary is, to endeavor to imitate her virtues ; therefore it would be well always to propose to ourselves the imitation of some virtue that corresponds to the festival; as, for example, on the feast of her Immaculate Conception, purity of intention; on her Nativity, renewal of the spirit, to throw off tepidity; on her Presentation, detachment from something to which we are most attached; on her Annunciation, humility in supporting contempt; on her Visitation, charity towards our neighbor, in giving alms, or at least in praying for sinners; on her Purification, obedience to Superiors; and in fine, on the Feast of her Assumption, let us endeavor to detach ourselves from the world, do all to prepare ourselves for death, and regulate each day of our lives as if it was to be our làst.

6. Besides going to Communion on the day of the feast, it would be well to ask leave from our confessor to go more frequently during the novena. Father Segneri used to say, that we cannot honor Mary better than

with Jesus. She herself revealed to a holy soul (as Father Crasset relates),[1] that we can offer her nothing that is more pleasing to her than the Holy Communion; for in that Holy Sacrament it is that Jesus gathers the fruit of his Passion in our soul. Hence it appears that the Blessed Virgin desires nothing so much of her clients as Communion; saying, *Come, eat my bread, and drink the wine which I have mingled for you.*[2]

7. Finally on the day of the feast, after Communion, we must offer ourselves to the service of this divine Mother, and ask of her the grace to practise the virtue, or whatever other grace we had proposed to ourselves, during the novena. It is well every year to choose, amongst the feasts of the Blessed Virgin, one for which we have the greatest and most tender devotion; and for this one to make a very special preparation by dedicating ourselves anew, and in a more particular manner, to her service, choosing her for our Sovereign Lady, Advocate, and Mother.* Then we must ask her pardon for all our negligence in her service during the past year, and promise greater fidelity for the next; and conclude by begging her to accept us for her servants, and to obtain us a holy death.

III.

The Rosary and the Office of Our Blessed Lady.

It is well known that the devotion of the most holy rosary was revealed to St. Dominic by the divine Mother herself, at a time when the saint was in affliction, and bewailing, with his Sovereign Lady, over the Albigen-

---

[1] *Vér. Dév.* p. 2, tr. 6, pr. 6.

[2] "Venite. comedite panem meum, et bibite vinum quod miscui vobis."—*Prov.* ix. 5.

---

* At the end of this book will be found two formulas for this dedication—the one for a single person, the other for a family.

sian heretics, who were at that time doing great mischief to the Church. The Blessed Virgin said to him: "This land will always be sterile until rain falls on it." St. Dominic was then given to understand that this rain was the devotion of the rosary, which he was to propagate. This the saint indeed did, and it was embraced by all Catholics; so much so that, even to the present day, there is no devotion so generally practised by the faithful of all classes as that of the rosary. What is there that modern heretics, Calvin, Bucer, and others, have not said to throw discredit on the use of beads? But the immense good that this noble devotion has done to the world is well known. How many, by its means, have been delivered from sin! how many led to a holy life! how many to a good death, and are now saved! To be convinced of this, we need only read the many books that treat on the subject. Suffice it to know that this devotion has been approved by the Church, and that the Sovereign Pontiffs have enriched it with indulgences.* The rosary should also be said with devotion;

---

* The holy author here enumerates the principal indulgences that had been attached to the devotion of the Rosary up to the time in which he wrote. Conformably to his intention we here indicate summarily those that we can gain at the present time, according to the *Raccolta.*

An indulgence of one hundred days for every *Our Father* and every *Hail Mary* is granted to all the faithful who with devotion and at least contrite heart, shall say either the whole Rosary of fifteen decades, or a third part of it, that is five decades. And if they recite the whole or at least five decades for every day for a year, they can gain a plenary indulgence on any day of their choice after confession and Communion.

Besides, *an indulgence of ten years and ten times forty days* to those who recite the Rosary of five decades in company with others, either in public or in private. And if persons have the habit of thus reciting it at least three times a week they can gain a *plenary indulgence* on the last Sunday of every month, under the usual conditions. A *plenary indulgence* may be gained by saying five decades before the Blessed Sacrament, either exposed or in the tabernacle.

and here we may call to mind what the Blessed Virgin said to St. Eulalia, "that she was better pleased with five decades said slowly and devoutly than with fifteen said in a hurry and with little devotion." [1] It is, therefore, well to say the rosary kneeling, before an image of Mary; and, before each decade, to make an act of love to Jesus and Mary, and ask them for some particular grace. It is also preferable to say it with others rather than alone.

II. As to the little office of the Blessed Virgin, which is said to have been composed by St. Peter Damian,

[1] *Men. Cist.* 11 *Maii.*

There are many special indulgences for the month of October.

These different indulgences are applicable to the souls in purgatory. To gain them we must have a rosary that has been blessed by a priest who has the power to bless it; and in reciting it we must meditate on the mysteries of the birth, the Passion, and the resurrection of our Lord Jesus Christ in the following order for the fifteen decades, each composed of an *Our Father,* ten *Hail Marys,* and one *Glory be to the Father:*

Joyful mysteries: The annunciation, the visitation, the birth, the presentation and finding of Jesus in the temple.

Sorrowful mysteries: The sufferings of Jesus in the garden, the scourging, the crowning with thorns, the carrying of the cross, the crucifixion.

Glorious mysteries: The resurrection, the ascension, the coming of the Holy Ghost, the assumption of the Blessed Virgin, her coronation in heaven.

When we recite only five decades, we meditate according to our devotion on the joyful, the sorrowful, or the glorious mysteries; those who are unable to meditate on these divine mysteries may gain the indulgence by merely saying the rosary devoutly. The decades may be said separately provided they are said in one day.

We must here observe that the faithful who are members of the Confraternity of the holy Rosary can gain many other indulgences, either by reciting the rosary, or by performing other good works. The indulgences of the Crosier beads of *five hundred days* for every *Our Father* and every *Hail Mary* can be gained simultaneously with the Dominican indulgences, if the beads have both blessings.

Pius V. granted indulgences to those who recited it, which are now replaced by those of Leo XIII. and the Blessed Virgin has many times shown how acceptable this devotion is to her; as may be seen in Father Auriemma's little work.[1]

She is also much pleased with the Litany of Loretto, for reciting which there is an indulgence of three hundred days each time; and for those who say it every day, a plenary indulgence on Mary's five principal festivals,—the Immaculate Conception, Nativity, Annunciation, Purification, and Assumption, on the usual conditions. The hymn, *Ave maris Stella,* "Hail Star of the Sea," is also very pleasing to Mary; she desired St. Bridget to say it every day;[2] but still more is she pleased with the *Magnificat;* for we then praise her in the very words in which she herself praised God.

IV.

Fasting.

There are many devout clients of Mary who, to honor her, fast on bread and water on Saturdays, and the vigils of her feasts.

It is well known that Saturday is dedicated by the holy Church to Mary, because, as St. Bernard says, on that day, the day after the death of her Son, she remained constant in faith.[3] Therefore Mary's clients are careful to honor her on that day by some particular devotion, and especially by fasting on bread and water, as did St. Charles Borromeo, Cardinal Tolet, and so many others. Neithard, Bishop of Bamberg, and Father Joseph Arriaga, of the Society of Jesus, took no food at all on that day.

---

[1] *Aff. p.* 1, c. 8.

[2] *Rev. extr.* c. 8.

[3] "Per illud triste Sabbatum stetit in fide; propter quod aptissime tota Ecclesia, diem Sabbati per totius anni circulum celebrare consuevit."—*Lib. de Pass.* c. 2.

The great graces that the Mother of God has dispensed to those who do this are recorded by Father Auriemma in his little work.[1] Let one example suffice: it is that of a famous captain of brigands, who, on account of this devotion, was preserved in life after his head had been cut off, and was thus enabled to make his confession ; for the unfortunate creature was in a state of sin. After confession he declared that, on account of this devotion, the Blessed Virgin had obtained for him so great a grace, and immediately expired.

It would not, then, be anything very great, for a person who pretends to be devout to Mary, and particularly for one who has perhaps already deserved hell, to offer her this fast on Saturdays. I affirm that those who practise this devotion can hardly be lost; not that I mean to say that if they die in mortal sin the Blessed Virgin will deliver them by a miracle, as she did this bandit: these are prodigies of divine mercy which very rarely occur, and it would be the height of folly to expect eternal salvation by such means; but I say, that for those who practise this devotion, the divine Mother will make perseverance in God's grace easy, and obtain them a good death. All the members of our little Congregation, who are able to do so, practise this devotion. I say those who are able to do so; for if our health does not permit it, at least we should on Saturdays content ourselves with one dish, or observe an ordinary fast, or abstain from fruit, or something for which we have a relish. On Saturdays we should always practise some devotion in honor of our Blessed Lady, receive holy Communion, or at least hear Mass, visit an image of Mary, wear a hair-cloth, or something of that sort. But at least `on the vigils of her seven principal festivals, her clients should offer her this fast either on bread and water, or honor her otherwise as best they can.

[1] *Aff.* p. 1, c. 17.

V.

The Visiting of the Images of Mary.

Father Segneri says,[1] that the devil did not know how to repair his losses in the overthrow of idolatry better than by attacking sacred images through the instrumentality of heretics. But the holy Church has defended them even with the blood of martyrs; and the divine Mother has shown by prodigies how pleasing to her are the visits paid to her images.

St. John Damascene had his hand cut off for having defended by his writings the images of Mary; but his sovereign Lady miraculously restored it to him. Father Spinelli relates,[2] that in Constantinople a veil that covered an image of the Blessed Virgin on every Saturday drew itself aside, and after vespers again closed of its own accord. The veil of an image of our Blessed Lady, visited by St. John of God, was once withdrawn in a similar manner; so much so that the sacristan thinking that the saint was a robber kicked him; but his foot instantly withered.[3]

Hence all Mary's clients often visit with great affection her images and the churches dedicated in her honor. These are precisely, according to St. John Damascene, the cities of refuge in which we can find safety from temptations, and the chastisements that we have deserved for our sins. The first thing that the Emperor St. Henry used to do, on entering a city, was to visit a church of our Blessed Lady. Father Thomas Sanchez used never to return home without having visited some church of Mary.

Let us not think it too much to visit our Queen every

[1] *Div. di M.* p. 2, c. 3.
[2] *M. Deip.* c. 29, n. 17.
[3] *Boll.* 8 *Mart. Vit.* 2. c. 2.

day in some church or chapel, or even in our own house, where for this purpose it would be well to have in a retired part a little oratory, with her image, which should be kept decorated with drapery, flowers, tapers, or lamps; and before it we should also recite her litany, the rosary, etc. For this purpose I have published a little book (which has already been reprinted eight times), of visits to the Blessed Sacrament as well as to the Blessed Virgin, for every day in the month. Some devout client of Mary could also have one of her feasts celebrated in a church or chapel, with greater solemnity than it otherwise would be, and have it preceded by a novena, with exposition of the Blessed Sacrament, and even with sermons.

Here, however, it is well to relate a fact recorded by Father Spinelli,[1] in his book of "Miracles of the Madonna." In the year 1611, on the vigil of Pentecost, an immense concourse of people had assembled at the celebrated sanctuary of Mary, at Montevergine. The people had profaned the feast with dances, excesses, and immodest conduct, when suddenly it was discovered that fire was bursting forth from the house of amusement in which they were assembled, and in less than an hour and a half it was reduced to ashes, and more than four hundred persons lost their lives. Five persons who escaped deposed on oath that they had seen our Blessed Lady herself set fire to the place with two torches. After this, I entreat the clients of Mary to keep away as much as possible from such sanctuaries during festivals, and also, as far as they can, to prevent others from going there; for on such occasions the devil gains more profit than the Blessed Virgin derives honor by it. Let those who have this devotion go at a time when there is no concourse of people.

[1] *Tr. de Exempl.* n. 62.

VI.

The Scapular.

As men esteem it an honor to have persons who wear their livery, so also is our Blessed Lady pleased that her clients should wear her scapular, as a mark that they have dedicated themselves to her service, and that they are members of the household of the Mother of God. Modern heretics, as usual, ridicule this devotion; but the holy Church has approved it by many Bulls and indulgences. Fathers Crasset and Lezzana,[1] speaking of the scapular of Mount Carmel, relate that towards the year 1251 the Blessed Virgin appeared to St. Simon Stock, an Englishman, and giving him the scapular, said, that all who should wear it would be saved from eternal damnation. She said, "Receive, my beloved son, this scapular of thy Order, the badge of my confraternity, a privilege granted to thee and to all Carmelites: whoever dies clothed with it will not suffer eternal flames." Moreover, Father Crasset relates that Mary appeared to Pope John XXII., and commanded him to make it known that all those who should wear this scapular would be delivered from purgatory on the Saturday after their death ; and this he did by a Bull, which was afterwards confirmed by Alexander V., Clement VII., and other Pontiffs. Paul V., as we have remarked in the first part of this work,[2] gives us to understand the same thing, and seems to explain the Bulls of his predecessors, and prescribes in his the conditions on which the indulgences may be gained. These conditions are: that each one should observe the chastity required in his state of life, and the recitation of the little office of the Blessed Virgin; those who cannot do so must be exact in keeping

---

[1] *Mar. Patr.* c. 5.　　　　　　　　　[2] Page 235.

the fast days prescribed by the Church, and abstain from meat on Wednesdays and Saturdays.

The indulgences, moreover, which are annexed to the scapular of Mount Carmel, of the Seven Dolors of our Lady, of the Blessed Trinity, and especially of the Immaculate Conception, are innumerable, as well partial as plenary, both in life and for the hour of death. For my own part, I have been careful to receive all these scapulars.* To that of the Immaculate Conception in particular very great indulgences have been attached by various sovereign pontiffs.

VII.

Confraternities of our Blessed Lady.

Some disapprove of confraternities, because they sometimes give rise to quarrels, and because many join them for temporal purposes. But as churches and the sacraments are not condemned because there are many who make a bad use of them, neither should confraternities be condemned. The sovereign pontiffs, so far from condemning them, have approved and highly commended them, and also enriched them with many indulgences. St. Francis de Sales,[1] with great earnestness, exhorts all seculars to join them. What pains, moreover, did not St. Charles Borromeo take to establish and multiply these confraternities. In his synods, he particularly recommends confessors to engage their penitents to join them.[2] And with good reason; for these sodalities, especially those of our Blessed Lady,

[1] *Introd.* p. 2, c. 15.

[2] "Confessor pro viribus suadebit, ut alicui societati pœnitentes adscribantur."—*Act. Med.* t. i. p. 4. *Instr. conf.*

---

* At present these four Scapulars are usually fastened to one another, and many persons add to them the Scapular of the Passion and that of the Sacred Hearts of Jesus and Mary.—ED.

are so many Noah's arks, in which poor seculars find a
refuge from the deluge of temptations and sins which
inundate the world. We, from the experience of our
missions, well know the utility of these confraternities.
As a rule, a man who does not attend the meetings of a
confraternity commits more sins than twenty men who
do attend them. A confraternity can well be called *a
tower of David; a thousand bucklers hang upon it—all the
armor of valiant men.*[1] The reason that confraternities do
so much good is, that in them the members acquire
many weapons of defence against hell, and put in practice the requisite means of preservation in divine grace,
which are seldom made use of by seculars who are not
members of these confraternities.

1. In the first place, one means of salvation is, to
meditate on the eternal truths: *Remember thy last end, and
thou shalt never sin.*[2] How many are lost because they
neglect to do this! *With desolation is all the land made
desolate; because there is none that considereth in his heart.*[3]
But those who frequent the meetings of their confraternities are led to think of these truths by the many
meditations, lectures, and sermons they there hear: *My
sheep hear my voice.*[4]

2. To save one's soul, prayer is necessary: *Ask, and you
shall receive;*[5] this the members of the confraternities do
constantly. God also hears their prayers the more
readily; for he has himself said, that he grants graces
more willingly to prayers offered up in common: *If two
of you shall consent upon earth concerning anything whatsoever*

---

[1] "Turris David ; . . mille clypei pendent ex ea, omnis armatura
fortium."—*Cant*. iv. 4.

[2] "Memorare novissima tua, et in æternum non peccabis."—*Ecclus*. vii. 40.

[3] "Desolatione desolata est omnis terra, quia nullus est qui recogitet
corde."—*Jerem*. xii. 11.

[4] "Oves meæ vocem meam audiunt."—*John*, x. 27.

[5] "Petite, et accipietis."—*Ib*. xvi. 24.

they shall ask it, it shall be done to them by my Father:[1] on which St. Ambrose says, that "many who are weak, when united become strong; and it is impossible that the prayers of so many should not be heard."[2]

3. In confraternities the sacraments are most likely to be frequented, both on account of the rules and the example which is given by the other members. And thus perseverance in grace is more easily obtained, the sacred Council of Trent having declared, that holy Communion is "an antidote whereby we may be freed from daily faults, and be preserved from mortal sins."[3]

4. Besides the frequentation of the sacraments in these confraternities, many acts of mortification, humility, and charity towards the sick brethren and the poor, are performed. Well would it be if this holy custom of assisting the sick-poor of the place were introduced into all confraternities.

5. We have already said how profitable it is for our salvation to serve the Mother of God: and what else do the members do in the confraternity but serve her? How much is she not praised there! How many prayers are not there offered to her! From the very beginning, the brothers are consecrated to her service; they choose her in an especial manner for their sovereign Lady and Mother; they are inscribed in the book of the children of Mary; hence, as they are her servants and children in an especial manner, in an especial manner are they treated by her, and she protects them in life and in death. So that a member of a confraternity of Mary can say, *Now all good things came to me together with it.*[4]

---

[1] "Si duo ex vobis consenserint super terram de omni re, quamcumque petierint, fiet illis a Patre meo."—*Matt.* xviii. 19.

[2] "Multi minimi, dum congregantur unanimes, fiunt magni; et multorum preces impossibile est ut non impetrent."—*In. Rom.* xv.

[3] "Tamquam antidotum, quo liberemur a culpis quotidianis, et a peccatis mortalibus præservemur."—*Sess.* 13, c. 2.

[4] "Venerunt autem mihi omnia bona pariter cum illa."—*Wisd.* vii. 11.

Each member should therefore pay attention to two things: First of all, the object that he should have in view should be no other than to serve God and his Mother Mary, and save his soul; secondly, not to allow worldly affairs to prevent his attendance at the meeting on the appointed days; for he has there to attend to the most important business that he has in the world, which is his eternal salvation. He should also endeavor to draw as many others as he can to join the confraternity, and especially to bring back those members who have left it.

O with what terrible chastisements has our Lord punished those who have abandoned the confraternity of our Blessed Lady! There was a brother who did so in Naples; and when he was exhorted to return, he answered, "I will do so when my legs are broken, and my head is cut off." He prophesied; for, a short time afterwards, some enemies of his broke his legs and cut off his head.[1]

On the other hand, the members who persevere have both their temporal and spiritual wants provided for by Mary. *All her domestics are clothed with double garments.*[2] Father Auriemma[3] relates how many special graces Mary grants to members of the confraternity, both in life and in death, but more particularly in death. Father Crasset[4] gives an account of a young man, who, in the year 1586, was dying. He fell asleep; but afterwards waking, he said to his confessor, O Father, I have been in great danger of damnation, but our Blessed Lady rescued me. The devils presented my sins before our Lord's tribunal, and they were already preparing to drag me to hell; but the Blessed Virgin came and said to them: "Whither are you taking this young man? What business have you with a servant of mine, who has

---

[1] *Sarnelli, Congr.* p. 1, § 14.

[2] "Omnes domestici ejus vestiti sunt duplicibus."—*Prov.* xxxi. 21.

[3] *Aff.* p. 2, c. 4.

[4] *Vér. Dév. p.* 2, tr. 6, pr. 5.

served me so long in my confraternity? The devils fled, and thus was I delivered from their hands." The same author also relates, that another brother had also, at the point of death, a great battle with hell; but at length, having conquered, filled with joy, he exclaimed: "O what a blessing it is to serve the holy Mother in her confraternity!" and thus filled with consolation, he expired. He then adds, that in Naples, when the Duke of Popoli was dying, he said to his son: "Son, know that the little good that I have done in this life, I attribute to my confraternity. Hence, I have no greater treasure to leave thee than the confraternity of Mary. I now value more having been one of its members, than being Duke of Popoli."

VIII.

The Alms Given in Mary's Honor.

Clients of the Blessed Virgin are accustomed to give alms to the poor in honor of the divine Mother, especially on Saturdays.

That holy shoemaker, of whom St. Gregory speaks in his dialogues [1] (his name was Deusdedit), used on Saturdays to distribute all his earnings of the past week to the poor. Hence, a holy soul in a vision saw a sumptuous palace, which God was preparing in heaven for this servant of Mary, but its construction only went on on Saturdays. St. Gerard never refused anything at any time for which he was asked in Mary's name. Father Martin Guttierez, of the Society of Jesus, did the same, and in consequence acknowledged that he had never asked Mary for a grace which he had not obtained. This servant of hers having been put to death by the Huguenots, the divine Mother appeared to

[1] L. 4, c. 36.

his companions, accompanied by virgins, who, by her direction, wrapped the body in linen, and carried it away. St. Eberhard, bishop of Saltzburg, practised the same devotion, and, on account of it, a holy monk saw him as a child in the arms of Mary, who said: "This is my son Eberhard, who never denied me anything." [1] Alexander of Hales, who had the same devotion, being once asked, in the name of Mary, by a Franciscan lay brother, to join the Order, immediately complied, gave up the world, and became a friar.

Let, therefore, no client of the Blessed Virgin think it too much to give a trifling alms every day in her honor, and to increase it on Saturdays. If they can do nothing else, they should at least perform some other act for the love of Mary; such as visiting the sick, praying for sinners, and for the souls in purgatory, etc. Works of mercy are very pleasing to the heart of this Mother of Mercy.

IX.

Frequent Recourse to Mary.

Of all devotions, there is none so pleasing to our Mother as that of having frequent recourse to her intercession, seeking her help in all our wants; for example, when we have to give or ask advice, in dangers, afflictions, and temptations; and particularly in temptations against purity. The divine Mother will then certainly deliver us, if we have recourse to her by saying the antiphon, "We fly to thy patronage," etc.; or with the "Hail Mary;" or by only invoking the most holy name of Mary, which has particular power against the devils.

[1] "Hic est filius meus Eberardus, qui nihil mihi unquam negavit."
—*Boll. 22 Jun. Vit.* c. 4.

Blessed Santi, of the Order of St. Francis, being once tempted with an impure thought, had recourse to Mary: she immediately appeared to him, and placing her hand on his breast delivered him.

It is also useful on these occasions to kiss or press to our heart our rosary or scapular, or to look at an image of the Blessed Virgin.

It is well also to know that Pius X. granted three hundred days' indulgence to those who pronounce the names of Jesus and Mary, and seven years and seven quarantines for the three names of Jesus, Mary and Joseph.

X.

Several other Practices in Honor of Mary.

1. To say or hear Mass, or to have Mass said, in honor of the Blessed Virgin. It is true that the holy sacrifice of the Mass can be offered to God alone, to whom it is offered principally as an acknowledgment of his supreme dominion. But the sacred Council of Trent [1] says that this does not prevent it from being, at the same time, offered to God in thanksgiving for the graces granted to the saints and to his most holy Mother, that whilst we are mindful of them, they may deign to intercede for us. And for this reason at Mass we say, "That it may avail to their honor, but to our salvation." [2] Our Blessed Lady herself revealed to a holy soul, that this devotion of offering the Mass, as also of saying the "Our Father," the "Hail Mary," and "Glory be to the Father" three times, in honor of the Most Holy Trinity, and in Thanksgiving for the graces granted to her, was most pleasing to her; for the Blessed Virgin, being un-.

---

[1] *Sess.* 22, *cap.* 3.
[2] "Ut illis proficiat ad honorem, nobis autem ad salutem."

able to thank our Lord for all the precious gifts he has bestowed on her, rejoices greatly when her children help her to thank God.

2. To reverence the saints who are more nearly related to Mary, as St. Joseph, St. Joachim, and St. Anne. The Blessed Virgin herself recommended a certain nobleman to be devout towards her mother, St. Anne. We should also honor the saints who were most devoted to the divine Mother, such as St. John the Evangelist, St. John the Baptist, St. Bernard, St. John Damascene the defender of her images, St. Ildephonsus the defender of her virginity, etc.

3. To read every day a book that treats of the glories of Mary; to preach, or least to try to instil into all, and particularly our relatives, devotion to the divine Mother. The Blessed Virgin once said to St. Bridget, "Take care that thy children are also my children." To pray every day for the most devoted clients of Mary, both living and dead.

We should also remember the many indulgences granted by sovereign pontiffs to those who in various ways honor the Queen of heaven. 1. To whoever says, "Blessed be the holy and immaculate conception of the Blessed Virgin Mary, Mother of God," Leo XIII. granted for each time an indulgence of three hundred days. 2. For the Litany of Loretto, three hundred days' indulgence. 3. For the names of Jesus and Mary, three hundred days' indulgence and for the names of Jesus, Mary and Joseph, seven years and seven quarantines.[1] Here, for the convenience of devout souls, I will indicate other indulgences granted by sovereign pontiffs for other devotions. 1. For hearing Mass when specially granted. 2. For making an act of contrition

[1] *Raccolta.*

Benedict XV. granted three hundred days and for an act of love: "My God, I love Thee," three hundred days. 3. To those who say the invocation: "O Mary, Queen of light, enlighten sinners and bring them to the heart of thy divine Son," three hundred days' indulgence. 4. To those who meditate for at least a quarter of an hour every day, Benedict XIV. granted many indulgences, and a plenary one once a month, on condition of approaching the sacraments of Penance and the Holy Eucharist. 5. To those who say the prayer *Anima Christi*, three hundred days' indulgence. 6. To those who accompany the holy Viaticum, five years and five times forty days, if without a wax-light; and if with one, seven years and seven quarantines: those who cannot accompany it, but say a "Pater" and an "Ave" for the intention of the sovereign pontiff, one hundred days. For a brief visit and adoration at the altar of the Blessed Sacrament on first entering a church, made before anything else, three hundred days, as also for every exterior act of reverence when passing a church or a chapel where the Blessed Sacrament is reserved. 8. To priests who before saying Mass say the prayer *Ego volo celebrare missam*, fifty days.

The Raccolta gives very many other indulgences. Those who endeavor to gain these indulgences must be careful to dispose themselves by an act of contrition. I omit other devotions which may be found in other books, such as those of the seven joys, of the twelve privileges of Mary, and the like; and conclude in the beautiful words of St. Bernardine of Sienna:

"O Lady, blessed amongst all women, thou art the honor of the human race, and the salvation of our people. Thy merits have no limits, and thou hast full power over all creatures. Thou art the Mother of God, the sovereign Lady of the world, and the Queen of heaven. Thou art the dispenser of all graces, and the ornament of the holy Church. Thou art the model of the just, the consolation of the saints, and the root of our salvation. Thou art the joy of paradise, the gate of heaven, the glory of God. Behold, we have announced thy praises. We beseech thee, then, O Mother of Mercy, to supply for our weakness, to excuse our presumption, to accept our services, to bless our labors, by imprinting thy love in the hearts of all; that after having honored and loved thy Son on earth, we may praise him and bless him forever in heaven. Amen." [1]

CONCLUSION.

And with this, my dear reader and brother, lover of our Mother Mary, I bid you farewell, and say: Continue with joy to honor and love this good Lady, and endeavor also to cause her to be loved by as many as you can: and doubt not, but be fully persuaded, that if you persevere until death in true devotion to Mary, your salvation is certain. I conclude, not that I should not still have much to say on the glories of this great Queen, but lest I should tire you. The little that I have written will be more than sufficient to make you desire this great treasure, devotion towards the Mother of God, which she will fully reward by her powerful patronage. Accept, then, the desire which I have had in this work, to lead you to salvation and to sanctity, by inflaming you with love and ardent devotion to this most amiable Queen. And should you find that in this I have somewhat helped you by my book, as a charity I beg that you will recommend me to Mary, and ask her for me the grace which I ask her for you, that we may one day be together at her feet, in company with all her other dear children.

And to thee do I turn in conclusion, O Mother of my Lord, and my Mother Mary. I beseech thee graciously to accept my poor labors, and the desire which I have had to see thee praised and loved by all. Thou well

[1] *Pro Fest. V. M.* s. 13, a. 2, c. 3.

knowest how ardently I have desired to complete this little work of thy Glories before the end of my life, which is already drawing to its close. But now I die happy, leaving this book on earth, which will continue to praise and preach thee as I have endeavored to do during the years which have passed since my conversion, which through thee I obtained from God. O immaculate Mary, I recommend all those who love thee to thee, and especially those who read this little book; and more particularly those who have the charity to recommend me to thee. O Lady, grant them perseverance, make them all saints, and thus lead them all united to praise thee in heaven. O my most sweet Mother, it is true that I am only a poor sinner, but I glory in loving thee, and hope great things from thee, and amongst others to die loving thee. I trust that in the agonies of death, when the devil will put my sins before me, that in the first place the Passion of Jesus, and then thy intercession, will strengthen and enable me to leave this miserable life in the grace of God, that so I may go and love him, and thank thee, my Mother, for all eternity. Amen.

Lovely Rose, if thou dost deign
  Love to lavish still on me,
Grant my heart such love to gain
  That it die for love of thee.

My Lady, grant this grace to me,
  To love thee until death:
And when I die, to call on thee
  Still with my latest breath.

My hope art thou, O Mary blest,
  Sweet star of life's dark sea;
Ah, guide me safe to port of rest,
  And open heaven to me.

Live Jesus, Mary Joseph, and Teresa!

Meditations.*

I.

Novena to the Blessed Virgin.

Or, Meditations on the Litany of Loretto, for the nine days preceding each of the principal Festivals of the Divine Mother.

MEDITATION I.

I.

Sancta Maria, ora pro nobis. "HOLY MARY, pray for us." Since, in the Litany of our Blessed Lady, the Church teaches us to ask this good Mother so many times to pray for us, it will be well before meditating upon the titles by which she is invoked, to consider the great power which her prayers have with God. Blessed is that person for whom Mary prays. Jesus rejoices when his most Beloved Mother prays to him, that he may have the pleasure of granting her all she asks. One day St. Bridget heard Jesus speak to Mary and say, "My Mother, thou well knowest that I cannot do otherwise than grant thy prayers; therefore, ask of me what thou wilt."[1] And he then added, "Since thou, when on earth, didst deny me nothing, it is becoming, now that I am in heaven, that I should deny thee nothing that thou askest me."[2] St. Bernard says, "To be heard by the Son is to be graciously heard."[3] Mary has only to

---

[1] *Rev.* l. 6, c. 23.　　　　　　　[2] *Ib.* l. 1, c. 24.

[3] "A Filio audiri est exaudiri."—*Paciucch. In Sal. Ang. exc.* 20.

---

* These meditations were not composed by the holy author for the *Glories of Mary.* We have, however, placed them here in the order of the complete works.

speak, and her Son grants her all that she asks. Let us, therefore, pray to this divine Mother, without ceasing, if we wish to secure our eternal salvation; and let us address her in the words of St. Andrew of Crete:

"We beseech thee, therefore, O Holy Virgin, to grant us the help of thy prayers with God; prayers that are more precious than all the treasures of the world; prayers that obtain for us a very great abundance of graces; prayers that confound all enemies, and triumph over their strength."[1]

II.

Sancta Maria. "HOLY MARY." The name of Mary is a name of salvation. This name came not of earth, but from heaven: hence St. Epiphanius says, that it was not given to Mary by her parents, but was imposed on her by the express will of God. Therefore it is that, after the name of Jesus, the name of Mary is above every other name; for God has filled it with grace and sweetness, that every blessing may be obtained by him who names it. St. Bernard says, "O Mary, thou canst not be named without inflaming the heart of him who does so with love for thee."[2] Blessed Henry Suso used to exclaim, "O Mary, what must thou thyself be, since thy very name is so amiable and gracious?"[3] That name is filled with blessings. St. Bonaventure says,[4] that the name of Mary cannot be invoked without profit to him who does so. Above all, this name has power to overcome the temptations of hell.

Ah, my Lady, had I always invoked thee in my temptations, I should not have fallen. For the future I will never cease to invoke thee, saying, "Mary, help me; Mary, succor me." And do thou obtain me the grace always to invoke thee in time of spiritual danger.

[1] *In Dorm. S. M.* s. 3.
[2] *Depr. ad Glor. V.*
[3] *Dial. c.* 16.
[4] *Spec. B. V. lect.* 9.

III.

Sancta Dei Genitrix. "HOLY MOTHER OF GOD."—If the prayers of the saints are very powerful with God, how great must be the power of those of Mary! The former are the prayers of servants, the latter the prayers of a mother. St. Antoninus says that the prayers of Mary have the force of a command with Jesus Christ.[1] Hence he concludes, that it is impossible for the Son not to grant a grace for which the Mother asks.[2] St. Bernard, therefore, exhorts us to ask for every grace which we desire from God through Mary. "Let us seek for grace, and seek it by Mary." And why? "Because she is a mother, and is always graciously heard."[3]

O great Mother of God, pray to Jesus for me. Behold the miseries of my soul, and pity me. Pray, and never cease to pray, until thou seest me safe in Paradise. O Mary, thou art my hope; abandon me not. "Holy Mother of God, pray for us."

MEDITATION II.

I.

Mater divinæ gratiæ. "MOTHER OF DIVINE GRACE."— St. Anselm calls Mary "the Mother of all graces;"[4] and Blessed Raymond Jordano, "The treasurer of divine grace."[5] Hence St. Bernardine of Sienna writes, that "all the gifts and graces that we receive from God are dispensed by the hands of Mary, to whom, when, and as she pleases."[6] This she herself says: *With me are riches*

---

[1] "Oratio Deiparæ habet rationem imperii."

[2] "Impossibile est eam non exaudiri."—P. 4, t. 15, c. 17, § 4.

[3] "Quia Mater est, et frustrari non potest."—*De Aquæd.*

[4] "Mater gratiarum."—*Psalt. B. V.* p. 2.

[5] "Thesauraria gratiarum."—*Cont. de V. M. in prol.*

[6] "Omnia dona et gratiæ, quibus vult, quando vult, et quomodo vult, per manus ipsius administrantur."—*Pro Fest. S. V.* s. 5, c. 8.

. . . *that I may enrich them that love me.*[1] "Our Lord has deposited all the riches of his graces in my hands, that I may enrich those who love me."

Then, my Queen, if I love thee, I no longer shall be poor as I am. After God, I love thee above all things; do thou obtain me greater tenderness and love for thy goodness. St. Bonaventure[2] tells me that all whom thou willest are saved; therefore will I address thee with the same saint, "O salvation of all who call upon thee, save me from hell;" but first of all, save me from sin, which alone can take me to hell.

II.

Mater purissima. "MOTHER MOST PURE."—This Virgin Mother, all fair and pure, renders all her servants pure and chaste. St. Ambrose writes, that when Mary was on earth her presence alone inspired all those who looked at her with a love of purity.[3] She was called a lily amongst thorns : *As the lily among thorns, so is my love among the daughters.*[4] "All other virgins," says Denis the Carthusian, "were thorns either to themselves or to others; but the Blessed Virgin was so neither to herself nor to others, for she inspired all those upon whom she looked with pure and holy affections."[5] Frigenius, who wrote the life of St. Thomas Aquinas, relates that it was an ordinary saying of the saint, that "even the images of this chaste turtle-dove extinguish sensual desires in those who look at them with devotion." The Venerable John D'Avila says, "that many who were tempted

---

[1] "Mecum sunt divitiæ . . . ut ditem diligentes me."—*Prov.* viii. 18.

[2] *Cant. p. Psalt.*

[3] "Tanta erat Mariæ gratia, ut, etiam quos viseret, integritatis insigne conferret."—*Inst. virg.* c. 7.

[4] "Sicut lilium inter spinas, sic Amica mea inter filias."—*Cant.* ii. 2.

[5] *In Cant.* a. 8.

against purity had preserved themselves chaste by devotion to our Blessed Lady." [1] O, how especially powerful is the name of Mary in conquering all temptations to this vice !

O most pure Mary, deliver me from it. Grant that in my temptations I may always have recourse to thee, and invoke thee as long as the temptation lasts.

III.

Mater inviolata. "MOTHER UNDEFILED."—Mary was that spotless woman who always appeared beautiful and without stain in the eyes of God: *Thou art all fair, O my love, and there is not a spot in thee.* [2] Hence she was made the sinner's peacemaker, as she is called by St. Ephrem, "Hail, peacemaker of the whole world!" [3] This she also says herself in the sacred Canticles, *I am become in His presence as one finding peace.* [4] St. Gregory says, [5] "that if a rebel appeared before his offended king to appease him, instead of doing so he would provoke him to greater anger." Hence Mary being destined to treat of peace between God and men, it was not becoming that she should appear as a sinner and as an accomplice in Adam's sin; and therefore our Lord preserved her from every stain.

Ah, my immaculate Queen, fair dove, and the beloved of God, disdain not to cast thine eyes on the many stains and wounds of my soul: see me, and pity me. God, who loves thee so much, denies thee nothing; and thou knowest not how to refuse those who have recourse to thee. O Mary, to thee I have recourse; pity me. "Mother inviolate, pray for us."

---

[1] *Audi fil.* c. 14.

[2] "Tota pulchra es, Amica mea, et macula non est in te."—*Cant.* iv. 7.

[3] "Ave, orbis Conciliatrix."—*De Laud. Dei Gen.*

[4] "Facta sum coram eo quasi pacem reperiens."—*Cant.* viii. 10.

[5] *Past.* p. i. c. 11.

MEDITATION III.

I.

Mater amabilis. "MOTHER MOST AMIABLE."—Richard of St. Laurence says, "that Mary was amiable in the eyes of God himself."[1] Mary was so beautiful in the eyes of God that he was enamoured of her beauty. *How beautiful art thou, my love! how beautiful thou art!*[2] Hence he called her his only dove, his only perfect one: *One is my dove; my perfect one is but one.*[3] "It is certain," as Father Suarez says,[4] "that God loved Mary more than all the other saints together; and with reason; for she alone loved God more than all men, and all angels have ever loved him."

O most beautiful Mary, O most amiable Mary, thou hast gained the heart of God; take also my poor heart, and make me a saint. I love thee; in thee is my confidence. "Most amiable Mother, pray for us."

II.

Mater Salvatoris. "MOTHER OF OUR REDEEMER."—St. Bonaventure calls Mary "the Mediatress of our salvation;"[5] and St. John Damascene "the Saviour in a certain manner of the world."[6] For two reasons Mary can be called the Saviour of the world and our Mediatress; that is, the mediatress of grace, as Jesus Christ is the mediator of justice. First, on account of the consent which she gave at the Incarnation of the Eternal Word; for by that consent, St. Bernardine says, "she procured

[1] "Fuit Beata Virgo amabilis oculis ipsius Dei."—*De Laud. B. M.* l. 5.

[2] "Quam pulchra es, Amica mea! quam pulchra es!"—*Cant.* iv. 1.

[3] "Una est columba mea, perfecta mea."—*Cant.* vi. 8.

[4] *De Inc.* p. 2, d. 18, s. 4.

[5] "Maria, Mediatrix nostræ salutis."—*Spec. B. V. lect.* 9.

[6] "Salvatrix mundi."—*Men. Græc.* 15 *Aug.*

us salvation." [1]   Secondly, by the consent which Mary
gave to the death of her Son, in which she expressed her
willingness that he should be sacrificed on the cross for
our salvation.

I remind thee, then, O Mother of my Saviour, that
thou didst once offer the life of the Son to God; save
me now by thy intercession.

III.

Virgo veneranda.   "VIRGIN MOST VENERABLE."—St.
Anselm says, "that when we say that Mary is the
Mother of God, we speak of a dignity which is above
every other dignity that can be named or thought of,
after that of God;" therefore he says, "O Lady, nothing
equals thee; for all is either above thee, and this is God
alone, or beneath thee, and this is all that is not God." [2]
In fine, St. Bernardine writes, "that God alone can
know the greatness of Mary." [3]   Blessed Albert the
Great says, "that Mary could not be more closely united
to God without becoming God." [4]   This great Mother
of God is, then, indeed worthy of our veneration, since
God himself could not have made her greater than he
did when he made her his Mother.

O Mother of God, my Mother Mary, I venerate thee,
and would wish thee to be venerated by all hearts, as
the exalted Lady that thou art.   Pity a poor sinner who
loves thee, and trusts in thee.   "Virgin most venerable,
pray for us."

[1] "Per hunc consensum, omnium salutem procuravit."—*Pro Fest.
V. M.* s. 8, a. 2, c. 2.

[2] *De Conc. B. M. V.*

[3] "Tanta fuit perfectio Virginis, ut soli Deo cognoscenda reserve
tur."—*Pro Fest. V. M.* s. 4, a. 3, c. 1.

[4] "Magis Deo conjungi non potuit, nisi fieret Deus."

MEDITATION IV.

I.

Virgo prædicanda. "VIRGIN MOST RENOWNED."—The Holy Church proclaims that this divine Mother is "most worthy of every praise;" [1] for, as St. Ildephonsus says, "all praise that is given to the Mother redounds to the honor of the Son." [2] With reason, then, did St. George of Nicomedia declare, "that God accepts the praises which are lavished on Mary, as if they were bestowed on himself." [3] The Blessed Virgin promises Paradise to him who endeavors to make her known and loved: *they that explain me, shall have life everlasting.* [4] Therefore, Richard of St. Laurence writes, that "all who honor her in this world will be honored by her in the next." [5] St. Anselm says, "that as Mary, by becoming the Mother of God was the means of the salvation of sinners, so are sinners saved by proclaiming her praises." [6] All cannot be preachers, but all can praise her, and speak to relatives and friends in familiar conversation of the merits of Mary, of her powers and mercy, and thus lead them to devotion towards this divine Mother.

O Queen of Heaven, from this time forward I am determined to do all that I can to cause thee to be venerated and loved by all. Accept my desire, and help me to execute it; in the mean time inscribe me in the number of thy servants, and never permit me again to become a slave of Lucifer.

[1] "Omni laude dignissima."

[2] "Redundat ad Filium, quód impenditur Matri."—*De Virginit. S. M.* c. 12.

[3] "Tuam enim gloriam Creator existimat esse propriam."—*Or. in Ingr. B. V.*

[4] "Qui elucidant me, vitam æternam habebunt."—*Ecclus.* xxiv. 31.

[5] "Glorificavit in futuro honorificantes se in præsenti."—*De Laud. B. M.* l. 2, p. 1.

[6] *De Excell. V.* c. 1.

II.

Virgo potens. "VIRGIN MOST POWERFUL."—And who amongst the saints is as powerful with God as his most holy Mother? She obtains all that she pleases. "Thou willest," says St. Bernard, "and all is done."[1] St. Peter Damian even says, "that when Mary asks graces from God, she does not ask, but, so to say, commands,[2] for her Son honors her by refusing her nothing."[3] Thus does the Son honor his beloved Mother by granting her whatever she asks, even in favor of sinners. Hence St. Germanus says, "Thou, O Mother of God, art omnipotent to save sinners, and needest no other recommendation with God, for thou art the Mother of true life."[4]

O Mary, thou canst make me a saint; I rely on thee.

III.

Virgo clemens. "VIRGIN MOST MERCIFUL."—Mary is as clement and merciful toward those who have recourse to her intercession as she is powerful with God. St. Bernard says, "that since the power to save us cannot be wanting to Mary, as she is the Mother of God, so neither can the will be wanting to her, for she is our Mother."[5] Who is there that ever had recourse to Mary and was abandoned? "Let him cease to praise thy mercy," says the same St. Bernard, "who remembers having ever invoked thee without being graciously heard."[6] St. Bonaventure writes, "that Mary has so great a desire to be invoked by us, that she may dis-

[1] "Velis tu, et omnia fient."
[2] "Accedis, non rogans, sed imperans."
[3] "Nam Filius, nihil negans, honorat te."—*In Nat. B. V.* s. 1.
[4] *In Dorm. B. V.* s. 2.
[5] "Nec facultas ei deesse poterit, nec voluntas.—*In Assumpt.* s. 1.
[6] "Sileat misericordiam tuam, si quis te invocatam meminerit defuisse."—*Ibid.* s. 4.

pense her favors-to us in greater abundance, that she is not only offended by those who speak ill of her, but also by those who neglect to ask her for graces."[1] Thus, to obtain her help, we are not obliged to pray much to this Mother of Mercy; it is enough to ask for it with confidence. "Her mercy," says Richard of St. Victor, "comes to our aid before we invoke it:"[2] and he tells us why: "It is because she cannot know and see our miseries without relieving them."[3]

See, then, O Mary, see my miseries and help me. "Virgin most merciful, pray for us."

MEDITATION V.

I.

Virgo fidelis. "VIRGIN MOST FAITHFUL."—Blessed is he who by his prayers watches by the gate of Mary, as the poor wait at the door of the rich to obtain relief. *Blessed is the man*, Mary says, *that heareth me, and that watcheth daily at my gates.*[4] O that we were as faithful to serve this divine Mother as she is faithful to relieve us when we pray to her! Mary promises that all who serve and honor her shall be free from sin and obtain eternal life: *They that work by me shall not sin. They that explain me shall have life everlasting.*[5] She invites all to have recourse to her, and promises them every grace that they desire: *In me is all grace of the way and of the truth; in me is all hope of life and of virtue; come over to me, all ye that desire me.*[6] St. Laurence Justinian applies to Mary that

---

[1] "In te, Domina, peccant, non solum qui tibi injuriam irrogant, sed etiam qui te non rogant."

[2] "Velocius occurrit ejus pietas, quam invocetur."

[3] "Non potest miserias scire, et non subvenire."—*In Cant.* c. 23.

[4] "Beatus homo qui audit me, et qui vigilat ad fores meas quotidie."—*Prov.* viii. 34.

[5] "Qui operantur in me, non peccabunt. Qui elucidant me, vitam æternam habebunt."—*Ecclus.* xxiv. 30.

[6] "In me gratia omnis viæ et veritatis; in me omnis spes vitæ et virtutis. Transite ad m. ...."—*Ibid.* 25.

other text of Ecclesiasticus, *her bands are a healthful binding;*[1] and then adds, "wherefore bands, unless to bind her servants, that they may not stray in the fields of sin."[2] Mary binds her servants, that they may not give themselves too much liberty, which would cause their ruin.

O Mother of God, in thee do I place all my confidence; thou must preserve me from falling any more into sin. My Lady, abandon me not, obtain me the grace rather to die than to lose the grace of God.

II.

Causa nostræ lætitiæ. "CAUSE OF OUR JOY."—As the dawn is a cause of joy, after the darkness and gloom of night, so was the birth of Mary, who is our dawn, a cause of joy to the world, which, before the coming of Jesus Christ, had been, for four thousand years, immersed in the darkness of sin. A holy Father says, "that in the birth of Mary the dawn appeared."[3] The dawn is the forerunner of the sun, and Mary was the precursor of the Incarnate Word, the Sun of Justice, the Redeemer, who, by his death, delivered us from eternal death. With reason the Church sings, on the Nativity of Mary, "Thy birth, O holy Mother of God, announced joy to the whole world."[4] And as Mary was the beginning of our joy, so is she also its completion; for St. Bernard says, "that Jesus Christ deposited the whole price of our redemption in the hands of Mary; that every grace which we receive, we may receive it from her."[5]

---

[1] "Vincula illius, alligatura salutaris."—*Ecclus.* vi. 31.

[2] "' Vincula,' quibus ligamur, ne discurramus per campos licentiæ.' "—*De Laud. B. M.* l. 2, p. 3.

[3] "Nata Virgine, surrexit aurora."—*De Assumpt.*

[4] ' Nativitas tua, Dei genitrix Virgo, gaudium annuntiavit universo mundo."—*Off. Nat. B. M. V.*

[5] "Redempturus humanum genus, pretium universum contulit in Mariam, ut, si quid salutis in nobis est ab illa noverimus redundare."—*De Aquæd*

O Mother of God, thou art my joy and my hope; for thou deniest thy graces to no one, and thou obtainest all that thou willest from God.

III.

Vas insigne devotionis. "VESSEL OF SINGULAR DEVOTION."—Devotion, as St. Thomas [1] teaches, consists in the readiness with which our will conforms itself to the will of God. This was the principal virtue which rendered his most Holy Mother so dear to God. This also was the signification of the answer which our Lord gave to the woman who called the womb which bore him blessed:

Yea rather, blessed are they that hear the word of God and keep it. [2] By this, according to Venerable Bede, our Lord meant that Mary was more blessed by the union of her will with that of God than by being his Mother. That flower which always turns towards the sun is a real type of Mary. The divine will was alone the aim and satisfaction of the heart of Mary; as she herself proclaimed, *My spirit hath rejoiced in God my Saviour.* [3]

O blessed art thou my Lady, who wast always, and in all, united to the divine will. Obtain for me the grace to spend the rest of my life in constant conformity to the will of God.

MEDITATION VI.

I.

Rosa mystica. "MYSTICAL ROSE."—Of Mary it is said in the sacred Canticles, that she was the enclosed Garden of God, *My sister, my spouse, is a garden enclosed.* [4] St. Bernard writes, "that our Lord planted all the flowers

---

[1] 2. 2, q. 82, a. 1.
[2] "Quinimo beati, qui audiunt verbum Dei et custodiunt illud."—*Luke*, xi. 28.
[3] "Et exsultavit spiritus meus in Deo salutari meo."
[4] "Hortus conclusus, soror mea sponsa."—*Cant.* iv. 12.

which adorn the Church in this garden; and amongst others the violet of humility, the lily of purity, and the rose of charity." [1] "A rose is red, and of a fiery color," says Blessed Raymond Jordano, "which denotes love of God and of our neighbor;" [2] therefore, on account of the ardent love with which the heart of Mary was always inflamed towards God and us, she is called a rose. And where can we find an advocate who is more earnest in the affair of our salvation, or who loves us more than Mary? "We acknowledge," says St. Augustine of her, "that one alone is solicitous for us in heaven." [3]

O my dear Mother, could I but love thee as thou lovest me! I will not, however, cease to do all that I can to honor and love thee. My most sweet Lady, do thou obtain for me grace to be faithful to thee.

II.

Turris Davidica. "TOWER OF DAVID."—Mary is called in the sacred Canticles the Tower of David: *Thy neck is as the tower of David; a thousand bucklers hang upon it; all the armor of valiant men.* [4] St. Bernardine says, that the tower of David stood on high, that is, on Sion; therefore Mary is called the tower of David, to denote the height of the perfection of this great creature: "As Sion was a very elevated spot, so was the Blessed Virgin most exalted." [5] Therefore of Mary it is said in the Psalms, that the very beginning of her sanctity was more exalted than the mountains: *The foundations thereof are in the*

---

[1] *Depr. ad glor. V.*

[2] Rosa rubicunda, per Dei et proximi charitatem; nam igneus color designat charitatem."—*Op. plen. de V.* p. 14, *cont.* 43.

[3] "Te solam, O Maria! pro Sancta Ecclesia sollicitam præ omnibus Sanctis scimus."—*Ap. S. Bonav. Spec. B. V. lect.* 6.

[4] "Sicut Turris David collum tuum."—*Cant.* iv. 4.

[5] "Sion locus erat eminentissimus, sic Beata Virgo altissima."—*Pro Fest. V. M.* s. 4, a. 2, c. 3.

holy mountains:[1] St. Gregory[2] explains it to mean that the divine Mother was more holy in the first moment of her life than any of the saints were at the moment of their death

Ah, my Queen and Mother, I rejoice in thy greatness, and am willing rather-to sacrifice my life than that thy glory should be diminished in the least degree, were such a thing possible. O that I could only by shedding every drop of my blood cause all nations of the earth to adore and love thee as the greåt Lady which thou art!

III.

Turris eburnea. "TOWER OF IVORY."—Thus is Mary also called. *Thy neck is as a tower of ivory.*[3] Mary is called a neck; for she is the mystic neck through which the vital spirits, that is, the divine help which preserves in us the life of grace, are transmitted from Jesus Christ the Head to us the faithful, who are members of the mystic body of the Church. St. Bernardine says, "The life-giving graces flow from Christ the Head, through the Blessed Virgin, into his mystic body."[4] The saint then adds, "that from the time when Mary conceived the Incarnate Word, she received the great honor from God, that no one should receive any grace otherwise than through her hands. In fine, ivory is greatly esteemed and is strong. Hence the Abbot Rupert writes of Mary, "that as a tower of ivory she is beloved by God, and terrible to the devil."[5]

Then, O my sovereign Lady, because thou art so beloved of God, thou canst obtain us every grace; and be-

[1] " Fundamenta ejus in montibus sanctis."—*Ps.* lxxxvi. 1.

[2] *In* 1 *Reg.* i.

[3] " Collum tuum sicut turris eburnea."—*Cant.* vii. 4.

[4] " Per Virginem a capite Christo vítales gratiæ in ejus corpus mysticum transfunduntur."—*Pro Fest. V. M.* s. 5, c. 8.

[5] " Sicut turris eburnea, Deo amabilis, diabolo terribilis."—*In Cant* l. 6.

cause thou art terrible to the evil spirits, thou canst delivers us from all their snares. Have mercy on us, who glory in living under thy protection.

MEDITATION VII.

I.

Domus aurea. "HOUSE OF GOLD."—Gold is a symbol of love. Therefore Blessed Albert the Great calls Mary "a golden temple of charity."[1] And with reason; for St. Thomas says, that "as all in the temple was covered with gold, so was everything in the beautiful soul of Mary filled with sanctity."[2] Mary was the house of gold which Eternal Wisdom, that is, the divine Word, chose for his dwelling on earth: *Wisdom hath built herself a house.*[3] "This House of God," says Richard of St. Laurence, "is so rich that it can relieve all our wants."[4]

O Mary, thou lovest God so much, and therefore thou desirest to see him loved by all. This is the grace which above all others I ask of thee, and which I hope from thee; obtain me great love for God.

II.

Fœderis arca. "ARK OF THE COVENANT."—Hesychius calls Mary "an ark more spacious than that of Noah;"[5] for in the ark of Noah only two animals of every kind were received, but under the mantle of Mary the just and sinners find place. This was one day revealed to St. Gertrude;[6] for she saw a multitude of wild beasts,

---

[1] "Templum aureum charitatis."—*Bibl. Mar.* 3 *Reg.* n. 4.

[2] "Nihil erat in Templo quod non auro tegeretur; nihil erat in Virgine, quod non sanctitate plenum esset."—*S. in Purif. ex Ep.*

[3] "Sapientia ædificavit sibi domum."—*Prov.* ix. 1.

[4] "Domus Dei, cujus tanta est abundantia, quod nostram potest replere inopiam."—*De Laud. B. M.* l. 12.

[5] "Arca Noe largior."—*De S. M. Deip. hom.* 2.

[6] *Insin.* l. 4, c. 50

lions, leopards, and the like, that took refuge under the mantle of Mary; and she not only did not drive them away, but with her benign hands caressed them, that they might not flee away. The animals that entered the ark remained animals; but sinners who are received under the mantle of Mary do not remain sinners. She is certain to change their hearts, and to render them agreeable to God. The Blessed Virgin herself said to St. Bridget, "However much a man may have sinned, if he returns to me with a real purpose of amendment, I am ready at once to receive him; neither do I pay attention to the sins with which he is laden; but only to the good disposition in which he comes; and then I do not disdain to anoint and heal his wounds, for I am called and truly am the Mother of Mercy." [1]

O Mother of Mercy, will I then say to thee, in the words of St. Bernard, "Remember that it has never been heard of in any age, that any sinner who had recourse to thee was rejected by thee." I, a miserable sinner, have recourse to thee and trust in thee.

III.

Janua cœli. "GATE OF HEAVEN."—Mary is called the "Gate of Heaven," because, as St. Bonaventure declares, "no one can enter heaven unless by Mary, as through a door." [2] Our Queen says, *My power is in Jerusalem.* [3] Richard of St. Laurence adds: "Commanding what I will and introducing whom I will." [4] I can obtain whatever I please for my clients, and introduce all whom I please into paradise. Hence St. Bonaventure writes, that "those who enjoy the favor of Mary are recognized

---

[1] *Rev.* l. 2, c. 23:—l. 6, c. 117.

[2] "Nullus potest cœlum intrare, nisi per Mariam transeat, tamquam per portam."—*In Luc.* i.

[3] "In Jerusalem potestas-mea."—*Ecclus.* xxiv. 15.—*In Miss. B. V.*

[4] "Impetrandi quod volo, et, quos volo, introducendi."—*De Laud. B. M.* l. 4.

by the citizens of heaven; and those who bear her stamp, that is, have the grace to be her servants, are inscribed in the Book of Life." [1] For this reason, Bernardine de Bustis [2] calls Mary "the Book of Life," and says that whoever, by this devotion, is written in this book, is certain to be saved.

Ah, my Mother, in thee do I repose my hope of eternal salvation. I love thee; do thou save me; never allow a servant of thine who loves thee to go to blaspheme thee in hell.

MEDITATION VIII.

I.

Stella matutina. " Morning Star."—St. John Damascene calls Mary "the Star which indicates the rising of the sun." [3] As the morning star precedes the sun, so does devotion towards the most Blessed Virgin precede the sun of divine grace; for St. Germanus says [4] that "devotion in a soul towards Mary is a sign either that it is already in a state of grace, or that it will very soon be so." Our Lady is also called "the Star of the Sea" by the Church; for, as St. Thomas explains it, "as mariners, in tempestuous weather, are guided by the star of the sea into port, so are souls guided by Mary over the sea of this world into Paradise." [5] Hence St. Bernard warns us, saying, "If you do not wish to be lost in the storm of temptations, turn not your eyes from this star of salvation." [6] He then continues, "if you follow Mary, you

---

[1] *Psalt. maj. Ps.* xci.

[2] *Marial.* p. 2, s. 2.

[3] " Stella demonstrans solem."—*Men. Græc.* 15 *Mart.*

[4] *De Zona Deip*

[5] "Sicut per stellam maris navigantes diriguntur ad portum, ita Christiani diriguntur per Mariam ad gloriam."—*In Sal. Ang.*

[6] " Ne avertas oculos a fulgore hujus Sideris, si non vis obrui procellis."

will not go astray; if Mary protects you, you cannot fear to be lost; if Mary favors you, you will reach Paradise." [1]

II.

Salus infirmorum. "HEALTH OF THE WEAK."—Mary is called by St. Simon Stock " the medicine of sinners;" [2] and by St. Ephrem, not only medicine, but health itself: " Robust health for those who have recourse to her." [3] Hence those who have recourse to Mary not only find in her a remedy, but health itself; and this she herself promises to all who seek her: *He that shall find me shall find life, and shall have salvation from the Lord.* [4] Neither let us fear that, on account of the bad odor of our wounds, she may refuse to take care of us: she is our Mother; and as a mother does not shrink from dressing the wound of her child, neither does this celestial physician refuse to hear servants who have recourse to her. Wherefore St. Bernard says, " O Mother of God, thou dost not disdain a sinner, however loathsome he may be: if he sends up his sighs to thee, thou wilt deliver him with thine own hand from despair." [5]

III.

Refugium peccatorum. "REFUGE OF SINNERS."—Thus is Mary called by St. Germanus; he says, " She is the ever-ready refuge of sinners." [6] Yes, of all sinners; for, as the Abbot of Celles says, " she can despise no sinner, but receives all, and welcomes all, the moment they have

---

[1] " Ipsam sequens, non devias; ipsa protegente, non metuis; ipsa propitia, pervenis."—*De Laud. V. M. hom.* 2.

[2] " Peccatorum medicina."

[3] " Salus firma recurrentium ad eam."—*De Laud. Dei Gen.*

[4] " Qui me invenerit, inveniet vitam, et hauriet salutem a Domino."—*Prov.* viii. 35.

[5] *Depr. ad Glor. V.*

[6] " Refugium paratissimum peccatorum."—*De Zona Deip.*

recourse to her."[1]   Hence St. John Damascene affirms, that Mary is not only the refuge of the innocent, but also of the wicked, who implore her protection: " I am a city of refuge to all who fly to me."[2]   Therefore St. Bonaventure says to her: "Thou embracest with maternal affection a sinner who is even despised by the whole world, nor dost thou cease thine embrace until thou hast reconciled him with his judge."[3]   By this the saint gives us to understand, that a sinner being hated by God is also odious and abominable to all creatures; but if he has recourse to Mary, the refuge of sinners, not only she does not despise him, but embraces him with affection, and does not leave him until her Son Jesus Christ, who is our Judge, has forgiven him.

Since, then, O my Lady, thou art the refuge of all sinners, thou art also my refuge.   Thou, who despisest no one who has recourse to thee, despise me not, who recommend myself to thee: "Refuge of sinners, pray for us." O Mary, pray for us, and save us."

MEDITATION IX.

I.

Consolatrix afflictorum.   "COMFORTRESS OF THE AFFLICTED."—St. Germanus says, " O Mary, who, after thy Son, is as solicitous for the whole human race as thou art ? who protects us in our trials as thou dost !"[4]   Who,

---

[1] "Tu es tutissimum refugium , a te nullus peccator despicitur; omnes peccatores recipis, nec moram in hoc facis."—*Op. plen. de V.* p. 9, *cont.* 14.

[2] " Civitas refugii omnium ad eam confugientium."—*De Dorm. B. M.* s. 2.

[3] " Peccatorem toti mundo despectum materno affectu amplecteris; nec deseris, quousque Judici miserum reconcilies."—*Spec. B. V. lect.* 5.

[4] " Quis, post Filium tuum, curam gerit generis humani, sicut tu ? quis ita nos defendit in nostris afflictionibus ?"—*De Zona Deip.*

O Mary, watches over our interests as thou dost? who is solicitous as thou art for us in our afflictions? "No," replies St. Antoninus; "no saint can be found who compassionates us in our miseries as does this most tender Lady, the Blessed Virgin Mary." [1] And as the miseries which afflict us the most are disorders of the soul, Blessed Henry Suso calls Mary "the most faithful comfortress of sinners." [2] We need only show Mary the wounds of our souls, and she immediately helps us by her prayers, and consoles us. Nay, even as Richard of St. Victor writes, her compassion anticipates our wants, and she relieves us before we invoke her. [3] Let us say, then, with St. Bonaventure:

"O Mary, console us always, but especially at the hour of our death: come at that last hour and receive our souls, and present them thyself to thy Son, who will judge us."

II.

Auxilium Christianorum. "HELP OF CHRISTIANS."—St. John Damascene calls Mary "the prepared and always ready help of Christians, by which they are delivered from dangers." [4] The help of Mary is, as St. Cosmas of Jerusalem [5] writes, "all-powerful to deliver us from sin and hell." St. Bernard, [6] addressing Mary, says, "Thou art an invincible warrior in defence of thy servants, fighting against the devils who assail them." For this reason she is called an army in the sacred Canticles: *thou art . . . terrible as an army set in array.* [7]

[1] "Non reperitur aliquis Sanctorum ita compati infirmitatibus nostris, sicut Mulier hæc, Beata Virgo Maria."—*P.* 4, t. 15, c. 2.

[2] "Consolatrix fidelissima peccatorum."—*Dial.* c. 16.

[3] "Velocius occurrit quam invocetur."—*In Cant.* c. 23.

[4] "Auxilium promptum et paratum Christianorum, eripiens nos a periculis."—*Paracl. B. V.*

[5] *Hymn.* 6, *in depr. ad Deip.*

[6] "Tu Bellatrix egregia."—*Depr. ad Glor. V.*

[7] "Terribilis ut castrorum acies ordinata."—*Cant.* vi. 3.

Ah, my Queen, had I always had recourse to thee, I should never have been conquered by my enemies; henceforth thou shalt be my strength: in my temptations I will always have recourse to thee; from thee do I hope for victory.

III.

Regina Martyrum. "QUEEN OF MARTYRS."—With reason is Mary called the Queen of Martyrs, for her martyrdom in the death of her Son on the cross exceeded the sufferings of all the martyrs. *There stood by the cross of Jesus His Mother.*[1] Mothers fly from their children when they see them dying and are unable to help them. Mary did not fly, but remained with Jesus until she saw him expire. *She stood by the cross*, and whilst Jesus was in his agony she offered the life of her Son to the Eternal Father for our salvation; but in doing so she also was in an agony, and experienced a torment greater than any death.

O my afflicted Mother, be graciously pleased, by the merit of the sorrows which thou didst endure at the foot of the cross, to obtain for me true sorrow for my sins, and love for Jesus my Redeemer; and by the sword which transpierced thy heart when thou didst see him bow down his head and expire, I beseech thee to help me at the hour of my death, and then to obtain me eternal salvation, that I may love thee with thy Jesus forever.

[1] "Stabat autem juxta crucem Jesu Mater ejus."—*John*, xix. 25.

II.

MEDITATIONS FOR THE SEVEN PRINCIPAL FEASTS OF THE BLESSED VIRGIN.

I.

The Feast of the Immaculate Conception.

December 8.

I.

IT was indeed becoming that the three divine Persons should preserve Mary from original sin.

It was becoming that the Father should do so, because Mary was his first-born daughter. As Jesus was the first-born of God, *the first-born of every creature,*[1] so also was Mary, the destined Mother of God, always considered by him as his first-born daughter by adoption, and therefore he always possessed her by his grace: *The Lord possessed me in the beginning of His ways.*[2] For the honor, therefore, of his Son, it was becoming that the Father should preserve his Mother from every stain of sin. It was also becoming that he should do so, because he destined this his daughter to crush the head of the infernal serpent, who had seduced man, as we read in Genesis, *she shall crush thy head.*[3] How, then, could he permit that she should first be the slave of this infernal serpent? Moreover, Mary was also destined to become the advocate of sinners; therefore it was also becoming that God should preserve her from sin, that she might not appear guilty of the same fault as men for whom she was to intercede.

[1] " Primogenitus omnis creaturæ."—*Col.* i. 15.
[2] " Dominus possedit me in initio viarum suarum."—*Prov.* viii. 22.
[3] " Ipsa conteret caput tuum."—*Gen.* iii. 15.

II.

It was becoming that the Son should have an immaculate Mother. He himself chose Mary for his Mother. It is impossible to believe that a son who could have a queen for his mother would choose a slave. How, then, can we imagine that the Eternal Word, who could have an ever-immaculate Mother, and one who had always been a friend of God, would have one defiled by sin, and at one time the enemy of God? Moreover, as an ancient author says, "the flesh of Christ is the flesh of Mary." [1] The Son of God would have felt horror to have taken flesh of a St. Agnes, a St. Gertrude, or of a St. Teresa, because these holy virgins were defiled by sin before baptism; and therefore the devil could then have reproached him with being clothed with flesh which had once been subject to him. But as Mary was always pure and immaculate, our Lord felt no horror at becoming man in her chaste womb.[2] Besides, St. Thomas says,[3] that "Mary was preserved from every actual sin, even venial;" for otherwise she would not have been a becoming Mother of God; but how much less would she have been so, had she been defiled by original sin, which renders the soul hateful to God?

III.

It was becoming the Holy Ghost, that this his most beloved spouse should be immaculate. As men who had already fallen into sin were to be redeemed, he willed that this his spouse should be redeemed in a more noble way; that is, by being preserved from falling into sin. And since God preserved the body of Mary after her death, how much more should we believe that he pre-

[1] "Caro Jesu caro est Mariæ."—*Lib. de Assumpt.* c. 5.
[2] "Non horruisti Virginis uterum."—*Hymn. Te Deum.*
[3] P. 3, q. 27, a. 4.

served her soul from the corruption of sin? Hence the divine Spouse calls her, in the sacred Canticles, *an enclosed garden, a sealed fountain;*[1] for an enemy never entered the blessed soul of Mary. Therefore he praised her, calling her all beautiful, always his friend, and all pure: *Thou art all fair, O my love, and there is not a spot in thee.*[2]

Ah, my most beautiful Lady, I rejoice in seeing thee, by thy purity and thy beauty, so dear to God. I thank God for having preserved thee from every stain. My Queen, since thou art so loved by the most Holy Trinity, disdain not to cast thine eyes on my soul, which is so defiled by sin, that, seeing it, thou mayest obtain for me pardon and eternal salvation from God. Behold me, and change me. Thou, by thy sweetness, hast drawn so many hearts to thy love, draw also my heart, that henceforward it may love no other than God and thee. Thou well knowest that I have placed all my hopes in Thee, my dear Mother; abandon me not. Help me always with thine intercession in life, and especially at the hour of my death; grant that I may die invoking and loving thee, that I may love thee forever in Paradise.

II.

The Feast of the Purification.

The Presentation of Jesus in the Temple.

February 2.

I.

When the time had come in which, according to the law, Mary was to be purified in the Temple, and to present Jesus to the Eternal Father, she, accompanied by St. Joseph, directed her steps towards Jerusalem. Joseph took two turtle-doves, which were to be offered, and Mary took her beloved infant. She took the divine

---

[1] *Cant.* iv. 12.

[2] "Tota pulchra es, Amica mea, et macula non est in te."—*Ibid.* 7.

Lamb to offer it to God, as a token of the great sacrifice which he would one day accomplish on the cross.

My God, I also unite my sacrifice to that of Mary; I offer Thee Thy Incarnate Son; and by his merits I beseech Thee to grant me Thy grace. I do not deserve it; but Jesus sacrificed himself to Thee to obtain it for me. For the love of Jesus, then, have mercy on me.

II.

Behold, Mary entered the Temple, and in the name of the whole human race made the oblation of her Son. But, especially on this day, Jesus offered himself to his Eternal Father. "Behold me, O Father," he said; "to Thee do I consecrate my whole life; Thou hast sent me into the world to save it: accept my blood and my life; I offer them without reserve to Thee, for the salvation of the world."

Unfortunate should I have been, my Dear Redeemer, hadst Thou not satisfied the divine justice for me. I thank Thee with my whole soul, and I love Thee with my whole heart. And whom shall I love, if I do not love a God who sacrificed his life for me?

III.

This sacrifice was more precious in the sight of God than if all men and angels had offered him their lives. Yes, because it was in this offering of Jesus alone that the Eternal Father received infinite honor and an infinite satisfaction. Jesus Christ said one day to Blessed Angela of Foligno, "I offered myself for thee, that thou mightest offer thyself to me."

Yes, my Jesus, since Thou hast offered Thy life to Thy Eternal Father for me, I offer my life and my entire self to Thee. Hitherto, with the greatest ingratitude, I have despised Thee; but Thou hast promised no more to remember the outrages of a sinner who repents of having offended Thee. My Jesus, I grieve for having offended Thee, and wish that I could die of grief. I was dead by sin ; from Thee I hope for life, and my life shall be to love Thee, O Infinite Good. Make me love Thee; I ask for nothing more. Dispense the riches of this world to those who desire them; I desire nothing but the treasure of Thy love. My Jesus, Thou alone art sufficient for me. O Queen and my Mother Mary, through thee do I hope for every grace.

III.

The Feast of the Annunciation.

March 25.

i.

When God was pleased to send his Son on earth that by becoming man he might redeem lost man, he chose for him a Virgin Mother, who, amongst all virgins, was the most pure, the most holy, and the most humble. Behold, whilst Mary was in her poor dwelling, beseeching God to send the promised Redeemer, an angel stood before her and saluted her, saying, *Hail, full of grace ; the Lord is with thee ; blessed art thou among women.*[1] And what was the conduct of this humble Virgin when she heard so honorable a salutation ? She was not elated, but was silent and troubled, considering herself indeed unworthy of such praises: *she was troubled at his saying.*[2]

O Mary, thou art so humble, and I am so filled with pride ; obtain for me holy humility.

II.

Think you that these praises caused Mary at least to suspect that she might be the destined Mother of the

[1] " Ave, gratia Plena ! Dominus tecum; benedicta tu in mulieri-bus."—*Luke*, i. 28.

[2] " Quæ cum audisset, turbata est in sermone ejus."

Redeemer? No; they only caused her to conceive a great fear of herself; so much so, indeed, that the angel had to encourage her: *Fear not, Mary ; for thou hast found grace with God.*[1] He then announced to her that she was the chosen Mother of the Redeemer of the world : *Behold thou shalt conceive in thy womb, and shalt bring forth a Son, and thou shalt call his name Jesus.*[2]

Blessed art thou, O Mary ; how dear wast thou to God, and how dear art thou still to him! Have pity on me.

III.

"And now, O holy Virgin," says St. Bernard,[3] "why dost thou delay thy consent? The Eternal Word awaits it to clothe himself with flesh and become thy Son. We also await it, who in misery are condemned to eternal death. If thou consentest, and acceptest to become his Mother, we shall be made free. Quickly, O Lady, answer. Delay not the salvation of the world, which depends on thy consent." But let us rejoice, for Mary already hears the angel : *Behold the handmaid of the Lord ; be it done to me according to thy word.*[4] "Behold," she says, "the slave of the Lord, who is bound to do all that her Lord commands." If he chooses a slave for his Mother, it is not she who is to be praised, but the goodness of that Lord alone, who is thus graciously pleased to honor her.

O most humble Mary, thou by this thy humility didst so enamour thy God that thou didst draw him to thee, so as to become thy Son and our Redeemer. I know that thy Son refuses thee nothing that thou askest him.

[1] " Ne timeas, Maria; invenisti enim gratiam apud Deum."

[2] " Ecce concipies in utero et paries Filium, et vocabis nomen ejus Jesum."

[3] *De Laud. V. M. hom.* 4.

[4] " Ecce ancilla Domini; fiat mihi secundum verbum tuum."

13

Ask him to forgive all the offences that I have committed against him ; ask him to grant me perseverance until death. In fine, recommend my soul to him ; for thy recommendations meet with no denial from a Son who loves thee so much. O Mary, thou hast to save me ; thou art my hope.

IV.

The Feast of the Visitation.

July 2.

I.

Mary set out from Nazareth to go to the city of Judea, in which St. Elizabeth resided ; a distance, according to Broccardus, of upwards of seventy miles, or at least seven days' journey. Her spouse St. Joseph alone accompanied her. The holy and tender Virgin hastened her steps, as St. Luke tells us : *Mary, rising up in those days, went into the hill country with haste.*[1] Tell us, O holy Lady, why didst thou undertake so long and arduous a journey, and why didst thou so hasten thy steps ? "I went," she replies, "to exercise my office of charity : I went to console a family."

Since, then, O great Mother of God, thy office is to console and dispense graces to souls, ah, be graciously pleased also to visit and console my soul. Thy visit sanctified the house of Elizabeth : come, O Mary, and sanctify me also.

II.

Behold, the Blessed Virgin already arrived at the house of Elizabeth. She was the Mother of God, but yet she was the first to salute Elizabeth : *And she entered . . . and saluted Elizabeth.*[2] Elizabeth, enlightened

[1] "Abiit in montana cum festinatione."—*Luke,* i. 39.
[2] "Intravit, . . . et salutavit Elisabeth."

by God, knew that the divine Word had become man, that he had become the Son of Mary ; therefore she called her blessed amongst women, and blessed the divine fruit which she carried in her womb : *Blessed art thou among women, and blessed is the fruit of thy womb.*[1] At the same time, filled with confusion and joy, she exclaimed : *And whence is this to me, that the Mother of my Lord should come to me?*[2] But what does the humble Mary reply to these words? She says : *My soul doth magnify the Lord ;*[3] as if she had said, "Ah, Elizabeth, thou dost praise me ; but I praise my God, who hath been graciously pleased to exalt me, who am his poor servant, to the dignity of being his Mother :" *He hath regarded the humility of His handmaid.*[4]

O most holy Mary, since thou dispensest so many graces to those who ask thee for them, I beseech thee to grant me thy humility. Thou esteemest thyself as nothing before God ; but I am worse than nothing, for I am a sinner. Thou canst make me humble ; do so, for the love of that God who made thee his Mother.

III.

But what took place at the first sound of the voice of Mary saluting Elizabeth? *When Elizabeth heard the salutation of Mary, the infant leaped in her womb, and Elizabeth was filled with the Holy Ghost.*[5] The infant John exulted with joy on account of the divine grace which was then conferred upon him. Elizabeth was filled with the Holy Ghost ; and Zachary, the father of the Baptist, had shortly afterwards the consolation of recovering his speech.

[1] " Benedicta tu inter mulieres, et benedictus Fructus ventris tui."
[2] " Et unde hoc mihi, ut veniat Mater Domini mei ad me ?"
[3] " Magnificat anima mea Dominum."
[4] " Respexit humilitatem ancillæ suæ."
[5] " Ut audivit salutationem Mariæ Elisabeth, exsultavit infans in utero ejus; et repleta est Spiritu Sancto Elisabeth."

It is indeed, true, O my Queen and Mother, that it is through thee that divine graces are dispensed, and through thee that souls are sanctified. Then, my own most dear Queen, do not forget me thy poor servant; for I love thee and have placed all my hopes in thee. Thy prayers are ever graciously heard by God, who loves thee so much. Hasten, therefore, my mother; pray for me, and make me a saint.

V.

The Feast of the Assumption.

August 15.

I.

Mary died; but how did she die? She died entirely detached from all created things; she died consumed by that divine love which during her whole life had always inflamed her most holy heart.

O holy Mother, thou hast already left the earth; do not forget us miserable pilgrims who remain in this valley of tears, struggling against so many enemies who wish to drag us to hell. Ah, by the merits of thy precious death be graciously pleased to obtain us detachment from earthly things, the forgiveness of our sins, love of God, and holy perseverance; and when the hour of death arrives, help us from heaven with thy prayers, and obtain for us that we may kiss thy feet in Paradise.

II.

Mary died, and her most pure body was carried by the holy Apostles and placed in the sepulchre, where it was guarded by angels for three days; after which it was transported to Paradise; but her beautiful soul entered the blessed kingdom at the very moment in which she expired, accompanied by innumerable angels, and also accompanied by her Son himself. When she had entered heaven, she humbly presented herself before God, adored him, and with immense feeling thanked him for the many graces which he had bestowed upon her. God embraced her, blessed her, and declared her Queen of the universe, exalting her above all the angels and saints.' But now, if, as the Apostle says, the human mind cannot comprehend the immense glory which God has prepared in heaven for his servants who have loved him in this world, how great must be the glory which he bestowed on this most holy Mother, who on earth loved him more than all the saints and angels, and loved him with all her strength ; so that when Mary entered heaven she alone could say to God, " O Lord, if on earth I did not love Thee as much as Thou deservedst, at least I loved Thee as much as I could love Thee."

III.

Let us rejoice with Mary at the glory with which God has enriched her. Let us also rejoice for ourselves; for at the same time that Mary was made Queen of the world, she was also made our advocate. She is so compassionate an advocate, that she accepts the causes of all sinners who recommend themselves to her; and she also has so great power with our judge, that she gains all causes which she defends.

Our Queen and advocate, our salvation is in thy hands if thou prayest for us, we shall be saved. Only tell thy Son that thou willest that we should be with thee in Paradise. He refuses thee nothing that thou askest. O Mary, our life, our sweetness, and our hope, pray to Jesus for us.

¹ " Exaltata est sancta Dei Genitrix super choros Angelorum ad cœlestia regna."—*Off. de Assumpt.*

VI.

The Feast of the Nativity

September 8.

I.

Before the birth of Mary the world was lost in the darkness of sin. "Mary was born and the dawn arose," says a holy Father.[1] Of Mary it had already been said: *Who is she that cometh forth as the morning rising?*[2] As the earth rejoices when the dawn appears, because it is the precursor of the sun, so also when Mary was born the whole world rejoiced, because she was the precursor of Jesus Christ, the Sun of Justice, who being made her Son, came to save us by his death; hence the Church sings, "Thy nativity, O Virgin Mother of God, announced joy to the whole world; for from thee arose the Sun of Justice, who has given us life eternal."[3] So that when Mary was born, our remedy, our consolation, and our salvation came into the world; for through Mary we received our Saviour.

II.

This child being, then, destined to become the Mother of the Eternal Word, God enriched her with so great grace, that in the first moment of her Immaculate Conception her sanctity exceeded that of all the saints and angels together, for she received grace of a higher order —one that corresponded to the dignity of Mother of God.

[1] "Nata Virgine, surrexit aurora."—*Serm. de Assumpt.*

[2] "Quæ est ista, quæ progreditur quasi aurora consurgens?"—*Cant.* vi. 9.

[3] "Nativitas tua, Dei Genitrix Virgo, gaudium annuntiavit universo mundo; ex te enim ortus est Sol justitiæ. Christus Deus noster, qui . . donavit nobis vitam sempiternam."—*Off. de Nat. B V*

O holy child! O full of grace! I, miserable sinner that I am, salute and adore thee. Thou art the béloved one, the delight of God; pity me, who on account of my sins have been hateful and abominable in his sight. Thou, O most pure Virgin, knewest from thy very childhood so well how to gain the heart of God, that he never did and never will refuse thee anything, and grants thee all that thou askest. My hopes are therefore in thee; recommend me to thy Son, and I shall be saved.

III.

When Mary was destined to be the Mother of God, she was also destined to become the mediatress between God and sinners. Hence the angelic St. Thomas says " that Mary received sufficient grace to save all men," [1] and therefore St. Bernard calls her " a full aqueduct, that of her plenitude we all may partake." [2]

O my Queen, mediatress of sinners, perform thy office; intercede for me. My sins shall not prevent me from trusting in thee, O great Mother of God; no, I trust in thee; and so great is my confidence, that were my salvation in my own hands, I could place it in thine. O Mary, receive me under thy protection; for that is all my desire.

VII.

The Feast of the Presentation.

November 21.

I.

The holy Mary child had hardly attained the age of three years when she entreated her holy parents to take

---

[1] *Expos. in Sal. Ang.*

[2] " Plenus aquæductus, ut accipiant cæteri de ejus plenitudine."— *De Aquæd.*

her to the Temple, according to the promise which they had made. The appointed day having arrived, the immaculate young Virgin left Nazareth with St. Joachim and St. Ann; a choir of angels also accompanied that holy child, who was destined to become the mother of their Creator. "Go," says St. Germanus, "go, O Blessed Virgin, to the house of the Lord, to await the coming of the Holy Ghost, who will make thee the Mother of the Eternal Word." [1]

II.

When the holy company had reached the Temple of Jerusalem, the blessed child turned to her parents, and kneeling, kissed their hands, asked their blessing, and, without looking back, ascended the steps of the Temple, and renouncing all earthly things, and all that the world could give her, she offered and consecrated herself without reserve to God. The life of Mary in the Temple was thenceforward but one continual exercise of love and offering of her whole self to her Lord. She advanced from hour to hour, nay, even from moment to moment, in all virtues, fortified, it is true, by divine grace, but always exerting herself with her whole strength to correspond to this grace. Mary herself said, in a vision to St. Elizabeth of Hungary, "Thou thinkest, perhaps, that I obtained grace and virtues without effort. Know that I received no graces from God without great labor, constant prayer, ardent desires, and many tears and mortifications."

III.

Thus in the Temple the tender Virgin Mary prayed without ceasing. And seeing that the human race was lost and hateful to God, she principally prayed for the coming of the Messiah, and ardently desired to be the

[1] *Encom. in S. Deip.*

servant of the happy virgin who was to become the mother of God. But, O holy Lady, know that on account of thy prayers the Son of God hastens his coming into the world to redeem the world; and moreover know that thou art that blessed one who art chosen to be the Mother of thy Creator.

O beloved of God, most holy child, thou prayest for all: pray also for me. Thou didst consecrate thy entire self from thy very childhood to the love of thy God: obtain that I, during the time that I have yet to be on earth, may live for God alone. On this day, in union with thee, I renounce all creatures, and consecrate myself to the love of my Lord. I also offer myself to thee, my Queen, to serve thee always. Accept me as thy servant in an especial manner, and obtain me the grace to be always faithful to thee and to thy Son, that I may one day praise thee, and love thee for all eternity in heaven.

We shall find this subject more developed in three meditations at the end of the preceding volume, page 456.

Acts of Consecration to Mary.

I.

Dedication of One's Self to Mary.

Most holy Virgin Mary, Mother of God, I, N., although most unworthy to be thy servant, yet moved by thy wonderful compassion, and by my desire to serve thee, now choose thee, in presence of my guardian angel and of the whole celestial court, for my especial Lady, Advocate, and Mother: and I firmly purpose always to love and serve thee for the future, and to do whatever I can to induce others to love and serve thee also. I beseech thee, O Mother of God, and my most compassionate and loving Mother, by the blood which thy Son shed for me, to receive me into the number of thy servants, to be thy child and servant forever. Assist me in all my thoughts, words, and actions in every moment of my life, so that every step that I take, and every breath that I draw, may be directed to the greater glory of my God ; and through thy most powerful intercession, may I never more offend my beloved Jesus, but may I glorify him, and love him in this life, and love thee, my most beloved and dear Mother, and thus love thee and enjoy thee in heaven for all eternity. Amen.

My Mother Mary, I recommend my soul to thee, and especially at the hour of my death.

II.

Dedication of a Family to Mary.

Most Blessed Virgin, Immaculate Queen and our Mother Mary, refuge and consolation of all miserable creatures ; prostrate before thy throne, with my whole

family, I choose thee for my Lady, Mother, and Advocate with God. I dedicate myself, with all who belong
to me, forever to thy service, and beseech thee, O Mother
of God, to receive us into the number of thy servants,
by taking us all under thy protection, helping us in life,
and still more at the hour of our death. O Mother of
Mercy, I appoint thee as Lady and Ruler of my whole
house, of my relatives, of my interests, and of all my
affairs. Disdain not to take charge of them : dispose of
all as it pleases thee. Bless me then, and all my family,
and do not permit that any of us should offend thy Son.
Do thou defend us in temptations, deliver us from dangers, provide for us our necessities, counsel us in our
doubts, comfort us in our afflictions, assist us in our infirmities, and especially in the sorrows of death. Never
allow the devil to glory in having in his chains any of
us who are now consecrated to thee ; but grant that we
may go to heaven to thank thee, and together with
thee to praise and love Jesus our Redeemer for all eternity. Amen. Thus may it be.

Prayers to Mary for Every Day in the Week.*

SUNDAY.

To obtain the Forgiveness of Our Sins.

BEHOLD, O Mother of God, at thy feet a miserable sinner, a slave of hell, who has recourse to thee and trusts in thee. I do not deserve that thou shouldst even look at me; but I know that thou, having seen thy Son die for the salvation of sinners, hast the greatest desire to help them. I hear all call thee the refuge of sinners, the hope of those who are in despair, and the help of the abandoned. Thou art, then, my refuge, my hope, and my help. Thou hast to save me by thy intercession. Help me, for the love of Jesus Christ; extend thy hand to a miserable creature who has fallen, and recommends himself to thee. I know that thy pleasure is to help a sinner to thy utmost; help me, therefore, now that thou canst do so. By my sins I have lost divine grace, and with it my soul; I now place myself in thy hands. Tell me what I must do to recover the favor of my Lord, and I will immediately do it. He sends me to thee that thou mayst help me; and he wills that I should

---

* These prayers, written before the "Glories of Mary," were printed with the "Visits to the Blessed Sacrament" in the year 1745, and inserted later in an abridged form in the *Rule of Life*, chap. ii. § 7.

The sovereign Pontiff, Pius VII., by a rescript, June 21, 1808, granted *an indulgence of three hundred days*, once a day, to all the faithful who with at least contrite heart and devotion shall say, on the days assigned, together with the *Hail Mary* three times, these prayers, to make some reparation for the many blasphemies uttered against her not only by unbelievers, but also by bad Christians. A *plenary indulgence*, once a month, to all who having said these prayers every day for a month, as directed above, if being truly penitent, after confession and Communion, they pray to God for holy Church. These indulgences, both plenary and partial, were confirmed forever by his Holiness Pope Pius IX., by a rescript June 18, 1876.—ED.

have recourse to thy mercy, that not only the merits of thy Son, but also that thy intercession may help me to save my soul. To thee, then, I have recourse; do thou, who prayest for so many others, pray also to Jesus for me. Ask him to pardon me, and he will forgive me; tell him that thou desirest my salvation, and he will save me; show how thou canst enrich those who trust in thee. Amen. Thus I hope, thus may it be.

MONDAY.

To obtain Holy Perseverance.

O Queen of Heaven, I, who was once a miserable slave of Lucifer, now dedicate myself to thee, to be thy servant forever; I offer myself to honor thee, and serve thee during my whole life; do thou accept me, and refuse me not, as I should deserve. O my Mother, in thee have I placed all my hopes, from thee do I expect every grace. I bless and thank God, who in his mercy has given me this confidence in thee, which I consider a pledge of my salvation. Alas, miserable wretch that I am, I have hitherto fallen, because I have not had recourse to thee. I now hope that, through the merits of Jesus Christ and thy prayers, I have obtained pardon. But I may again lose divine grace; the danger is not past. My enemies do not sleep. How many new temptations have I still to conquer! Ah, my most sweet Lady, protect me, and permit me not again to become their slave: help me at all times. I know that thou wilt help me, and that with thy help I shall conquer, if I recommend myself to thee; but this is what I fear—I fear that in time of danger I may neglect to call upon thee, and thus be lost. I ask thee, then, for this grace; obtain that, in the assaults of hell, I may always have recourse to thee, saying, Mary, help me. My Mother, permit me not to lose my God.

TUESDAY.

To obtain a Good Death.

O Mary, how shall I die? Even now, that I think of my sins, and of that decisive moment on which my salvation or eternal damnation depends, of that moment in which I must expire and be judged, I tremble and am confounded. O my most sweet Mother, my hopes are in the blood of Jesus Christ and in thy intercession. O comfortress of the afflicted, do not, then, abandon me, cease not to console me in that moment of so great affliction. If I am now so tormented by remorse for sins committed, the uncertainty of pardon, the danger of relapse, and the rigor of divine justice, what will become of me then? Unless thou helpest me, I shall be lost. Ah, my Lady, before death obtain me great sorrow for my sins, thorough amendment, and fidelity to God during the remainder of my life. And when my last moment arrives, O Mary, my hope, help me in the great distress in which I shall then be; encourage me, that I may not despair at the sight of my sins, which the devil will place before me. Obtain that I may then invoke thee more frequently; so that I may expire with thy most sweet name and that of thy beloved Son on my lips. Nay more, my Lady, but forgive my boldness, before I expire do thou come thyself and comfort me with thy presence. Thou hast granted this favor to so many of thy devout servants, I also desire and hope it. I am a sinner, it is true; I do not deserve so great a favor; but I am thy servant, I love thee and have full confidence in thee. O Mary, I shall expect thee; do not disappoint me of this consolation. At least, if I am not worthy of so great a favor, do thou help me from heaven, that I may leave this life loving God and thee, to love thee eternally in Paradise.

WEDNESDAY.

To obtain Deliverance from Hell.*

My most beloved Lady, I thank thee for having delivered me from hell as many times as I have deserved it by my sins.

---

* Besides the indulgences mentioned above, page 202, the same Pontiff, Pius VII., by a decree, May 15, 1821, granted an indulgence of *three hundred days*, once a day, to those who, with at least contrite heart and devotion, shall say this prayer, together with the *Salve Regina.* "Hail, O Queen," three times. Moreover, a *plenary indulgence*, once a month, to all who practise this devotion, every day for a month, on any day when, being truly penitent, after confession and Communion, they pray for some time, for the intention of his Holiness. These indulgences are also applicable to the souls in purgatory.—ED.

Miserable creature that I was, I was once condemned to that prison, and perhaps already, after the first sin, the sentence would have been put into execution, if thou, in thy compassion, hadst not helped me. Thou, without even being asked by me, and only in thy goodness, didst restrain divine Justice; and then, conquering my obduracy, thou didst draw me to have confidence in thee. O, into how many other sins should I have afterwards fallen, in the dangers in which I have been, hadst not thou, my loving Mother, preserved me by the graces which thou didst obtain for me! Ah, my Queen, continue to guard me from hell; for what will thy mercy, and the favors which thou hast shown me, avail me if I am lost? If I did not always love thee, now at least—after God—I love thee above all things. Never allow me to turn my back on thee and on God, who, by thy means, has granted me so many graces. My most amiable Lady, never allow me to have the misfortune to hate thee and curse thee for all eternity in hell. Wilt thou endure to see a servant of thine, who loves thee, lost? O Mary, what sayest thou? I shall be lost if I abandon thee. But who can ever more have the heart to leave thee? How can I ever forget the love thou hast borne me? My Lady, since thou hast done so much to save me, complete the work, continue the aid. Wilt thou help me? But what do I say? If at a time when I lived forgetful of thee thou didst favor me so much, how much more may I not hope for now that I love thee and recommend myself to thee! No, he can never be lost who recommends himself to thee; he alone is lost who has not recourse to thee. Ay, my Mother, leave me not in my own hands, for I should then be lost; grant that I may always have recourse to thee. Save me, my hope, save me from hell; but, in the first place, save me from sin, which alone can condemn me to it.

THURSDAY.

To obtain Heaven.

O Queen of Paradise, who reignest above all the choirs of angels, and who art the nearest of all creatures to God, I, a miserable sinner, salute thee from this valley of tears, and beseech thee to turn thy compassionate eyes towards me, for whichever side they turn they dispense graces. See, O Mary, in how many dangers I now am, and shall be as long as I live in this world, of losing my soul, of losing heaven and God. In thee, O Lady, I have placed all my hopes. I love thee, and sigh to go soon to see thee, and praise thee in heaven. Ah, Mary, when will be that happy day on which I shall see myself safe at thy feet, and contemplate my Mother who has done so much for my salvation? When shall I kiss that hand which has delivered me so many times from hell, and has dispensed me so many graces, when, on account of my sins, I deserved to be hated and abandoned by all? My Lady, in life I have been very ungrateful to thee; but if I reach heaven, I shall no longer be ungrateful: there I shall love thee as much as I can in every moment for all eternity, and shall make amends for my ingratitude by blessings and thanking thee forever. I thank God with my whole heart, who gives me firm confidence in the blood of Jesus Christ and in thee, and in the conviction that thou wilt save me; that thou wilt deliver me from my sins; that thou wilt give me light and strength to execute the divine will; and, in fine, that thou wilt lead me to the gate of Paradise. Thy servants have hoped for all this, and not one of them was deceived. No, neither shall I be deceived. O Mary, my full confidence is that thou hast to save me. Beseech thy Son Jesus, as I also beseech him, by the merits of his Passion, to preserve and always increase this confidence in me, and I shall be saved.

FRIDAY.
To obtain Love towards Her and Jesus Christ.

O Mary, I already know that thou art the most noble, the most sublime, the most pure, the most beautiful, the most benign, the most holy—in a word, the most amiable of all creatures. O that all knew thee, my Lady, and loved thee as thou dost merit! But I am consoled when I remember that in heaven and on earth there are so many happy souls who live enamoured of thy goodness and beauty. Above all, I rejoice that God himself loves thee alone more than he loves all men and angels together. My most amiable Queen, I, a miserable sinner, love thee also; but I love thee too little. I desire a greater and more tender love towards thee; and this thou must obtain for me, since to love thee is a great mark of predestination, and a grace which God only grants to those whom he will save.

I see also, my Mother, that I am indeed under great obligations to thy Son. I see that he merits infinite love. Thou, who desirest nothing else but to see him loved, hast to obtain me this grace above all others; obtain me great love for Jesus Christ. Thou obtainest all that thou willest from God; ah, then, be graciously pleased to obtain me the grace to be so united to the divine will that I may never more be separated from it. I do not ask of thee earthly goods, honors, or riches. I ask thee for that which thy heart desires most for me. I wish to love my God. Is it possible that thou refusest to second this my desire, which is so pleasing to thee? Ah no, thou already helpest me; already thou prayest for me. Pray, pray, and cease not to pray until thou seest me safe in heaven, beyond the possibility of ever more losing my Lord, and certain to love him forever, together with thee, my dearest Mother.

SATURDAY.

To obtain Her Patronage.

O my most holy Mother. I see the graces which thou hast obtained for me; and I see the ingratitude of which I have been guilty towards thee. An ungrateful soul is no longer worthy of favors; but I will not on this account distrust thy mercy, which is greater than my ingratitude. O my great advocate, pity me. Thou dispensest all the graces which God grants to us miserable creatures, and for this purpose he has made thee so powerful, so rich, and so benign. He has done so, that thou mightest succor us in our miseries. Ah, Mother of mercy, leave me not in my poverty. Thou art the advocate of the most miserable and guilty criminals who have recourse to thee; defend me also, who recommend myself to thee. Say not that my cause is too difficult to be gained; for all causes, however desperate, when defended by thee are gained. In thy hands, then, do I place my eternal salvation; to thee do I intrust my soul: it was lost; thou, then, by thy intercession hast to save it. I wish to be inscribed amongst thy most devoted servants; reject me not. Thou seekest the miserable, to relieve them; abandon me not, who am a wretched sinner, and who have recourse to thee. Speak for me; thy Son does all that thou askest him. Take me under thy protection; that is all that I ask. Yes; for if thou protectest me, I fear nothing. I do not fear my sins; for thou wilt obtain me a remedy for the evil they have done me. I do not fear the devils; for thou art more powerful than all hell. I do not even fear Jesus my Judge himself; for by a single prayer of thine he is appeased. I only fear that by my negligence I may cease to recommend myself to thee, and thus be lost. It is true that these graces are too great for me, who have not deserved them; but they are not too great for thee, who art so much loved by God. Hence he grants thee all that thou askest. Thou hast only to speak, and he denies thee nothing. Pray, then, to Jesus for me; tell him that thou protectest me; and then he is sure to pity me. My Mother, in thee too I do trust; in this hope I shall live in peace, and in it I wish to die.

Live Jesus our love, and Mary our hope!

Little Rosary in Honor of the Seven Dolors of Mary.

Deus, in adjutorium meum intende.—Domine, ad adjuvandum me festina. Gloria Patri et Filio et Spiritui Sancto.—Sicut erat in principio, et nunc et semper, et in sæcula sæculorum. Amen.

Incline unto mine aid, O God ! O Lord ! make haste to help me. Glory be to the Father, and to the Son, and to the Holy Ghost. As it was in the beginning, is now and ever shall be, world without end. Amen.

My Mother! share thy grief with me,
And let me bear thee company
To mourn thy Jesus' death with thee.

I.

I pity thee, O afflicted Mother, on account of the first sword of sorrow that pierced thee, when in the Temple all the outrages which men would inflict on thy beloved Jesus were presented before thee by St. Simeon, and which thou already knewest by the sacred Scriptures ; outrages which were to cause him to die before thine eyes, on that infamous cross, exhausted of his blood, abandoned by all, and thyself unable to defend or help him. By that bitter knowledge, then, which for so many years afflicted thy heart, I beseech thee, my Queen, to obtain me the grace that during my life and at my death I may ever keep the Passion of Jesus and thy sorrows impressed on my heart.

Our Father once, Hail Mary seven times, and the Strophe, are repeated after each Dolor.

II.

I pity thee, my afflicted Mother, for the second sword which pierced thee, when, soon after his birth, thou didst behold thy innocent Son threatened with death by those very men for whose salvation he had come into the world ; so that in the darkness of night thou wast obliged to fly secretly with him into Egypt. By the many hardships, then, which thou, a delicate young woman, in company with thine exiled Child, didst endure in so long and fatiguing a journey through rough and desert countries, and during thy residence in Egypt, where, being unknown and a stranger, thou didst live for so many years in poverty and contempt,—I beseech thee, my beloved Lady, to obtain for me grace to suffer with patience until death, in thy company, the trials of this miserable life ; that I may thus in the next escape the eternal punishments of hell, which I have deserved.

Our Father, etc.

III.

I pity thee, my sorrowful Mother, on account of the third sword which pierced thee in the loss of thy dear Son Jesus, who remained absent from thee in Jerusalem for three days. No longer seeing thy Beloved by thy side, and not knowing the cause of his absence, I can well imagine, my loving Queen, that during those nights thou didst not repose, and didst only sigh for him, who was all thy treasure. By the sighs, then, of those three days, for thee too long and bitter, I beseech thee to obtain me the grace, that I may never lose my God; that so, always clinging to him, I may leave the world united to him.

Our Father, etc.

IV.

I pity thee, my sorrowful Mother, for the fourth sword which pierced thee, in seeing thy Son condemned to death, bound with cords and chains, covered with blood and wounds, crowned with a wreath of thorns, falling under the weight of a heavy cross which he carried on his wounded shoulders, going as an innocent Lamb to die for love of us. Thine eyes met his, and his met thine; and your glances were as so many cruel arrows, which wounded your loving hearts. By this great sorrow, then, I beseech thee to obtain me the grace to live in all things resigned to the will of my God, and to carry my cross cheerfully in company with Jesus, until my last breath.

Our Father, etc.

v.

I pity thee, my afflicted Mother, for the fifth sword which pierced thee, when on Mount Calvary thou didst behold thy beloved Son Jesus slowly dying before thy eyes, amid so many torments and insults, on that hard bed of the cross, where thou couldst not administer him even the least of those comforts that are granted to the greatest criminals at the hour of death. I beseech thee, by the agony which thou, my most loving Mother, didst endure together with thy dying Son, and by the sadness which thou didst feel, when, for the last time, he spoke to thee from the cross and bade thee farewell, and left all of us, in the person of St. John, to thee as thy children; but that constancy with which thou didst then see him bow down his head and expire, I beseech thee to obtain me the grace, from thy crucified love, to live and die crucified to all earthly things, that I may spend my life for God alone, and thus one day enter Paradise to enjoy him face to face.

Our Father, etc.

VI.

I pity thee, my afflicted Mother, for the sixth sword which pierced thee, when thou didst see the sweet heart of thy Son pierced through and through. He was already dead, and had died for those ungrateful creatures, who, even after his death, were not satisfied with the torments they had inflicted upon him. By this cruel sorrow, then, which was all thine, I beseech thee to obtain me the grace to dwell in the heart of Jesus, wounded and opened for me; in that heart, I say, which is the beautiful abode of love, in which all souls who love God repose; and that, living there, I may never think of or love anything but God. Most sacred Virgin, thou canst obtain this for me; from thee do I hope for it.

Our Father, etc.

VII.

I pity thee, my afflicted Mother, for the seventh sword which pierced thee on seeing thy Son in thy arms already dead, no longer fair and beautiful as thou didst receive him in the stable of Bethlehem, but covered with blood, livid and all lacerated with wounds, so that even his bones were seen; thou didst then say, " My Son, my Son, to what has love reduced Thee !" And when he was borne to the sepulchre, thou wouldst thyself accompany him, and place him with thy own hands in the tomb; and bidding him the last farewell, thou didst leave thy loving heart buried with thy Son. By this martyrdom of thy beautiful soul, do thou obtain me, O Mother of fair love, the forgiveness of the offences which I have committed against my beloved God, and of which I repent with my whole heart. Do thou defend me in temptations, do thou assist me at the moment of my death, that, saving my soul through the merits of Jesus and thine, I may one day, after this miserable exile, go to Paradise to-sing the praises of Jesus and of thee for all eternity. Amen.

Our Father, etc.

Ora pro nobis, Virgo dolorosis-
sima!—Ut digni efficiamur pro-
missionibus Christi.

O God, at whose Passion, ac-
Pray for us, O most sorrowful
Virgin:—That we may be made
worthy of the promises of Christ.

Oremus.

Let us pray.

Deus, in cujus passione, secun-
dum Simeonis prophetiam, dul-
cissimam animam gloriosae Vir-
ginis et Matris Mariae doloris
gladius pertransivit, concede pro-
pitius, ut, qui dolores ejus ven-
erando recolimus, passionis tuae
effectum felicem consequamur.
Qui vivis et regnas in saecula
saeculorum. Amen.

cording to the prophecy of Simeon, a sword of sorrow did pierce
through the most sweet soul of
the glorious Virgin and Mother
Mary; grant that we, who com-
memorate and reverence her dolors, may experience the blessed
effect of Thy Passion, who livest
and reignest world without end.
Amen.

Benedict XIII. granted two hundred days' indulgence for every
"Our Father" and every "Hail Mary," to those who recite the little
Rosary of the Seven Dolors,* in the churches of the Servites of Mary.
He also granted the same favor to all who recite it in any place
whatever, on Fridays or any day during Lent. To those who recite
it on other days he granted one hundred days for every "Our
Father" and "Hail Mary." To those who recite it entire, seven
years and seven quarantines. A plenary indulgence once a month
on the usual conditions.

---

* This chaplet is divided into seven parts, each being composed
of an *Our Father* and seven times *Hail Mary,* in honor of the seven
principal sorrows of Mary, the Mother of God. To gain the indulgences that are attached to it and that have been largely increased
by Clement XII. it should have been duly blessed for this purpose,
and whilst reciting it one must reflect on the sorrows of the Blessed
Virgin, according to one's capacity, and add at the end the *Hail
Mary* three times in honor of the tears that she shed during these
sorrows. The seven parts may be said separately provided they are
said in one day.—ED.

Little Rosary of Mary Immaculate,

V. *Deus, in adjutorium meum intende.*

R. *Domine, ad adjuvandum me festina.*

Gloria Patri et Filio et Spiritui Sancto.—Sicut erat in principio, et nunc, et semper, et in sæcula sæculorum. Amen.

V. Incline unto .mine aid, O God.

R. O Lord, make haste to help me.

Glory be to the Father, and to the Son, and to the Holy Ghost : as it was in the beginning, is now, and ever shall be, world without end. Amen.

After this an " Our Father" is recited, in honor of the Eternal Father, and in thanksgiving for all the graces bestowed on Mary, and is followed by four " Hail Marys." The same is repeated in honor of the Son, and again in honor of the Holy Ghost.

After each " Hail Mary" are added these words :

" May the Immaculate Conception of Mary be ever praised !"

After each fourth " Hail Mary" is recited the following verse :

As 'mid the thorns the lily fair
Art thou, Virgin Immaculate,
From sin preserved by Him whose care
Did thee His Mother blest create.

We conclude with the following Verse and Prayer.*

Immaculata Conceptio Sanctæ Mariæ Virginis.

Quæ serpentis caput virgineo pede contrivit.

The Holy Virgin Mary conceived without sin.

The Virgin's foot hath bruised the serpent's head.

---

* We give the Verse and Prayer of the proper Office that is recited at the present time: this St. Alphonsus would himself have done.

The little Chaplet .of the Immaculate Conception, to which Pope Pius IX. attached indulgences in 1855, is composed of fifteen beads that are divided into three parts, and is recited in the following manner. We first make the sign of the Cross, and then add for each part

Oremus.

Let us pray.

Deus, qui, per Immaculatam Virginis Conceptionem, dignum Filio tuo habitaculum praeparasti: quaesumus ut, qui ex morte ejusdem Filii tui praevisa, eam ab omni labe praeservasti, nos quoque mundos ejus intercessione ad te pervenire concedas. Per eundem Christum Dominum nostrum. Amen.

O God, who didst cause that a virgin should be conceived without sin, to the end that she might be made a meet dwelling-place for Thy dear Son; O God, who through the precious death of the same Thy Son foreseen by Thee, didst keep her clean from all stain,—hear us, we beseech Thee, and grant that by her prayers we also, who are presently defiled, may finally be made pure, and so with her attain unto Thee. Through the same Christ our Lord. Amen.

the ejaculatory prayer: "Blessed be the holy and Immaculate Conception of the most Blessed Virgin Mary;" one *Our Father*, four *Hail Marys*, and one *Glory*, etc. An *indulgence of three hundred days* is granted if one recites it with at least a contrite heart; and if one recites it every day, *a plenary indulgence* each month on condition that one confesses and receives Holy Communion. These indulgences are applicable to the souls in purgatory. No beads are necessary nor need they be blessed.—ED.

𝕷𝖎𝖙𝖙𝖑𝖊 𝕮𝖍𝖆𝖕𝖑𝖊𝖙 𝖔𝖋 𝖙𝖍𝖊 𝕭𝖑𝖊𝖘𝖘𝖊𝖉 𝕿𝖗𝖎𝖓𝖎𝖙𝖞

IN HONOR OF THE BLESSED VIRGIN.

The Blessed Virgin revealed to a devout soul that she was much pleased at being honored by her servants with the following devotion : *

I render Thee thanks, O Eternal Father! for the power that Thou hast given to Mary, Thy daughter.

Our Father, Hail Mary, Glory be to the Father, etc.

I render Thee thanks, O Eternal Son ! for the wisdom that Thou hast given to Mary, Thy Mother.

Our Father, Hail Mary, Glory be to the Father, etc.

I render Thee thanks, O Eternal Spirit ! for the love that Thou hast given to Mary, Thy Spouse.

Our Father, Hail Mary, Glory be to the Father, etc.

---

* See what is said of this on page 613. This pious practice and the prayers that follow have served, in the first Italian editions, usually very compact, to fill up here and there a page where there was a blank. We have here collected and arranged them.—ED.

Various Prayers to Mary.

I

Prayer to obtain a Good Death.

O Mary, sweet refuge of poor sinners and my tender Mother! when my soul must depart from this world, by the grief that thou didst experience in being present at the death of thy divine Son on the Cross, I beseech thee to assist me with thy mercy. Banish from me the infernal enemies, and come then to take my soul and to present it to the Eternal Judge. My Queen, do not abandon me; it is thou who after Jesus must be my help at that dreadful moment. Ask thy Son that in his goodness he may grant me the grace to die while embracing thy feet, and to breathe forth my soul into his sacred wounds while saying: Jesus and Mary, I give you my heart and my soul.

II.

Abbreviated Prayer of St. Ephrem.

O Immaculate and wholly-pure Virgin Mary, Mother of God, Queen of the world, hope of those who are in despair: thou art the joy of the saints; thou art the peacemaker between sinners and God; thou art the advocate of the abandoned, the secure haven of those who are on the sea of the world; thou art the consolation of the world, the ransom of slaves, the comfortress of the afflicted, the salvation of the universe. O great Queen, we take refuge in thy protection; "We have no confidence but in thee, O most faithful Virgin." After God, thou art all my hope. We bear the name of thy servants; allow not the enemy to drag us to hell. I salute thee, O great mediatress of peace between men and God, Mother of Jesus our Lord, who is the love of all men and of God, to whom be honor and benediction with the Father and the Holy Ghost. Amen.

---

[1] *De Laud. Dei Gen.*

III.

Prayer of St. Bernard.

To thee we cry, O Queen of Mercy! return, that we may behold thee dispensing favors, bestowing remedies, giving strength. Show us thy compassionate looks, and we shall be saved.[1]

O sovereign Lady of all things, Saint of saints, our strength and refuge, God, as it were, of the world, glory of heaven, accept those who love thee; hear us, for thy Son honors thee and denies thee nothing.[2]

Ah, tender Mother! tell thy all-powerful Son that we have no more wine. We are thirsty after the wine of his love, of that marvellous wine that fills souls with a holy inebriation, inflames them, and gives them the strength to despise the things of this world and to seek with ardor heavenly goods.[3]

Thou art, O Mary! a field filled with treasures. Thou art full of virtues, full of graces. Thou didst appear on the earth as a shining and silver-gilt aurora. Exempt from every original stain, thou didst appear from the first instant endowed with the perfect use of reason and all inflamed with divine love. No; the enemy of salvation was never able to hurt thee, finding thee always surrounded by impenetrable bucklers, and fortified with all the arms that he feared. Thou alone didst possess all the perfections and all the merits of all the saints united.[4]

[1] " Ad te clamamus, Regina misericordiæ ! revertere, ut intueamur te largientem beneficia conferentem remedia, ponentem fortitudinem. Ostende nobis faciem miserationum tuarum, et salvi erimus." —*In Salve Reg.* §. 2.

[2] " Domina rerum, Sancta Sanctorum, Virtus nostra et Refugium, Decus mundi, Gloria cœli ! agnosce te diligentes. Audi nos, nam te Filius nihil negans honorat."—*In Salve Reg.* s. 3.

[3] " Domina ! dic pro nobis Filio tuo: Vinum non habent. Calix hujus vini inebrians quam præclarus est ! inebriat amor Dei ad contemptum mundi, calefacit, facit fortes, somnolentes ad temporalia, et ad invisibilia promptos."

[4] " Tu es Ager plenus. Plena virtutum, plena gratiarum. Tu processisti ut aurora lucida et rubicunda. Quia, superatis originalibus peccatis, nata es lucida cognitione veritatis et rubicunda amore virtutis. Nihil omnino profecit inimicus in te, eo quod mille clypei

Run, hasten, O Lady, and in thy mercy help thy sinful servant, who calls upon thee, and deliver him from the hands of the enemy.[1]

Who will not sigh to thee? We sigh with love and grief, for we are oppressed on every side. How can we do otherwise than sigh to thee, O solace of the miserable, refuge of outcasts, ransom of captives? We are certain that when thou seest our miseries, thy compassion will hasten to relieve us.[2]

O our sovereign Lady and our Advocate, commend us to thy Son. Grant, O blessed one, by the grace which thou hast merited, that he who through thee was graciously pleased to become a partaker of our infirmity and misery, may also, through thy intercession, make us partakers of his happiness and glory.[3]

IV.

Prayer of the Venerable Louis Blosius.

Ave, desperantium Spes, desti-tutorum Adjutrix, Maria, cujus honori tantum tribuit Filius, ut, quidquid petieris, mox impetres, quidquid volueris, mox fiat! Tibi regni cœlestis thesauri commissi sunt. Præsta, Domina, ut, inter procellas hujus vitæ, semper te attendam. Tuæ pietati commendo

Hail Mary, hope of those who are in despair, help of the destitute! Hail, thou whom thy Son so greatly honors, that whatever thou askest, thou dost at once obtain; whatever thou willest is at once done. To thee are the treasures of the kingdom of heaven intrusted. Grant, O Lady,

pependerunt ex te, omnis armatura fortium. Nihil est enim virtutis, quod in te non resplendeat; et quidquid singuli habuere Sancti, tu sola possedisti."—*In Salve Reg.* s. 4.

[1] "Curre, festina, Domina! et tuum nequissimum servum ad te clamantem parcendo adjuva, et eripe de manu hostis."

[2] "Quis ad te non suspirabit? Amore suspiramus et dolore; quomodo ergo ad te non suspirabimus, Solatium miserorum, Refugium expulsorum, Liberatio captivorum! Non dubitamus, quin, si nostras aspexeris miserias, non poterit tua miseratio suum retardare effectum." —*Med. in Salve Reg.*

[3] "O Domina nostra, Advocata nostra! tuo Filio nos commenda. Fac, o Benedicta! per gratiam quam invenisti, ut qui, te mediante, fieri dignatus est particeps infirmitatis et miseriæ nostræ, te quoque intercedente, participes faciat nos gloriæ et beatitudinis suæ."—*In Adv. D.* s. 2.

animam et corpus meum; dirige et protege me singulis horis atque momentis, o dulce Præsidium meum!

Ave, benignissima misericordiæ Mater! salve, veniæ Conciliatrix, optatissima Maria! Quis te non amet? Tu in rebus dubiis Lumen et in mæroribus Solatium, in angustiis Relevamen, in periculis et tentationibus Refugium; tu, post Unigenitum tuum, certa fidelium Salus. Beati, qui diligunt te, Domina! Inclina, quæso, aures tuæ pietatis precibus hujus servi tui, hujus miseri peccatoris, et caliginem vitiorum meorum radiis tuæ sanctitatis dissipa, ut tibi placeam.[1]

that amid the storms of this life I may always remember thee. To thy charitable mercy I commend my soul and body. O my sweet protectress, direct and protect me in every hour, in every moment of my life. Amen.

Hail, most benign Mother of Mercy! Hail, our Comfortress, Mary the desire of our hearts! who is there that loves thee not? Thou art our light in doubts, our comfort in sorrows, our relief in distress, our refuge in dangers and temptations. Thou, after thy only-begotten Son, art our certain salvation; blessed are those who love thee, O Lady. Incline, I beseech thee, the ears of thy compassion to the prayers of this thy servant, a miserable sinner, and dispel the darkness of my vices by the rays of thy sanctity, that I may please thee.

V.

Ejaculatory Prayers.

Mother of God, remember me.[2]

O Virgin and Mother, grant that I may always remember thee.[3]

Holy Virgin Mary, Mother of God, pray to Jesus for me.[3]

O Lady, grant that Jesus may never cast me off.[4]

O Mary, may my heart never cease to love thee, and my tongue never cease to praise thee.[5]

O Lady, by the love which thou bearest to Jesus, help me to love him.[6]

[1] *Par. An. Fid.* p. 2, c. 4.
[2] St. Francis Xavier.
[3] St. Philip Neri.
[4] St. Ephrem.
[5] St. Bonaventure.
[6] St. Bridget.

O Mary, be graciously pleased to make me thy servant.[1]

O Mary, I give myself to thee without reserve; do thou accept and preserve me.[2]

O Mary, abandon me not until death.[3]

Hail, Mary, my Mother.[4]

Holy Mary, my Advocate, pray for me.[5]

In thee from my whole heart I have placed my hope.[6]

It is not possible, O Lady, that thou shouldst abandon him who has placed his hopes in thee.[7]

Thou hast only to will our salvation, and then it is not possible that we should not obtain it.[8]

Hail, Daughter of God the Father; hail, Mother of God the Son; hail, Spouse of God the Holy Ghost; hail, Temple of the whole Trinity.[9]

> Thy name of Mary, to my ear
>   O Mother Mary, sounds more sweet
>   Than sweetest melody;
> It brings such peace and joy so dear,
>   That I would ever more repeat
>   A word so sweet to me.
>
>   O Virgin fair,
> What loveliness is thine!
> Mother Divine,
>   Such beauty rare
> Enslaves this heart of mine.

Deo gratias et Mariæ!—Thanks be to God and to Mary.

May all things be to the eternal glory of the most Holy Trinity and of Immaculate Mary.

LIVE ALWAYS JESUS OUR LOVE, AND MARY OUR HOPE, WITH ST. JOSEPH AND ST. TERESA OUR ADVOCATES!

[1] St. Jane Frances de Chantal.
[2] St. Mary Magdalene de Pazzi.
[3] Father Spinelli.
[4] Father Francis Brancaccio.
[5] Father Sertorio Caputo.
[6] St. John Damascene.
[7] St. Bernard.
[8] St. Anselm.
[9] Simon Garcia.

Acclamations in Praise of Mary.

O most sacred Virgin Mary, O Queen of angels, how beautiful, accomplished, and perfect has Heaven made thee! O that I could appear to God as thou appearest to me. Thou art so beautiful and gracious that with thy beauty thou ravishest hearts. When thou art seen, everything appears deformed, all beauty is eclipsed, every grace is lost sight of; as the stars disappear at the rising of the sun.

When thy tenderly devoted servant, St. John Damascene, contemplated thee, and when he saw that thou wast so beautiful, it seemed to him that thou hadst taken the flower and that which was best in every creature, and therefore he called thee "the loveliness of nature,"[1] the grace and comeliness of every creature. St. Augustine, the bright light of Doctors, contemplated thee, and thou didst appear to him so fair and beautiful, that he called thee the countenance of God, and it did not seem to him adulation.[2] Thy devout son Albert the Great[3] contemplated thee, and to him it seemed that all the graces and gifts that were in the most celebrated women of the old dispensation, were all in a much higher degree in thee; the golden mouth of Sarah, which smiling, rejoices heaven and earth; the sweet and tender look of the faithful Lia, with which thou didst soften the heart of God, hardened against sinners; the splendor of countenance of the beautiful Rachel, for with thy beauty thou dost eclipse the sun; the grace and demeanor of the discreet Abigail, by which thou

[1] "Venustas naturæ."—*In Nat. B. M.* s. 1.
[2] "Si formam Dei te appellem, digna existis."—S. 208, *E. B. app.*
[3] *De Laud. B. M.* l. 6, c. 9.

didst appease an angry God: the vivacity and strength of the valiant Judith, for by thy power and thy grace thou dost subdue the most ferocious hearts.

In fine, O sovereign Princess, from the immense ocean of thy beauty the beauty and grace of all creatures flowed forth as rivers. The sea learnt to curl its waves, and to wave its crystal waters from the golden hair, which gracefully floated over thy shoulders and ivory neck. The crystal fountains and their transparent depths learnt their tranquil and steady flow from the serenity of thy beautiful brow and placid countenance. The lovely rainbow, when in full beauty, learnt with studious care its graceful bend from thy eyebrows, thus better to send forth its rays of light. The morning star itself, and the sweet star at night, are sparks from thy beautiful eyes. The white lilies and ruby roses stole their colors from thy lovely cheeks. Envious purple and coral sigh for the color of thy lips. The most delicious milk and sweetest honey are distillations from the sweet honeycomb of thy mouth. The scented jasmine and fragrant Damasc rose stole their perfume from thy breath. The loftiest cedar and the most erect, the fairest cypress, were happy when they beheld their image in thy erect and lofty neck. The palm-tree, emulous and jealous, likened itself to thy noble stature. In fine, O Lady, every created beauty is a shadow and trace of thy beauty.

And thus I wonder not, O sovereign Princess, that heaven and earth place themselves under thy feet; for such are they, and thou art so great, that to be only under thy feet enriches them, and they esteem themselves happy and blessed in kissing them. Thus did the moon rejoice when the evangelist St. John saw her under thy feet, and the sun increased in splendor when it clothed thee with its rays of light. The Evangelist, blinded by the brilliancy of thy light, was lost in wonder and ravished out of himself at the sight of so stupendous a miracle of beauty, in which the beauty of heaven and earth was concentrated, and he said,[1] *There appeared a great sign in heaven.* A great miracle appeared in the heavens—a miracle which filled the angels with astonishment, and caused the earth to tremble. That miracle was a woman clothed from head to foot in light and splendor. The resplendent sun itself chose her for his Mother, and placed himself in her womb; the fair moon covers her feet as sandals edged with silver; a multitude of stars crown her brow, and, emulating one with another, bind her locks together, and form upon her head a diadem of precious gems: *and on her head a crown of twelve stars.*

Thus, O most sacred Virgin, the saints, considering thee in the midst of such splendor more beautiful than the sun, and more fair than the moon, which are the ornament and concentration of all beauty; and considering the acclamations of joy which attend thee in heaven, can never cease their astonishment at thy beauty, and can only exclaim and burst forth in acclamations of wonder and astonishment. St. Peter Damian exclaims in his admiration, "O holy and most holy of all saints, richest treasure of all sanctity." St. Bernard: "O admirable Virgin, O woman, honor of all women, the best, the greatest that the world ever possessed." St. Epiphanius: "O heaven, greater and vaster than the heavens themselves; O Virgin, truly full of grace." And the Catholic Church, in the name of all, exclaims, "O most clement, most pious, and most sweet Virgin Mary."

And I also, O heavenly Princess, with thy permission, although I am the least of thy servants, I will also make my acclamations of wonder and astonishment.

---

[1] "Signum magnum apparuit in cœlo; mulier amicta sole, et luna sub pedibus ejus, et in capite ejus corona stellarum duodecim."—*Apoc.* xii. 1.

O gracious and beautiful heaven, more vast than the heavens themselves, for they cannot contain God, who is immense, but he concealed himself in thy womb; O richest of all treasures, in which was deposited the treasure of our redemption; O Mother of sinners, under whose mantle we are defended; O consolation of the world, in which all who are afflicted, infirm, and disconsolate, find consolation; O beautiful eyes, which steal hearts; O coral lips, which imprison souls; O generous hands, filled with lilies, and which always distribute graces; O pure creature, who appearest a God, and whom I should have taken for a God, had not faith taught me that thou art not so, although thou hast a splendor, and I know not what of divine sovereignty; O great Lady, empress of heaven, enjoy for a thousand eternities the greatness of thy state, the immensity of thy greatness, and the happiness of thy glory. We only beseech thee, O compassionate Mother, not to forget us, who glory in being thy servants and children. And since in thee are deposited all graces, and the best and most privileged of all created things, grant, O Lady, that we, thy devout children, may be favored more beyond comparison than are all other men on earth. The whole world should know that the dear children of Mary are the best of heaven and earth: they are the spoilt children, who enjoy all the choicest possessions of their Mother; they are the beloved Benjamins, who, being caressed in the bosom of the Queen of Heaven, are doubly favored and doubly caressed by the Majesty of God. This I hope, O most beautiful Rachel; and this I am confident that thou wilt do, O sovereign Princess. In the name of what thou art, do it; for all heaven prostrate at thy feet beseeches thee, and with importunity asks it of thee. Say only yes, pronounce only a loving consent; be it done, be it done, *fiat, fiat !*

O men, of what are you thinking ? How can you love

earthly, deceitful, and lying creatures, which betray you and cause you to lose your souls, your bodies, Paradise, and God! And why do you not love the most loving, the most amiable, the most faithful Mary, who, after having enriched you with consolations and graces in this life, will obtain you from her divine beloved Son the eternal glory of Paradise?

O Mary, Mary more beautiful than all creatures, lovely after Jesus above all loves, more dear than all created things, gracious above every grace, pity this miserable heart of mine; miserable because it does not love thee; and it ought to love thee. Thou canst inflame it with thy holy love. Turn, O Mary, thy loving eyes upon me; look at me, and draw me to thee; and grant that after God I may love no other but thee, most gracious, most amiable Mary, Mother of Jesus, and my Mother.

HYMNS.

I.

A Soul the Lover of Mary.

I AM the lover of a Queen,
  Whose heart so sweet and kind doth prove,
  That seeing one who seeks her love,
She scouts him not though poor and mean.

She sits a Queen, with heavenly grace;
  But from her throne her gentle eyes
  Look down on him who humbly sighs
To see the beauty of her face.

This Virgin is so pure, that she
  Was chosen by the Eternal Word
  The Spouse, the Mother of our Lord;
And she has stol'n my heart from me.

Oh! could I but behold, one day,
  All hearts with love of her inflam'd,
  And hear her sweetest name proclaim'd
By every tongue in joyful lay!

Then in sweet harmony should flow,
  In every land through endless days;
  Praise be to Mary, ceaseless praise!
And praise to God who loved her so!

Let him who wills seek other love,
  If earthly beauty can rejoice
  His soul:—she only is my choice
Whose beauty ravished God above.

Then, Mary, stretch thy hand to me,
  Sweet loving Robber! seize thy prey:
  Take from my breast this heart away,
Which sighs and languishes for thee.

That fire of love into it pour
  With which thou ceasest not to burn,
  That my poor heart, like thine, may yearn
With love of Jesus evermore.

II.

Our Mother, Mary.

THOU art clement, thou art chaste,
  Mary, thou art fair;
Of all mothers sweetest, best,
  None with thee compare.

O Mother blest! whom God bestows
  On sinners and on just,
What joy, what hope, thou givest those
  Who in thy mercy trust!
                    Thou art clement, etc.

O heavenly Mother! Mistress sweet!
  It never yet was told
That suppliant sinner left thy feet
  Unpitied, unconsoled.
                    Thou art clement, etc.

O Mother pitiful and mild!
  Cease not to pray for me;
For I do love thee as a child,
  And sigh for love of thee.
                    Thou art clement, etc.

Most pow'rful Mother! all men know
  Thy Son denies thee nought;
Thou askest—wishest it—and, lo,
  His power thy will has wrought.
                    Thou art clement, etc.

Mother of Love! for me obtain,
  Ungrateful though I be,
To love that God who first could deign
  To show such love to me.
                    Thou art clement, etc.

III.

Invocation of Mary in time of Temptations.

HASTE, my Mother, run to help me;
　Mother, haste, do not delay;
See from hell the envious serpent
　Comes my trembling soul to slay.

Ah! his very look affrights me,
　And his cruel rage I fear;
Whither fly, if he attacks me?
　See him, see him coming near!

Lo! I faint away with terror,
　For if yet thou dost delay,
He will dart at me his venom;
　Then, alas! I am his prey.

Cries and tears have nought availed me,
　Spite of all I see him there;
Saints I call till I am weary,
　Still he stands with threatening air.

Now his mighty jaws are open,
　And his forkèd tongue I see;
Ah! he coils to spring upon me—
　Mother! hasten, make him flee.

Mary! yes, the name of Mary
　Strikes with dread my cruel foe;
Straight he flees as from the sunbeam
　Swiftly melts the winter's snow.

Now he's gone; but do thou ever
　Stay beside me, Mother dear;
Then the hellish fiend to tempt me
　Never more will venture near.

IV.

Aspirations to Mary.

KNOWEST thou, sweet Mary,
　　Whereto I aspire?
'Tis my hope to love thee,—
　　This is my desire.

I would e'er be near thee,
　　Queen most fair and sweet;
Do not, do not drive me
　　From my Mother's feet.

Then, O Rose most lovely!
　　Let me hear from thee,
Loving Mother! tell me
　　What thou wilt of me.

More I cannot offer,
Lo! I bring my heart;
Lovingly I give it,
　　Ne'er from thee to part.

Lady, thou didst take it,
　　'Tis no longer mine:
Long since thou didst love it,
　　And its love was thine!

Do not, then, forsake me,
　　Mother of sweet Love,
Till one day thou see me
　　Safe in heaven above.

Answers to Critics

I.

Reply to an Anonymous Writer, who Censured a Passage in the Glories of Mary.*

A BOOK entitled *Lamindi Pritanii redivivi Epistola parænetica ad P. Bened. Piazza*, printed in the course of last year (1755), having fallen into my hands, I found towards the end of it an appendix, in which the author, who is anonymous, criticises what I have written in the above-quoted part of my little work.[1] In it I maintain, with Father Piazza, that all graces come to us through the divine Mother, in opposition to that which the celebrated Louis Muratori wrote in his book called *Well-regulated Devotion*,[2] under the name of *Pritanius*.

The anonymous writer says that I am mistaken in my assertion, that Pritanius wrote that the proposition, that God grants no graces otherwise than through Mary, was hyperbolical and exaggerated, having dropped from the lips of some saints in the heat of fervor. Fearing that such might have been the case, I have again read the book; and I see that though Pritanius does not exactly join the above-mentioned words to the passage in which he speaks of the saints, yet from the context it is evident that he also refers it to the saints who have spoken on this subject.

[1] Vol. VII. ch. v. § 1.
[2] *Della Regolata Divozione.*

---

*The same critic, with considerable haughtiness and bitterness, found fault at the same time with the Moral Theology of our saint; the latter also sent him on this subject a reply that was solid as it was moderate.—ED.

Speaking of another proposition, that Mary commands in heaven, he says: "This and other similar expressions, which have dropped from the lips of some saints in their devout fervor, will not stand when examined by the rules of sound theology." Again, he says, "We must hear the Church, and not the hyperboles of a private author, even though he be a saint." He immediately afterwards adds, "We may also meet with some who assert that no grace comes to us from God otherwise than through the hands of Mary." Now remark the words, "We may also meet with some." He afterwards says, "To pretend that all the graces which we receive from God pass by Mary, would be a devout exaggeration."

But even supposing that the dead Pritanius did not say it, there is a living Pritanius who says it in his book (see No. 545), in which, amongst other things, he tells us that "sometimes the saints in praising the Blessed Virgin exaggerated, and used tropes." I now, therefore, answer him and say, that without doubt hyperbole, under which name tropes are included, cannot be taxed with untruth when it is evident from the context that it goes beyond the truth; as the case is when St. Peter Damian says that "Mary does not pray, but commands." [1] The same applies to St. Anselm, when he says that "she weeps in heaven for those who offend God." In such cases as these, in which there can be no mistake, tropes are lawful. But such is not the case in propositions in which the hyperbole is not evident, and therefore would be a real deception.

But let us come to the principal point in question. To prove it, I do not intend to bring forward the intrinsic reasons which would support it. I will only refer here to the reason which I adduced in my book, "that God is

[1] "Accedis, non solum rogans, sed imperans."—*In Nat. B. V e. I.*

thus pleased to honor his Beloved, who in life honored him so much." St. Thomas says that in "proportion to the graces they have merited, the saints can save many others; but that our Blessed Redeemer and his most Holy Mother merited so much grace that they can save all men."[1] Moreover, as she is the universal advocate of all men, it is becoming that all who are saved should obtain salvation by her means. Moreover—and this seems to me a more solid reason—as Mary co-operated by her charity, as St. Augustine says,[2] in the spiritual birth of the faithful, so also God wills that she should co-operate by her intercession in obtaining for them the life of grace in this world, and the life of glory in eternity. For this reason the Church makes us call her, without any limitation, "OUR LIFE" and "OUR HOPE."

But that which has made and still makes the greatest impression on my mind is, that I see this opinion maintained, not only by so many learned authors, but also by saints.

The anonymous writer believes he has in particular proved that St. Bernard never meant to assert that all graces come to us by the hands of Mary, but only that through her we received Jesus Christ, who is the source and plenitude of all graces. But I believe, on the other hand, that I shall here evidently prove the reverse of what I now add.

St. Bernard says that Mary received the plenitude of grace from God. Then explaining in what this plenitude consists, he says that it consists principally in the reception into herself of Jesus Christ, who is the source of all graces; but then he adds, that in consequence of this,

---

[1] "Magnum enim est in quolibet Sancto, quando habet tantum de gratia, quod sufficit ad salutem multorum; sed, quando haberet tantum, quod sufficeret ad salutem omnium, hoc esset maximum; et hoc est in Christo et in Beata Virgine."—*Exp. in Sal. Ang.*

[2] *De S. Virginit.* c. 6.

the Blessed Virgin received another plenitude, which is the plenitude of graces; that, as she is the mediatress of men with God, so she might herself dispense the graces to all men. The saint says, " Why should human frailty fear to approach Mary ? In her there is nothing severe, nothing terrible; she is all sweetness, offering milk and wool to all. Thank him, then, who has provided you with such a mediatress. She has made herself all to all, to the wise and to the foolish; by her most abundant charity she has made herself a debtor to all. She opens her merciful heart to all, that all may receive of her plenitude; the captive redemption, the sick health, the sinner pardon, the just grace, the angels joy, her Son flesh, that no one may hide himself from her heat."[1] Remark, therefore, the words, " that all may receive of her plenitude,"[2] for they clearly prove that St. Bernard here speaks, not of the first plenitude, which is Jesus Christ—otherwise he could not say that even her Son received his flesh of her plenitude—but of the second, or consequent fulness of grace, as we have already said, which Mary received from God, whereby to dispense to each one of us the graces which we receive. Remark also the words, " there is no one who hides himself from her heat."[3] Did any one receive graces otherwise than through Mary, he could hide himself from the heat of this sun; but St. Bernard says that no one can hide him-

---

[1] " Quid ad Mariam accedere trepidet humana fragilitas ? Nihil austerum in ea, nihil terribile; tota suavis est, omnibus offerens lac et lanam. Age gratias ei qui talem tibi Mediatricem providit. Omnibus omnia facta est, sapientibus et insipientibus copiosissima charitate Debitricem se fecit. Omnibus misericordiæ sinum aperit, ut de plenitudine ejus accipiant universi, captivus redemptionem, æger curationem, peccator veniam. justus gratiam, Angelus lætitiam, Filii persona carnis humanæ substantiam; ut non sit qui se abscondat a calore ejus."—*In Sign. magn.*

[2] "Ut de plenitudine ejus accipiant universi."

[3] "Ut non sit qui se abscondat a calore ejus."

self from the warmth of Mary. Elsewhere he says, "By
thee we have access to the Son, O blessed finder of grace,
bearer of life, and Mother of salvation, that we may receive him by thee, who through thee was given to us;" [1]
by which the saint clearly gives us to understand, that,
as we have access to the Father only through the Son,
who is the Mediator of justice, and who by his merits
obtain for us all graces, so also we only have access to
the Son by means of the Mother, who is the mediatress
of grace, and by her prayers obtains for us all the graces
that Jesus Christ has merited for us.

This is still better explained by that which the saint
afterwards says in a sermon of *the Aqueduct*, in the commencement of which he says, that Mary received the
first plenitude of grace from God, that is Jesus Christ,
in order that she might impart it to us also. But a little
further on he speaks clearly of the second plenitude of
graces which she received, consequently of the graces
which we receive through her prayers. The saint says,
"It is true that Mary obtained Jesus Christ, the source
of graces, from God ; but this perhaps does not fully
satisfy your desires ; for you would wish that she should
herself obtain for you, by her intercession, these graces
which Jesus Christ merited for you." [2] The saint then
passes on to exhort us never to cease to honor and have
recourse with great confidence to this divine Mother,
saying, that which we desire, God has already granted,
by depositing in Mary the plenitude of every blessing ;
that whatever we receive of hope, grace, and salvation
from God we may see that we have obtained it by the
means of Mary, who ascends overflowing with delights. [3]

[1] "Per te accessum habeamus ad Filium, O Inventrix gratiæ, Mater
salutis ! ut per te nos suscipiat, qui per te datus est nobis."—*In Adv.
D.* s. 2.

[2] "Verum id quidem, sed parum est, ni fallor, desideriis vestris."

[3] "Altius ergo intueamini quanto devotionis affectu a nobis eam

"She," the saint says, "is a garden of delights" (and remark that he is still speaking of the graces which are actually dispensed to us by Mary's hand), "upon which that divine south wind has not only breathed in passing, but has so filled with his balmy breath, that its perfumes, that is, the most precious gifts of graces, are sent forth on every side."[1] And in reference to the first text which I quoted, "There is no one who hides himself from her heat,"[2] the saint says : "Take away the sun, where will be the day ? Take away Mary, what will be left but the darkest night ?"[3]

The saint then continues to exhort us to recommend ourselves to Mary, and to take her as our advocate with Jesus Christ. He encourages us, saying, that if she prays for us, her Son is certain graciously to hear her ; for he hears his Mother, and the Father hears his Son,[4] and immediately adds, "My children, she is the sinner's ladder ; she is my greatest confidence ; she is the whole ground of my hope."[5] Here, when the saint calls her the sinner's ladder, and the whole ground of his hope, he certainly does so for no other reason than because he considers her as the intercessor for, and the dispenser of

voluerit honorari, qui totius boni plenitudinem posuit in Maria, ut proinde, si quid spei in nobis est, si quid gratiæ, si quid salutis, ab ea noverimus redundare, quæ ascendit deliciis affluens."

[1] " Hortus deliciarum, quem non modo afflaverit veniens, sed et perflaverit superveniens Auster ille divinus, ut undique fluant et effluant aromata ejus, charismata scilicet gratiarum."

[2] " Ut non sit qui se abscondat a calore ejus."

[3] " Tolle corpus hoc solare, quod illuminat mundum, ubi dies ? Tolle Mariam, hanc maris Stellam, quid nisi caligo et tenebræ relinquuntur ?"

[4] " Ad Mariam recurre ; non dubius dixerim, exaudietur ipsa pro reverentia sua : exaudiet utique Matrem Filius, et exaudiet Filium Pater."

[5] " Filioli, hæc peccatorum Scala, hæc mea maxima Fiducia, hæc tota Ratio spei meæ."

all graces. She is a ladder, and as we cannot reach the third step of the ladder unless we put our foot on the first, so neither can we reach God otherwise than by Jesus Christ ; nor Jesus Christ otherwise than by Mary. He then calls her his greatest confidence, and the whole ground of his hope : and why? Because God having willed that all graces should pass through Mary, he would have considered himself deprived of grace and hope, had he been deprived of her intercession.

He then exhorts us to do as he does; that is, to place all our hopes in Mary; giving us at the same time to understand that if Mary prays for us we are certain of salvation. For, as the Father cannot but graciously hear the Son, neither can the Son do otherwise than graciously hear his Mother. On the other hand, he tells us, that if Mary does not pray for us, we shall not obtain salvation; because she will not have provided us with grace, which is all that we require, and the only means by which we are saved. He then concludes, "What more can we desire? Let us seek for grace, and seek it by Mary; for that which she seeks she finds, and never meets with a refusal." [1]

Moreover, I have given in my book many other passages, with their references, as well from the writings of the saints as from other ancient and renowned authors; and I do not see how it is possible to explain them otherwise than according to our opinion. I will here simply give them together, without comment; and my reader may judge how far my opinion is correct.

St. Sophronius, in a sermon on the Assumption, for

[1] " Quid enim ? potestne Filius aut repellere aut sustinere repulsam ? non audire aut non audiri Filius potest ? Semper hæc inveniet gratiam, et sola est gratia, qua egemus. . . . Nimirum sola est gratia qua salvamur. Quid nos alia concupiscimus? Quæramus gratiam, et per Mariam quæramus; quia, quod quærit, invenit, et frustrari non potest."—*De Aquæd.*

merly attributed to St. Jerome, says, that "the plenitude of all grace, which was in Christ, came into Mary."[1]

St. Bernardine of Sienna, that "all graces of the spiritual life that descend from Christ, their head, to the faithful, who are his mystical body, are transmitted by the means of Mary." That "from the moment in which this Virgin Mother conceived the divine Word in her womb, she acquired a special jurisdiction, so to say, over all the gifts of the Holy Ghost; so that no creature has since received any grace from God, otherwise than by the hands of Mary." That "all gifts, all virtues, and all graces are dispensed by the hands of Mary, to whomsoever, when, and as she pleases."[2]

Again the same saint: "As God was pleased to dwell in the womb of this holy Virgin, she acquired, so to say, a kind of jurisdiction over all graces; for when Jesus Christ issued forth from her most sacred womb, all the streams of divine gifts flowed from her as from a celestial ocean." St. Bonaventure: "As the moon, which stands between the sun and the earth, transmits to this latter whatever she receives from the former, so does Mary pour out upon us who are in this world the heavenly graces which she receives from God." Again: "God will not save us without the intercession of Mary." Again: "As a child cannot live without a nurse to suckle it, so no one can be saved without the protection of Mary."[3]

---

[1] "In Christo fuit plenitudo gratiæ sicut in Capite influente, in Maria vero sicut in Collo transfundente."—*Contenson, Theol. ment.* t. 2, l. 10, d. 6, c. 1.

[2] "Per Virginem a Capite Christo vitales gratiæ in ejus Corpus mysticum transfunduntur. A tempore, quo virgo Mater concepit in utero Verbum Dei, quamdam, ut sic dicam, jurisdictionem obtinuit in omni Spiritus Sancti processione temporali; ita, quod nulla creatura aliquam a Deo obtinuit gratiam, nisi secundum ipsius piæ Matris dispensationem. Ideo omnia dona, virtutes, et gratiæ, quibus vult, quando vult, et quomodo vult, per ipsius manus dispensantur."—*Pro Fest. V. M.* s. 5, c. 8.

[3] "Cum tota natura divina intra Virginis uterum exstiterit, non

St. Ephrem says: "O most holy Virgin, receive us under thy protection, if thou wilt see us saved; for we have no hope of salvation but through thy means."[1]

St. Germanus: "What hope can we have of salvation, if thou dost abandon us, O Mary, who art the life of Christians?"[2]

St. Ildephonsus: "O Mary, God has decided on committing all good gifts that he has provided for men to thy hands; and therefore he has entrusted all treasures and riches of grace to thee."[3]

St. Antoninus: "Whoever asks and expects to find graces without the intercession of Mary, endeavors to fly without wings."[4]

St. Peter Damian: "All the treasures of the mercy of God are in her hands."[5]

Gerson: "She is our mediatress, through whose hands God has decreed that all that He gives to men should pass."[6]

timeo dicere quod in omnes gratiarum effluxus quamdam jurisdictionem habuerit hæc virgo, de cujus utero, quasi de quodam Divinitatis oceano, flumina emanant omnium gratiarum.—Sicut luna inter corpora cœlestia et terrena est media, et, quod ab illis accipit, ad inferiora refundit; sic et Virgo Regina inter nos et Deum est media, et gratiam ipsa nobis refundit."—*Spanner. Polyanth. litt. M.* t. 6.—"Ipse, sine ea, non salvabit te; quemadmodum infans sine nutrice non potest vivere, ita nec sine Domina nostra potes habere salutem."—*Cant. p. Psalt.*

[1] "Nobis non est alia quam a te fiducia, O Virgo sincerissima!"—*De Laud. Dei Gen.*

[2] "Si nos deserueris, quid erit de nobis, O vita christianorum!"—*De Zona Deip.*

[3] "Omnia bona quæ iillic summa Majestas decrevit facere, tuis manibus voluit commendare; commissi quippe sunt tibi thesauri et ornamenta gratiarum."—*De Cor. V.* c. 15.

[4] "Qui petit sine ipsa duce, sine alis tentat volare."—*P.* 4, *tit.* 15, c. 22, § 9.

[5] "In manibus tuis sunt thesauri miserationum Domini."—*De Nat. B. V.* s. 1.

[6] "Mediatrix nostra, per cujus manus Deus ordinavit dare ea quæ dat humanæ naturæ."—*S. de Annunc.*

The Abbot of Celles: "She is the dispenser of the divine graces: for her Son grants nothing but what passes through her hands." In another place he says: "Our salvation is in her hands." [1]

Cassian: "The salvation of all depends on their being favored and protected by Mary." St. Bernardine of Sienna says the same thing: "O Lady, since thou art the dispenser of all graces, our salvation is in your hands." [2]

Richard of St. Laurence: "Whatever graces God grants to His creatures, He wills that they should pass through the hands of His virgin Mother." [3] Elsewhere he supposes Jesus Christ saying: "No one comes to me unless my Mother draws him by her prayers." [4] Referring to the words of Proverbs: *She is like the merchant's ship,* he says: "In the sea of the world all are lost who are not received into this ship: therefore, as often as we see ourselves in danger of perishing in the midst of the waves of this sea, we should cry out to Mary: Lady, save us; we perish." [5] Again he says: "As we should fall into the abyss if the ground were withdrawn from under our feet, so does a soul deprived of the succor of Mary fall first into sin, and then into hell." [6]

[1] "Tu Dispensatrix es gratiarum divinarum; nihil concedit nobis Filius tuus, quin pertransierit per manus tuas."—*Op. plen. de B. V.* p. 9, *cont.* 14.—"Salus nostra in manu illius est."—*Cont. de V. M. in prol.*

[2] "Tota salus humani generis consistit in multitudine gratiæ Mariæ et favoris."—*Pelbart, Stell.* l. 12, p. 1, a. 3.—"Tu Dispensatrix omnium gratiarum."—*Pro Fest. V. M.* s. 13, a. 2, c. 3.

[3] "Deus quidquid boni dat creaturis suis, per manus Matris Virginis vult transire."—*De Laud. B. M.* l. 2, p. 3.

[4] "Nemo potest venire ad me, nisi Mater mea suis precibus traxerit eum."—*De Laud. B. M.* l. 12, p. 2.

[5] "In mare mundi submerguntur omnes illi quos non suscipit Nayis ista; ideo, quoties videmus insurgentes super nos fluctus hujus maris, clamare debemus ad Mariam: Domina! salva nos, perimus."—*Ibid.* l. 11.

[6] "Subtracta terra, statim descendimus in profundum; sic, subtracta

I add another argument, which has great weight with me; it is, that the greater part of the faithful have always recourse to the intercession of the divine Mother for all the graces which they desire: whence it appears that the above-mentioned pious belief is, we may almost say, the general belief of the Church. Of this very argument—that is, the general belief of the faithful—Petavius [1] makes use to prove the doctrine, which I consider certain, of the Immaculate Conception of Mary.* To conclude: the above belief, that all graces pass by the hands of Mary, seeming to me, as also to many other writers,—such as Segneri,[2] Paciucchelli,[3] Crasset,[4] Mendoza,[5] Nieremberg,[6] Poiré,[7] etc., —both very pious and very probable, I shall always rejoice that I have believed it and taught it to others, if for no other reason, at least because it inflames my devotion towards Mary; whereas the opposite opinion cools it, which is certainly not a slight evil.

nobis adjutorio Mariæ, statim labimur in peccatum, et inde in infernum."—*De Laud. B. M.* l. 8.

[1] *De Inc.* l. 14, c. 2, n. 10.   [2] *Div. di M.* p. 1, c. 5.
[3] *In Sal. Ang. exc.* 15.   [4] *Vér. Dév.* p. 1, tr. 1, q. 5.
[5] *Virid. s. erud.* l. 2, pr. 2.   [6] *De Aff. erga B. V.* c. 13.
[7] *Tr. Cour. tr.* 2, c. 10, §§ 2, 3.

---

* At that time the doctrine of the Immaculate Conception had not been defined as an article of faith.

II.

A Short Reply to the Extravagant Reform

Attempted by the Abbé Rolli; a Reform which is in Opposition to the Devotion and Love we owe to the Divine Mother.*

A DEVOUT and learned little work, by Father Ildephonsus Cardoni, of the order of Friars Minor, has lately fallen into my hands. In it the good Father refutes, with much learning, a book published by the Abbé Leoluca Rolli, under the title of *The New Project*, etc.,† in which he pretends to reform the various prayers and devotions of the Catholic Church in honor of the most Blessed Virgin Mary and other saints. For the honor of this Blessed Virgin, and out of the feeling of especial devotion which I have nourished towards her from my childhood, I have determined to give in an abbreviated form the contents of these two works; that is to say, the wicked propositions of the one, and the convincing arguments of the other.

I.

The Abbé Rolli, speaking of the miraculous translation by the angels of the holy House of Loretto from Nazareth into Dalmatia, and from Dalmatia to the property of a good lady named Laureta, in the diocese of Recanati, in the march of Ancona, and thence to a hill a mile and a half distant from that property, where it is now venerated,—the above-named Abbé calls the history of that translation "a story which is told," as if it was a

---

* This treatise was written by the holy Bishop about the year 1775, when he was nearly 80 years old.—See Tannoia, Book 4, ch. 3.

† *Il Novello Progetto*, etc.

fable ; whereas the illustrious Pontiff Benedict XIV., speaking, in his beautiful work on the feasts of Mary, of this holy house, calls it " the dwelling in which the divine Word assumed human flesh, and which was translated by the ministry of angels." He then adds, that "its authenticity is proved as well by ancient monuments and unbroken tradition as by the testimony of Sovereign Pontiffs, the common consent of the faithful, and the continual miracles which are there worked even to the present day." [1] In fact Tursellin, in his *History of the House of Loretto*, asserts that nearly all the Popes after Pius II. have spoken of its miraculous translation ; and Sixtus V., in the year 1583, instituted an order under the auspices of our Blessed Lady of Loretto. Notwithstanding this, the Abbé Rolli, without reason, seems to follow in the track of Launoy, Verger, Hospinien, and other Protestants who have denied the miraculous translation, and also Theodore Beza and the Calvinist David Pareus, who call the house of Loretto "the Lauretanian Idol." [2] But all these have been refuted with unanswerable evidence by many learned Catholic writers—Canisius, Turiano, and Gretser, as Theophilus Raynaud writes. [3] Turselin, on the authority of grave authors, relates the miracle, which is confirmed by Peter Giorgio, Jerome Angelita, and by John Bonifacio. He is referred to by Benedict XIV., [4] who writes, that even heretics, on entering this holy house, are converted, and impose silence on those who deny the miracle.

[1] "Conclave, ubi Verbum divinum humanam assumpsit carnem, Angelorum ministerio translatum est, ita adstipulantibus tum vetustis monumentis, perpetuaque traditione, tum Summorum Pontificum testimoniis, communi sensu fidelium, et continuis, quæ in dies eduntur, miraculis."—*De Fest.* l. 2, c. 16.

[2] "Idolum Lauretanum."

[3] *Hag. Lugd. tr.* 4, *antem.*

[4] *De Fest.* l. 2, c. 16.

II.

The Abbé Rolli then criticises the titles of " Tower of David," " Tower of Ivory," and "House of Gold,"[1] which in the litanies are bestowed on the Blessed Virgin. He calls them affected, almost ridiculous, and unmeaning. How are they unmeaning? They indeed mean a great deal ; for they denote the power with which the Mother of God defends her devout servants, and the ardent charity of her blessed soul, which rendered her worthy to become the temple of the Eternal Word ; as these titles are precisely explained by St. Bernard, St. Ephrem, Richard of St. Laurence, and others.

Afterwards speaking of the titles, " Mirror of Justice," " Refuge of Sinners," " Morning Star," and "Gate of Heaven,"[2] he says that a Catholic hearing these titles given to the Blessed Virgin must make an act of faith, and believe that they are only applicable to Jesus Christ, and not to Mary ; just as if they were prejudicial to faith. He, therefore, would wish all these litanies abolished, although they have been recited and sung in all churches of priests and religious for so many ages, and this with the approbation of many Pontiffs ; which also proves that these titles are not only not affected and ridiculous, but that they are filled with piety and tenderness towards our holy Queen, and thus excite us to greater confidence in her protection. Who can deny that these litanies, according to the established discipline of so many years, form a part of the public worship of the Church ?

The Abbé Rolli then takes great pains to discredit the custom which now exists of singing the Litany of Loretto when the Blessed Sacrament is exposed, and expressly

[1] " Turris Davidica, Turris eburnea, Domus aurea."
[2] " Speculum justitiæ, Refugium peccatorum, Stella matutina, Janua cœli."

calls it an abuse. In this he avails himself of the opinion of Louis Muratori, who in his book called *Well-regulated Devotion* [1] does not indeed, as the Abbé Rolli does, call it an abuse, but says that it would be worth while to consider whether it might not be better on this occasion to sing prayers immediately addressed to Jesus our Saviour. For my part I cannot understand how it is unbecoming to beg the divine Mother to offer her prayers for us to Jesus, exposed in the Blessed Sacrament. Every one knows that God has given us Jesus Christ, that we may have recourse to him as to our chief Mediator; but St. Bernard says that God has also given us Mary as an advocate with Jesus Christ: "Thou desirest an advocate with him? Have recourse to Mary; the Son will graciously hear His Mother." [2] In another place the same saint adds: "We need a mediator with Christ the Mediator, and we cannot find one more fitting than Mary." [3] He uses the words "we need;" that is, another mediator with Jesus Christ is necessary; not indeed with an absolute necessity, but with a moral one, to increase our confidence; for Jesus Christ alone is our Mediator by absolute necessity. St. Jerome, however, to take away any scruple that might arise when we have recourse to Mary, says that we must go to her, not as to the author of grace (as Calvin falsely said), but only as to an intercessor; and that for this reason we say, "Have mercy on us" to Jesus Christ; but to the Blessed Virgin and the saints we say, "Pray for us." [4] Thus did St. Jerome convince Vigilantius on this point.

[1] *Ch.* 22.
[2] "Advocatum habere vis et ad ipsum? ad Mariam recurre; exaudiet utique Matrem Filius."—*De Aquæd.*
[3] "Opus est Mediatore ad Mediatorem istum; nec alter nobis utilior quam Maria."—*In Sign. magn.*
[4] "Miserere nobis"—"Ora pro nobis."

III.

The Abbé Rolli is not satisfied with calling the titles bestowed on the Blessed Virgin in the Litany of Loretto affected, almost ridiculous, and unmeaning, but he has also the boldness to attack the sacred Antiphon, "Hail, Holy Queen," although he knows that the Holy Church has approved it, by making its recitation in the canonical hours obligatory on all in choir. Luther had already said that this prayer was scandalous, and gave the Blessed Virgin the attributes of God. The heretic Peter Martyr also wrote, that as Jesus Christ was our only Mediator, it was injurious to Him to admit Mary as our advocate and mediatress. Our Abbé Rolli is not ashamed, in his *New Project*, when speaking of the "Salve Regina," to write these words: "Out of blind respect and party spirit the titles given to the Virgin in the 'Salve Regina' are retained." He says, moreover, that Brother Herman Contractus, whom *he* believes to have been its author, called the divine Mother "Our Hope" and "Our Advocate,"[1] only in simple piety and devotion, since Jesus Christ alone is our only Hope and our only Advocate. It may well be said that this way of speaking differs little from what the above-quoted heretic Peter Martyr said. But since St. Epiphanius calls the Blessed Virgin our Mediatress, which is the same thing as advocate, and St. Ephrem[2] calls her the hope of those who are in despair, how does the Abbé Rolli dare to assert that "these titles are only retained out of blind respect and party spirit"? The Church, then, permits the prayer "Salve Regina" out of blind respect and party spirit!

IV.

The Abbé Rolli then leaves the Litany and the "Salve Regina," and goes on to speak of the devotions of the

[1] " Spes nostra—Advocata nostra."   [2] " Spes desperantium."

scapular, rosary, cords, and girdles of other saints, calling them all trifling, and, so to say, useless ; when, on
the other hand, we know that the Sovereign Pontiffs
have approved of these devotions, and enriched them
with indulgences. The learnei Papebroeck calls those
persons wicked who deny that the Sovereign Pontiffs
have approved the devotion of devoutly wearing the
scapular of Mary by many favors, and that God has approved it by many benefits.[1] Bzovius[2] also, and the
Bollandists,[3] speak in high terms of praise of the rosary
of Mary, which has also been greatly praised by Leo X.,
St. Pius V., Gregory XIII., Sixtus V., and many other
Pontiffs. Of such religious devotions the learned Pouget
writes : " Those who blame them, in their ignorance
blaspheme."[4]

The Abbé Rolli next vents his fury against those
Christians who practise these devotions when in a state
of sin, in the hope of receiving mercy from God through
their means. He exclaims, " Such devotees are all
damned." In this, as I have already remarked, he takes
Lamindus Pritanius for his master, that is, Louis Muratori, who, in his book, *Well-regulated Devotion*, says :
that " if a Christian, living at enmity with God, trusts
that, on account of the confidence which he has in the
Blessed Virgin, she by her intercession will not allow him
to be surprised by sudden death, and that he will have
time to make his peace with God, or hopes for some
temporal benefit ; such a hope is injurious, superstitious,

---

[1] " Improbus porro sit, qui negat multis Romanorum Pontificum
gratiis ac privilegiis ornatam, multis etiam divinis beneficiis compro-
batam esse Scapularis Mariani devote gestandi religionem."—*Resp.* p.
2, *ad* a. 20, n. 28.

[2] *A.D.* 1213.

[3] 4 *Aug. Vit. S. Dom. comm. præv.* § 19.

[4] " Qui ista vituperant, ' Quæcunque ignorant, blasphemant '"—
Inst. cath. p. 3. s. 2, c. 10, § 2.—*Jud.* x.

and contrary to the teaching of the Church, and is wholly to be rejected."

But in this Pritanius and Rolli are in direct opposition to Cardinal Bellarmin, quoted by Benedict XIV. in his book *De Festis.*[1] Cardinal Bellarmin[2] writes, "that devotions performed in a state of sin, if they do not justify, they at least dispose the soul to obtain justification through the merits of the divine Mother or of other saints." But that which is of the greatest weight, and fully condemns them, is the doctrine of the master of theologians, St. Thomas, who teaches that "the devotions of the faithful, although performed in a state of sin, if they do not suffice to obtain their salvation, yet they obtain them three things: first, they accustom them to pious works; secondly, they obtain them temporal blessings; and thirdly, they dispose them for the reception of divine grace."[3] The same angelic Doctor also teaches "that although the prayer of a sinner is not in itself worthy of grace, nevertheless it obtains it through the pure mercy of God."[4] He then adds, that "it is possible that the prayer of a sinner, even without an efficacious (that is, a firm and enduring) purpose of amendment, may be granted, out of the infinite mercy of God, provided that he is not in so obstinate a state of mind as constantly to reject every exhortation to repentance."[5]

---

[1] *De Fest.* l. 2, c. 6.

[2] *De Pœn.* l. 2, c. 7.

[3] "Opera ista ad triplex bonum valent: ad temporalium consecutionem, ad dispositionem ad gratiam, et ad assuefactionem bonorum operum."—*Suppl.* q. 14, a. 4.

[4] "Orationem peccatoris Deus audit, non quasi ex justitia, sed ex pura misericordia."—2. 2, q. 83, a. 16.

[5] "Fieri potest ut, ex infinita Dei misericordia, peccatoris oratio exaudiatur, etiam sine proposito (efficaci nimirum ac stabili) emendandæ vitæ; dummodo non tam obstinato sit animo, ut omne pœnitentiæ consilium perpetuo abjecerit."—*De Fest.* l. 2, c. 6.

Pritanius or Muratori also says another thing in his book. He asserts that "when the Blessed Virgin and the saints pray for us, they do not offer their own merits, but only the efficacy of the merits of Jesus Christ." But in this he has been fully refuted by the learned Don Constantine Gaudio, in his book entitled *Defence of the Spotless Devotion, etc.*[1]

The same Pritanius, in another part of his book, says, "One reason may be alleged, which is, that our prayers will have more power when accompanied by those of the Holy Mother." But he gives himself an inconsistent answer, and one that in no way corresponds to his learning. He says, "This reason proves too much, and therefore proves nothing; otherwise it would never be fitting to pray to Jesus without joining to our prayers the incession of Mary." O God, what an answer! Then it would be unbecoming always to join to our prayers the intercession of Mary when we address ourselves to Jesus Christ? while the Council of Trent teaches "that it is good and useful earnestly to invoke the saints."[2] But if the intercession of the saints, and especially that of Mary, is good and useful, it is also good and useful always to obtain it. Therefore St. Bernard advises and exhorts all to ask for graces from God, and to ask for them through Mary; for Mary's prayers to God are the prayers of a Mother, and therefore are never refused. The saint says, "Let us seek for grace, and seek it by Mary; for she is a Mother, and cannot ask in vain."[3] How strange is this! Louis Muratori, whom I have always venerated, was celebrated throughout Europe, as it appears from his beautiful life, which has been so well

---

[1] *Difesa dell' illibata divozione, etc.*, contro di Lamindo Pritanio.

[2] "Bonum atque utile esse suppliciter eos invocare."—*Sess.* 25, *de Invoc. Sanct.*

[3] "Quæramus gratiam, et per Mariam quæramus; quia frustrari non potest."—*De Aquæd.*

written by his nephew; yet in many parts of his works, as we have already seen, he does not show that piety towards the Mother of God which would have become such a soul as his.

There is no need for me to write at greater length on the propositions above referred to. That which moved me to write the little I have on this subject, was that I saw the devout prayers and titles commonly given to Mary in her litanies and in the "Salve Regina" held up to discredit: and also I heard those devotions of the scapular and the rosary of Mary called trifling, which, in fact, are so religious, and which have been dear to me from my childhood. However, should any one wish to see the reform which the Abbé Rolli pretended to introduce in all these things refuted at length and fully, he can read the work of the Friar Minor Father Cardoni, to which I referred at the beginning of this short treatise.

INDEX.

Index.

DOLORS of Mary, little Rosary of, 662; indulgenced chaplet, 666.

DOMENICA OF PARADISE, her history, 348.

E

ELLEN, a sinner converted by the recitation of the Rosary, 86.

ELPHINSTONE, a young Scotchman, 54.

EMINGO, Blessed, began his sermons with the praises of Mary, 31.

ESKILL, ST., Archbishop of Lunden, Sweden, his history, 78.

ESTHER—figure of Mary, 40.

EUCHARIST, it is not improper to chant the Litany of Loretto before the Blessed Sacrament that is exposed, 697.

EXAMPLES of devotion to the Mother of God, counsel in regard to undue criticism, 16; love and devotion towards the Blessed Virgin, 54, 63, 104, 106, 117, 246, 348, 421, 437; preaching of her praises, 31, 32; visits to her churches and images, 68, 136, 389, 523, 604; recitation of the "Hail Mary," 229, 371, 593; and of the Rosary, 86, 236, 599; of the "Angelus," 595; of the "Stabat," 531; recourse to her protection, 44, 77, 91, 96, 116, 128, 138, 150, 164, 175, 189, 208, 334, 389; invocation and power of her name, 94, 148, 150, 261, 263, 270, 271; her mercy and her goodness, 44, 77, 175, 198, 208, 270; she wishes that we should not fear to ask too much of her, 242; her power against demons, 101, 103, 149, 150; she obtains conversion and a happy death for sinners that do not cease to recommend themselves to her, 103, 128, 189, 214, 218, 229, 258, 371; she preserves from hell certain sinners that died in a state of damnation, 227; woe be to those that cease to honor her, 334; pictures of the Immaculate Conception, 315; devotion to her dolors, 478, 479, 498, 516, 523, 531, 536; scapular, 404; fasting on Saturdays, 523, 602; alms, 611; other sacrifices made for the love of her, 164, 236; confraternities, 610; perseverance in devotion to her, 592; she loves obedience, 578.

F

FAITH of the Blessed Virgin, 564.

FASTING in honor of Mary, 597, 602.

FRANCIS DE SALES, his temptation and his deliverance from it, 138.

G

GERMAINE COUSIN, St., note, 69.

GRACE, grandeur of the grace received by Mary from the beginning, 318; all graces come through her mediation, 25, 80, 111, 158, 376, 684; she is pleased when we thank God for the graces bestowed upon her, 613.

Index.

H

HELL, the Mother of God preserves us from it, 220; sometimes even after dying in sin; 226; prayer to Mary to be preserved from it, 657.

HOPE of Mary, or her confidence in God, 568.

HUMILITY, eulogy and practice of this virtue considered in the Blessed Virgin, 547.

I

INDULGENCES, various, 595, 600, 601, 602, 606, 613, 614, 655, 657, 666, 667.

J

JEROME, EMILIAN, ST., his conversion and his life, 517.

JESUS, contradicted in everything, 495; he is pleased when we compassionate his Mother in her sorrows, 478.

JOACHIM PICCOLOMINI, Blessed, his devotion to the Mother of Sorrows and her reward, 523.

JOHN OF GOD, St., visited by the Blessed Virgin at his death, 106.

L

LAWRENCE ST., martyr, his courage in sufferings, 473.

LEONARD, Friar, his devotion to the Mother of God at his death, 63.

LITANY of the Blessed Virgin, indulgence, 602; meditations, 618; answer to critics, 697.

LORETTO, the holy house of, its miraculous translation, 695.

LOVE for Jesus and Mary, prayer to obtain it, 659. Divine love, see *charity*.

M

MARK and MARCELLINUS, Sts., suffered with joy for Jesus Christ, 473.

MARY, first-born daughter of God, 288; spouse of the Holy Ghost, 304; how the Saviour raised her by making her his Mother, 362; and in crowning her in heaven, 424; she is the most perfect of creatures, 318; our model in all virtues, 546; one cannot praise her too much, 29; her humility, 353, 392, 445, 547; merits that she acquired in the beginning, 329, 337, 342; then by consecrating herself to God in the Temple, 340, 343, 456; and in offering up her divine Son, 392; her faith, 564; her hope and her confidence in God, 568; her charity towards God, 554; even sleep did not hinder her from actually loving God, 558; her love for Jesus, 475, 511; her charity towards the sinner, 561; her chastity, 571; her voluntary poverty, 575; her obedience, 578; her spirit of meditation and of prayer, 584; her love for

Index.

Index.

P

R

S

T

Index.

V

Z

ORDER FORM

O.B.L. VICTORY MISSION
REV. RONALD L. TANGEN
RR #2 BOX 25
BROOKINGS, S.D.
605-693-3983

Gentlemen:

Please send me _____ copies of THE GLORIES
OF MARY. Enclosed is my payment in the amount of

_____

Name _____

Street _____

City _____

State _____ Zip _____

Donations for these books will be as follows:

QUANTITY PRICES

1 copy:	$3.00	25 copies:	$2.00 ea.
5 copies:	3.00 ea.	100 copies:	1.50 ea.
10 copies:	2.50 ea.	500 copies:	1.25 ea.
	1,000 or more copies: 1.00 ea.		

Please include check or money order.